W9-BMX-753

Public Records Online

The National Guide to Private & Government Online Sources of Public Records

Public Records Online

The National Guide to Private & Government Online Sources of Public Records
Fourth Edition

©2003 By Facts on Demand Press
206 West Julie Drive, Suite 2
Tempe, AZ 85283
(800) 929-3811

ISBN: 1-889150-37-1
Edited by Michael L. Sankey and Peter J. Weber.
Cover Design by Robin Fox & Associates

Cataloging-in-Publication Data

Public Records Online : the national guide to private &
    government online sources of public records / [edited by
    Michael L. Sankey and Peter J. Weber].—4th ed.
        p. cm.
        ISBM: 1-889150-37-1

        1. Electronic public records–United States—
        Directories. 2. Information services industries—United
        States–Directories. I. Sankey, Michael L., 1949-
        II. Weber, Peter J. (Peter Julius), 1952-

    JK468.P76P83 2000   352.3'87'0973
                                         QB100-700981

Contents

Section I - Public Records Primer   5

51 STATE CHAPTERS...

Section III - Private Database Vendors   407

Appendix   511

A SPECIAL THANK YOU!

The goal of Public Records Online, now it is 4th edition, is to present a current and comprehensive picture of the regulations and procedures for online access to public records. This cannot be done without the help of a certain group people.

Therefore, we wish to acknowledge and extend a special thank you to:

- All the government administrators and information systems personnel at the 4,500+ government agencies profiled in the book; and

- The database vendors working in the private sector who compile the extensive databases and gateways profiled herein.

Our sincere thanks, from Fact on Demand Press, to all of you for taking the time and having the interest to help us assemble this collection of facts. Your valuable assistance is a direct reflection of the accuracy of this publication.

Thank you!

The research staff at Facts on Demand Press
Helen Doornbos
Bill Roberts
Annette Talley
Peter J. Weber
Mark Sankey
Michael Sankey

Introduction

Complex and Mysterious?

The access to and use of current public records is one of the fundamental pillars of our democratic society.

Yet, the words "Public Records" often convey a complex, almost mysterious source of information that is perceived as difficult to access, hard to decipher, and likely to be of interest only to private investigators and reporters.

This view could not be further from the reality!

The Doorway to Online Public Records

Today there are literally thousands of public records and public information sources accessible by anyone with a computer and a modem. With this rapid growth it becomes necessary for online users to understand what information is available and what information is not, to know how the information is gathered and stored, and to know who "has" the information and where it is located.

This book is your key to opening the door to online public records information. Whether you surf the World Wide Web, connect via modem to a court's computer system or utilize a company's dial-up system, *Public Records Online* is your gateway to the world of online records research.

The information you desire is probably out there somewhere. You need only find its particular "trail." To that end, this book has been designed to be your tour guide when traveling the trail of online information. With this book in hand you've made the first step on your trip.

Now, we suggest that you read the beginning chapters to fully prepare you for your journey. Once you are familiar with the cyber scenery, you will need only to scan the chapters and sources to find the right "trail" to take.

Our goal is to also provide you with a complete **Public Records Primer**—so you can understand what you need, where it might be, and how to access that information like a pro.

Your Access to 6500 Government Agencies and Private Vendors

Herein, we will examine online trails that begin or are maintained at the federal, state, county, and in certain instances, the city and town level. *Public Records Online* is especially useful for these applications:

> Background Investigation
>
> Competitive Intelligence
>
> Legal Research
>
> Locating People
>
> Locating Assets
>
> Pre-Employment and Tenant Screening
>
> Process Serving
>
> Skiptracing
>
> Genealogy

The Information Trail

Whether you are new at searching public records or not, there are a myriad of issues that must be considered and questions that must be answered if you are to become an effective, efficient user of the online tools now available.

Finding information is not an easy process; *Public Records Online* aims to make it so. To this end, *Public Records Online* reveals where records are kept, outlines access requirements and gives searching hints so that you can explore the depths of the public record industry.

Equipped with the information contained in these pages you can find the facts, gain access to the information you need, and even track your own "information trail!"

How This Book Is Organized

Public Records Online is organized into four Sections--

1. Public Record Primer

2. Government Online Sources

3. Private Database Vendors

4. Appendix

The Public Record Primer

The purpose of the Public Record Primer section is to assist the reader in knowing *where categories of records can be found* and *how to search.* The Primer contains many searching hints and is an excellent overall source of information that will especially help those not familiar with searching government records, whether online or not.

An important segment of this section is the discussion of privacy issues including public information vs. personal information and how records enter the public domain. The Primer is not limited to a discussion of only online records, but to all public records and public information.

The **Searching Other Federal Records Online** chapter contains an excellent article (on page 58-65) contributed by Alan Schlein, author of *Find it Online!* (Facts on Demand Press). Mr. Schlein presents a unique dissertation about the best federal government Internet sites for finding usual information quickly and efficiently.

Another important chapter is **When to Use a Public Record Vendor** (starting on page 69). This chapter contains a wealth of information about commercial public record vendors, especially those who offer online access to records.

Government Online Sources

Individual state chapters have been compiled into an easy to use format that details what is available online. Free online access and fee-based systems are denoted, with the type or category of records available. Five sub-chapters or sections are presented in this order:

1. State Public Record Agencies

2. State Licensing and Regulatory Boards

3. Federal Courts (US District and Bankruptcy)

4. County Courts

5. County Recorder Offices

Be sure to review the introductions and Online Access Notes found at the beginning of each state's County Courts and County Recorder's Office sections. This is a good place to find out about statewide online systems.

Private Database Vendors

The third section of *Public Records Online* includes two chapters:

Vendor Information Index–This index consists of 28 Public Record Information Categories. The vendors are listed alphabetically within each category. Each listing includes geographic coverage area and the name of proprietary databases or gateways offered.

Vendor Profiles–Read full profiles of each company. Includes proprietary products, clientele restrictions, and contact information.

The Appendix

The Appendix consists of these items:

Trade Associations–A list of trade associations connected to the public information industry and their web sites.

Editors' Choices -- 11 Great Web Sites–A short list of web sites to visit and use.

Section I

Public Record Primer

Public Records Unveiled

Definition of Public Records

The strict **definition** of **public records** is—

> *"Those records maintained by government agencies that are open without restriction to public inspection, either by statute or by tradition."*

If access to a record that is held by a government agency is restricted in some way, then it is not a public record.

Accessibility Paradox

Adding to the mystique of government records is the accessibility paradox. For example, in some states a specific category of records is severely restricted, and therefore those records are not "public," while the very same category of records may be 100% open in other states. Among these categories are criminal histories, vehicle ownership records and worker's compensation records.

At times, you will see the following box printed on pages throughout this book. We are not trying to fill up space. As your public record searching takes you from state-to-state or county-to-county, this is the one important adage to keep in mind.

Editor's Tip: Just because records are maintained in a certain way in your state or county do not assume that any other county or state does things the same way that you are used to.

Public vs. Private vs. Personal

Before reading further, let's define types of records held by government or by private industry. Of course, not all information about a company or individual is public. The boundaries between public and private information are not well understood, and continually undergo intense scrutiny. The following is an introduction to the subject from a viewpoint of a professional record searcher.

Public Record

Public records are records of **incidents** or **actions** filed or recorded with a government agency for the purpose of notifying others about the matter—the "public." The **deed** to your house recorded at the county recorder's office is a public record—it is a legal requirement that you record with the county recorder. Anyone requiring details about your property may review or copy the documents.

Public Information

Your **telephone listing** in the phone book is public information; that is, you freely furnished the information to ease the flow of commercial and private communications.

Personal Information

Any information about a person or business that the person or business might consider private and confidential in nature, such as your **Social Security Number**, is personal information. Such information will remain private to a limited extent unless it is disclosed to some outside entity that could make it public. **Personal information may be found in either public records or in public information.**

How Personal Information Enters the Public Domain

Many people confuse the three categories above, lump them into one and wonder how "big brother" accumulated so much information about them. Therefore, these distinctions are important. The reality is that **much of this information is given willingly**.

Actually, there are two ways that personal information can enter the public domain—statutory and voluntary. In a **voluntary** transaction, you **share** personal information of your own free will. In a **statutory** transaction, you **disclose** personal information because the law requires you to.

The confusion of terms used today feeds the increasing conflict between privacy advocates and commercial interests. This, in turn, is driving legislation towards more and more **restrictions** on the **dissemination of personal information**—the same personal information that, in fact, is willingly shared by most people and companies in order to participate in our market economy.

Where Public Records are Held

There are two places you can find public records—

1. at a government agency

2. within the database of a private company

Government agencies maintain records in a variety of ways. While many state agencies and highly populated county agencies are computerized, many others use microfiche, microfilm, and paper to store files and indexes. Agencies that have converted to computer will not necessarily place complete file records on their system; they are more apt to include only an index, pointer or summary data to the files.

Private enterprises develop their databases in one of two ways: they buy the records in bulk from government agencies; or they send personnel to the agencies and compile this information by using a copy machine or keying information into a laptop computer. The database is then available for internal use or for resale purposes. An example of such a company is *Superior Information* (800 848-0489). Superior maintains a very comprehensive database of civil judgments, tax liens, Uniform Commercial Code filings and bankruptcy data gathered from the Mid-Atlantic States.

Editor's Tip: Public records purchased and/or compiled by private companies for resale purposes must follow the same access and restriction regulations as the related government jurisdiction.

The Common Methods Used to Access Public Records

The following is a look at the various methods available to access public records.

Visit in Person

This is easy if you live close by. Many courthouses and recorders offices have free access terminals open to the public. Certain records, such as corporate or UCC (Uniform Commercial Code) records generally found at the Secretary of State, can be viewed or pulled for free, but will incur a fee for copies. A signed release is a common requirement for accessing motor vehicle and criminal records.

Mail, Fax, or Telephone

Although some agencies permit phone or fax requests, the majority of agencies prefer mail requests. Some agencies consider fax requesting to be an expedited service that incurs higher fees. Agencies that permit telephone requests may merely answer "Yes" or "No" to questions such as "Does John Doe have a civil court case in his name?" We have indicated when telephone and fax requesting is available, as well as the extent of the service.

Online and the Internet

The Internet may be a free means to certain agency records or may be the conduit to a subscription or commercial site. This commercial online access method of public records is much more prevalent at the state level compared to the county level. Many agencies, such as DMVs, make the information available to pre-approved, high volume, ongoing accounts. Typically, this access involves fees and a specified, minimum amount of usage.

However, there is a definite trend of certain agencies posting public record data on the Internet for free. Two examples are Secretary of State offices (whose records include corporation, UCC and tax liens) and county/city tax assessor offices (whose records reveal property ownership). Usually this information is limited to name indexes and summary data, rather than document images. In addition, a growing number of state licensing boards are posting their membership lists on the net (although addresses and phone numbers of the licensed individuals typically are not listed).

Also, the Internet is a good place to find *general* information about government agencies. Many web sites enable one to download, read and/or print current forms, policies and regulations.

Hire Someone Else

As mentioned previously, one method to access public records is from a vendor. These companies must comply with state and federal laws, thus if the government agency will not a release a record, chances are a vendor company will not either. There are a variety of types of companies that can be hired to perform record searches. An excellent, quick source to find the right vendor for a particular need is www.publicrecordsources.com or *The Directory of Local Court & County Record Retrievers*.

Bulk or Database Purchases

Many agencies offer programs to purchase all or parts of their database for statistical or commercial purposes. The restrictions vary widely from state to state, even within the same record type or category. Typically, records are available (to those who qualify) in the following media types; magnetic tapes, FTP, cartridges, paper printouts, labels, disks, CDs, microfiche and/or microfilm. Throughout the individual state chapters, we have indicated where these bulk purchases are available, to whom, and for what purposes as well as the costs involved.

Using the Freedom of Information Act and Other Acts

The Federal Freedom of Information Act has no bearing on state, county or local government agencies because these agencies are subject to that state's individual act. Further, the government agencies profiled in this book generally already have systems in place to release information and the act is not needed. However, if you are trying to obtain records from agencies beyond the scope of this book, there are many useful Internet sites that will give you the information you need to complete such a request. We can recommend these sites:

www.epic.org/open_gov/rights.html

www.usdoj.gov/04foia/

Fees, Charges, and Usage

Public records are not necessarily free of charge, certainly not if they are maintained by private industry. Remember that **public records are records of incidents or transactions**. These incidents can be civil or criminal court actions, recordings, filings or occurrences such as speeding tickets or accidents. **It costs money** (time, salaries, supplies, etc.) **to record and track these events**. Common charges found at the government level include copy fees (to make copies of the document), search fees (for clerical personnel to search for the record), and certification fees (to certify that a document as being accurate and coming from the particular agency). Fees can vary from $.10 per page for copies to a $25.00 search fee for government personnel to do the actual look-up. Some government agencies will allow you to walk in and view records at no charge. Fewer will release information over the phone for no fee.

Commercial online access of government-held records usually costs less money on a per record basis than non-online. A key to purchasing public records online direct from some government agencies is the frequency of usage requirements. Many agencies require a minimum amount of requests per month or per session. Certainly, it does not make economic sense to spend a lot of money on programming and set-up fees if you intend on ordering only five records per month. You would be better off to do the search by more conventional methods (mail, visit in person) or hire a search vendor. Going direct online to the source is not always the least expensive option!

If a private enterprise is in the business of maintaining a public records database, it generally does so to offer these records for resale. Typical clients include financial institutions, the legal industry, the insurance industry, and pre-employment screening firms among others. Usually, records are sold via online access or on a CD-ROM.

Also, there are a number of public record search firms—companies that will do a name search—for a fee. These companies do not warehouse the records, but search on demand for a specific name.

Private companies usually offer different price levels based on volume of usage, while government agencies have one price per category, regardless of the amount of requests.

A Few Myths About Searching Public Records Online

The availability of online public records is not as widespread as one might think. According to our research, only *25% of public records can be found online*. Most of the county agencies offering online access are the recorders' offices and tax assessors. You will not find an abundance of criminal and civil court records, except at the federal court level.

At the state level, UCC Filing and corporation and business ownership records are frequently found online. A strong word of caution—many government online sources should not be used as the sole search for true due diligence needs, such as compliance with the Fair Credit Reporting Act. Many government web sites offering online record access include a warning or disclosure statement that the data can have errors and/or should be used for informational purposes only.

The last section of this book examines over 200 private companies that offer online access to their proprietary databases (or gateways) of public record information. Keep in mind they present many records that may not be otherwise found online via the government online sources.

Public Record & Public Information Categories

The following descriptions of the record categories fall into our definitions of either "public records" or "public information."

In considering these definitions, keep the following points in mind:

- Very little government record information is truly open to the public. Even presumably harmless information is subject to restrictions somewhere in the US. Likewise items that you believe should be highly confidential are probably considered "public information" in one or more states.

- Just because your state or county has certain rules, regulations and practices regarding the accessibility and content of public records does not mean that any other state or county follows the same rules.

Business Records

Each state maintains basic information about businesses that register with them for the purpose of making their business name public and protecting its uniqueness. A number of states offer this information online. In fact, there is a trend for state agencies to use the Internet as a means to provide this information. The amount of business information collected by government agencies varies widely from state to state. Much, but not all, of the information collected by government agencies is open to public inspection. For example, annual reports are not available in some states, yet may be available for a fee in others.

As in many other categories, private companies purchase and/or compile a database for resale via online. Fees are based on volume.

Below are summaries of the main types of business records.

Corporation Records (found at the state level)

Checking to see if a corporation is incorporated is considered a "**status check.**" The information that results from a status check typically includes the date of incorporation, status, type, registered agent and, sometimes, officers or directors. This is a good way to find the start of a paper trail and/or to find affiliates of the subject of your search. Some states permit status checks over the telephone.

If available, articles of incorporation (or amendments to them) as well as copies of annual reports may also provide useful information about a business or business owner. However, corporate records may *not* be a good source for a business address because most states allow corporations to use a registered agent as their address for service of process.

Partnership Records (found at the state level)

Some state statutes require registration of certain kinds of partnerships at the state level. Sometimes, these partner names and addresses may be available from the same office that handles corporation records. Some states have a department created specifically to administer limited partnerships and the records associated with them. These filings provide a wealth of information about other partners. Such information can be used to uncover other businesses that may be registered as well.

Limited Liability Companies (found at state level)

A newer form of business entity, similar to a corporation but has the favorable tax characteristics of a partnership, is known as the Limited Liability Company (LLC). An LLC is legal in most every state. An offspring of this, which many states now permit, is the Limited Liability Partnership (LLP).

Trademark & Trade Name (found at state or county levels)

"Trade names" and "trademarks" are relative terms. A trademark may be known as a "service mark." Trade names may be referred to as "fictitious names," "assumed names," or "DBAs." States (or counties) will not let two entities register and use the same or close to the same name or trademark

Typically, the agency that oversees corporation records usually maintains the files for trademarks and/or trade names. Most states will allow verbal status checks of names or worded marks. Some states will administer "fictitious names" at the state level while county agencies administer "trade names," or vice versa.

Patents & Copyrights (found at federal level)

The federal government controls copyrights and patents. Several private companies maintain online searchable databases of trademarks, service marks, and patents.

The filing for public review of trademarks and patents is designed to protect these assets from copying.

Sales Tax Registrations (found at state level)

Any individual or firm that sells applicable goods or services to an end-user is required to register with the appropriate state agency. Such registration is necessary to collect applicable sales tax on the goods and services, and to ensure remittance of those taxes to the state.

45 states collect some sort of sales tax on a variety of goods and services. Of these, 38 will at the very least confirm that a tax permit exists. Each sales tax registrant is given a special state tax permit number, which may be called by various names, including tax ID number or seller's permit number. These numbers are not to be confused with the federal employer identification number.

SEC & Other Financial Data

The Federal Securities and Exchange Commission (SEC) is the public repository for information about publicly held companies. These companies are required to share their material facts with existing and prospective stockholders. See page 56 for information about the SEC database EDGAR.

Private companies, on the other hand, are not subject to public scrutiny. Their financial information is public information only to the extent that the company itself decides to disclose information.

Lien and Security Interest Records

Liens filed by the government and others against individuals and businesses without their consent. Liens are filed, according to a state's law, either at a state agency or county recorder's office. Some states require filing at both locations.

Mortgages and UCC liens are voluntary liens accepted by a borrower in order to obtain financing. Involuntary liens, on the other hand, arise by action of law against a person or business owing a debt that would otherwise be unsecured. The federal and state governments file tax liens when there is a failure to pay income or withholding taxes. Another example: a contractor can file a mechanic's lien to be first in line to receive payment for materials used on a job.

States that offer online access to corporate records generally make their lien records available online also. While there is less likelihood of finding this information online at the local government level, a limited number of local recorder offices make the information available online.

> **Editor's Tip:** Liens are a very competitive arena for private companies offering online access. There are several nationwide databases available as well as a number of strong regional companies who offer this information online to their clientele.

Uniform Commercial Code (found at state and county or city levels)

All 50 states and the District of Columbia have passed a version of the model Uniform Commercial Code (UCC). UCC filings are used to record liens in financing transactions such as equipment loans, leases, inventory loans, and accounts receivable financing. The Code allows potential lenders to be notified that certain assets of a debtor are already used to secure a loan or lease. *Therefore, examining UCC filings is an excellent way to find bank accounts, security interests, financiers, and assets.*

Revised Article 9 of the Code (see page 37) made significant changes to the location of filings and records. Prior to July 2001, of the 7.5 million new UCC financing statements filed annually, 2.5 million were filed at the state level; 5 million were filed at the local level. Now, less than 3% of filings are done so at the local level. Although there are significant variations among state statutes, the state level is usually a good starting place to uncover liens filed against an individual or business.

Tax Liens (found at state and county or city levels)

The federal government and every state have some sort of taxes, such as those associated with sales, income, withholding, unemployment, and/or personal property. When these taxes go unpaid, the appropriate state agency can file a lien on the real or personal property of the subject. ***Normally, the state agency that maintains UCC records also maintains tax liens.***

Individuals vs. Businesses

Tax liens filed against individuals are frequently maintained at separate locations from those liens filed against businesses. For example, a large number of states require liens filed against businesses to be filed at a central state location (i.e., Secretary of State's office) and liens against individuals to be filed at the county level (i.e., Recorder, Register of Deeds, Clerk of Court, etc.).

State vs. Federal Liens

Liens on a company may not all be filed in the same location. A federal tax lien will not necessarily be filed (recorded) at the same location/jurisdiction as a lien filed by the state. This holds true for both individual liens and as well as business liens filed against personal property. Typically, state tax liens on personal property will be found where UCCs are filed. ***Tax liens on real property will be found where real property deeds are recorded***, with few exceptions. Unsatisfied state and federal tax liens may be renewed if prescribed by individual state statutes. However, once satisfied, the time the record will remain in the repository before removal varies by jurisdiction.

Real Estate and Tax Assessor (found at county and local levels)

Traditionally, real estate records are public so that everyone can know who owns what property. Liens on real estate must be public so a buyer knows all the facts. The county (or parish) recorder's office is the record source. However, many private companies purchase entire county record databases and create their own database for commercial purposes. This information is generally sold online or in some form of bulk medium such as magnetic tape.

This category of public record is perhaps the fastest growing in regards to freely accessible over the Internet, form both the government and private sectors. We have indicated all the recorder offices that offer web **name queries;** many more offer location searches (using maps and parcel numbers to locate an address).

Bankruptcies (found at federal court level)

This entails case information about people and businesses that have filed for protection under the bankruptcy laws of the United States. Only federal courts handle bankruptcy cases. Many types of financial records maintained by government agencies are considered public records; bankruptcy records, unlike some other court records, are in this class of fully open court records. There are several private companies that compile databases with names and dates of these records.

The federal government offers online access to bankruptcy records through its PACER system. Turn to page 49 for details on this relatively inexpensive access mode.

Court Records

Criminal Records (found at state level, county courts, and federal courts)

There are over 7,000 courts in the US that maintain a database of criminal records. The courts generally submit records of major misdemeanors, felony arrest records and convictions to a central state repository. The states in turn submit criminal record activity to the FBI's National Crime Information Center (which is not open to the public).

Generally, criminal record information at the courthouse is open to the public. Not all state agencies open their criminal records to the public. Of those states that *will* release records to the public, many require fingerprints or signed release forms. The information that *could be* disclosed on the report includes the arrest record, criminal charges, fines, sentencing and incarceration information. In states where records are not released, the best places to search for criminal record activity is at the city or county level with the county or district court clerk. Many of these searches can be done with a phone call.

A handful of states offer the public online access to a central criminal record repository. However, a number of states maintain a central repository of court records open to online access, as you will find in the Government Sources Section.

Other sources of criminal record information come from the state corrections (prison) agencies, and the states' Sexual Offender Registries. Many of these sources are online, as you will find in the next section of this book.

There are a few private companies purchase local records to create databases for resale. Their "online access" of criminal record information usually involves 24-48 hour service, unless they are connected to one of the state court systems, such as in Washington or Maryland. Turn to the Appendix for an excellent article titled "National" Criminal History Database--Issues and Opportunities in Pre-Employment Screening.

Editor's Note: For detailed information about the access and use of criminal records, see BRB Publication's *Criminal Records Book*.

Litigation & Civil Judgments (found at county, local, and federal courts)

Actions under federal laws are found at US District Courts. Actions under state laws are found within the state court system at the county level. Municipalities also have courts. Records of civil litigation case and records about judgments are often collected by commercial database vendors.

There are a several state court systems and a number of local courts that offer online access. These agencies are profiled in the Government Online Sources Section of this book.

There are a number of private companies who create databases of this information for online access by their clients. These companies have the option of purchasing a tape from the government agency or sending personnel with laptop computers to manually gather case information at the courthouse.

For more information about searching, please refer to the Searching County Court Records chapter starting on page 26.

Other Court Records

The local court system offers a myriad of other record types including probate, juvenile, eviction, and domestic relations. Usually, these records are handled by separate courts or by court divisions within the county. Again, please refer to the Searching County Court Records chapter.

Motor Vehicle Records

Driving History Records (found at state level, but, on occasion, accessible at county level)

The retrieval industry often refers to driving records as "MVRs." Typical information on an MVR might include full name, address, Social Security Number, physical description and date of birth along with the conviction and accident history. Also, the license type, restrictions and/or endorsements can provide background data on an individual.

In recent years there have been major changes regarding the release of motor vehicle data to the public. This is a direct result of the Driver's Privacy Protection Act (DPPA). States must differentiate between *permissible users* (14 are designated in DPPA) and *casual requesters* to determine who may receive a record and/or how much personal information is reported on the record. For example, if a state DMV chooses to sell a record to a "casual requester," the record can contain personal information (address, etc.) only with the consent of the subject.

All states offer an electronic means to obtain some type of motor vehicle information, usually by online access or magnetic tape. Over 40 states offer online retrieval to approved accounts. Access is not always immediate; some states require a wait of up to four hours before retrieving the data. In many instances, a minimum order requirement must be agreed to before an online access account is permitted.

Pay particular attention to the restriction requirements mentioned in this category throughout this publication. Refer to pages 66-68 for more information about DPPA and the permissible uses. Also, for those interested in extensive, detailed information about either driver or vehicle records, refer to BRB Publication's *The MVR Book*.

Editor's Tip: Driver history (MVR) information can be ordered online from many search firms throughout the country. However, only a handful of companies have the ability to directly access multiple state DMVs. Most public record search firms and specialty firms buy MVRs from one of these companies and then resell them to clients.

Vehicle & Vessel Ownership, Registration, VINs, Titles, & Liens (found at state and, on occasion, at county level)

State repositories of vehicle/vessel registration and ownership records hold a wide range of information. Generally, record requesters submit a name to uncover vehicle(s) owned or submit vehicle information to obtain an owner's name and address. However, this category of record information is also subject to the DPPA as described above.

The original language of DPPA required the states to offer an "opt out" option to drivers and vehicle owners, if they (the states) sold marketing lists or individual records to casual requesters (those requesters not specifically mentioned in DPPA). Public Law 106-69 reversed this. Effective June 1, 2000, states automatically opt out all individuals, unless the individual specifically asks to be included. While nearly all states have this "opt in" procedure in place, very few individuals request to be placed on marketing lists and such.

Passage of Public Law 106-69 was dramatic since it essentially did away with sales of:

- marketing lists;

- records (with addresses and other personal information) to "casual" requesters;

- record databases to information vendors and database compilers (except for vehicle recall purposes, etc.)

Accident Reports (found at state level or local level)

The State Police or Department of Public Safety usually maintains accident reports. For the purposes of this publication, "accident records" are designated as those prepared by the investigating officer. Copies of a *citizen's* accident report are not usually available to the public and are not reviewed herein. Typical information found on a state accident report includes drivers' addresses and license numbers as well as a description of the incident. Accidents investigated by local officials or minor accidents where the damage does not exceed a reporting limit (such as $1,000), are not available from state agencies. When state DMV's hold accident reports, they follow the DPPA guidelines with regards to record requests.

Other Important Records on Individuals & Businesses

Addresses & Telephone Numbers

This category of online information may be obtained from either government or private sources. As the most elementary of public information categories, address and telephone numbers are no longer considered restricted information by most people. Even though you have an unlisted telephone number, it still can be found if you have listed that number on, for example, a voter registration card or magazine subscription form.

Some government agencies offer customized lists for sale. Typical types of agencies include those holding motor vehicle, voter registration, corporation filings, or business license records.

Private companies develop databases of addresses and telephone numbers in two ways. They may do this in the normal course of business, such as phone companies, credit card companies, or credit bureaus. Or, they may purchase and merge government and/or private company databases to create their own database. They then sell this "new database" online in a batch format, perhaps on CD-ROM. These companies must be careful to follow any restrictions that government agencies may place on the release of the data. For example, Experian collects information about vehicle owners to supply vehicle manufacturers with address and telephone data for vehicle recalls. Experian also sells information from that same database for direct marketing purposes, but only if state regulations permit.

The Internet is filled with people-finder sites; most search engines have one, which is an excellent way to do a national white-pages search.

GED Records (found at state level)

By contacting the state offices that oversee GED Records, one can verify whether someone truly received a GED certificate for the high school education equivalency. These records are useful for pre-employment screening or background checking purposes. Few GED agencies offer online access to records, but most state agencies will verify over the phone the existence of a GED certificate. Many even offer copies of transcripts free-of-charge. When doing a record search, you must know the name of the student at the time of the test and a general idea of the year and test location. GED Records are *not* useful when trying to locate an individual.

Licensing & Business Registration (found at state boards)

Occupational licenses and business registrations contain a plethora of information readily available from various state agencies. A common reason to call these agencies is to corroborate professional or industry credentials. Often, a telephone call to the agency may secure an address and phone number.

For more information, turn to pages 42-45 for the chapter Searching State Occupational Licensing Boards.

Medical

Medical record Information about an individual's medical status and history are summarized in various repositories that are accessible only to authorized insurance and other private company employees. Medical information is neither public information nor closed record. Like credit information, it is not meant to be shared with anyone, unless you give authorization.

Military

Each branch maintains its own records. Much of this, such as years of service and rank, is open public record. However, some details in the file of an individual may be subject to restrictions on access—approval by the subject may be required.

For more information about military records, turn to page 57.

Voter Registration (found at state & county levels)

Voting Registration Records are a good place to find addresses and voting history, and can generally be viewed at the local level.

Every state has a central election agency or commission, and most have a central repository of voter information collected from the county level agencies. The degree or level of accessibility to these records varies widely from state to state. Over half of the states will sell portions of the registered voter database, but only 10 states permit individual searching by name. Most states only allow access for political purposes such as "Get Out the Vote" campaigns or compilation of campaign contribution lists. Nearly every state and local agency blocks the release of Social Security Numbers and telephone numbers found on these records.

Several private companies purchase databases from states wherein voter registration information is "open," and make that data available online. Profiles of these companies are included in this book.

Vital Records: Birth, Death, Marriage, & Divorce Records (found at state & county levels)

Copies of vital record certificates are needed for a variety of reasons—social security, jobs, passports, family history, litigation, lost heir searching, proof of identity, etc. Most states understand the urgency of these requests, and many offer an expedited service. A number of states will take requests over the phone if you use a credit card. Searchers must also be aware that in many instances certain vital records are *not* kept at the state level. The searcher must then turn to city and county record repositories to find the information needed.

Most states offer expedited fax ordering, requiring the use of a credit card, through the services of an outside vendor known as VitalChek. This independent company maintains individual fax order telephone lines at each state office they service. Whether it is behind the scenes or not, ordering vital records by fax typically involves VitalChek in some manner. Also, their web site www.vitalchek.com offers a means to place an online order for a vital record from many states, but results are still mailed.

Older vital records are usually found in the state archives. There is an excellent web site of extensive historical genealogy-related databases at http://ancestry.com/mainv.htm. Another source of historical vital record information is the Family History Library of the Church of Jesus Christ of Latter Day Saints (located at 35 NW Temple, Salt Lake City 84150). They have millions of microfilmed records from church and civil registers from all over the world.

Workers' Compensation Records (found at state level)

Research at state workers' compensation boards is generally limited to determining if an employee has filed a claim and/or obtaining copies of the claim records themselves. With the passage of the Americans with Disabilities Act (ADA) in the early 1990s, using information from workers' compensation boards for pre-employment screening was virtually eliminated. However, a review of workers' compensation histories may only be conducted after a conditional job offer has been made and when medical information is reviewed. The legality of performing this review is subject to individual state statutes, which vary widely. Access to this information is generally restricted to those who have a direct interest in the case. Only a handful of states consider the non-medical portion of their Workers Compensation records to be unrestricted open public record. Few offer the information online.

Several companies purchase and combine entire state databases to create a proprietary database for resale, which may be available online.

Additional Record Sources Worth Reviewing

Aviation Records

Records about pilots and ownership & registration of aircraft are often used by private investigators when doing a background report or looking for assets. Pilots are licensed and aircraft is registered with the Federal Aviation Association (FAA) whose web site is www.faa.gov. Go the Private Database Vendors Indices for a list of private companies offering access to pilot and aircraft records.

Education & Employment

Information about an employee's or prospective employee's schooling, training, education, and jobs is important to any employer. Learning institutions maintain their own records of attendance, completion and degree/certification granted. Also, employers will confirm certain information about former employees. This is an example of private information that becomes public by voluntary disclosure. As part of your credit record, this information would be considered restricted. If, however, you disclose this information to Who's Who, or to a credit card company, it becomes public information.

Environmental

Information about hazards to the environment is critical. There is little tradition and less law regarding how open or restricted information is at the state and local (recorder's office) levels. Most information on hazardous materials, soil composition, even OSHA inspection reports is public record. But many federal web sites have removed information since 9-11.

OSHA stands for Occupational Safety & Health Administration, which is part of the US Department of Labor. Their web site is www.osha.gov/.

Another federal government source is the US Environmental Protection Agency found at www.epa.gov/records/. According to Author Alan Schlein (*Find it Online*) the EPA "…no longer allows direct access to the Envirofacts databases, which explain what toxic chemicals are found in water, hazardous waste, toxic waste, and Superfund sites, and is broken down by community. The EPA had originally created the database to provide the public with direct access to the wealth of information contained in its databases. The public is no longer able to access the information."

State Legislation & Regulations

Telephone numbers, costs and procedures for obtaining copies of passed and pending bills are listed under the heading "Legislation." Most state legislative bodies offer free Internet access to bill text and status, some even offer subject queries. Notwithstanding federal guidelines, the state legislatures and legislators control the policies and provisions for the release of state held information. Every year there is a multitude of bills introduced in state legislatures that would, if passed, create major changes in the access and retrieval of records and personal information.

Tenant History

This, like credit history, is another example of a combination of public and proprietary information collected by private businesses for the purpose of tracking an element of personal life important to an industry—in this case the housing rental industry. Database vendors often collect rental history records from property managers and owners. The records are often shared within the industry on a restricted online basis according to disclosure rules set by the companies themselves. Another important part of a Tenant History is a search for eviction notices (forcible detainers) at the local courts. Again, these court records are entered into a vendor's database for re-sale.

A list of vendors who have created a proprietary database is found at the back of the Private Database Vendors Section.

Credit Information and Social Security Numbers

Social Security Numbers

The Social Security Number (SSN) is the subject of a persistent struggle between privacy rights groups and various business interests. The truth is that many individuals gave up the privacy of their number by writing it on a voter registration form, product registration form, or any of a myriad of other voluntary disclosures made over the years. It is probable that a good researcher can still legally find the SSN of anyone (along with at least an approximate birth date) with some ease. In the past, a major source of finding a SSN was in the "header" of a credit report. But not any more, see below.

Credit Information

Credit data is derived from financial transactions of people or businesses. **Private companies maintain this information; government only regulates access.** Certain credit information about individuals is restricted by law, such as the Fair Credit Reporting Act, at the federal level and by even more restrictive laws in many states. Credit information about businesses is not restricted by law and is fully open to anyone who requests (pays for) it.

A credit report essentially has two parts—the credit header and the credit history. A credit header is essentially the upper portion of a credit report containing the Social Security Number, age, phone number, last several addresses, and any AKAs. Recently, access to credit header information (see below) has been closed to most business entities.

> **Editor's Tip:** Keep in mind that a business' credit information is not restricted by law and is fully open to anyone who requests and pays for it.

Credit Header Ban Went Into Effect July 1st, 2001

July 1st, 2001 was an important date for skiptracers, fraud investigators, and other businesses that rely on "credit headers." This information has always been available without the consent of the individual (subject). Per a federal court ruling, beginning July 1st 2001, access to credit header information was treated in the same manner as access to credit reports—there has to be permission granted by the individual.

The basis of this ban is traced to the Gramm-Leach-Bliley Act (GLB). Section 502 of this act prohibits a financial institution from disclosing nonpublic personal information about a consumer to non-affiliated third parties, unless a consumer has elected not to opt out from disclosure. Trans Union and other members of the Individual References Services Group (IRSG), among others, filed suit in an effort to keep this information open for "appropriate commercial purposes." The ruling, dated April 30th, denied this argument. The sale of credit headers seemed to be on borrowed time anyway—originally, the ban was to begin November 2000. However, due to the lawsuits and action involving the FTC, a provision changed the start of the ban until July 1st, 2001.

Impact of Changes

The impact of the ruling (and an FTC opinion) was far ranging. The ruling restricted credit bureaus from selling the above-mentioned data to information vendors who compile their own proprietary databases. But there are some alternatives to those business entities that rely on this type of public record information. The data is grandfathered. Provider companies that purchased files from the credit bureaus can continue to sell the data to their customers. Although data will never be updated from the credit bureaus, the existing data can still be used without the restrictions imposed by the ruling.

According to our friends at Merlin Information Services, TransUnion has created the only IRSG compliant "Super File" known as the TUCS file. This file contains identifying information such as Social Security Numbers and dates of birth, obtained from financial institutions before GLB went into effect on July 1, 2001. Since that date, the file has been updated from public record sources, phone listings and postal change of address information.

The Gramm-Leach-Bliley Act did not deny access to public record sources or databases that may contain age, SSN, phone, prior addresses, and AKAs. The Act only forbid financial institutions from disclosing this data. Therefore, those businesses that were shut-off from credit headers, had to investigate alternative sources of public records.

Searching County Court Records

Some Court Basics

Before trudging into a courthouse and demanding to view a document, you should first be aware of some basic court procedures. Whether the case is filed in a state, municipal, or federal court, each case follows a similar process.

The term "County Courts," as used in this publication, refers to those courts of original jurisdiction (trial courts) within each state's court system that handle...

Felonies	Generally defined as crimes punishable by one year or more of jail time
Civil Actions	For money damages (usually greater than $3,000)
Probate	Estate matters
Misdemeanors	Generally defined as minor infractions with a fine or minimal jail time
Evictions	Landlord/tenant actions
Small Claims	Actions for minor money damages (generally under $3,000)

A *civil case* usually commences when a plaintiff files a complaint with a court against defendants. The defendants respond to the complaint with an answer. After this initial round, there may be literally hundreds of activities before the court issues a judgment. These activities can include revised complaints and their answers, motions of various kinds, discovery proceedings (including depositions) to establish the documentation and facts involved in the case. All of these activities are listed on a **docket sheet**, which may be a piece of paper or a computerized index.

Once the court issues a judgment, either party may appeal the ruling to an appellate division or court. In the case of a money judgment, the winning side can usually file it as a judgment lien with the county recorder. Appellate divisions usually deal only with legal issues and not the facts of the case.

In a *criminal case*, the plaintiff is a government jurisdiction. The Government brings the action against the defendant for violation of one or more of its statutes.

In a *bankruptcy case,* which can be heard only in federal courts, there is neither defendant nor plaintiff. Instead, the debtor files voluntarily for bankruptcy protection against creditors, or the creditors file against the debtor in order to force the debtor into involuntary bankruptcy.

State Court Structure

The secret to determining where a state court case is located is to understand how the court system is structured in that particular state. The general structure of all state court systems has four parts:

Appellate courts   Limited jurisdiction trial courts

Intermediate appellate courts   General jurisdiction trial courts

The two highest levels, appellate and intermediate appellate courts, only hear cases on appeal from the trial courts. Opinions of these appellate courts are of interest primarily to attorneys seeking legal precedents for new cases.

General jurisdiction trial courts usually handle a full range of civil and criminal litigation. These courts usually handle felonies and larger civil cases.

Limited jurisdiction trial courts come in two varieties. First, many limited jurisdiction courts handle smaller civil claims (usually $10,000 or less), misdemeanors, and pretrial hearing for felonies. Second, some of these courts, sometimes called special jurisdiction courts, are limited to one type of litigation, for example the Court of Claims in New York, which only handles liability cases against the state.

Some states, for instance Iowa, have consolidated their general and limited jurisdiction court structure into one combined court system. In other states there may be a further distinction between state-supported courts and municipal courts. In New York, for example, nearly 1,300 Justice Courts handle local ordinance and traffic violations, including DWI.

Generalizations should not be made about where specific types of cases are handled in the various states. Misdemeanors, probate, landlord/tenant (eviction), domestic relations, and juvenile cases may be handled in either or both the general and limited jurisdiction courts. To help you locate the correct court to perform your search in, this publication specifically lists the types of cases handled by each court.

How Courts Maintain Records

Case Numbering

When a case is filed, it is assigned a case number. This is the primary indexing method in every court. Therefore, in searching for case records, you will need to know—or find—the applicable case number. If you have the number in good form already, your search should be fast and reasonably inexpensive.

You should be aware that case numbering procedures are not consistent throughout a state court system. One district may assign numbers by district while another may assign numbers by location (division) within the district, or by judge. Remember: case numbers appearing in legal text citations may not be adequate for searching unless they appear in the proper form for the particular court in which you are searching.

The Docket Sheet

Information from cover sheets and from documents filed as a case goes forward is recorded on the docket sheet. The docket sheet then contains an outline of the case history from initial filing to its current status. While docket sheets differ somewhat in format, the basic information contained on a docket sheet is consistent from court to court. All docket sheets contain:

- Name of court, including location (division) and the judge assigned;

- Case number and case name;

- Names of all plaintiffs and defendants/debtors;

- Names and addresses of attorneys for the plaintiff or debtor;

- Nature and cause (e.g., statute) of action.

Computerization

Most courts are computerized, which means that the docket sheet data is entered into a computer system. Within a state or judicial district, the courts *may* be linked together via a single computer system.

Docket sheets from cases closed before the advent of computerization may not be in the computer system. For pre-computer cases, most courts keep summary case information on microfilm, microfiche, or index cards.

Case documents are not generally available on computer because courts are still experimenting with and developing electronic filing and imaging of court documents. Generally, documents are only available to be copied by contacting the court where the case records are located.

Searching State Courts Online

Online searching is generally limited to a copy of the courts' docket sheets (see above). Most courts are computerized in-house, which means that the docket sheet data is entered into a computer system of the courthouse itself. Checking a courthouse's computer index is the quickest way to find if case records exist online.

A growing number of state courts provide electronic access to their records, as you will see on the Table on pages 40-41. Details to these systems are found in the Government Online Sources Section. For example, in Alabama, Maryland, Minnesota, New Mexico, Oregon, Washington, and Wisconsin where "statewide" online systems are available, you still need to understand (1) the court structure in that state, (2) which particular courts are included in their online system, and (3) what types of cases are included.

Without proper consideration of these variables, these online systems are subject to misuse, which can lead to disastrous consequences like failing to discover that an applicant for a security guard position is a convicted burglar.

If Records Are Not Available Online

If you need copies of case records, court personnel may make copies for you for a fee, or you may be able to make copies yourself if the court allows. Also, court personnel may certify the document for you for a fee. Perhaps due to a shortage of staff or fear of litigation, some courts that previously would conduct searches of criminal records on behalf of the public are no longer making that service available. Typically, these courts do one of two things. In some states, such as Kentucky, the courts refer the searcher to a state agency that maintains a database combining individual court records (which may not be very current). In other states, such as Nebraska, the courts simply refuse to conduct searches, leaving the searcher with no choice but to use a local retrieval firm or other individual to conduct the search on his or her behalf.

Court Record Searching Tips

Learn the Index & Record Systems

Most civil courts index records by both plaintiffs as well as the defendants, but some only index by the defendant name. A plaintiff search is useful, for example, to determine if someone is especially litigious.

During the past decade, thousands of courts have installed computerized indexing systems. The year when computer indexing started in each of these courts is indicated in the profile of most of the automated courts. Computerized systems are considerably faster and easier to search, allowing for more indexing capability than the microfilm and card indexes that preceded them.

Understand the Search Requirements

There is a strong tendency for courts to overstate their search requirements. For civil cases, the usual reasonable requirement is a defendant (or plaintiff) name—full name if it is a common name—and the time frame to search—e.g., 1993-2002. For criminal cases, the court may require more identification, such as date of birth (DOB), to ascertain the correct individual. Other information "required" by courts— such as Social Security Number (SSN)—is often just "helpful" to narrow the search on a common name. Further, we have indicated when certain pieces of information may be helpful but are not required.

Be Aware of Restricted Records

Most courts have a number of types of case records, such as juvenile and adoptions, which are not released without a court order. These types are indicated in each profile.

Other Court Search Tips

- Watch for name variations from state to state. Do not assume that the structure of the court system in another state is anything like your own. In one state, the Circuit Court may be the highest trial court whereas in another it is a limited jurisdiction court. Examples are: (1) New York, where the Supreme Court is not very "supreme," and the downstate court structure varies from upstate; and (2) Tennessee, where circuit courts are in districts.

- In many instances two types of courts within a county (e.g., circuit and district) are combined. When phoning or writing these courts, we recommend that your request specifically state in your request that you want both courts included in the search.

- Be aware that the number of courts that no longer conduct name searches has risen. For these courts, you must hire a local retriever, directly or through a search company, to search for you. It should be noted that usually these courts still take specific document copy requests by mail. Because of long mail turnaround times and court fees, local retrievers are frequently used even when the court will honor a request by mail. A court's entry indicates if it is one of the many to offer a public access terminal, free of charge, to view case documents or indexes.

- When searching for case records, keep in mind that many of the higher level courts also handle appeals from lower courts.

- Where more than one court has jurisdiction for a particular kind of civil case, the minimum and maximum claim fields clarify whether there is overlapping jurisdiction in the state. In most states, the lower and upper court civil claim limits dovetail nicely between the court levels, so you can readily tell which court has the type of civil case you are concerned about.

- If you send requests by mail, send a self-addressed, stamped envelope (SASE). This may very well insure quicker service.

Searching Recording Office Records

The Lowdown on Recorded Documents

Documents filed and record at local county, parish, city or town offices represent some of the best opportunities to gain access to open public records, especially if you are searching online. If you are lucky enough to live in close proximity, you can visit your local office and, for free, view records. Recorded documents are also one of the most available types of public records that can be viewed or obtain via online and through the Internet.

Real Estate

As mentioned previously, real estate records are public so that everyone can know who owns what property. Liens on real estate must be public so a buyer knows all the facts. The county (or parish or city) recorder's office is the source. Also, access is also available from many private companies that purchase entire county record databases and create their own database for commercial purposes.

Uniform Commercial Code (UCC)

UCC filings are to personal property what mortgages are to real estate property. UCCs are in the category of financial records that must be fully open to public scrutiny so that other potential lenders are on notice about which assets of the borrower have been pledged as collateral.

As with tax liens, UCC recordings are filed, according to state law, either at the state or local (county, town, parish) level. Until June 30, 2001, liens on certain types of companies required dual filing (must file at BOTH locations, thus records can be searched at BOTH locations). As of July 1, 2001, UCC filings other than those that go into real estate records are no longer filed at the local filing offices in most states, but older filings can still be located there until 2008. As with real estate records, there are a number of private companies who have created their own databases for commercial resale.

A Great Source of Information

Although recorded documents are a necessity to making an informed business-related decision, they are also a virtual treasure trove of data. UCC filing documents will you the names and addresses of creditors and debtors, describe the asset offered for collateral, the date of the filing, and whether or note the loan has been satisfied. This information contained on the statements can lead an experience investigator to other roads done the information trail. For example, if the collateral is a plane or a vessel, this will lead to registration records or if the debtor is a business, other names on the filing may lead to other traceable business partners or ventures.

Recording Office Searching Rules

The general rules for background searching of UCC records are as follows:

- *Except in local filing states, a search at the state level is adequate to locate all UCC records on a subject.*

- *Mortgage record searches will include any real estate related UCC filings.*

See pages 36-37 for discussions of special collateral rules.

Due diligence searching, however, usually demands searching the local records in dual filing states as well.

The County Rule

Where to search for recorded documents usually isn't a difficult problem to overcome in everyday practice. In most states, these transactions are recorded at one designated recording office in the county where the property is located.

We call this the "County Rule." It applies to types of public records such as real estate recordings, tax liens, Uniform Commercial Code (UCC) filings, vital records, and voter registration records. However, as with most government rules, there are a variety of exceptions, which are summarized here.

The Exceptions

The five categories of exceptions to the County Rule (or Parish Rule, if searching in Louisiana) are listed below (the details are listed in the chart to follow)—

- Special Recording Districts (AK, HI)

- Multiple Recording Offices (AL, AR, IA, KY, ME, MA, MS, TN)

- Independent Cities (MD, MO, NV, VA)

- Recording at the Municipal Level (CT, RI, VT)
- Identical Names—Different Place (CT, IL, MA, NE, NH, PA, RI, VT, VA)

The Personal Property Problem and the Fifth Exception

The real estate recording system in the US is self-auditing to the extent that you generally cannot record a document in the wrong recording office. However, many documents are rejected for recording because they are submitted to the wrong recording office. There are a number of reasons why this occurs, one of which is the overlap of filing locations for real estate and UCC.

Finding the right location of a related UCC filing is a different and much more difficult problem from finding a real estate recording. In the majority of states, the usual place to file a UCC financing statement is at the Secretary of States office—these are called central filing states. In the dual and local filing states, the place to file, in addition to the central filing office, is usually at the same office where your real estate documents are recorded. However, where there are identical place names referring to two different places, it becomes quite confusing, so hence, the fifth exemption.

The County Rule—Exceptions Chart

Each of these five categories of recording exceptions is summarized below by state.

AL	Four counties contain two separate recording offices. They are Barbour, Coffee, Jefferson, and St. Clair.
AK	The 23 Alaskan counties are called boroughs. However, real estate recording is done under a system that was established at the time of the Gold Rush (whenever that was) of **34 Recording Districts**. Some of the Districts are identical in geography to boroughs, such as the Aleutian Islands, but other boroughs and districts overlap. Therefore, you need to know which recording district any given town or city is located in.
AR	Ten counties contain two separate recording offices. They are Arkansas, Carroll, Clay, Craighead, Franklin, Logan, Mississippi, Prairie, Sebastian, and Yell.
CT	There is **no county recording** in this state. All recording is done at the city/town level. Lenders persist in attempting to record or file documents in the counties of Fairfield, Hartford, Litchfield, New Haven, New London, Tolland, and Windham related to property located in other cities/towns because each of these cities/towns bears the same name as a Connecticut county.
HI	All recording is done at one central office.

IL	Cook County has separate offices for real estate recording and UCC filing.
IA	Lee county has two recording offices.
KY	Kenton County has two recording offices. Jefferson County has a separate office for UCC filing.
LA	Louisiana counties are called **Parishes**. One parish, St. Martin, has two non-contiguous segments.
ME	Aroostock and Oxford counties have two separate recording offices.
MD	The City of Baltimore has its own separate recording office.
MA	Berkshire and Bristol counties each has three recording offices. Essex, Middlesex and Worcester counties each has two recording offices. Cities/towns bearing the same name as a county are Barnstable, Essex, Franklin, Hampden, Nantucket, Norfolk, Plymouth, and Worcester. UCC financing statements on personal property collateral are submitted to cities/towns, while real estate recording is handled by the counties.
MS	Ten counties contain two separate recording offices. They are Bolivar, Carroll, Chickasaw, Harrison, Hinds, Jasper, Jones, Panola, Tallahatchie, and Yalobusha.
MO	The City of St. Louis has its own recording office.
NE	Fifteen counties have separate offices for real estate recording and for UCC filing.
NH	Cities/towns bearing the same name as a county are Carroll, Grafton, Hillsborough, Merrimack, Strafford, and Sullivan. UCC financing statements on personal property collateral are submitted to cities/towns, while real estate recording is handled by the counties.
NV	Carson City has its own recording office.
PA	Each county has a separate recording office and prothonotary office. UCC financing statements on personal property are submitted to the prothonotary, and real estate documents are submitted to the recorder.
RI	There is **no county recording** in this state. All recording is done at the city/town level. Lenders persist in attempting to record or file documents in the counties of Bristol, Newport, and Providence related to property located in other cities/ towns because each of these cities/towns bears the same name as a Rhode Island county.
TN	Sullivan County has two separate recording offices.

VT	There is **no county recording** in this state. All recording is done at the city/town level. Lenders persist in attempting to record or file documents in the counties of Addison, Bennington, Chittenden, Essex, Franklin, Grand Isle, Orange, Rutland, Washington, Windham, and Windsor related to property located in other cities/towns because each of these cities/towns bears the same name as a Vermont county. Adding to the confusion, there are four place names in the state that refer to both a city and a town: Barre, Newport, Rutland, and St. Albans.
VA	There are 41 independent cities in Virginia. Twenty-seven have separate recording offices. The following 15 share their filing offices with the surrounding county:

INDEPENDENT CITY	*FILE IN*
Bedford	Bedford County
Covington	Alleghany County
Emporia	Greenville County
Fairfax	Fairfax County
Falls Church	Arlington or Fairfax County
Franklin	Southhampton County
Galax	Carroll County
Harrisonburg	Rockingham County
Lexington	Rockbridge County
Manassas	Prince William County
Manassas Park	Prince William County
Norton	Wise County
Poquoson	York County
South Boston	Halifax County
Williamsburg	James City County

Online Searching For Asset/Lien Records

A growing number of county government jurisdictions provide online access to recorded documents and they can be found in the Government Online Sources Section. Many are fee sites, but the number of free sites available via the Internet is increasing.

Keep in mind there are a number of private companies who compile and maintain these records and offer them for resale, and they offer the most comprehensive source. Look for a list of these companies in the Index portion of the Private Database Vendors Section.

Special Categories of Collateral

Real Estate Related UCC Collateral

A specific purpose of lien statutes under both the UCC and real estate laws is to put a buyer or potential secured creditor on notice that someone has a prior security interest in real or personal property. UCC financing statements are to personal property what mortgages or deeds of trust are to real property.

One problem addressed by the UCC is that certain types of property have the characteristics of both real and personal property. In those instances, it is necessary to have a way to provide lien notice to two different categories of interested parties: those who deal with the real estate aspect of the property and those who deal with the "personal" aspect of the property.

In general, our definition of real estate related UCC collateral is any property that in one form is attached to land, but that in another form is not attached. For the sake of simplicity, we can define the characteristics of two broad types of property that meet this definition:

Property that is initially attached to real property, but then is separated.
Three specific types of collateral have this characteristic: *minerals* (including oil and gas), *timber*, and *crops*. These things are grown on or extracted from land. While they are on or in the ground they are thought of as real property, but once they are harvested or extracted they become personal property. Some states have a separate central filing system for crops.

Property that is initially personal property, but then is attached to land, generally called ***fixtures***.
Equipment such as telephone systems or heavy industrial equipment permanently affixed to a building are examples of fixtures. It is important to realize that what is a fixture, like beauty, is in the eye of the beholder, since it is a vague concept at best.

UCC financing statements applicable to real estate related collateral must be filed where the real estate and mortgage records are kept, which is generally at the county level—except in Connecticut, Rhode Island and Vermont, where the Town/City Clerk maintains these records. The chart gives the titles of the local official who maintains these records.

Consumer Goods

Among the state-to-state variations, some states required filing where real estate is filed for certain consumer goods. However, as of July 1, 2001 all non-realty related UCC filings in most states, including consumer goods, now go only to the central filing office in the state.

Equipment Used in Farming Operations

Until recently, 33 states required only local filing for equipment used in farming operations. However as of July 1, 2001, all non-realty-related UCC filing has been centralized.

Searching Note

If you are looking for information on subjects that might have these types of filings against them, a search of county records may still be revealing even if you would normally search only at the state level.

The Importance of Revised Article 9

Revised Article 9

On July 1, 2001, Revised Article 9 became law in 46 states and the District of Columbia, with 4 states adopting the law later; Alabama (January 1, 2002), Connecticut (October 1, 2001), Florida (January 1, 2002) and Mississippi (January 1, 2002). Under this new law, most UCC filings will go to the state where a business is organized, not where the collateral or chief executive offices are located. Thus, you will find new filings against IBM only in Delaware (IBM and many other public companies are Delaware corporations), and not in New York or in any other states where it has branch offices. Therefore, you will need to know where a company is organized in order to know where to find new UCC filings against it.

The place to file against individuals is the state where the person resides.

However, the new law does not apply to federal tax liens, which are still generally filed where the chief executive office is located. IBM's chief executive offices, for example, may still be in New York State.

As stated above, realty-related UCC filings continue to go to land recording offices where the property is located.

Old Article 9

Under old Article 9, Uniform Commercial Code financing statements and changes to them might be filed at two or three government agencies in each state, depending upon the type of collateral involved in the transaction. Each state's UCC statute contained variations on a nationally recommended Model Act. Each variation is explained below. You will still need to know about where UCC filings are located under old Article 9 because the transition period to Revised Article 9 is five years long. UCC filings on record before July 1, 2001 remain effective until they lapse, which is generally five years from initial filing date.

A lot of UCC filings against IBM, for example, made before July 1, 2001 will still be on record in New York's central filing office, and may also be found in county filing offices since New York was a dual filing state, as explained below.

Under old Article 9, 33 states were central filing states. Central filing states are those where most types of personal property collateral require filing of a UCC financing statement only at a central filing location within that state.

Under old Article 9, five states had statewide UCC database systems. Some of these systems are still in effect under Revised Article 9. Minnesota and **Wisconsin** were central filing states with a difference: UCC financing statements filed at the county level are also entered into a statewide database. In **North Dakota** UCC financing statements may be filed at either the state or county level, and all filings are entered into a statewide database. In **Louisiana**, **Nebraska**, and **Georgia**, UCC financing statements may be filed with **any** county (parish). Under Revised Article 9, Minnesota has established a county/state system like North Dakota in all but six county offices, and Nebraska is now a central filing state. In each of these six states the records are entered into a central, statewide database that is available for searching in each county, as well as at the state agency (no state agency in Louisiana or Georgia).

Under old Article 9, eight states required dual filing of certain types of UCC financing statements. The usual definition of a dual filing state is one in which financing statements containing collateral such as inventory, equipment or receivables *must* be filed in *both* a central filing office, usually with the Secretary of State, and in a local (county) office where the collateral or business is located. The three states below were also dual filing states, with a difference. Under Revised Article 9, no dual filing is required within a state

Under old Article 9, the filing systems in three states, MA, NH, and PA, can be described as triple filing because the real estate portion of the filings goes to an office separate from the UCC filing offices. In Massachusetts and New Hampshire, UCC filings were submitted to the town/city while real estate filings go to the county. In Pennsylvania, county government was separated into the Prothonotary for UCC filings and the Recorder for real estate filings. The local filing offices for non-realty-related UCC filings no longer take filings under Revised Article 9, but they will continue to perform searches of the old records.

Some counties in other states do have separate addresses for real estate recording, but this is usually just a matter of local departmentalization.

Under old Article 9, Kentucky and Wyoming were the only *local filing only* states. In both of these states a few filings were also found at the state level because filings for out of state debtors went to the Secretary of State. And in Wyoming, filings for Wyoming debtor accounts receivable and farm products require dual filing. However, under Revised Article 9, all filings have been centralized.

Searching Hints — State Agencies

Types of Records Available

Each state has government agencies that maintain records in each of the following categories—

Corporation Records	Workers' Compensation Records
Criminal Records	Sales Tax Registrations
Federal Tax Liens	Vehicle & Ownership Records
Fictitious or Assumed Names	Death Records
Incarceration Records	Sexual Offender Records
Limited Liability Company Records	Divorce Records
Limited Partnership Records	Marriage Records
State Tax Liens	State Investigated Accident Reports
Trademark, Trade Name	Birth Records
Uniform Commercial Code Filings	Driver Records
Vessel Records	Certain Occupational Licensing

Certain of these categories are more apt to offer online access, and some rarely do. For definitions, descriptions and comments about online accessibility of these categories see the Online Information Categories section starting on 13.

Each state chapter in the Government Sources Section begins with the state's web site as well as those of the Attorney General and the State Archives. These are excellent starting points to answer questions about topics or agencies not covered in this book.

State Agency Online Public Record Table

Codes

O	Open to Public – No Charge
$$	Commercial Access – Fees Involved
O-$$	Two Systems (fee & free) *or* Free Index with Fees for Record Copies
S	Severe Access Restrictions (Signed Authorization, etc.)
L	Available Only at Local Level
P	Partial Database Available

Note: If **blank**, then not available online to the public

State	Criminal Records	Prison Records	Sexual Offender	Driver Records	UCC Records	Corp. Records	State Courts
Alabama			O	$$-S	O	O	
Alaska	O-P		O	$$-S	O	O	O-P
Arizona			O	$$-S	O	O-$$	O-P
Arkansas		O		$$-S		O	
California				$$-S	O-$$	O	
Colorado	$$			$$-S	O	O	O-P
Connecticut				$$-S	O	O	O-P
Delaware			O	$$-S			
Dist. of Columbia			O	$$-S	O		
Florida	$$	O	O	$$-S	O	O	
Georgia		O	O	$$-S	$$	O-$$	
Hawaii						O	O
Idaho			O	$$-S	O-$$	O	
Illinois	$$	O	O	$$-S		O-$$	
Indiana	$$	O	O	$$-S	O-$$	O-$$	
Iowa					O	O	O
Kansas			O	$$-S	$$	$$	
Kentucky		O	O	$$-S	O	O	
Louisiana			O	$$-S	$$	O-$$	
Maine				$$-S	O-$$	O	
Maryland			O	$$-S	O	O	O-P
Massachusetts				$$-S	O-$$	O-$$	S
Michigan	$$	O	O	$$-S		O	
Minnesota			O	$$-S	O-$$	O-$$	

State	Criminal Records	Prison Records	Sexual Offender	Driver Records	UCC Records	Corp. Records	State Courts
Mississippi			O	$$-S	O-$$	O	
Missouri				$$-S	O-$$	O	O-P
Montana				$$-S	$$	O	
Nebraska		O	O	$$-S	$$	$$	
Nevada		O		$$-S	$$	O	
New Hampshire				$$-S			
New Jersey			O	$$-S	O-$$	O-$$	$$
New Mexico			O	$$-S	O	O	O-P
New York		O	O	$$-S		O-$$	$$-P
North Carolina		O	O	$$-S	O	O	
North Dakota			O	$$-S	O-$$	O	
Ohio		O		$$-O	O	O	
Oklahoma		O			O		O-P
Oregon	$$				O-$$	O-$$	$$
Pennsylvania	$$	O		$$-S	O	O	
Rhode Island				$$-S		O	O
South Carolina	$$		O	$$-S	O	O	
South Dakota			O	$$-S	$$	O	
Tennessee			O	$$-S	O	O	
Texas	$$		O	$$-S	O-$$	O-$$	
Utah			O	$$-S	O-$$	O-$$	$$
Vermont		O		$$-S	O	O	
Virginia	$$-S		O	$$-S			O-P
Washington	$$				$$	O	$$
West Virginia			O	$$-S		O	
Wisconsin	$$		O	$$-S	O-$$	O	O-P
Wyoming			O	$$-S	$$	O	

Codes

O   Open to Public – No Charge
$$ Commercial Access – Fees Involved
O-$$ Two Systems (fee & free) *or* Free Index with Fees for Record Copies
S   Severe Access Restrictions (Signed Authorization, etc.)
L   Available Only at Local Level
P   Partial Database Available
Note: If **blank**, then not available online to the public

Searching State Occupational Licensing Boards

The Privacy Question

While some agencies consider this information private and confidential, most agencies freely release at least some basic data over the phone or by mail.

Our research indicates that many agencies appear to make their own judgments regarding what specifically is private and confidential in their files. For example, approximately 45% of the agencies indicate that they will disclose adverse information about a registrant, and many others will only disclose selected portions of the information or merely verify a credential.

In any event, the basic rule to follow when you contact a licensing agency is to **ask for the specific kinds of information available.**

What Information May Be Available

An agency may be willing to release part or all of the following—

- Field of Certification
- Status of License/Certificate
- Date License/Certificate Issued
- Date License/Certificate Expires
- Current or Most Recent Employer

- Social Security Number
- Address of Subject
- Complaints, Violations or Disciplinary Actions

The License Searchable Online List

Within the Government Online Sources Section, for each state there is a list of boards and their corresponding URLs that offer **free Internet access** to their records. This means that you can do a name search or query from this web site.

The list of online access boards is one of the fastest growing and most frequently changing categories of public information.

Searching Tips

Of course, not all licensing boards offer Internet access to search for the licensees. Here are some tips to keep in mind if you must call or write to a licensing board.

Some Agencies Charge Fees

Several trends are observed when verifying search fees of the various licensing agencies. They are—

1. There is no charge to verify if a particular person is licensed; this can usually be done by phone.

2. The fee for copies or faxes ranges from $.25 to $2.00.

3. A fee of $5 to $20 usually applies to written requests. This is due to the fact that written certifications give more information than verbal inquiries, i.e. disciplinary action, exam scores.

4. A fee that is $25 or more is typically for a list of licensed professionals. For example, a hospital might need a roster of registered nurses in a certain geographic area.

Distinguish the Type of Agency

Within the agency category listings, it is important to note that there are five general types of agencies. When you are verifying credentials, you should be aware of what distinguishes each type, which in turn could alter the questions you ask.

Private Certification

Private Licensing and Certification—requires a proven level of minimum competence before license is granted. These professional licenses separate the true "professions" from the third category below. In many of these professions, the certification body, such as the American Institute of Certified Public Accountants, is a private association whereas the licensing body, such as the New York State Education Department, is the licensing agency. Also, many professions may provide additional certifications in specialty areas.

State Certification

State Licensing & Certification—requires certification through an *examination* and/or other *requirements supervised* directly *by the state* rather than by a private association.

By Individual

Individual Registration—required if an individual intends to offer specified products or services in the designated area, but does not require certification that the person has met minimum requirements. An everyday example would be registering a handgun in a state that does not require passing a gun safety course.

By Business

Business Registration—required if a business intends to do business or offer specified products or services in a designated area, such as registering a liquor license. Some business license agencies require testing or a background check. Others merely charge a fee after a cursory review of the application.

Special Permits

Permits—give the grantee specific permission to do something, whether it is to sell hot-dogs on the corner or to put up a three story sign. Permits are usually granted at the local level rather than the state level of government.

Other Forms of Licensing & Registration

Although the state level is where much of the licensing and registration occurs, you should be aware of other places you may want to search.

Local Government Agencies

Local government agencies at both the **county** and **municipal levels** require a myriad of business registrations and permits in order to do business (construction, signage, etc.) within their borders. Even where you think a business or person, such as a remodeling contractor, should have local registrations you want to check out, it is still best to start at the state level.

County Recording Office and City Hall

If you decide to check on local registrations and permits, call the offices at both the county—try the **county recording office**—and municipal level—try **city hall**—to find out what type of registrations may be required for the person or business you are checking out.

Like the state level, you should expect that receiving basic information will only involve a phone call and that you will not be charged for obtaining a status summary.

Professional Associations

As mentioned above, many professional licenses are based on completion of the requirements of professional associations. In addition, there are *many professional designations* from such associations that *are not recognized as official licenses by government*. Other designations are basic certifications in fields that are so specialized that they are not of interest to the states, but rather only to the professionals within an industry. For example, if your company needs to hire an investigator to check out a potential fraud against you, you might want to hire a CFE—Certified Fraud Examiner—who has met the minimum requirements for that title from the Association of Certified Fraud Examiners.

Other Media

Mail Lists & Databases

Many agencies make their lists available in reprinted or computer form, and a few maintain online access to their files. If you are interested in the availability of licensing agency information in bulk (e.g. mailing lists, magnetic tapes, disks) or online, call the agency and ask about formats that are available.

Online Searching & CD-ROMS

A number of private vendors also compile lists from these agencies and make them available online or on CD-ROM. We do not necessarily suggest these databases for credential searching. Be sure to first find out if they are complete, up-to-date, and contain all the information you can obtain directly from the licensing agency. These databases are extremely valuable as a general source of background information on an individual or company that you wish to do business with.

Searching Federal Court Records

In addition to detailing how to obtain Federal Court information, another objective of this publication is to show searchers how the Federal Court system has evolved during the past few years. One problem searchers encounter is that older records may be in a different form or in a different location from newer records. For example, a searcher can go astray trying to find bankruptcy cases in Ohio unless they know about changes in Dayton.

One development that continues to change the fundamental nature of Federal Courts case record access is, of course, computerization. Now, every Federal Court in the United States has converted to a computerized index.

Federal Court Structure

The Federal Court system includes three levels of courts, plus some special courts, described as follows—

Supreme Court of the United States

The Supreme Court of the United States is the court of last resort in the United States. It is located in Washington, DC, where it hears appeals from the United States Courts of Appeals and from the highest courts of each state.

United States Court of Appeals

The United States Court of Appeals consists of thirteen appellate courts that hear appeals of verdicts from the courts of general jurisdiction. They are designated as follows:

The Federal Circuit Court of Appeals hears appeals from the US Claims Court and the US Court of International Trade. It is located in Washington, DC.

The District of Columbia Circuit Court of Appeals hears appeals from the district courts in Washington, DC as well as from the Tax Court.

Eleven geographic **Courts of Appeals**—each of these appeal courts covers a designated number of states and territories. The chart on the pages 53-55 lists the circuit numbers (1 through 11) and location of the Court of Appeals for each state.

United States District Courts

The United States District Courts are the courts of general jurisdiction, or trial courts, and are subdivided into two categories—

The District Courts are courts of general jurisdiction, or trial courts, for federal matters, excluding bankruptcy. Essentially, this means they hear cases involving federal law and cases where there is diversity of citizenship. Both **civil** and **criminal** cases come before these courts.

The Bankruptcy Courts generally follow the same geographic boundaries as the US District Courts. There is at least one bankruptcy court for each state; within a state there may be one or more judicial districts and within a judicial district there may be more than one location (division) where the courts hear cases. While civil lawsuits may be filed in either state or federal courts depending upon the applicable law, all bankruptcy actions are filed with the US Bankruptcy Courts.

Special Courts/Separate Courts

The Special Courts/Separate Courts have been created to hear cases or appeals for certain areas of litigation demanding special expertise. Examples include the US Tax Court, the Court of International Trade and the US Claims Court.

How Federal Trial Courts are Organized

At the federal level, all cases involve federal or US constitutional law or interstate commerce. The task of locating the right court is seemingly simplified by the nature of the federal system—

- All court locations are based upon the plaintiff's county of domicile.

- All civil and criminal cases go to the US District Courts.

- All bankruptcy cases go to the US Bankruptcy Courts.

However, a plaintiff or defendant may have cases in any of the 500 court locations, so it is really not all that simple to find them.

There is at least one District and one Bankruptcy Court in each state. In many states there is more than one court, often divided further into judicial districts—e.g., the State of New York consists of four judicial districts, the Northern, Southern, Eastern and Western. Further, many judicial districts contain more than one court location (usually called a division).

The Bankruptcy Courts generally use the same hearing locations as the District Courts. If court locations differ, the usual variance is to have fewer Bankruptcy Court locations.

Case Numbering

When a case is filed with a federal court, a case number is assigned. This is the primary indexing method. Therefore, in searching for case records, you will need to know or find the applicable case number. If you have the number in good form already, your search should be fast and reasonably inexpensive.

You should be aware that case numbering procedures are not consistent throughout the Federal Court system: one judicial district may assign numbers by district while another may assign numbers by location (division) within the judicial district or by judge. Remember that case numbers appearing in legal text citations may not be adequate for searching unless they appear in the proper form for the particular court.

All the basic civil case information that is entered onto docket sheets, and into computerized systems like PACER (see below), starts with standard form JS-44, the Civil Cover Sheet, or the equivalent.

Docket Sheet

As in the state court system, information from cover sheets, and from documents filed as a case goes forward, is recorded on the **docket sheet**, which then contains the case history from initial filing to its current status. While docket sheets differ somewhat in format, the basic information contained on a docket sheet is consistent from court to court. As noted earlier in the state court section, all docket sheets contain:

- Name of court, including location (division) and the judge assigned;

- Case number and case name;

- Names of all plaintiffs and defendants/debtors;

- Names and addresses of attorneys for the plaintiff or debtor;

- Nature and cause (e.g., US civil statute) of action;

- Listing of documents filed in the case, including docket entry number, the date and a short description (e.g., 12-2-92, #1, Complaint).

Assignment of Cases and Computerization

Traditionally, cases were assigned within a district by county. Although this is still true in most states, the introduction of computer systems to track dockets has led to a more flexible approach to case assignment, as is the case in Minnesota and Connecticut. Rather than blindly assigning all cases from a county to one judge, their districts are using random numbers and other logical methods to balance caseloads among their judges.

This trend may appear to confuse the case search process. Actually, the only problem that the searcher may face is to figure out where the case records themselves are located. Finding cases has become significantly easier with the wide availability of PACER from remote access and on-site terminals in each court location with the same district-wide information base.

Computerized Indexes are Available

Computerized courts generally index each case record by the names of some or all the parties to the case—the plaintiffs and defendants (debtors and creditors in Bankruptcy Court) as well as by case number. Therefore, when you search by name you will first receive a listing of all cases in which the name appears, both as plaintiff and defendant.

Electronic Access to Federal Courts

Numerous programs have been developed for electronic access to Federal Court records. In recent years the Administrative Office of the United States Courts in Washington, DC has developed three innovative public access programs: VCIS, PACER, and the Case Management/ Electronic Case Files (CM/ECF) project. The most useful program for online searching is PACER.

PACER

PACER, the acronym for **P**ublic **A**ccess to **E**lectronic **C**ourt **R**ecords, provides docket information online for open cases at **all US Bankruptcy courts** and **most US District courts**. Access is via either a commercial dial-up system (user fee of $.60 a minute) or through the Internet (user fee is $.07 per page). Cases for the US Court of Federal Claims are also available.

Each court controls its own computer system and case information database; therefore, there are some variations among jurisdictions as to the information offered.

Sign-up and technical support is handled at the PACER Service Center in San Antonio, Texas 800-676-6856. You can sign up for all or multiple districts at once. In many judicial districts, when you sign up for PACER access, you will receive a PACER Primer that has been customized for each district. The primer contains a summary of how to access PACER, how to select cases, how to read case numbers and docket sheets, some searching tips, who to call for problem resolution, and district specific program variations.

A continuing problem with PACER is that each court determines when records will be purged and how records will be indexed, leaving you to guess how a name is spelled or abbreviated and how much information about closed cases your search will uncover. A PACER search for anything but open cases **cannot** take the place of a full seven-year search of the federal court records available by written request from the court itself or through a local document retrieval company. Many districts report that they have closed records back a number of years, but at the same time indicate they purge docket items every six months.

Before Accessing PACER, Search the "National" US Party/Case Index

It is no longer necessary to call each court in every state and district to determine where a debtor has filed bankruptcy, or if someone is a defendant in Federal litigation. National and regional searches of district and bankruptcy filings can be made with one call (via modem) to the US Party/Case Index.

The US Party/Case Index is a national index for U.S. district, bankruptcy, and appellate courts. This index allows searches to determine whether or not a party is involved in federal litigation almost anywhere in the nation.

The US Party/Case Index provides the capability to perform national or regional searches on party name and Social Security Number in the bankruptcy index, party name and nature of suit in the civil index, and party name in the criminal and appellate indices.

The search will provide a list of case numbers, filing locations and filing dates for those cases matching the search criteria. If you need more information about the case, you must obtain it from the court directly or through that court's individual PACER system.

You may access the US Party/Case Index by dialup connection or via the Internet. The Internet site for the US Party/Case Index is http://pacer.uspci.uscourts.gov. The toll-free dial-up number for the US Party/Case Index is 800-974-8896. For more information, call the PACER service center at 800-676-6856.

In accordance with Judicial Conference policy, most courts charge a $.60 per minute access fee for the traditional dial-up service or $.07 per page for Internet service.

RACER

RACER stands for Remote Access to Court Electronic Records. Accessed through the Internet, RACER offers access to the same records as PACER. At present, searching RACER is free in a few courts, but normally the fee structure is $.07 per page.

Miscellaneous Online Systems

Some courts have developed their own online systems. In addition to RACER, Idaho's Bankruptcy and District Courts have other searching options available on their web site.

Likewise, the Southern District Court of New York offers CourtWeb, which provides information to the public on selected recent rulings of those judges who have elected to make information available in electronic form.

Case Management/Electronic Case Files (CM/ECF)

Electronic Case Files (ECF) is a prototype system for the filing of cases electronically. This service, initially introduced in January 1996, enables participating attorneys and litigants to electronically submit pleadings and corresponding docket entries to the court via the Internet thereby eliminating substantial paper handling and processing time. ECF permits any interested parties to instantaneously access the entire official case docket and documents on the Internet of selective civil and bankruptcy cases within these jurisdictions.

The federal judiciary's Case management/Electronic Case Files (CM/ECF) project is designed to replace the aging electronic docketing and case management systems in more than 200 bankruptcy, district and appellate courts by 2005. CM/ECF will provide the capability for courts to have case file documents in electronic format and to accept filings over the Internet. Forty-seven federal courts are currently operational as we go to press, and another group of courts are in the process of implementing CM/ECF.

It is important to note that when you search ECF, you are ONLY searching cases that have been filed electronically. A case may not have been filed electronically through CM-ECF, so you must still conduct a search using PACER if you want to know if a case exists.

One important feature of this system is their National Locator, known as the United States Party Index. This is a name search, used to locate the specific court where records are available.

For further information about CM/ECF visit http://pacer.psc.uscourts.gov/cmecf./index.html.

VCIS

Another important system is **VCIS** (Voice Case Information System). Nearly all of the US Bankruptcy Court judicial districts provide **VCIS**, a means of accessing information regarding open bankruptcy cases by merely using a touch-tone telephone. There is no charge. Individual names are entered last name first with as much of the first name as you wish to include. For example, Carl R. Ernst could be entered as ERNSTC or ERNSTCARL. Do not enter the middle initial. Business names are entered as they are written, without blanks.

The VCIS System, like the PACER System, has become pervasive and now covers open cases for all but a few US Bankruptcy Court locations. Each Bankruptcy Court profile includes that court's VCIS phone number.

Federal Courts Searching Hints

- VCIS should *only* be used to locate information about open cases. Do not attempt to use VCIS as a substitute for a PACER search.

- Since this publication includes the counties of jurisdiction for each court, the list of counties in each Court's profile is a good starting point for determining where case records may or may not be found.

- Before performing a general PACER search to determine whether cases exist under a particular plaintiff, debtor, or defendant name, first be certain to review that Court's profile, which will show the earliest dates of case records available on the PACER. Also, searchers need to be sure that the Court's case index includes all cases, open and closed, for that particular period. Be aware that some courts purge older, closed cases after a period of time, making such a PACER search incomplete. (Wherever known, this publication indicates within the court profiles the purge timeframe for PACER records. Times vary from court to court and state to state.)

- Experience shows that court personnel are typically not aware of — nor concerned about — the types of searches performed by readers of this publication. Court personnel often focus on only open cases, whereas a searcher may want to know as much about closed cases as open ones. Thus, court personnel are sometimes fuzzy in answering questions about how far back case records go on PACER, and whether closed cases have been purged. If you are looking for cases older than a year or two, there is no substitute for a real, on-site search performed by the court itself or by a local search expert (if the court allows full access to its indexes).

- Some courts may be more willing than others to give out information by telephone. This is because most courts have converted from the old card index system to fully computerized indexes, which are easily accessible, while on the phone.

Federal Records Centers and the National Archives

After a federal case is closed, the documents are held by Federal Courts themselves for a number of years, then stored at a designated Federal Records Center (FRC). After 20 to 30 years, the records are then transferred from the FRC to the regional archives offices of the National Archives and Records Administration (NARA). The length of time between a case being closed and its being moved to an FRC varies widely by district. Each court has its own transfer cycle and determines access procedures to its case records, even after they have been sent to the FRC.

When case records are sent to an FRC, the boxes of records are assigned accession, location and box numbers. These numbers, which are called case locator information, **must be obtained from the originating court in order to retrieve documents from the FRC.**

Some courts will provide such information over the telephone, but others require a written request. This information is now available on PACER in certain judicial districts. The Federal Records Center for each state is listed as follows:

State	Circuit	Appeals Court	Federal Records Center
AK	9	San Francisco, CA	Anchorage (Some records are in temporary storage in Seattle)
AL	11	Atlanta, GA	Atlanta
AR	8	St. Louis, MO	Fort Worth
AZ	9	San Francisco, CA	Los Angeles
CA	9	San Francisco, CA	Los Angeles (Central & Southern CA) San Francisco (Eastern & Northern CA)
CO	10	Denver, CO	Denver
CT	2	New York, NY	Boston
DC		Washington, DC	Washington, DC
DE	3	Philadelphia, PA	Philadelphia
FL	11	Atlanta, GA	Atlanta
GA	11	Atlanta, GA	Atlanta
GU	9	San Francisco, CA	San Francisco
HI	9	San Francisco, CA	San Francisco
IA	8	St. Louis, MO	Kansas City, MO
ID	9	San Francisco, CA	Seattle
IL	7	Chicago, IL	Chicago
IN	7	Chicago, IL	Chicago
KS	10	Denver, CO	Kansas City, MO
KY	6	Cincinnati, OH	Atlanta
LA	5	New Orleans, LA	Fort Worth
MA	1	Boston, MA	Boston
MD	4	Richmond, VA	Philadelphia
ME	1	Boston, MA	Boston
MI	6	Cincinnati, OH	Chicago
MN	8	St. Louis, MO	Chicago

State	Circuit	Appeals Court	Federal Records Center
MO	8	St. Louis, MO	Kansas City, MO
MS	5	New Orleans, LA	Atlanta
MT	9	San Francisco, CA	Denver
NC	4	Richmond, VA	Atlanta
ND	8	St. Louis, MO	Denver
NE	8	St. Louis, MO	Kansas City, MO
NH	1	Boston, MA	Boston
NJ	3	Philadelphia, PA	New York
NM	10	Denver, CO	Denver
NV	9	San Francisco, CA	Los Angeles (Clark County, NV) San Francisco (Other NV counties)
NY	2	New York, NY	New York
OH	6	Cincinnati, OH	Chicago; Dayton has some bankruptcy
OK	10	Denver, CO	Fort Worth
OR	9	San Francisco, CA	Seattle
PA	3	Philadelphia, PA	Philadelphia
PR	1	Boston, MA	New York
RI	1	Boston, MA	Boston
SC	4	Richmond, VA	Atlanta
SD	8	St. Louis, MO	Denver
TN	6	Cincinnati, OH	Atlanta
TX	5	New Orleans, LA	Fort Worth
UT	10	Denver, CO	Denver
VA	4	Richmond, VA	Philadelphia
VI	3	Philadelphia, PA	New York
VT	2	New York, NY	Boston
WA	9	San Francisco, CA	Seattle
WI	7	Chicago, IL	Chicago
WV	4	Richmond, VA	Philadelphia
WY	10	Denver, CO	Denver

Notes to the Chart:

GU is Guam, PR is Puerto Rico, and VI is the Virgin Islands.

According to some odd logic, the following Federal Records Centers are not located in the city named above, but are actually somewhere else. Below are the exceptions:

Atlanta—in East Point, GA

Boston—in Waltham, MA

Los Angeles—in Laguna Niguel, CA

New York—in Bayonne, NJ

San Francisco—in San Bruno, CA

Searching Other Federal Records Online

EDGAR

EDGAR, the Electronic Data Gathering Analysis, and Retrieval system was established by the Securities and Exchange Commission (SEC) to allow companies to make required filing to the SEC by direct transmission. As of May 6, 1996, all public domestic companies are required to make their filings on EDGAR, except for filings made to the Commission's regional offices and those filings made on paper due to a hardship exemption.

EDGAR is an extensive repository of US corporation information and it is available online.

What Information is Available on EDGAR?

Companies must file the following reports with the SEC:

- 10-K, an annual financial report including audited year-end financial statements.

- 10-Q, a quarterly report, unaudited.

- 8K - a report detailing significant or unscheduled corporate changes or events.

- Securities offering and trading registrations and the final prospectus.

The list above is not conclusive. There are other miscellaneous reports filed, including those dealing with security holdings by institutions and insiders. Access to these documents provides a wealth on information.

How to Access EDGAR Online

EDGAR is searchable online at: www.sec.gov/edgar.shmtl. A number of private vendors offer access to EDGAR records. LEXIS/NEXIS acts as the data wholesaler or distributor on behalf of the government. LEXIS/NEXIS sells data to information retailers, including it's own NEXIS service.

Aviation Records

The Federal Aviation Association (FAA) is the US government agency with the responsibility of all matters related to the safety of civil aviation. The FAA, among other functions, provides the system that registers aircraft, and documents showing title or interest in aircraft. Their web site, at www.faa.gov, is the ultimate source of aviation records, airports and facilities, safety regulations, and civil research and engineering.

The Aircraft Owners and Pilots Association is the largest organization of its kind with a 340,000 members. Their web site is www.aopa.org and is an excellent source of information regarding the aviation industry.

Another excellent source of aircraft information is *Jane's World Airlines* at www.janes.com.

Military Records

This topic is so broad that there can be a book written about it, and in fact there is! *The Armed Forces Locator Directory* from MIE Publishing (800-937-2133) is an excellent source. The book, now in its 8th edition, covers every conceivable topic regarding military records. Their web site www.militaryusa.com offers free access to some useful databases.

The Privacy Act of 1974 (5 U.S.C. 552a) and the Department of Defense directives require a written request, signed and dated, to access military personnel records. For further details, visit the NPRC site listed below.

Military Internet Sources

There are a number of great Internet sites that provide valuable information on obtaining military and military personnel records. The National Personnel Records Center (NPRC), maintained by the National Archives and Records Administration is www.nara.gov/regional/mpr.html. This site is full of useful information and links. Other excellent sites include:

www.army.mil	The official site of the US Army
www.af.mil	The official site of the US Air Force
www.navy.mil	The official site of the US Navy
www.usmc.mil	The official site of the US Marine Corps
www.ngb.dtic.mil	The official site of the National Guard
www.uscg.mil	The official site of the US Coast Guard

US Government Gateways…by Alan Schlein

The remainder of this Chapter was written and contributed by online pioneer and award winning journalist Alan M. Schlein, author of Find It Online.

We sincerely thank Alan for permitting the use of his material in Public Records Online. *Alan can be reached at his* www.deadlineonline.com. *Check out his web site—it is a great source with lots of useful links!*

In the U.S., almost every federal government agency is online. There's a nationwide network of depository libraries, including the enormous resources of the National Archives (www.nara.gov), the twelve presidential libraries, and four national libraries (the Library of Congress, the National Agricultural Library, the National Library of Education and the National Library of Medicine). There are almost 5000 government web sites from more than forty-two U.S. departments and agencies.

Because there are so many government web sites, you may need to turn to the hundreds of web sites, called *government gateways*, that organize and link government sites, in order to find the starting point for your research. Some gateways are simply collections of links. Others provide access to bulletin boards of specific government agencies so that you find and contact employees with specific knowledge. Guides are becoming increasingly important in light of the growing number of reports and publications that aren't printed any more, but simply posted online.

Best US Government Gateways (listed alphabetically)

Documents Center

www.lib.umich.edu/govdocs/index.html

Documents Center is a clearinghouse for local, state, federal, foreign, and international government information. It is one of the more comprehensive online searching aids for government information on the Internet and especially useful as a meta-site of meta-sites.

Federal Web Locators

www.infoctr.edu/fwl/

This web locator is really two sites in one: a federal government web site at www.infoctr.edu/fwl and a separate site that tracks federal courts at www.infoctr.edu/fwl/fedweb.juris.htm, both of which are browsable by category or by keyword. Together they provide links to thousands of government agencies and departments.

FedLaw

http://fedlaw.gsa.gov

FedLaw is an extremely broad resource for federal legal and regulatory research containing 1,600+ links to law-related information. It has very good topical and title indices that group web links into hundreds of subjects. The site is operated by the General Services Administration (GSA).

Fedstats

www.fedstats.gov

This is a terrific collection of statistical sites from the federal government and a good central clearinghouse for other federal statistics sites.

FedWorld Information Network

www.fedworld.gov

FedWorld helps you search over thirty million U.S. government pages. It is a massive collection of 15,000 files and databases of government sites, including bulletin boards that can help you identify government employees with expertise in a broad range of subjects. A surprising number of these experts will take the time to discuss questions from the general public.

FirstGov

www.firstgov.gov

Responding to the need for a central clearinghouse of U.S. federal government sites, the U.S. government developed FirstGov and linked every federal agency to its site as well as every state government. It has an easy-to-use search tool, allowing you to specify if you want federal or state agencies and to easily locate business regulations and vital records. It also lets you look for federal government phone numbers and email addresses. This is an easy-to-use starting point, powered by the FAST/AllTheWeb search engine. Also, check out the FAQs of the U.S. government for questions and answers about the U.S. government at www.faq.gov.

Google's Uncle Sam

www.google.com/unclesam

Google's Uncle Sam site is a search engine geared to looking at U.S. government sites. It's an easy-to-use tool if you know what you are looking for.

Govbot – Government Search Engine

http://ciir.cs.umass.edu/ciirdemo/Govbot

Developed by the Center for Intelligent Information Retrieval, Govbot's searchable keyword index of government web sites is limited to sites with a top-level domain name ending in.gov or.mil.

Healthfinder

www.healthfinder.gov

This is a great starting point for health-related government information.

InfoMine: Scholarly Internet Resource Collections

http://lib-www.ucr.edu

InfoMine provides collections of scholarly Internet resources, best for academics. It is one of the best academic resources anywhere, from the librarians at the University of California Riverside. Its Government Information section is easily searchable by subject. It has detailed headings and its resource listings are very specific. Since the site is run by a university, some of its references are limited to student use only.

SearchGov.com

www.searchgov.com

A private company that has an effective search for U.S. government sites.

Speech & Transcript Center

http://gwis2.circ.gwu.edu/~gprice/speech.htm

This site links directly to web sites containing transcripts of speeches. Pulled together by former George Washington University reference librarian and Invisible Web author Gary Price, it encompasses government resources, business leaders, and real audio. A large section is devoted to U.S. and international government speech transcripts – including Congressional hearings, testimony and transcripts.

U.S. Federal Government Agencies Directory

www.lib.lsu.edu/gov/fedgov.html

This directory of federal agencies is maintained by Louisiana State University and links to hundreds of federal government Internet sites. It's divided by branch and agency and is very thorough, but focus on your target because it's easy to lose your way or become overwhelmed en route.

U.S. Government Information

www-libraries.colorado.edu/ps/gov/us/federal.htm

This is a gem of a site from the University of Colorado and a good starting point. It's not as thorough as the LSU site above, but still very valuable.

Best US Government Web Sites

U.S. tax dollars are put to good and visible use here. A few of the government's web pages are excellent. Some can be used in lieu of commercial tools, but only if you have the time to invest.

A few of the top government sites – the Census and the Securities and Exchange Commission – are models of content and presentation. They are very deep, very thorough, and easy to use. If only the rest of the federal government would follow suit. Unfortunately, the best of the federal government is just that: the best. Not all agencies maintain such detailed and relevant resources.

Following are the crown jewels of the government's collection, in ranked order:

U.S. Census Bureau

www.census.gov

Without question, this is the U.S. government's top site. It's saturated with information and census publications – at times overwhelmingly so – but worth every minute of your time. A few hours spent here is a worthwhile investment for almost anyone seeking to background a community, learn about business, or find any kind of demographic information. You can search several ways: alphabetically by subject, by word, by location, and by geographic map. The only problem is the sheer volume of data.

One feature, the Thematic Mapping System, allows users to extract data from Census CD-ROMs and display them in maps by state or county. You can create maps on all kinds of subjects – for example, tracking violent crime to farm income by region. The site also features the Statistical Abstract of the U.S. with a searchable index at www.census.gov/statab/www/stateabs.html.

The potential uses of census data are infinite. Marketers use it to find community information. Reporters search out trends by block, neighborhood or region. Educators conduct research. Businesses evaluate new business prospects. Genealogists trace family trees – though full census data isn't available for seventy-two years from the date the census is taken. You can even use it to identify ideal communities in which to raise a family. Jennifer LaFleur, now at The St. Louis Post-Dispatch did a story while at The San Jose Mercury News using the census site to find eligible bachelors in specific areas of San Jose. Additional census resources include:

1990 U.S. Census LOOKUP

http://venus.census.gov/cdrom/lookup/

Census Tract Street Locator

http://tier2.census.gov/ctsl/ctsl.htm

Census FactFinder

http://factfinder.census.gov

Census Industry Statistics

www.censusgov/main/www/industries.html

U.S. Securities and Exchange Commission (SEC)

www.sec.gov

Only the Census site is better than the SEC site, which is a first-rate, must-stop place for information shopping on U.S. companies. Its EDGAR database search site at www.sec.gov/edaux/searches.htm is easy to use and provides access to documents that companies and corporations are required to file under regulatory laws.

The SEC site is a great starting point for information about specific companies and industry trends. The SEC requires all publicly-held corporations and some large privately-held corporations to disclose detailed financial information about their activities, plans, holdings, executives' salaries and stakes, legal problems and so forth.

Library of Congress (LOC)

www.loc.gov

This site is an extraordinary collection of documents. Thomas, the Library's Congressional online center site at http://thomas.loc.gov provides an exhaustive collection of congressional documents, including bill summaries, voting records and the full Congressional Record, which is the official record of Congressional action. This LOC site also links to many international, federal, state and local government sites. You can also access the library's more than five million records online, some versions in full-text and some in abstract form. Though the library's entire 121 million item collection is not yet available online, the amount online increases daily. In addition to books and papers, it includes an extensive images collection ranging from Frank Lloyd Wright's designs to the Dead Sea Scrolls to the world's largest online collection of baseball cards. The Library of Congress also has a terrific collection of international information on its web site at www.loc.gov/rr/ international/portals.html.

Superintendent of Documents Home Page (GPO)

www.access.gpo.gov/su_docs

The GPO is the federal government's primary information printer and distributor. All federally funded information from every agency is sent here, which makes the GPO's holdings priceless. Luckily, the GPO site is well-constructed and easy to use. For example, it has the full text of the Federal Register, which lists all federal regulations and proposals, and full-text access to the Congressional Record. The GPO also produces an online version of the Congressional Directory, providing details on every congressional district, profiles of members, staff profiles, maps of every district and historical documents about Congress. This site will expand exponentially over the next few years, as the number of materials go out of print and online. GPO Access also allows you to electronically retrieve much of the bureaucratic paper in Washington, electronically, from the Government Printing Office including searching more than seventy databases and indices. If you need some help finding things, use the topic-specific finder at this site.

National Technical Information Service (NTIS)

www.ntis.gov

The best place to find federal government reports related to technology and science. NTIS is the nation's clearinghouse for unclassified technical reports of government-sponsored research. NTIS collects, indexes, abstracts, and sells U.S. and foreign research – mostly in science, technology, behavioral, and social science data.

IGnet

www.ignet.gov

This is a truly marvelous collection of reports and information from the Inspector Generals of about sixty federal agency departments. They find waste and abuse within government agencies. It is well worth checking when starting research on government-related matters.

General Accounting Office GAO Reports

www.gao.gov/decisions/decision.htm

The Comptroller General Opinions from the last sixty days are posted on this GAO web site.

These reports and opinions are excellent references. For historical opinions back to 1996 go to www.access.gpo.gov/su_docs/aces/aces170.shtml.

White House
www.whitehouse.gov

This site wouldn't make this list if not for its economic statistics page and the transcript of every official action the U.S. President takes at www.whitehouse.gov/news/. Unfortunately, as with many government sites, its primary focus is in promoting itself.

DefenseLINK – U.S. Department of Defense (DOD)
www.defenselink.mil

This is the brand-name site for Pentagon-related information. There's a tremendous amount of data here – categorized by branch of service – including U.S. troop deployments worldwide. And to the Pentagon's credit they've made this a very easy site to use.

Defense Technical Information Center (DTIC)
www.dtic.mil

The DTIC site is loaded with links and defense information – everything from contractors to weapon systems. It even includes de-classified information about the Gulf War. It is the best place to start for defense information. You can even find a list of all military-related contracts, including beneficiary communities and the kinds of contracts awarded. The only problem with the site is there's no search engine to make it easy to find information.

Bureau of Transportation Statistics
www.bts.gov

The U.S. Department of Transportation's enormous collection of information about every facet of transportation. There's a lot of valuable material here including the Transportation Statistics Annual Report. It also holds financial data for airlines and searchable databases containing information about fatal accidents and on-time statistics for airlines, which can be narrowed to your local airport.

National Archives And Records Administration
www.nara.gov

A breathtaking collection of research online, for example the National Archives has descriptions of more than 170,000 documents related to the Kennedy assassination. It also contains a world-class database holding descriptions of more than 95,000 records held by the Still Picture and Motion Picture, Sound and Video Branches. This site also links to the twelve Presidential Archives with their records of every person ever mentioned in Executive Branch correspondence. You can view an image of the original document. The Archives

Research Center Online has great collections of family history/genealogy research and veteran's service records.

usgovsearch

www.usgovsearch.com

This site may be retooling under a new URL. In conjunction with the National Technical Information Service, search engine company Northern Light has created one of the most thorough search tools for finding government-related information. Usgovsearch is a strong rival to the U.S. government run FirstGov.gov. With Divines Inc.'s recent purchase of Northern Light, it is unclear how long this will stay an inexpensive site. You can search the Web using usgovsearch but you can also get information from Northern Light's low-cost Special Collections resources. It allows you to run searches and find out the inter-relationships among agencies. Most of the material can be found elsewhere for free, but for speed and thoroughness usgovsearch is excellent. With the special collections between US$1 and US$4 per article, it is a very useful and inexpensive tool.

Federal Consumer Information Center National Contact Center

www.info.gov

While this is largely a telephone service that gets more than a million calls a year, this web site tries to provide a way through the maze of federal agencies. It includes a clearinghouse of phone numbers for all federal agencies, state, and local government sites as well.

SciTechResources.gov

www.scitechresources.gov

This is a tremendous directory of about 700 science and technology resources on U.S. government sites from the U.S. Department of Commerce, National Technical and Information Service.

Motor Vehicle Records and the Driver's Privacy Protection Act

The Driver's Privacy Protection Act Title XXXI—Protection of Privacy of Information in State Motor Vehicle Records—was attached as an amendment to the Violent Crime Control Act of 1994 and was signed by President Clinton late in that summer. The intent of the DPPA is to protect the personal privacy of persons licensed to drive by prohibiting certain disclosures of information maintained by the states. This federal mandate declared that the federal government had the right to restrict or prohibit the release of personal information of persons licensed to drive or own motor vehicles. States were given three years to comply.

The profiles of the state motor vehicle departments throughout this book may refer to DPPA and permissible users. Therefore, we are printing a copy of the Act's permissible uses.

Personal Information and the Permissible Uses

The Act prohibits disclosure of personal information from the driver history, vehicle registration, title files held by state DMVs, except for 14 specific "permissible uses." The Act's definition of Personal Information is..

"..information that identifies an individual, including an individual's photograph, social security number, driver identification number, name, address (but not the 5-digit zip code), telephone number, and medical or disability information, but does not include information on vehicular accidents, driving violations, and driver's status."

The permissible uses do, in general, permit ongoing, legitimate businesses and individuals to obtain full record data, but with added compliance procedures. The following text, taken directly from the Act, details these 14 Permissible Uses—

§2721. Prohibition on release and use of certain personal information from State motor vehicle records "(a) IN GENERAL.--Except as provided in subsection (b), a State department of motor vehicles, and any officer, employee, or contractor, thereof, shall not knowingly disclose or otherwise make available to any person or entity personal information about any individual obtained by the department in connection with a motor vehicle record.

"(b) PERMISSIBLE USES.--Personal information referred to in subsection (a) shall be disclosed for use in connection with matters of motor vehicle or driver safety and theft, motor vehicle emissions, motor vehicle product alterations, recalls, or advisories, performance monitoring of motor vehicles and dealers by motor vehicle manufacturers, and removal of non-owners records from the original owner records of motor vehicle manufacturers to carry out the purposes of the Automobile Information Disclosure Act, the Motor Vehicle Information and Cost Saving Act, the National Traffic and Motor Vehicle Safety Act of 1966, the Anti-Car Theft Act of 1992, and the Clean Air Act, and may be disclosed as follows:

"(1) For use by any government agency, including any court or law enforcement agency, in carrying out its functions, or any private person or entity acting on behalf of a Federal, State, or local agency in carrying out its functions.

"(2) For use in connection with matters of motor vehicle or driver safety and theft; motor vehicle emissions; motor vehicle product alterations, recalls, or advisories; performance monitoring of motor vehicles, motor vehicle parts and dealers; motor vehicle market research activities, including survey research; and removal of non-owner records from the original owner records of motor vehicle manufacturers.

"(3) For use in the normal course of business by a legitimate business or its agents, employees, or contractors, but only--

"(A) to verify the accuracy of personal information submitted by the individual to the business or its agents, employees, or contractors; and

"(B) if such information as so submitted is not correct or is no longer correct, to obtain the correct information, but only for the purposes of preventing fraud by, pursuing legal remedies against, or recovering on a debt or security interest against, the individual.

"(4) For use in connection with any civil, criminal, administrative, or arbitral proceeding in any Federal, State, or local court or agency or before any self-regulatory body, including the service of process, investigation in anticipation of litigation, and the execution or enforcement of judgments and orders, or pursuant to an order of a Federal, State, or local court.

"(5) For use in research activities, and for use in producing statistical reports, so long as the personal information is not published, redisclosed, or used to contact individuals.

"(6) For use by any insurer or insurance support organization, or by a self-insured entity, or its agents, employees, or contractors, in connection with claims investigation activities, antifraud activities, rating or underwriting.

"(7) For use in providing notice to the owners of towed or impounded vehicles.

"(8) For use by any licensed private investigative agency or licensed security service for any purpose permitted under this subsection.

"(9) For use by an employer or its agent or insurer to obtain or verify information relating to a holder of a commercial driver's license that is required under the Commercial Motor Vehicle Safety Act of 1986 (49 U.S.C. App. 2710 et seq.)

"(10) For use in connection with the operation of private toll transportation facilities.

"(11) For any other use in response to requests for individual motor vehicle records if the State has obtained the express consent of the person to whom such personal information pertains.

"(12) For bulk distribution for surveys, marketing or solicitations if if the State has obtained the express consent of the person to whom such personal information pertains.

"(13) For use by any requester, if the requester demonstrates it has obtained the written consent of the individual to whom the information pertains.

"(14) For any other use specifically authorized under the law of the State that holds the record, if such use is related to the operation of a motor vehicle or public safety.

"(c) RESALE OR REDISCLOSURE.--An authorized recipient of personal information (except a recipient under subsection (b)(11) or (12) may resell or redisclose the information only for a use permitted under subsection (b) (but not for uses under subsection (b) (11) or (12). An authorized recipient under subsection (b)(11) may resell or redisclose personal information for any purpose. An authorized recipient under subsection (b)(12) may resell or redisclose personal information pursuant to subsection (b)(12). Any authorized recipient (except a recipient under subsection (b)(11)) that resells or rediscloses personal information covered by this title must keep for a period of 5 years records identifying each person or entity that receives information and the permitted purpose for which the information will be used and must make such records available to the motor vehicle department upon request.

"(d) WAIVER PROCEDURES.--A State motor vehicle department may establish and carry out procedures under which the department or its agents, upon receiving a request for personal information that does not fall within one of the exceptions in subsection (b), may mail a copy of the request to the individual about whom the information was requested, informing such individual of the request, together with a statement to the effect that the information will not be released unless the individual waives such individual's right to privacy under this section.

When to Use a Public Record Vendor

Hiring Someone to Obtain the Record

There are five main categories of public record professionals: distributors and gateways; search firms; local document retrievers; investigative firms; and information brokers.

Distributors and Gateways (Proprietary Database Vendors)

Distributors are automated public record firms who combine public sources of bulk data and/or online access to develop their own database product(s). Primary Distributors include companies that collect or buy public record information from its original source and reformat the information in some useful way. They tend to focus on one or a limited number of types of information, although a few firms have branched into multiple information categories.

Gateways are companies that either compile data from or provide an automated gateway to Primary Distributors. Gateways thus provide "one-stop shopping" for multiple geographic areas and/or categories of information.

Companies can be *both* Primary Distributors and Gateways. For example, a number of online database companies are both primary distributors of corporate information and also gateways to real estate information from other Primary Distributors

Search Firms

Search firms are companies that furnish public record search and document retrieval services through outside online services and/or through a network of specialists, including their own employees or correspondents (see Retrievers below). There are three types of Search Firms.

Search Generalists offer a full range of search capabilities in many public record categories over a wide geographic region. They may rely on gateways, primary distributors and/or networks of retrievers. They combine online proficiency with document retrieval expertise.

Search Specialists focus either on one geographic region—like Ohio—or on one specific type of public record information—like driver/vehicle records.

Application Specialists focus on one or two types of services geared to specific needs. In this category are pre-employment screening firms and tenant screening firms. Like investigators, they search many of the public record categories in order to prepare an overall report about a person or business.

Local Document Retrievers

Local document retrievers use their own personnel to search specific requested categories of public records usually in order to obtain documentation for legal compliance (e.g., incorporations), for lending, and for litigation. The retriever or his/her personnel goes directly to the agency to look up the information. A retriever may be relied upon for strong knowledge in a local area, whereas a search generalist has a breadth of knowledge and experience in a wider geographic range. Usually they do not review or interpret the results or issue reports as investigators do, but rather return documents with the results of searches. They tend to be localized, but there are companies that offer national or regional services with a network of retrievers and/or correspondents.

> **Editor's Note:** The 700+ members of the **Public Record Retriever Network (PRRN)** can be located by and counties served at www.brbpub.com/PRRN. This organization sets industry standards for the retrieval of public record documents and operates under a Code of Professional Conduct. Using one of these record retrievers is an excellent way to access records in those jurisdictions that do not offer online access.

Private Investigation Firms

Investigators use public records as tools rather than as ends in themselves, in order to create an overall, comprehensive "picture" of an individual or company for a particular purpose. They interpret the information they have gathered in order to identify further investigation tracks. They summarize their results in a report compiled from all the sources used.

Many investigators also act as Search Firms, especially as tenant or pre-employment screeners, but this is a different role from the role of Investigator per se, and screening firms act very much like investigators in their approach to a project. In addition, an investigator may be licensed, and may perform the types of services traditionally thought of as detective work, such as surveillance.

Information Brokers

There is one additional type of firm that occasionally utilizes public records. **Information Brokers** (IB) gather information that will help their clients make informed business decisions. Their work is usually done on a custom basis with each project being unique. IBs are extremely knowledgeable in online research of full text databases and most specialize in a particular subject area, such as patent searching or competitive intelligence. The Association of Independent Information Professionals (AIIP), at www.aiip.org, has over 700 experienced professional information specialist members from 21 countries.

Which Type of Vendor is Right for You?

With all the variations of vendors and the categories of information, the obvious question is; "How do I find the right vendor for the public record information I need?" Before you start calling every interesting online vendor that catches your eye, you need to narrow your search to the **type** of vendor for your needs. To do this, ask yourself the following questions—

What is the Frequency of Usage?

If you have on-going, recurring requests for a particular type of information, it is probably best to choose a different vendor then if you have infrequent requests. Setting up an account with a primary distributor, such as LEXIS or Westlaw will give you an inexpensive per search fee, but the monthly minimum requirements will be prohibitive to the casual requester, who would be better off finding a vendor who accesses or is a gateway to one of these vendors.

What is the Complexity of the Search?

The importance of hiring a vendor who understands and can interpret the information in the final format increases with the complexity of the search. Pulling a corporation record in Maryland is not difficult, but doing an online criminal record search in Maryland, when only a portion of the felony records are online, is not so easy.

Thus, part of the answer to determining which vendor or type of vendor to use is to become conversant with what is (and is not) available from government agencies. Without knowing what is available (and what restrictions apply), you cannot guide the search process effectively. Once you are comfortable knowing the kinds of information available in the public record, you are in a position to find the best method to access needed information.

What are the Geographic Boundaries of the Search?

A search of local records close to you may require little assistance, but a search of records nationally or in a state 2,000 miles away will require seeking a vendor who covers the area you need to search. Many national primary distributors and gateways combine various local and state databases into one large comprehensive system available for searching. However, if your record searching is narrowed by a region or locality, then an online source that specializes in a specific geographic region (like Superior Information Services in NJ) may be an alternative to a national vendor. Keep in mind that many national firms allow you to order a search online, even though results cannot be delivered immediately and some hands-on local searching is required.

Of course, you may want to use the government agency online system if available for the kind of information you need.

10 Questions to Ask a Public Records Vendor
(Or a Vendor Who Uses Online Sources)

The following discussion focuses specifically on automated sources of information because many valuable types of public records have been entered into a computer and, therefore, require a computer search to obtain reliable results. The original version of the text to follow was written by **Mr. Leroy Cook.** Mr. Cook is the founder and Director of ION and The Investigators Anywhere Resource Line (800-338-3463, http://ioninc.com). Mr. Cook has graciously allowed us to edit the article and reprint it for our readers.

1. Where does he or she get the information?

You may feel awkward asking a vendor where he or she obtained the information you are purchasing. The fake Rolex watch is a reminder that even buying physical things based on looks alone—without knowing where they come from—is dangerous.

Reliable information vendors *will* provide verification material such as the name of the database or service accessed, when it was last updated, and how complete it is.

It is important that you know the gathering process in order to better judge the reliability of the information being purchased. There *are* certain investigative sources that a vendor will not be willing to disclose to you. However, that type of source should not be confused with the information that is being sold item by item. Information technology has changed so rapidly that some information vendors may still confuse "items of information" with "investigative reports." Items of information sold as units are *not* investigative reports. The professional reputation of an information vendor is a guarantee of sorts. Still, because information as a commodity is so new, there is little in the way of an implied warranty of fitness.

2. How long does it take for the new information or changes to get into the system?

Any answer *except* a clear, concise date and time or the vendor's personal knowledge of an ongoing system's methods of maintaining information currency is a reason to keep probing. In view of the preceding question, this one might seem repetitive, but it *really* is a different issue. Microfiche or a database of records may have been updated last week at a courthouse or a DMV, but the department's computer section may also be working with a three-month backlog. In this case, a critical incident occurring one month ago would *not* show up in the information updated last week. The importance of timeliness is a variable to be determined by you, but to be truly informed you need to know how "fresh" the information is. Ideally, the mechanism by which you purchase items of information *should* include an update or statement of accuracy—as a part of the reply—*without* having to ask.

3. What are the searchable fields? Which fields are mandatory?

If your knowledge of "fields" and "records" is limited to the places where cattle graze and those flat, round things that play music, you *could* have a problem telling a good database from a bad one. An MVR vendor, for example, should be able to tell you that a subject's middle initial is critical when pulling an Arizona driving record. You don't have to become a programmer to use a computer and you needn't know a database management language to benefit from databases, *but* it is very helpful to understand how databases are constructed and (*at the least*) what fields, records, and indexing procedures are used.

As a general rule, the computerized, public-record information world is not standardized from county to county or from state to state; in the same way, there is little standardization within or between information vendors. Look at the system documentation from the vendor. The manual should include this sort of information.

4. How much latitude is there for error (misspellings or inappropriate punctuation) in a data request?

If the vendor's requirements for search data appear to be concise and meticulous, then you're probably on the right track. Some computer systems will tell (or "flag") an operator when they make a mistake such as omitting important punctuation or using an unnecessary comma. Other systems allow you to make inquiries by whatever means or in whatever format you like—and then tell you the requested information has *not* been found. In this instance, the desired information may *actually* be there, but the computer didn't understand the question because of the way in which it was asked. It is easy to misinterpret "no record found" as "there is no record." Please take note that the meanings of these two phrases are quite different.

5. What method is used to place the information in the repository and what error control or edit process is used?

In some databases, information may be scanned in or may be entered by a single operator as it is received and, in others, information may be entered *twice* to allow the computer to catch input errors by searching for non-duplicate entries. You don't have to know *everything* about all the options, but the vendor selling information in quantity *should.*

6. How many different databases or sources does the vendor access *and* how often?

The chance of obtaining an accurate search of a database increases with the frequency of access and the vendor's/searcher's level of knowledge. If he or she only makes inquiries once a month—and the results are important—you may need to find someone who sells data at higher volume. The point here is that it is better to find someone who specializes in the type of information you are seeking than it is to utilize a vendor who *can* get the information, but actually specializes in another type of data.

7. Does the price include assistance in interpreting the data received?

A report that includes coding and ambiguous abbreviations may look impressive in your file, but may not be too meaningful. For all reports, except those you deal with regularly, interpretation assistance can be *very* important. Some information vendors offer searches for information they really don't know much about through sources that they only use occasionally. Professional pride sometimes prohibits them from disclosing their limitations—until *you* ask the right questions.

8. Do vendors "keep track" of requesters and the information they seek (usage records)?

This may not seem like a serious concern when you are requesting information you're legally entitled to; however, there *is* a possibility that your usage records could be made available to a competitor. Most probably, the information itself is *already* being (or will be) sold to someone else, but you may not necessarily want *everyone* to know what you are requesting and how often. If the vendor keeps records of who-asks-what, the confidentiality of that information should be addressed in your agreement with the vendor.

9. Will the subject of the inquiry be notified of the request?

If your inquiry is sub rosa or if the subject's discovery of the search could lead to embarrassment, double check! There are laws that mandate the notification of subjects when certain types of inquiries are made into their files. If notification is required, the way it is accomplished could be critical.

10. Is the turnaround time and cost of the search made clear at the outset?

You should be crystal clear about what you expect and/or need; the vendor should be succinct when conveying exactly what will be provided and how much it will cost. Failure to address these issues can lead to disputes and hard feelings.

These are excellent questions and concepts to keep in mind when searching for the right public record vendor to meet your needs.

Section II

Government Online Sources

Individual state chapters have been compiled into an easy to use format that details what is available online. Free online access and fee-based systems are denoted, with the type or category of records available. Five sub-chapters or sections are presented in this order:

1. State Public Record Agencies

2. State Licensing and Regulatory Boards

3. County Courts

4. County Recorder & Assessor Offices

5. Federal Courts (US District and Bankruptcy)

Be sure to review the introductions and Online Access Notes found at the beginning of each state's County Courts and County Recorder and Assessor Office sections. This is a good place to find out about statewide online systems.

Editor's Tip: Just because records are maintained in a certain way in your state or county do not assume that any other county or state does things the same way that you are used to.

Capital:	Montgomery Montgomery County	Home Page	www.state.al.us
Time Zone:	CST	Attorney General	www.ago.state.al.us
Number of Counties:	67	Archives	www.archives.state.al.us

State Level ... Major Agencies

Criminal Records

Online: The State Court Administration provides records over its State Judicial Online System (SJIS) at www.alacourt.org. See the "County Level ... Courts" Section, Online Notes, page 79.

Corporation Records, Limited Partnership Records, Limited Liability Company Records, Limited Liability Partnerships, Trade Names, Trademarks/Servicemarks

Secretary of State, Corporations Division, PO Box 5616, Montgomery, AL 36103-5616 (Courier: 11 S Union St, Ste 207, Montgomery, AL 36104); 334-242-5324, 334-242-5325 (Trademarks), 334-240-3138 (Fax), 8AM-5PM.

www.sos.state.al.us

The web site has free searches of corporate and business records. Search individual files for Active Names at http://arc-sos.state.al.us/CGI/SOSCRP01.MBR/INPUT.

Uniform Commercial Code, Federal Tax Liens, State Tax Liens

UCC Division, Secretary of State, PO Box 5616, Montgomery, AL 36103-5616 (Courier: 11 South Union St, Suite 207, Montgomery, AL 36104); 334-242-5231, 8AM-5PM.

www.sos.state.al.us/sosinfo/inquiry.cfm

The agency has UCC information available to search at the web address; there is no fee. You can search by name or file number.

Sexual Offender Registry

Sex offender data is maintained by the Alabama Bureau of Investigations who can be reached at 334-260-1100. Free searching of records is available online at www.gsiweb.net. Missing persons and felony fugitives are also listed here.

Driver Records

Department of Public Safety, Driver Records-License Division, PO Box 1471, Montgomery, AL 36102-1471 (Courier: 502 Dexter Ave, Montgomery, AL 36104); 334-242-4400, 334-242-4639 (Fax), 8AM-5PM.

www.dps.state.al.us/

Alabama offers real time processing access via the AAMVAnet 3270 Terminal Connection. There is a minimum order requirement of 500 requests per month. Fee is $5.75 per record. Requesters must provide their own connection device and terminal emulation software.

Legislation Records

www.legislature.state.al.us

There is a free service on the Internet for bill text, status, history, voting, audio of Senate, and Code of Alabama.

State Level ... Occupational Licensing

Abortion/Reproductive Health Center .... www.adph.org/providers/
Ambulatory Surgery Center .... www.adph.org/providers/
Architect .... www.alarchbd.state.al.us/rostersearch/rostersearch.asp
Assisted Living Facility/Unit .... www.adph.org/providers/
Attorney .... www.alabar.org/page.cfm?page=im_include/im_dirSearch.cfm
Birthing Center .... www.adph.org/providers/
Cerebral Palsy Center .... www.adph.org/providers/
Electrical Contractor .... www.aecb.state.al.us/Search/new_search.asp
Electrician, Journeyman .... www.aecb.state.al.us/Search/new_search.asp
Engineer/Engineer in Training .... www.bels.state.al.us/LicenseeSearch/searchmenu.asp
Forester .... http://home.earthlink.net/~pbsears/foresters.html
Home Builder .... www.hblb.state.al.us/Lic_Search/search.asp
Home Health Agency .... www.adph.org/providers/
Home Inspector .... www.sos.state.al.us/sosinfo/inquiry.cfm
Hospice .... www.adph.org/providers/
Hospital .... www.adph.org/providers/
Hospital, Rural Primary Care .... www.adph.org/providers/
Independent Clinical/Physiological Lab .... www.adph.org/providers/
Insurance Adjuster .... www.aldoi.org/licenseesearch.htm
Insurance Agent .... www.aldoi.org/licenseesearch.htm
Insurance Broker/Producer .... www.aldoi.org/licenseesearch.htm
Insurance Company .... www.aldoi.org/companysearch.htm
Insurance Corporation/Partnership .... www.aldoi.org/companysearch.htm
Massage Therapist www.adeca.state.al.us/soicc/soicc/WebSTAR3.0/SOICC/LicOcc/massage.html
Medical Doctor .... www.albme.org/verification.htm
Mental Health Center .... www.adph.org/providers/
Notary Public .... www.sos.state.al.us/sosinfo/inquiry.cfm
Nursing Home .... www.adph.org/providers/
Nursing Home Administrator .... www.alboenha.state.al.us/logon.html
Optometrist .... www.odfinder.org/LicSearch.asp
Physical Therapist/Therapist Asst .... www.pt.state.al.us/License/searchform.asp
Preneed Sales Agent .... www.aldoi.org/licenseesearch.htm
Public Accountant-CPA .... www.asbpa.state.al.us/register/register.asp
Real Estate Appraiser .... http://reab.state.al.us/appraisers/searchform.asp
Real Estate Broker .... www.arec.state.al.us/search.asp
Real Estate Salesperson/Agent .... www.arec.state.al.us/search.asp
Rehabilitation Center .... www.adph.org/providers/
Reinsurance Intermediary .... www.aldoi.org/licenseesearch.htm
Renal Disease (End Stage) Treatment Ctr. .... www.adph.org/providers/
Sleep Disorder Center .... www.adph.org/providers/
Social Worker .... www.abswe.state.al.us/Lic_Search/search.asp
Surplus Line Broker .... www.aldoi.org/licenseesearch.htm
Surveyor, Land .... www.bels.state.al.us/LicenseeSearch/searchmenu.asp
X-ray (Portable) Supplier .... www.adph.org/providers/

County Level ... Courts

Court Administration: Director of Courts, 300 Dexter Ave, Montgomery, AL, 36104; 334-242-0300; www.alacourt.org

Court Structure: Circuit Courts are the courts of general jurisdiction; District Courts have limited jurisdiction in civil matters. These courts are combined in all but eight larger counties. Barbour, Coffee, Jefferson, St. Clair, Talladega, and Tallapoosa Counties have two court locations within the county. Jefferson County (Birmingham), Madison (Huntsville), Marshall, and Tuscaloosa Counties have separate criminal divisions for Circuit and/or District Courts.

Online Access Note: In the past, the state offered a commercial remote access to the State Judicial Information System (SJIS), but they are no longer adding new users. Instead they are recommending new users to contact a designated private vendor. For more information visit their web site at www.alacourt.com; note that fees are involved. State Supreme Court and Appellette decisions are available at www.alalinc.net.

Baldwin County
Probate Court *Probate Records*
Online access to probate property records is available free at www.deltacomputersystems.com/al/al05/probatea.html.

Calhoun County
Circuit Court *Sex Offender Records*
The County sex offender registry is online at www.calhouncountysheriff.org/html/Framsex.html. From Sept. 1999 forward only.

Mobile County
District Court *Probate Records*
Access to the Probate court's recordings database is available free at www.mobilecounty.org/probatecourt/recordssearch.htm.

Russell County
Circuit & District Court *Sex Offender Records*
The county sex offender registry if available free at www.rcso.org/sex2.htm.

County Level ... Recorders & Assessors

Recording Office Organization: 67 counties, 71 recording offices. The recording officer is the Judge of Probate. Four counties have two recording offices-Barbour, Coffee, Jefferson, and St. Clair. The entire state is in the Central Time Zone (CST). Federal and state tax liens on personal property of businesses are filed with the Secretary of State. Other federal and state tax liens are filed with the county Judge of Probate. Counties do not perform separate tax lien searches although the liens are usually filed in the same index with UCC financing statements.

Online Access Note: There is no statewide system, but a limited number of counties offer free online access to recorded documents.

Baldwin County   *Property, Deed, Recording, UCC Records*
www.probate.co.baldwin.al.us
Access to recordings, deeds, and UCCs is available at the web site, see the "Recording" box. Also, Online access to probate's property information is available free at www.deltacomputersystems.com/al/al05/probatea.html.

Jefferson County (Birmingham Division)   *Property Tax, Unclaimed Property Records*
Access to the property tax due database is available free at http://tc.jeffcointouch.com/taxcollection/HTML/index.asp. No name searching. Also, access to the unclaimed property list is available free at www.jeffcointouch.com/unclaimed/alpha.asp?section=directory

Mobile County   *Deed, UCC, Property, Incs, Marriage Records*
http://mobile-county.net/probate
Access to the Probate court's recordings database are available free at www.mobilecounty.org/probatecourt/recordssearch.htm.
Marriages are in a separate index.

Morgan County   *Property, Appraisal Records*
Access is available free at www.deltacomputersystems.com/AL/AL52/INDEX.html

St. Clair County (Southern Congressional District)   *Property, Appraisal Records*
Access is available free at www.deltacomputersystems.com/AL/AL59/INDEX.html

Tuscaloosa County   *Real Estate, Lien, UCC, Grantor/Grantee, Probate, Marriage Records*
www.tuscco.com
Access to the records database is available free at www.tuscco.com/RecordsRoom/Records.htm. Also included are searches for
mortgages, incorporations, bonds, discharges, exemptions

Federal Courts in Alabama...

Standards for Federal Courts: The universal PACER sign-up number is 800-676-6856. Find PACER and the Party/Case Index on
the Web at http://pacer.psc.uscourts.gov. PACER dial-up access is $.60 per minute. Also, courts offering internet access via RACER,
PACER, Web-PACER or the new CM-ECF charge $.07 per page fee unless noted as free.

US District Court -- Middle District of Alabama
Home Page: www.almd.uscourts.gov
PACER: Case records are available back to 1994. Records are purged every 18 months. New records are available online after 1 day.
PACER URL: http://pacer.alnd.uscourts.gov. Document images available.
Dothan Division counties: Coffee, Dale, Geneva, Henry, Houston.
Montgomery Division counties: Autauga, Barbour, Bullock, Butler, Chilton, Coosa, Covington, Crenshaw, Elmore, Lowndes,
Montgomery, Pike.
Opelika Division counties: Chambers, Lee, Macon, Randolph, Russell, Tallapoosa.

US Bankruptcy Court -- Middle District of Alabama
Home Page: www.almb.uscourts.gov
PACER: NIBS court. Use of PC Anywhere V4.0 recommended. Case records are available back to case 89-02000. Records are
purged every 6 months. New civil records are available online after 2-3 days.   **PACER URL:** WebPacer is available online at
https://ecf.almb.uscourts.gov. Document images available.
Electronic Filing: Electronic filing information is available online at https://ecf.almb.uscourts.gov. **Also:** access via phone on VCIS
(Voice Case Information System) is available: 334-954-3868.
Montgomery Division counties: Autauga, Barbour, Bullock, Butler, Chambers, Chilton, Coffee, Coosa, Covington, Crenshaw, Dale,
Elmore, Geneva, Henry, Houston, Lee, Lowndes, Macon, Montgomery, Pike, Randolph, Russell, Tallapoosa.

US District Court -- Northern District of Alabama
Home Page: www.alnd.uscourts.gov
PACER: Case records are available back to 1994. Records are purged every 18 months. New records are available online after 1 day.
PACER URL: http://pacer.alnd.uscourts.gov. Document images available.
Birmingham Division counties: Bibb, Blount, Calhoun, Clay, Cleburne, Greene, Jefferson, Pickens, Shelby, Sumter, Talladega,
Tuscaloosa.
Florence Division counties: Colbert, Franklin, Lauderdale.
Gadsden Division counties: Cherokee, De Kalb, Etowah, Marshall, St. Clair.
Huntsville Division counties: Cullman, Jackson, Lawrence, Limestone, Madison, Morgan.
Jasper Division counties: Fayette, Lamar, Marion, Walker, Winston.

US Bankruptcy Court -- Northern District of Alabama
Home Page: www.alnb.uscourts.gov
PACER: Case records are available back to October 31, 1976. New civil records are available online after 1 day.   **PACER URL:**
http://pacer.alnb.uscourts.gov. **Also:** access via phone on VCIS (Voice Case Information System) is available: 877-466-8879.

Anniston Division counties: Calhoun, Cherokee, Clay, Cleburne, De Kalb, Etowah, Marshall, St. Clair, Talladega.
Birmingham Division counties: Blount, Jefferson, Shelby.
Decatur Division counties: Colbert, Cullman, Franklin, Jackson, Lauderdale, Lawrence, Limestone, Madison, Morgan. The part of Winston County North of Double Springs is handled by this division.
Tuscaloosa Division counties: Bibb, Fayette, Greene, Lamar, Marion, Pickens, Sumter, Tuscaloosa, Walker, Winston. The part of Winston County North of Double Springs is handled by Decatur Division.

US District Court -- Southern District of Alabama

Home Page: www.als.uscourts.gov
PACER: Toll-free access: 800-622-9392. Local access phone: 334-694-4672. Case records are available back to 1993. New records are available online after 1 day. **PACER URL:** http://pacer.alsd.uscourts.gov.
Other Online Access: Search records on the Internet using RACER; connect via the link at www.als.uscourts.gov. Access fee is $.07 per page.
Mobile Division counties: Baldwin, Choctaw, Clarke, Conecuh, Escambia, Mobile, Monroe, Washington.
Selma Division counties: Dallas, Hale, Marengo, Perry, Wilcox.

US Bankruptcy Court -- Southern District of Alabama

Home Page: www.alsb.uscourts.gov
PACER: Case records are available back to 1993. New civil records are available online after 1 day.
Electronic Filing: Electronic filing information is available online at https://ecf.alsb.uscourts.gov.
Other Online Access: Check www.alsb.uscourts.gov/EFiling.htm for latest ECF updates. **Also:** access via phone on VCIS (Voice Case Information System) is available: 334-441-5637.
Mobile Division counties: Baldwin, Choctaw, Clarke, Conecuh, Dallas, Escambia, Hale, Marengo, Mobile, Monroe, Perry, Washington, Wilcox.

Editor's Tip: Just because records are maintained in a certain way in your state or county do not assume that any other county or state does things the same way that you are used to.

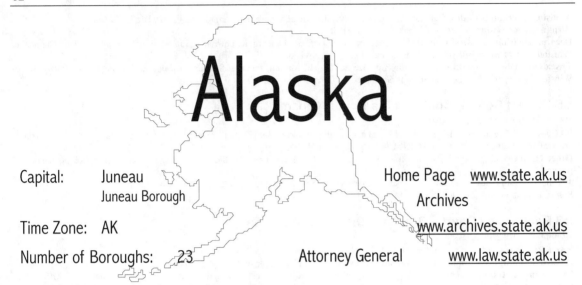

Capital:	Juneau	Home Page	www.state.ak.us
	Juneau Borough	Archives	
Time Zone:	AK		www.archives.state.ak.us
Number of Boroughs:	23	Attorney General	www.law.state.ak.us

State Level ... Major Agencies

Criminal Records

Department of Public Safety, Records and Identification, 5700 E Tudor Rd, Anchorage, AK 99507; 907-269-5765, 907-269-5091 (Fax), 8AM-4:30PM.

www.dps.state.ak.us

Name searching of limited trial court records and calendars are available free online at www.state.ak.us/courts/names.htm. As a pilot program, the records are not complete, though all courts with electronic capabilities contribute some records. This excludes many of the smaller outlying courts. Name search gives case number only.

Sexual Offender Registry

Sex offender data is available online at www.dps.state.ak.us/nSorcr/asp/.

Corporation Records, Trademarks/Servicemarks, Fictitious Name, Assumed Name, Limited Partnership Records, Limited Liability Company Records, Limited Liability Partnership Records

Corporation Section, Department of Community & Econ Dev, PO Box 110808, Juneau, AK 99811-0808 (Courier: 150 Third Street Rm 217, Juneau, AK 99801); 907-465-2530, 907-465-3257 (Fax), 8AM-5PM.

www.dced.state.ak.us/bsc/corps.htm

At the web site, one can access status information on corps, LLCs, LLP, LP (all both foreign and domestic), registered and reserved names, as well as trademark information. There is no fee. **Other options:** For bulk purchase, the requester must use a third party. Call 907-465-2530 for more information.

Uniform Commercial Code

UCC Central File Systems Office, State Recorder's Office, 550 West 7th Ave #1200A, Anchorage, AK 99501-3564; 907-269-8873, 907-269-8899, 8AM-3:30PM.

www.dnr.state.ak.us/ssd/ucc/index.cfm

One can search by granter-grantee name, date, document number or dcoument type at www.dnr.state.ak.us/ucc/search. There is no fee. **Other options:** Bulkmedia of the entire UCC database can be purchased from the State Recorder's Office (907-269-8881).

Driver Records

Division of Motor Vehicles, Driver's Records, 2760 Sherwood Lane #B, Juneau, AK 99801; 907-465-4361 (Motor Vehicle Reports Desk), 907-465-4363 (Licensing), 907-465-5509 (Fax), 8AM-5PM.

www.state.ak.us/dmv

Online access costs $5.00 per record. Inquiries may be made at any time, 24 hours a day. Batch inquiries may call back within thirty minutes for responses. Search by the first four letters of driver's name, license number and date of birth. At present, there is only one phone line available for users; you may experience a busy signal.

Legislation Records

www.legis.state.ak.us

All information, including statutes, is available from the Internet site.

State Level ... Occupational Licensing

Acupuncturist	www.dced.state.ak.us/occ/search3.htm
Alcohol Establishment	www.abc.revenue.state.ak.us/Feb%2002%20Operating.xls
Anesthetist (Dental), General/Permit	www.dced.state.ak.us/occ/search3.htm
Architect	www.dced.state.ak.us/occ/search3.htm
Athletic Promoter	www.dced.state.ak.us/occ/search3.htm
Athletic Trainer	www.dced.state.ak.us/occ/search3.htm
Audiologist/Hearing Aid Dealer	www.dced.state.ak.us/occ/search3.htm
Bail Bondsman	www.dced.state.ak.us/ins/apps/InsLicStart.cfm
Barber	www.dced.state.ak.us/occ/search3.htm
Barber Shop Owner/School/Instructor	www.dced.state.ak.us/occ/search3.htm
Big Game Guide/Assistant/Transporter	www.dced.state.ak.us/occ/search3.htm
Boxer	www.dced.state.ak.us/occ/search3.htm
Boxing Physician	www.dced.state.ak.us/occ/search3.htm
Boxing/Wrestling Personnel	www.dced.state.ak.us/occ/search3.htm
Chiropractor	www.dced.state.ak.us/occ/search3.htm
Collection Agency/Operator	www.dced.state.ak.us/occ/search3.htm
Concert Promoter	www.dced.state.ak.us/occ/search3.htm
Construction Contractor	www.dced.state.ak.us/occ/search3.htm
Contractor, Civil/Elect./Mech./Mining/Petrol.	www.dced.state.ak.us/occ/search3.htm
Contractor, Residential	www.dced.state.ak.us/occ/search3.htm
Cosmetologist/Hairdresser	www.dced.state.ak.us/occ/search3.htm
Cosmetology Shop Owner/School/Instructor	www.dced.state.ak.us/occ/search3.htm
Counselor, Professional	www.dced.state.ak.us/occ/OccStart.cfm
Dental Hygienist	www.dced.state.ak.us/occ/search3.htm
Dentist/Dental Examiner	www.dced.state.ak.us/occ/search3.htm
Dietitian/Nutritionist	www.dced.state.ak.us/occ/OccStart.cfm
Drug Distributor/Drug Room	www.dced.state.ak.us/occ/search3.htm
Electrical Administrator	www.dced.state.ak.us/occ/search3.htm
Employment Agency Operator/Agency Permit	www.dced.state.ak.us/occ/search3.htm
Engineer	www.dced.state.ak.us/occ/search3.htm
Esthetician	www.dced.state.ak.us/occ/search3.htm
Funeral Director/Establishment	www.dced.state.ak.us/occ/search3.htm
Geologist	www.dced.state.ak.us/occ/search3.htm
Guide Outfitter, Hunting	www.dced.state.ak.us/occ/search3.htm
Hearing Aid Dealer	www.dced.state.ak.us/occ/search3.htm
Independent Adjuster	www.dced.state.ak.us/ins/apps/InsLicStart.cfm
Insurance Agent, Managing General	www.dced.state.ak.us/ins/apps/InsLicStart.cfm
Insurance Occupation	www.dced.state.ak.us/ins/apps/InsLicStart.cfm
Insurance Producer	www.dced.state.ak.us/ins/apps/InsLicStart.cfm
Lobbyist/Lobbyist Employer	www.state.ak.us/local/akpages/ADMIN/apoc/lobcov.htm
Marriage & Family Therapist	www.dced.state.ak.us/occ/OccStart.cfm

Mechanical Administrator www.dced.state.ak.us/occ/search3.htm
Medical Doctor/Surgeon www.dced.state.ak.us/occ/search3.htm
Midwife .... www.dced.state.ak.us/occ/OccStart.cfm
Mortician/Embalmer www.dced.state.ak.us/occ/search3.htm
Naturopathic Physician www.dced.state.ak.us/occ/search3.htm
Nurse/Nurse Anesthetist/Nurse-RN/LPN www.dced.state.ak.us/occ/search3.htm
Nurses' Aide www.dced.state.ak.us/occ/search3.htm
Nursing Home Administrator www.dced.state.ak.us/occ/search3.htm
Occupational Therapist/Assistant www.dced.state.ak.us/occ/search3.htm
Optician, Dispensing www.dced.state.ak.us/occ/search3.htm
Optometrist www.dced.state.ak.us/occ/search3.htm
Osteopathic Physician www.dced.state.ak.us/occ/search3.htm
Paramedic www.dced.state.ak.us/occ/search3.htm
Parenteral Sedation (Dental) www.dced.state.ak.us/occ/search3.htm
Pharmacist/Pharmacist Intern www.dced.state.ak.us/occ/search3.htm
Pharmacy www.dced.state.ak.us/occ/search3.htm
Physical Therapist/Assistant www.dced.state.ak.us/occ/search3.htm
Physician Assistant www.dced.state.ak.us/occ/search3.htm
Pilot, Marine www.dced.state.ak.us/occ/search3.htm
Podiatrist www.dced.state.ak.us/occ/search3.htm
Psychologist/Psychological Assistant www.dced.state.ak.us/occ/search3.htm
Public Accountant-CPA .... www.dced.state.ak.us/occ/OccStart.cfm
Real Estate Agent/Broker/Assoc. www.dced.state.ak.us/occ/search3.htm
Real Estate Appraiser www.dced.state.ak.us/occ/search3.htm
Referee .... www.dced.state.ak.us/occ/OccStart.cfm
Reinsurance Intermediary Broker/Mgr. .... www.dced.state.ak.us/ins/apps/InsLicStart.cfm
Social Worker .... www.dced.state.ak.us/occ/OccStart.cfm
Social Worker, Clinical .... www.dced.state.ak.us/occ/OccStart.cfm
Surplus Line Broker .... www.dced.state.ak.us/ins/apps/InsLicStart.cfm
Surveyor, Land www.dced.state.ak.us/occ/search3.htm
Underground Storage Tank Worker/Contr. www.dced.state.ak.us/occ/search3.htm
Vessel Agent www.dced.state.ak.us/occ/search3.htm
Veterinarian/Veterinary Technician www.dced.state.ak.us/occ/search3.htm
Wrestler .... www.dced.state.ak.us/occ/OccStart.cfm

County Level ... Courts

Court Administration: Office of the Administrative Director, 303 K St, Anchorage, AK, 99501; 907-264-0547; www.state.ak.us/courts/

Court Structure: Alaska is not organized into counties, but rather into 15 boroughs (3 unified home rule municipalities that are combination borough and city, and 12 boroughs) and 12 home rule cities, which do not directly coincide with the 4 Judicial Districts into which the judicial system is divided, that is, judicial boundaries cross borough boundaries.

Online Access Note: You may name search the nearly statewide Alaska Trial Courts database at www.state.ak.us/courts/names.htm. This includes only those courts with electronic indexing and access. This database is updated quarterly; records do not go back beyond 1990. Search results give case number and court only, and index gives only the name used on the first pleading; no index updates. The home web page also gives access to Supreme Court and Appellate opinions.

Fairbanks North Star Borough

Superior & District Court (4th District) *Civil and Criminal Records*
www.state.ak.us/courts/courtdir.htm
Access to the previous 6 months of Fairbanks civil court records are available free at
www.state.ak.us/courts/akct.htm. Click on "trial courts."

County Level ... Recorders & Assessors

Recording Office Organization: The 23 Alaskan counties are called boroughs. However, real estate recording is done under a system of 34 recording districts that was established at the time of the Gold Rush. Some of the Districts are identical in geography to boroughs, such as the Aleutian Islands, but other boroughs and districts overlap. Therefore you need to know which recording district any given town or city is located in. A helpful web site is www.dnr.state.ak.us/recorders/findYourDistrict.htm. All state and federal tax liens are filed with the District Recorder. Districts do not perform separate tax lien searches.

The entire state except the Aleutian Islands is in the Alaska Time Zone (AK).

Online Access Note: Online access to the state recorder's office database from the Dept. of Natural Resources is available free at www.dnr.state.ak.us/recorders/search. This includes property information, liens, deeds, bankruptcies and more. Images are not available although the index goes as far back as the mid-1970's depending on the recording district involved. Also, a DNR "land records" database is searchable at www.dnr.state.ak.us/cgi-bin/lris/landrecords. Finally, UCCs may be searched at www.dnr.state.ak.us/ucc/search.

Statewide *Real Estate, UCC Records*

Online access is available on the statewide DNR system at www.dnr.state.ak.us/recorders/search. Index goes back to mid-1970's depending on the recording district involved. Images are not available.

Fairbanks District *Real Estate, UCC Records*

www.co.fairbanks.ak.us

Access to the City of Fairbanks Property database is available for free online at www.co.fairbanks.ak.us/database/aurora/default.asp.

Juneau District *Real Estate, UCC Records*

www.juneau.org/cbj/index.php

Access to City of Juneau Property Records database is available free online at www.juneau.lib.ak.us/assessordata/assessor.asp. Also includes link access to Juneau rentals data and the Records home page.

Kenai District *Assessor, Real Estate, UCC Records*

www.dnr.state.ak.us/ssd/recoff/default.htm

Access to Kenai Peninsula Borough Assessing Dept. Public Information Search Page is available free at www.borough.kenai.ak.us/assessingdept/Parcel_QUERY/SEARCH.HTM.

Federal Courts in Alaska...

Standards for Federal Courts: The universal PACER sign-up number is 800-676-6856. Find PACER and the Party/Case Index on the Web at http://pacer.psc.uscourts.gov. PACER dial-up access is $.60 per minute. Also, courts offering internet access via RACER, PACER, Web-PACER or the new CM-ECF charge $.07 per page fee unless noted as free.

US District Court -- District of Alaska

Home Page: www.akd.uscourts.gov

PACER: Toll-free access: 888-271-6212. Local access phone: 907-677-6178. Case records are available back to 1987. Records are purged every 6 months. New records are available online after 1 day.

Other Online Access: Court does not participate in the U.S. party case index.

Anchorage Division counties: Aleutian Islands-East, Aleutian Islands-West, Anchorage Borough, Bristol Bay Borough, Kenai Peninsula Borough, Kodiak Island Borough, Matanuska-Susitna Borough, Valdez-Cordova.

Fairbanks Division counties: Bethel, Fairbanks North Star Borough, North Slope Borough, Northwest Arctic Borough, Southeast Fairbanks, Wade Hampton, Yukon-Koyukuk.

Juneau Division counties: Haines Borough, Juneau Borough, Prince of Wales-Outer Ketchikan, Sitka Borough, Skagway-Hoonah-Angoon, Wrangell-Petersburg.

Ketchikan Division counties: Ketchikan Gateway Borough.

Nome Division counties: Nome.

US Bankruptcy Court -- District of Alaska

Home Page: http://www2.akb.uscourts.gov/mainpage.htm

PACER: Case records are available back to July 1991. Records are purged 6 months. New civil records are available online after 2 days. **PACER URL:** http://pacer.akb.uscourts.gov. Document images available.

Electronic Filing: Electronic filing information is available online at https://ecf.akb.uscourts.gov.

Other Online Access: The RACER system has been replaced by the ECF/PACER system. Access fee is $.07 per page. **Also:** access via phone on VCIS (Voice Case Information System) is available: 888-878-3110, 907-271-2658

Anchorage Division counties: All boroughs and districts in Alaska.

Editor's Tip: Remember, Alaska has its own time zone. Alaska time is one hour earlier than Pacific Standard Time, and four hours earlier than Eastern Standard Time.

Also not that Alaska's Aleutian Islands are in the Hawaii Time Zone, which is one hour earlier than Alaska Time.

Capital: Phoenix   Home Page   www.state.az.us
                Maricopa County   Archives

Time Zone: MST (no DST)   www.dlapr.lib.az.us/archives

Number of Counties: 15   Attorney General   www.attorneygeneral.state.az.us

State Level ... Major Agencies

Corporation Records, Limited Liability Company Records

Corporation Commission, 1300 W Washington, Phoenix, AZ 85007; 602-542-3026 (Status), 602-542-3285 (Annual Reports), 602-542-3414 (Fax), 8AM-5PM.

www.cc.state.az.us

The web site provides free access to all corporation information. Also, a commercial online system, called STARPAS, functions 24 hours a day, 7 days a week. The initial set-up fee is $36.00 and access costs $.30 per minute. Call 602-542-0685 for a sign-up package.

Trademarks/Servicemarks, Trade Names, Limited Partnership Records

Secretary of State, Trademarks/Tradenames/Limited Partnership Division, 1700 W Washington, 7th Floor, Phoenix, AZ 85007; 602-542-6187, 602-542-7386 (Fax), 8AM-5PM.

www.sosaz.com

Trade names, trademarks, and registered names (partnerships) can be searched for free at www.sosas.com/business_services/trademakrand tradenames.htm. **Other options:** Bulk purchase is available on microfiche.

Uniform Commercial Code, Federal Tax Liens, State Tax Liens

UCC Division, Secretary of State, 1700 W Washington, 7th Floor, Phoenix, AZ 85007 (Courier: Customer Service Center, 14 North 18th Ave, Phoenix, AZ 85007); 602-542-6178, 602-542-7386 (Fax), 8AM - 5PM.

www.sosaz.com

UCC records can be searched for free over the web site. Searching can be done by debtor, secured party name, or file number. From this site you can also pull down a weekly microfiche file of filings (about 10 megabytes). Note there are 2 searches - a pre 07/01/01 search of the old database, and a strict Revised Article 9 which is current up within 4 days of present. **Other options:** Email requests are accepted. Microfilm of filings is available for purchase.

Sexual Offender Registry

Sex offender data is maintained by the Department of Public Safety's Sex Offender Cummunity Notification Unit. Free online searching is available at www.azsexoffender.com or call 602-255-0611.

Driver Records

Motor Vehicle Division, Record Services Section, PO Box 2100, Mail Drop 539M, Phoenix, AZ 85001-2100 (Courier: Customer Records Services, 1801 W Jefferson, Rm 111, Phoenix, AZ 85007); 602-255-0072, 8AM-5PM.

www.dot.state.az.us/MVD/mvd.htm

Arizona's online system is interactive and open 24 hours daily. Fee is $3.00 per record. This system is primarily for those requesters who qualify per DPPA. For more information call 602-712-7235. **Other options:** Overnight magnetic tape-to-tape ordering available.

Vehicle Ownership, Vehicle Identification

Motor Vehicle Division - Director's Office, Record Services Section, PO Box 2100, Mail Drop 504M, Phoenix, AZ 85001-2100 (Courier: Customer Records Services, 1801 W Jefferson, Rm 111, Phoenix, AZ 85007); 602-712-8420, 8AM-5PM.

www.dot.state.az.us/MVD/mvd.htm

Online access is offered only to permissible users. Fee is $3.00 per record. The system is open 24 hours a day, seven days a week. For more information, call 602-712-7235.

Legislation Records

www.azleg.state.az.us

Most information, beginning with 1997, is available through the Internet (i.e. bill text, committee minutes, committee assignments, member bios, etc.). There is no fee. **Other options:** Name, address, and office # lists are available at no charge. Roll call vote histories of individuals per year are available at $.10 per page.

State Level ... Occupational Licensing

Advance Fee Loan Broker	www.azbanking.com/Lists/Lists.htm
Appraiser, Real/Personal Property	www.asc.gov/content/category1/appr_by_state.asp
Architect	www.btr.state.az.us
Assayer	www.btr.state.az.us
Attorney	www.azbar.org/MemberFinder/MF_Search.cfm
Bank	www.azbanking.com/Lists/BA_List.HTML
Bank	www.azbanking.com/Lists/Lists.htm
Behavioral Health Emergency/Residential Service	www.hs.state.az.us/als/databases/index.html
Behavioral Outpatient Clinic	www.hs.state.az.us/als/databases/index.html
Behavioral Outpatient Rehab Center	www.hs.state.az.us/als/databases/index.html
Charity	www.sosaz.com/scripts/Charity_Search.dll
Chiropractor	www.azchiroboard.com/dir.html
Collection Agency	www.azbanking.com/Lists/Lists.htm
Consumer Lender	www.azbanking.com/Lists/Lists.htm
Contractor	www.rc.state.az.us/clsc/AZROCLicenseQuery
Counselor, Professional	http://aspin.asu.edu/~azbbhe/directory/listing.html
Court Reporter	www.supreme.state.az.us/cr/CRcertlist2001.htm
Credit Union	www.azbanking.com/Lists/Lists.htm
Day Care Establishment	www.hs.state.az.us/als/databases/index.html
Debt Management	www.azbanking.com/Lists/Lists.htm
Degree Program (Vocational)	http://azppse.state.az.us/directory.html
Engineer	www.btr.state.az.us
Escrow Agent	www.azbanking.com/Lists/Lists.htm
Funeral Preneed Trust Company	www.azbanking.com/Lists/Lists.htm
Geologist	www.btr.state.az.us
Hearing Aid Dispenser	www.hs.state.az.us/als/databases/index.html
Home Inspector	www.btr.state.az.us
Landscape Architect	www.btr.state.az.us
Liquor Producer	www.azll.com/query.htm
Liquor Retail Co-Operative/Agent/Mgr. (Retail)	www.azll.com/query.htm
Liquor Wholesaler	www.azll.com/query.htm

Lobbyist	www.sos.state.az.us/scripts/Lobbyist_Search.dll
Marriage & Family Therapist	http://aspin.asu.edu/~azbbhe/directory/listing.html
Medical Doctor, Intern/Resident	www.bomex.org/getlicense.asp
Money Transmitter	www.azbanking.com/Lists/Lists.htm
Mortgage Banker, Commercial	www.azbanking.com/Lists/Lists.htm
Mortgage Banker/Broker	www.azbanking.com/Lists/Lists.htm
Motor Vehicle Dealer/Sales Finance	www.azbanking.com/Lists/Lists.htm
Naturopathic Physician	www.npbomex.az.gov/lic.html
Notary Public	www.sosaz.com/scripts/Notary_Search.dll
Optometrist	www.asbo.state.az.us
Pawn Shop	www.azbanking.com/Lists/DPC_List.HTML
Pesticide Company	www.sb.state.az.us/pdf/codir.pdf
Physician Assistant	www.bomex.org/getlicense.asp
Post-Secondary Education Institution	http://azppse.state.az.us/directory.html
Post-Secondary Vocational Program, Private	http://azppse.state.az.us/directory.html
Premium Finance Company	www.azbanking.com/Lists/Lists.htm
Property Tax Agent	www.appraisal.state.az.us/Directory/taxagent.html
Psychologist	http://psychboard.az.gov/dir.html
Public Accountant-CPA	www.accountancy.state.az.us
Public Accounting Firm-CPA/PA	www.accountancy.state.az.us
Real Estate Appraiser	www.appraisal.state.az.us/Directory/appr1.html
Real Estate Broker/Salesperson	www.re.state.az.us/db.html
Real Estate Firm	www.re.state.az.us/db.html
Sales Finance Company	www.azbanking.com/Lists/Lists.htm
Social Worker	http://aspin.asu.edu/~azbbhe/directory/listing.html
Substance Abuse Counselor	http://aspin.asu.edu/~azbbhe/directory/listing.html
Surveyor, Land	www.btr.state.az.us
Telemarketing Firm	www.sosaz.com/scripts/TS_Search_engine.cgi
Trust Company	www.azbanking.com/Lists/Lists.htm
Trust Division of Chartered Fin. Inst.	www.azbanking.com/Lists/Lists.htm

County Level ... Courts

Court Administration: Administrative Office of the Courts, Arizona Supreme Court Bldg, 1501 W Washington, Phoenix, AZ, 85007; 602-542-9301; www.supreme.state.az.us/

Court Structure: The Superior Court is the court of general jurisdiction. Justice, and Municipal courts generally have separate jurisdiction over certain case types. Most courts will search their records by plaintiff or defendant. Estate cases are handled by Superior Court.

Online Access Note: The Arizona Judicial Branch offers Public Access to Court Case Information, a valuable online service providing a resource for information about court cases from 137 out of 180 superior, justice, and municipal courts in Arizona. Access information includes: detailed case information, i.e., case type, charges, filing and disposition dates; the parties in the case, not including victims and witnesses; and the court mailing address and location. Go to www.supreme.state.az.us/publicaccess/.

The Maricopa and Pima county courts maintain their own systems but will also, under current planning, be part of ACAP. These two counties provide ever-increasing online access to the public.

Apache County
Superior Court *Civil and Criminal Records*
Online access to records is free at www.supreme.state.az.us/publicaccess/.

Online access to records is free at www.supreme.state.az.us/publicaccess for these Justice Courts:
Chinle Justice Court -- Puerco Justice Court -- Round Valley Justice Court -- St John's Justice Court

Cochise County
Superior Court *Civil and Criminal Records*
www.co.cochise.az.us/Court/Crtclerk.htm
Online access to records is free at www.supreme.state.az.us/publicaccess/.

Online access to records is free at www.supreme.state.az.us/publicaccess for these Justice Courts:
Benson Justice Court -- Bisbee Justice Court -- Bowie Justice -- Douglas Justice Court -- Sierra Vista Justice -- Willcox Justice Court

Coconino County
Superior Court *Civil and Criminal Records*
Online access to records is free at www.supreme.state.az.us/publicaccess/. In addition, the site provides records for these Justicee
Courts: Flagstaff Justice Court -- Fredonia Justice Court -- Page Justice Court -- Williams Justice Court

Gila County
Superior Court *Civil and Criminal Records*
Online access to records is free at www.supreme.state.az.us/publicaccess/. In addition, the site provides records for these Justicee
Courts: Globe Regional Justice Court -- Payson Justice Court -- Winkleman Justice Court

Graham County
Superior Court *Civil and Criminal Records*
Online access to records is free at www.supreme.state.az.us/publicaccess/. In addition, the site provides records for these Justicee
Courts: Justice Court Precinct #1 -- Pima Justice Court Precinct #2

Greenlee County
Superior Court *Civil and Criminal Records*
Online access to records is free at www.supreme.state.az.us/publicaccess/. In addition, the site provides records for these Justicee
Courts: Justice Court Precinct #1 -- Justice Court Precinct #2

La Paz County
Superior Court *Civil and Criminal Records*
www.co.la-paz.az.us/courts.htm
Online access to records is free at www.supreme.state.az.us/publicaccess/. In addition, the site provides records for these Justicee
Courts: Parker Justice Court -- Quartzsite Justice Court -- Salome Justice Court

Maricopa County
Superior Court *Civil and Criminal Records*
www.superiorcourt.maricopa.gov
Online access is available free at www.superiorcourt.maricopa.gov/docket/public_new.html. Case file can be printed. Online access to
records is free at www.supreme.state.az.us/publicaccess for these Justice Courts: Buckeye Justice Court -- Gila Bend Justice Court --
Glendale Justice Court -- Maryvale Justice Court -- North Valley Justice Court -- Peoria Justice Court -- Scottsdale Justice Court --
Tolleson Justice Court -- Wickenburg Justice Court

Navajo County
Superior Court *Civil and Criminal Records*
Online access to records is free at www.supreme.state.az.us/publicaccess/. In addition, the site provides records for these Justicee
Courts: Holbrook Justice Court -- Kayenta Justice Court -- Pinetop-Lakeside Justice Court -- Show Low Justice Court -- Snowflake
Justice Court -- Winslow Justice Court

Pima County
Superior Court *Civil and Criminal Records*
www.cosc.co.pima.az.us
Online access to superior court records is available free at www.cosc.co.pima.az.us/record_search/. Cases without dispositions are not
included online.

Pima County Consolidated Justice Court *Civil and Criminal Records*
http://jp.co.pima.az.us

Online access is free http://geronimo.jp.co.pima.az.us/casesearch/. You can search docket information for civil, criminal or traffic cases by name, docket or citation number.

Online access to records is free at www.supreme.state.az.us/publicaccess for these Justice Courts: Ajo Justice Court Civil -- Green Valley Justice Court

Pinal County
Superior Court *Civil and Criminal Records*
www.co.pinal.az.us/clerksc
Online access to records is free at www.supreme.state.az.us/publicaccess/. In addition, the site provides records for these Justicee Courts: Apache Junction Justice Court -- Casa Grande Justice Court -- Eloy Justice Court -- Florence Justice Court -- Mammoth Justice Court -- Maricopa Justice Court -- Oracle Justice Court -- Superior/Kearny Justice Court

Santa Cruz County
Superior Court *Civil and Criminal Records*
http://sccazcourts.org
Online access to records is free at www.supreme.state.az.us/publicaccess/. In addition, the site provides records for these Justicee Courts: East Santa Cruz County Justice Court - Precinct #2 -- Santa Cruz Justice Court

Yavapai County
Superior Court *Civil and Criminal Records*
Free access to Superior Court records at www.supreme.state.az.us/publicaccess/. In addition, the site provides records for these Justicee Courts: Bagdad Justice Court -- Bagdad-Yarnell Justice Court -- Mayer Justice Court -- Seligman Justice Court -- Verde Valley Justice Court

Yuma County
Superior Court *Civil and Criminal Records*
Online access to records is free at www.supreme.state.az.us/publicaccess/. In addition, the site provides records for these Justicee Courts: Somerton Justice Court -- Wellton Justice Court -- Yuma Justice Court

County Level ... Recorders & Assessors

Recording Office Organization: 15 counties, 16 recording offices (The Navajo Nation in NE Arizona is the sixteenth). The recording officer is the County Recorder. Recordings are usually placed in a Grantor/Grantee index. The entire state is in the Mountain Time Zone (MST) and does not change to daylight savings time. Note that no less than four new zip codes have added in recent years: 480 and 623 for east and west Phoenix Metro area respectively, 520 for south and southeastern state, and 924 for west and north of state. Federal and state tax liens on personal property of businesses are filed with the Secretary of State. Other federal and state tax liens are filed with the County Recorder. Several counties will do a separate tax lien search.

Online Access Note: A number of county assessor offices offer online access. The Secretary of State offers online access to UCC records at www.sosaz.com/scripts/UCC_Search.dll.

Apache County   *Real Estate, Recording Records*
www.co.apache.az.us/Recorder/index.htm
Access to the Apache County Recorder Query Index are available free at www.co.apache.az.us/Recorder/index/query.asp.

Coconino County   *Recording, Grantor/Grantee, Real Estate Records*
http://co.coconino.az.us/recorder/
Access to county iCRIS system is available free at http://coco-criswf.infomagic.net/splash.jsp. Registration is required. Documents are $1.00 to print, signup and request documents at 800-793-6181. Online records go back to 1983; images back to 3/1999.

Maricopa County   *Real Estate, Lien Records*

http://recorder.maricopa.gov

Access is available by direct dial-up or on the Internet. Dial-up access requires one-time set-up fee of $300 plus $.06 per minute. Dial-up hours are 8am-10pm M-F, 8-5 S-S. Records date back to 1983. For additional information, contact Linda Kinchloe at 602-506-3637. Also, access to the County Recorder's database is available free at http://recorder.maricopa.gov/recdocdata. Records go back to 1983. Also, access to the Assessor database is available free at www.maricopa.gov/assessor/default.asp. Residential data is available. Also, perform name/parcel/property tax appeal lookups free on the SBOE site at www.sboe.state.az.us/cgi-bin/name_lookup.pl.

Mohave County   *Real Estate, Grantor/Grantee, Lien, Assessor Records*

www.co.mohave.az.us

Access to the Recorder's System is available free at http://icris.co.mohave.az.us/splash.jsp. Registration and password is required. Also, online access to the Assessor's property database is available free (no registration) at www.co.mohave.az.us/1moweb/depts_files/assessor_files/assessdata.asp. A sales history database is also here. Also, the treasurer's tax sale parcel search is available at www.co.mohave.az.us/1moweb/depts_files/treasure_files/about_treasure.htm. You may also search restaurant inspections at the main web site.

Navajo County   *Property, Assessor, Grantor/Grantee, Recording, UCCs Records*

www.co.navajo.az.us

Access to the recorder's database of land inormation, UCCs and Grantor/Grantee indexes is available free at http://iris.co.navajo.az.us/irisonweb. Also, access to the property assessor database if available free at www.co.mohave.az.us./navajo/assessor/assessdatalink.asp.

Pima County   *Assessor, Real Estate, Lien, Recording Records*

www.recorder.co.pima.az.us

Access to the recorder's Research Records database is available free at www.recorder.co.pima.az.us/research.html. Click "Enter Here" and use the word "public" for user name and password. Also, records on the Pima County Tax Assessor database are available free online at www.asr.co.pima.az.us/apiq/index.html. Also, a name/parcel/property tax lookup may be performed free on the SBOE site at www.sboe.state.az.us/cgi-bin/name_lookup.pl. Also, search by parcel number on the Treasurer's tax inquiry database at www.to.co.pima.az.us/inquiry.html.

Pinal County   *Grantor/Grantee, Tax Bill, Tax Lien, Tax Sales Records*

http://co.pinal.az.us

Access to the county recorder's index is available free at http://co.pinal.az.us/recorder/docsearch.asp. Also, online access to the county treasurer's database of tax liens, tax bills, and tax sales is available free at http://co.pinal.az.us/treasurer. Click on appropriate "Tax Searches" button.

Yavapai County   *Assessor, Real Estate, Recording Records*

www.co.yavapai.az.us/departments/recorder/RecorderMain.asp

Access to the recording office iCRIS database is available free at http://icris.co.yavapai.az.us/splash.jsp. Records from 1976 to present; images from 1986 to present. Also, assessor and land records on the County Geographic Information Systems (GIS) database are available free online at www.co.yavapai.az.us/departments/gis/gisOnlineApps.asp. To search, choose a "session" in the "Locate Property Information" box.

Federal Courts in Arizona...

Standards for Federal Courts: The universal PACER sign-up number is 800-676-6856. Find PACER and the Party/Case Index on the Web at http://pacer.psc.uscourts.gov. PACER dial-up access is $.60 per minute. Also, courts offering internet access via RACER, PACER, Web-PACER or the new CM-ECF charge $.07 per page fee unless noted as free.

US District Court -- District of Arizona

Home Page: www.azd.uscourts.gov

PACER: Toll-free access: 888-372-5707. Local access phone: 602-322-7194. Case records are available back to 1992. Records are purged every 12 months. New records are available online after 1-3 days. **PACER URL:** http://pacer.azd.uscourts.gov.

Phoenix Division counties: Gila, La Paz, Maricopa, Pinal, Yuma. Some Yuma cases handled by San Diego Division of the Southern District of California.

Prescott Division counties: Apache, Coconino, Mohave, Navajo, Yavapai.

Tucson Division counties: Cochise, Graham, Greelee, Pima, Santa Cruz. The Globe Division was closed effective January 1994, and all case records for that division are now found here.

US Bankruptcy Court -- District of Arizona

Home Page: www.azb.uscourts.gov

PACER: Toll-free access: 800-556-9230. Local access phone: 602-640-5832. Use of PC Anywhere v4.0 suggested. Additional password is bkc. Case records are available back to 1986. Records are purged every six months. New civil records are available online after 1 week. **PACER URL:** http://pacer.azb.uscourts.gov.

Electronic Filing: Electronic filing information is available online at http://pacer.psc.uscourts.gov/bk/azbh.html. **Also:** access via phone on VCIS (Voice Case Information System) is available: 602-640-5820.

Phoenix Division counties: Apache, Coconino, Maricopa, Navajo, Yavapai.

Tucson Division counties: Cochise, Gila, Graham, Greenlee, Pima, Pinal, Santa Cruz.

Yuma Division counties: La Paz, Mohave, Yuma.

Editor's Tip: Arizona, which is on Mountain Standard Time, does not observe Daylight Savings Time rules. Thus, from the first Sunday in April to the last Sunday in October, nearly all Arizona locations will have the same clock time as Pacific Daylight Time, the same time as in California, Oregon, Nevada and Washington.

There are exceptions. Some Arizona Indian Reservation offices may observe Daylight Savings Time. Most notable is the Navajo Indian Reservation in northeastern Arizona. The Navajos observe DST. This does not include the Hopi Indian Reservation, which incidentally is surrounded by the Navajos. This has been known to create a problem in Tuba City, AZ where hospitals may be an hour different than government offices when DST is in effect.

Arkansas

Capital:	Little Rock Pulaski County	Home Page	www.state.ar.us
Time Zone:	CST	Attorney General	www.ag.state.ar.us
Number of Counties:	75	Archives	www.ark-ives.com

State Level ... Major Agencies

Corporation Records, Fictitious Name, Limited Liability Company Records, Limited Partnerships

Secretary of State, Corporation Department-Aegon Bldg, 501 Woodlane, Rm 310, Little Rock, AR 72201-1094; 501-682-3409, 888-233-0325, 501-682-3437 (Fax), 8AM-5PM.

www.sosweb.state.ar.us/corps

The Internet site permits free searching of corporation records. You can search by name, registered agent, or filing number. **Other options:** Bulk release of records is available for $.50 per page. Contact Julie Butler at 501-682-3409 for details.

Trademarks/Servicemarks

Secretary of State, Trademarks Section-Aegon Bldg, 501 Woodlane, #310, Little Rock, AR 72201; 501-682-3409, 888-233-0325, 501-682-3437 (Fax), 8AM-5PM.

www.sosweb.state.ar.us/corps/trademk

Searching is available at no fee over the Internet site. Search by name, owner, city, or filing number. You can also search via email at corprequest@sosmail.state.ar.us. **Other options:** Records can be provided in bulk for $.50 per page. Contact Julie Butler at 501-682-3409 for details.

Incarceration Records

www.accessarkansas.org/doc/

The online access is limited to current inmates only. Location, ADC number, physical Identifiers and sentencing information, release dates are released.

Workers' Compensation Records

Workers Compensation Department, 324 Spring Street, PO Box 950, Little Rock, AR 72203-0950; 501-682-3930, 800-622-4472, 501-682-6761 (Fax), 8AM-4:30PM M-F.

www.awcc.state.ar.us

To perform an online claim search, one must be a subscriber to the Information Network of Arkansas (INA). Records are from May 1, 1997 forward. There is an annual $50 subscriber fee to INA. For more information, visit the web site at www.state.ar.us/ina.html.

Driver Records

Department of Driver Services, Driving Records Division, PO Box 1272, Room 1130, Little Rock, AR 72203-1272 (Courier: 1900 W 7th, #1130, Little Rock, AR 72201); 501-682-7207, 501-682-7908, 501-682-2075 (Fax), 8AM-4:30PM.

www.accessarkansas.org/dfa/driverservices/

Access is available through the Information Network of Arkansas (INA). The system offers both batch and interactive service. The system is only available to INA subscribers who have statutory rights to the data. The record fee is $8.00, or $11.00 for commercial drivers. Visit www.state.ar.us/ina.html. **Other options:** High volume requesters use magnetic tape-to-tape for overnight access.

Legislation Records

www.arkleg.state.ar.us

Search through the Internet site listed above, you may also search by subject matter.

State Level ... Occupational Licensing

Agriculture Education	www.as-is.org/directory/search_lic.html
Architect	www.state.ar.us/arch/search.html
Asbestos Abatement Inspector	www.adeq.state.ar.us/compsvs/webmaster/databases.htm
Asbestos Abatement Management Planner	www.adeq.state.ar.us/compsvs/webmaster/databases.htm
Asbestos Abatement Training Provider	www.adeq.state.ar.us/compsvs/webmaster/databases.htm
Asbestos Removal Worker	www.adeq.state.ar.us/compsvs/webmaster/databases.htm
Attorney	http://courts.state.ar.us/attylist/new/
Bank	www.sosweb.state.ar.us/corps/bkin
Business Education Teacher	www.as-is.org/directory/search_lic.html
Career Education Coordinator	www.as-is.org/directory/search_lic.html
Career Orientation Teacher	www.as-is.org/directory/search_lic.html
Cemetery, Perpetual Care	www.ark.org/arsec/database/dbsearch.cgi?dbname=7&limit=20&listall=ON
Child Care Provider	www.state.ar.us/childcare/search.html
Chiropractor	www.accessarkansas.org/asbce/search.html
Contractor	www.state.ar.us/clb/search.html
Cosmetologist	www.accessarkansas.org/cos/search.php
Cosmetology Instructor	www.accessarkansas.org/cos/search.php
Counselor, Professional	www.state.ar.us/abec/search.php
Dental Hygienist	www.asbde.org
Dentist	www.asbde.org
Electrologist	www.accessarkansas.org/cos/search.php
Electrolysis Instructor	www.accessarkansas.org/cos/search.php
Embalmer/Embalmer Apprentice	www.accessarkansas.org/fdemb/
Engineer/Engineer in Training	www.accessarkansas.org/pels/search.html
Fire Equipment Inspector	www.arfireprotection.org/roster/index.html
Fire Extinguisher Repairer	www.arfireprotection.org/roster/index.html
Fire Extinguisher Sprinkler Inspector	www.arfireprotection.org/roster/index.html
Funeral Director/Apprentice	www.accessarkansas.org/fdemb/
Funeral Home/Crematory	www.accessarkansas.org/fdemb/
Home Inspector	www.sosweb.state.ar.us/corps/homeinsp
Insurance Agency	www.sosweb.state.ar.us/corps/bkin
Insurance Sales Agent	www.accessarkansas.org/insurance/license/search.php
Investment Advisor	www.ark.org/arsec/database/search.html
Landscape Architect	www.state.ar.us/arch/search.html
Lobbyist	www.sosweb.state.ar.us/elect.html
Manicurist	www.accessarkansas.org/cos/search.php
Marriage & Family Therapist	www.state.ar.us/abec/search.php
Midwife Nurse	www.accessarkansas.org/nurse/registry/index.html
Mortgage Loan Broker/Company	www.ark.org/arsec/database/search.html
Motor Vehicle Dealer/Salesperson, New	www.armvc.com/mfg_dist/search.php
Motor Vehicle Mfg/Rep, New	www.armvc.com/mfg_dist/search.php

Notary Public .... www.sosweb.state.ar.us/corps/notary
Nurse/ Nurse-LPN .... www.accessarkansas.org/nurse/registry/index.html
Nurse Anesthetist .... www.accessarkansas.org/nurse/registry/index.html
Optician.. www.ark.org/directory/detail2.cgi?ID-1050
Optometrist... www.odfinder.org/LicSearch.asp
Public Accountant-CPA .... www.accessarkansas.org/asbpa
Real Estate Appraiser .... www.asc.gov/content/category1/appr_by_state.asp
Real Estate Broker................................... www.accessarkansas.org/arec/db/
Real Estate Sales Agent............................. www.accessarkansas.org/arec/db/
School Counselor .... www.as-is.org/directory/search_lic.html
School Principal/Admin/Super.................... www.as-is.org/directory/search_lic.html
Securities Agent .... www.ark.org/arsec/database/search.html
Securities Broker/Dealer............................ www.ark.org/arsec/database/search.html
Social Worker.. www.state.ar.us/swlb/search/index.html
Solid Waste Facility Operator .... www.adeq.state.ar.us/compsvs/webmaster/databases.htm
Surveyor, Land .... www.accessarkansas.org/pels/search.html
Surveyor-in-Training................................ www.accessarkansas.org/pels/search.html
Teacher... www.as-is.org/directory/search_lic.html
Waste Water Treatment Plant Operator......... www.adeq.state.ar.us/compsvs/webmaster/databases.htm

County Level ... Courts

Court Administration: Administrative Office of Courts, 625 Marshall St, Justice Bldg, Little Rock, AR, 72201; 501-682-9400; http://courts.state.ar.us

Court Structure: Circuit Courts are the courts of general jurisdiction and are arranged in 28 circuits. County Courts are, fundamentally, administrative courts dealing with county fiscal issues. For all intents and purposes, Circuit and County Courts are combined. And by abolishing the distinction between law and equity case types, the legislature allowed the former Chancery Courts to be absorbed into the Circuit Courts as of 1/2002. As of 8/2/97, the civil limit raised to $5000 in limited jurisdiction District Courts. As of 7/1/2001, Municipal Courts are known as District Courts.

Online Access Note: There is a very limited internal online computer system at the Administrative Office of Courts. The home web page gives online access to Supreme and Appellate opinions.

Benton County
Circuit Court *Civil and Criminal Records*
www.co.benton.ar.us
Civil court docket information is available free online at http://64.217.42.130:5061. Use "option" 21.

County Level ... Recorders & Assessors

Recording Office Organization: 75 counties, 85 recording offices. The recording officer is the Clerk of Circuit Court, who is Ex Officio Recorder. Ten counties have two recording offices - Arkansas, Carroll, Clay, Craighead, Franklin, Logan, Mississippi, Prairie, Sebastian, and Yell. The entire state is in the Central Time Zone (CST). Federal tax liens on personal property of businesses are filed with the Secretary of State. Other federal and all state tax liens are filed with the Circuit Clerk. Many counties will perform separate tax lien searches. Search fees are usually $6.00 per name.

Online Access Note: There is no statewide access. Benton county offers records via their web site. Also, there is a commercial system available for a limited number of participating counties. Registration and logon is required, the signup fee is $200 minimum plus $.10 per minute usage. For signup or information call 479-631-8054 or visit www.arcountydata.com.

Editor's Note: A private vendor has placed access to 15 participating counties at www.arcountydata.com. The counties are: Baxter County - Carroll County (Eastern District) - Carroll County (Western District) - Craighead County (Western District) - Faulkner County - Fulton County - Izard County - Lonoke County - Pope County - Pulaski County - Saline County - Sebastian County (Fort Smith District) - Sebastian County (Southern District) - Sharp County - Stone County - White County.

Benton County *Real Estate, Lien, Deeds, Plats, Property Tax Records*

www.co.benton.ar.us
County Assessor, tax collector, medical liens, plats and circuit court information is available free online at http://64.217.42.130:5061. Also, registration and logon is required to search all participating counties at www.arcountydata.com. Signup fee is $200 minimum plus $.10 per minute usage. For signup or information call 479-631-8054 or visit www.arcountydata.com. Also, online access to property records is available by subscription at www.recordsusa.com. Credit card, username and password is required; choose either monthly or per-use plan. Visit the web site or call Lisa at 601-264-7701 for information.

Desha County *Real Estate, Recording Records*

Access to county recorder records is available by subscription at www.recordsusa.com. Credit card, username and password is required; choose either monthly or per-use plan. Visit the web site or call Lisa at 601-264-7701 for information.

Drew County *UCC, Land Records*

UCC and Land Records are available by subscription at www.recordsusa.com. Credit card, username and password is required; choose either monthly or per-use plan. Visit the web site or call Lisa at 601-264-7701 for information.

Federal Courts in Arkansas...

Standards for Federal Courts: The universal PACER sign-up number is 800-676-6856. Find PACER and the Party/Case Index on the Web at http://pacer.psc.uscourts.gov. PACER dial-up access is $.60 per minute. Also, courts offering internet access via RACER, PACER, Web-PACER or the new CM-ECF charge $.07 per page fee unless noted as free.

US District Court -- Eastern District of Arkansas

Home Page: www.are.uscourts.gov
PACER: Toll-free access: 800-371-8842. Local access phone: 501-324-6190. Case records are available back to 1987-89. Records are purged every five years. New records are available online after 1 day.
Other Online Access: Search records on the Internet using RACER at www.are.uscourts.gov/perl/bkplog.html. Access fee is $.07 per page.
Batesville Division counties: Cleburne, Fulton, Independence, Izard, Jackson, Sharp, Stone.
Helena Division counties: Cross, Lee, Monroe, Phillips, St. Francis, Woodruff.
Jonesboro Division counties: Clay, Craighead, Crittenden, Greene, Lawrence, Mississippi, Poinsett, Randolph.
Little Rock Division counties: Conway, Faulkner, Lonoke, Perry, Pope, Prairie, Pulaski, Saline, Van Buren, White, Yell.
Pine Bluff Division counties: Arkansas, Chicot, Cleveland, Dallas, Desha, Drew, Grant, Jefferson, Lincoln.

US Bankruptcy Court -- Eastern District of Arkansas

Home Page: www.areb.uscourts.gov
PACER: Case records are available back to May 1989. Records are purged every six months. New civil records are available online after 1 day.
Electronic Filing: Electronic filing information is available online at https://ecf.areb.uscourts.gov. **Also:** access via phone on VCIS (Voice Case Information System) is available: 800-891-6741, 501-918-5555
Little Rock Division counties: Same counties as included in Eastern District of Arkansas, plus the counties included in the Western District divisions of El Dorado, Hot Springs and Texarkana. All bankruptcy cases in Arkansas prior to mid-1993 were heard here.

US District Court -- Western District of Arkansas

Home Page: www.arwd.uscourts.gov
PACER: Sign-up number is 501-783-6833. Case records are available back to September 1990. Records are purged every five years. New records are available online after 1 day.
Other Online Access: PACER via email offers case information directly to your emailbox. Visit www.arwd.uscourts.gov/mailform.html and input the information you are looking for; results sent to you by email. Court does not participate in the U.S. party case index.

El Dorado Division counties: Ashley, Bradley, Calhoun, Columbia, Ouachita, Union.
Fayetteville Division counties: Benton, Madison, Washington.
Fort Smith Division counties: Crawford, Franklin, Johnson, Logan, Polk, Scott, Sebastian.
Hot Springs Division counties: Clark, Garland, Hot Springs, Montgomery, Pike.
Texarkana Division counties: Hempstead, Howard, Lafayette, Little River, Miller, Nevada, Sevier.

US Bankruptcy Court -- Western District of Arkansas

Home Page: www.arb.uscourts.gov

Same counties as included in the US District Court - Western District of Arkansas except that counties included in the divisions of El Dorado and Texarkana are heard in Little Rock.

PACER: Case records are available back to May 1989. Records are purged every six months. New civil records are available online after 1 day.

Electronic Filing: Electronic filing information is available online at https://ecf.arwb.uscourts.gov. **Also:** access via phone on VCIS (Voice Case Information System) is available: 800-891-6741, 501-918-5555

Fayetteville Division counties: Same counties as included in the Western District of Arkansas except that counties included in the divisions of El Dorado and Texarkana are heard in Little Rock.

Editor's Tip: Just because records are maintained in a certain way in your state or county do not assume that any other county or state does things the same way that you are used to.

California

Capital: Sacramento
Sacramento County

Time Zone: PST

Number of Counties: 58

Home Page www.state.ca.us
Attorney General
http://caag.state.ca.us

Archives www.ss.ca.gov/archives/archives.htm

State Level ... Major Agencies

Corporation Records, Limited Liability Company Records, Limited Partnerships, Limited Liability Partnerships,

Secretary of State, Information Retrieval/Certification Unit, 1500 11th Street, 3rd Fl, Sacramento, CA 95814; 916-657-5448 (Corps), 916-653-3794 (LLCs), 916-653-3365 (Partnerships), 8AM-4:30PM.

www.ss.ca.gov

The web site offers access to more than 2 million records including corporation, LLC, LP and LLP. Information available includes status, file number, date of filing and agent for service of process. Please note the file is updated weekly (not daily).

Uniform Commercial Code, Federal Tax Liens, State Tax Liens

UCC Division, Secretary of State, PO Box 942835, Sacramento, CA 94235-0001 (Courier: 1500 11th St, 2nd Fl, Sacramento, CA 95814); 916-653-3516, 8AM-5PM.

www.ss.ca.gov

Direct Access provides dial-up searching via PC and modem. This provides limited search capabilities, it's primary use is to verify filings. The data available conatins names and file dates, but not colateral. Fees range from $1-3 dollars, depending on type of search. Each page scroll is $.25. Requesters operate from a prepaid account.

Sales Tax Registrations

Board of Equalization, Sales and Use Tax Department, PO Box 942879, Sacramento, CA 94279-0001; 916-445-6362, 800-400-7115 (In California Only), 916-324-4433 (Fax), 8AM-5PM.

www.boe.ca.gov

Birth Certificates

State Department of Health Svcs, Office of Vital Records, PO Box 730241, Sacramento, CA 94244-0241 (Courier: 304 S Street, Sacramento, CA 95814); 916-445-2684 (Recording), 916-445-1719 (Attendant), 800-858-5553 (Fax), 8AM-4:30PM.

www.dhs.ca.gov/chs

Birth records from 1905-1995 can be accessed at http://userdb.rootsweb.com/ca/birth/search.cgi. The site is maintained by a private entity, but the data is provided by this agency.

Driver Records

Department of Motor Vehicles, Information Services Branch, PO Box 944247, Mail Station G199, Sacramento, CA 94244-2470; 916-657-8098, 916-657-6525 (Driver Licensing), 916-657-5564 (Requester Accounts), 8AM-5PM.

www.dmv.ca.gov

The department offers online access, but a $10,000 one-time setup fee is required. The fee is $2.00 per record. The system is open 24 hours, 7 days a week. For more information call 916-657-5582. **Other options:** Employers and regulatory agencies may monitor their drivers in the Pull Notice Program. The DMV informs the organization when there is activity on enrolled drivers. Call 916-657-6346 for details.

Vehicle Ownership, Vehicle Identification, Vessel Ownership, Vessel Registration

Department of Motor Vehicle, Office of Information Services, PO Box 944247, MS-G199, Sacramento, CA 94244-2470; 916-657-8098 (Walk-in/Mail-in Phone), 916-657-7914 (Commercial Accounts), 916-657-6739 (Vessel Registration), 916-657-5583 (Fax), 8AM-5PM.

www.dmv.ca.gov

24 hour online access is limited to certain Authorized Vendors. Requesters are may not use the data for direct marketing, solicitation, nor resell for those purposes. A bond is required and very high fees are involved. For more information, call Sue Jefferson at 916-657-5582. **Other options:** California offers delivery of registration information on magnetic tape, disk or paper within special parameters. Release of information is denied for commercial marketing purposes.

Legislation Records

www.leginfo.ca.gov

The Internet site has all legislative information back to 1993. The site also gives access to state laws.

State Level ... Occupational Licensing

Acupuncturist	www.acupuncture.ca.gov
Air Conditioning Contractor	http://www2.cslb.ca.gov/CSLB_LIBRARY/Name+Request.asp
Alarm Company	www.dca.ca.gov/bsis/lookup.htm
Alarm Company Employee/Manager	www.dca.ca.gov/bsis/lookup.htm
Animal Health Technician	www.vmb.ca.gov/2licensg/lic1list.htm
Architect	www.cab.ca.gov/Templates/querysearch.cfm
Athletic Event Manager/Promoter/Matchmaker	www.dca.ca.gov/csac/directories.htm
Attorney	www.calsb.org/MM/SBMBRSHP.HTM
Automobile Dealer/Repair	www.smogcheck.ca.gov/stdPage.asp?Body=/Consumer/verify_a_license.htm
Bank	www.sbd.ca.gov/directry/db.asp
Baton Training Facility/Instructor	www.dca.ca.gov/bsis/lookup.htm
Boxer	www.dca.ca.gov/csac/directories.htm
Brake & Lamp Adjuster	www.smogcheck.ca.gov/stdPage.asp?Body=/Consumer/verify_a_license.htm
Brake Station	www.smogcheck.ca.gov/stdPage.asp?Body=/Consumer/verify_a_license.htm
Building Contractor, General-Class B	http://www2.cslb.ca.gov/CSLB_LIBRARY/Name+Request.asp
Cabinet & Millwork	http://www2.cslb.ca.gov/CSLB_LIBRARY/Name+Request.asp
Cemetery, Cemetery Broker/Sales Agent	www.dca.ca.gov/cemetery/lookup.htm
Clinic Pharmaceutical Permit	www.pharmacy.ca.gov/license_lookup.htm
Concrete Contractor/Company	http://www2.cslb.ca.gov/CSLB_LIBRARY/Name+Request.asp
Continuing Education Provider	www.bbs.ca.gov/weblookup.htm
Contractor	www.cslb.ca.gov
Court Reporter (Certified Shorthand Reporter)	www.courtreportersboard.ca.gov
Credit Union	www.sbd.ca.gov/directry/cu.asp
Cremated Remains Disposer	www.dca.ca.gov/cemetery/lookup.htm
Crematory	www.dca.ca.gov/cemetery/lookup.htm

Dental Assistant	www.comda.ca.gov/licensestatus.html
Dental Assistant, Extended Function	www.comda.ca.gov/licensestatus.html
Dental Hygienist	www.comda.ca.gov/licensestatus.html
Dentist	www.dbc.ca.gov/License.html
Drug Wholesaler/Drug Room	www.pharmacy.ca.gov/license_lookup.htm
Drywall	http://www2.cslb.ca.gov/CSLB_LIBRARY/Name+Request.asp
Earthwork & Paving	http://www2.cslb.ca.gov/CSLB_LIBRARY/Name+Request.asp
Educational Psychologist	www.bbs.ca.gov/weblokup.htm
Electrical (General) & Electric Sign	http://www2.cslb.ca.gov/CSLB_LIBRARY/Name+Request.asp
Electronics & Appliance Repair	http://www2.dca.ca.gov/pls/wllpub/wllquery$.startup
Elevator Installation	http://www2.cslb.ca.gov/CSLB_LIBRARY/Name+Request.asp
Embalmer/Embalmer Apprentice	www.dca.ca.gov/cemetery/lookup.htm
Engineer (Various)	www.dca.ca.gov/pels/l_lookup.htm
Fencing	http://www2.cslb.ca.gov/CSLB_LIBRARY/Name+Request.asp
Firearm Permit	www.dca.ca.gov/bsis/lookup.htm
Firearm Training Facility/Instructor	www.dca.ca.gov/bsis/lookup.htm
Flooring & Floor Covering	http://www2.cslb.ca.gov/CSLB_LIBRARY/Name+Request.asp
Fumigation	www.dca.ca.gov/pestboard/lookup.htm
Funeral Director/Establishment	www.dca.ca.gov/cemetery/lookup.htm
Funerary Training Establishment/Apprentice	www.dca.ca.gov/cemetery/lookup.htm
Geologist	www.dca.ca.gov/geology/lookup/
Geologist, Engineering	www.dca.ca.gov/geology/lookup/
Geophysicist	www.dca.ca.gov/geology/lookup/
Glazier	http://www2.cslb.ca.gov/CSLB_LIBRARY/Name+Request.asp
Hearing Aid Dispenser	www.dca.ca.gov/hearingaid/
Heating & Warm-Air Ventilating	http://www2.cslb.ca.gov/CSLB_LIBRARY/Name+Request.asp
Horse Racing Entity	www.chrb.ca.gov/license_search.htm
Horse Racing Occupation	www.chrb.ca.gov/license_search.htm
Hospital Exemptee	www.pharmacy.ca.gov/license_lookup.htm
Hydrogeologist	www.dca.ca.gov/geology/lookup/
Hypodermic Needle & Syringe Distributor	www.pharmacy.ca.gov/license_lookup.htm
Industrial Loan Company, Premium	www.sbd.ca.gov/directry/pf.asp
Insulation & Accoustical Contractor	http://www2.cslb.ca.gov/CSLB_LIBRARY/Name+Request.asp
Insurance Adjuster	www.insurance.ca.gov/LIC/Licensestatus.htm
Insurance Agent/Broker	www.insurance.ca.gov/LIC/Licensestatus.htm
Insurance Company	www.insurance.ca.gov/docs/FS-CompanyProfiles.htm
Lamp Station	www.smogcheck.ca.gov/stdPage.asp?Body=/Consumer/verify_a_license.htm
Landscape Architect	www.latc.dca.ca.gov/Licensee/search.htm
Landscaping	http://www2.cslb.ca.gov/CSLB_LIBRARY/Name+Request.asp
Lobbyist/Lobbyist Firm/Employer	http://cal-access.ss.ca.gov/Lobbying/
Locksmith/Locksmith Company	www.dca.ca.gov/bsis/lookup.htm
Marriage & Family Therapist	www.bbs.ca.gov/weblokup.htm
Masonry	http://www2.cslb.ca.gov/CSLB_LIBRARY/Name+Request.asp
Medical Doctor/Surgeon	www.docboard.org/ca/df/casearch.htm
Money Orders/Payment Instruments Issuer	www.sbd.ca.gov/directry/pi.asp
Nurse	www.rn.ca.gov/online/online.htm
Optometrist	www.optometry.ca.gov/search.asp
Optometry Branch Office	www.optometry.ca.gov/search.asp
Optometry Fictitious Name Practice	www.optometry.ca.gov/search.asp
Ornamental Metal	http://www2.cslb.ca.gov/CSLB_LIBRARY/Name+Request.asp
Painting & Decorating	http://www2.cslb.ca.gov/CSLB_LIBRARY/Name+Request.asp
Parking & Highway Improvement	http://www2.cslb.ca.gov/CSLB_LIBRARY/Name+Request.asp
Patrol Operator, Private	www.dca.ca.gov/bsis/lookup.htm
Pest Control Field Rep./Operator	www.dca.ca.gov/pestboard/lookup.htm
Pesticide Applicator	www.dca.ca.gov/pestboard/lookup.htm
Pharmacist/Pharmacist Intern	www.pharmacy.ca.gov/license_lookup.htm
Pharmacy	www.pharmacy.ca.gov/license_lookup.htm
Pharmacy Technician	www.pharmacy.ca.gov/license_lookup.htm
Physician Assistant	www.docboard.org/ca/df/casearch.htm
Plastering	http://www2.cslb.ca.gov/CSLB_LIBRARY/Name+Request.asp

Plumber	http://www2.cslb.ca.gov/CSLB_LIBRARY/Name+Request.asp
Podiatrist	www.docboard.org/ca/df/casearch.htm
Private Investigator	www.dca.ca.gov/bsis/lookup.htm
Psychiatric Technician	www.bvnpt.ca.gov/licverif.htm
Psychological Assistant	www.psychboard.ca.gov
Psychologist	www.psychboard.ca.gov
Real Estate Broker/Corporation	www.dre.ca.gov/licstats.htm
Real Estate Sales Agent	www.dre.ca.gov/licstats.htm
Refrigeration	http://www2.cslb.ca.gov/CSLB_LIBRARY/Name+Request.asp
Repossessor Agency/Mgr./Employee	www.dca.ca.gov/bsis/lookup.htm
Respiratory Care Practitioner	www.rcb.ca.gov/activercps.htm
Roofing Contractor	http://www2.cslb.ca.gov/CSLB_LIBRARY/Name+Request.asp
Sanitation System	http://www2.cslb.ca.gov/CSLB_LIBRARY/Name+Request.asp
Savings & Loan Association	www.sbd.ca.gov/directry/sl.asp
Security Guard/Armored Car Guard	www.dca.ca.gov/bsis/lookup.htm
Service Contract Seller (Appliance)	http://www2.dca.ca.gov/pls/wllpub/wllquery$.startup
Sheet Metal	http://www2.cslb.ca.gov/CSLB_LIBRARY/Name+Request.asp
Smog Check Station	www.smogcheck.ca.gov/stdPage.asp?Body=/Consumer/verify_a_license.htm
Smog Check Technician	www.smogcheck.ca.gov/stdPage.asp?Body=/Consumer/verify_a_license.htm
Social Worker, Clinical	www.bbs.ca.gov/weblokup.htm
Social Worker, Clinical Associate	www.bbs.ca.gov/weblokup.htm
Solar Energy	http://www2.cslb.ca.gov/CSLB_LIBRARY/Name+Request.asp
Specialty Contractor-Class C	http://www2.cslb.ca.gov/CSLB_LIBRARY/Name+Request.asp
Steel, Reinforcing & Structural	http://www2.cslb.ca.gov/CSLB_LIBRARY/Name+Request.asp
Supervising Physician	www.docboard.org/ca/df/casearch.htm
Surveyor, Land	www.dca.ca.gov/pels/l_lookup.htm
Swimming Pool	http://www2.cslb.ca.gov/CSLB_LIBRARY/Name+Request.asp
Tax Education Provider	www.ctec.org/html/approved_education_providers_.html
Teacher	https://teachercred.ctc.ca.gov/teachers/index.jsp
Termite Control	www.dca.ca.gov/pestboard/lookup.htm
Thrift & Loan Company	www.sbd.ca.gov/directry/tl.asp
Tile Contractor, Ceramic & Mosaic	http://www2.cslb.ca.gov/CSLB_LIBRARY/Name+Request.asp
Travelers Checks Issuer	www.sbd.ca.gov/directry/tc.asp
Trust Company	www.sbd.ca.gov/directry/trust.asp
Veterinarian	www.vmb.ca.gov/2licensg/lic1list.htm
Veterinary Food/Animal Drug Retailer	www.pharmacy.ca.gov/license_lookup.htm
Veterinary Hospital	www.vmb.ca.gov/2licensg/lic1list.htm
Vocational Nurse	www.bvnpt.ca.gov/licverif.htm
Water Well Driller	http://www2.cslb.ca.gov/CSLB_LIBRARY/Name+Request.asp

County Level ... Courts

Court Administration: Administrative Office of Courts, 455 Golden Gate Ave, San Francisco, CA, 94102; 415-865-4200; www.courtinfo.ca.gov

Court Structure: In July, 1998, the judges in individual counties were given the opportunity to vote on unification of superior and municipal courts within their respective counties. By late 2000, all counties had voted to unify these courts. Courts that were formally Municipal Courts are now known as Limited Jurisdiction Superior Courts. In some counties, superior and municipal courts were combined into one superior court. Civil under $25,000 is a Limited Civil Court, over $25,000 is an Unlimited Civil Court, and if both are over and under, then the court is a Combined Civil Court. It is important to note that Limited Courts may try minor felonies not included under our felony definition. Due to its large number of courts, the Los Angeles County section is arranged uniquely in this book. Each Branch or Division of the Los Angeles Superior Court is given by name, which usually indicates its general jurisdictional and geographic boundary.

Online Access Note: There is no statewide online computer access available, internal or external. However, a number of counties have developed their own online access sytems and provide Internet access at no fee. Also, www.courtinfo.ca.gov contains very useful information about the state court system.

Alameda County

Superior Court North Branch - Superior Court Pleasanton Branch - Superior Court South Branch/Hayward - Alameda Branch Superior Court Berkeley/Albany Superior Court Civil - Fremont Superior Court - Hayward Superior Court - Livermore/Pleasanton/Dublin Superior Court - Oakland/Piedmont/Emeryville Superior Court - Oakland/Piedmont/Emeryville Superior Court Criminal *Civil Records*
www.co.alameda.ca.us/courts/index.shtml
Online access to calendars, limited civil case summaries and complex litigations are available free from Register of Actions/Domain Web at the web site. Search limited cases by number; litigations by case name or number.

Contra Costa County

Superior Court *Civil Records*
www.co.contra-costa.ca.us
There is a free remote dial-up system for civil, probate and county law records. Call 925-646-2479 for details.

Walnut Creek Branch *Civil and Probate Records*
Pittsburg Branch *Civil and Probate Records*
Richmond Superior Court *Civil and Probate Records*
www.co.contra-costa.ca.us
There is a free remote dial-up system for civil, probate and family law records. Call 925-646-2479 for sign-up.

Fresno County

Superior Court *Civil, Probate, Family, Small Claim Records*
www.fresno.ca.gov/2810/default.htm
Online access to civil, probate, family, small claims cases is available free at www.fresno.ca.gov/2810/SJVAP/CourtConnect.asp. You must enter a Fresno county zip code to enter.

Clovis Division - Coalinga Division - Firebaugh Division - Fowler Division - Kerman Division - Kingsburg Division - Reedley Division - Sanger Division - Selma Division - Superior Court *Civil, Probate, Family, Small Claim Records*
www.fresno.ca.gov/2810/default.htm
Online access to civil, probate, family, small claims cases is available free at www.fresno.ca.gov/2810/SJVAP/CourtConnect.asp. You must enter a Fresno county zip code to enter.

Los Angeles County

Los Angeles Superior Court - Central District *Civil and Probate Records*

Alhambra Superior Court - Northeast District *Civil Records*

Beverly Hills Superior Court - West District *Civil Records*

Burbank Superior Court - North Central District *Civil Records*

Citrus Superior Court - East District *Civil Records*

Compton Superior Court - South Central District *Civil Records*

Culver City Superior Court - West District *Civil Records*

Downey Superior Court - Southeast District *Civil Records*

East Los Angeles Superior Court - Central District *Civil Records*

Glendale Superior Court - NorthCentral District *Civil Records*

Huntington Park Superior Court - Southeast District *Civil Records*

Inglewood Superior Court - Southwest District *Civil Records*

Lancaster Superior Court - North District *Civil Records*

Long Beach Superior Court - South District *Civil Records*

Los Cerritos (Bellflower) Superior Court - Southeast District *Civil Records*

Malibu Superior Court - West District *Civil Records*

Norwalk Superior Court - Southeast District *Civil Records*

Palmdale Superior Court - North District *Civil Records*

Pasadena Superior Court - Northeast District *Civil Records*

Pomona Superior Court - East District *Civil Records*

Redondo Beach Superior Court - Southwest District *Civil Records*

Rio Hondo Superior Court - East District *Civil Records*

San Fernando Superior Court - North Valley District *Civil and Criminal Records*

San Pedro Superior Court - South District *Civil Records*

Santa Anita Superior Court - Northeast District *Civil Records*

Santa Clarita Superior Court - North Valley District *Civil Records*

Santa Monica Superior Court - West District *Civil Records*

South Gate Superior Court - Southeast District *Civil Records*

Torrance Superior Court - Southwest District *Civil Records*

Van Nuys Superior Court - Northwest District *Civil Records*

West Los Angeles Superior Court - West District *Civil Records*

Whittier Superior Court - Southeast District *Civil Records*

www.lasuperiorcourt.org

Online access to all these **Los Angeles County** Courts is available free at www.lasuperiorcourt.org. Court location, case number required to search. Available for civil, small claims, probate and unlawful detainer records.

Marin County
Superior Court *Civil and Criminal Records*
www.co.marin.ca.us/courts
Online access to the current court calendar is available free at www.co.marin.ca.us/depts/MC/main/courtcal/name.cfm. Online Access to the active criminal calendar is the same as civil.

Monterey County
Superior Court - Monterey Branch *Civil Records*
Superior Court - Salinas Division *Criminal Records*
King City Division - Consolidated Trial Court *Civil and Criminal Records*
Marina Division *Civil Records*
www.co.monterey.ca.us/court
Online access to calendars and current cases is available free online at www.co.monterey.ca.us/court/calendar.asp.

Orange County
Superior Court - *Civil Records*
Superior Court - Criminal Operations *Criminal Records*
Central Orange County Superior Court - Limited Jurisdiction *Civil and Criminal Records*
Harbor - Laguna Hills Superior Court - Civil Division *Civil Records*
Harbor - Laguna Niguel Superior Court - Criminal Division *Criminal Records*
Harbor - Newport Beach Superior Court *Civil and Criminal Records*
North Orange County Superior Court *Civil and Criminal Records*
West Orange County Superior Court *Civil and Criminal Records*
www.occourts.org
Online access is to be available in 2002 at www.occourts.org/caseinfo.asp.

Riverside County
Superior Court - Civil Division *Civil and Probate Records*
Superior Court - Criminal Division *Criminal Records*
www.co.riverside.ca.us/depts/courts
The Automated Case Management System is the pay system for Riverside County Superior Courts for Internet access, but the intent is to make record searching free on the Internet eventually. Records date back to 1984 and include civil, criminal, family law, probate & traffic case information for all Riverside/Indio Courts. For further information, call 909-955-5945.

Banning Division - Superior Court *Civil and Criminal Records*
Blythe Division - Superior Court *Civil and Criminal Records*
Corona Branch - Superior Court *Civil and Criminal Records*
Hemet Division - Superior Court *Civil and Criminal Records*
Indio Division - Superior Court *Civil and Criminal Records*
Lake Elsinore Division - Superior Court *Civil Records*
Palm Springs Division - Superior Court *Criminal Records*
Perris Branch - Superior Court *Civil and Criminal Records*
Temecula Branch - Superior Court *Civil Records*
Moreno Valley Branch - Superior Court *Civil Records*
www.co.riverside.ca.us/depts/courts
For the preceding courts, see Superior Court Main Division (above) for online information.

Sacramento County
Superior Court *Civil and Criminal Records*
www.saccourt.com
All court records for the county are available free on the Internet at www.saccourt.com.

Galt Division - South Sacramento Superior Court Elk Grove Branch - Walnut Grove Branch *Civil/Criminal Records*
www.saccourt.com
All civil records for Sacramento County are available free on the Internet at www.saccourt.com. Online access for criminal records is the same as civil.

San Bernardino County
Central District - Superior Court *Civil Records and Probate Notes; Daily Criminal Dockets*
Rancho Cucamonga District - Superior Court
Central Division Branch - Superior Court
www.sbcounty.gov/courts/
Online access to weekly "Probate Notes" is available free at www.co.san-bernardino.ca.us/courts/probate/default.htm. Only the daily criminal docket is available free at the court main web site.

Shasta County
Superior Court *Criminal Records*
Burney Branch - Superior Court *Criminal Records*
www.shastacourts.com
Online access to the criminal division index is available free at www.shastacourts.com/criminal.shtml. Also, the Integrated Justice System Access at www.shastacourts.com/access.shtml is limited to attorneys involved on county cases.

Solano County
Superior Court - *Civil Records*
Superior Court *Criminal Records*
Vallejo Branch - Superior Court *Civil and Criminal Records*
www.solanocourts.com
Online access to civil records is available free at the web site; click on "Court Connect." Online access to criminal records is available free at the web site; click on "Court Connect.".

Ventura County
Ventura Superior Court *Civil and Criminal Records*
http://courts.countyofventura.org
Access to civil court records 10/93-present is available free online at http://courts.countyofventura.org/civcase/case_home.asp. Search by defendant or plaintiff name, case number, or date. Access to criminal court records available free online at http://courts.countyofventura.org/vent_frameset_puba.htm. There are several indices to search.

East County Superior Court *Civil and Criminal Records*
http://courts.countyofventura.org
Access to civil court records 10/93-present is available free online at the web site. Search by defendant or plaintiff name, case number, or date. Access to criminal court records available free online at the web site. There are two indices to search.

County Level ... Recorders & Assessors

Recording Office Organization: 58 counties, 58 recording offices. The recording officer is the County Recorder. Recordings are usually located in a Grantor/Grantee or General index. The entire state is in the Pacific Time Zone (PST). Federal and state tax liens on personal property of businesses are filed with the Secretary of State. Other federal and state tax liens are filed with the County Recorder. Some counties will perform separate tax lien searches. Fees vary for this type of search.

Online Access Note: A number of counties offer aonline access to assessor and real estate information. The system in Los Angeles is a commercial subscription system.

Alameda County   *Assessor Records*
www.co.alameda.ca.us
Access to the Property Value and Tax Information database is available free online at www.co.alameda.ca.us/aswpinq.

Amador County   *Recording, Fictitious Name, Birth, Death, Marriage Records*
Access to the county clerk database is available free at www.criis.com/amador/official.htm. There is a free "test" recorder grantor/grantee "images" search page at www.criis.com/amador_test.html.

Butte County   *Real Estate, Fictitious Name, Marriage, Birth, Death, Recording Records*
www.buttecounty.net
Access to the County Recorder's database of official documents is free at http://clerk-recorder.buttecounty.net/election/index.html.
Records go back to 1988.

Calaveras County   *Property Records*
Access to the GIS Project of property information is available free at www.co.calaveras.ca.us/departments/gisproj.html. Click on "The
Parcel Information System."

Contra Costa County   *Recording, Fictitious Business Name, Marriage, Death, Birth Records*
www.co.contra-costa.ca.us/depart/elect/Rindex.html
Recorder office records back to 1996 are available free at www.criis.com/contracosta/srecord_current.shtml. County Birth records are
at www.criis.com/contracosta/sbirth.shtml. County Death records are at www.criis.com/contracosta/sdeath.shtml. Fictitious Business
names are at www.criis.com/contracosta/sfictitious.shtml. Marriage records are at www.criis.com/contracosta/smarriage.shtml.

El Dorado County   *Real Estate, Personal Property, Vital Statistic, Fictitious Name Records*
www.co.el-dorado.ca.us/countyclerk/
Access to the Recorder's index is available free on the Internet at http://main.co.el-dorado.ca.us/CGI/WWB012/WWM501/R. Records
go back to 1949. Official records on the County Recorder database are available free on the Internet at http://main.co.el-
dorado.ca.us/CGI/WWB012/WWM501/C. Search by date range and name or document number. County vital statistics - births,
deaths, non-confidential marriages, and fictitious names - are available free on the Internet at http://main.co.el-
dorado.ca.us/CGI/WWB012/WWM500/C.

Fresno County   *Assessor, Birth, Death, Marriage Records*
www.fresno.ca.gov/0420/recorders_web/index.htm
Recording office records on the county recorder database are available free at
http://assessor.fresno.ca.gov/fresno/srecord_oracle.shtml. County Birth Records are at
http://assessor.fresno.ca.gov/fresno/sbirth_oracle.shtml. County death records are at
http://assessor.fresno.ca.gov/fresno/sdeath_oracle.shtml. Marriage records are at
http://assessor.fresno.ca.gov/fresno/smarriage_oracle.shtml.

Inyo County   *Recording, Fictitious Name, Birth, Death, Marriage Records*
Access to the county clerk database may be available free at www.criis.com/inyo/official.shtml.

Kern County   *Assessor, Property Tax, Fictitious Business Name, Vital Statistic, Recording, Real Estate Records*
www.co.kern.ca.us/recorder
Records on the County of Kern Online Assessor database are available free online at
http://assessor.co.kern.ca.us/kips/property_search.asp. Birth, Death, Marriage records may be purchased through Vitalchek at
www.vitalchek.com. Also, search county clerk's fictitious business name database free at www.co.kern.ca.us/ctyclerk/dba/default.asp.
The recorders database of deeds is available free at http://recorder.co.kern.ca.us/kips/property_search.asp. Also, search the treasurer
database for fictious business names and property tax assessment information free at http://kerndata.com. Online maps also available.

Lassen County   *Real Estate, Recording Records*
http://clerk.lassencounty.org
Access to the county recorder database is available free at http://icris.lassencounty.org. Registration is required. Recorded documents
go back to 7/1985. Vital statistics back to 7/12/1999.

Los Angeles County   *Assessor, Fictitious Business Name, Inmates Records*
http://regrec.co.la.ca.us
Search county inmates at http://pajis.lasd.org/ajis_search.cfm. For assessments use the PDB Inquiry System dial-up service; $100.00
monthly plus $1.00 per inquiry, also $75 sign-up fee for 3-year dial-up. Usage fee is $6.50 per hour or $.11 per minute. Send
registration request to Data Systems Spvr2 Tech Admin, LA County Assessor's, 500 W Temple St Rm 293, LA, CA 90012. Further
info: 213-974-3237 or visit http://assessor.co.la.ca.us/outsidesales/online.asp. Tax info line: 213-974-3838. Also, property and
assessor information (no name searching) is available free online at http://assessor.co.la.ca.us/DataMaps/pais.asp. Search the map or
by address. Search for county Fictitious Names free online at http://regrec.co.la.ca.us/fbn/FBN.cfm.

Marin County   *Real Estate, Property Tax, Grantor/Grantee, Recording, Vital Statistic Records*
www.co.marin.ca.us/depts/AR/main/index.cfm
Search the county Grantor/Grantee index free at www.co.marin.ca.us/depts/AR/RiiMs/index.asp. Also, search the property tax database at www.co.marin.ca.us/depts/AR/COMPASS/index.asp but there is no name searching. Also, search the real estate sales lists by month and year by selecting the year. Also, search the vital records for document index number at www.co.marin.ca.us/depts/AR/VitalStatistics/index.asp. Birth records go back to 1967; deaths to 1979. Marriages go back to 1948.

Modoc County   *Recording, Fictitious Name, Birth, Death, Marriage Records*
Access to the county clerk database may be available free at www.criis.com/modoc/official.shtml.

Nevada County   *Recording, Fictious Name, Birth, Death, Marriage Records*
http://recorder.co.nevada.ca.us
Access to the county clerk database is available free at www.criis.com/nevada/official.shtml.

Orange County   *Grantor/Grantee, Deed, Lien, Judgment Records*
Orange County Grantor/Grantee records are available free online at http://cr.ocgov.com/grantorgrantee/.

Placer County   *Recording, Fictitious Name, Birth, Death, Marriage Records*
www.placer.ca.gov/clerk/clerk.htm
Recorder office records are available free at the web site. County Birth records are at www.criis.com/placer/sbirth.shtml. County Death records are at www.criis.com/placer/sdeath.shtml. County Marriage records are at www.criis.com/placer/smarriage.shtml. County Fictitious Business Names are at www.criis.com/placer/sfictitious.shtml.

Riverside County   *Assessor, Property Tax, Fictitious Name, Grantor/Grantee Records*
http://riverside.asrclkrec.com
Property tax information from the County Treasurer database is available free from EZproperty.com on the internet at https://riverside.ca.ezgov.com/ezproperty/review_search.jsp. Also, access to the county fictitious name database and Grantor/Grantee index is available at http://riverside.asrclkrec.com/OS.asp. The FBN search is free; a fee is charged for documents from the Grantor/Grantee index.

Sacramento County   *Assessor, Recording, Grantor/Grantee, Deed, Business License Records*
www.co.sacramento.ca.us
Access to the Dept. of Finance Clerk-recorder assessment database is available free at www.erosi.saccounty.net/Inputs.asp. Online records go back to 1965. Also, clerk recorder data is soon to be available online at www.criis.com/sacramento/official.shtml and may include Fictitious Names, Birth, Death, Marriages. Also, search City of West Sacramento business licenses at www.ci.west-sacramento.ca.us/cityhall/departments/finance/buslic/blfind.cfm

San Bernardino County   *Recorder, Assessor, Fictitious Name Records*
www.co.san-bernardino.ca.us
Records on the County Assessor database are available free on the Internet at www.co.san-bernardino.ca.us/tax/trsearch.asp. For automated call distribution, call 909-387-8306; for fictitious names information, call 909-386-8970. Fictitious business names are also available online at www.co.san-bernardino.ca.us/ACR/RecSearch.htm. Also, the Auditor/Controller Grantor/Grantee recording index is available free at www.co.san-bernardino.ca.us/ACR/or/recsearch.asp.

San Diego County   *Assessor, Fictitious Name, Real Estate, Grantor/Grantee, Inmates, Most Wanted, Warrant, Sex Offender, Pets, Missing Children, Tax Sale Records*
www.co.san-diego.ca.us
Records on the County Assessor/Recorder/County Clerk Online Services site are available free online at www.co.san-diego.ca.us/cnty/cntydepts/general/assessor/online.html including fictitious business names, indexes, maps, property information. Grantee/grantor index search by name for individual record data at http://arcc.co.san-diego.ca.us/services/grantorgrantee. Also, online search inmates at http://199.106.18.5/waar/waar.html. Also, search www.sdcounty.ca.gov/general/online.html for most wanted, warrants, sex offenders, found pet, missing children, tax sales, real estate.

San Francisco County   *Property Tax, Recording, Fictitious Name, Birth, Death, Marriage Records*
Access to the City Property Tax database is available free at https://cityservices.sfgov.org/serv/ttx_pt. No name searching; and address or Block/lot # is required. Also, online accessto recording, birth, death, marriage and fictitious name records on the county clerk database may be available free at www.criis.com/sanfrancisco/official.htm. Fictitious business names are also searchable at http://cityservices.sfgov.org/serv/clerk_fbn.

San Mateo County *Property Tax, Fictitious Name, Voter Registration Records*
www.care.co.sanmateo.ca.us
Records on the county property taxes and fictitious names databases are available free online at
www.care.co.sanmateo.ca.us/frames/our_office/ceo_d.htm. Search by address, city or parcel ID#. Also, a voter registration
confirmation site is available free; birthdate and address required. There is also a secured property search, but no name searching.

Santa Barbara County *Assessor Records*
www.sb-democracy.com
Access to assessor online property info system (OPIS) in available free at the web site with parcel #. Records go back 10 years.
Database is free to view but only subscribers will be able to download. Full access requires registration. Contact Larry Herrera for an
account. herrera@co.santa-barbara.ca.us

Santa Clara County *Recording, Grantor/Grantee, Marriage, Death Records*
www.clerkrecordersearch.org
Access to the County Clerk-Recorder database is available free at the web site.

Santa Cruz County *Assessor, Property Tax, Fictitious Business Name, Recording, Deed, Judgment,*
Vital Statistic Records
www.co.santa-cruz.ca.us/rcd/
Access to the assessor's parcel information data is available free at http://sccounty01.co.santa-cruz.ca.us/ASR/. No name searching.
Also, search for property information using the GIS map at http://gis.co.santa-cruz.ca.us. Also, search the recorder's fictitious business
names free at http://sccounty01.co.santa-cruz.ca.us/clerkrecorder/Asp/FBNInquiry.asp. Also, access to the recorder's official records
is avaialble free at http://sccounty01.co.santa-cruz.ca.us/clerkrecorder/Asp/ORInquiry.asp. Online indexes go back to 1978. Births,
Deaths, and Marriages are also searchable back to 1984.

Shasta County *Assessor Records*
www.co.shasta.ca.us
Records on the City of Redding Parcel Search By Parcel Number Server are available free at
http://cor400.ci.redding.ca.us/nd/gow3lkap.ndm/input. CA state law has removed owner names.

Solano County *Property Tax, Recording, Deed, Judgment, Lien Records*
www.solanocounty.com
Search the treasurer/tax collector/county clerk property database ifree at www.solanocounty.com/treasurer/propquery.asp. Also, the
recorder's index is to be online in late 2002; see www.solanocounty.com/assessrecord/.

Stanislaus County *Recording, Fictitious Name, Birth, Death, Marriage Records*
www.co.stanislaus.ca.us
Recorder office records are available free at www.criis.com/stanislaus/srecord_current.shtml. County Birth records are at
www.criis.com/stanislaus/sbirth.shtml. Death records are at www.criis.com/stanislaus/sdeath.shtml. Marriage records are at
www.criis.com/stanislaus/smarriage.shtml. County Fictitious Business Name records are at www.criis.com/stanislaus/sfictitious.shtml.

Trinity County *Vital Statistic Records*
www.trinitycounty.org/Departments/assessor-clerk-elect/clerkrecorder.htm
Access to the Recorder's vital statistics database is available free at http://halfile.trinitycounty.org. For user name, enter "vital"; leave
password field empty.

Tulare County *Recording, Deed, Judgment, Lien, Vital Statistic, Fictitious Name Records*
www.co.tulare.ca.us
Search the recorders database including births, marriages, deaths free at http://209.78.90.65/riimsweb/orinquiry.asp.

Ventura County *Recording, Fictitious Name, Birth, Death, Marriage Records*
www.ventura.org/assessor/index.html
Access to the county clerks database is available free at www.criis.com/ventura/official.htm.

Yolo County *Assessor, Birth, Death, Marriage, Fictitious Business Name Records*
www.yolocounty.org/org/Recorder
Access to recordings on the county clerk database are available free at www.criis.com/yolo/srecord_current.shtml. County Birth
records are at www.criis.com/yolo/sbirth.shtml. County Death records are at www.criis.com/yolo/sdeath.shtml. Marriage records are

at www.criis.com/yolo/smarriage.shtml. County Fictitious Business Name records are at www.criis.com/yolo/sfictitious.shtml. Also, City of Davis business licenses are free at www.city.davis.ca.us/ed/business/

Federal Courts in California...

Standards for Federal Courts: The universal PACER sign-up number is 800-676-6856. Find PACER and the Party/Case Index on the Web at http://pacer.psc.uscourts.gov. PACER dial-up access is $.60 per minute. Also, courts offering internet access via RACER, PACER, Web-PACER or the new CM-ECF charge $.07 per page fee unless noted as free.

US District Court -- Central District of California

Home Page: www.cacd.uscourts.gov
PACER: Case records are available back to 1993. New records are available online after 2 days.   **PACER URL:** http://pacer.cacd.uscourts.gov. Document images available.
Electronic Filing: Electronic filing information is available online at (CM/ECF available late 2002).
Opinions Online: Court opinions are available online at www.cacd.uscourts.gov.
Los Angeles (Western) Division counties: Los Angeles, San Luis Obispo, Santa Barbara, Ventura.
Riverside (Eastern) Division counties: Riverside, San Bernardino.
Santa Ana (Southern) Division counties: Orange.

US Bankruptcy Court -- Central District of California

Home Page: www.cacb.uscourts.gov
PACER: Toll-free access: 800-257-3887. Local access phone: 213-620-0031. Case records are available back to 1992. Records are purged once a year. New civil records are available online after 1 day.   **PACER URL:** http://pacerla.cacb.uscourts.gov. Document images available.
Other Online Access: WebPACER Dial-up Networking is available at IP address of 156.131.137.252. **Also:** access via phone on VCIS (Voice Case Information System) is available: 213-894-4111.
Los Angeles Division counties: Los Angeles (certain Los Angeles ZIP Codes are shared with San Fernando Valley Division.).
Riverside (East) Division counties: Riverside, San Bernardino.
San Fernando Valley Division counties: Los Angeles (certain Los Angeles ZIP Codes are shared with Los Angeles Division), Ventura.
Santa Ana Division counties: Orange.
Santa Barbara (Northern) Division counties: San Luis Obispo, Santa Barbara, Ventura. Certain Ventura ZIP Codes are assigned to the new office in San Fernando Valley.

US District Court -- Eastern District of California

Home Page: www.caed.uscourts.gov
PACER: Toll-free access: 800-530-7682. Local access phone: 916-498-6567. Case records are available back to 1990 (some earlier). Records are purged at varying intervals. New records are available online after 1 day.   **PACER URL:** http://pacer.caed.uscourts.gov. Document images available.
Opinions Online: Court opinions are available online at www.caed.uscourts.gov.
Other Online Access: Search records on the Internet using RACER at https://racer.caed.uscourts.gov/. Access fee is $.07 per page.
Fresno Division counties: Fresno, Inyo, Kern, Kings, Madera, Mariposa, Merced, Stanislaus, Tulare, Tuolumne.
Sacramento Division counties: Alpine, Amador, Butte, Calaveras, Colusa, El Dorado, Glenn, Lassen, Modoc, Mono, Nevada, Placer, Plumas, Sacramento, San Joaquin, Shasta, Sierra, Siskiyou, Solano, Sutter, Tehama, Trinity, Yolo, Yuba.

US Bankruptcy Court -- Eastern District of California

Home Page: www.caeb.uscourts.gov
PACER: Case records are available back to August 1990. Records are purged every six months. New civil records are available online after 1 day.   **PACER URL:** http://pacer.caeb.uscourts.gov/pacerhome.html. **Also:** access via phone on VCIS (Voice Case Information System) is available: 916-551-2989.
Fresno Division counties: Fresno, Inyo, Kern, Kings, Madera, Mariposa, Merced, Tulare. Three Kern ZIP Codes, 93243 and 93523-24, are handled by San Fernando Valley in the Central District.
Modesto Division counties: Calaveras, San Joaquin, Stanislaus, Tuolumne. The following ZIP Codes in San Joaquin County are handled by the Sacramento Division: 95220, 95227, 95234, 95237, 95240-95242, 95253, 95258, and 95686. Mariposa and Merced counties were transferred to the Fresno Division as of January 1, 1995.

Sacramento Division counties: Alpine, Amador, Butte, Colusa, El Dorado, Glenn, Lassen, Modoc, Mono, Nevada, Placer, Plumas, Sacramento, Shasta, Sierra, Siskiyou, Solano, Sutter, Tehama, Trinity, Yolo, Yuba. This court also handles the following ZIP Codes in San Joaquin County: 95220, 95227, 95234, 95237, 95240-95242, 95253, 95258 and 95686.

US District Court -- Northern District of California

Home Page: www.cand.uscourts.gov
PACER: Toll-free access: 888-877-5883. Local access phone: 415-522-2144. Case records are available back to 1984. Records are purged every six months. New records are available online after 1 day. **PACER URL:** http://pacer.cand.uscourts.gov.
Electronic Filing: Electronic filing information is available online at https://ecf.cand.uscourts.gov.
Other Online Access: ECF cases data back to 4/2001.
Oakland Division counties: Alameda, Contra Costa(Note: Cases may be filed here or at San Francisco Div.; records available electronically at either; the 1st number of the case number indicates the file location: 3=SF, 4=Oak., 5=SJ.
San Francisco Division counties: Del Norte, Humboldt, Lake, Marin, Mendocino, Napa, San Francisco, San Mateo, Sonoma(Note: Cases may be filed here or at Oakland Div; records available electronically at either; the 1st number of the case number indicates the file location: 3=SF, 4=Oak., 5=SJ.
San Jose Division counties: Monterey, San Benito, Santa Clara, Santa Cruz.

US Bankruptcy Court -- Northern District of California

Home Page: www.canb.uscourts.gov
PACER: Toll-free access: 888-773-8548. Local access phone: 415-268-4832. Case records are available back to 1993. Records are purged every six months to one year. New civil records are available online after 1 day.
PACER URL: http://pacer.canb.uscourts.gov.
Electronic Filing: (Currently in the process of implementing CM/ECF). **Also:** access via phone on VCIS (Voice Case Information System) is available: 800-570-9819, 415-705-3160
Oakland Division counties: Alameda, Contra Costa.
San Francisco Division counties: San Francisco, San Mateo.
San Jose Division counties: Monterey, San Benito, Santa Clara, Santa Cruz.
Santa Rosa Division counties: Del Norte, Humboldt, Lake, Marin, Mendocino, Napa, Sonoma.

US District Court -- Southern District of California

Home Page: www.casd.uscourts.gov
PACER: Toll-free access: 888-241-9760. Local access phone: 619-557-7138. Case records are available back to 1990. New records are available online after 1 day. **PACER URL:** http://pacer.casd.uscourts.gov. Document images available.
Other Online Access: A computer bulletin board is accessible at 619-557-6779.
San Diego Division counties: Imperial, San Diego. Court also handles some cases from Yuma County, AZ.

US Bankruptcy Court -- Southern District of California

Home Page: www.casb.uscourts.gov
PACER: Toll-free access: 800-870-9972. Local access phone: 619-557-6875. Case records are available back to 1989. Records are purged every six months. New civil records are available online after 3 days. **PACER URL:** http://pacer.casb.uscourts.gov. Document images available.
Electronic Filing: Electronic filing information is available online at http://ecf.casb.uscourts.gov. **Also:** access via phone on VCIS (Voice Case Information System) is available: 619-557-6521.
San Diego Division counties: Imperial, San Diego.

Capital: Denver
                Denver County   Home Page   www.state.co.us

Time Zone: MST   Attorney General   www.ago.state.co.us

Number of Counties: 64   Archives   www.archives.state.co.us

State Level ... Major Agencies

Criminal Records

Bureau of Investigation, State Repository, Identification Unit, 690 Kipling St, Suite 3000, Denver, CO 80215; 303-239-4208, 303-239-5858 (Fax), 8AM-4:30PM.

http://cbi.state.co.us

There is a remote access system available called the Electronic Clearance System (ECS). This is an overnight batch system, open M-F from 7AM to 4PM. The fee is $5.50 per record. There is no set-up fee, but requesters must register and meet quotas. Billing is monthly. For more information, call 303-239-4233.

Corporation Records, Trademarks/Servicemarks, Fictitious Name, Limited Liability Company Records, Assumed Name

Secretary of State, Business Division, 1560 Broadway, Suite 200, Denver, CO 80202; 303-894-2200 x2 (Business Entities), 900-555-1717 (Status-Name), 303-894-2242 (Fax), 7:30AM-5PM.

www.sos.state.co.us

The Sec. of State's Business Record Search page offers free searching of corporate names and associate information at www.sos.state.co.us/pubs/business/main.htm.

Uniform Commercial Code, Federal Tax Liens, State Tax Liens

Secretary of State, UCC Division, 1560 Broadway, Suite 200, Denver, CO 80202; 303-894-2200, 303-869-4864 (Fax), 7:30AM-5PM.

www.sos.state.co.us

There is free record searching at this agency's web site.

Sales Tax Registrations, Trade Names

Revenue Department, Taxpayers Services Office, 1375 Sherman St, Denver, CO 80261 (Courier: 1625 Broadway, Ste 805, Denver, CO 80261); 303-232-2416, 303-866-3211 (Fax), 8AM-4:30PM.

www.revenue.state.co.us

You can search trade names at www.businesstax.state.co.us/pgBusTax.htm. You can verfiy a sales tax license or exemption number at www.taxview.state.co.us. **Other options:** Tradename lists are available on diskette, tape or paper.

Birth Certificates, Death Records, Marriage Certificates, Divorce Records

Department of Public Health & Environment, Vital Records Section HSVR-A1, 4300 Cherry Creek Dr S, Denver, CO 80246-1530; 303-756-4464 (Recorded Message), 303-692-2224 (Credit Card Ordering), 303-692-2234, 800-423-1108 (Fax), 8:30AM-4:30PM.

www.cdphe.state.co.us/hs/certs.asp

Records can be ordered online from a state designated vendor - VitalChek. Go to www.vitalchek.com/default.asp

Legislation Records

www.state.co.us/gov_dir/stateleg.html

The web site gives access to bills, status, journals from the last two sessions, and much more.

State Level ... Occupational Licensing

Acupuncturist	www.dora.state.co.us/pls/real/ARMS_Search.Set_Up
Architect	www.dora.state.co.us/pls/real/ARMS_Search.Set_Up
Architectural Firm	www.dora.state.co.us/pls/real/ARMS_Search.Set_Up
Audiologist	www.dora.state.co.us/pls/real/ARMS_Search.Set_Up
Barber	www.dora.state.co.us/pls/real/ARMS_Search.Disclaimer_Page
Chiropractor	www.dora.state.co.us/pls/real/ARMS_Search.Disclaimer_Page
Cosmetician	www.dora.state.co.us/pls/real/ARMS_Search.Disclaimer_Page
Cosmetologist	www.dora.state.co.us/pls/real/ARMS_Search.Disclaimer_Page
Counselor, Professional	www.dora.state.co.us/pls/real/ARMS_Search.Disclaimer_Page
Credit Union	www.dora.state.co.us/Financial-Services/homeregu.html#credit
Dental Hygienist	www.dora.state.co.us/pls/real/ARMS_Search.Disclaimer_Page
Dentist	www.dora.state.co.us/pls/real/ARMS_Search.Disclaimer_Page
Electrical Contractor	www.dora.state.co.us/pls/real/ARMS_Search.Disclaimer_Page
Electrician Journeyman/Master	www.dora.state.co.us/pls/real/ARMS_Search.Disclaimer_Page
Engineer/Engineer in Training	www.dora.state.co.us/pls/real/ARMS_Search.Disclaimer_Page
Family Therapist	www.dora.state.co.us/pls/real/ARMS_Search.Disclaimer_Page
Hearing Aid Dealer	www.dora.state.co.us/pls/real/ARMS_Search.Set_Up
Insurance Agency	www.dora.state.co.us/pls/real/INS_Agent.Search_Form
Insurance Company	www.dora.state.co.us/pls/real/INS_Company.Search_Form
Insurance Producer	www.dora.state.co.us/pls/real/INS_Agent.Search_Form
Land Surveyor	www.dora.state.co.us/pls/real/ARMS_Search.Disclaimer_Page
Land Surveyor Intern	www.dora.state.co.us/pls/real/ARMS_Search.Disclaimer_Page
Lobbyist	www.sos.state.co.us/pubs/bingo_raffles/new2001lobbyist_dir.htm
Manicurist	www.dora.state.co.us/pls/real/ARMS_Search.Disclaimer_Page
Manufactured Housing Dealer	www.dola.state.co.us/doh/Documents/dealers.htm
Manufactured Housing Mfg.	www.dola.state.co.us/doh/Documents/parkt.htm
Marriage Therapist	www.dora.state.co.us/pls/real/ARMS_Search.Disclaimer_Page
Medical Doctor	www.dora.state.co.us/pls/real/ARMS_Search.Disclaimer_Page
Midwife	www.dora.state.co.us/pls/real/ARMS_Search.Disclaimer_Page
Nurse	www.dora.state.co.us/pls/real/ARMS_Search.Disclaimer_Page
Nurses' Aide	www.dora.state.co.us/pls/real/ARMS_Search.Disclaimer_Page
Nursing Care Facility	www.dora.state.co.us/pls/real/ARMS_Search.Set_Up
Nursing Home Administrator	www.dora.state.co.us/pls/real/ARMS_Search.Set_Up
Optometrist	www.dora.state.co.us/pls/real/ARMS_Search.Disclaimer_Page
Outfitter	www.dora.state.co.us/pls/real/ARMS_Search.Disclaimer_Page
Pharmacist/Pharmacist /Intern	www.dora.state.co.us/pls/real/ARMS_Search.Disclaimer_Page
Pharmacy	www.dora.state.co.us/pls/real/ARMS_Search.Disclaimer_Page
Physical Therapist	www.dora.state.co.us/pls/real/ARMS_Search.Disclaimer_Page
Physician Assistant	www.dora.state.co.us/pls/real/ARMS_Search.Disclaimer_Page
Plumber Journeyman/Master/Residential	www.dora.state.co.us/pls/real/ARMS_Search.Disclaimer_Page
Podiatrist	www.dora.state.co.us/pls/real/ARMS_Search.Disclaimer_Page
Psychologist	www.dora.state.co.us/pls/real/ARMS_Search.Disclaimer_Page
Public Accountant-CPA	www.dora.state.co.us/pls/real/ARMS_Search.Disclaimer_Page

Real Estate Appraiser	www.dora.state.co.us/pls/real/re_estate_home
Real Estate Broker/Salesperson	www.dora.state.co.us/pls/real/re_estate_home
River Outfitter	www.dora.state.co.us/pls/real/ARMS_Search.Disclaimer_Page
Savings & Loan Association	www.dora.state.co.us/Financial-Services/homeregu.html#savings
Securities Broker	http://pdpi.nasdr.com/pdpi/disclaimer_frame.htm
Securities Dealer	http://pdpi.nasdr.com/pdpi/disclaimer_frame.htm
Social Worker	www.dora.state.co.us/pls/real/ARMS_Search.Disclaimer_Page
Stock Broker	http://pdpi.nasdr.com/pdpi/disclaimer_frame.htm
Veterinarian	www.dora.state.co.us/pls/real/ARMS_Search.Disclaimer_Page
Veterinary Student	www.dora.state.co.us/pls/real/ARMS_Search.Disclaimer_Page

County Level ... Courts

Court Administration: State Court Administrator, 1301 Pennsylvania St, Suite 300, Denver, CO, 80203; 303-861-1111; www.courts.state.co.us

Court Structure: The District and County Courts have overlapping jurisdiction over civil cases involving less than $15,000. District and County Courts are combined in most counties. Combined courts usually search both the civil or criminal indexes for a single fee. Municipal courts only have jurisdiction over traffic, parking, and ordinance violations.

Online Access Note: There is no official government system, but we can mention a unique commercial system. As a result of an initiative of the Colorado Judicial Branch, all district courts and all county courts except Denver County Court are available on the Internet at www.cocourts.com. Real-time records include civil, civil water, small claims, domestic, felony, misdemeanor, and traffic cases and can be accessed by name or case number. Court records go as far back as 1995. There is a fee for this subscription Internet access, generally $5.00 per search and there are discounts for volume users. Contact Jeff Mueller, Major Accounts, by telephone at 866-COCOURT, or by email at Jeffm@cocourts.com.

Denver County

County Court - Civil Division *Civil Records*
www.courts.state.co.us/district/02nd/dcadmn02.htm
Online searching of Denver County Civil Division court cases is available at www.denvergov.org/civilcourts.asp. Search by name, business name, or case number.

Teller County

4th District & County Courts *Civil and Criminal Records*
www.tellercountycourts.com/
Online access to civil and criminal records is available at www.cocourts.com. Also, a record request form is available to download at https://33.securedata.net/gofourth/pub_data_req_form.htm.

Editor's Note: See the text above about a private, statewide access system.

County Level ... Recorders & Assessors

Recording Office Organization:
63 counties, 63 recording offices. The recording officer is the County Clerk and Recorder. The entire state is in the Mountain Time Zone (MST). Federal and some state tax liens on personal property are filed with the Secretary of State. Other federal and state tax liens are filed with the County Clerk and Recorder. Many counties will perform tax lien searches, usually at the same fees as UCC searches.

On November 15, 2001, Broomfield City and County came into existence, derived from portions of Adams, Boulder, Jefferson and Weld counties. County offices are located at 1 Descombes Dr, Broomfield, CO 80020; 303-469-3301; hours 8AM-5PM. To determine if an address is in Broomfield, parcel search by address at www.co.broomfield.co.us/centralrecords/assessor.shtml.

Online Access Note:
To date, over 20 Colorado Counties offer free access to property assessor records. At the state level, the Secretary of State offers web access to UCCs and the Department of Revenue offers trade name searches. See the State Agencies section for details.

Adams County   *Assessor, Property Records*
Records from the Adams County Assessor database are available free online at www.co.adams.co.us/gis/html/QuickSearchFSIE.htm. Also, search property information on the GIS mapping page for free at www.co.adams.co.us/gis/

Arapahoe County   *Assessor Records*
www.co.arapahoe.co.us
Records on the Arapahoe County Assessor database are available free online at www.co.arapahoe.co.us/as/ResForm.htm.

Boulder County   *Assessor, Property Tax, Voter Registration Records*
www.co.boulder.co.us
Search the assessor's property database for free at www.co.boulder.co.us/assessor/disclaimer.htm. No name searching. Also, the county treasurer has data available electronically and on microfiche; Alpha index by owner name is $25.00 per set. Also, search property tax records at www.co.boulder.co.us/treas/disclaim.htm. No name searching. Also, search voter registration at www.co.boulder.co.us. Click on "Check your Voter Registration." Name and DOB required.

Broomfield County   *Real Estate, Assessor Records*
www.co.broomfield.co.us
Access to the assessor property database is available free at http://ims.ci.broomfield.co.us/website/htmlviewer/Parcelsearch/. Search by address or parcel ID only.

Denver County   *Assessor Records*
www.denvergov.org
Records on the Denver City and Denver County Assessor database are available free online at www.denvergov.org/realproperty.asp.

Douglas County   *Assessor, Property Records*
www.douglas.co.us/assessor
Records on the county assessor database are available free at www.douglas.co.us/assessor.

Eagle County   *Assessor, Property, Sales Grantor/Grantee Records*
www.eagle-county.com/dept.htm
Records on the County Assessor-Treasurer databases are available free online at www.eagle-county.com/Goodturns/assessor/search.asp?.

El Paso County   *Assessor Records*
www.co.el-paso.co.us or www.elpasoco.com
Records on the county Assessor database are available free online at http://land.elpasoco.com/default.htm.

Grand County   *Property, Assessor, Grantor/Grantee, Recording Records*
www.gcgovernment.com
Access to the Clerk&Recorder database is available free at www.gcpermit.com/clerks/. Also, the accessor database is available free at www.gcpermit.com/assessor/ Also, property ownership information is available free at www.co.grand.co.us/Assessor/Download_Page.html.

Jefferson County   *Assessor, Property, Grantor/Grantee, Deed, Judgment, Recording Records*
http://206.247.49.21/ext/dpt/officials/clkrec/index.htm
Records on the county Assessor database are available free online at http://206.247.49.21/ext/dpt/officials/assessor/index.htm. Also, search the recorder's Grantor/Grantee index for free at http://ww4.co.jefferson.co.us/crint/disclaimer.htm.

La Plata County   *Assessor Records*
www.laplatainfo.com
Records on the county Assessor database are available free online at www.laplatainfo.com/search2.html.

Larimer County   *Property Tax, Assessor, Treasurer, UCC, Deed, Judgment, Recording, Voter Registration Records*
www.larimer.org
Search the county Public Record Databases for free at www.larimer.org/databases/index.htm

Logan County   *Assessor, Real Estate Records*
www.loganco.gov/departments.htm
Access to the Assessor's Property Search database is available free at www.loganco-assessor.org/search.asp?.

Mesa County   *Assessor, Real Estate, Property Tax Records*
www.co.mesa.co.us
Records on the county Assessor database are available free online at http://205.169.141.11/Assessor/Database/netsearch.html. Any search is by address or parcel #. You may also do parcel searches at http://mcweb.co.mesa.co.us/imd/gis/autoFrame.htm. There is also a GIS-mapping search page for property information at http://198.204.117.70/maps/index.htm. Also, an interactive Voice Response System lets callers access real property information at 970-256-1563. Fax back service is available. Also, search the Treasurer's Tax Status Information database at http://205.169.141.11/Treasurer/Database/NETSearch.HTML#Top.

Park County   *Assessor Records*
www.parkco.org
Records on the county Assessor database are available free online at www.parkco.org/Search2.asp? including tax information, owner, address, building characteristics, legal and deed information.

Pitkin County   *Assessor, Inmates Records*
www.pitkingov.com
Records on the county Assessor database are available free online at www.mitchandco.com/realestate/pitkin/index.cfm. Also, the sheriff's current inmate list is available free at www.pitkin-sheriff.com/inmate/jailcip.html.

Pueblo County   *Assessor, Real Estate Records*
www.co.pueblo.co.us/index2.htm
Access to the county assessor database is available free at http://pueblocountyassessor.org/FrontPage.html.

Routt County   *Real Estate, Assessor, Treasurer Records*
www.co.routt.co.us/clerk
Records on the county Assessor/Treasurer Property Search database are available free online at http://pioneer.yampa.com/asp/assessor/search.asp?. Records on the Routt County Clerk and Recorder Reception Search database are available free online at http://pioneer.yampa.com/asp/clerk/search.asp?.

Teller County   *Real Estate, Grantor Index, Assessor, Property Tax Records*
www.co.teller.co.us
Access the county clerk real estate database for free at http://data.co.teller.co.us/AsrData/wc.dll?Doc~GrantSearch Also, the assessor database is available free at http://data.co.teller.co.us/AsrData/wc.dll?AsrDataProc~OwnerNameSearch.

Weld County   *Real Estate Records*
www.co.weld.co.us
Search property information on the map server database available at the web site. Click on the "Property Information and mapping" button then search by name.

Federal Courts in Colorado...

Standards for Federal Courts: The universal PACER sign-up number is 800-676-6856. Find PACER and the Party/Case Index on the Web at http://pacer.psc.uscourts.gov. PACER dial-up access is $.60 per minute. Also, courts offering internet access via RACER, PACER, Web-PACER or the new CM-ECF charge $.07 per page fee unless noted as free.

US District Court -- District of Colorado

Home Page: www.co.uscourts.gov
PACER: Toll-free access: 888-481-7027. Local access phone: 303-335-2335. Case records are available back to 1990. Records are purged on a varying schedule. New records are available online after 1 day. **PACER URL:** http://pacer.cod.uscourts.gov.
Denver Division counties: All counties in Colorado.

US Bankruptcy Court -- District of Colorado

Home Page: www.co.uscourts.gov
PACER: Case records are available back to July 1981. New civil records are available online after 1 day. **PACER URL:** http://pacer.cob.uscourts.gov.
Electronic Filing: Electronic filing information is available online at https://ecf.cob.uscourts.gov. **Also:** access via phone on VCIS (Voice Case Information System) is available: 303-844-0267.
Denver Division counties: All counties in Colorado.

Editor's Tip: Just because records are maintained in a certain way in your state or county do not assume that any other county or state does things the same way that you are used to.

Connecticut

Capital:	Hartford	Home Page	www.state.ct.us
	Hartford County		
Time Zone:	EST	Attorney General	www.cslib.org/attygenl
Number of Counties:	8	Archives	www.cslib.org/archives.htm

State Level ... Major Agencies

Corporation Records, Limited Partnership Records, Trademarks/Servicemarks, Limited Liability Company Records

Secretary of State, Commercial Recording Division, 30 Trinity St, Hartford, CT 06106; 860-509-6001, 860-509-6069 (Fax), 8:30AM-4:30PM.

www.sots.state.ct.us

Click on the CONCORD option at the web site for free access to corporation and UCC records. The system is open from 7AM to 11PM. You can search by business name only.

Uniform Commercial Code, Federal Tax Liens, State Tax Liens

UCC Division, Secretary of State, PO Box 150470, Hartford, CT 06115-0470 (Courier: 30 Trinity St, Hartford, CT 06106); 860-509-6004, 860-509-6069 (Fax), 8:30AM-4PM.

www.sots.state.ct.us

Records may be accessed at no charge on the Internet. Click on the CONCORD option. The system is open 7AM to 11PM.

Driver Records

Department of Motor Vehicles, Copy Records Unit, 60 State St., Wethersfield, CT 06161-0503; 860-263-5154, 8:30AM-4:30PM T-F.

www.ct.gov/dmv/site/default.asp

Online access is provided to approved businesses that enter into written contract. The contract requires a prepayment with minimum hits annually and a surety bond. Fee is $5.00 per record. The address is part of the record. For more information, call 203-805-6093. **Other options:** Magnetic tape ordering is available for approved users, call 203-805-6093 for details.

Vehicle Ownership, Vehicle Identification

Department of Motor Vehicles, Copy Record Unit, 60 State St, Wethersfield, CT 06161-1896; 860-263-5154, 8:AM-4:30PM T- F.

www.ct.gov/dmv/site/default.asp

Vehicle record information is available on a volume basis to approved businesses that enter into a written agreement. The contract requires an annual fee and a surety bond. For more information, call 203-805-6093.

Legislation Records

www.cga.state.ct.us/default.asp

From the web site you can track bills, find update or status, and print copies of bills. Also, you can request via email at billroom@cslib.org.

State Level ... Occupational Licensing

Acupuncturist	www.state.ct.us/dph/scripts/hlthprof.asp
Alcohol/Drug Counselor	www.state.ct.us/dph/scripts/hlthprof.asp
Antenna Service Dealer/Technician	www.dcpaccess.state.ct.us/DCPPublic/LicenseLookup.asp
Appraiser, MVPD	www.state.ct.us/cid/license/licweb1.asp
Appraiser, MVR	www.state.ct.us/cid/license/licweb1.asp
Architect	www.dcpaccess.state.ct.us/DCPPublic/LicenseLookup.asp
Architectural Firm	www.dcpaccess.state.ct.us/DCPPublic/LicenseLookup.asp
Asbestos Professional	www.state.ct.us/dph/scripts/hlthprof.asp
Athletic Promoter	www.dcpaccess.state.ct.us/DCPPublic/LicenseLookup.asp
Audiologist	www.state.ct.us/dph/scripts/hlthprof.asp
Automobile Insurance Adjuster	www.state.ct.us/cid/license/licweb1.asp
Bail Bond Agent	www.state.ct.us/cid/license/licweb1.asp
Bank	www.state.ct.us/dob/pages/banklist.htm
Bank & Trust Company	www.state.ct.us/dob/pages/bcharter.htm
Bank Branch	www.state.ct.us/dob/pages/branch1.htm
Barber	www.state.ct.us/dph/scripts/hlthprof.asp
Bedding Mfg/Renovation	www.dcpaccess.state.ct.us/DCPPublic/LicenseLookup.asp
Boxer	www.dcpaccess.state.ct.us/DCPPublic/LicenseLookup.asp
Building Contractor	www.dcpaccess.state.ct.us/DCPPublic/LicenseLookup.asp
Casualty Adjuster	www.state.ct.us/cid/license/licweb1.asp
Check Cashing Service	www.state.ct.us/dob/pages/chckcash.htm
Chiropractor	www.state.ct.us/dph/scripts/hlthprof.asp
Collection Agency	www.state.ct.us/dob/pages/collect.htm
Collection Agency, Consumer	www.state.ct.us/dob/pages/collect.htm
Cosmetologist	www.state.ct.us/dph/scripts/hlthprof.asp
Counselor, Professional	www.state.ct.us/dph/scripts/hlthprof.asp
Credit Union	www.state.ct.us/dob/pages/culist.htm
Debt Adjuster	www.state.ct.us/dob/pages/debtadj.htm
Dental Anes/Conscious Sedation Permittee	www.state.ct.us/dph/scripts/hlthprof.asp
Dentist/Dental Hygienist	www.state.ct.us/dph/scripts/hlthprof.asp
Dietician/Nutritionist	www.state.ct.us/dph/scripts/hlthprof.asp
Electrical Contractor/Inspector	www.dcpaccess.state.ct.us/DCPPublic/LicenseLookup.asp
Electrical Journeyman/Apprentice	www.dcpaccess.state.ct.us/DCPPublic/LicenseLookup.asp
Electrical Sign Installer	www.dcpaccess.state.ct.us/DCPPublic/LicenseLookup.asp
Electrician	www.dcpaccess.state.ct.us/DCPPublic/LicenseLookup.asp
Electrologist/Hypertricologist	www.state.ct.us/dph/scripts/hlthprof.asp
Electronics Service Dealer/Technician	www.dcpaccess.state.ct.us/DCPPublic/LicenseLookup.asp
Elevator Inspector/Mechanic	www.dcpaccess.state.ct.us/DCPPublic/LicenseLookup.asp
Embalmer	www.state.ct.us/dph/scripts/hlthprof.asp
Emergency Medical Service Professional	www.state.ct.us/dph/scripts/hlthprof.asp
Emergency Medical Technician	www.state.ct.us/dph/scripts/hlthprof.asp
Engineer	www.dcpaccess.state.ct.us/DCPPublic/LicenseLookup.asp
Fire Protection Inspector/Contractor	www.dcpaccess.state.ct.us/DCPPublic/LicenseLookup.asp
Funeral Director	www.state.ct.us/dph/scripts/hlthprof.asp
Funeral Home	www.state.ct.us/dph/scripts/hlthprof.asp
Glazier	www.dcpaccess.state.ct.us/DCPPublic/LicenseLookup.asp
Hairdresser	www.state.ct.us/dph/scripts/hlthprof.asp
Hearing Instrument Specialist	www.state.ct.us/dph/scripts/hlthprof.asp
Heating, Piping & Cooling Contractor/Journeyman	www.dcpaccess.state.ct.us/DCPPublic/LicenseLookup.asp
Homeopathic Physician	www.state.ct.us/dph/scripts/hlthprof.asp

Hypertrichologist	www.state.ct.us/dph/scripts/hlthprof.asp
Insurance Adjuster/Public Adjuster	www.state.ct.us/cid/license/licweb1.asp
Insurance Agent, Fraternal	www.state.ct.us/cid/license/licweb1.asp
Insurance Agent/Broker/Consultant	www.state.ct.us/cid/license/licweb1.asp
Insurance Appraiser	www.state.ct.us/cid/license/licweb1.asp
Insurance Company/Producer	www.state.ct.us/cid/license/licweb1.asp
Interior Designer	www.dcpaccess.state.ct.us/DCPPublic/LicenseLookup.asp
Land Surveyor Firm	www.dcpaccess.state.ct.us/DCPPublic/LicenseLookup.asp
Lead Planner/Project Designer	www.state.ct.us/dph/scripts/hlthprof.asp
Lead Professional	www.state.ct.us/dph/scripts/hlthprof.asp
Liquor License	www.dcpaccess.state.ct.us/DCPPublic/LicenseLookup.asp
Loan Company, Small	www.state.ct.us/dob/pages/smalloan.htm
Lobbyist	www.ethics.state.ct.us/publicinfo.htm
Marriage & Family Therapist	www.state.ct.us/dph/scripts/hlthprof.asp
Massage Therapist	www.state.ct.us/dph/scripts/hlthprof.asp
Medical Doctor	www.state.ct.us/dph/scripts/hlthprof.asp
Medical Response Technician	www.state.ct.us/dph/scripts/hlthprof.asp
Midwife	www.state.ct.us/dph/scripts/hlthprof.asp
Mobile Home Park/Seller	www.dcpaccess.state.ct.us/DCPPublic/LicenseLookup.asp
Money Forwarder	www.state.ct.us/dob/pages/$forward.htm
Mortgage (1st) Broker/Lender	www.state.ct.us/dob/pages/1stmtg.htm
Mortgage (2nd) Broker/Lender	www.state.ct.us/dob/pages/2ndmtg.htm
Naturopathic Physician	www.state.ct.us/dph/scripts/hlthprof.asp
Nurse	www.state.ct.us/dph/scripts/hlthprof.asp
Nurse, Advance Registered Practice	www.state.ct.us/dph/scripts/hlthprof.asp
Nurse-LPN	www.state.ct.us/dph/scripts/hlthprof.asp
Nursing Home Administrator	www.state.ct.us/dph/scripts/hlthprof.asp
Occupational Therapist/Assistant	www.state.ct.us/dph/scripts/hlthprof.asp
Optical Shop	www.state.ct.us/dph/scripts/hlthprof.asp
Optician	www.state.ct.us/dph/scripts/hlthprof.asp
Optometrist	www.state.ct.us/dph/scripts/hlthprof.asp
Osteopathic Physician	www.state.ct.us/dph/scripts/hlthprof.asp
Paramedic	www.state.ct.us/dph/scripts/hlthprof.asp
Pharmacist/Pharmacist Intern	www.dcpaccess.state.ct.us/DCPPublic/LicenseLookup.asp
Pharmacy	www.dcpaccess.state.ct.us/DCPPublic/LicenseLookup.asp
Physical Therapist/Assistant	www.state.ct.us/dph/scripts/hlthprof.asp
Physician Assistant	www.state.ct.us/dph/scripts/hlthprof.asp
Pipefitter	www.dcpaccess.state.ct.us/DCPPublic/LicenseLookup.asp
Plumber	www.dcpaccess.state.ct.us/DCPPublic/LicenseLookup.asp
Podiatrist	www.state.ct.us/dph/scripts/hlthprof.asp
Psychologist	www.state.ct.us/dph/scripts/hlthprof.asp
Public Service Technician	www.dcpaccess.state.ct.us/DCPPublic/LicenseLookup.asp
Radiographer	www.state.ct.us/dph/scripts/hlthprof.asp
Real Estate Appraiser	www.dcpaccess.state.ct.us/DCPPublic/LicenseLookup.asp
Real Estate Broker/Salesperson	www.dcpaccess.state.ct.us/DCPPublic/LicenseLookup.asp
Reinsurance Intermediary	www.state.ct.us/cid/license/licweb1.asp
Respiratory Care Practitioner	www.state.ct.us/dph/scripts/hlthprof.asp
Sales Finance Company	www.state.ct.us/dob/pages/salefinc.htm
Sanitarian	www.state.ct.us/dph/scripts/hlthprof.asp
Savings & Loan Association Bank	www.state.ct.us/dob/pages/bcharter.htm
Savings Bank	www.state.ct.us/dob/pages/bcharter.htm
Sheet Metal	www.dcpaccess.state.ct.us/DCPPublic/LicenseLookup.asp
Social Worker	www.state.ct.us/dph/scripts/hlthprof.asp
Solar Energy Contractor/Journeyman	www.dcpaccess.state.ct.us/DCPPublic/LicenseLookup.asp
Speech Pathologist	www.state.ct.us/dph/scripts/hlthprof.asp
Sprinkler Layout Technician	www.dcpaccess.state.ct.us/DCPPublic/LicenseLookup.asp
Subsurface Sewage Cleaner/Installer	www.state.ct.us/dph/scripts/hlthprof.asp
Surplus Line Broker	www.state.ct.us/cid/license/licweb1.asp
Surveyor, Land	www.dcpaccess.state.ct.us/DCPPublic/LicenseLookup.asp
Veterinarian	www.state.ct.us/dph/scripts/hlthprof.asp

Weigher...www.dcpaccess.state.ct.us/DCPPublic/LicenseLookup.asp
Weights & Measures Dealer/Repairer/Regulator..........www.dcpaccess.state.ct.us/DCPPublic/LicenseLookup.asp
Well Driller...www.dcpaccess.state.ct.us/DCPPublic/LicenseLookup.asp
Wrestler/Wrestling Manager...www.dcpaccess.state.ct.us/DCPPublic/LicenseLookup.asp

County Level ... Courts

Court Administration: Chief Court Administrator, 231 Capitol Av, Hartford, CT, 06106; 860-757-2100; www.jud.state.ct.us

Court Structure: The Superior Court is the sole court of original jurisdiction for all causes of action, except for matters over which the probate courts have jurisdiction as provided by statute. The state is divided into 13 Judicial Districts, 20 Geographic Area Courts, and 14 Juvenile Districts. The Superior Court - comprised primarily of the Judicial District Courts and the Geographical Area Courts - has five divisions: Criminal, Civil, Family, Juvenile, and Administrative Appeals. When not combined, the Judicial District Courts handle felony and civil cases while the Geographic Area Courts handle misdemeanors, and some handle small claims.

Online Access Note: The Judicial Branch provides access to civil and family records via the Internet, located online at www.jud2.state.ct.us (click on "Party Name Inquiry"). The site contains party name search, assignment lists, and calendars. Also, questions about the fuller commercial system available through Judicial Information Systems should be directed to the CT JIS Office at 860-282-6500. There is currently no online access to criminal records; however, criminal and motor vehicle data is available for purchase in database format.

There are no known courts that independently offer access to their records.

County Level ... Recorders & Assessors

Recording Office Organization: 8 counties and 170 towns/cities. There is no county recording in this state. The recording officer is the Town/City Clerk. Be careful not to confuse searching in the following towns/cities as equivalent to a countywide search: Fairfield, Hartford, Litchfield, New Haven, New London, Tolland, and Windham. The entire state is in the Eastern Time Zone (EST). All federal and state tax liens on personal property are filed with the Secretary of State. Federal and state tax liens on real property are filed with the Town/City Clerk. Towns will not perform tax lien searches.

Online Access Note: A number of towns offer free access to assessor information. The State's Municipal Public Access Initiative has produced a web site of Town and Municipality general information at www.munic.state.ct.us.

Fairfield County

Brookfield Town   *Assessor Records*
Search the town assessor database at http://data.visionappraisal.com/BrookfieldCT/. Free registration for full data.

Danbury City   *Assessor Records*
Search the city assessor database at http://data.visionappraisal.com/DanburyCT/. Free registration for full data.

Fairfield Town   *Assessor Records*
Search the town assessor database at http://data.visionappraisal.com/FairfieldCT/. Free registration for full data.

Stamford City   *Assessor, Real Estate, Personal Property Records*
www.cityofstamford.org/Welcome.htm

Access to the city tax assessor database is available free online at www.cityofstamford.org/Tax/main.htm. A land records index should be online in Fall, 2001.

Westport Town   *Assessor Records*
www.ci.westport.ct.us/govt/services
Access to the 2000 assessments database is available free at
www.ci.westport.ct.us/govt/services/finance/assessor/default.asp.

Hartford County

Enfield Town   *Tax Sales Records*
Searchthe town's tax sale list free at www.enfield.org/Link_Tax.htm. Use Control+F and search for name.

Glastonbury Town   *Property Records*
www.glasct.org
Search town property information free on the GIS Interactive Mapping site at www.glasct.org/isa/intermaps.html. Click on "Property Information (Parcels)."

Granby Town   *Assessor Records*
Search the town assessor's database at http://data.visionappraisal.com/GranbyCT. Free registration for full data.

Manchester Town   *Assessor Records*
www.ci.manchester.ct.us/Town_Clerk/index.htm
Search Town assessor database at http://data.visionappraisal.com/ManchesterCT. Free registration required for full access.

Suffield Town   *Assessor Records*
Search the town assessor's database at http://data.visionappraisal.com/SuffieldCT. Free registration required for full access.

Wethersfield Town   *Assessor Records*
www.wethersfieldct.com/govt.htm
Search the town assessor's grand list free at www.wethersfieldct.com/assess/service.htm. No name searching; download as ascii or Excel file format.

Windsor Locks Town   *Assessor Records*
Search the town assessor database at http://data.visionappraisal.com/WINDSORLOCKSCT/. Free registration for full data.

Windsor Town   *Assessor, Real Estate Records*
www.townofwindsorct.com
Search the town clerk's Recording database free at www.townofwindsorct.com/records.htm. Records go back to 1991; plan is to go back to 1970. Also, search the town assessor's Taxpayer Information System database at http://data.visionappraisal.com/WINDSORCT/. Free egistration required for full access.

Litchfield County

New Milford Town   *Assessor Records*
www.newmilford.org/agencies/home.htm
Search the town assessor database at http://data.visionappraisal.com/NewMilfordCT/. Free registration required for full access.

Middlesex County

Chester Town   *Assessor Records*
Search the Assessor's Taxpayer Inform. System database at http://data.visionappraisal.com/ChesterCT. Free registration for full data.

Middlefield Town   *Assessor Records*
www.munic.state.ct.us/MIDDLEFIELD/contents.htm
Search town assessor database at http://data.visionappraisal.com/MiddlefieldCT/. Free registration required for full data.

Old Saybrook Town   *Real Estate Records*
www.oldsaybrookct.com
Real Estate records on the Assessor's database are available free online at http://209.150.7.14/assessor/index.cfm.

New Haven County
Hamden Town   *Assessor Records*
Search the town assessor's database at http://data.visionappraisal.com/hamdenct. Free registration required for full access.

Madison Town   *Assessor Records*
Search Town assessor database at http://data.visionappraisal.com/MadisonCT/. Free Registration required for full access.

Milford City   *Assessor Records*
Search the city assessor's database at http://data.visionappraisal.com/milfordct/. Free registration required for full data.

Naugatuck Town   *Assessor Records*
Search the town assessor database at http://data.visionappraisal.com/NaugatuckCT/. Free registration required for full data.

New Haven City   *Assessor Records*
Search the city assessor database at http://data.visionappraisal.com/NewhavenCT/. Free registration required for full data.

West Haven City   *Assessor Records*
Search town assessor's database at http://data.visionappraisal.com/Westhavenct/. Free registration required for full access.

Woodbridge Town   *Assessor Records*
www.munic.state.ct.us/woodbridge/townclerk.html
Search town assessor's database at http://data.visionappraisal.com/woodbridgeCT. Free registration required for full data.

New London County
Colchester Town   *Assessor Records*
Search the town assessor database at http://data.visionappraisal.com/ColchesterCT/. Free registration for full data.

East Lyme Town   *Assessor Records*
Search the town assessor database at http://data.visionappraisal.com/EastLymeCT/. Free registration for full data.

New London City   *Assessor Records*
Search the city assessor's database at http://data.visionappraisal.com//NewLondonCT. Free registration required for full access.

Norwich City   *Assessor Records*
Search the city assessor's database at http://data.visionappraisal.com/NorwichCT. Free registration required for full data.

Old Lyme Town   *Assessor Records*
Search the town Assessor's database at http://data.visionappraisal.com/OLDLYMECT. Free registration required for full access.

Tolland County
Columbia Town   *Assessor Records*
Search the town assessor database at http://data.visionappraisal.com/ColumbiaCT/. Free registration for full data.

Windham County
Thompson Town   *Assessor Records*
Search the town assessor database at http://data.visionappraisal.com/ThompsonCT/. Free registration for full data.

Federal Courts in Connecticut...

Standards for Federal Courts: The universal PACER sign-up number is 800-676-6856. Find PACER and the Party/Case Index on the Web at http://pacer.psc.uscourts.gov. PACER dial-up access is $.60 per minute. Also, courts offering internet access via RACER, PACER, Web-PACER or the new CM-ECF charge $.07 per page fee unless noted as free.

US District Court -- District of Connecticut

Home Page: www.ctd.uscourts.gov

PACER: Toll-free access: 800-292-0658. Local access phone: 203-773-2451. Case records are available back to November 1, 1991. New records are available online after 1 day. **PACER URL:** http://pacer.ctd.uscourts.gov.

Bridgeport Division counties: Fairfield (prior to 1993). Since January 1993, cases from any county may be assigned to any of the divisions in the district.

Hartford Division counties: Hartford, Tolland, Windham (prior to 1993). Since 1993, cases from any county may be assigned to any of the divisions in the district.

New Haven Division counties: Litchfield, Middlesex, New Haven, New London (prior to 1993). Since 1993, cases from any county may be assigned to any of the divisions in the district.

US Bankruptcy Court -- District of Connecticut

Home Page: www.ctb.uscourts.gov

PACER: Case records are available back to 1979. Records are purged every 6 months. New civil records are available online after 1 day. **PACER URL:** http://pacer.ctb.uscourts.gov. Document images available.

Electronic Filing: (Currently in the process of implementing CM/ECF). **Also:** access via phone on VCIS (Voice Case Information System) is available: 800-800-5113, 860-240-3345

Bridgeport Division counties: Fairfield.

Hartford Division counties: Hartford, Litchfield, Middlesex, Tolland, Windham.

New Haven Division counties: New Haven, New London.

Delaware

Capital:	Dover Kent County	Home Page	www.state.de.us
Time Zone:	EST	Archives	www.state.de.us/sos/dpa
Number of Counties:	3	Attorney General	www.state.de.us/attgen

State Level ... Major Agencies

Birth Certificates, Death Records, Marriage Certificates

Department of Health, Office of Vital Statistics, PO Box 637, Dover, DE 19903 (Courier: William Penn & Federal Sts, Jesse Cooper Bldg, Dover, DE 19901); 302-739-4721, 302-736-1862 (Fax), 8AM-4:30PM (Counter closes at 4:20 PM).

www.deph.org/vs.htm

Access available at vitalchek.com, a state designated vendor.

Sexual Offender Registry

The State Bureau of Investigations oversees the sexual offender records. Free public access is available online at www.state.de.us/dsp/sexoff/search.htm.

Driver Records

Division of Motor Vehicles, Driver Services, PO Box 698, Dover, DE 19903 (Courier: 303 Transportation Circle, Dover, DE 19901); 302-744-2506, 302-739-2602 (Fax), 8AM-4:30PM M-T-TH-F; 12:00PM-8PM W.

www.delaware.gov/yahoo/DMV

Online searching is single inquiry only, no batch request mode is offered. Searching is done by driver's license number or name and DOB. A signed contract application and valid "business license" is required. Access is provided 24 hours daily through a 900 number at a fee of $1.00 per minute, plus the $4.00 per record fee. For more information, call 302-744-2606. **Other options:** Tape-to-tape is offered for high volume, batch requesters. Also, the state will release data from the driver license file on tapes or cartridges, but this cannot be resold.

Vehicle Ownership, Vehicle Identification

Division of Motor Vehicles, Correspondence Section, PO Box 698, Dover, DE 19903 (Courier: 303 Transportation Circle, Dover, DE 19901); 302-744-2511, 302-739-2042 (Fax), 8:30AM-4:30PM M-T-TH-F; 12-8PM W.

www.delaware.gov/yahoo/DMV

There is an additional $1.00 per minute fee for using the online "900 number" system. Records are $4.00 each. The system is single inquiry mode and open from 8 AM to 4:30 PM, except on Wed. from noon to 8PM. For more information, call 302-744-2606. This program is strictly monitored and not available for non-permissible uses. **Other options:** Bulk information can be obtained on a customized basis in tape, cartridge or paper format. However, the purpose of the request is carefully screened and information cannot be resold.

Legislation Records

www.legis.state.de.us

Access information at the Internet site, no fee.

State Level ... Occupational Licensing

Engineer	www.dape.org
Engineering Firm	www.dape.org
Optometrist	www.odfinder.org/LicSearch.asp
Real Estate Appraiser	www.asc.gov/content/category1/appr_by_state.asp
School Admin. Supervisor/Asst.	www.doe.state.de.us/EduDir/EduDirStart.asp
School Counselor	www.doe.state.de.us/EduDir/EduDirStart.asp
School Principal/Superintendent	www.doe.state.de.us/EduDir/EduDirStart.asp
Teacher	www.doe.state.de.us/EduDir/EduDirStart.asp

County Level ... Courts

Court Administration: Administrative Office of the Courts, PO Box 8911, Wilmington, DE, 19899; 302-577-2480; http://courts.state.de.us/supreme/index.htm

Court Structure: Superior Courts have jurisdiction over felonies and all drug offenses, the Court of Common Pleas has jurisdiction over all misdemeanors. Court of Chancery handles corporation and equity matters, as well as probate and estates. Guardianships are handled by the Register of Wills, corporate matters such as equity disputes and injunctions are handled by the Clerk of Chancery.

Online Access Note: Only Supreme Court Final Orders and opinions are available at http://courts.state.de.us/supreme/opinions.htm.

An online system called CLAD, developed by Mead Data Central and the New Castle Superior Court, is currently available in Delaware. CLAD contains only toxic waste, asbestos, and class action cases. However, based on CLAD's success, Delaware may pursue development of online availability of other public records by working in conjunction with private information resource enterprises.

There are no known courts that independently offer online access to their records.

County Level ... Recorders & Assessors

Recording Office Organization: Delaware has 3 counties and 3 recording offices. The recording officer is the County Recorder in both jurisdictions. Delaware is in the Eastern Time Zone (EST). Federal tax liens on personal property of businesses are filed with the Secretary of State. Other federal and all state tax liens on personal property are filed with the County Recorder. Copy and certification fees vary.

Online Access Note: There is no statewide access to recorder or assessor information.

New Castle County   *Real Estate, Property Assessor Records*
www.co.new-castle.de.us
Records on the City of New Castle Geographic Information System database are available free online at www.2isystems.com/newcastle/Search2.CFM. County property information can also be found at www.co.new-castle.de.us/LandUse/LandUse1.htm. No name searching.

Federal Courts in Delaware...

Standards for Federal Courts: The universal PACER sign-up number is 800-676-6856. Find PACER and the Party/Case Index on the Web at http://pacer.psc.uscourts.gov. PACER dial-up access is $.60 per minute. Also, courts offering internet access via RACER, PACER, Web-PACER or the new CM-ECF charge $.07 per page fee unless noted as free.

US District Court -- District of Delaware
Home Page: www.ded.uscourts.gov
PACER: Toll-free access: 888-793-9488. Local access phone: 302-573-6651. Case records are available back to January 1991. Records are purged every few years (not since 1/91). New records are available online after 2 days.   **PACER URL:** http://pacer.ded.uscourts.gov.
Opinions Online: Court opinions are available online at www.lawlib.widener.edu/pages/deopind.htm.
Wilmington Division counties: All counties in Delaware.

US Bankruptcy Court -- District of Delaware
Home Page: www.deb.uscourts.gov
PACER: Case records are available back to 1991. Records are purged every four years. New civil records available online after 1 day.
Electronic Filing: Electronic filing information is available online at https://ecf.deb.uscourts.gov/.
Other Online Access: Online access to WebPacer is available free at www.deb.uscourts.gov/wconnect/wc.dll?usbcn_racer~main.
Also: access via phone on VCIS (Voice Case Information System) is available: 888-667-5530, 302-573-6233
Wilmington Division counties: All counties in Delaware.

District of Columbia

Time Zone: EST   Home Page   www.washingtondc.gov

State Level ... Major Agencies

Uniform Commercial Code, Federal Tax Liens, State Tax Liens

UCC Recorder, District of Columbia Recorder of Deeds, 515 D Street NW, Washington, DC 20001; 202-727-0400, 202-727-7114, 8:15AM-4:45PM.

http://countyrecords.landata.com/WashDC/

Search by name or document number at the web site. Registration is required but there is no fee. It is the intent of the Washington DC Recorder of Deeds to sell document images through this site in the near future.

Sexual Offender Registry

The Sex Offender Registry is maintained by the Police Department. Records are available for searching at http://mpdc.dc.gov/serv/sor/impreminder.shtm.

Driver Records

Department of Motor Vehicles, Driver Records Division, 301 "C" St, NW, Rm 1000, Washington, DC 20001; 202-727-6761, 202-727-5000 (General), 8:15AM-4PM M-T-TH-F; 8:15AM-7:00PM W.

www.dmv.washingtondc.gov/main.shtm

Online requests are taken throughout the day and are available in batch the next morning after 8:15 am. There is no minimum order requirement. Fee is $5.00 per record. Billing is a "bank" system which draws from pre-paid account. Requesters are restricted to high volume, ongoing users. Each requester must be approved and sign a contract. For more information, call 202-727-5692.

Legislation Records

www.dccouncil.washington.dc.us

Bill text and status may be reviewed at the Internet site.

State Level ... Occupational Licensing

Acupuncturist .... http://dchealth.dc.gov/prof_license/services/search_licensing.asp
Addiction Counselor .... http://dchealth.dc.gov/prof_license/services/search_licensing.asp
Attorney .... www.dcbar.org/memberlookup/searchform.cfm
Chiropractor .... http://dchealth.dc.gov/prof_license/services/search_licensing.asp
Counselor, Professional .... http://dchealth.dc.gov/prof_license/services/search_licensing.asp
Dance Therapist .... http://dchealth.dc.gov/prof_license/services/search_licensing.asp
Dental Hygienist .... http://dchealth.dc.gov/prof_license/services/search_licensing.asp
Dentist .... http://dchealth.dc.gov/prof_license/services/search_licensing.asp
Dietitian/Nutritionist .... http://dchealth.dc.gov/prof_license/services/search_licensing.asp
Investment Advisor .... http://disr.washingtondc.gov/services/licenseing_security_prof/index.shtm
Investment Advisor Representative .... http://disr.washingtondc.gov/services/licenseing_security_prof/index.shtm
Massage Therapist .... http://dchealth.dc.gov/prof_license/services/search_licensing.asp
Medical Doctor .... http://dchealth.dc.gov/prof_license/services/search_licensing.asp
Midwife Nurse .... http://dchealth.dc.gov/prof_license/services/search_licensing.asp
Naturopath .... http://dchealth.dc.gov/prof_license/services/search_licensing.asp
Nurse Anesthetist .... http://dchealth.dc.gov/prof_license/services/search_licensing.asp
Nurse, Clinical .... http://dchealth.dc.gov/prof_license/services/search_licensing.asp
Nurse, Licensed Practical .... http://dchealth.dc.gov/prof_license/services/search_licensing.asp
Nurse-LPN .... http://dchealth.dc.gov/prof_license/services/search_licensing.asp
Nursing Home Administrator .... http://dchealth.dc.gov/prof_license/services/search_licensing.asp
Occupational Therapist .... http://dchealth.dc.gov/prof_license/services/search_licensing.asp
Optometrist .... www.odfinder.org/LicSearch.asp
Osteopath .... http://dchealth.dc.gov/prof_license/services/search_licensing.asp
Pharmacist .... http://dchealth.dc.gov/prof_license/services/search_licensing.asp
Physical Therapist .... http://dchealth.dc.gov/prof_license/services/search_licensing.asp
Physician Assistant .... http://dchealth.dc.gov/prof_license/services/search_licensing.asp
Podiatrist .... http://dchealth.dc.gov/prof_license/services/search_licensing.asp
Psychologist .... http://dchealth.dc.gov/prof_license/services/search_licensing.asp
Real Estate Appraiser .... www.asc.gov/content/category1/appr_by_state.asp
Recreational Therapist .... http://dchealth.dc.gov/prof_license/services/search_licensing.asp
Respiratory Care .... http://dchealth.dc.gov/prof_license/services/search_licensing.asp
Securities Agent .... http://disr.washingtondc.gov/services/licenseing_security_prof/index.shtm
Securities Broker/Dealer .... http://disr.washingtondc.gov/services/licenseing_security_prof/index.shtm
Social Worker .... http://dchealth.dc.gov/prof_license/services/search_licensing.asp

County Level ... Courts

Court Administration: Executive Office, 500 Indiana Av NW, Room 1500, Washington, DC, 20001; 202-879-1700; www.dcsc.gov

Court Structure: The Superior Court in DC is divided into 17 divisions, 4 of which are: Criminal, Civil, Family, and Tax-Probate. The Tax-Probate Division of the Superior Court handles probate. Eviction is part of the court's Landlord and Tenant Branch (202-879-4879)..

Online Access Note: The Superior Court and Court of Appeals offer access to opinions at www.dcbar.org. Limited cases (those filed electronically) are available at www.dcbar.org/dcsc/efiling.html.

District of Columbia
Superior Court - Civil Division *Civil Records*
www.dcbar.org/dcsc/
Limited cases are available free via the e-Filing Project. Attorneys and legal professionals participating in the project must register for the CourtLink eFile service either by logging onto www.courtlink.com or calling 1-888-529-7587. See also www.dcbar.org/dcsc/efiling.html.

County Level ... Recorders & Assessors

Recording Office Organization: District of Columbia is in the Eastern Time Zone (EST). Federal tax liens on personal property of businesses are filed with the Secretary of State. Other federal and all state tax liens on personal property are filed with the Recorder.

Online Access Note: Search the recorders database at http://countyrecords.landata. com/WashDC. Registration is required; images are available for free, temporarily. Also, search the real property tax database for free at http://cfo.washingtondc.gov/services/tax/property/database.shtm.

District of Columbia *Real Estate, Assessor, Recording, Deed, Judgment, Lien, UCC Records - see above.*

Federal Courts in District of Columbia...

Standards for Federal Courts: The universal PACER sign-up number is 800-676-6856. Find PACER and the Party/Case Index on the Web at http://pacer.psc.uscourts.gov. PACER dial-up access is $.60 per minute. Also, courts offering internet access via RACER, PACER, Web-PACER or the new CM-ECF charge $.07 per page fee unless noted as free.

US District Court -- District of Columbia
Home Page: www.dcd.uscourts.gov
PACER: Toll-free access: 888-253-6878. Local access phone: 202-273-0606. New records are available online after. **PACER URL:** http://pacer.dcd.uscourts.gov.
Electronic Filing: Electronic filing information is available online at https://ecf.dcd.uscourts.gov.
Opinions Online: Court opinions are available online at www.dcd.uscourts.gov.

US Bankruptcy Court -- District of District of Columbia
Home Page: www.dcb.uscourts.gov
PACER: Toll-free access: 888-289-2414. Local access phone: 202-273-0630. Case records are available back to 1991. Records are purged every six months. New civil records are available online after 2 days. **PACER URL:** http://pacer.dcb.uscourts.gov.
Electronic Filing: (Currently in the process of implementing CM/ECF). **Also:** access via phone on VCIS (Voice Case Information System) is available: 202-273-0048.

Capital:	Tallahassee Leon County	Home Page	www.state.fl.us
Time Zone:	EST/CST	Attorney General	http://legal.firn.edu
# of Counties:	67	Archives	http://dlis.dos.state.fl.us/barm/

State Level ... Major Agencies

Criminal Records

Florida Department of Law Enforcement, User Services Bureau, PO Box 1489, Tallahassee, FL 32302 (Courier: 2331 Phillip Rd, Tallahassee, FL 32308); 850-410-8109, 850-410-8107, 850-410-8201 (Fax), 8AM-5PM.

www.fdle.state.fl.us/index.asp

Criminal history information from 1967 forward may be ordered over the Department Program Internet site at www2.fdle.state.fl.us. A $15.00 fee applies. Juvenile records from 10/1994 forward are also available. Credit card ordering will return records to your screen or via email.

Sexual Offender Registry

The Florida Department of Law Enforcement maintains a Sexual Offender/Predator Search System for access to sexual offenders and predators. The data is available online at www.fdle.state.fl.us/sexual_predators.

Incarceration Records

Search the inmate database at www.dc.state.fl.us/inmateinfo/inmateinfomenu.asp.

Corporation Records, Limited Partnership Records, Limited Liability Company Records, Trademarks/Servicemarks, Fictitious Names, Federal Tax Liens

Division of Corporations, Department of State, PO Box 6327, Tallahassee, FL 32314 (Courier: 409 E Gaines St, Tallahassee, FL 32399); 850-488-9000 (Telephone Inquires), 850-245-6053 (Copy Requests), 850-245-6056 (Annual Reports), 8AM-5PM.

www.sunbiz.org

The state's excellent Internet site gives detailed information on all corporate, trademark, limited liability company and limited partnerships (from 01/96): fictitious names (from 01/97); and lien records (from 01/97). **Other options:** The state offers record purchases on microfiche sets and on CD disks.

Uniform Commercial Code

UCC Filings, C/O Image API, PO Box 5588, Tallahassee, FL 32314 (Courier: 2670 Executive Center Circle W, #100, Tallahassee, FL 32301); 850-222-8526, 850-487-6013 (Fax), 8AM-5PM.

www.floridaucc.com/

The state Internet site allows access for no charge. Search by name or document number, for records 1997 to present. Tax Liens are not included with UCC filing information. **Other options:** Microfilm reels and CD's of images are available for bulk purchase requesters. Call for more information.

Driver Records

Division of Drivers Licenses, Bureau of Records, PO Box 5775, Tallahassee, FL 32314-5775 (Courier: 2900 Apalachee Pky, MS90, Neil Kirkman Bldg, Tallahassee, FL 32399); 850-488-0250, 850-487-7080 (Fax), 8AM-5PM.

www.hsmv.state.fl.us

Online requests are sold on on interactive basis for $2.10 per record. The state differentiates between high and low volume users. Requesters with 5,000 or more records per month are considered Network Providers. Call 850-488-6264 to become a Provider. Requesters with less than 5,000 requests per month (called Individual Users) are directed to a Provider. A list of providers is found at the web site. Check the status of any Florida Driver License free at http://www2.hsmv.state.fl.us/dlstatus.html. Simple enter the driver license number. **Other options:** The state will process magnetic tape requests. Also, they will provide customized database searches of the license information. Call 850-487-4467 for more details.

Vehicle Ownership, Vehicle Identification

Division of Motor Vehicles, Information Research Section, Neil Kirkman Bldg, A-126, Tallahassee, FL 32399; 850-488-5665, 850-921-6122, 850-488-8983 (Fax), 8AM-4:30PM.

www.hsmv.state.fl.us

Florida has contracted to release vehicle information through approved Network Providers. Accounts must first be approved by the state. For each record accessed, the charge is $.50 plus a transactional fee, and the subscriber fee. Users must work from an estimated 2 1/2 month pre-paid bank. New subscribers must complete an application with the Department 850-488-6710. **Other options:** A user may obtain ownership information by county or statewide vehicle class code basis. For more information, call the Motor Vehicle Data Listing Information Services at 850-488-46710.

Legislation Records

www.leg.state.fl.us/Welcome/index.cfm

Their Internet site contains full text of bills and a bill history session outlining actions taken on bills. The site is updated every day at 11 PM. Records go back to 1998. There is a more extensive online information service available. This system also includes information on lobbyists. Fees are involved, call 850-488-4371.

State Level ... Occupational Licensing

Acupuncturist	www.doh.state.fl.us/irm00praes/praslist.asp
Air Ambulance	www.doh.state.fl.us/ems/emslookup.html
Air Conditioning Contractor	www.state.fl.us/oraweb/owa/www_dbpr2.qry_lic_menu
Alarm System Contractor	https://www.myfloridalicense.com/licensing/wl11.jsp?SID=
Alcoholic Beverage Permit	https://www.myfloridalicense.com/licensing/wl11.jsp?SID=
Ambulance Service	www.doh.state.fl.us/ems/emslookup.html
Asbestos Remover/Contractor	www.state.fl.us/oraweb/owa/www_dbpr2.qry_lic_menu
Asbestos Surveyor Consultant	www.state.fl.us/oraweb/owa/www_dbpr2.qry_lic_menu
Assisted Living Facility	www.floridahealthstat.com/qs/owa/facilitylocator.facllocator
Athletic Agent	https://www.myfloridalicense.com/licensing/wl11.jsp?SID=
Athletic Trainer	www.doh.state.fl.us/irm00praes/praslist.asp
Attorney	www.flabar.org/newflabar/findlawyer.html
Auction Company	www.state.fl.us/oraweb/owa/www_dbpr2.qry_lic_menu
Auctioneer	www.state.fl.us/oraweb/owa/www_dbpr2.qry_lic_menu
Bank	www.dbf.state.fl.us/cf/dogi/Inst_search.cfm
Barber/Barber Assistant/Barber Shop	https://www.myfloridalicense.com/licensing/wl11.jsp?SID=
Boxer	https://www.myfloridalicense.com/licensing/wl11.jsp?SID=
Building Code Administrator	https://www.myfloridalicense.com/licensing/wl11.jsp?SID=
Building Contractor	www.state.fl.us/oraweb/owa/www_dbpr2.qry_lic_menu

Building Inspector	https://www.myfloridalicense.com/licensing/wl11.jsp?SID=
Chiropractor	www.doh.state.fl.us/irm00praes/praslist.asp
Clinical Lab Personnel	www.doh.state.fl.us/irm00praes/praslist.asp
Collection Agency	https://ssl.dbf.state.fl.us/cf/lic/pubinqry/pub2/index.cfm
Community Association Manager	https://www.myfloridalicense.com/licensing/wl11.jsp?SID=
Company in Receivership	www.doi.state.fl.us/Receiver/indextest.html
Construction Business	www.state.fl.us/oraweb/owa/www_dbpr2.qry_lic_menu
Contractor, General	www.state.fl.us/oraweb/owa/www_dbpr2.qry_lic_menu
Cosmetologist, Hair Braider, Nails/Salon	https://www.myfloridalicense.com/licensing/wl11.jsp?SID=
Credit Union	www.dbf.state.fl.us/cf/dogi/Inst_search.cfm
Crematory	https://www.myfloridalicense.com/licensing/wl11.jsp?SID=
Dentist/Dental Assistant	www.doh.state.fl.us/irm00praes/praslist.asp
Dietician/Nutritionist	www.doh.state.fl.us/irm00praes/praslist.asp
Doctor, Limited License	www.doh.state.fl.us/irm00praes/praslist.asp
Electrical Contractor	www.state.fl.us/oraweb/owa/www_dbpr2.qry_lic_menu
Electrologist/Electrologist Facility	www.doh.state.fl.us/irm00praes/praslist.asp
Elevator Certificates of Operation	https://www.myfloridalicense.com/licensing/wl11.jsp?SID=
Embalmer	https://www.myfloridalicense.com/licensing/wl11.jsp?SID=
Emerg. Insect Sting Treatment	www.doh.state.fl.us/ems/emslookup.html
Emergency Medical Technician	www.doh.state.fl.us/ems/emslookup.html
Finance Company, Consumer	https://ssl.dbf.state.fl.us/cf/lic/pubinqry/pub3/index.cfm
Financial Institution	www.dbf.state.fl.us/cf/dogi/Inst_search.cfm
Firearms Instructor	http://licgweb.dos.state.fl.us/access/individual.html
Firearms License, Statewide	http://licgweb.dos.state.fl.us/access/individual.html
Food Services Establishment	https://www.myfloridalicense.com/licensing/wl11.jsp?SID=
Funeral Director, Funeral Home	https://www.myfloridalicense.com/licensing/wl11.jsp?SID=
Geologist/Geology Firm	https://www.myfloridalicense.com/licensing/wl11.jsp?SID=
Health Facility	www.floridahealthstat.com/qs/owa/facilitylocator.facllocator
Hearing Aid Specialist	www.doh.state.fl.us/irm00praes/praslist.asp
Home Health Care Agency	www.floridahealthstat.com/qs/owa/facilitylocator.facllocator
Hospital	www.floridahealthstat.com/qs/owa/facilitylocator.facllocator
Hotel/Restaurant	https://www.myfloridalicense.com/licensing/wl11.jsp?SID=
Installment Seller, Retail	www.dbf.state.fl.us/licensing/
Insurance Adjuster/Agent/Title Agent	www.doi.state.fl.us/Data/AAR/index.htm
Insurance-related Company	www.doi.state.fl.us/Consumers/indextest.html
International Bank Office	www.dbf.state.fl.us/cf/dogi/Inst_search.cfm
Kickboxer	https://www.myfloridalicense.com/licensing/wl11.jsp?SID=
Lab License	www.floridahealthstat.com/qs/owa/facilitylocator.facllocator
Liquor Store	https://www.myfloridalicense.com/licensing/wl11.jsp?SID=
Lobbyist/Principal	www.leg.state.fl.us/lobbyist/index.cfm
Lodging Establishment	https://www.myfloridalicense.com/licensing/wl11.jsp?SID=
Marriage & Family Therapist	www.doh.state.fl.us/irm00praes/praslist.asp
Massage Therapist/School/Facility	www.doh.state.fl.us/irm00praes/praslist.asp
Mechanical Contractor	www.state.fl.us/oraweb/owa/www_dbpr2.qry_lic_menu
Medical Doctor	www.doh.state.fl.us/irm00praes/praslist.asp
Medical Faculty Certificate	www.doh.state.fl.us/irm00praes/praslist.asp
Mental Health Counselor	www.doh.state.fl.us/irm00praes/praslist.asp
Midwife	www.doh.state.fl.us/irm00praes/praslist.asp
Mortgage Broker School	https://ssl.dbf.state.fl.us/cf/lic/mbschools/index.cfm
Mortgage Broker/Firm	https://ssl.dbf.state.fl.us/cf/lic/pubinqry/pub1/index.cfm
Motel/Restaurant	https://www.myfloridalicense.com/licensing/wl11.jsp?SID=
Nail Specialist	https://www.myfloridalicense.com/licensing/wl11.jsp?SID=
Naturopath	www.doh.state.fl.us/irm00praes/praslist.asp
Notary Public	http://notaries.dos.state.fl.us/not001.html
Nuclear Radiology Physicist	www.doh.state.fl.us/irm00praes/praslist.asp
Nurse	www.doh.state.fl.us/irm00praes/praslist.asp
Nurse, Practical	www.doh.state.fl.us/irm00praes/praslist.asp
Nursing Assistant	www.doh.state.fl.us/irm00praes/praslist.asp
Nursing Home Administrator	www.doh.state.fl.us/irm00praes/praslist.asp
Nutrition Counselor	www.doh.state.fl.us/irm00praes/praslist.asp

Occupational Therapist	www.doh.state.fl.us/irm00praes/praslist.asp
Optician/Optician Apprentice	www.doh.state.fl.us/irm00praes/praslist.asp
Optometrist	www.doh.state.fl.us/irm00praes/praslist.asp
Orthotist/Prosthetist	www.doh.state.fl.us/irm00praes/praslist.asp
Osteopathic Physician/Limited Osteopathic Physician	www.doh.state.fl.us/irm00praes/praslist.asp
Paramedic	www.doh.state.fl.us/ems/emslookup.html
Pari-Mutuel Wagering	https://www.myfloridalicense.com/licensing/wl11.jsp?SID=
Pedorthist	www.doh.state.fl.us/irm00praes/praslist.asp
Pest Control Operator	www.safepesticideuse.com/safety/Search/CompanySearch.asp
Pesticide Applicator	www.safepesticideuse.com/safety/Search/PersonSearch.asp
Pesticide Applicator (Commercial, Private, Public)	http://safepesticideuse.com/safety/default.htm
Pesticide Dealer	http://safepesticideuse.com/safety/default.htm
Pharmacist, Consulting	www.doh.state.fl.us/irm00praes/praslist.asp
Pharmacist/Pharmacist Intern	www.doh.state.fl.us/irm00praes/praslist.asp
Physical Therapist/Assistant	www.doh.state.fl.us/irm00praes/praslist.asp
Physician Assistant	www.doh.state.fl.us/irm00praes/praslist.asp
Physicist, Medical	www.doh.state.fl.us/irm00praes/praslist.asp
Pilot, State/Deputy	https://www.myfloridalicense.com/licensing/wl11.jsp?SID=
Plumbing Contractor	www.state.fl.us/oraweb/owa/www_dbpr2.qry_lic_menu
Polygraph Examiner	www.floridapolygraph.org/members.html
Private Investigator/Agency	http://licgweb.dos.state.fl.us/access/individual.html
Psychologist/Limited License Psychologist	www.doh.state.fl.us/irm00praes/praslist.asp
Public Accountant-CPA	https://www.myfloridalicense.com/licensing/wl11.jsp?SID=
Racing, Dog/Horse	https://www.myfloridalicense.com/licensing/wl11.jsp?SID=
Real Estate Appraiser	www.state.fl.us/oraweb/owa/www_dbpr2.qry_lic_menu
Real Estate Broker/Salesperson	www.state.fl.us/oraweb/owa/www_dbpr2.qry_lic_menu
Recovery Agent School/Instructor/Mgr.	http://licgweb.dos.state.fl.us/access/agency.html
Recovery Agent/Agency/Intern	http://licgweb.dos.state.fl.us/access/agency.html
Respiratory Care Therapist/Provider	www.doh.state.fl.us/irm00praes/praslist.asp
Roofing Contractor	www.state.fl.us/oraweb/owa/www_dbpr2.qry_lic_menu
Sales Finance Company	www.dbf.state.fl.us/licensing/
Savings & Loan Association, Charter	www.dbf.state.fl.us/cf/dogi/Inst_search.cfm
School Psychologist	www.doh.state.fl.us/irm00praes/praslist.asp
Security Officer School	http://licgweb.dos.state.fl.us/access/agency.html
Security Officer/Instructor	http://licgweb.dos.state.fl.us/access/individual.html
Social Worker, Clinical	www.doh.state.fl.us/irm00praes/praslist.asp
Solar Energy Contractor	www.state.fl.us/oraweb/owa/www_dbpr2.qry_lic_menu
Speech-Language Pathologist/Audiologist	www.doh.state.fl.us/irm00praes/praslist.asp
Surveyor, Mapping	https://www.myfloridalicense.com/licensing/wl11.jsp?SID=
Swimming Pool/Spa Contractor	www.state.fl.us/oraweb/owa/www_dbpr2.qry_lic_menu
Talent Agency	https://www.myfloridalicense.com/licensing/wl11.jsp?SID=
Therapeutic Radiologic Physician	www.doh.state.fl.us/irm00praes/praslist.asp
Tobacco Wholesale	https://www.myfloridalicense.com/licensing/wl11.jsp?SID=
Trust Company	www.dbf.state.fl.us/cf/dogi/Inst_search.cfm
Underground Utility Contractor	www.state.fl.us/oraweb/owa/www_dbpr2.qry_lic_menu
Veterinarian/Veterinary Establishment	https://www.myfloridalicense.com/licensing/wl11.jsp?SID=
Yacht & Ship Broker/Salesman	https://www.myfloridalicense.com/licensing/wl11.jsp?SID=

County Level ... Courts

Court Administration: Office of State Courts Administrator, Supreme Court Bldg, 500 S Duval, Tallahassee, FL, 32399-1900; 850-922-5082; www.flcourts.org/

Court Structure: All counties have combined Circuit and County Courts. The Circuit Court is the court of general jurisdiction.

Online Access Note: There is a statewide, online computer system for internal use only; there is no statewide external access available nor planned currently. A number of courts do offer online access to the public, usually this is through the Clerk of the Circuit Court. However, the Florida Legislature mandated that court documents must be imaged and available for inspection over a publicly available website. In response to concerns of identity theft and fraud, the Florida Legislature recently passed new laws concerning privacy of public documents on public web sites. These laws now make it possible for certain of these documents viewed on the Clerk web sites to be either redacted of sensitive information or in some cases removed completely. The Clerk of the Circuit Court cannot place an image or copy of the following documents on a publicly available Internet web site for general public display: Military discharges; Death certificates; Court files, records or papers relating to Family Law, Juvenile Law or Probate Law cases.

Alachua County

Circuit & County Courts *Civil and Criminal Records*

www.alachuaclerk.org

Search Circuit's open cases free at http://circuit8.org/case/index.html by division; password required. Contact court for information, 352-374-3636. Civil records can be searched by name or case number. County Clerk online access is available free at www.clerk-alachua-fl.org/clerk/pubrec.html.

Baker County

Circuit & County Courts *Criminal Records*

http://circuit8.org

Access to the circuit-wide criminal quick lookup available at http://circuit8.org/golem/gencrim.html. Account and password is required; restricted usage.

Bradford County

Circuit Court *Criminal Records*

http://circuit8.org

Access to the circuit-wide criminal quick lookup available at http://circuit8.org/golem/gencrim.html. Account and password is required; restricted usage.

County Court *Civil Records*

www.bradford-co-fla.org/

Access to court records from the County Clerk is available free at www.myfloridacounty.com/services/officialrecords_intro.shtml.

Brevard County

Circuit Court *Civil and Criminal Records*

www.clerk.co.brevard.fl.us

Access county court records free from FACTSweb at www.clerk.co.brevard.fl.us/pages/facts1.htm. Online records back to 1988 can be searched by name, case number or citation number.

Broward County

Circuit & County Courts *Civil and Criminal Records*

www.17th.flcourts.org

The county clerk online fee system is being replaced by a web system. The web allows basic information free at www.browardclerk.org/bccoc2/default.asp. Search by name or case number or case type. The "Premium Access" for detailed case information requires a fee, registration and password. Call 954-831-5654 for information or visit the web site.

Charlotte County
Circuit & County Courts - *Civil and Probate Records*
http://co.charlotte.fl.us/clrkinfo/clerk_default.htm
Online access to civil and probate records is available by subscription, see the web site. Original payment is $186.00 ($150 refundable) plus a usage fee based on number of transactions. Allows printing of copies. For more information, call 941-637-4848.

Circuit & County Courts - *Criminal Records*
http://co.charlotte.fl.us/clrkinfo/clerk_default.htm
Online access to criminal records available by subscription or free; see the web site. The full subscription requires an original payment of $186.00 ($150 refundable) plus a usage fee based on number of transactions. Allows printing of copies. For more information, call 941-637-2199. The free access at http://co.charlotte.fl.us/public/public_access.htm requires that you provide a name and birthdate.

Clay County
Circuit Court *Civil Records*
County Court *Civil and Criminal Records*
http://clerk.co.clay.fl.us
Online access to records is available at no fee from web site. Click on "Online Information." Online records go back to 1992. This free web service takes the place of the commercial system.

Collier County
Circuit and County Courts *Civil, Probate, and Criminal Records*
www.clerk.collier.fl.us
Online access is now available free at www.clerk.collier.fl.us/clerkspublicac/Default.htm. Records include probate, traffic and domestic. Criminal records access is now available free at www.clerk.collier.fl.us/clerkspublicac/Default.htm.

Columbia County
Circuit & County Courts *Civil Records*
Limited online access to Clerk of Circuit Court's database is available free at www.columbiaclerk.com/Public_Re cords/public_records.html. Search by name, file number or document type.

Dade County
Circuit & County Courts *Civil Records*
http://jud11.flcourts.org
Two sources exist. Subscription online access requires $125.00 setup fee, $52.00 monthly and $.25 per minute after the first 208 minutes each month. Docket information can be searched by case number or name. Call 305-596-8148 for more information. Also, online access to civil court records on the county clerk database are available free at www.metro-dade.com/clerk/Public-Records/disclaimer.asp.

Circuit & County Courts - *Criminal Records*
http://jud11.flcourts.org
Fees for criminal online access requires $125.00 setup, $52.00 per month for the first 208 minutes and a $.25 per minute charge thereafter. Searching is by name or case number. Call 305-596-8148 for more information.

Duval County
Circuit & County Courts *Civil Records*
www.coj.net/pub/clerk/default.htm
Two sources are available. Online access requires $100.00 setup fee, but no access charges. For more information, call 904-630-1212 x5115. Also, court records and more are available free at the Clerk of Circuit Court search site at www.coj.net/legal/officialrecords/.

Circuit & County Courts *Criminal Records*
www.coj.net/pub/clerk/default.htm
 Online access to criminal records requires $100.00 setup fee, but no access charges. Records go back to 1992. For more information, call Leslie Peterson at 904-630-1212 x5115.

Escambia County
Circuit & County Courts *Civil, Probate and Criminal Records*
www.clerk.co.escambia.fl.us
Access to criminal, civil, family and probate court records is available free at www.clerk.co.escambia.fl.us/public_records.html. Search by name, citation, or case number. Small claims, traffic, and marriage data also available.

Flagler County

Circuit & County Courts *Civil Records*

http://clerk.co.flagler.fl.us

Online access to the Clerk of Circuit Court index is available at www.myfloridacounty.com. Search free; documents are $1 per page.

Gadsden County

Circuit & County Courts *Civil and Criminal Records*

www.clerk.co.gadsden.fl.us

Online access to civil court records are available free from the County Clerk at www.clerk.co.gadsden.fl.us.

Hernando County

Circuit & County Courts *Civil and Criminal Records*

www.clerk.co.hernando.fl.us/

Online access to court records is now available free at www.clerk.co.hernando.fl.us/disclaimer.asp. Online records may go as far back as 1/1983. Your browser must be Javascript enables (MS Explorer 4.0 or above).

Highlands County

Circuit & County Courts *Civil, Probate, Small Claims*

www.jud10.org

Online access to county clerk records available free at www.clerk.co.highlands.fl.us/highlands.fl/civil-records-search.jsp. Also includes small claims, probate, and tax deeds.

Hillsborough County

Circuit & County Courts *Civil, Probate, Domestic, and Criminal Records*

www.hillsclerk.com

Online access requires $50.00 set-up/software fee plus initial $50.00 towards access charges of $.20 per minute. Probate, traffic and domestic records are included. Call the help desk at 813-276-8100, Ext. 7000 for more information.

Indian River County

Circuit & County Courts *Civil and Criminal Records*

Online access to county recordings index is available free at http://bdc.co.indian-river.fl.us. Records go back to 1983. Full access to court records is available via the clerk's subscription service. Fee is $200.00 per month. For information about free and fee access, call Gary at 772-567-8000 x216.

Jackson County

Circuit & County Courts *Civil Records*

www.jacksonclerk.com

Online access to civil record indices is available free from myfloridacounty.com at www.jacksonclerk.com.

Lake County

Circuit & County Courts *Civil Records*

www.lakecountyclerk.org/default1.asp

Online access to Clerk of Court records available free at www.lakecountyclerk.org/services.asp?subject=Online_Court_Records. County civil records go back to 1985; Circuit records go back to 9/1984. Also, marriage licenses back to 2000 available at the main web site. Also, recordings, liens, and judgments on the Circuit Clerk web site are available.

Lee County

Circuit & County Courts *Civil, Probate, Small Claim, and Criminal Records*

www.leeclerk.org

The fee system has been replaced by free Internet access at the web site. Registration required. Online records go back to 1988. Call 239-335-2975 for more information. Includes traffic, felony, misdemeanor, civil, small claims and probate.

Leon County

Circuit & County Courts *Civil and Criminal Records*

www.clerk.leon.fl.us

Also, you may search cases and "High Profile Cases" (re: Election 2000) at www.clerk.leon.fl.us under "Search Court Databases." Registration required.

Levy County

Circuit & County Courts *Civil and Criminal Records*

http://circuit8.org

Online access to the Clerk of Circuit Court recording records available free at www.levyclerk.com/Public_Records/
Public_Records.html. Access to the circuit-wide criminal quick lookup available at http://circuit8.org/golem/gencrim.html. Account
and password is required; restricted usage.

Manatee County

Circuit & County Courts *Civil and Criminal Records*

www.manateeclerk.com

A subscription online service is available for $50 plus $60 per user fee advance; for sign-up information visit the web site. Also, court
records the Circuit clerk's office are available free at www.manateeclerk.com/mpa/cvweb.asp.

Marion County

Circuit & County Courts *Civil Records*

www.marioncountyclerk.org

Online access to county clerk civil records available free online at www.marioncountyclerk.org/Courts/factsweb.htm. Search by name
or case number. The site's time default field must be used.

Martin County

Circuit & County Courts *Civil and Criminal Records*

www.martin.fl.us/GOVT/co/clerk

Online access to civil case information on the records division database available free at http://clerk-web.martin.fl.us/wb_or1. Also
includes small claims, recordings, other document types. Criminal records indexed form 01/01/86, and images from 11/01/93.

Monroe County

Circuit & County Courts *Civil and Criminal Records*

www.co.monroe.fl.us

Online access to civil cases if available free at www.clerk-of-the-court.com/searchCivilCases.asp. Online access to criminal records is
available free at www.clerk-of-the-court.com/searchCriminalCases.asp. Includes traffic cases online.

Okaloosa County

Circuit & County Courts *Civil, Probate, and Criminal Records*

www.clerkofcourts.cc

Two options are available. Access to the full online system requires monthly fee of $100.00. Searching is by name or case number.
Records also include probate, traffic and domestic records. For more information, call 850-689-5821. Also, civil criminal, probate,
child support, traffic, and marriage licenses records available free on the internet at www.clerkofcourts.cc/orsearch/contract.htm.

Orange County

Circuit & County Courts *Civil and Criminal Records*

http://orangeclerk.ocfl.net

The Teleclerk countywide remote online system has been replaced by the free iclerk system at
http://orangeclerk1.onetgov.net/restricted/iclerk/index.htm. Set your browser "privacy" to "low. Use "public" as username and
password. For more information, call 407-836-2060. This court also accepts email requests.

County Court - Apopka Branch *Civil and Criminal Records*
County Court - NE Orange Division *Civil and Criminal Records*
County Court #3 *Civil and Criminal Records*

http://orangeclerk.ocfl.net

The Teleclerk countywide remote online system has been replaced by the free iclerk system at
http://orangeclerk1.onetgov.net/restricted/iclerk/index.htm. Set your browser "privacy" to "low. Use "public" as username and
password. For more information, call 407-836-2060.

Osceola County

Circuit Court *Civil Records*
Circuit & County Courts - Criminal Division *Criminal Records*
County Court *Civil Records*

www.ninja9.net

www.osceolaclerk.com
Online access to court records available free at www.osceolaclerkcourt.org/search.htm. Includes party index and case summary searching.

Palm Beach County
Circuit & County Courts - Civil Division *Civil, Probate, Small Claims, Criminal Records*
Circuit & County Courts - Criminal Division *Criminal Records*
www.pbcountyclerk.com
Access to the countywide remote online system requires $145 setup and $65 per month fees. Civil index goes back to '88. Records also include probate, traffic and domestic. Contact Betty Jones at 561-355-6783 or M. McArthur at 561-355-6846 for information. Also, online access to the 15th judicial circuit records available at http://web3172.co.palm-beach.fl.us/aemasp/default.asp. Registration and password is required.

Pasco County
Circuit & County Courts *Civil, Crminal and Probate Records*
www.jud6.org
Online access to Clerk of Court records via the Internet is to be available in late 2001. Current access to the countywide remote online system requires a $100 deposit, $50 annual fee and $10 monthly minimum. There is a $.10 per screen charge. Probate records also available. Call 352-521-4201 for more information.

Pinellas County
Circuit & County Courts - Civil Division *Civil and Probate Records*
Criminal Justice Center *Criminal Records*
County Court - Criminal Division *Criminal Records*
www.jud6.org
Access to the countywide remote online system requires $60 fee plus $5.00 per month and $.05 per screen. Civil index goes back to 1972. Contact Sue Maskeny at 727-464-3779 for information. Includes probate and traffic records.

Polk County
Circuit & County Courts *Civil and **Criminal** Records*
www.polk-county.net/clerk/clerk.html
Two options are available. Online access to the complete database requires $150 setup fee and $.15 per minute charge with a $50 minimum per quarter. Call 863-534-7575 for more information. Second, case index information back to 1990 available free from the County Clerk's web site at www.polk-county.net/clerk/Public_Records/Public_index.html. Includes land and lien searching.

Putnam County
Circuit & County Courts *Civil and Criminal Records*
Access to the countywide criminal online system requires $400 setup fee and $40. monthly charge plus $.05 per minute over 20 hours. Criminal records go back to 1972. System includes civil and real property records. Contact Ryel Christiansen to register; 386-329-0361 or 386-329-0249.

St. Johns County
Circuit & County Courts *Civi, Criminal and Probate Records*
www.co.st-johns.fl.us
Access to the countywide remote online system requires $200 setup fee plus a monthly fee of $50. Searching is by name or case number. Call Mark Dearing at 904-823-2333 x361 for more information. Also, online access to the county Clerk of Circuit Court recording database available free at www.co.st-johns.fl.us/Const-Officers/Clerk-of-Court/doris/searchdocs.asp. Includes civil and probate records.

St. Lucie County
Circuit & County Courts *Civil Records*
Online access to civil records is to be online by 2003 at http://public.slcclerkofcourt.com. Case tracking should also be available. Bond record tracking is available.

Circuit & County Courts *Criminal Records*
www.martin.fl.us/GOVT/co/schack
Online access to bonds, traffic and misdemeanor records is available free at http://public.slcclerkofcourt.com. Online records go back to 7/6/1992. Felony records are to be online in 2002. Case tracking should also be available.

Sarasota County
Circuit & County Courts *Civil and Probate Records*
www.clerk.co.sarasota.fl.us
Civil and DV case records from the Clerk of Circuit Court database are available free online at
www.clerk.co.sarasota.fl.us/civilapp/civilinq.asp. Criminal, probate and domestic records are also available. Probate court records are
available at www.clerk.co.sarasota.fl.us/probapp/probinq.asp.

Circuit & County Courts *Criminal Records*
www.clerk.co.sarasota.fl.us
Criminal case records from the Clerk of the Circuit Court database available free online at
www.clerk.co.sarasota.fl.us/crimdisclaim.htm. Civil, probate and domestic records are also available.

Seminole County
Circuit & County Courts *Civil Records*
www.18thcircuit.state.fl.us
Access to the County Clerk's online records available free at www.seminoleclerk.org/OfficialRecords. Search by name, clerk's file
number, or book & page.

Suwannee County
Circuit & County Courts *Civil and Criminal Records*
www.suwanneeclerkofcourt.com
Online access to County Clerk of Circuit Court records is available at the web site.

Union County
Circuit & County Courts *Criminal Records*
http://circuit8.org
 Access to the circuit-wide criminal quick lookup available at http://circuit8.org/golem/gencrim.html. Account and password is
required; restricted usage.

Volusia County
Circuit & County Courts *Civil and Probate Records*
www.clerk.org
Access to the countywide remote online system requires $125 setup fee plus a $25 monthly fee. Windows required. Search by name or
case number. Call Tom White 904-736-5915 for more information. Criminal, probate and traffic records are also available.

Circuit & County Courts *Criminal and Traffic Records*
www.clerk.org
Two access methods are available. Access to the Clerk of Circuit Courts database of Citation Violations and 24-hour Arrest Reports is
available free at www.clerk.org/publicrecords/or.tshtml. Access to the countywide criminal online system requires $125 setup fee plus
a $25 monthly. Windows required. Search by name or case number back to 1988. Call 904-822-5710 for more information. Civil,
probate and traffic records are also available.

Walton County
Circuit & County Courts *Civil, Probate, Domestic, and Criminal Records*
www.co.walton.fl.us/clerk/
Access to the county online system requires a setup fee of at least $30 plus $100 monthly. System includes probate, traffic, domestic
and criminal data. Search by name or case number. Call David Langford for more information, 850-892-8115. Also, the web site
offers access to civil record indices.

Washington County
Circuit & County Courts *Civil Records*
Online access to the Clerk of Circuit Court index is available at www.myfloridacounty.com. Search free; documents are $1 per page.

County Level ... Recorders & Assessors

Recording Office Organization: 67 counties, 67 recording offices. The recording officer is the Clerk of the Circuit Court. All transactions are recorded in the "Official Record," a grantor/grantee index. Some counties will search by type of transaction while others will return everything on the index. 57 counties are in the Eastern Time Zone (EST) and 10 are in the Central Time Zone (CST). Federal tax liens on personal property of businesses are filed with the Secretary of State. All other federal and state tax liens on personal property are filed with the county Clerk of Circuit Court. Usually tax liens on personal property are filed in the same index with UCC financing statements and real estate transactions. Most counties will perform a tax lien as part of a UCC search.

Online Access Note:
There are numerous county agencies that provide online access to records. Free online access to fifty-one county Circuit Clerks of Courts database records is available at www.myfloridacounty.com/services/officialrecords_intro.shtml.

On or after October 1, 2002, any person preparing or filing a document for recording in the Official Record may not include a social security number in such document unless required by law. The Clerk of the Circuit Court cannot place an image or copy of the following documents on a publicly available Internet web site for general public display: Military discharges; Death certificates; Court files, records or papers relating to Family Law, Juvenile Law or Probate Law cases.

Any person has the right to request the Clerk/County Recorder to redact/remove his Social Security Number from an image or copy of an Official Record that has been placed on such Clerk/County Recorder's publicly available Internet web site.

Alachua County   *Property Appraiser, Real Estate, Lien, Vital Statistic, Recording Records*
www.clerk-alachua-fl.org
Access to the Clerk of Courts recording database are available free at www.clerk-alachua-fl.org/clerk/pubrec.html. Records go back to 1/1993. Also, search the County Property Search page free online at www.acpafl.org/services/search/search.asp. There is also a sales search here. Also, online access to the state recorders' meta-search site is available free at www.myfloridacounty.com. Click on Official Records.

Baker County   *Real Estate, Lien, Recording Records*
Search the state recorders' meta-search site for free at www.myfloridacounty.com. Click on Official records.

Bay County   *Property Tax, Real Estate, Tax Lien, Recording Records*
www.baycoclerk.com
Access to the Clerk of the Circuit Court Recordings database is available free at www.clerk.co.bay.fl.us/orsearch. Records go back to 1/1987. Also, search the property appraiser database free at http://bcpa.elementaldata.com/search.asp; the tax collector at http://bctc.elementaldata.com/disclaimer.asp. Also, property information from the Assessor database is free online at http://bcpa.co.bay.fl.us/database.htm. Also, online access to the state recorders' meta-search site is available free at www.myfloridacounty.com. Click on Official Records.

Bradford County   *Real Estate, Appraisal, Deed, Judgment, Marriage, Lien, Court Records*
Access to the recorders database is available free at www.mybradfordcounty.com. Click on "Official Records." Also, search the property appraiser database at www.bradfordappraiser.com/Search_F.asp. Also, online access to the state recorders' meta-search site is available free at www.myfloridacounty.com. Click on Official Records.

Brevard County   *Property Appraiser, Real Estate, Lien, Marriage, Recording, Tax Sale Records*
www.clerk.co.brevard.fl.us
Access to the Circuit Clerk's tax lien (1981-95), land records (1995 to present) and marriage records is free at www.clerk.co.brevard.fl.us/pages/pubrec9.htm. Indexed records from 1/1981 to 9/30/1995 are at http://crystalweb1.clerk.co.brevard.fl.us/Indexing/f_indexing.cfm. Also, property tax records are available free at www.brevardpropertyappraiser.com/asp/disclaimer.asp. Search by name or map. Also, tax deed sales are listed free at www.clerk.co.brevard.fl.us/taxdeed/taxdeed.htm

Broward County   *Property Appraiser, Real Estate, Lien, Recording, Occupational License Records*

www.broward.org/records

Access to the county records Public Search database 1978-present is available free at http://205.166.161.12/oncoreweb/start/disclaim.asp. Additionally, professional users may register and receive a password for additional access options. Also, Property Appraiser records are available free online at www.bcpa.net/search.htm. Also, search the occupational license database at www.co.broward.fl.us/rise.htm.

Calhoun County   *Real Estate, Lien, Deed, Judgment, Recording Records*

www.calhounclerk.com

Search the state recorders' meta-search site for free at www.myfloridacounty.com. Click on Official Records.

Charlotte County   *Property Appraiser, Real Estate, Lien, Recording Records*

www.co.charlotte.fl.us

Property records are available free online at www.ccappraiser.com/record.asp. Sales records are also available here and at the tax collector database, which is free at www.cctaxcol.com/record.asp?. Also, recordings from the county clerk database are available free online at http://208.47.160.70. Search by book/page or grantor/grantee. A subscription service (CASWEB) is also available, which includes images, court records, recordings, etc. Bulk database record purchases, by year, are also available. Also, online access to the state recorders' meta-search site is available free at www.myfloridacounty.com. Click on Official Records.

Citrus County   *Property Appraiser, Real Estate, Lien, Recording, Marriage Records*

www.clerk.citrus.fl.us

Access to the Clerk of Circuit Court records is available free at www.clerk.citrus.fl.us/hart_wwwroot/. Search Marriage License records free online at www.clerk.citrus.fl.us/marrsearch.asp. Search by first and last name. Also, Property records are available free online at www.pa.citrus.fl.us/ccpaask.html. Also, online access to the state recorders' meta-search site is available free at www.myfloridacounty.com. Click on Official Records.

Clay County   *Appraiser, Real Estate, Lien, Recording Records*

http://clerk.co.clay.fl.us

The county clerk of circuit court allows free online access to recording records at http://clerk.co.clay.fl.us/Disclaimer_page.htm. This replaces the commercial system. Records go back to 1990 Also, the Clay County Property Appraiser's office records are available free at www.ccpao.com/ccpao/ccpao.asp?page=Disclaimer. Search by name, street name and number, or real estate number. Also, search tangible personal property free on the tax collector database at www.ccpao.com/tpp/. Online access to the state recorders' meta-search site is available free at www.myfloridacounty.com. Click on Official Records.

Collier County   *Property Appraiser, Real Estate, Lien, UCC, Vital Statistic, Recording, Tax Sales, Wanted/Missing Person Records*

www.clerk.collier.fl.us

Access to records on the Property Appraiser database are available free online at www.collierappraiser.com/Disclaimer.asp. The sheriff's wanted and missing persons lists are at www.colliersheriff.org. Online access to clerk of courts court records, lien, real estate, UCCs and vital records is available free at www.clerk.collier.fl.us/clerkspublicac/Default.htm. Records include probate, traffic and domestic. Lending agency information is available. Also, Online access to the state recorders' meta-search site is available free at www.myfloridacounty.com. Click on Official Records. Tax deeds sales data is free at www.clerk.collier.fl.us/OfficialRecords/Tax_Deeds/Tax%20Deeds.htm

Columbia County   *Real Estate, Lien, Recording, Probate, Property Tax Records*

www.columbiaclerk.com

Access to the Clerk of Circuit Courts recording database is available free at www.mycolumbiacounty.com. Search by name, book/page, file number of document type. Also, online access to the state recorders' meta-search site is available free at www.myfloridacounty.com. Click on Official Records. Also, search the tax rolls at for free at www.columbiataxcollector.com/collectmax/collect30.asp

Dade County   *Property Appraiser, Real Estate, Lien, Recording, Marriage, Tax Deed Sale Records*

www.metro-dade.com/clerk

Three sources available. Record access to 11 databases requires an initial setup fee is $125 and a minimum monthly fee of $52 for 208 minutes of use, $.25 ea. add'l minute. Records date back to 1975. Includes property appraisal, building permits, tax collection and other data. Contact 305-596-8148 for information. There's a 2nd subscription service for county recorder only for $50 per month at www.co.miami-dade.fl.us/public-records/features.asp. Third, recorder records are available free at www.co.miami-dade.fl.us/public-records/default.asp. Appraiser records are available free online at www.co.miami-dade.fl.us/pa/record.htm. Tax deed sales: www.co.miami-dade.fl.us/clerk/Tax-Deeds/home.htm.

De Soto County *Real Estate, Lien, Recording, Property Tax Records*

Search the state recorders' meta-search site for free at www.myfloridacounty.com. Click on Official Records. Also, access to the property appraiser data is available free at http://qpublic.net/desoto/search.html

Dixie County *Real Estate, Lien, Recording Records*

Search the state recorders' meta-search site for free at www.myfloridacounty.com. Click on Official Records.

Duval County *Property Appraiser, Real Estate, Lien, Recording, Grantor/Grantee, Vital Statistic Records*

www.ci.jax.fl.us

Access to the Clerk of Circuit Court and City of Jacksonville Official Records (a grantor/grantee index) is available free at http://apps1.coj.net/legal/officialrecords/. Also, the County Property Appraiser offers free access to property records for Duval County and City of Jacksonville at http://pawww.coj.net/pub/property/lookup.htm. Also, online access to the state recorders' meta-search site is available free at www.myfloridacounty.com.

Escambia County

Property Appraiser, Real Estate, Lien, Recording, Marriage, Property Tax, Tax Sale Records

www.clerk.co.escambia.fl.us

Access to the Clerk of Court Public Records database is available free at www.clerk.co.escambia.fl.us/public_records.html. This includes grantor/grantee index and marriage, traffic and court records. Also, online access to the tax collector's Property Tax Inquiry database is available free online at http://ectc.co.escambia.fl.us/ectc/index2.html. Click on ECTC Online then on "Cyber-Tax." Tax sale information is also available. Also, search the property appraiser real estate records at www.escpa.org/searchform.asp.

Flagler County *Property Appraiser, Recording, Real Estate, Lien Records*

http://clerk.co.flagler.fl.us

Official records from the clerk's index are to be online in 2002. The index is now available on CD-rom for $31.39. For information, contact Judy Daughtry at 386-437-7434. Also, online access to the state recorders' meta-search site is available free at www.myflaglercounty.com. Click on Official Records. Also, property information from the tax appraiser is available free at www.qpublic.net/flagler/search.html.

Franklin County *Real Estate, Lien, Recording Records*

www.franklinclerk.com

Search the state recorders' meta-search site for free at www.myfloridacounty.com. Click on Official Records.

Gadsden County *Real Estate, Recording, Judgment, Deed, Lien, Vital Statistic, Property Appraiser Records*

www.clerk.co.gadsden.fl.us

Access to the official records index is available free at www.clerk.co.gadsden.fl.us/OfficialRecords/. Index records go back to 1985. Provides index numbers only. Also, access to the property appraiser database is available free at www.qpublic.net/gadsden/search.html.

Gilchrist County *Real Estate, Property Appraiser, Lien, Recording Records*

www.co.gilchrist.fl.us/cophone

Access to the property appraiser database is available free at www.qpublic.net/gilchrist/search.html. Sales searches are also available. Also, Online access to the state recorders' meta-search site is available free at www.myfloridacounty.com. Click on Official Records.

Glades County *Real Estate, Lien, Recording Records*

Search the state recorders' meta-search site for free at www.myfloridacounty.com. Click on Official Records.

Gulf County *Real Estate, Lien, Deed, Judgment, Marriage, Death, Recording Records*

www.gulfclerk.com

Search the state recorders' meta-search site for free at www.myfloridacounty.com. Click on Official Records.

Hamilton County *Real Estate, Lien, Recording Records*

Search the state recorders' meta-search site for free at www.myfloridacounty.com. Click on Official Records.

Hardee County *Real Estate, Recording, Lien, Property Appraiser Records*

Search the state recorders' meta-search site for free at www.myfloridacounty.com. Click on Official Records. Also, online assess to the property appraiser data is available free at www.hardeecounty.net/cfaps/appraiser/propform.cfm.

Hendry County   *Real Estate, Lien, Recording Records*

Search the state recorders' meta-search site for free at www.myfloridacounty.com. Click on Official Records. Also, access the property appraiser database at http://dev.hendryprop.com/GIS/Search_F.asp.

Hernando County   *Property Appraiser, Real Estate, Lien, Marriage, Recording Records*

www.co.hernando.fl.us
Access to the clerk; Official Records database is now available free at www.clerk.co.hernando.fl.us/disclaimer.asp. Your browser must be Javascript enabled. Includes recordings, marriages, and court records. Also, the county now offers 2 levels of the Public Inquiry System Property Appraiser Real Estate database - Easy Search & Real Time Search - free online at www.co.hernando.fl.us/pa/propsearch.htm. Search by owner, address, or parcel key. Also, Online access to the state recorders' meta-search site is available free at www.myfloridacounty.com. Click on Official Records.

Highlands County   *Property Appraiser, Personal Property, Real Estate, Lien, Recording Records*

www.clerk.co.highlands.fl.us
Property appraiser records are available free online at www.appraiser.co.highlands.fl.us/search.html; tangible personal property records are available. Also, online access to the recorders' meta-search site is available at www.myflorida.com. Click on Official Records. Also, online access to deeds, mortgages, judgments from the county recording database are available free at www.clerk.co.highlands.fl.us/highlands.fl/official-records-search.jsp. Records go back to 1983. Also, online access to the county tax collector database is available free at www.collector.co.highlands.fl.us/search/index.html.

Hillsborough County   *Property Appraiser, Personal Property, Real Estate, Lien, Deed, Recording Records*

www.hillsclerk.com
Property appriaser records are available free at www.hcpafl.org/disclaimer.html. Receive owner data, legal, sales, value summaries. Also, access to state recorders' search site is available at www.myfloridacounty.com. Click on official records. Also, the clerk's recordings can be searched free at http://publicrecord.hillsclerk.com. The County also offers access to county court, real estate, and lien records through a fee online service. Courts, traffic and domestic records included. Access is $.25 per minute or $5.00 per month, whichever is greater, plus a $50.00 one-time set-up fee with software. Contact the help desk at 813-276-8100 x7000 for more information.

Holmes County   *Real Estate, Lien, Recording Records*

Search the state recorders' meta-search site for free at www.myfloridacounty.com. Click on Official Records.

Indian River County   *Property Appraiser, Real Estate, Lien, Vital Statistic Records*

http://indian-river.fl.us
Appraiser information is free, but only some of the recording office information is. Appraiser records are available free online at http://ircpa.irene.net/search.html. Online access to recording indexes on the Clerk of the Circuit Court database are available free at http://bdc.co.indian-river.fl.us. Records go back to 1983. Full real estate, lien and court and vital records are available from the Clerk of the Circuit Court at the fee site, subscription is $200 per month. For information about free and fee access, call 772-567-8000 x216.

Jackson County   *Real Estate, Lien, Recording, Marriage, Death, Probate Records*

www.jacksoncountyclerk.com
Access to the Clerk of Circuit Court Official Records database is available free at www.jacksonclerk.com. Images will go back to 5/1996 Also, online access to the state recorders' meta-search site is available free at www.myfloridacounty.com. Click on Official Records.

Jefferson County   *Property, Real Estate, Lien, Recording Records*

http://co.jefferson.fl.us
Access to the Property Appraiser database is available free at http://qpublic.net/jefferson/search.html. Sales searches are also available. Also, online access to the Clerk of Circuit Court recordings database is available free at www.myjeffersoncounty.com. Also, online access to the state recorders' meta-search site is available free at www.myfloridacounty.com. Click on Official Records.

Lafayette County   *Real Estate, Lien, Recording Records*

www.lafayetteclerk.com
Search the state recorders' meta-search site for free at www.myfloridacounty.com. Click on Official Records.

Lake County   *Property Appraiser, Real Estate, Lien, Marriage, Recording Records*

www.lakecountyclerk.org
The new county clerk official records database is available free online at www.lakecountyclerk.org/services.asp?subject=Online_Official_Records. Records go as far back as 1974. Includes court records.

Also, records on the County Property Assessor database are available free online at www.lakecopropappr.com/search.asp. Also, marriage records back to 11/2000 are available at www.lakecountyclerk.org/departments.asp?subject=Marriage_Licenses. Also, online access to the state recorders' meta-search site is available free at www.myfloridacounty.com. Click on Official records.

Lee County *Property Appraiser, Real Estate, Occupational License, Lien, Recording Records*
http://leeclerk.org/index.asp

Access to the appraiser database is available free at www.property-appraiser.lee.fl.us/Queries/FindParcel.htm, or the tax roll database at www.leetc.com/Taxes/default.asp. Also, access to the county "license" database is available at www.leetc.com/OccupationalLicense/default.asp. Also, search the clerk of circuit court data at http://leeclerk.org/SearchOfficialRecords.htm. Records go back to 1988. Also a subscription service ($50 set-up, $25 per month) allows full access to clerk's records. Also, online access to the state recorders' meta-search site is available free at www.myfloridacounty.com. Click on Official Records.

Leon County *Property Appraiser, Real Estate, Lien, Marriage, Recording, Permit, Foreclosure Records*
www.clerk.leon.fl.us

Real Estate, lien, and foreclosure records from the County Clerk are available free online at www.clerk.leon.fl.us. Lending agency information is also available. Also, access to full document images requires user name and password, plus $100 per month. Property Appraiser database records are available free at www.co.leon.fl.us/propappr/search.cfm. Also, online access to the state recorders' meta-search site is available free at www.myfloridacounty.com. Click on Official Records. Also, search the county tax collector tax rolls database free at http://dta.co.leon.fl.us/tax/default.asp. Also, search the county "permits" database at www.tlcgis.org/tallahassee. Search marriages at http://cvweb.clerk.leon.fl.us/index_marriage.html.

Levy County *Real Estate, Lien, Recording Records*
www.levyclerk.com

Access to the Clerk of Circuit Court recording database are available free at http://63.144.218.154/scripts/LevyClerk.exe?K. Search by name, book/page, file number or document type. Also, online access to the state recorders' meta-search site is available free at www.myfloridacounty.com. Click on Official Records. Also, access to the property appraiser data is available free at www.qpublic.net/levy/search.html.

Liberty County *Real Estate, Lien, Recording Records*
www.libertyclerk.com

Search the state recorders' meta-search site for free at www.myfloridacounty.com. Click on Official Records.

Madison County *Real Estate, Lien, Recording, Property Appraiser Records*

Search the state recorders' meta-search site for free at www.myfloridacounty.com. Click on Official records. Also, access to the property appraiser's rpoperty cards and sale databases is available free at www.madpa.org/db/disclaimer.asp.

Manatee County *Appraiser, Real Estate, Lien, Vital Statistic, Recording Records*
www.clerkofcourts.com

Several sources exist. Real estate and recordings records are available free from the Clerk of Circuit Court and Comptroller's database at www.clerkofcourts.com/PubRec/RecordedDocs/ormain.htm. Also, Online access to the state recorders' meta-search site is available free at www.myfloridacounty.com. Click on Official Records. Also, Property Appraiser records are available free online at www.manateepao.com. On the 4th county online system, real estate and vital records are available at no fee to view, but you are limited to 2 hours access. Lending agency information is available. Call Martha Pope at 941-741-4051 for information.

Marion County *Property Appraiser, Real Estate, Lien, Marriage, Recording Records*
www.marioncountyclerk.org

Records on the County Clerk of Court records database are available free online at www.marioncountyclerk.org. Also, records on the Marion County Property Appraiser database are available online free at www.propappr.marion.fl.us. Also, online access to the state recorders' meta-search site is available free at www.myfloridacounty.com. Click on Official Records.

Martin County *Property Appraiser, Real Estate, Lien, Recording, Personal Property Records*
www.martin.fl.us/GOVT

Access to the clerk of the circuit court recordings database are available free online at http://clerk-web.martin.fl.us/wb_or1. Also, records on the county property appraiser database are available free online at http://paoweb.martin.fl.us. Choose from "Online Property Searches." Personal property searches are also available. The county tax collector data files are available free online at www.martin.fl.us/GOVT/co/tax/search. Also, online access to the state recorders' meta-search site is available free at www.myfloridacounty.com.

Monroe County   *Recording, Real Estate, Deed, Lien Records*
www.co.monroe.fl.us
Access to the clerk of circuit courts database is available free at www.clerk-of-the-court.com/searchOfficialRecords.asp.

Nassau County   *Real Estate, Lien, Recording Records*
www.nassauclerk.com
Search the state recorders' meta-search site for free at www.myfloridacounty.com. Click on Official Records. Also, the recorders database is available free at www.nassauclerk.com/county/official_records_login.htm.

Okaloosa County   *Property Appraiser, Real Estate, Lien, Recording, Vital Statistic Records*
Several databases are available. Access to Okaloosa County online system requires a monthly usage fee of $100. No addresses listed. Lending agency information, traffic and domestic records are. For information, contact Don Howard at 850-689-5821. Online access to land records is available free at www.clerkofcourts.cc/orsearch/contract.htm. Access to marriage records is available free at www.clerkofcourts.cc/marsearch/marriage.asp. Property Appraiser records are available free online at www.okaloosapa.com/search.html. Also, online access to the state recorders' meta-search site is available free at www.myfloridacounty.com.

Okeechobee County   *Property Appraiser Records*
Search the statewide recording database via www.myfloridacounty.com. Documents are free to view, but there is a fee to order. Access to the property appraiser database is available free at http://www2.okeechobeepa.com/GIS/Search_F.asp.

Orange County   *Property Appraiser, Recording, Real Estate, Lien, Vital Statistic, Land Sales, Personal Property Records*
www.occompt.com
Real Estate, Lien, and Marriage records on the county Comptroller database are available free at www.occompt.com/2002/records.html. Lending Agency information is available. Also, property records on the Property Appraiser database are available free at www.ocpafl.org/docs/disclaimer.html. At this main site, click on "Record Searches." Also search Tangible Personal Property records and residential sales.

Osceola County   *Real Estate, Property Appraiser Records*
www.osceolaclerk.com
Access to the county Clerk of Circuit Court database features court records only at this time; see www.osceolaclerkcourt.org. Search by party name. While property appraiser records are soon to be available free online at www.property-appraiser.com/records.htm, you may currently purchase property data from the county information system database. For information, call 407-343-3700. Data is delivered in either 8mm data cartridges, CD-ROM, or 3.5" diskettes. Fees vary; tax roll data is available for $75.00. Also, land records may be available online at www.osceolaclerkrecording.org.

Palm Beach County   *Property Appraiser, Real Estate, Lien, Recording, Vital Statistic Records*
www.co.palm-beach.fl.us
Access to the clerk of circuit court recording database are available free at www.pbcountyclerk.com/records_home.html. Records go back to 1968; includes marriage records 1979 to present. Images go back to 1993. They are planning a subscription full-index system and also CD-Roms of indexes as far back as 1968. Also, records on the county Property Appraiser database are available free online at www.co.palm-beach.fl.us/papa.

Pasco County   *Property Appraiser, Real Estate, Lien, Vital Statistic, Recording, Occ License Records*
http://pascogov.com
Several sources available. Access to real estate, liens, marriage records requires a $25 annual fee plus a $50 deposit. Billing rate is $.05 per minute, $.03 evenings. For information, call 352-521-4529. There is a fax back service. Also, free internet access to indexes is at www.pascoclerk.com. Click on "records." Also, online access to the state recorders' meta-search site is available at www.myfloridacounty.com. Click on Official records. Also, property records on the Property Appraiser database are available free at http://appraiser.pascogov.com. Sales data and maps are available. Search tax records and occupational licences free at http://taxcollector.pascogov.com.

Pinellas County   *Property Appraiser, Real Estate, Lien, Judgment, Recording, Tax Deed Sale, Traffic/Boating Fine Records*
http://clerk.co.pinellas.fl.us/recsonl.htm
Assessor/property records are available free online at www.pao.co.pinellas.fl.us/search2.html. Also, tax deed sales indexes are avaialble free at http://clerk.co.pinellas.fl.us/recsonl.htm. Also, the county clerk of circuit court's recordings are available free online

at http://clerk.co.pinellas.fl.us. Click on official records or probate under "E-business." Also, online access to the state recorders' meta-search site is available free at www.myfloridacounty.com. Click on Official Records. Search traffic and boating fines at https://pubtitleu.co.pinellas.fl.us/credit/accountspayable/CourtChargeIntro.jsp.

Polk County *Property Appraiser, Real Estate, Lien, Vital Statistic, Recording, Personal Property Records*
www.polk-county.net
Search the county clerk database at www.polk-county.net/clerk/clerk.html for free court records, deeds, mortgages, plats, marriages, resolutions. For copies of documents, call 863-534-4524. Fee is $1.00 per page. Also, property and personal property records from the County Property Appraiser database are available free at www.polkpa.org.

Putnam County *Real Estate, Lien, Recording, Tax Assessor, Occ License, Warrant Records*
www.putnam-fl.com/clk/
Access to the county clerk database requires a $400 setup fee and monthly charge of $40 plus $.05 per minute over 20 hours. Includes civil court records and real property records back to 10/1983. For information, call 904-329-0353. Also, online access to the state recorders' meta-search site is available free at www.myfloridacounty.com. Click on Official Records. Also, the sheriff;s warrant list is at www.putnamsheriff.org/warrant.htm. Also, search the online tax rolls at www.putnam-fl.com/app/disclaimer.htm. No name searching. Also, searchthe treasurer's tax rolls and occupational licensing at www.putnam-fl.com/txc/onlineinquiry.htm.

St. Johns County *Property Appraiser, Real Estate, Lien, Recording, Civil Records*
www.co.st-johns.fl.us
Access to the county Clerk of Circuit Court recording database is available free at www.co.st-johns.fl.us/Const-Officers/Clerk-of-Court/doris/searchdocs.asp. Search by name, parcel ID, instrument type. Includes civil and probate records, UCCs. Also, online access to the state recorders' meta-search site is available free at www.myfloridacounty.com. Click on Official Records.

St. Lucie County *Property Appraiser, Real Estate, Lien, Recording, Marriage, Fictitious Name Records*
www.stlucieco.gov
Access to the clerk of circuit courts database of recordings, deeds, liens, mortgages, marriages, fictitious names is available free at http://public.slcclerkofcourt.com. Business searching is also available for a small fee. Also, online access to the state recorders' meta-search site is available free at www.myfloridacounty.com. Click on Official Records. Also, property appraiser records are available free online at www.paslc.org. Click on the "real property database" or "interactive map."

Santa Rosa County *Property Appraiser, Real Estate, Lien, Recording Records*
www.srcpa.org
Property records are available free at www.srcpa.org/property.php or at the main Property Appraiser page click on "Record Search." Also, online access to the state recorders' meta-search site is available free at www.myfloridacounty.com. Click on Official Records.

Sarasota County *Property Appraiser, Real Estate, Lien, Vital Statistic, Recording Records*
www.clerk.co.sarasota.fl.us
Access to the Clerk of Circuit Court recordings database are available free at www.clerk.co.sarasota.fl.us/online.htm. Includes civil, criminal, and traffic court indexes. Also search indexes at www.clerk.co.sarasota.fl.us/isol/. Marriage licenses may be searched free by groom/bride name, license #, or date. Probate records are also available. Online access to the state recorders' meta-search site is available free at www.myfloridacounty.com. Click on Official Records. Also, records on the Property Appraiser database are available free online at www.sarasotaproperty.net/scpa_recs.htm; includes subdivision/condominium sales.

Seminole County *Property Appraiser, Real Estate, Lien, Recording Records*
www.seminoleclerk.org
The county clerk of circuit court's recordings database is available free at http://officialrecords.seminoleclerk.org/NV_Records/. Also, property appraisal records are available free online at www.scpafl.org/pls/web/web.seminole_county_disclaimer. There is also a map search.

Sumter County *Real Estate, Lien, Recording Records*
Search the state recorders' meta-search site for free at www.myfloridacounty.com. Click on Official records.

Suwannee County *Real Estate, Lien, Recording, Property Tax Records*
www.suwanneeclerkofcourt.com
Access of the county clerk of circuit database is available free at www.suwanneeclerkofcourt.com/court/kiosk.html. Also, search the tax collector database free at www.suwanneecountytax.com/collectmax/collect30.asp.

Taylor County   *County Commissioner Records*
http://taco.perryfl.com
Access to county commission records is available free at http://taco.perryfl.com/search.htm. Online records go back to 1988.

Union County   *Real Estate, Lien, Recording Records*
Search the state recorders' meta-search site for free at www.myfloridacounty.com. Click on Official records.

Volusia County
Property Appraiser, Real Estate, Lien, Vital Statistic, Recording, Citation Violation, Arrest Records
www.clerk.org
Property records are available free online at www.clerk.org/publicrecords/or.tshtml. Indexes go back to 3/1996; will soon have documents back to 1990. Volusia County also offers full Real Estate, Lien, and vital records on a commercial Internet site. The initial set up fee is $125 with a flat monthly fee of $25. For information, contact the clerk. Also, search the 24-arrest ledger and citations back to 1990 at www.clerk.org/publicrecords/cv.tshtml. Enter your name to access. Also, online access to the state recorders' meta-search site is available free at www.myfloridacounty.com. Click on Official records. Also, search the property appraiser database free at http://webserver.vcgov.org/vc_search.html.

Wakulla County   *Real Estate, Lien, Recording, Property Appraiser Records*
The state recorders' meta-search site is available free at www.myfloridacounty.com. Click on Official records. Also, search the property appraiser database free at http://wakulla.acsgrm.com/Property_Search.php.

Walton County   *Real Estate, Lien, Vital Statistic, Grantor/Grantee Records*
www.co.walton.fl.us/clerk
Records back to 1/1976 on the County Clerk database are available free online at www.co.walton.fl.us/clerk/or/ordisclm.htm. This has taken the place of the commercial system. Also, property appraiser records are available free at
www.co.walton.fl.us/propertyappraiser/taxsearch/

Washington County   *Recording, Deed, Judgment, Lien Records*
www.myflorida.com
Search the state recorders' meta-search site for free at www.myfloridacounty.com. Click on Official Records.

Federal Courts in Florida...

Standards for Federal Courts: The universal PACER sign-up number is 800-676-6856. Find PACER and the Party/Case Index on the Web at http://pacer.psc.uscourts.gov. PACER dial-up access is $.60 per minute. Also, courts offering internet access via RACER, PACER, Web-PACER or the new CM-ECF charge $.07 per page fee unless noted as free.

US District Court -- Middle District of Florida
Home Page: www.flmd.uscourts.gov
PACER: Toll-free access: 888-815-8701. Local access phone: 813-301-5820. Case records are available back to 1989-90. Records are purged three years after case closed. New records are available online after 1 day. **PACER URL:** http://pacer.flmd.uscourts.gov.
Fort Myers Division counties: Charlotte, Collier, De Soto, Glades, Hendry, Lee.
Jacksonville Division counties: Baker, Bradford, Clay, Columbia, Duval, Flagler, Hamilton, Nassau, Putnam, St. Johns, Suwannee, Union.
Ocala Division counties: Citrus, Lake, Marion, Sumter.
Orlando Division counties: Brevard, Orange, Osceola, Seminole, Volusia.
Tampa Division counties: Hardee, Hernando, Hillsborough, Manatee, Pasco, Pinellas, Polk, Sarasota.

US Bankruptcy Court -- Middle District of Florida
Home Page: www.flmb.uscourts.gov
PACER: Case records are available back to 1981. Records are purged every year. New civil records are available online after 1 week.
Electronic Filing: (Currently in the process of implementing CM/ECF).
Other Online Access: Court does not participate in the U.S. party case index. **Also:** access via phone on VCIS (Voice Case Information System) is available: 904-232-1313.
Jacksonville Division counties: Baker, Bradford, Citrus, Clay, Columbia, Duval, Flagler, Hamilton, Marion, Nassau, Putnam, St. Johns, Sumter, Suwannee, Union, Volusia.

Orlando Division counties: Brevard, Lake, Orange, Osceola, Seminole.
Tampa Division counties: Charlotte, Collier, De Soto, Glades, Hardee, Hendry, Hernando, Hillsborough, Lee, Manatee, Pasco, Pinellas, Polk, Sarasota.

US District Court -- Northern District of Florida

Home Page: www.flnd.uscourts.gov

PACER: Toll-free access: 800-844-0479. Local access phone: 850-942-8897. Case records are available back to 1992. Records are purged three years after case closed. New records are available online after 2 days. **PACER URL:** http://pacer.flnd.uscourts.gov.
Gainesville Division counties: Alachua, Dixie, Gilchrist, Lafayette, Levy. Records for cases prior to July 1996 are maintained at the Tallahassee Division.
Panama City Division counties: Bay, Calhoun, Gulf, Holmes, Jackson, Washington.
Pensacola Division counties: Escambia, Okaloosa, Santa Rosa, Walton.
Tallahassee Division counties: Franklin, Gadsden, Jefferson, Leon, Liberty, Madison, Taylor, Wakulla.

US Bankruptcy Court -- Northern District of Florida

Home Page: www.flnb.uscourts.gov/

PACER: Sign-up number is 904-435-8475. Toll-free access: 888-765-1751. Local access phone: 850-444-0189. Use of PC Anywhere V4.0 recommended. Password is bkc for version 7.5; password is bkcpc for version 8.0 Case records are available back to September 1985. Records are purged when cases are closed. New civil records are available online after 2 days. **PACER URL:** http://pacer.flnb.uscourts.gov. **Also:** access via phone on VCIS (Voice Case Information System) is available: 850-942-8358.
Pensacola Division counties: Escambia, Okaloosa, Santa Rosa, Walton.
Tallahassee Division counties: Alachua, Bay, Calhoun, Dixie, Franklin, Gadsden, Gilchrist, Gulf, Holmes, Jackson, Jefferson, Lafayette, Leon, Levy, Liberty, Madison, Taylor, Wakulla, Washington.

US District Court -- Southern District of Florida

Home Page: www.flsd.uscourts.gov

PACER: Toll-free access: 800-372-8846. Local access phone: 305-536-7265. Case records are available back to August 1990. Records are purged three years after case closed. New records are available online after 1 day. **PACER URL:** http://pacer.flsd.uscourts.gov. Document images available.
Fort Lauderdale Division counties: Broward.
Fort Pierce Division counties: Highlands, Indian River, Martin, Okeechobee, St. Lucie.
Key West Division counties: Monroe.
Miami Division counties: Dade.
West Palm Beach Division counties: Palm Beach.

US Bankruptcy Court -- Southern District of Florida

Home Page: www.flsb.uscourts.gov

PACER: Toll-free access: 888-443-0081. Local access phone: 305-536-7492. Case records are available back to 1986. Records are purged every six months. New civil records are available online after 1 day. **PACER URL:** http://pacer.flsb.uscourts.gov/login.html.
Also: access via phone on VCIS (Voice Case Information System) is available: 800-473-0226, 305-536-5979
Miami Division counties: Broward, Dade, Highlands, Indian River, Martin, Monroe, Okeechobee, Palm Beach, St. Lucie. Cases may also be assigned to Fort Lauderdale or to West Palm Beach.

Capital:	Atlanta
	Fulton County
Time Zone:	EST
Number of Counties:	159

Home Page   www.state.ga.us

Attorney General

         www.law.state.ga.us

Archives   www.sos.state.ga.us/archives

State Level ... Major Agencies

Corporation Records, Limited Partnership Records, Limited Liability Partnerships, Limited Liability Company Records

Secretary of State, Corporation Division, 315 W Tower, #2 ML King Drive, Atlanta, GA 30334-1530; 404-656-2817, 404-651-9059 (Fax), 8AM-5PM.

www.sos.state.ga.us/corporations

Records are available from the corporation database on the Internet site above or The corporate database can be searched by entity name or registered agent for no fee. Document Image and certificates are available for a $10.00 fee at www.ganet.org/services/corp/corpsearch.shtml. Major credit cards accepted. Other services include name reservation, filing procedures, downloading of forms/applications.

Trademarks/Servicemarks

Secretary of State, Trademark Division, 2 Martin Luther King, Room 315, W Tower, Atlanta, GA 30334; 404-656-2861, 404-657-6380 (Fax), 8AM-5PM.

www.sos.state.ga.us/corporations/trademarks.htm

A record database is searchable from the web site.

Uniform Commercial Code

Superior Court Clerks' Cooperative Authority, 1875 Century Blvd, #100, Atlanta, GA 30345; 404-327-9058, 404-327-7877 (Fax), 9AM-5PM.

http://www2.gsccca.org

Online access is available for regular, ongoing requesters. There is a monthly charge of $9.95 and a $.25 fee per image. Billing is monthly. The system is open 24 hours daily. The online service also includes real estate indexes and images. Minimum baud rate is 9600; 28.8 is supported. Information from 01/01/95 forward is available. Call 800-304-5175 or 404-327-9058 for a subscription package. **Other options:** The entire UCC Central Index System can be purchased on a daily, weekly, biweekly basis. For more information, contact the Director's office.

Sexual Offender Registry

The state sexual offender data is available at www.state.ga.us/gbi/disclaim.html. There is no fee.

Incarceration Records

Information on current and former inmates is available at www.dcor.state.ga.us.

Driver Records

Department of Motor Vehicle Safety, Driver's Services Section, MVR Unit, PO Box 80447, Conyers, GA 30013 (Courier: 2206 East View Parkway, Conyers, GA 30013); 678-413-8441, 8AM-3:30PM.

www.dmvs.ga.gov

Through the coordinated efforts of the GA Department of Motor Vehicle Safety and the Georgia Technology Authority, driving records are now available via the Internet for "certified users, including insurance, employers, and car rental companies. Requesters must complete several applications and user agreement forms. The fees are $5.00 for a three-year record and $7.00 for a seven-year record. For further information, visit: https://online.dmvs.ga.gov/mvr/begin.asp.

Legislation Records

www.legis.state.ga.us

The Internet site listed above has bill information. Also, you can search at www.ganet.org/services/leg

Voter Registration

Secretary of State, Elections Division, 2 Martin Luther King Dr SE, Suite 1104, Atlanta, GA 30334; 404-656-2871, 404-651-9531 (Fax), 8AM-5PM.

www.sos.state.ga.us/elections

Name and DOB needed to search registration information at the web site. Go to "Poll Locator." The results will provide address and district-precinct information, no SSNs released. **Other options:** CDs, Internet files, disks, and paper lists are available for purchase for non-commercial purposes. Look at the web site for pricing.

State Level ... Occupational Licensing

Acupuncturist	www.medicalboard.state.ga.us/bdsearch/index.html
Air Conditioning Contractor	https://secure.sos.state.ga.us/myverification/
Architect	https://secure.sos.state.ga.us/myverification/
Athletic Agent	https://secure.sos.state.ga.us/myverification/
Athletic Trainer	https://secure.sos.state.ga.us/myverification/
Auctioneer/Auction Dealer	https://secure.sos.state.ga.us/myverification/
Audiologist	https://secure.sos.state.ga.us/myverification/
Bank	www.ganet.org/dbf/other_institutions.html
Barber/Barber Shop	https://secure.sos.state.ga.us/myverification/
Cardiac Technician	www.medicalboard.state.ga.us/bdsearch/index.html
Charity	www.sos.state.ga.us/securities/charitysearch.htm
Check Casher/Seller	www.ganet.org/dbf/other_institutions.html
Chiropractor	https://secure.sos.state.ga.us/myverification/
Contractor, General	https://secure.sos.state.ga.us/myverification/
Cosmetologist/Cosmetology Shop	https://secure.sos.state.ga.us/myverification/
Counselor	https://secure.sos.state.ga.us/myverification/
Credit Union	www.ganet.org/dbf/other_institutions.html
Dental Hygienist	https://secure.sos.state.ga.us/myverification/
Dentist	https://secure.sos.state.ga.us/myverification/
Detox Specialist	www.medicalboard.state.ga.us/bdsearch/index.html
Dietitian	https://secure.sos.state.ga.us/myverification/
Drug Whlse/Retail/Mfg (Hospital)	https://secure.sos.state.ga.us/myverification/

EDP - Electronic Data Processor .... www.ganet.org/dbf/other_institutions.html
Electrical Contractor .... https://secure.sos.state.ga.us/myverification/
Embalmer .... https://secure.sos.state.ga.us/myverification/
Engineer .... https://secure.sos.state.ga.us/myverification/
Esthetician .... https://secure.sos.state.ga.us/myverification/
Family Therapist .... https://secure.sos.state.ga.us/myverification/
Forester .... https://secure.sos.state.ga.us/myverification/
Funeral Director/Apprentice .... https://secure.sos.state.ga.us/myverification/
Funeral Establishment .... https://secure.sos.state.ga.us/myverification/
Geologist .... https://secure.sos.state.ga.us/myverification/
Hearing Aid Dealer/Dispenser .... https://secure.sos.state.ga.us/myverification/
Holding Company/Representative Office .... www.ganet.org/dbf/other_institutions.html
Insurance Agent .... www.inscomm.state.ga.us/AGENTS/AgentStatus.asp
Interior Designer .... https://secure.sos.state.ga.us/myverification/
Landscape Architect .... https://secure.sos.state.ga.us/myverification/
Low Voltage Contractor .... https://secure.sos.state.ga.us/myverification/
Manicurist .... https://secure.sos.state.ga.us/myverification/
Marriage Counselor .... https://secure.sos.state.ga.us/myverification/
Medical Doctor .... www.medicalboard.state.ga.us/bdsearch/index.html
Mortgage Institution .... www.ganet.org/dbf/mortgage.html
Nail Care .... https://secure.sos.state.ga.us/myverification/
Nuclear Pharmacist .... https://secure.sos.state.ga.us/myverification/
Nurse-LPN .... https://secure.sos.state.ga.us/myverification/
Nurse-RN .... https://secure.sos.state.ga.us/myverification/
Nursing Home Administrator .... https://secure.sos.state.ga.us/myverification/
Occupational Therapist/Assistant .... https://secure.sos.state.ga.us/myverification/
Optician, Dispensing .... https://secure.sos.state.ga.us/myverification/
Optometrist .... https://secure.sos.state.ga.us/myverification/
Osteopathic Physician .... www.medicalboard.state.ga.us/bdsearch/index.html
Paramedic .... www.medicalboard.state.ga.us/bdsearch/index.html
Pesticide Applicator .... www.kellysolutions.com/ga/Applicators/index.htm
Pesticide Contractor/Employee .... www.kellysolutions.com/ga/Applicators/index.htm
Pharmacist .... https://secure.sos.state.ga.us/myverification/
Pharmacy School, Clinic Researcher .... https://secure.sos.state.ga.us/myverification/
Physical Therapist/Therapist Asst .... https://secure.sos.state.ga.us/myverification/
Physician Assistant .... www.medicalboard.state.ga.us/bdsearch/index.html
Plumber Journeyman/Contractor .... https://secure.sos.state.ga.us/myverification/
Podiatrist .... https://secure.sos.state.ga.us/myverification/
Poison Pharmacist .... https://secure.sos.state.ga.us/myverification/
Private Detective .... https://secure.sos.state.ga.us/myverification/
Psychologist .... https://secure.sos.state.ga.us/myverification/
Public Accountant-CPA .... https://secure.sos.state.ga.us/myverification/
Real Estate Appraiser .... www.asc.gov/content/category1/appr_by_state.asp
Rebuilder (Motor Vehicle) .... https://secure.sos.state.ga.us/myverification/
Respiratory Care Practitioner .... www.medicalboard.state.ga.us/bdsearch/index.html
Salvage Pool Operator .... https://secure.sos.state.ga.us/myverification/
Salvage Yard Dealer .... https://secure.sos.state.ga.us/myverification/
School Librarian .... https://secure.sos.state.ga.us/myverification/
Security Agency .... https://secure.sos.state.ga.us/myverification/
Security Guard .... https://secure.sos.state.ga.us/myverification/
Social Worker .... https://secure.sos.state.ga.us/myverification/
Speech-Language Pathologist .... https://secure.sos.state.ga.us/myverification/
Surveyor, Land .... https://secure.sos.state.ga.us/myverification/
Used Car Dealer .... https://secure.sos.state.ga.us/myverification/
Used Car Parts Dist. .... https://secure.sos.state.ga.us/myverification/
Utility Contractor .... https://secure.sos.state.ga.us/myverification/
Veterinarian/Veterinary Technician .... https://secure.sos.state.ga.us/myverification/
Waste Water-related Occupation .... https://secure.sos.state.ga.us/myverification/

County Level ... Courts

Court Administration:
Court Administrator, 244 Washington St SW, Suite 550, Atlanta, GA, 30334; 404-656-5171; www.georgiacourts.org/aoc/index.html

Court Structure:
Georgia's Superior Courts are arranged in 49 circuits of general jurisdiction, and these assume the role of a State Court if the county does not have one. The 69 State Courts, like Superior Courts, can conduct jury trials, but are limited jurisdiction. Each county has a Probate, a Juvenile, and a Magistrate Court; the latter has jurisdiction over civil actions under $15,000, also one type of misdemeanor related to passing bad checks. Magistrate Courts also issue arrest warrants and set bond on all felonies. Probate courts can, in certain cases, issue search and arrest warrants, and hear miscellaneous misdemeanors.

Online Access Note:
Several counties have Internet access to records. There is no online access available statewide, although one is being planned.

Cherokee County
Magistrate Court *Civil Records*
www.cccourt.com
Search the magistrate court database online at www.ncourt.com/search.html#database.

Cobb County
Superior Court *Civil and Criminal Records*
www.cobbgasupctclk.com/index.htm
Civil or criminal indexes of Clerk of Superior Court are available free online at the web site. Search by name, type or case number. The data is updated every Friday.

Dougherty County
Superior & State Court *Civil and Criminal Records*
Magistrate Court *Civil Records*
Probate Court *Probate Records*
www.dougherty.ga.us/
Access to civil and criminal court docket data available free at the web site. The same system permits access to probate, tax, deeds, and death certificate records.

Gwinnett County
Superior & State Court *Civil and Criminal Records*
www.gwinnettcourts.com/courts/Supcourt.htm
Online access to court case party index is available free online at www.gwinnettcourts.com/misc/casendx.htm. Search by name or case number.

Magistrate Court *Civil Records*
www.gwinnettcourts.com/courts/Magcourt.htm
Online access to court case party index is available free at www.gwinnettcourts.com/misc/casendx.htm.

Probate Court *Probate Records*
www.gwinnettcourts.com/courts/Procourt.htm
Search Probate records by name for free at the web site; click on "Data Search."

County Level ... Recorders & Assessors

Recording Office Organization: 159 counties, 159 recording offices. The recording officer is the Clerk of Superior Court. All transactions are recorded in a "General Execution Docket." The entire state is in the Eastern Time Zone (EST). All tax liens on personal property are filed with the county Clerk of Superior Court in a "General Execution Docket" (grantor/grantee) or "Lien Index." Most counties will not perform tax lien searches.

Online Access Note: Georgia's Superior Court Clerk's Cooperative Authority (GSCCCA) at www.gsccca.org/search offers access on a subscription basis for ongoing users, or a free four hour trial for casual requesters. The system includes a UCC Index with records back to 1/1995; Real Estate Deed Index back to 1/1999; Notary Public Index and Plat Index. Subscription is $9.95 per month per user for unlimited use and $.25 for each page printed. You may submit UCC Certified Search requests online. The charge for certified searches is $10 per debtor name.

Clayton County   *Real Estate, UCC, Notary Records*
www.co.clayton.ga.us/superior_court/clerk_of_courts/
Search real estate, UCC, and Notary records free at www.co.clayton.ga.us/superior_court/clerk_of_courts

Cobb County   *Real Estate, Grantor/Grantee Records*
www.cobbgasupctclk.com
Property records on the County Superior Court Clerk web site are available free online at www.cobbgasupctclk.com/index.htm. Search by name, address, land description, instrument type, or book & page. You may also search court records. Also, see www2.gsccca.org for online access to Deed and UCC indexes.

De Kalb County   *RE Deeds, UCC Records*
See www.gsccca.org for online access to Deed and UCC indexes. Also, search tax commissioner property tax data for free at https://dklbweb.dekalbga.org/taxcommissioner/PropertyTaxMain2.htm. Click on "Make/View Property Tax Payment." No name searching.

Dougherty County   *Real Estate, Personal Property, Tax, Courts, Deed, Mortgage, Tax Assessor, Personal Property, UCC, Death, Divorce, Trade Name Records*
www.albany.ga.us
Access to the clerk of courts Dept. of Deeds public menu is available at www.albany.ga.us/exec/site/?mid=231. Click on "clerk of courts record system" or "county/city tax records system." The tax records system has personal property, deeds, assessments. See www.gsccca.org for online access to Deed and UCC indexes.

Fayette County   *Assessor, Real Estate Records*
www.admin.co.fayette.ga.us
Records on the County Assessor database are available free on the GIS-mapping site at www.fayettecountymaps.com/disclaimer.htm. Also, See www2.gsccca.org for online access to Deed and UCC indexes.

Glynn County   *Assessor, Property, Recording, UCC Records*
Access to the county assessor property tax records is available free on the GIS mapping web site at http://maps.binarybus.com/glynn/disclaimer.asp. Also see www2.gsccca.org for online access to Deed and UCC indexes.

Gwinnett County   *Property, Deed, UCC, Judgment Records*
www.gwinnettcourts.com
See www.gsccca.org for online access to Deed, Plat and UCC indexes. Deed records go back to 1999; UCCs to1995. Also, search for civil court judgments at www.gwinnettcourts.com/misc/casendx.htm.

Houston County   *Assessor, Real Estate Records*
www.houstoncountyga.com
Access to the assessor's Mapguide database is available free at www.assessor.houstoncountyga.org. The Autodesk MapGuide viewer is available to download. Also see www2.gsccca.org for online access to Deed and UCC indexes.

McIntosh County   *Deed (2000-present), UCC, Notary Records*
Call 800-304-5175 to subscribe to UCCs and Deed indexes. See www.gsccca.org for online access to Deed and UCC indexes.

Oglethorpe County   *UCC, Real Estate Records*
UCC and real estate records are available online from the Oglethorpe County Clerk for a monthly subscription fee of $9.95 plus $.25 per printed page. Guest accounts are available. For information and to open an account, call 404-327-9058. Also, see www2.gsccca.org for online access to Deed and UCC indexes.

Federal Courts in Georgia...

Standards for Federal Courts: The universal PACER sign-up number is 800-676-6856. Find PACER and the Party/Case Index on the Web at http://pacer.psc.uscourts.gov. PACER dial-up access is $.60 per minute. Also, courts offering internet access via RACER, PACER, Web-PACER or the new CM-ECF charge $.07 per page fee unless noted as free.

US District Court -- Middle District of Georgia
Home Page: www.gamd.uscourts.gov
PACER: Toll-free access: 888-234-3839. Local access phone: 912-752-8170. Case records are available back to January 1991. Records are purged never. New records are available online after 1-2 days. **PACER URL:** http://pacer.gamd.uscourts.gov.
Albany/Americus Division counties: Baker, Ben Hill, Calhoun, Crisp, Dougherty, Early, Lee, Miller, Mitchell, Schley, Sumter, Terrell, Turner, Webster, Worth. Ben Hill and Crisp were transfered from the Macon Division as of October 1, 1997.
Athens Division counties: Clarke, Elbert, Franklin, Greene, Hart, Madison, Morgan, Oconee, Oglethorpe, Walton. Closed cases before April 1997 are located in the Macon Division.
Columbus Division counties: Chattahoochee, Clay, Harris, Marion, Muscogee, Quitman, Randolph, Stewart, Talbot, Taylor.
Macon Division counties: Baldwin, Ben Hill, Bibb, Bleckley, Butts, Crawford, Crisp, Dooly, Hancock, Houston, Jasper, Jones, Lamar, Macon, Monroe, Peach, Pulaski, Putnam, Twiggs, Upson, Washington, Wilcox, Wilkinson. Athens Division cases closed before April 1997 are also located here.
Thomasville Division counties: Brooks, Colquitt, Decatur, Grady, Seminole, Thomas.
Valdosta Division counties: Berrien, Clinch, Cook, Echols, Irwin, Lanier, Lowndes, Tift.

US Bankruptcy Court -- Middle District of Georgia
Home Page: www.gamb.uscourts.gov
PACER: Toll-free access: 800-546-7343. Local access phone: 912-752-3551. Case records are available back to March 1990 (some back to 1985). Records are purged except last 12 months. New civil records are available online after 1 day. **PACER URL:** http://pacer.gamb.uscourts.gov.
Electronic Filing: (Currently in the process of implementing CM/ECF). **Also:** access via phone on VCIS (Voice Case Information System) is available: 800-211-3015, 912-752-8183
Columbus Division counties: Berrien, Brooks, Chattahoochee, Clay, Clinch, Colquitt, Cook, Decatur, Echols, Grady, Harris, Irwin, Lanier, Lowndes, Marion, Muscogee, Quitman, Randolph, Seminole, Stewart,Talbot, Taylor, Thomas, Tift.
Macon Division counties: Baldwin, Baker, Ben Hill, Bibb, Bleckley, Butts, Calhoun, Clarke, Crawford, Crisp, Dooly, Dougherty, Early, Elbert, Franklin, Greene, Hancock, Hart, Houston, Jasper, Jones, Lamar, Lee, Macon, Madison, Miller, Mitchell, Monroe, Morgan, Oconee, Oglethorpe, Peach, Pulaski, Putnam, Schley, Sumter, Terrell, Turner, Twiggs, Upson, Walton, Washington, Webster, Wilcox, Wilkinson, Worth.

US District Court -- Northern District of Georgia
Home Page: www.gand.uscourts.gov
PACER: Toll-free access: 800-801-6932. Local access phone: 404-730-9668. Case records are available back to August 1992. Records are purged on a varied schedule. New records are available online after 1 day. **PACER URL:** http://pacer.gand.uscourts.gov.
Atlanta Division counties: Cherokee, Clayton, Cobb, De Kalb, Douglas, Fulton, Gwinnett, Henry, Newton, Rockdale.
Gainesville Division counties: Banks, Barrow, Dawson, Fannin, Forsyth, Gilmer, Habersham, Hall, Jackson, Lumpkin, Pickens, Rabun, Stephens, Towns, Union, White.
Newnan Division counties: Carroll, Coweta, Fayette, Haralson, Heard, Meriwether, Pike, Spalding, Troup.
Rome Division counties: Bartow, Catoosa, Chattooga, Dade, Floyd, Gordon, Murray, Paulding, Polk, Walker, Whitfield.

US Bankruptcy Court -- Northern District of Georgia

Home Page: www.ganb.uscourts.gov

PACER: Toll-free access: 800-436-8395. Local access phone: 404-730-3264. Case records are available back to August 1986. Records are purged never. New civil records are available online after 2 days.

Electronic Filing: Electronic filing information is available online at http://ecf.ganb.uscourts.gov. **Also:** access via phone on VCIS (Voice Case Information System) is available: 800-510-8284, 404-730-2866

Atlanta Division counties: Cherokee, Clayton, Cobb, DeKalb, Douglas, Fulton, Gwinnett, Henry, Newton, Rockdale.

Gainesville Division counties: Banks, Barrow, Dawson, Fannin, Forsyth, Gilmer, Habersham, Hall, Jackson, Lumpkin, Pickens, Rabun, Stephens, Towns, Union, White.

Newnan Division counties: Carroll, Coweta, Fayette, Haralson, Heard, Meriwether, Pike, Spalding, Troup.

Rome Division counties: Bartow, Catoosa, Chattooga, Dade, Floyd, Gordon, Murray, Paulding, Polk, Walker, Whitfield.

US District Court -- Southern District of Georgia

Home Page: www.gasd.uscourts.gov

PACER: Toll-free access: 800-801-6934. Local access phone: 912-650-4046. Document images available. Case records are available back to June 1995. New records are available online after 1 day. **PACER URL:** http://pacer.gasd.uscourts.gov. Document images available.

Augusta Division counties: Burke, Columbia, Glascock, Jefferson, Lincoln, McDuffie, Richmond, Taliaferro, Warren, Wilkes.

Brunswick Division counties: Appling, Camden, Glynn, Jeff Davis, Long, McIntosh, Wayne.

Dublin Division counties: Dodge, Johnson, Laurens, Montgomery, Telfair, Treutlen, Wheeler.

Savannah Division counties: Bryan, Chatham, Effingham, Liberty.

Statesboro Division counties: Bulloch, Candler, Emanuel, Evans, Jenkins, Screven, Tattnall, Toombs.

Waycross Division counties: Atkinson, Bacon, Brantley, Charlton, Coffee, Pierce, Ware.

US Bankruptcy Court -- Southern District of Georgia

Home Page: www.gas.uscourts.gov

PACER: Toll-free access: 800-295-8679. Local access phone: 912-650-4190. Document images available on Pacer. Case records are available back to August 1986. Records are purged annually. New records are available online after. **PACER URL:** http://pacer.gasb.uscourts.gov. This appears to be a homogenization of RACER and PACER; the fee is $.07 per page.

Other Online Access: Court does not participate in the U.S. party case index.

Augusta Division counties: Bulloch, Burke, Candler, Columbia, Dodge, Emanuel, Evans, Glascock, Jefferson, Jenkins, Johnson, Laurens, Lincoln, McDuffie, Montgomery, Richmond, Screven, Taliaferro, Tattnall, Telfair, Toombs, Treutlen, Warren, Wheeler, Wilkes.

Savannah Division counties: Appling, Atkinson, Bacon, Brantley, Bryan, Camden, Charlton, Chatham, Coffee, Effingham, Glynn, Jeff Davis, Liberty, Long, McIntosh, Pierce, Ware, Wayne.

Editor's Tip: Just because records are maintained in a certain way in your state or county do not assume that any other county or state does things the same way that you are used to.

Hawaii

Capital:	Honolulu	Home Page	www.state.hi.us
	Honolulu County		
Time Zone:	HT	Attorney General	www.state.hi.us/ag
Number of Counties:	4	Archives	www.state.hi.us/dags/archives

State Level ... Major Agencies

Corporation Records, Trade Name, Limited Partnership Records, Assumed Name, Trademarks/Servicemarks, Limited Liability Company Records, Limited Liability Partnerships

Business Registration Division, PO Box 40, Honolulu, HI 96810 (Courier: 1010 Richard St, 1st Floor, Honolulu, HI 96813); 808-586-2727, 808-586-2733 (Fax), 7:45AM-4:30PM.

www.businessregistrations.com

Online access is available through the Internet or via modem dial-up at 808-587-4800. There are no fees, the system is open 24 hours. For assistance during business hours, call 808-586-1919. Also, business names searching is available free online at www.ehawaiigov.com. Business license searching is available free at www.ehawaiigov.org/serv/taxpayer. Search by name, ID number of DBA name.

Legislation Records

www.capitol.hawaii.gov

To dial online for current year bill information line, call 808-296-4636. Or, access the information through the Internet site. There is no fee, the system is up 24 hours.

State Level ... Occupational Licensing

Acupuncturist	www.ehawaiigov.org/serv/pvl
Architect	www.ehawaiigov.org/serv/pvl
Auction	www.ehawaiigov.org/serv/pvl
Bank/Bank Agencies/Offices	www.state.hi.us/dcca/dfi/regulated.html
Barber Shop	www.ehawaiigov.org/serv/pvl
Barber/Barber Apprentice	www.ehawaiigov.org/serv/pvl
Beauty Operator/School/Shop	www.ehawaiigov.org/serv/pvl
Cemetery	www.ehawaiigov.org/serv/pvl
Chiropractor	www.ehawaiigov.org/serv/pvl
Collection Agency	www.ehawaiigov.org/serv/pvl

Condominium Hotel Operator .... www.ehawaiigov.org/serv/pvl
Condominium Managing Agent .... www.ehawaiigov.org/serv/pvl
Contractor .... www.ehawaiigov.org/serv/pvl
Cosmetologist .... www.ehawaiigov.org/serv/pvl
Credit Union .... www.state.hi.us/dcca/dfi/regulated.html
Dental Hygienist .... www.ehawaiigov.org/serv/pvl
Dentist .... www.ehawaiigov.org/serv/pvl
Drug (Prescription) Dist./Whlse. .... www.ehawaiigov.org/serv/pvl
Elected Officials Financial Disclosure .... www.state.hi.us/ethics/noindex/pubrec.htm
Electrician .... www.ehawaiigov.org/serv/pvl
Electrologist .... www.ehawaiigov.org/serv/pvl
Elevator Mechanic .... www.ehawaiigov.org/serv/pvl
Emergency Medical Personnel .... www.ehawaiigov.org/serv/pvl
Employment Agency .... www.ehawaiigov.org/serv/pvl
Engineer .... www.ehawaiigov.org/serv/pvl
Escrow Company .... www.state.hi.us/dcca/dfi/regulated.html
Financial Services Loan Company .... www.state.hi.us/dcca/dfi/regulated.html
Hearing Aid Dealer/Fitter .... www.ehawaiigov.org/serv/pvl
Insurance Adjuster .... www.ehawaiigov.org/serv/hils
Insurance Agent/Solicitor .... www.ehawaiigov.org/serv/hils
Landscape Architect .... www.ehawaiigov.org/serv/pvl
Lobbyist .... www.state.hi.us/ethics/noindex/pubrec.htm
Marriage & Family Therapist .... www.ehawaiigov.org/serv/pvl
Massage Therapist/Establishment .... www.ehawaiigov.org/serv/pvl
Mechanic .... www.ehawaiigov.org/serv/pvl
Medical Doctor .... www.ehawaiigov.org/serv/pvl
Mortgage Broker/Solicitor .... www.ehawaiigov.org/serv/pvl
Motor Vehicle Dealer/Broker/Seller .... www.ehawaiigov.org/serv/pvl
Motor Vehicle Repair Dealer .... www.ehawaiigov.org/serv/pvl
Naturopathic Physician .... www.ehawaiigov.org/serv/pvl
Nurse .... www.ehawaiigov.org/serv/pvl
Nursing Home Administrator .... www.ehawaiigov.org/serv/pvl
Occupational Therapist .... www.ehawaiigov.org/serv/pvl
Optician, Dispensing .... www.ehawaiigov.org/serv/pvl
Optometrist .... www.ehawaiigov.org/serv/pvl
Osteopathic Physician .... www.ehawaiigov.org/serv/pvl
Pest Control Field Rep./Operator .... www.ehawaiigov.org/serv/pvl
Pharmacist/Pharmacy .... www.ehawaiigov.org/serv/pvl
Pharmacy, Out-of-State .... www.ehawaiigov.org/serv/pvl
Physical Therapist .... www.ehawaiigov.org/serv/pvl
Physician Assistant .... www.ehawaiigov.org/serv/pvl
Plumber .... www.ehawaiigov.org/serv/pvl
Podiatrist .... www.ehawaiigov.org/serv/pvl
Port Pilot .... www.ehawaiigov.org/serv/pvl
Private Detective .... www.ehawaiigov.org/serv/pvl
Private Detective/Investigation Agency .... www.ehawaiigov.org/serv/pvl
Psychologist .... www.ehawaiigov.org/serv/pvl
Public Accountant-CPA .... www.ehawaiigov.org/serv/pvl
Real Estate Appraiser .... www.ehawaiigov.org/serv/pvl
Real Estate Broker/Seller .... www.ehawaiigov.org/serv/pvl
Savings & Loan Association .... www.state.hi.us/dcca/dfi/regulated.html
Savings Bank .... www.state.hi.us/dcca/dfi/regulated.html
Security Guard/Agency .... www.ehawaiigov.org/serv/pvl
Social Worker .... www.ehawaiigov.org/serv/pvl
Speech Pathologist/Audiologist .... www.ehawaiigov.org/serv/pvl
Surveyor, Land .... www.ehawaiigov.org/serv/pvl
Timeshare .... www.ehawaiigov.org/serv/pvl
Travel Agency .... www.ehawaiigov.org/serv/pvl
Trust Company .... www.state.hi.us/dcca/dfi/regulated.html
Veterinarian .... www.ehawaiigov.org/serv/pvl

County Level ... Courts

Court Administration: Administrative Director of Courts, Judicial Branch, 417 S King St, Honolulu, HI, 96813; 808-539-4900; www.courts.state.hi.us

Court Structure: Hawaii's trial level is comprised of Circuit Courts (with Family Courts) and District Courts. These trial courts function in four judicial circuits: First (Oahu), Second (Maui/Molokai/Lanai), Third (Hawaii County), and Fifth (Kauai/Niihau) The Fourth Circuit was merged with the Third in 1943.

Circuit Courts are general jurisdiction and handle all jury trials, felony cases, and civil cases over $20,000, also probate and guardianship. The District Court handles criminal cases punishable by a fine and/or less then 1-yr imprisonment and some civil cases up to $20,000, also landlord/tenant and DUI cases.

Online Access Note: Free online access to Circuit Court and family court records is available at the web site www.courts.state.hi.us (click on "Search Court Records"). Search by name or case number. These records are not considered "official" for FCRA compliant searches.

Hawaii County
3rd Circuit Court Legal Documents Section *Civil and Criminal Records*
www.courts.state.hi.us
Online access to Circuit Court and family court records available free at the web site. Search by name or case number. Records go back to early 1900s.

Honolulu County
1st Circuit Court *Civil and Criminal Records*
www.courts.state.hi.us/index.jsp
Online access to Circuit Court & family court records available free at www.courts.state.hi.us/hod/judstart.htm. Search by name or case number. Records go back to 1984.

Kauai County
5th Circuit Court *Civil and Criminal Records*
www.courts.state.hi.us
Online access to Circuit Court and family court records available free at the web site. Search by name or case number. Records go back to 1984.

Maui County
2nd Circuit Court *Civil and Criminal Records*
www.courts.state.hi.us
Online access to Circuit Court & family court records available free at the web site. Search by name or case number. Records go back to 1984.

County Level ... Recorders & Assessors

Recording Office Organization: All UCC financing statements, tax liens, and real estate documents are filed centrally with the Bureau of Conveyances located in Honolulu. The entire state is in the Hawaii Time Zone (HT).

Online Access Note: There is no statewide access to recorder or assessor information.

Bureau of Conveyances *Property Records*

Property records on the Hawaii County property assessor records are available free at www.hawaiipropertytax.com. Maui Assessor Property records are available free at www.mauipropertytax.com. There is also a Maui property lookup at http://gil.co.maui.hi.us/kivanet/2/land/lookup/index.cfm?fa=dslladdr.

Federal Courts in Hawaii...

Standards for Federal Courts: The universal PACER sign-up number is 800-676-6856. Find PACER and the Party/Case Index on the Web at http://pacer.psc.uscourts.gov. PACER dial-up access is $.60 per minute. Also, courts offering internet access via RACER, PACER, Web-PACER or the new CM-ECF charge $.07 per page fee unless noted as free.

US District Court -- District of Hawaii

Home Page: www.hid.uscourts.gov

PACER: Case records are available back to October 1991. Records are purged never. New civil records are available online after 1 day. New criminal records are available online after 3 days. **PACER URL:** http://pacer.hid.uscourts.gov.

Honolulu Division counties: All counties.

US Bankruptcy Court -- District of Hawaii

Home Page: www.hib.uscourts.gov

PACER: Toll-free access: 888-853-3766. Local access phone: 808-522-8118. Use of PC Anywhere v4.0 suggested. Additional password is "pals" Case records are available back to 1987. Records are purged varies. New civil records are available online after 1 day. **PACER URL:** http://pacer.hib.uscourts.gov. Document images available.

Electronic Filing: (Currently in the process of implementing CM/ECF). **Also:** access via phone on VCIS (Voice Case Information System) is available: 808-522-8122.

Honolulu Division counties: All counties.

Capital:	Boise		Home Page	www.state.id.us
	Ada County			
Time Zone:	MST/PST		Archives	http://idahohistory.net
Number of Counties:	44		Attorney General	http://www2.state.id.us/ag/

State Level ... Major Agencies

Corporation Records, Limited Partnerships, Trademarks/Servicemarks, Limited Liability Companys, Limited Liability Partnerships, Assumed Names

Secretary of State, Corporation Division, PO Box 83720, Boise, ID 83720-0080 (Courier: 700 W Jefferson, Boise, ID 83720); 208-334-2301, 208-334-2080 (Fax), 8AM-5PM.

www.idsos.state.id.us

Business Entity Searches at www.accessidaho.org/apps/sos/corp/search.html is a free Internet service open 24 hours daily. **Other options:** There are a variety of formats and media available for bulk purchase requesters. Requesters can subscribers to a monthly CD update.

Uniform Commercial Code, Federal Tax Liens, State Tax Liens

UCC Division, Secretary of State, PO Box 83720, Boise, ID 83720-0080 (Courier: 700 W Jefferson, Boise, ID 83720); 208-334-3191, 208-334-2847 (Fax), 8AM-5PM.

www.idsos.state.id.us

There is a free limited search at https://www.accessidaho.org/secure/sos/liens/search.html. We recommend professional searchers to subscribe to the extensive commercial service at this site. There is a $75 annual fee and possible transaction fees. **Other options:** A summary data file on current filing is available on 4mm data tape.

Sexual Offender Registry

The Bureau of Identification restricts access to the online Sex Offender Registry to those authorized by law. Registration and password is required at www.isp.state.id.us/. This service is provided to those agencies qualifying under Idaho Code 18-8283 (c) for special lists; schools and non-profit organizations.

Driver Records

Idaho Transportation Department, Driver's Services, PO Box 34, Boise, ID 83731-0034 (Courier: 3311 W State, Boise, ID 83703); 208-334-8736, 208-334-8739 (Fax), 8:30AM-5PM.

http://www2.state.id.us/itd/dmv/ds.htm

Idaho offers online access (CICS) to the driver license files through its portal provider, Access Idaho. Fee is $5.50 per record. For more information, call 208-332-0102 or visit www.accessidaho.org. **Other options:** Idaho offers bulk retrieval of basic drivers license information with a signed contract. For information, call 208-334-8601

Vehicle Ownership, Vehicle Identification

Idaho Transportation Department, Vehicle Services, PO Box 34, Boise, ID 83731-0034 (Courier: 3311 W State St, Boise, ID 83707); 208-334-8773, 208-334-8542 (Fax), 8:30AM-5PM.

http://www2.state.id.us/itd/dmv/vs.htm

Idaho offers online and batch access to registration and title files through its portal provider, Access Idaho. Records are $4.00 each plus an additional convenience fee. For more information, call 208-332-0102. **Other options:** Idaho offers bulk retrieval of registration, ownership, and vehicle information with a signed contract. For more information, call 208-334-8601.

Legislation Records

http://www2.state.id.us/legislat/legislat.html

Statutes, bill information, and subject index are available from the web site. They also will answer questions via email. (kford@lso.state.id.us)

State Level ... Occupational Licensing

Applicator, Commercial/Private	www.agri.state.id.us/agresource/_agtechlookup/querylic.asp
Attorney	http://www2.state.id.us/isb/mem/attorney_roster.asp
Bank	http://finance.state.id.us/industry/bank_info.asp
Boiler Inspector	www.accessidaho.org/public/dbs/safety/search.html
Collection Agency/Collector	http://finance.state.id.us/industry/statutes_confin.asp?Chapter=CAA
Community Action Program	www.puc.state.id.us/consumer/helplist.pdf
Contractor, Public Works	www.accessidaho.org/public/dbs/pubworks/search.html
Credit Union	http://finance.state.id.us/industry/creditunion_section.asp
Dental Hygienist	http://www2.state.id.us/isbd/search.htm
Dentist	http://www2.state.id.us/isbd/search.htm
Electrical Inspector/Contr./Apprentice/Journeyman	www.accessidaho.org/public/dbs/electrical/search.html
Engineer	http://www2.state.id.us/ipels/pelsnumb.htm
Finance Company	http://finance.state.id.us/consumer/concredit_section.asp
Guide	http://www2.state.id.us/oglb/oglbhome.htm
Investment Advisor	http://finance.state.id.us/industry/securities_resources.asp?resource=IARR
Lobbyist	www.idsos.state.id.us/elect/lobbyist/lobinfo.htm
Manufactured Commercial Building	www.accessidaho.org/public/dbs/building/search.html
Manufactured Homes & Housing	www.accessidaho.org/public/dbs/building/search.html
Manufactured Housing Dealer/Broker/Mfg	www.accessidaho.org/public/dbs/building/search.html
Mortgage Broker/Banker	http://finance.state.id.us/industry/mortgage_section.asp
Mortgage Company	http://finance.state.id.us/industry/mortgage_section.asp
Mortician/Mortician Resident Trainee	http://www2.state.id.us/ibol/ibollicense_Search.cfm
Optometrist	www.odfinder.org/LicSearch.asp
Oral Surgeon	http://www2.state.id.us/isbd/search.htm
Orthodontist	http://www2.state.id.us/isbd/search.htm
Outfitter	http://www2.state.id.us/oglb/oglbhome.htm
Pesticide Applicator/Operator/Dealer/Mfg	www.agri.state.id.us/QueryLic.htm
Plumbing Insp./Contr./Apprentice/Journeyman	www.accessidaho.org/public/dbs/plumbing/search.html
Public Accountant-CPA	http://www2.state.id.us/boa/HTM/license.htm
Public Accountant-LPA	http://www2.state.id.us/boa/HTM/license.htm
Real Estate Appraiser	www.asc.gov/content/category1/appr_by_state.asp
Savings & Loan Association	http://finance.state.id.us/industry/bank_section.asp
Securities Broker/Dealer/Seller/Issuer	http://finance.state.id.us/industry/securities.asp
Surveyor, Land	http://www2.state.id.us/ipels/pelsnumb.htm
Trust Company	http://finance.state.id.us/consumer/bank_info.asp
Utility Pay Stations	www.puc.state.id.us/consumer/paystations.htm

County Level ... Courts

Court Administration: Administrative Director of Courts, Supreme Court Building, 451 W State St, Boise, ID, 83720; 208-334-2246; http://www2.state.id.us/judicial/

Court Structure: The District Court oversees felony and most civil cases. Small claims are handled by the Magistrate Division of the District Court. Probate is handled by the Magistrate Division of the District Court.

Online Access Note: There is no statewide computer system offering external access. ISTARS is a statewide intra-court/intra-agency system run and managed by the State Supreme Court. All counties are on ISTARS, and all courts provide public access terminals on-site.

Canyon County
District & Magistrate Courts *Civil Records*
www.the3rdjudicialdistrict.com
A daily court calendar is available at the web site.

County Level ... Recorders & Assessors

Recording Office Organization: 44 counties, 44 recording offices. The recording officer is the County Recorder. Many counties utilize a grantor/grantee index containing all transactions recorded with them. 34 counties are in the Mountain Time Zone (MST), and 10 are in the Pacific Time Zone (PST). Until 07/01/98, state tax liens were filed at the local county recorder. Now they are filed with the Secretary of State who has all active case files. Federal tax liens on personal property of businesses are filed with the Secretary of State. Other federal tax liens are filed with the county recorder. Some counties will perform a combined tax lien search while others will not perform tax lien searches.

Online Access Note: Several have web access to assessor records. Also, the Secretary of State's office offers online access to UCCs.

Ada County   *Assessor, Property Records*
Search the property assessor database for free at www.adacountyassessor.org.

Canyon County   *Assessor, Property Records*
www.canyoncounty.org
Access to the Assessor and Treasurer's databases requires $35 registration/setup fee and 150 yearly fee. For subscription information, email clane@canyoncounty.org or call 208-454-7401 or visit the web site.

Kootenai County   *Property, Recording, Unclaimed Property Records*
www.co.kootenai.id.us/default.asp
Access to the county mapping/recording database is available free at www.co.kootenai.id.us/departments/mapping. No name searching.

Federal Courts in Idaho...

Standards for Federal Courts: The universal PACER sign-up number is 800-676-6856. Find PACER and the Party/Case Index on the Web at http://pacer.psc.uscourts.gov. PACER dial-up access is $.60 per minute. Also, courts offering internet access via RACER, PACER, Web-PACER or the new CM-ECF charge $.07 per page fee unless noted as free.

US District Court -- District of Idaho

Home Page: www.id.uscourts.gov

PACER: New civil records are available online after 2 days. New criminal records are available online after 1 day.

Opinions Online: Court opinions are available online at www.id.uscourts.gov.

Other Online Access: Search records online using RACER. Currently the system is free; visit www.id.uscourts.gov/doc.htm. Court does not participate in the U.S. party case index.

Boise Division counties: Ada, Adams, Blaine, Boise, Camas, Canyon, Cassia, Elmore, Gem, Gooding, Jerome, Lincoln, Minidoka, Owyhee, Payette, Twin Falls, Valley, Washington.

Coeur d' Alene Division counties: Benewah, Bonner, Boundary, Kootenai, Shoshone.

Moscow Division counties: Clearwater, Latah, Lewis, Nez Perce.

Pocatello Division counties: Bannock, Bear Lake, Bingham, Bonneville, Butte, Caribou, Clark, Custer, Franklin, Fremont, Idaho, Jefferson, Lemhi, Madison, Oneida, Power, Teton.

US Bankruptcy Court -- District of Idaho

Home Page: www.id.uscourts.gov

PACER: Sign-up number is 208-334-9342. Case records are available back to September 1990. Records are purged immediately when case closed. New civil records are available online after 1 day.

Opinions Online: Court opinions are available online at www.id.uscourts.gov.

Other Online Access: Search records online using RACER. Currently the system is free; visit www.id.uscourts.gov/doc.htm. Court does not participate in the U.S. party case index. **Also:** access via phone on VCIS (Voice Case Information System) is available: 208-334-9386.

Boise Division counties: Ada, Adams, Blaine, Boise, Camas, Canyon, Cassia, Elmore, Gem, Gooding, Jerome, Lincoln, Minidoka, Owyhee, Payette, Twin Falls, Valley, Washington.

Coeur d' Alene Division counties: Benewah, Bonner, Boundary, Kootenai, Shoshone.

Moscow Division counties: Clearwater, Idaho, Latah, Lewis, Nez Perce.

Pocatello Division counties: Bannock, Bear Lake, Bingham, Bonneville, Butte, Caribou, Clark, Custer, Franklin, Fremont, Jefferson, Lemhi, Madison, Oneida, Power, Teton.

Editor's Tip: The nine northern-most counties of Idaho are on Pacific Standard Time. The counties are Bonner, Boundary, Kootenai, Benewah, Shoshone, Latah, Clearwater, Nez Pierce and the northern half of Idaho County. The remainder of the state is on Mountain Standard Time.

Illinois

Capital: Springfield
          Sangamon County

Time Zone: CST

# of Counties: 102

Home Page   www.state.il.us

Attorney General   www.ag.state.il.us

Archives   www.sos.state.il.us/departments/archives/archives.html

State Level ... Major Agencies

Criminal Records

Illinois State Police, Bureau of Identification, 260 N Chicago St, Joliet, IL 60432-4075; 815-740-5216, 8AM-4PM M-F.

www.isp.state.il.us

Online access costs $7.00 per name. Upon signing an interagency agreement with ISP and establishing a $200 escrow account, users can submit inquiries over modem. Replies with convictions are returned by mail. Clear records can be returned via email, by request. Modem access is available from 7AM-4PM M-F, excluding holidays. Users must utilize LAPLINK version 6.0 or later. For more information on the Modem Porgram, call 815-740-5164.

Sexual Offender Registry

The state police also maintain the sex offender data for the state. The information may be searched online for no charge at http://samnet.isp.state.il.us/ispso2/sex_offenders/index.asp and also at http://12.17.79.4.

Incarceration Records

Information on current inmates is available is online from the Department of Corrections. Visit www.idoc.state.il.us. Location, conviction information, physical identifiers, and release dates are reported.

Corporation Records, Limited Partnership Records, Trade Names, Assumed Name, Limited Liability Company Records

Department of Business Services, Corporate Department, 330 Howlett Bldg, 3rd Floor, Copy Section, Springfield, IL 62756 (Courier: 501 S 2nd St, Springfield, IL 62756); 217-782-7880, 217-782-9521 (Name Availability), 217-782-4528 (Fax), 8AM-4:30PM.

www.sos.state.il.us

The web site gives free access to corporate and LLC records (no not-for-profit records). Search Corporate/LLC records at www.cyberdriveillinois.com/departments/business_services/corpstart.html. A commercial access program is also available. Fees vary. Potential users must submit in writing the purpose of the request. Submit to: Barbara Vincen, Dept. of Business Srvs, 330 Howlett Bldg, Springfield, IL 62756. Also, call 217-558-2116 for more information. **Other options:** List or bulk file purchases are available. Call 217-558-2116 for more information.

> **Editor's Note:** The Illinois Driver Services Department recently started a Pilot Project for online access to driving records. At this time the program is only available to those users who currently order at least 200 records per day.

Death Records

IL Department of Public Health, Division of Vital Records, 605 W Jefferson St, Springfield, IL 62702-5097; 217-782-6554, 217-782-6553 (Instructions), 217-523-2648 (Fax), 8AM-5PM.

www.idph.state.il.us/vital/vitalhome.htm

No online access available from this agency. However, the state archives database of Illinois Death Certificates 1918-1950 is available free at www.cyberdriveillinois.com/departments/archives/genealogy/forms/idphdeathsrch.html.

Legislation Records

www.legis.state.il.us

The Legislative Information System is available for subscription through a standard modem. The sign-up fee is $500.00 which includes 100 free minutes of access. Thereafter, access time is billed at $1.00 per minute. The hours of availability are 8 AM - 10 PM when in session and 8 AM - 5 PM when not in session, M-F. Contact Craig Garret at 217- 782-4083 to set-up an account. The Internet site offers free access but the state has a disclaimer which says the site should not be relied upon as an official record of action. **Other options:** A prepayment of $500.00 is required to obtain a printed copy of all bills.

State Level ... Occupational Licensing

Architect	www.dpr.state.il.us/licenselookup/default.asp
Athletic Trainer	www.dpr.state.il.us/licenselookup/default.asp
Attorney	www.iardc.org/lawyersearch.html
Bank	www.obre.state.il.us/CBT/REGENTY/Institution.asp?Inst=1
Barber	www.dpr.state.il.us/licenselookup/default.asp
Bilingual Teacher, Transitional	https://isbes1.isbe.net/tciscertificateinquiry/default.asp
Check Printer	www.obre.state.il.us/CBT/REGENTY/BTREGCHK.HTM
Chiropractor	www.dpr.state.il.us/licenselookup/default.asp
Collection Agency	www.dpr.state.il.us/licenselookup/default.asp
Controlled Substance Registrant	www.dpr.state.il.us/licenselookup/default.asp
Corporate Fiduciary	www.obre.state.il.us/CBT/REGENTY/usa.asp?State=N
Cosmetologist	www.dpr.state.il.us/licenselookup/default.asp
Counselor/Clinical Professional Counselor	www.dpr.state.il.us/licenselookup/default.asp
Dentist/Dental Hygienist	www.dpr.state.il.us/licenselookup/default.asp
Dietitian/Nutrition Counselor	www.dpr.state.il.us/licenselookup/default.asp
Drug Distributor, Wholesale	www.dpr.state.il.us/licenselookup/default.asp
Early Childhood Teacher	https://isbes1.isbe.net/tciscertificateinquiry/default.asp
Engineer	www.dpr.state.il.us/licenselookup/default.asp
Engineer, Structural	www.dpr.state.il.us/licenselookup/default.asp
Environmental Health Practitioner	www.dpr.state.il.us/licenselookup/default.asp
Esthetician	www.dpr.state.il.us/licenselookup/default.asp
Funeral Director/Embalmer	www.dpr.state.il.us/licenselookup/default.asp
High School Teacher	https://isbes1.isbe.net/tciscertificateinquiry/default.asp
HMO	www.state.il.us/INS/healthInsurance/HMO_by_County.htm
Insurance Producer	http://163.191.40.50:8080/ins/imsfor
Interior Designer	www.dpr.state.il.us/licenselookup/default.asp
Landscape Architect	www.dpr.state.il.us/licenselookup/default.asp
Lead Contractor	http://app.idph.state.il.us/Envhealth/Lead/Leadcnt.asp
Lead Risk Assessor/Inspector/Supervisor	http://app.idph.state.il.us/Envhealth/lead/Leadinsp.asp
Lead Training Provider	http://app.idph.state.il.us/Envhealth/lead/Leadinsp.asp
Liquor License, Retail/Dist./Mfg.	http://www2.state.il.us/lcc/license_search.asp
Lobbyist	www.cyberdriveillinois.com/cgi-bin/index/lobbysrch.s
Long Term Care Insurance Company	www.state.il.us/INS/ship/LTC_2002.pdf
Marriage & Family Therapist	www.dpr.state.il.us/licenselookup/default.asp

Medical Corporation	www.dpr.state.il.us/licenselookup/default.asp
Medical Doctor/Physician Assistant	www.dpr.state.il.us/licenselookup/default.asp
Mortgage Banker/Broker	www.obre.state.il.us/MBLookup/MBLookup.htm
Nail Technician	www.dpr.state.il.us/licenselookup/default.asp
Naprapath	www.dpr.state.il.us/licenselookup/default.asp
Nurse	www.dpr.state.il.us/licenselookup/default.asp
Nursing Home Administrator	www.medicare.gov/Nursing/Overview.asp
Occupational Therapist	www.dpr.state.il.us/licenselookup/default.asp
Optometrist	www.dpr.state.il.us/licenselookup/default.asp
Osteopathic Physician	www.dpr.state.il.us/licenselookup/default.asp
Pawnbroker	www.obre.state.il.us/CBT/REGENTY/Pawn.asp?County=N
Pharmacist/Pharmacy	www.dpr.state.il.us/licenselookup/default.asp
Physical Therapist	www.dpr.state.il.us/licenselookup/default.asp
Podiatrist	www.dpr.state.il.us/licenselookup/default.asp
Polygraph - Deception Detection Examiner	www.dpr.state.il.us/licenselookup/default.asp
Private Detective	www.dpr.state.il.us/licenselookup/default.asp
Private Security Contractor	www.dpr.state.il.us/licenselookup/default.asp
Psychologist	www.dpr.state.il.us/licenselookup/default.asp
Public Accountant-CPA	www.dpr.state.il.us/licenselookup/default.asp
Real Estate Appraiser	www.obre.state.il.us/lookup_c/
Real Estate Broker	www.obre.state.il.us/lookup_c/
Real Estate Salesperson	www.obre.state.il.us/lookup_c/
Roofer	www.dpr.state.il.us/licenselookup/default.asp
Sawmill	www.dnr.state.il.us/conservation/forestry/2002/SAWMILL.htm
Shorthand Reporter	www.dpr.state.il.us/licenselookup/default.asp
Social Worker	www.dpr.state.il.us/licenselookup/default.asp
Special Teacher	https://isbes1.isbe.net/tciscertificateinquiry/default.asp
Speech-Language Pathologist/Audiologist	www.dpr.state.il.us/licenselookup/default.asp
Substitute Teacher	https://isbes1.isbe.net/tciscertificateinquiry/default.asp
Surveyor, Land	www.dpr.state.il.us/licenselookup/default.asp
Teacher	https://isbes1.isbe.net/tciscertificateinquiry/default.asp
Trust Company	www.obre.state.il.us/CBT/REGENTY/BTREG.HTM
Veterinarian	www.dpr.state.il.us/licenselookup/default.asp

County Level ... Courts

Court Administration: Administrative Office of Courts, 222 N LaSalle 13th Floor, Chicago, IL, 60601; 312-793-3250.

Court Structure: Illinois is divided into 22 judicial circuits; 3 are single county: Cook, Du Page (18th Circuit) and Will (12th Circuit). The other 19 circuits consist of 2 or more contiguous counties. The Circuit Court of Cook County is the largest unified court system in the world. Its 2300-person staff handles approximately 2.4 million cases each year. The civil part of the various Circuit Courts in Cook County is divided as follows: under $30,000 are "civil cases" and over $30,000 are "civil law division cases." Probate is handled by the Circuit Court in all counties.

Online Access Note: While there is no statewide public online system available, a number of Illinois Circuit Courts offer online access. And, Judici.com offers free searching for a growing number of counties; the Judici.com home page also offers a commercial subscription service for multi-county searching.

Adams County
Circuit Court *Civil and Criminal Records*
www.co.adams.il.us
Online access to 8th Circuit Clerk of Court records available free at www.circuitclerk.co.adams.il.us/. Search by name, case or docket number.

Bureau County
Circuit Court *Civil and Criminal Records*

www.bccirclk.gov

Online access to judicial circuit records is available to local attorney firms and retrievers. The service is free. Call Clerk's office for details, 815-872-0027.

Carroll County
Circuit Court *Civil, Probate, Small Claim and Criminal Records*

Free access to criminal, civil, small claims, probate and traffic records available at www.judici.com/IL008015J/index.html.

Champaign County
Circuit Court *Civil and Criminal Records*

www.cccircuitclerk.com

Access to the remote online system called PASS requires a setup fee and annual user fee. Online case records go back to '92. Fee is $200 per year plus $25 per user; there are separate reduced fees for law firms and non-profits organizations. Contact Jo Kelly at 217-384-3767 for subscription information.

Cook County
Circuit Court - Chicago District 1 *Civil and Criminal Records*
Bridgeview District 5 *Civil and Criminal Records*
Markham District 6 *Civil and Criminal Records*
Maywood District 4 *Civil and Criminal Records*
Rolling Meadows District 3 *Civil and Criminal Records*
Skokie District 2 *Civil and Criminal Records*

www.cookcountyclerkofcourt.org

Online case searching for limited case information - case snapshots - is available free online at www.cookcountyclerkofcourt.org/Terms/terms.html. Search by name, case number or court date. Information includes parties (up to 3), attorneys, case type, the filing date, the ad damnum (amount of damages sought), division and district, and most current court date. Criminal records online are misdemeanor records only.

Grundy County
Circuit Court *Civil Records*

Online access to judicial circuit records should be available in 2002 for local attorney firms and retrievers. Service is free. Call the Clerk's office at 815-941-3256 for details.

Jackson County
Circuit Court *Civil, Probate, Small Claim, and Criminal Records*

www.circuitclerk.co.jackson.il.us

Free access to criminal, civil, small claims, probate and traffic records available at http://circuitclerk.co.jackson.il.us/.

Jo Daviess County
Circuit Court *Civil, Probate, Small Claim, and Criminal Records*

Free access to criminal civil, small claims, probate and traffic records available at www.judici.com/IL043015J/index.html.

La Salle County
Circuit Court *Civil and Criminal Records*

Online access to Judicial Circuit records requires a $200 setup fee (waived for not-for-profits) and $.10 per minute usage fee. Call the Clerk's office at 815-434-8671 for details.

Lee County
Circuit Court *Civil, Probate, Small Claim, and Criminal Records*

Free access to criminal, civil, small claims, probate and traffic records available at www.judici.com/IL052025J/index.html.

Logan County
Circuit Court *Civil, Probate, Small Claim, and Criminal Records*
www.co.logan.il.us/circuit_clerk/
Online access to criminal civil, small claims, probate and traffic records is available free at http://co.logan.il.us/circuit_clerk/. Click on search court cases.

McHenry County
Circuit Court *Civil, Probate, Domestic, and Criminal Records*
www.mchenrycircuitclerk.org
Access to records on the remote online system requires $750 license fee plus $50 per month. Records date back to 1991. Civil, criminal, probate, traffic, and domestic records are available. For more information, call 815-334-4193.

Macon County
Circuit Court *Civil and Criminal Records*
www.court.co.macon.il.us
Access to court records is available free online at the web site 24-hrs a day. Search docket information back to 04/96.

Montgomery County
Circuit Court *Civil and Criminal Records*
www.courts.montgomery.k12.il.us
Online access to court records is available at www.courts.montgomery.k12.il.us/CaseInfo.htm. Search by name or case number.

Ogle County
Circuit Court *Civil, Probate, Small Claim, and Criminal Records*
www.oglecounty.org/marty/circuitclerk.html
Free access to criminal, civil, small claims, probate and traffic records available at www.oglecounty.org. Click on "Search for Case Information."

Pike County
Circuit Court *Civil, Probate, Small Claim, and Criminal Records*
Free access to criminal, civil, small claims, probate and traffic records available at www.judici.com/IL075015J/index.html.

Rock Island County
Circuit Court *Civil, Probate, Domestic, and Criminal Records*
www.co.rock-island.il.us/Government/CircuitClk/CircuitClk.html
Access to records on the remote online system requires $200 setup fee plus a $1.00 per minute for access. Civil, criminal, probate, traffic, and domestic records can be accessed by name or case number.

Stephenson County
Circuit Court *Civil, Probate, Small Claim, and Criminal Records*
htto://www.judici.com
Free access to criminal, civil, small claims, probate and traffic records available at www.judici.com/IL089015J/index.html,

Winnebago County
Circuit Court *Civil and Criminal Records*
www.cc.co.winnebago.il.us
Online access to court records is via a subscription service; fee is $10 per month. Visit www.cc.co.winnebago.il.us/caseinfo.asp?P=I or call Wendi at 815- 987-3073 for information.

County Level ... Recorders & Assessors

Recording Office Organization: 102 counties, 103 recording offices. Cook County had separate offices for real estate recording and UCC filing until June 30, 2001. As of that date the UCC filing office only searches for pre-existing UCCs, and no longer takes new UCC filings. The recording officer is the Recorder of Deeds. Many counties utilize a grantor/grantee index containing all transactions. The entire state is in the Central Time Zone (CST). Federal tax liens on personal property of businesses are filed with the Secretary of State. Other federal and all state tax liens on personal property are filed with the County Recorder.

Online Access Note: A limited number of counties offer online access. There is no statewide system.

Cook County   *Property Tax Records*
www.cookcountyassessor.com
Records on the County Assessor Residential Assessment Search database are available free online at www.cookcountyassessor.com/startsearch.html. Search residential or non-residential properties.

Cook County Recorder   *Recorder, Deed, Grantor/Grantee, Heirs Records*
Search the DIMS database of the recordings since 10/1985; registration and fees apply. Includes Treasurer's Current Year Tax System (APIN) and DuPageCounty Recorder. Registration response form is at www.cookctyrecorder.com/remoteform.htm. Also, you may purchase the real estate transfer list; $100 per year on disk ($50 if you pick-up at agency.) Also, search the treasurer's heirs database free at www.cookcountytreasurer.com/info/estates/.

> **Editor's Note:** We have listed the Cook County Assessor and the Cook County Recorder as separate entries.

De Kalb County   *Real Estate, Lien Records*
The De Kalb County online system requires a $350 subscription fee, with a per minute charge of $.25, $.50 if printing. Records date back to 1980. Lending agency information is available. For further information, contact Sheila Larson at 815-895-7152.

Du Page County   *Real Estate, Lien, Tax Assessor Records*
www.dupageco.org/recorder/index.html
For access to the Du Page County database one must lease a live interface telephone line from a carrier to establish a connection. Additionally, there is a fee of $.05 per transaction. Records date back to 1977. For information, contact Fred Kieltcka at 630-682-7030. Free access via the Internet may now be available; visit the web site. Online access to the sheriff's sex offenders, most wanted, and deadbeat parents lists are available free at www.co.dupage.il.us/sheriff/

Gallatin County   *Property Records*
Search for propety information on the GIS-mapping site for free at www.co.gallatin.mt.us/GIS/index.htm. No name searching.

Henry County   *Assessor Records*
www.henrycty.com/recorder/index.html
Access to the assessor database is available free at www.henrycty.com/assessor/search.asp. Also, the county most wanted/fugitive list is available at www.henrycty.com/sheriff/fugitives.html.

La Salle County   *Real Estate, Assessor Records*
www.lasallecounty.org/Final/contents2.htm
Assessor/property records on the County Assessor database are available online at www.lasallecounty.org/cidnet/asrpfull.htm. Registration and password required; there is a $200.00 per year fee, plus per minute charges. For information, phone 815-434-8233. Also, last 2 years assessment data can be accessed online free at www.lasallecounty.org/contents3.htm. Parcel number is required.

McHenry County *Assessor/Treasurer Records*
Records on the County Treasurer Inquiry site are available free online at http://209.172.155.14/cidnet.publictre1.htm.

McLean County   *Assessor, Property, Treasurer Tax Bill, Sex Offender, Assumed Name Records*
www.mclean.gov/
Access to the county Tax Bill Information Lookup database is available free at www.mclean.gov/Treasurer/2ndInstallmentSearch.asp. No name searching; parcel number or street name and city required. Also, access to the Township of Normal assessor database is available free at www.normaltownship.org/Assessor/ParcelSearch.php. No name searching; parcel number or address required. Also, search the sex offender data at www.mclean.gov/sheriff/SexOffenderPage.htm. Also, search the assumed named list at www.mclean.gov/CountyClerk/CountyClerkAssumedNamesMain.asp. Search election officials by precinct at the web site.

Stark County   *Unclaimed Funds Records*
www.starkcourt.org
Access to the county clerk of courts unclaimed funds database are available at www.starkcourt.org/cgi-bin/starkcrt/pdfarchive/uf_pdflist.cgi. File is in pdf format.

Wayne County   *Assessor, Property Records*
http://assessor.wayne.il.us/Index.html
Records on the Wayne Township Assessor Office database are available free online at http://assessor.wayne.il.us/OPID.html. Also, an advanced search feature (fee) is available for subscribers. This includes legal, assessment, sales history, buildings and other information.

Winnebago County   *Property, UCC Records*
Access to county land and UCC records is available free at www.landaccess.com.

Federal Courts in Illinois...

Standards for Federal Courts: The universal PACER sign-up number is 800-676-6856. Find PACER and the Party/Case Index on the Web at http://pacer.psc.uscourts.gov. PACER dial-up access is $.60 per minute. Also, courts offering internet access via RACER, PACER, Web-PACER or the new CM-ECF charge $.07 per page fee unless noted as free.

US District Court -- Central District of Illinois
Home Page: www.ilcd.uscourts.gov
PACER: Toll-free access: 800-258-3678. Local access phone: 217-492-4997. Case records are available back to 1995. Records are purged after 5-7 years. New records are available online after 1 day. **PACER URL:** http://pacer.ilcd.uscourts.gov.
Danville/Urbana Division counties: Champaign, Coles, Douglas, Edgar, Ford, Iroquois, Kankakee, Macon, Moultrie, Piatt, Vermilion.
Peoria Division counties: Bureau, Fulton, Hancock, Knox, Livingston, McDonough, McLean, Marshall, Peoria, Putnam, Stark, Tazewell, Woodford.
Rock Island Division counties: Henderson, Henry, Mercer, Rock Island, Warren.
Springfield Division counties: Adams, Brown, Cass, Christian, De Witt, Greene, Logan, Macoupin, Mason, Menard, Montgomery, Morgan, Pike, Sangamon, Schuyler, Scott, Shelby.

US Bankruptcy Court -- Central District of Illinois
Home Page: www.ilcb.uscourts.gov
PACER: Toll-free access: 800-454-9893. Local access phone: 217-492-4260. Case records are available back to 1989-90. Records are purged immediately when case is closed. New civil records are available online after 2 days. **PACER URL:** http://pacer.ilcb.uscourts.gov. **Also:** access via phone on VCIS (Voice Case Information System) is available: 800-827-9005, 217-492-4550
Danville Division counties: Champaign, Coles, Douglas, Edgar, Ford, Iroquois, Kankakee, Livingston, Moultrie, Piatt, Vermilion.
Peoria Division counties: Bureau, Fulton, Hancock, Henderson, Henry, Knox, Marshall, McDonough, Mercer, Peoria, Putnam, Rock Island, Stark, Tazewell, Warren, Woodford.
Springfield Division counties: Adams, Brown, Cass, Christian, De Witt, Greene, Logan, Macon, Macoupin, Mason, McLean, Menard, Montgomery, Morgan, Pike, Sangamon, Schuyler, Scott, Shelby.

US District Court -- Northern District of Illinois

Home Page: www.ilnd.uscourts.gov

PACER: Toll-free access: 800-621-7029. Local access phone: 312-408-7777. Case records are available back to 1988. Records are purged varies. New records are available online after 1-2 days. **PACER URL:** http://pacer.ilnd.uscourts.gov. Document images available.

Chicago (Eastern) Division counties: Cook, Du Page, Grundy, Kane, Kendall, Lake, La Salle, Will.

Rockford Division counties: Boone, Carroll, De Kalb, Jo Daviess, Lee, McHenry, Ogle, Stephenson, Whiteside, Winnebago.

US Bankruptcy Court -- Northern District of Illinois

Home Page: www.ilnb.uscourts.gov

PACER: Toll-free access: 888-541-1078. Local access phone: 312-408-5101. Document images available on Pacer. Case records are available back to July 1, 1993. Records are purged never. New civil records are available online after 1 day. **PACER URL:** Online access to PACER/RACER is available at the web site. Access fee is 7 cents per document.

Electronic Filing: (Currently in the process of implementing CM/ECF).

Other Online Access: Case Image Viewing is available from 5 a.m. to 11:59 p.m. CST at www.ilnb.uscourts.gov/casenotice.htm. Access fee is $.07 per page. **Also:** access via phone on VCIS (Voice Case Information System) is available: 888-232-6814, 312-408-5089

Chicago (Eastern) Division counties: Cook, Du Page, Grundy, Kane, Kendall, La Salle, Lake, Will.

Rockford Division counties: Boone, Carroll, De Kalb, Jo Daviess, Lee, McHenry, Ogle, Stephenson, Whiteside, Winnebago.

US District Court -- Southern District of Illinois

Home Page: www.ilsd.uscourts.gov

PACER: Case records are available back to 1985. Records are purged when deemed necessary. New civil records are available online after 1 day. New criminal records are available online after 1-2 days. **PACER URL:** http://pacer.ilsd.uscourts.gov.

Benton Division counties: Alexander, Clark, Clay, Crawford, Cumberland, Edwards, Effingham, Franklin, Gallatin, Hamilton, Hardin, Jackson, Jasper, Jefferson, Johnson, Lawrence, Massac, Perry, Pope, Pulaski, Richland, Saline, Union, Wabash, Wayne, White, Williamson. Cases may also be allocated to the Benton Division.

East St Louis Division counties: Bond, Calhoun, Clinton, Fayette, Jersey, Madison, Marion, Monroe, Randolph, St. Clair, Washington. Cases for these counties may also be allocated to the Benton Division.

US Bankruptcy Court -- Southern District of Illinois

Home Page: www.ilsb.uscourts.gov

PACER: Case records are available back to January 1989. Records are purged as deemed necessary. New civil records are available online after 1 day. **PACER URL:** http://pacer.ilsb.uscourts.gov.

Electronic Filing: Electronic filing information is available online at https://ecf.ilsb.uscourts.gov. **Also:** access via phone on VCIS (Voice Case Information System) is available: 800-726-5622, 618-482-9365

Benton Division counties: Alexander, Edwards, Franklin, Gallatin, Hamilton, Hardin, Jackson, Jefferson, Johnson, Massac, Perry, Pope, Pulaski, Randolph, Saline, Union, Wabash, Washington, Wayne, White, Williamson.

East St Louis Division counties: Bond, Calhoun, Clark, Clay, Clinton, Crawford, Cumberland, Effingham, Fayette, Jasper, Jersey, Lawrence, Madison, Marion, Monroe, Richland, St. Clair.

Capital: Indianapolis
Marion County

Time Zone: EST/CST

Number of Counties: 92

Home Page www.state.in.us

Attorney General

www.in.gov/attorneygeneral

Archives www.in.gov/icpr/

State Level ... Major Agencies

Criminal Records

Indiana State Police, Central Records, IGCN - 100 N Senate Ave Room 302, Indianapolis, IN 46204-2259; 317-232-8266, 8AM-4:30PM.

www.IN.gov/isp/

Subcribers to accessIndiana can obtain limited records for $22.50 per search. Go to www.in.gov/isp/lch/centralsearch.html.

Sexual Offender Registry

Sex offender data is available online at www.state.in.us/serv/cji_sor, and maintained by the Indiana Department of Corrections. Phone requests can be made to 317-232-1233.

Incarceration Records

Search online at www.in.gov/indcorrection; provide either full name or inmate number.

Corporation Records, Limited Partnerships, Fictitious Name, Assumed Name, Limited Liability Company Records, Limited Liability Partnerships

Corporation Division, Secretary of State, 302 W Washington St, Room E018, Indianapolis, IN 46204; 317-232-6576, 317-233-3387 (Fax), 8AM-5:30PM M-F.

www.IN.gov/sos/

This subscription service is available from the Access Indiana Information Network (AI) gateway on the Internet. There is no fee to view a partial record, but $1.00 to view a screen containing the registered agent and other information. Go to www.ai.org. **Other options:** Monthly lists of all new businesses are available online, as are bulk data and specialized searches.

Uniform Commercial Code

UCC Division, Secretary of State, 302 West Washington St, Room E-018, Indianapolis, IN 46204; 317-233-3984, 317-233-3387 (Fax), 8AM-5:30PM.

www.in.gov/sos/business/ucc.html

You may browse lien records at https://www.ai.org/sos/bus_service/online_ucc/browse/default.asp. There is no charge. An offical search may be performed online via an AccessIndiana account for $3.00 per record (plus $4.40 for use of credit card, if desired). Plans are underway to offer filing services also.

Birth Certificates

State Department of Health, Vital Records Office, PO Box 7125, Indianapolis, IN 46206-7125 (Courier: 2 N. Meridian, Indianapolis, IN 46204); 317-233-2700, 317-233-7210 (Fax), 8:15AM-4:45PM.

www.in.gov/isdh/index.htm

Records may be ordered online via the web site, but the requester must still fax a photo copy of an ID before the record request is processed.

Driver Records

BMV-Driving Records, 100 N Senate Ave, Indiana Government Center North, Room N405, Indianapolis, IN 46204; 317-232-6000 x2, 8:15AM-4:30PM.

www.in.gov/bmv/

Access Indiana Information Network (AIIN) is the state owned interactive information and communication system which provides batch and interactive access to driving records. There is an annual $50.00 fee. Online access costs $5.00 per record. For more information, call AIIN at 317-233-2010 or go to www.ai.org

Vehicle Ownership, Vehicle Identification, Vessel Ownership, Vessel Registration

Bureau of Motor Vehicles, Records, 100 N Senate Ave, Room N404, Indianapolis, IN 46204; 317-233-6000, 8:15AM-4:45PM.

www.in.gov/bmv/

The Access Indiana Information network (AIIN) at 317-233-2010 is the state appointed vendor. The fee is $5.00 per record plus an annual fee of $50.00. Visit www.ai.org for more information. **Other options:** Bulk record requests are not available from Indiana.

Legislation Records

www.in.gov/legislative/

All legislative information is available over the Internet. The Indiana Code is also available.

State Level ... Occupational Licensing

Athletic Trainer	www.state.in.us/hpb/mlvs/index.html
Audiologist	www.state.in.us/hpb/mlvs/index.html
Child Care Center	www.carefinderindiana.org/carefinder/LicStatus.htm
Child Care Home	www.carefinderindiana.org/carefinder/LicStatus.htm
Child Care Provider	www.carefinderindiana.org/carefinder/LicStatus.htm
Chiropractor	www.state.in.us/hpb/mlvs/index.html
Collection Agency	www.in.gov/serv/sos_securities
Dental Hygienist	www.state.in.us/hpb/mlvs/index.html
Dentist	www.state.in.us/hpb/mlvs/index.html
Dietitian	www.state.in.us/hpb/mlvs/index.html
Emergency Medical Technician	www.state.in.us/hpb/mlvs/index.html
Environmental Health	www.state.in.us/hpb/mlvs/index.html
Hazardous Waste Facility/Handler	www.in.gov/idem/land/permits/lists/index.html

Health Services Administrator.......................................www.state.in.us/hpb/mlvs/index.html
Hearing Aid Dealer...www.state.in.us/hpb/mlvs/index.html
Hypnotist...www.state.in.us/hpb/mlvs/index.html
Insurance Agent/Consultant ....www.in.gov/idoi/
Investment Advisor ....www.in.gov/serv/sos_securities
Loan Brokers...www.in.gov/serv/sos_securities
Marriage & Family Therapist ....www.state.in.us/hpb/mlvs/index.html
Medical Doctor..www.state.in.us/hpb/mlvs/index.html
Mental Health Counselor...www.state.in.us/hpb/mlvs/index.html
Midwife Nurse...www.state.in.us/hpb/mlvs/index.html
Notary Public ....www.ai.org/serv/sos_notary
Nurse...www.state.in.us/hpb/mlvs/index.html
Nurse-RN/LPN...www.state.in.us/hpb/mlvs/index.html
Nursing Home Administrator ....www.state.in.us/hpb/mlvs/index.html
Occupational Therapist ....www.state.in.us/hpb/mlvs/index.html
Optometrist..www.state.in.us/hpb/mlvs/index.html
Osteopathic Physician ....www.state.in.us/hpb/mlvs/index.html
Pharmacist/Pharmacist Intern ....www.state.in.us/hpb/mlvs/index.html
Physical Therapist/Therapist Asst ....www.state.in.us/hpb/mlvs/index.html
Physician ....www.state.in.us/hpb/mlvs/index.html
Physician Assistant...www.state.in.us/hpb/mlvs/index.html
Podiatrist ....www.state.in.us/hpb/mlvs/index.html
Polygraph Examiner ....www.indianapolygraphassociation.com
Psychologist ....www.state.in.us/hpb/mlvs/index.html
Real Estate Appraiser ....www.asc.gov/content/category1/appr_by_state.asp
Respiratory Care Practitioner ....www.state.in.us/hpb/mlvs/index.html
Securities Broker/Dealer...www.in.gov/serv/sos_securities
Securities Sales Agent ....www.in.gov/serv/sos_securities
Social Worker..www.state.in.us/hpb/mlvs/index.html
Social Worker, Clinical ....www.state.in.us/hpb/mlvs/index.html
Solid Waste Facility ....www.in.gov/idem/land/permits/lists/index.html
Speech Pathologist ....www.state.in.us/hpb/mlvs/index.html
Teacher..http://dew4.doe.state.in.us/LIC/license.html
Veterinarian...www.state.in.us/hpb/mlvs/index.html
Waste Tire Processor/Transporter...............................www.in.gov/idem/land/permits/lists/index.html
Yard Waste Composting Facility................................www.in.gov/idem/land/permits/lists/index.html

County Level ... Courts

Court Administration: State Court Administrator, 115 W Washington St Suite 1080, Indianapolis, IN, 46204; 317-232-2542; www.IN.gov/judiciary

Court Structure: There are 92 judicial circuits with Circuit Courts or Combined Circuit and Superior Courts. In addition, there are 48 City Courts and 25 Town Courts. County Courts are gradually being restructured into divisions of the Superior Courts. Note that Small Claims in Marion County are heard at the township and records are maintained at that level. The Circuit Court Clerk/County Clerk in every county is the same individual and is responsible for keeping all county judicial records. However, it is recommended that, when requesting a record, the request indicate which court heard the case (Circuit, Superior, or County).

Online Access Note: There is no statewide online access system available to the public. Three counties do offer online access to records.

Delaware County
Circuit Court *Criminal Records*
www.dcclerk.org

Online access to criminal records from 1850 to 1950 only is available free at www.munpl.org/Main_Pages/documents.htm, the Muncie Public Library web site.

Marion County

Circuit & Superior Court *Civil and Criminal Records*

www.indygov.org/clerk

Access to civil and criminal records is at www.civicnet.net. A $50 setup fee gives free access to index, but file copy fees vary from $2.-$5. Non-subscribers may use a credit card and search for $4.50 per name. Criminal records go back to 1988.

Tippecanoe County

Circuit, Superior & County Court *Civil and Criminal Records*

www.county.tippecanoe.in.us

Online access to court records through CourtView are available free online at http://court.county.tippecanoe.in.us/pa/pa.htm.

County Level ... Recorders & Assessors

Recording Office Organization: 92 counties, 92 recording offices. The recording officer is the County Recorder (or the Circuit Clerk for state tax liens on personal property). Many counties utilize a "Miscellaneous Index" for tax and other liens. 81 counties are in the Eastern Time Zone (EST), and 11 are in the Central Time Zone (CST). All federal tax liens on personal property are filed with the County Recorder. State tax liens on personal property are filed with the Circuit Clerk who is in a different office from the Recorder. Most counties will not perform tax lien searches.

Online Access Note: Very few county agencies offer online access. The most notable is the subscription service offered by Marion County at www.civicnet.net.

Elkhart County   *Real Estate, Lien, Tax Assessor Records*

www.elkhartcountygov.com/administrative

Access to Elkhart County records is available for an annual fee of $50. plus a minimum of $20 per month of use. The minimum fee allows for 2 hours access, and additional use is billed at $10 per hour. Lending agency information is available. For information, call at 574-535-6777.

Marion County   *Real Estate, Lien Records*

Access to Marion County online records requires a $200 set up fee, plus an escrow balance of at least $100 must be maintained. Additional charges are $.50 per minute, $.25 display charge for first page; $.10 each add'l page. Records date back to 1987; images from 2/24/93. Federal tax liens and UCC information are available. For information, contact Mike Kerner at 317-327-4587.

St. Joseph County   *Land, Most Wanted Records*

www.indico.net/counties/STJOSEPH/

Access to county land information is available via a private company using Tapestry at https://www.landrecords.net/. Registration and credit card required; casual requesters permitted. Also, access to the county sheriff most wanted list is at www.skyenet.net/cstoppers/mostwanted/mostwant.html

Tippecanoe County   *Property Records*

http://county.tippecanoe.in.us

Access to property information on the county gis-mapping site is available free at http://gis.county.tippecanoe.in.us/gis/app12/index.html

Vanderburgh County   *Property Records*

www.assessor.evansville.net

Records on the County Assessor Property database are available free online at www.assessor.evansville.net/disclaim.htm.

Wayne County   *Marriage Records*

www.co.wayne.in.us/offices

Marriage records are being added irregularly to the web site at www.co.wayne.in.us/marriage/retrieve.cgi. Records are from 1811 forward, with recent years being added.

Federal Courts in Indiana...

Standards for Federal Courts: The universal PACER sign-up number is 800-676-6856. Find PACER and the Party/Case Index on the Web at http://pacer.psc.uscourts.gov. PACER dial-up access is $.60 per minute. Also, courts offering internet access via RACER, PACER, Web-PACER or the new CM-ECF charge $.07 per page fee unless noted as free.

US District Court -- Northern District of Indiana

Home Page: www.innd.uscourts.gov

PACER: Toll-free access: 800-371-8843. Local access phone: 574-246-8200. Case records are available back to 1994. Records are purged as deemed necessary. New records are available online after 2 days. **PACER URL:** http://pacer.innd.uscourts.gov.

Fort Wayne Division counties: Adams, Allen, Blackford, DeKalb, Grant, Huntington, Jay, Lagrange, Noble, Steuben, Wells, Whitley.

Hammond Division counties: Lake, Porter.

Lafayette Division counties: Benton, Carroll, Jasper, Newton, Tippecanoe, Warren, White.

South Bend Division counties: Cass, Elkhart, Fulton, Kosciusko, La Porte, Marshall, Miami, Pulaski, St. Joseph, Starke, Wabash.

US Bankruptcy Court -- Northern District of Indiana

Home Page: www.innb.uscourts.gov

PACER: Toll-free access: 888-917-2237. Local access phone: 574-968-2270. Case records are available back to 1992. Records are purged every 6 months. New civil records are available online after 2 days. **PACER URL:** http://pacer.innb.uscourts.gov.

Electronic Filing: (Currently in the process of implementing CM/ECF). **Also:** access via phone on VCIS (Voice Case Information System) is available: 800-755-8393, 574-236-8814

Fort Wayne Division counties: Adams, Allen, Blackford, DeKalb, Grant, Huntington, Jay, Lagrange, Noble, Steuben, Wells, Whitley.

Hammond at Gary Division counties: Lake, Porter.

Hammond at Lafayette Division counties: Benton, Carroll, Jasper, Newton, Tippecanoe, Warren, White.

South Bend Division counties: Cass, Elkhart, Fulton, Kosciusko, La Porte, Marshall, Miami, Pulaski, St. Joseph, Starke, Wabash.

US District Court -- Southern District of Indiana

Home Page: www.insd.uscourts.gov

Electronic Filing: (Currently in the process of implementing CM/ECF).

Other Online Access: Search records for free on the Internet; visit www.insd.uscourts.gov/casesearch.htm to search. Court does not participate in the U.S. party case index.

Evansville Division counties: Daviess, Dubois, Gibson, Martin, Perry, Pike, Posey, Spencer, Vanderburgh, Warrick.

Indianapolis Division counties: Bartholomew, Boone, Brown, Clinton, Decatur, Delaware, Fayette, Fountain, Franklin, Hamilton, Hancock, Hendricks, Henry, Howard, Johnson, Madison, Marion, Monroe, Montgomery, Morgan, Randolph, Rush, Shelby, Tipton, Union, Wayne.

New Albany Division counties: Clark, Crawford, Dearborn, Floyd, Harrison, Jackson, Jefferson, Jennings, Lawrence, Ohio, Orange, Ripley, Scott, Switzerland, Washington.

Terre Haute Division counties: Clay, Greene, Knox, Owen, Parke, Putnam, Sullivan, Vermillion, Vigo.

US Bankruptcy Court -- Southern District of Indiana

Home Page: www.insb.uscourts.gov

PACER: Sign-up number is 317-229-3845. Case records are available back to 1988. Records are purged every 3 months. New civil records are available online after 2-3 days. **PACER UR:** www.insb.uscourts.gov. Click on "Case Search." Registration and fees now required. The free case lookup system is no longer found.

Other Online Access: Court does not participate in the U.S. party case index. **Also:** access via phone on VCIS (Voice Case Information System) is available: 800-335-8003.

Evansville Division counties: Daviess, Dubois, Gibson, Martin, Perry, Pike, Posey, Spencer, Vanderburgh, Warrick.

Indianapolis Division counties: Bartholomew, Boone, Brown, Clinton, Decatur, Delaware, Fayette, Fountain, Franklin, Hamilton, Hancock, Hendricks, Henry, Howard, Johnson, Madison, Marion, Monroe, Montgomery, Morgan, Randolph, Rush, Shelby, Tipton, Union, Wayne.

New Albany Division counties: Clark, Crawford, Dearborn, Floyd, Harrison, Jackson, Jefferson, Jennings, Lawrence, Ohio, Orange, Ripley, Scott, Switzerland, Washington.

Terre Haute Division counties: Clay, Greene, Knox, Owen, Parke, Putnam, Sullivan, Vermillion, Vigo.

Capital: Des Moines
                Polk County

Time Zone: CST

Number of Counties: 99

Home Page   www.state.ia.us

Attorney General   www.state.ia.us/government/ag

Archives   www.iowahistory.org

State Level ... Major Agencies

Criminal Records

Division of Criminal Investigations, Bureau of Identification, Wallace State Office Bldg, Des Moines, IA 50309; 515-281-4776, 515-281-7996, 515-242-6297 (Fax), 8AM-4:30PM.

www.state.ia.us/government/dps/dci/crimhist.htm

Although this agency does not offer online access, there is online free access to the statewide Iowa Judicial System courts database at www.judicial.state.ia.us/online_records/

Sexual Offender Registry

The Iowa Sex Offender Registry, maintained by the Division of Criminal Investigations, can be searched at www.state.ia.us/government/dps/dci/isor/ and at www.iowasexoffender.com. Only high-risk offenders are listed. The entire database may be searched at a local police or sheriff's department.

Corporation Records, Limited Liability Company Records, Fictitious Name, Limited Partnership Records, Trademarks/Servicemarks

Secretary of State, Corporation Div., 2nd Fl, Hoover Bldg, Des Moines, IA 50319; 515-281-5204, 515-242-5953 Fax, 8AM-4:30PM.

www.sos.state.ia.us

For free searching, go to www.sos.state.ia.us/corp/corp_search.asp. **Other options:** The state will sell the records in database format. Call the number listed above and ask for Karen Ubaldo for more information.

Uniform Commercial Code, Federal Tax Liens

UCC Division, Secretary of State, Hoover Bldg, 2nd Floor, Des Moines, IA 50319; 515-281-5204, 515-242-5953 (Other Fax Line), 515-242-6556 (Fax), 8AM-4:30PM.

www.sos.state.ia.us

All computerized information on or before June 30, 2001 is available online at www.sos.state.ia.us/UCC_Search/UccOld_Search.asp. There is no fee at this "UCC Archive" site. For computerized records online from July 1, 2001 to present, you may search at www.sos.state.ia.us/UCC_Search/UCC_Search.asp

Sales Tax Registrations

Department of Revenue, Taxpayer Services Division, Hoover State Office Bldg, Des Moines, IA 50306-0465; 515-281-3114, 515-242-6487 (Fax), 8AM-4PM.

www.state.ia.us/tax

One may check the status of a permit online, but the permit number is needed (no name searching). **Other options:** The agency will provide the database on lists, fees vary from $20.00 to $45.00.

Legislation Records

www.legis.state.ia.us

Access is available through the Legislative Computer Support Bureau web site. **Other options:** The state sells a weekly summary called the Session Brief. The fee is $10.60.

State Level ... Occupational Licensing

Acupuncturist	www.docboard.org/ia/find_ia.htm
Apiary	www.agriculture.state.ia.us/apiary.html
Architect	www.state.ia.us/government/com/prof/search.htm
Bank	www.idob.state.ia.us
Credit Union	www.iacudiv.state.ia.us/Public/fieldofmembership/membersearch.htm
Debt Management Company	www.idob.state.ia.us/license/lic_default.htm
Delayed Deposit Service Business	www.idob.state.ia.us/license/lic_default.htm
Engineer	www.state.ia.us/government/com/prof/search.htm
Finance Company	www.idob.state.ia.us/license/lic_default.htm
Landscape Architect	www.state.ia.us/government/com/prof/lands/lanscros.htm
Medical Doctor	www.docboard.org/ia/find_ia.htm
Money Transmitter	www.idob.state.ia.us/license/lic_default.htm
Mortgage Banker/Broker	www.idob.state.ia.us/license/lic_default.htm
Mortgage Loan Service	www.idob.state.ia.us/license/lic_default.htm
Notary Public	www.sos.state.ia.us/NotaryWeb
Nurse	www.state.ia.us/nursing/Licensure.html
Nurse, Advance Registered Practice	www.state.ia.us/nursing/Licensure.html
Nurse-LPN	www.state.ia.us/nursing/Licensure.html
Optometrist	www.odfinder.org/LicSearch.asp
Osteopathic Physician	www.docboard.org/ia/find_ia.htm
Public Accountant-CPA	www.state.ia.us/government/com/prof/search.htm
Real Estate Appraiser	www.state.ia.us/government/com/prof/search.htm
Real Estate Broker/Salesperson	www.state.ia.us/government/com/prof/search.htm
Surveyor, Land	www.state.ia.us/government/com/prof/search.htm
Trust Company	www.idob.state.ia.us/license/lic_default.htm

County Level ... Courts

Court Administration: State Court Administrator, State Capitol, Des Moines, IA, 50319; 515-281-5241; www.judicial.state.ia.us

Court Structure: The District Court is the court of general jurisdiction. Most courts do not do searches and recommend either in person searches or use of a record retriever. Courts that accept written search requests usually require an SASE. Most courts have a public access terminal for access to that court's records.

Online Access Note: Criminal, civil, probate, traffic and appellate information is available from all 99 counties in Iowa at www.judicial.state.ia.us/online_records/. The Iowa Courts Online site is providing basic case information for no charge; a more extensive fee portion will be available in the near future. Name searches are available on a statewide or specific county basis. While this is an excellent site with much information, there is one important consideration to keep in mind: although records are updated daily, the historical records offered are not from the same starting date on a county-by-county basis. Over 40% of the counties do not go back more than 7 years.

Statewide Access – All Counties

Criminal, civil, probate, traffic and appellate information is available from all 99 counties in Iowa at www.judicial.state.ia.us/online_records/. See the information above for details.

County Level ... Recorders & Assessors

Recording Office Organization: 99 counties, 100 recording offices. Lee County has two recording offices. The recording officer is the County Recorder. Many counties utilize a grantor/grantee index containing all transactions recorded with them. The entire state is in the Central Time Zone (CST). Federal tax liens on personal property of businesses are filed with the Secretary of State. Other federal and all state tax liens on personal property are filed with the County Recorder. County search practices vary widely but most provide some sort of tax lien search for $6.00 per name.

Online Access Note: A few counties offer online access. There is no statewide access to county recorder data.

Buena Vista County   *Property Assessor, Ag Sales, Jail Inmate, Accident, Incident Records*

Search the property assessor and Ag sales databases for free at www.co.buena-vista.ia.us/assessors/. No name searching. Also, search the jail inmates list for free at www.bvsheriff.com/jailroster/index.html. also, search accident/incident reports for free at www.bvsheriff.com/accident-incident/index.html.

Emmet County   *Real Estate Records*

Access to real estate records on the county database are available free at www.emmet.org/pmc. Also, the GIS mapping database may be searched. Includes parcel report, survey section grid, parcel maps, and more. Search the "Parcel Data" link by owner name, parcel ID, or address.

Marshall County   *Assessor, Property Records*

www.co.marshall.ia.us
Access to the accessor's property record card system is available free at www.co.marshall.ia.us/assessor/prcsystem.html.

Polk County   *Assessor, Property Records*

www.co.polk.ia.us
Access to the Polk County assessor database is available free at www.co.polk.ia.us/departments/assessor/assessor.htm. Search by property or by sales.

Pottawattamie County   *Real Estate, Property, Residential Sales Records*

www.pottco.org
Records on the Pottawattamie County Courthouse/Council Bluffs property database are available free at www.pottco.org. Search by owner name, address, or parcel number. Records of the Pottawattamie County Assessor "Residential Sales" database are available free online at www.pottco.org/htdocs/assessor.html.

Sioux County   *Tax Sales Records*

Search the treasurer's delinquent tax list for free at www.court-house.co.sioux.ia.us/pdf/taxlist.pdf. Site may be down.

Story County   *Assessor Records*

www.storycounty.com/departments.html
Records on the county assessor database are available free online at www.storyassessor.org/pmc/query.asp.

Federal Courts in Iowa...

Standards for Federal Courts: The universal PACER sign-up number is 800-676-6856. Find PACER and the Party/Case Index on the Web at http://pacer.psc.uscourts.gov. PACER dial-up access is $.60 per minute. Also, courts offering internet access via RACER, PACER, Web-PACER or the new CM-ECF charge $.07 per page fee unless noted as free.

US District Court -- Northern District of Iowa

Home Page: www.iand.uscourts.gov

PACER: Sign-up number is 800-676-5856. Toll-free access: 888-845-4528. Local access phone: 319-362-3256. Case records are available back to November 1992. New records are available online after 1 day. **PACER URL:** http://pacer.iand.uscourts.gov.

Electronic Filing: Electronic filing information is available online at (CM/ECF available Summer, 2002).

Cedar Rapids Division counties: Benton, Cedar, Cerro Gordo, Grundy, Hardin, Iowa, Jones, Linn, Tama.

Dubuque Division counties: Allamakee, Black Hawk, Bremer, Buchanan, Chickasaw, Clayton, Delaware, Dubuque, Fayette, Floyd, Howard, Jackson, Mitchell, Winneshiek.

Sioux City Division counties: Buena Vista, Cherokee, Clay, Crawford, Dickinson, Ida, Lyon, Monona, O'Brien, Osceola, Plymouth, Sac, Sioux, Woodbury.

US Bankruptcy Court -- Northern District of Iowa

Home Page: www.ianb.uscourts.gov **PACER URL:** http://pacer.ianb.uscourts.gov. Document images available.

Electronic Filing: Electronic filing information is available online at https://ecf.ianb.uscourts.gov. **Also:** access via phone on VCIS (Voice Case Information System) is available: 800-249-9859, 319-362-9906

Cedar Rapids Division counties: Allamakee, Benton, Black Hawk, Bremer, Buchanan, Buena Vista, Butler, Calhoun, Carroll, Cedar, Cerro Gordo, Cherokee, Chickasaw, Clay, Clayton, Crawford, Delaware, Dickinson, Dubuque, Emmet, Fayette, Floyd, Franklin, Grundy, Hamilton, Hancock, Hardin,Howard, Humboldt, Ida, Iowa, Jackson, Jones, Kossuth, Linn, Lyon, Mitchell, Monona, O'Brien, Osceola, Palo Alto, Plymouth, Pocahontas, Sac, Sioux, Tama, Webster, Winnebago, Winneshiek, Woodbury, Worth, Wright.

US District Court -- Southern District of Iowa

Home Page: www.iasd.uscourts.gov

PACER: Case records are available back to mid 1989. Records are purged every six months. New records are available online after 3 days. **PACER URL:** http://pacer.iasd.uscourts.gov. Document images available.

Other Online Access: The RACER system is now administered by PACER. Fee is $.07 per page.

Council Bluffs (Western) Division counties: Audubon, Cass, Fremont, Harrison, Mills, Montgomery, Page, Pottawattamie, Shelby.

Davenport (Eastern) Division counties: Henry, Johnson, Lee, Louisa, Muscatine, Scott, Van Buren, Washington.

Des Moines (Central) Division counties: Adair, Adams, Appanoose, Boone, Clarke, Clinton, Dallas, Davis, Decatur, Des Moines, Greene, Guthrie, Jasper, Jefferson, Keokuk, Lucas, Madison, Mahaska, Marion, Marshall, Monroe, Polk, Poweshiek, Ringgold, Story, Taylor, Union, Wapello, Warren, Wayne.

US Bankruptcy Court -- Southern District of Iowa

Home Page: www.iasb.uscourts.gov

PACER: Toll-free access: 800-597-5917. Local access phone: 515-284-6466. Case records are available back to June 1987. Records are purged every six months. New civil records are available online after 1 day.

Electronic Filing: (Currently in the process of implementing CM/ECF).

Other Online Access: Search records on the Internet using RACER at https://racer.iasb.uscourts.gov/perl/bkplog.html. Access fee is $.07 per page. **Also:** access via phone on VCIS (Voice Case Information System) is available: 888-219-5534, 515-284-6427

Des Moines Division counties: Adair, Adams, Appanoose, Audubon, Boone, Cass, Clarke, Clinton, Dallas, Davis, Decatur, Des Moines, Fremont, Greene, Guthrie, Harrison, Henry, Jasper, Jefferson, Johnson, Keokuk, Lee, Louisa, Lucas, Madison, Mahaska, Marion, Marshall, Mills, Monroe,Montgomery, Muscatine, Page, Polk, Pottawattamie, Poweshiek, Ringgold, Scott, Shelby, Story, Taylor, Union, Van Buren, Wapello, Warren, Washington, Wayne.

Capital:	Topeka Shawnee County	Home Page	www.state.ks.us
Time Zone:	CST/MST	Attorney General	www.ink.org/public/ksag
Number of Counties:	105	Archives	http://hs4.kshs.org

State Level ... Major Agencies

Sexual Offender Registry, Mosted Wanted List

Kansas Bureau of Investigation, Criminal Records Division, 1620 SW Tyler, Crim. History Record Sec., Topeka, KS 66612-1837; 785-296-8200, 785-296-6781 (Fax), 8AM-5PM.

www.kbi.state.ks.us

Offender data is available online at www.accesskansas.org/apps/kbi.search.. A Kansas "Mosted Wanted" list is available at www.accesskansas.org/kbi/mw.htm. Other options: Currently constructing web site that allows record checks for criminal records with credit card payment system.

Corporation Records, Limited Partnerships, Limited Liability Company Records

Secretary of State, Memorial Hall, 120 SW 10th Av, 1st Fl, Topeka, KS 66612-1594; 785-296-4564, 785-296-4570 (Fax), 8AM-5PM.

www.kssos.org/corpwelc.html

Corporate data can be ordered from the AcessKansas, a state sponsored interface at www.accesskansas.org/corporations. You must have a subscription that entails a $60.00 annual fee. There is no fee to search or view records, but there is a fee to order copies of certificates or good standings. Search by individual or company name, key word, date, or organizational number.

Uniform Commercial Code, Federal Tax Liens, State Tax Liens

UCC Division, Secretary of State, Memorial Hall, 120 SW 10th Av, Topeka, KS 66612; 785-296-1849, 785-296-3659 (Fax), 8-5PM.

www.kssos.org/uccwelc.html

Online service is provided by AccessKansas. The system is open 24 hours daily. There is an annual fee. Network charges are $.10 a minute unless access is through their Internet site at www.accesskansas.org which has no network fee. UCC records are $8.00 per record. This is the same online system used for corporation records. For more information, call at 800-4-KANSAS. **Other options:** AccessKansas also provides records in a bulk or database format.

Driver Records, Accident Reports

Department of Revenue, Driver Control Bureau, PO Box 12021, Topeka, KS 66612-2021 (Courier: Docking State Office Building, 915 Harrison, Rm 100, Topeka, KS 66612); 785-296-3671, 785-296-6851 (Fax), 8AM-4:45PM.

www.ksrevenue.org/dmv/driverinfo.html

Kansas has contracted with the Information Network of Kansas (INK) (800-452-6727) to service all electronic media requests of driver license histories. INK offers connection through an "800 number" or at www.accesskansas.org. The fee per record is $5.00 for batch requests or $5.50 if single inquiry. There is an initial $75 subscription fee and an annual $60 fee to access records from INK. The system is open 24 hours a day, 7 days a week. Batch requests are available at 7:30 am (if ordered by 10 pm the previous day). **Other options:** Tape-to-tape request records are available on an overnight basis through INK.

Vehicle Ownership, Vehicle Identification

Division of Vehicles, Title and Registration Bureau, 915 Harrison, Rm 155, Topeka, KS 66612; 785-296-3621, 785-296-3852 (Fax), 8AM-4:45PM.

www.ksrevenue.org/dmv/

Online batch inquires are $3.00 per record; online interactive requests are $5.00 per record. Visit www.accesskansas.org for a complete description of the AccessKansas (800-452-6727), the state authorized vendor. There is an initial $75 subscription fee and an annual $60 fee to access records from AccessKansas. **Other options:** The state has several programs available to sell data in bulk format. Contact Donnita Thoma at the Dept of Revenue's Bureau of Policy and Research.

Legislation Records

www.ink.org

The web site has bill information for the current session. The site also contains access to the state statutes.

State Level ... Occupational Licensing

Alcohol/Drug Counselor	www.ksbsrb.org/verification.html
Architect	www.state.ks.us/public/ksbtp/roster.html
Athletic Trainer	www.docboard.org/ks/df/kssearch.htm
Chiropractor	www.docboard.org/ks/df/kssearch.htm
Counselor, Professional	www.ksbsrb.org/verification.html
Dental Hygienist	www.accesskansas.org/cgi-bin/dental/verification/index.cgi
Dentist/Dental Hygienist	www.accesskansas.org/cgi-bin/dental/verification/index.cgi
Engineer	www.state.ks.us/public/ksbtp/roster.html
Funeral Establishment	www.accesskansas.org/ksbma/listings.html
Geologist	www.state.ks.us/public/ksbtp/roster.html
Insurance Company	www.ksinsurance.org/company/main.html
Landscape Architect	www.state.ks.us/public/ksbtp/roster.html
Lobbyist	www.kssos.org/election/Lobbyist/lbSearch.asp
Marriage & Family Therapist	www.ksbsrb.org/verification.html
Medical Doctor	www.docboard.org/ks/df/kssearch.htm
Mortician	www.accesskansas.org/ksbma/listings.html
Occupational Therapist/Assistant	www.docboard.org/ks/df/kssearch.htm
Optometrist	www.odfinder.org/LicSearch.asp
Osteopathic Physician	www.docboard.org/ks/df/kssearch.htm
Physical Therapist/Assistant	www.docboard.org/ks/df/kssearch.htm
Physician Assistant	www.docboard.org/ks/df/kssearch.htm
Podiatrist	www.docboard.org/ks/df/kssearch.htm
Psychologist	www.ksbsrb.org/verification.html
Public Accountant-CPA	www.ink.org/public/ksboa
Real Estate Appraiser	www.ink.org/public/kreab/appraisdir.html
Respiratory Therapist	www.docboard.org/ks/df/kssearch.htm
Social Worker	www.ksbsrb.org/verification.html
Surveyor, Land	www.state.ks.us/public/ksbtp/roster.html

County Level ... Courts

Court Administration: Judicial Administrator, Kansas Judicial Center, 301 SW 10th St, Topeka, KS, 66612; 785-296-2256; www.kscourts.org

Court Structure: The District Court is the court of general jurisdiction. There are 110 courts in 31 districts in 105 counties. If an individual in Municipal Court wants a jury trial, the request must be filed de novo in a District Court. Many Kansas courts do not do criminal record searches and will refer any criminal requests to the Kansas Bureau of Investigation. The Kansas Legislature's Administrative Order 156 (Fall, 2000) allows Courts to charge up to $12.00 per hour for search services, though courts may set their own search fees, if any.

Online Access Note: Commercial online access is available for District Court Records in 4 counties - Johnson, Sedgwick, Shawnee, and Wyandotte - through Access Kansas, part of the Information Network of Kansas (INK) Services. Franklin and Finney counties may be available early in 2003. A user can access INK through their Internet site at www.accesskansas.org or via a dial-up system. The INK subscription fee is $75.00, and the annual renewal fee is $60.00. There is no per minute connect charge but there is a transaction fee. Other information from INK includes Drivers License, Title, Registration, Lien, and UCC searches. For additional information or a registration packet, call 800-4-KANSAS (800-452-6727).

The Kansas Appellate Courts offer free online access to case information at www.kscourts.org.

Anderson County
District Court *Civil and Criminal Records*
www.kscourts.org/dstcts/4dstct.htm
Current court calendars are available free online at www.kscourts.org/dstcts/4andckt.htm. Online access to criminal calendars is the same as civil.

Coffey County
District Court *Civil, Probate, Marriage, and Criminal Records*
www.kscourts.org/dstcts/4dstct.htm
Current court calendars are available free online at www.kscourts.org/dstcts/4codckt.htm. Probate and marriage records are accessible at the web site.

Douglas County
District Court *Civil and Criminal Records*
www.douglas-county.com/District_Court/dc.asp
Online access via Internet to district court records is available for $180.00 annual fee and $60.00 set-up fee. For further information and registration, contact Beverly at 785-832-5299.

Johnson County
District Court *Civil Records*
www.jocoks.com/jococourts/index.htm
Index online through AccessKansas. See www.accesskansas.org for subscription information. Current court calendars for civil and criminal are available free online at www.kscourts.org/dstcts/4frdckt.htm.

Osage County
District Court *Civil and Criminal Records*
www.kscourts.org/dstcts/4dstct.htm
Current court calendars are available free online at www.kscourts.org/dstcts/4osdckt.htm.

Sedgwick County
District Court *Civil, Probate and Criminal Records*
http://distcrt18.state.ks.us/
Access to the remote online system requires a $225 setup fee, $49 monthly fee and small transaction fee. The system also includes probate, traffic, domestic, and criminal cases. For more information, call 316-383-7563.

Shawnee County
District Court *Civil and Criminal Records*
www.shawneecourt.org
Index online through INK of Kansas. See www.ink.org for subscription information. Also, online access to county court records available free at www.shawneecourt.org/doe/index.html.. Also find "viewing restricted" domestic documents here. Online access to criminal records is the same as civil.

Wyandotte County
District Court *Civil and Criminal Records*
Access to the remote online system requires specific software and $20 setup fee. Transactions are $.05 each. For more information call 913-573-2885.

County Level ... Recorders & Assessors

Recording Office Organization: 105 counties, 105 recording offices. The recording officer is the Register of Deeds. Many counties utilize a "Miscellaneous Index" for tax and other liens, separate from real estate records. 100 counties are in the Central Time Zone (CST) and 5 are in the Mountain Time Zone (MST). Federal tax liens on personal property of businesses are filed with the Secretary of State. Other federal tax liens and all state tax liens on personal property are filed with the county Register of Deeds. Most counties automatically include tax liens on personal property with a UCC search. Tax liens on personal property may usually be searched separately for $8.00 per name.

Online Access Note:
A few counties have online access, there is no statewide system.

Barton County *Assessor Records*
www.bartoncounty.org
Access to the County 2002 Property value list by address and name is available at www.bartoncounty.org/values/Propvalues.htm.

Douglas County *Property Appraiser, Real Estate Records*
www.douglas-county.com
Two non-government Internet sites provide free access to records from the Douglas County Assessor. Find County Property Appraiser records at www.douglas-county.com/value. Douglas County property valuations can be found at http://hometown.lawrence.com/valuation/valuation.cgi.

Johnson County *Property Appraiser, Tax Sales, Land Records*
www.jocoks.com
Records on the Johnson County Kansas Land Records database are available free online at http://appraiser.jocoks.com/disclaim.html. At the bottom of the Disclaimer page, click on "Yes". No name searching. Also, search the tax sales list for free at www.jocoks.com/countyclerk/taxsale/salenone.htm. Also, there is an online mapping service at http://aims.jocoks.com/products.htm.

Sedgwick County *Real Estate, Lien, Tax Assessor Records*
www.co.sedgwick.ks.us/dept.htm
Records are available two ways. Records on the Sedgwick County online system are available for a set up fee of $225, with a $49 monthly fee, and a per transaction charge of $.03-$.04. Lending agency information is available. For information, call John Zukovich at 316-383-7384. A sex offender registry list is available on the Web at the county departments page. County Treasurer & Appraiser database records are available free online at www.co.sedgwick.ks.us/Appraiser/RealProperty.htm. Search by city, street numbers or street name for property tax/appraisal information. No name searching.

Shawnee County *Property Appraiser Records*
www.co.shawnee.ks.us
Search residential or commercial property appraisal data at www.co.shawnee.ks.us/Appraiser_Web/appraiser.html. Search residential by name; commericial by address.

Wyandotte County　　*Real Estate, Lien, Property Appraisal Records*
County records are available online, and property tax records are available on dial-up. The dial-up services requires a $20 set up fee, with a $5 monthly fee and $.05 each after the first 100 transactions. Lending agency information is available. For information, contact Louise Sachen at 913-573-2885. Records from the County Assessor Tax database are available free on the Internet at www.courthouseusa.com/wyanadd.htm. Search by street number and name, but no name searching.

Federal Courts in Kansas...

Standards for Federal Courts: The universal PACER sign-up number is 800-676-6856. Find PACER and the Party/Case Index on the Web at http://pacer.psc.uscourts.gov. PACER dial-up access is $.60 per minute. Also, courts offering internet access via RACER, PACER, Web-PACER or the new CM-ECF charge $.07 per page fee unless noted as free.

US District Court -- District of Kansas
Home Page: www.ksd.uscourts.gov
PACER: Toll-free access: 800-898-3078. Local access phone: 316-269-6284. Case records are available back to 1991. Records are purged never. New civil records are available online after 2 days. New criminal records are available online after 3 days. **PACER URL:** http://pacer.ksd.uscourts.gov.
Electronic Filing: Electronic filing information is available online at (CM/ECF available late 2002).
Kansas City Division counties: Atchison, Bourbon, Brown, Cherokee, Crawford, Doniphan, Johnson, Labette, Leavenworth, Linn, Marshall, Miami, Nemaha, Wyandotte.
Topeka Division counties: Allen, Anderson, Chase, Clay, Cloud, Coffey, Dickinson, Douglas, Franklin, Geary, Jackson, Jewell, Lincoln, Lyon, Marion, Mitchell, Morris, Neosho, Osage, Ottawa, Pottawatomie, Republic, Riley, Saline, Shawnee, Wabaunsee, Washington, Wilson, Woodson.
Wichita Division counties: All counties in Kansas. Cases may be heard from counties in the other division.

US Bankruptcy Court -- District of Kansas
Home Page: www.ksb.uscourts.gov
PACER: Toll-free access: 800-613-7052. Local access phone: 316-269-6258. Case records are available back to 1988. Records are purged every 6 months. New civil records are available online after 1 day. **PACER URL:** http://pacer.ksb.uscourts.gov. Document images available.
Electronic Filing: (Currently in the process of implementing CM/ECF). **Also:** access via phone on VCIS (Voice Case Information System) is available: 800-827-9028, 316-269-6668
Kansas City Division counties: Atchison, Bourbon, Brown, Cherokee, Comanche, Crawford, Doniphan, Johnson, Labette, Leavenworth, Linn, Marshall, Miami, Nemaha, Wyandotte.
Topeka Division counties: Allen, Anderson, Chase, Clay, Cloud, Coffey, Dickinson, Douglas, Franklin, Geary, Jackson, Jewell, Lincoln, Lyon, Marion, Mitchell, Morris, Neosho, Osage, Ottawa, Pottawatomie, Republic, Riley, Saline, Shawnee, Wabaunsee, Washington, Wilson, Woodson.
Wichita Division counties: Barber, Barton, Butler, Chautauqua, Cheyenne, Clark, Comanche, Cowley, Decatur, Edwards, Elk, Ellis, Ellsworth, Finney, Ford, Gove, Graham, Grant, Gray, Greeley, Greenwood, Hamilton, Harper, Harvey, Haskell, Hodgeman, Jefferson, Kearny, Kingman, Kiowa,Lane, Logan, Mcpherson, Meade, Montgomery, Morton, Ness, Norton, Osborne, Pawnee, Phillips, Pratt, Rawlins, Reno, Rice, Rooks, Rush, Russell, Scott, Sedgwick, Seward, Sheridan, Smith, Stafford, Stanton, Stevens, Sumner, Thomas, Trego, Wallace, Wichita.

Capital:	Frankfort Franklin County	Home Page	www.state.ky.us
Time Zone:	EST/CST	Attorney General	www.law.state.ky.us
Number of Counties:	120	Archives	www.kdla.state.ky.us

State Level ... Major Agencies

Corporation Records, Limited Partnerships, Assumed Name, Limited Liability Company Records

Secretary of State, Corporate Records, PO Box 718, Frankfort, KY 40602-0718 (Courier: 700 Capitol Ave, Room 156, Frankfort, KY 40601); 502-564-7330, 502-564-4075 (Fax), 8AM-4PM.

www.sos.state.ky.us

The Internet site, open 24 hours, has a searchable database with over 340,000 KY businesses. The site also offers downloading of filing forms. **Other options:** Monthly lists of new corporations are available for $50.00 per month.

Trademarks/Servicemarks

Secretary of State, Trademarks Section, 700 Capitol Ave, Suite 152, Frankfort, KY 40601; 502-564-2848 x442, 502-564-1484 (Fax), 8AM-4:30PM.

www.sos.state.ky.us

Free, searchable database at www.kysos.com/trademarks/tmstart.asp.

Uniform Commercial Code

UCC Division, Secretary of State, PO Box 1470, Frankfort, KY 40602-0718 (Courier: 363C Versailles Rd, Mare Manor, Frankfort, KY 40601); 502-573-0265, 502-573-0259 (Fax), 8AM-4:30PM.

www.kysos.com

UCC record searching is offered free of charge at the web site. Search by debtor name, or file number. SSNs are withheld from the online system. Pre-paid accounts may be established for those requiring copies or certified documents.

Sexual Offender Registry

The state sexual offender list is available online at http://kspsor.state.ky.us/. The database is maintained by the Kentucky State Police.

Incarceration Records

Information on current and former inmates is available at www.cor.state.ky.us. Location, physical identifiers, conviction and sentencing information, and release dates are reported.

Death Records

Department for Public Health, Vital Statistics, 275 E Main St - IE-A, Frankfort, KY 40621-0001; 502-564-4212, 502-227-0032 (Fax), 8AM-3PM.

http://publichealth.state.ky.us/vital.htm

In cooperation with the University of Kentucky, there is a searchable death index at http://ukcc.uky.edu:80/~vitalrec/. This is for non-commercial use only. Records are from 1911 through 1992. Also, there is a free genealogy site at http://vitals.rootsweb.com/ky/death/search.cgi. Death Indexes from 1911-2000 are available. You may search by surname, given name, place of death, residence, or year.

Marriage Certificates, Divorce Records

Department for Public Health, Vital Statistics, 275 E Main St - IE-A, Frankfort, KY 40621-0001; 502-564-4212, 502-227-0032 (Fax), 8AM-3PM.

http://publichealth.state.ky.us/vital.htm

In cooperation with the University of Kentucky, a searchable index is available on the Internet at http://ukcc.uky.edu:80/~vitalrec/. The index runs from 1973 through 1993. This is for non-commercial use only. **Other options:** Contact Libraries and Archives.

Driver Records

Division of Driver Licensing, State Office Bldg, MVRS, 501 High Street, 2nd Floor, Frankfort, KY 40622; 502-564-6800 x2250, 502-564-5787 (Fax), 8AM-4:30PM.

www.kytc.state.ky.us

There are two systems. Permissible use requesters who need personal information can order by batch, minimum order is 150 requests per batch. Input received by 3 PM will be available the next morning. Fee is $3.00 per record and billing is monthly. Call for details to subscribe. Records without personal information can be obtained at www.kydirect.net. The $3.00 fee applies and up to 50 records can be ordered and received immediately.

Vehicle Ownership, Vehicle Identification

Department of Motor Vehicles, Division of Motor Vehicle Licensing, State Office Bldg, 3rd Floor, Frankfort, KY 40622; 502-564-4076 (Title History), 502-564-3298 (Other Requests), 502-564-1686 (Fax), 8AM-4:30PM.

www.kytc.state.ky.us

Online access costs $2.00 per record. The online mode is interactive. Title, lien and registration searches are available. Records include those for mobile homes. For more information, contact Gale Warfield at 502-564-4076. **Other options:** Kentucky has the ability to supply customized bulk delivery of vehicle registration information. The request must be in writing with the intended use outlined. For more information, call 502-564-3298.

Legislation Records

www.lrc.state.ky.us

The web site has an extensive searching mechanism for bills, actions, summaries, and statutes.

State Level ... Occupational Licensing

Alcohol/Drug Counselor	https://kyeasupt1.state.ky.us/OPB/BrdWebSearch.asp?BRD=4
Architect	http://kybera.com/roster.shtml
Art Therapist	https://kyeasupt1.state.ky.us/OPB/BrdWebSearch.asp?BRD=5
Athlete Agent	https://kyeasupt1.state.ky.us/OPB/BrdWebSearch.asp?BRD=19
Athletic Manager	https://kyeasupt1.state.ky.us/OPB/BrdWebSearch.asp?BRD=17

Athletic Trainer	https://kyeasupt1.state.ky.us/OPB/BrdWebSearch.asp?BRD=17
Auctioneer, Livestock, Limited	http://weba.state.ky.us/genericsearch/LicenseSearch.asp?AGY=3
Auctioneer, Tobacco, Limited	http://weba.state.ky.us/genericsearch/LicenseSearch.asp?AGY=3
Auctioneer/Auctioneer Apprentice	http://weba.state.ky.us/genericsearch/LicenseSearch.asp?AGY=3
Boxer/Boxing Professional	https://kyeasupt1.state.ky.us/OPB/BrdWebSearch.asp?BRD=17
Counselor, Pastoral	https://kyeasupt1.state.ky.us/OPB/BrdWebSearch.asp?BRD=3
Counselor, Professional	https://kyeasupt1.state.ky.us/OPB/BrdWebSearch.asp?BRD=6
Dental Hygienist	http://dentistry.state.ky.us/search.htm
Dentist	http://dentistry.state.ky.us/search.htm
Dietitian/Nutritionist	https://kyeasupt1.state.ky.us/OPB/BrdWebSearch.asp?BRD=8
Engineer	http://kyboels.state.ky.us/SearchRoster.asp
Engineer/Land Surveyor Firm	http://kyboels.state.ky.us/SearchRoster.asp
Geologist	www.state.ky.us/agencies/finance/boards/geology/pages/geol.html
Geologists, Recently Registered	www.state.ky.us/agencies/finance/boards/geology/pages/newgeo.htm
Hearing Instrument Specialist	https://kyeasupt1.state.ky.us/OPB/BrdWebSearch.asp?BRD=15
Insurance Agent	www.doi.state.ky.us/kentucky/search/agent/
Insurance CE Provider	www.doi.state.ky.us/kentucky/search/provider/
Insurance Company/Insurer	www.doi.state.ky.us/kentucky/search/company/
Marriage & Family Therapist	https://kyeasupt1.state.ky.us/OPB/BrdWebSearch.asp?BRD=9
Mortgage Broker	www.dfi.state.ky.us/aspscripts/mort_brokers.asp
Mortgage Loan Company	www.dfi.state.ky.us/aspscripts/mort_company.asp
Nursing Home Administrator	https://kyeasupt1.state.ky.us/OPB/BrdWebSearch.asp?BRD=10
Occupational Therapist/Assistant	https://kyeasupt1.state.ky.us/OPB/BrdWebSearch.asp?BRD=16
Ophthalmic Dispenser/Optician/Apprentice	https://kyeasupt1.state.ky.us/OPB/BrdWebSearch.asp?BRD=11
Optometrist	http://web.state.ky.us/GBC/LicenseSearch.asp?AGY=8
Proprietary Education School	https://kyeasupt1.state.ky.us/OPB/BrdWebSearch.asp?BRD=18
Psychologist	https://kyeasupt1.state.ky.us/OPB/BrdWebSearch.asp?BRD=7
Public Accountant-CPA	http://cpa.state.ky.us/Locate.html
Real Estate Appraiser	www.asc.gov/
Real Estate Broker	http://weba.state.ky.us/realestate/LicenseeLookUp.asp
Real Estate Brokerage/Firm	http://weba.state.ky.us/realestate/FirmLookUp.asp
Real Estate Sales Associate	http://weba.state.ky.us/realestate/LicenseeLookUp.asp
Social Worker	https://kyeasupt1.state.ky.us/OPB/BrdWebSearch.asp?BRD=2
Speech-Language Pathologist/Audiologist	https://kyeasupt1.state.ky.us/OPB/BrdWebSearch.asp?BRD=13
Surveyor, Land	http://kyboels.state.ky.us/SearchRoster.asp
Veterinarian	https://kyeasupt1.state.ky.us/OPB/BrdWebSearch.asp?BRD=14
Wrestler/Wrestling Professional	https://kyeasupt1.state.ky.us/OPB/BrdWebSearch.asp?BRD=17

County Level ... Courts

Court Administration: Administrative Office of Courts, 100 Mill Creek Park, Frankfort, KY, 40601; 502-573-2350; www.kycourts.net

Court Structure: The Circuit Court is the court of general jurisdiction and the District Court is the limited jurisdiction court. Most of Kentucky's counties combined the courts into one location and records are co-mingled.

Online Access Note: There are statewide, online computer systems called SUSTAIN and KyCourts available for internal judicial/state agency use only. No courts offer online access to records. However, you may search daily court calendars by county for free at http://dockets.kycourts.net. Also, you may search online for circuit court dockets (limited) on the supreme court search page at http://162.114.20.136/dockets. These are only the cases open before the Supreme Court.

There are no known courts that independently offer access to their records.

County Level ... Recorders & Assessors

Recording Office Organization: 120 counties, 122 recording offices. The recording officer is the County Clerk. Kenton County has two recording offices. Jefferson County had a separate office for UCC filing until June 30, 2001; that office now only searches for filings up to that date. 80 counties are in the Eastern Time Zone (EST) and 40 are in the Central Time Zone (CST). All federal and state tax liens on personal property are filed with the County Clerk, often in an "Encumbrance Book." Most counties will not perform tax lien searches.

Online Access Note: A number of counties offer free access to assessor records. Several other counties offer commercial systems. There is no statewide system.

Boone County *Real Estate, Lines, UCC, Assessor, Marriage Records*
www.boonecountyclerk.com
Access to the county clerk database is available through eCCLIX, a fee-based service; $200.00 sign-up and $65.00 monthly. Records go back to 1989; images to 1998. For information, see the web site or call 502-266-9445.

Boyd County *Real Estate, Lien Records*
Access to the County Clerk online records requires a $10 monthly usage fee. The system operates 24 hours daily; records date back to 1/1979. Lending agency information is available. For information, contact Maxine Selbee or Kathy Fisher at 606-739-5166.

Fayette County *Property, Crime Map Records*
Search the GIS-property mapping site by address at http://arcims.lfucg.com/maps/zoning/viewer.htm. No name searching. Also, search the interactive crime map at http://crimewatch.lfucg.com.

Jefferson County Clerk *Property, Assessor Records*
Access to the county property valuation administrator's Assessment Roll is available free at www.pvalouky.org/.

Kenton County (1st District) *Property Appraiser Records*
www.kentonpva.com
Access to the county Property Valuation database is available at www.kentonpva.com. Click on "Property Data." Search for free by using "Guest Access." For full, professional property data you may subscribe; fee for user name/ password is $50. per month

Kenton County (2nd District) *Property Appraiser Records*
www.kentonpva.com
Access to the county Property Valuation database is available free at www.kentonpva.com/pvacat/catsearch.htm.

Oldham County *Real Estate, Lien, UCC, Assessor, Marriage Records*
http://oldhamcounty.state.ky.us
Access to the county clerk database is available through eCCLIX, a fee-based service; $200.00 sign-up and $65.00 monthly. Records go back, generally, to 1980. UCC images to 2/97. Real estate instruments back to 1/95. Marriages back to 1980. For information, see the web site or call 502-266-9445.

Warren County *Real Estate, Lien, UCC, Assessor, Marriage Records*
http://warrencounty.state.ky.us
Access to the county clerk database is available through eCCLIX, a fee-based service; $200.00 sign-up and $65.00 monthly. Records go back to 1989; images to 1998. For information, see the web site or call 502-266-9445.

Federal Courts in Kentucky...

Standards for Federal Courts: The universal PACER sign-up number is 800-676-6856. Find PACER and the Party/Case Index on the Web at http://pacer.psc.uscourts.gov. PACER dial-up access is $.60 per minute. Also, courts offering internet access via RACER, PACER, Web-PACER or the new CM-ECF charge $.07 per page fee unless noted as free.

US District Court -- Eastern District of Kentucky

Home Page: www.kyed.uscourts.gov

PACER: Toll-free access: 800-361-0442. Local access phone: 606-233-2787. Case records are available back to September 1991. Records are purged never. New records are available online after 1 day. **PACER URL:** http://pacer.kyed.uscourts.gov.

Ashland Division counties: Boyd, Carter, Elliott, Greenup, Lawrence, Lewis, Morgan, Rowan.

Covington Division counties: Boone, Bracken, Campbell, Gallatin, Grant, Kenton, Mason, Pendleton, Robertson.

Frankfort Division counties: Anderson, Carroll, Franklin, Henry, Owen, Shelby, Trimble.

Lexington Division counties: Bath, Bourbon, Boyle, Clark, Estill, Fayette, Fleming, Garrard, Harrison, Jessamine, Lee, Lincoln, Madison, Menifee, Mercer, Montgomery, Nicholas, Powell, Scott, Wolfe, Woodford. Lee and Wolfe counties were part of the Pikeville Division before 10/31/92. Perry became part of Pikeville after 1992.

London Division counties: Bell, Clay, Harlan, Jackson, Knox, Laurel, Leslie, McCreary, Owsley, Pulaski, Rockcastle, Wayne, Whitley.

Pikeville Division counties: Breathitt, Floyd, Johnson, Knott, Letcher, Magoffin, Martin, Perry, Pike. Lee and Wolfe Counties were part of this division until 10/31/92, when they were moved to the Lexington Division.

US Bankruptcy Court -- Eastern District of Kentucky

Home Page: www.kyeb.uscourts.gov

PACER: Case records are available back to July 1992. Records are purged every six months. New civil records are available online after 1 day. **PACER URL:** http://pacer.kyeb.uscourts.gov.

Electronic Filing: Electronic filing information is available online at https://ecf.kyeb.uscourts.gov/. **Also:** access via phone on VCIS (Voice Case Information System) is available: 800-998-2650, 606-233-2657

Lexington Division counties: Anderson, Bath, Bell, Boone, Bourbon, Boyd, Boyle, Bracken, Breathitt, Campbell, Carroll, Carter, Clark, Clay, Elliott, Estill, Fayette, Fleming, Floyd, Franklin, Gallatin, Garrard, Grant, Greenup, Harlan, Harrison, Henry, Jackson, Jessamine, Johnson, Kenton, Knott, Knox, Laurel, Lawrence, Lee, Leslie, Letcher, Lewis, Lincoln, Madison, Magoffin, Martin, Mason, McCreary, Menifee, Mercer, Montgomery, Morgan, Nicholas, Owen, Owsley, Pendleton, Perry, Pike, Powell, Pulaski, Robertson, Rockcastle, Rowan, Scott, Shelby, Trimble, Wayne, Whitley, Wolfe, Woodford.

US District Court -- Western District of Kentucky

Home Page: www.kywd.uscourts.gov

PACER: Case records are available back to 1992. New records are available online after 1 day. Has converted the online WebPACER service over to nationwide PACER standards; click on "Court Records." Registration and fee required.

Electronic Filing: Electronic filing information is available online at www.kywd.uscourts.gov/scripts/usdckyw/ecf/ecf2.pl.

Opinions Online: Court opinions are available online at www.kywd.uscourts.gov.

Bowling Green Division counties: Adair, Allen, Barren, Butler, Casey, Clinton, Cumberland, Edmonson, Green, Hart, Logan, Metcalfe, Monroe, Russell, Simpson, Taylor, Todd, Warren.

Louisville Division counties: Breckinridge, Bullitt, Hardin, Jefferson, Larue, Marion, Meade, Nelson, Oldham, Spencer, Washington.

Owensboro Division counties: Daviess, Grayson, Hancock, Henderson, Hopkins, McLean, Muhlenberg, Ohio, Union, Webster.

Paducah Division counties: Ballard, Caldwell, Calloway, Carlisle, Christian, Crittenden, Fulton, Graves, Hickman, Livingston, Lyon, McCracken, Marshall, Trigg.

US Bankruptcy Court -- Western District of Kentucky

Home Page: www.kywb.uscourts.gov

PACER: Case records are available back to July 1992. Records are purged every six months. New civil records are available online after 1-2 days. **PACER URL:** http://pacer.kywb.uscourts.gov.

Electronic Filing: Electronic filing information is available online at https://ecf.kywb.uscourts.gov/. **Also:** access via phone on VCIS (Voice Case Information System) is available: 800-263-9385, 502-625-7391

Louisville Division counties: Adair, Allen, Ballard, Barren, Breckinridge, Bullitt, Butler, Caldwell, Calloway, Carlisle, Casey, Christian, Clinton, Crittenden, Cumberland, Daviess, Edmonson, Fulton, Graves, Grayson, Green, Hancock, Hardin, Hart, Henderson, Hickman, Hopkins, Jefferson, Larue, Livingston, Logan, Lyon, Marion, Marshall, McCracken, McLean, Meade, Metcalfe, Monroe, Muhlenberg, Nelson, Ohio, Oldham, Russell, Simpson, Spencer, Taylor, Todd, Trigg, Union, Warren, Washington, Webster.

Capital:	Baton Rouge
	East Baton Rouge Parish
Time Zone:	CST
# of Parishes:	64

Home Page   www.state.la.us

Attorney General   www.ag.state.la.us

Archives   www.sec.state.la.us/archives/archives/archives-index.htm

State Level ... Major Agencies

Corporation Records, Limited Partnership Records, Limited Liability Company Records, Trademarks/Servicemarks

Commercial Division, Corporation Department, PO Box 94125, Baton Rouge, LA 70804-9125 (Courier: 8549 United Plaza Blvd, Baton Rouge, LA 70809); 225-925-4704, 225-925-4726 (Fax), 8AM-4:30PM.

www.sec.state.la.us

There are 2 ways to go: free on the Internet or pay. To view limited information on the web site, go to "Commercial Division, Corporations Section," then "Search Corporations Database." The pay system is $360 per year for unlimited access. Almost any communications software will work with up to a 14,400 baud rate. The system is open from 6:30 am to 11pm. For more information, call Brenda Wright at 225-922-2880. **Other options:** The state offers corporation, LLC, partnership, and trademark information on tape cartridges. For more info, call 225-925-4792.

Uniform Commercial Code

Secretary of State, UCC Records, PO Box 94125, Baton Rouge, LA 70804-9125; 800-256-3758, 225-342-7011 (Fax), 8AM-4:30PM.

www.sec.state.la.us/comm/ucc-index.htm

An annual $400 fee gives unlimited access to UCC filing information. The dial-up service is open from 6:30 AM to 11 PM daily. Minimum baud rate is 9600. Most any software communications program can be configured to work. For further information, call Brenda Wright at 225-922-2880 or visit the web site.

Sexual Offender Registry

Sex offender and child predator data is maintained by the State Police. Records are open to the public and available online at www.lasocpr.lsp.org/Static/Search.htm.

Driver Records

Dept of Public Safety and Corrections, Office of Motor Vehicles, PO Box 64886, Baton Rouge, LA 70896 (Courier: 109 S Foster Dr, Baton Rouge, LA 70806); 877-368-5463, 225-925-6388, 225-925-6915 (Fax), 8AM-4:30PM.

www.expresslane.org

There are two methods. The commercial requester, interactive mode is available from 7 AM to 9:30 PM daily. There is a minimum order requirement of 2,000 requests per month. A bond or large deposit is required. Fee is $6.00 per record. For more information, call 225-925-6032. The 2nd method is for individuals to order their own record from the Internet site at www.expresslane.org. The fee is $16.40 and requires a credit card. **Other options:** Tape ordering is available for batch delivery. Bulk database sales are available to permissible users.

Legislation Records

www.legis.state.la.us

The Internet site has a wealth of information about sessions and bills from 1997 forward.

State Level ... Occupational Licensing

Acupuncturist	www.lsbme.org/bmeSearch/licenseesearch.asp
Athletic Trainer	www.lsbme.org/bmeSearch/licenseesearch.asp
Bank	www.ofi.state.la.us/newbanks.htm
Bond For Deed Agency	www.ofi.state.la.us/newbfd.htm
Check Casher	www.ofi.state.la.us/newcheckcash.htm
Clinical Lab Personnel	www.lsbme.org/bmeSearch/licenseesearch.asp
Collection Agency	www.ofi.state.la.us/newcolagn.htm
Consumer Credit Grantor	www.ofi.state.la.us/newliclen.htm
Contractor, Commercial/Residential/General/Sub	www.lslbc.state.la.us/croster.asp
Counselor, Professional (LPC)	www.lpcboard.org/lpc_alpha_list.htm
Credit Repair Agency	www.ofi.state.la.us/newcredrep.htm
Credit Union	www.ofi.state.la.us/newcus.htm
Dentist/Dental Hygienist	www.lsbd.org/dentistsearch.asp
Dietitian	www.lbedn.org/licensee_database.asp
Drug Distributor, Wholesale	www.lsbwdd.org
Engineer	www.lapels.com/indv_reg.html
Exercise Physiologist, Clinical	www.lsbme.org/bmeSearch/licenseesearch.asp
Insurance Agent, LHA/PC/Broker	www.ldi.state.la.us/searchforms/searchform.asp
Land Surveyor	www.lapels.com/indv_reg.html
Lender	www.ofi.state.la.us/newliclen.htm
Lobbyist	www.ethics.state.la.us/lobs.htm
Medical Doctor	www.lsbme.org/bmeSearch/licenseesearch.asp
Midwife	www.lsbme.org/bmeSearch/licenseesearch.asp
Mortgage Lender/Broker, Residential	www.ofi.state.la.us/newrml.htm
Notary Public	www.sec.state.la.us/notary-pub/NTRINQ.htm
Notification Filer	www.ofi.state.la.us/newnotif.htm
Nutritionist	www.lbedn.org/licensee_database.asp
Occupational Therapist/Technologist	www.lsbme.org/bmeSearch/licenseesearch.asp
Optometrist	www.odfinder.org/LicSearch.asp
Osteopathic Physician	www.lsbme.org/bmeSearch/licenseesearch.asp
Pawnbroker	www.ofi.state.la.us/newpawn.htm
Physician Assistant	www.lsbme.org/bmeSearch/licenseesearch.asp
Podiatrist	www.lsbme.org/bmeSearch/licenseesearch.asp
Radiologic Technologist, Private	www.lsbme.org/bmeSearch/licenseesearch.asp
Real Estate Appraiser	www.lreasbc.state.la.us/appraiserinfo.htm
Respiratory Therapist/Therapy Technician	www.lsbme.org/bmeSearch/licenseesearch.asp
Savings & Loan	www.ofi.state.la.us/newcus.htm
Solicitor	www.ldi.state.la.us/searchforms/searchform.asp
Thrift & Loan Company	www.ofi.state.la.us/newthrift.htm
Vocational Rehabilitative Counselor	www.lrcboard.org/licensee_database.asp

County Level ... Courts

Court Administration: Judicial Administrator, Judicial Council of the Supreme Court, 1555 Poydras St #1540, New Orleans, LA, 70112; 504-568-5747; www.lasc.org

Court Structure: A District Court Clerk in each Parish holds all the records for that Parish. Each Parish has its own clerk and courthouse. A municipality may have a Mayor's Court; the mayor may hold trials, but nothing over $30.00, and there are no records.

Online Access Note: The online computer system named Case Management Information System (CMIS) is operating and development is continuing. It is for internal use only; there is no plan to permit online public access. However, Supreme Court opinions are currently available.

There are a number of Parishes that offer a means of remote online access to the public.

Caddo Parish

1st District Court *Civil and Criminal Records*

www.caddoclerk.com

Online access to civil records back to 1994 and name index back to 1984 are available through county dial-up service. Registration and $50 set-up fee and $30 monthly usage fee is required. Marriage and recording information is also available. For information and sign-up, call 318-226-6523. Online criminal name index goes back to '80; minutes to '84. Current calendar is also available.

Bossier Parish

26th District Court *Civil, Probate, Domestic, and Criminal Records*

www.ebrclerkofcourt.org

Access to the Parish Clerk of Court online records requires $50 setup fee and a $35 monthly flat fee. Civil, criminal, probate (1988 forward), traffic and domestic index information is available by name or case number. Call 318-965-2336 for more information.

East Baton Rouge Parish

19th District Court *Civil, Probate, and Criminal Records*

www.ebrclerkofcourt.org/

Online access to the clerk's database is available by subscription. Civil record indexes go back to '88; case tracking of civil and probate back to 1991. Setup fee is $100.00 plus $15.00 per month plus per-minute usage charges. VS Com software required. Call the MIS Dept at 225-389-5295 for information or visit the web site. Criminal case tracking goes back to 8/1990.

Jefferson Parish

24th District Court *Civil and Criminal Records*

www.clerkofcourt.co.jefferson.la.us

Online access is available through dial-up service. Initiation fee is $200, plus $85.00 monthly and $.25 per minute usage fee. Includes recordings, marriage index, and assessor rolls. For further information and sign-up, call 504-364-2908 or visit the web site and click on "Jeffnet."

Lafayette Parish

15th District Court *Civil and Criminal Records*

www.lafayetteparishclerk.com

Access to the remote online system requires $100 setup fee plus $15 per month and $.50 per minute. Civil index goes back to 1986. For more information, call Derek Comeaux at 337-291-6433.

Orleans Parish

Civil District Court *Civil Records*

New Orleans City Court *Civil Records*

www.orleanscdc.gov

CDC Remote provides access to civil cases from 1985 and First City Court cases back to 1988 as well as parish mortgage and conveyance indexes. The fee is $250 per year. Call 504-592-9264 for more information.

St. Landry Parish
27th District Court *Civil Records*

www.stlandry.org

Access to civil indexes and images is to be available at www.stlandry.org. Index and images go back to 1998.

St. Tammany Parish
22nd District Court *Civil and Criminal Records*

Remote online access to civil records is available from the Clerk of Court; fee is $.20 per minute with $100 initial setup fee. Modem and PC Anywhere is required. For information, call Kristie Howell at 985-898-2491.

Tangipahoa Parish
21st District Court *Civil Records*

www.tangiclerk.org

Online access to Parish notarial index records is available by free subscription (subject to change; expect fee for images and usage); images go back to 1/1990. Visit www.tangiclerk.org/OnlineServices/onlineservices.asp for information or call Alison Theard: 985-748-7404.

County Level ... Recorders & Assessors

Recording Office Organization: 64 parishes (not counties), 64 recording offices (One parish, St. Martin, has two non-contiguous segments). The recording officer is the Clerk of Court. Many parishes include tax and other non-UCC liens in their mortgage records. The entire state is in the Central Time Zone (CST). All federal and state tax liens are filed with the Clerk of Court. Parishes usually file tax liens on personal property in their UCC or mortgage records, and most will perform tax lien searches for varying fees. Some parishes will automatically include tax liens on personal property in a mortgage certificate search.

Online Access Note: A number of Parishes offer online access to recorded documents, most are commercial fee systems.

Caddo Parish   *Real Estate, Lien, Marriage Records*
www.caddoclerk.com

Access to the Parish online records requires a $50 set up fee plus a $30 monthly fee. Mortgages and indirect conveyances date back to 1981; direct conveyances date back to 1914. Lending agency information available. UCCs are at Sec. of State. Marriage licenses go back to 1937. For system information, contact Susan Twohig at 318-226-6523.

East Baton Rouge Parish   *Real Estate, Lien Records*
www.ebrclerkofcourt.org

Access to online records requires a $100 set up fee with a $5 monthly fee and $.33 per minute of use. Four years worth of data is kept active on the system. Lending agency information is available. For information, contact Wendy Gibbs at 225-398-5295. UCC information is located at the Secretary of State.

Iberia Parish   *Real Estate, Lien, Marriage, Divorce Records*

Access to the Parish online records requires a $50 monthly usage fee. Records date back to 1959. Lending agency information is available. For information, contact Mike Thibodeaux at 337-365-7282.

Jefferson Parish   *Real Estate, Assessor, Marriage, Civil Records*
www.clerkofcourt.co.jefferson.la.us

Access to the clerk's JeffNet database is available by subscription; set-up fee is $200.00 plus $8.50 monthly and $.25 per minute. Mortgage and conveyance images go back to 1990; index to 1967. Marriage and assessor records go back to 1992. For information, visit www.clerkofcourt.co.jefferson.la.us/jeffnet.htm or call the Court Information Systems at 504-364-2908.

Lafayette Parish   *Real Estate, Lien Records*
www.lafayetteparishclerk.com

Access to Parish online records requires a $100 set up fee plus $15 per month and $.50 per minute. Conveyances date back to 1936; mortgages to 1948; other records to 1986. Lending agency information is available. For information, contact Derek Comeaux at 337-291-6433. Tax and UCC lien information is for this parish only.

Orleans Parish   *Real Estate, Lien Records*

Access to the Parish online records requires a set up fee and $300 deposit for 1,200 minutes of usage, plus $.25 per minute. Records date back to 9/1987. No lending agency information is available. For information, contact John Rabb at 504-592-9264.

St. Landry Parish   *Recording, Deed, Judgment, Civil Court Records*

www.stlandry.org/index.htm

Access to the conveyances index and civil cases is to be available free at www.stlandry.org. Document images 1978-present.

St. Tammany Parish   *Real Estate, Lien Records*

Access to online records requires a $100 set up fee, plus $.30 per minute of use. Records date back to 1961; viewable images on conveyances back to 1985; mortgages to 8/93. For information, contact Mark Cohn at 504-898-2890 or Christy Howell at 504-898-2491. UCC lien information is with the Secretary of State.

Tangipahoa Parish   *Real Estate, Lien, Recording, Civil Records*

www.tangiclerk.org

Access to Parish online records requires registration and a $55 monthly fee. Record dates vary though most indexes go back to 1990. Lending agency information is available. For information, contact Alison Carona at 504-549-1611. Also, a mapping feature is being developed that includes assessor basic information; access will be free.

Federal Courts in Louisiana...

Standards for Federal Courts: The universal PACER sign-up number is 800-676-6856. Find PACER and the Party/Case Index on the Web at http://pacer.psc.uscourts.gov. PACER dial-up access is $.60 per minute. Also, courts offering internet access via RACER, PACER, Web-PACER or the new CM-ECF charge $.07 per page fee unless noted as free.

US District Court -- Eastern District of Louisiana

Home Page: www.laed.uscourts.gov

PACER: Toll-free access: 888-257-1175. Local access phone: 504-589-6714. Case records are available back to 1989. Records are purged every six months. New records are available online after 1-2 days. **PACER URL:** http://pacer.laed.uscourts.gov. Document images available.

New Orleans Division counties: Assumption Parish, Jefferson Parish, Lafourche Parish, Orleans Parish, Plaquemines Parish, St. Bernard Parish, St. Charles Parish, St. James Parish, St. John the Baptist Parish, St. Tammany Parish, Tangipahoa Parish, Terrebonne Parish, Washington Parish.

US Bankruptcy Court -- Eastern District of Louisiana

Home Page: www.laeb.uscourts.gov

PACER: Case records are available back to 1985. Records are purged every six months. New civil records are available online after 2 days. **PACER URL:** http://pacer.laeb.uscourts.gov.

Electronic Filing: Electronic filing information is available online at https://ecf.laeb.uscourts.gov. **Also:** access via phone on VCIS (Voice Case Information System) is available: 504-589-7879.

New Orleans Division counties: Assumption Parish, Jefferson Parish, Lafourche Parish, Orleans Parish, Plaquemines Parish, St. Bernard Parish, St. Charles Parish, St. James Parish, St. John the Baptist Parish, St. Tammany Parish, Tangipahoa Parish, Terrebonne Parish, Washington Parish.

US District Court -- Middle District of Louisiana

Home Page: www.lamd.uscourts.gov

PACER: Toll-free access: 800-616-8757. Local access phone: 225-389-3547. Case records are available back to October 1993. New records are available online after 1 day. **PACER URL:** http://pacer.lamd.uscourts.gov. Document images available.

Baton Rouge Division counties: Ascension Parish, East Baton Rouge Parish, East Feliciana Parish, Iberville Parish, Livingston Parish, Pointe Coupee Parish, St. Helena Parish, West Baton Rouge Parish, West Feliciana Parish.

US Bankruptcy Court -- Middle District of Louisiana

Home Page: www.lamb.uscourts.gov

PACER: Case records are available back to May 15, 1992. New civil records are available online after 1 day. **PACER URL:** http://pacer.lamb.uscourts.gov.

Electronic Filing: Electronic filing information is available online at https://ecf.lamb.uscourts.gov. **Also:** access via phone on VCIS (Voice Case Information System) is available: 504-382-2175.

Baton Rouge Division counties: Ascension Parish, East Baton Rouge Parish, East Feliciana Parish, Iberville Parish, Livingston Parish, Pointe Coupee Parish, St. Helena Parish, West Baton Rouge Parish, West Feliciana Parish.

US District Court -- Western District of Louisiana

Home Page: www.lawd.uscourts.gov

PACER: Toll-free access: 888-263-2679. Local access phone: 318-676-3958. Case records are available back to October 1993. Records are purged as deemed necessary. New records are available online after 1 day. **PACER URL:** https://pacer.lawd.uscourts.gov. Document images available.

Alexandria Division counties: Avoyelles Parish, Catahoula Parish, Concordia Parish, Grant Parish, La Salle Parish, Natchitoches Parish, Rapides Parish, Winn Parish.

Lafayette Division counties: Acadia Parish, Evangeline Parish, Iberia Parish, Lafayette Parish, St. Landry Parish, St. Martin Parish, St. Mary Parish, Vermilion Parish.

Lake Charles Division counties: Allen Parish, Beauregard Parish, Calcasieu Parish, Cameron Parish, Jefferson Davis Parish, Vernon Parish.

Monroe Division counties: Caldwell Parish, East Carroll Parish, Franklin Parish, Jackson Parish, Lincoln Parish, Madison Parish, Morehouse Parish, Ouachita Parish, Richland Parish, Tensas Parish, Union Parish, West Carroll Parish.

Shreveport Division counties: Bienville Parish, Bossier Parish, Caddo Parish, Claiborne Parish, De Soto Parish, Red River Parish, Sabine Parish, Webster Parish.

US Bankruptcy Court -- Western District of Louisiana

Home Page: www.lawb.uscourts.gov

PACER: Toll-free access: 888-523-1976. Local access phone: 318-676-4235. Case records are available back to 1992. New civil records are available online after 1 day. **PACER URL:** http://pacer.lawb.uscourts.gov. Document images available.

Electronic Filing: (Currently in the process of implementing CM/ECF). **Also:** access via phone on VCIS (Voice Case Information System) is available: 800-326-4026, 318-676-4234

Alexandria Division counties: Avoyelles Parish, Catahoula Parish, Concordia Parish, Grant Parish, La Salle Parish, Natchitoches Parish, Rapides Parish, Vernon Parish, Winn Parish.

Lafayette-Opelousas Division counties: Acadia Parish, Evangeline Parish, Iberia Parish, Lafayette Parish, St. Landry Parish, St. Martin Parish, St. Mary Parish, Vermilion Parish.

Lake Charles Division counties: Allen Parish, Beauregard Parish, Calcasieu Parish, Cameron Parish, Jefferson Davis Parish.

Monroe Division counties: Caldwell Parish, East Carroll Parish, Franklin Parish, Jackson Parish, Lincoln Parish, Madison Parish, Morehouse Parish, Ouachita Parish, Richland Parish, Tensas Parish, Union Parish, West Carroll Parish.

Shreveport Division counties: Bienville Parish, Bossier Parish, Caddo Parish, Claiborne Parish, De Soto Parish, Red River Parish, Sabine Parish, Webster Parish.

Capital: Augusta Kennebec County	Home Page www.state.me.us
Time Zone: EST	Attorney General www.state.me.us/ag
Number of Counties: 16	Archives www.state.me.us/sos/arc

State Level ... Major Agencies

Corporation Records, Limited Partnerships, Trademarks/Servicemarks, Assumed Name, Limited Liability Company Records, Limited Liability Partnerships

Secretary of State, Reports & Information Division, 101 State House Station, Augusta, ME 04333-0101; 207-624-7752, 207-624-7736 (Main Number), 207-287-5874 (Fax), 8AM-5PM.

www.state.me.us/sos/cec/corp

The Internet site gives basic information about the entity including address, corp ID, agent, and status. **Other options:** Lists of new entities filed with this office are available monthly.

Uniform Commercial Code, Federal Tax Liens, State Tax Liens

UCC Filing Section, Secretary of State, 101 State House Station, Augusta, ME 04333-0101 (Courier: Burton McCross State Office Bldg, 109 Sewell St, 4th Fl, Augusta, ME 04333); 207-624-7760, 207-287-5874 (Fax), 8AM-5PM.

www.state.me.us/sos/cec/corp/ucc.htm#fi111

Online access is available at https://www.informe.org/ucc/search/begin.shtml. There is a free name search, and reports may be ordered online, also. **Other options:** Farm products - buyers reports, secured party available in bulk.

Birth Certificates

Maine Department of Human Services, Vital Records, 221 State St, Station 11, Augusta, ME 04333-0011; 207-287-3181, 877-523-2659 (VitalChek), 207-287-1093 (Fax), 8AM-5PM.

www.state.me.us/dhs/welcome.htm

Pre-1892 records are available at the Internet at www.state.me.us/sos/geneology/homepage.html. **Other options:** Physical birth lists are available for purchase, excluding restricted information.

Death Records

Maine Department of Human Services, Vital Records, 221 State St, Station 11, Augusta, ME 04333-0011; 207-287-3181, 877-523-2659 (VitalChek), 207-287-1093 (Fax), 8AM-5PM.

www.state.me.us/dhs/welcome.htm

Both old and newer records are available at www.state.me.us/sos/arc/geneology/homepage.html. Death History records from the Maine State Archives are also available at http://thor.ddp.state.me.us/pls/archives/archdev.death_archive.search_form. Also, a free genealogy site at http://vitals.rootsweb.com/me/death/search.cgi has Death Indexes from 1960-1997. Search by surname, given name, place or year. **Other options:** Bulk file purchases are available, with the exclusion of restricted data.

Marriage Certificates

Maine Department of Human Services, Vital Records, 221 State St, Station 11, Augusta, ME 04333-0011; 207-287-3181, 877-523-2659 (VitalChek), 207-287-1093 (Fax), 8AM-5PM.

www.state.me.us/dhs/welcome.htm

Records are available at www.state.me.us/sos/arc/geneology/homepage.html from 1892-1966 and 1976-1996. Marriage History records from the Maine State Archives are available at http://thor.ddp.state.me.us/pls/archives/archdev.marriage_archive.search_form. **Other options:** Bulk file purchasing is available, with restricted data excluded.

Driver Records

Bureau of Motor Vehicles, Driver License Services, 29 State House Station, Augusta, ME 04333-0029; 207-624-9000, 8AM-5PM.

www.state.me.us/sos/bmv

Access is through InforME via the Internet. There is a $50.00 annual fee and records are $5.00 per request. Visit the web site for details and sign-up or call 207-621-2600. The state offers "Driver Cross Check" - a program of notification when activity occurs on a specific record. **Other options:** Maine will sell statewide or customized lists of license drivers via magnetic tape and other media for high volume users. Call 207-621-2600 for details.

Vehicle Ownership, Vehicle Identification

Department of Motor Vehicles, Registration Section, 29 State House Station, Augusta, ME 04333-0029; 207-624-9000 x52149, 207-624-9204 (Fax), 8AM-5PM M-F.

www.state.me.us/sos/bmv/

Maine offers online access to title and registration records via PC and modem. The system is open 24 hours daily. To set up an account, call 207-624-9264. Fee is $5.00 per record, annual registration is $50.00.

Legislation Records

http://janus.state.me.us/legis/

The web site offers bills, status, and access to text of state laws. **Other options:** A weekly list of LDs (legislative documents) is available.

State Level ... Occupational Licensing

Acupuncturist	http://pfr.informe.org/webquery/LicLookup.aspx
Aesthetician	http://pfr.informe.org/webquery/LicLookup.aspx
Alcohol/Drug Abuse Counselor	http://pfr.informe.org/webquery/LicLookup.aspx
Animal Medical Technician	http://pfr.informe.org/webquery/LicLookup.aspx
Appraiser, Residential Real Estate	http://pfr.informe.org/webquery/LicLookup.aspx
Architect	http://pfr.informe.org/webquery/LicLookup.aspx
Athletic Trainer	http://pfr.informe.org/webquery/LicLookup.aspx
ATV-All-Terrain Vehicle	www.state.me.us/ifw/index.html
Auctioneer	http://pfr.informe.org/webquery/LicLookup.aspx
Barber	http://pfr.informe.org/webquery/LicLookup.aspx
Boiler Contractor	http://pfr.informe.org/webquery/LicLookup.aspx
Boxer	http://pfr.informe.org/webquery/LicLookup.aspx
Charitable Solicitation	http://pfr.informe.org/webquery/LicLookup.aspx
Chiropractor	http://pfr.informe.org/webquery/LicLookup.aspx
Cosmetologist	http://pfr.informe.org/webquery/LicLookup.aspx
Counselor	http://pfr.informe.org/webquery/LicLookup.aspx

Dentist/ Dental Hygienist/ Dental Radiographer	www.mainedental.org/search.htm
Denturist	www.mainedental.org/search.htm
Dietitian	http://pfr.informe.org/webquery/LicLookup.aspx
Electrician	http://pfr.informe.org/webquery/LicLookup.aspx
Elevator/Tramway Contractor	http://pfr.informe.org/webquery/LicLookup.aspx
Employee Leasing Company	www.state.me.us/pfr/ins/emplease.htm
Engineer	http://professionals.maineusa.com/engineers/database.html
Forester	http://pfr.informe.org/webquery/LicLookup.aspx
Fund Raiser	http://pfr.informe.org/webquery/LicLookup.aspx
Funeral Home/ Funeral Service	http://pfr.informe.org/webquery/LicLookup.aspx
Geologist	http://pfr.informe.org/webquery/LicLookup.aspx
Hearing Aid Dealer/Fitter	http://pfr.informe.org/webquery/LicLookup.aspx
HMO	www.state.me.us/pfr/ins/inshmo.htm
Insurance Advisor	http://pfr.informe.org/webquery/LicLookup.aspx
Insurance Agent/Company	http://pfr.informe.org/webquery/LicLookup.aspx
Interior Designer	http://pfr.informe.org/webquery/LicLookup.aspx
Interpreter	http://pfr.informe.org/webquery/LicLookup.aspx
Kickboxer	http://pfr.informe.org/webquery/LicLookup.aspx
Landscape Architect	http://pfr.informe.org/webquery/LicLookup.aspx
Manicurist	http://pfr.informe.org/webquery/LicLookup.aspx
Manufactured Housing	http://pfr.informe.org/webquery/LicLookup.aspx
Marriage & Family Therapist	http://pfr.informe.org/webquery/LicLookup.aspx
Massage Therapist	http://pfr.informe.org/webquery/LicLookup.aspx
Medical Doctor	www.docboard.org/me/df/mesearch.htm
Naturopathic Physician	http://pfr.informe.org/webquery/LicLookup.aspx
Notary Public	www.state.me.us/sos/cec/rcn/notary/notlist.htm
Nursing Home Administrator	http://pfr.informe.org/webquery/LicLookup.aspx
Occupational Therapist	http://pfr.informe.org/webquery/LicLookup.aspx
Oil & Solid Fuel	http://pfr.informe.org/webquery/LicLookup.aspx
Optometrist	http://pfr.informe.org/webquery/LicLooKup.aspx
Osteopathic Physician/Phys. Assist.	www.docboard.org/me-osteo/df/index.htm
Osteopathic Resident/Intern	www.docboard.org/me-osteo/df/index.htm
Pastoral Counselor	http://pfr.informe.org/webquery/LicLookup.aspx
Pharmacist	http://pfr.informe.org/webquery/LicLookup.aspx
Physical Therapist	http://pfr.informe.org/webquery/LicLookup.aspx
Physician Assistant	www.docboard.org/me/df/mesearch.htm
Plumber	http://pfr.informe.org/webquery/LicLookup.aspx
Podiatrist	http://pfr.informe.org/webquery/LicLookup.aspx
Preferred Provider Organization	www.state.me.us/pfr/ins/insppo.htm
Psychologist	http://pfr.informe.org/webquery/LicLookup.aspx
Public Accountant-CPA	http://pfr.informe.org/webquery/LicLookup.aspx
Radiologic Technician	http://pfr.informe.org/webquery/LicLookup.aspx
Real Estate Appraiser, General	http://pfr.informe.org/webquery/LicLookup.aspx
Real Estate Appraiser/Trainee	http://pfr.informe.org/webquery/LicLookup.aspx
Real Estate Broker	http://pfr.informe.org/webquery/LicLookup.aspx
Re-insurer, Approved	http://pfr.informe.org/webquery/LicLookup.aspx
Respiratory Care Therapist	http://pfr.informe.org/webquery/LicLookup.aspx
Snowmobile	www.state.me.us/ifw/index.html
Social Worker	http://pfr.informe.org/webquery/LicLookup.aspx
Soil Scientist	http://pfr.informe.org/webquery/LicLookup.aspx
Speech Pathologist/Audiologist	http://pfr.informe.org/webquery/LicLookup.aspx
Substance Abuse Counselor	http://pfr.informe.org/webquery/LicLookup.aspx
Surplus Lines Company	http://pfr.informe.org/webquery/LicLookup.aspx
Surveyor, Land	http://pfr.informe.org/webquery/LicLookup.aspx
Utilization Review Entity	www.state.me.us/pfr/ins/insmedur.htm
Vendor, Itinerant/Transient	http://pfr.informe.org/webquery/LicLookup.aspx
Veterinarian/ Veterinary Technician	http://pfr.informe.org/webquery/LicLookup.aspx
Watercraft	www.state.me.us/ifw/index.html
Wrestler	http://pfr.informe.org/webquery/LicLookup.aspx

County Level ... Courts

Court Administration: State Court Administrator, PO Box 4820, Portland, ME, 04112; 207-822-0792; www.state.me.us/courts

Court Structure: The Superior Court is the court of general jurisdiction. Prior to year 2001, District Courts accepted civil cases involving claims less than $30,000. Now, District Courts have jurisdiction concurrent with that of the Superior Court for all civil actions except those cases vested in the Superior Court by statute. Both Superior and District Courts handle "misdemeanor" and "felony" cases, with jury trials being held in Superior Court only. Superior Court has exclusive jurisdiction over pleas or trials for murder cases.

Online Access Note: Development of a judicial computer system is in use statewide for all criminal and certain civil case types. The remainder of civil case types will be available statewide in the near future. The system is initially for judicial and law enforcement agencies and will not include public access in the near term. Some counties are online through a private vendor.

There are no known courts that independently offer access to their records.

County Level ... Recorders & Assessors

Recording Office Organization: 16 counties, 17 recording offices. The recording officer is the County Register of Deeds. Counties maintain a general index of all transactions recorded. Aroostock and Oxford Counties each have two recording offices. There are no county assessors; each town has its own. The entire state is in the Eastern Time Zone (EST). All tax liens on personal property are filed with the Secretary of State. All tax liens on real property are filed with the Register of Deeds.

Online Access Note: There is no statewide system. Several counties have developed their own system and a private vendor has placed assessor records from a number of towns on the Internet. Visit http://data.visionappraisal.com.

Androscoggin County *Real Estate, Tax Lien Records*
Access to the Registry index is available for a $50.00 annual fee and $.25 per minute. Indexes go back to 1976. For information and sign-up, contact Jeanine at 207-782-0191.

Cumberland County *Assessor, Property Sales Records*
Records on the Cape Elizabeth Town Assessor database are available free online at www.capeelizabeth.com/taxdata.html. Search by owner name, road and house number for Cape Elizabeth Town. Records on the Freeport Town Assessor property databases are available free online at www.freeportmaine.com/assessor/sendform.html. Also, search the Town of South Portland assessor database at http://data.visionappraisal.com/SouthPortlandME. Also, search the Town of Cumberland assessor data at http://data.visionappraisal.com/CumberlandME. The Gorham assessor is at http://data.visionappraisal.com/GorhamME.

Hancock County *Real Estate, Lines, UCC, Recording Records*
www.co.hancock.me.us/deeds2.html
Access to the county registry of deeds database at www.registryofdeeds.com requires registration. Viewing of records back to 1790 is free, but $1.25 per page to print. Register online. This site has had hacker problems; site of the infamous 3-monkeys. For information, visit www.registryofdeeds.com or call 888-833-3979.

Kennebec County *Assessor Records*
Records on the Winslow Town Property Records database are available free online at www.winslowmaine.org. Records on the Town of Waterville Assessor's Database are available free online at http://data.visionappraisal.com/WatervilleME/. User ID is required; registration is free.

Sagadahoc County   *Assessor Records*
www.cityofbath.com
Records on the City of Bath Assessor database are available free online at www.cityofbath.com/assessing/INDEX.HTM.

York County   *Assessor, Property Records*
www.raynorshyn.com/yorknet
Search the Town of Kennebunk assessor data free at www.kennebunk.maine.org/assessing/database/database.html. Search the Town of Eliot assessor data at http://data.visionappraisal.com/EliotME. Search the Town of York assessor data at www.yorkmaine.org/assess/accsel.html. There is also an avdanced search feature with land value and acres. Town of York assessor is also available at http://data.visionappraisal.com/YorkME. Free registration is required.

Federal Courts in Maine...

Standards for Federal Courts: The universal PACER sign-up number is 800-676-6856. Find PACER and the Party/Case Index on the Web at http://pacer.psc.uscourts.gov. PACER dial-up access is $.60 per minute. Also, courts offering internet access via RACER, PACER, Web-PACER or the new CM-ECF charge $.07 per page fee unless noted as free.

US District Court -- District of Maine
Home Page: www.med.uscourts.gov
PACER: Case records are available back to August 1991. Records are purged every 6 months. New records are available online after 1 day. **PACER URL:** https://pacer.med.uscourts.gov.
Electronic Filing: Electronic filing information is available online at (CM/ECF available Summer, 2002).
Bangor Division counties: Aroostook, Franklin, Hancock, Kennebec, Penobscot, Piscataquis, Somerset, Waldo, Washington.
Portland Division counties: Androscoggin, Cumberland, Knox, Lincoln, Oxford, Sagadahoc, York.

US Bankruptcy Court -- District of Maine
Home Page: www.meb.uscourts.gov
PACER: Toll-free access: 800-733-8797. Local access phone: 207-780-3268. Case records are available back to December 1988. Records are purged every two years. New civil records are available online after 1 day. **PACER URL:** http://pacer.meb.uscourts.gov.
Electronic Filing: Electronic filing information is available online at https://ecf.meb.uscourts.gov. **Also:** access via phone on VCIS (Voice Case Information System) is available: 800-650-7253, 207-780-3755
Bangor Division counties: Aroostook, Franklin, Hancock, Kennebec, Knox, Lincoln, Penobscot, Piscataquis, Somerset, Waldo, Washington.
Portland Division counties: Androscoggin, Cumberland, Oxford, Sagadahoc, York.

Capital:	Annapolis	Home Page	www.mec.state.md.us
	Anne Arundel County		
Time Zone:	EST	Attorney General	www.oag.state.md.us
Number of Counties:	23	Archives	www.mdarchives.state.md.us

State Level ... Major Agencies

Criminal Records

www.dpscs.state.md.us

The State Court Administrator's office has online access to criminal records from all state district courts, 3 circuit courts, and 1 city court. The system is available 24 hours daily. There is an annual $50 fee to register. Land records may also be accessed from this system. Call 410-260-1031 for a sign-up package.

Sexual Offender Registry

The Sexual Offender Registry is maintained by the Department of Public Safety. Names searches can be done by mail or e-mail, sor@dpscs.state.md.us. Be sure to provide your full name, address, and reason for the request. Visit www.dpscs.state.md.us/sor/ for free online access.

Corporation Records, Limited Partnerships, Trade Names, Limited Liability Company Records, Fictitious Name, Limited Liability Partnerships

Department of Assessments and Taxation, Corporations Division, 301 W Preston St, Room 801, Baltimore, MD 21201; 410-767-1340, 410-767-1330 (Charter Information), 410-333-7097 (Fax), 8AM-4:30PM.

www.dat.state.md.us/bsfd

The web site offers free searching for corporate name and trade name records. The site also includes real estate (cannot search by name) and UCC records. **Other options:** The state will release information in a bulk output format. Contact 410-561-9600 for details.

Trademarks/Servicemarks

Secretary of State, Trademarks Division, State House, Annapolis, MD 21401; 410-974-5531 x2, 410-974-5527 (Fax), 9AM-5PM.

www.sos.state.md.us

Online searching is available at the Internet site. Search can be by keyword in the description field, the service or product, the owner, the classification, or the mark name or keyword in the mark name. The site offers application forms to register, renew, or assign trade and service marks, and general information about registration. Click on "Trade & Service Marks." **Other options:** A computer printout of all marks registered, renewed or assigned within a 3 month period is available for $.05 per trademark.

Uniform Commercial Code

UCC Division-Taxpayer's Services, Department of Assessments & Taxation, 301 West Preston St, Baltimore, MD 21201; 410-767-1340, 410-333-7097 (Fax), 8AM-4:30PM.

http://sdatcert3.resiusa.org/ucc-charter/

The Internet site above offers free access to UCC index information. Also, there is a related site offering access to real property data for the whole state at www.dat.state.md.us/realprop. **Other options:** The agency has available for sale copies of public release master data files including corporation, real estate, and UCC. In addition, they can produce customized files on paper or disk. Visit the web site for more information.

Workers' Compensation Records

Workers Compensation Commission, 10 E Baltimore St, Baltimore, MD 21202; 410-864-5100, 410-864-5101 (Fax), 8AM-4:30PM.

www.charm.net/~wcc

Request for online hook-up must be in writing on letterhead. There is no search fee, but there is a $7.00 set-up fee, $5.00 monthly fee and a $.01-03 per minute connect fee assessed by Verizon or other provider. The system is open 24 hours a day to only in-state accounts. Write to the Commission at address above, care of Information Technology Division, or call Lili Joseph at 410-864-5119. **Other options:** This agency will sell its entire database depending on the use of the purchaser. Contact the commission for further information.

Driver Records

MVA, Driver Records Unit, 6601 Ritchie Hwy, NE, Glen Burnie, MD 21062; 410-787-7758, 8:15AM-4:30PM.

www.mva.state.md.us

The network is available 6 days a week, twenty-four hours a day to qualified and bonded individuals and businesses. Access is through PC and modem. The communication network is the Public Data Network (Bell Atlantic). Fee is $7.00 per record. Call Ms. Barbara Bentley at 410-768-7234 for account information.

Vehicle Ownership, Vehicle Identification

Department of Motor Vehicles, Vehicle Registration Division, Room 204, 6601 Ritchie Hwy, NE, Glen Burnie, MD 21062; 410-768-7520, 410-768-7653 (Fax), 8:15AM-4:30PM.

www.mva.state.md.us

The state offers vehicle and ownership data over the same online network utilized for driving record searches. Fee is $7.00 per record and line charges will be incurred. For more information, call 410-768-7234.

Legislation Records

http://mlis.state.md.us

The Internet site has complete information regarding bills and status.

State Level ... Occupational Licensing

Architectural Partnership/Corporation .... www.dllr.state.md.us/query/arch.html
Barber.. www.dllr.state.md.us/query/barber.html
Charity.. www.sos.state.md.us/sos/charity/html/search.html
Contractor.. www.dllr.state.md.us/query/home_imprv.html
Cosmetologist.. www.dllr.state.md.us/query/cosmet.html
Electrician, Master .... www.dllr.state.md.us/query/master_elec.html
Engineer, Examining.. www.dllr.state.md.us/query/stat_eng.html
Engineer, Professional.. www.dllr.state.md.us/query/prof_eng.html
Esthetician... www.dllr.state.md.us/query/cosmet.html
Forester.. www.dllr.state.md.us/query/forester.html
Fund Raising Counsel .... www.sos.state.md.us/sos/charity/html/psfrclist.html
Home Improvement Contractor/Salesperson .... www.dllr.state.md.us/query/home_imprv.html

HVACR Contractor..www.dllr.state.md.us/query/hvacr.html
Interior Designer..www.dllr.state.md.us/query/cert_int_des.html
Land Surveyor...www.dllr.state.md.us/query/land_surv.html
Landscape Architect...www.dllr.state.md.us/query/land_arch.html
Makeup Artist...www.dllr.state.md.us/query/cosmet.html
Medical Doctor..www.docboard.org/md/df/mdsearch.htm
Nail Technician...www.dllr.state.md.us/query/cosmet.html
Nurse-RN/LPN..http://63.72.31.185/
Nursing Assistant...http://63.72.31.185/
Optometrist...www.odfinder.org/LicSearch.asp
Plumber...www.dllr.state.md.us/query/plumb.html
Polygraph Examiner..http://polygraph.org/states/mpa/Members.htm
Precious Metals & Gem Dealer/Secondhand.....................www.dllr.state.md.us/query/sec_hand_deal.html
Public Accountant-CPA...www.dllr.state.md.us/query/cpa.html
Real Estate Agent..www.dllr.state.md.us/query/real_est.html
Real Estate Appraiser...www.dllr.state.md.us/query/real_est_app.html
Solicitor, Professional...www.sos.state.md.us/sos/charity/html/psfrclist.html
Subcontractor..www.dllr.state.md.us/query/home_imprv.html

County Level ... Courts

Court Administration:　　Court Administrator, Administrative Office of the Courts, 361 Rowe Blvd, Courts of Appeal Building, Annapolis, MD, 21401; 410-260-1400; www.courts.state.md.us

Court Structure:　　The Circuit Court is the highest court of record. Effective 10/1/98, the civil judgment limit increased from $20,000 to $25,000 at the District Court level. Certain categories of minor felonies are handled by the District Courts. However, all misdemeanors and felonies that require a jury trial are handled by Circuit Courts.

Online Access Note:　　An online computer system -- see www.courts.state.md.us/dialup.html -- called the Judicial Information System (JIS) or (SJIS) provides dial-up access to civil and criminal case information from the following:

> **All District Courts** - All civil and all misdemeanors

> **All Circuit Courts Civil** - All Circuit Courts civil records are online through JIS.

> **Circuit Courts Criminal -** Three courts are on JIS - Anne Arundel County, Carroll County, and Baltimore City Court

> Inquiries may be made to: the District Court traffic system for case information data, calendar information data, court schedule data, or officer schedule data; the District Court criminal system for case information data or calendar caseload data; the District Court civil system for case information data, attorney name and address data; the land records system for land and plat records. There is an annual $50.00 for JIS dial-up access, which must be included with the application. For additional information or to receive a registration packet, write or call Judicial Information Systems, Security Administrator, 2661 Riva Rd., Suite 900, Annapolis, MD 21401, 410-260-1031, or visit the web site above.

County Level ... Recorders & Assessors

Recording Office Organization: 23 counties and one independent city -- 24 total recording offices. The recording officer is the Clerk of the Circuit Court. Baltimore City has a recording office separate from the county of Baltimore. The entire state is in the Eastern Time Zone (EST). All tax liens are filed with the county Clerk of Circuit Court. Counties will not perform tax lien name searches.

Online Access Note: Search statewide property records data free online at http://sdatcert3.resiusa.org/rp_rewrite/. No name searching.

Also, online access to county tax records is available at www.taxrecords.com Land survey, condominium and survey plats is available free by county at www.plats.net. Use username "Plato" and password "plato#". No name searching.

Also, the MD state Dept. of Planning offers MDPropertyview with property maps/parcels and assessments on the web or CD-Rom. Registration is required. Visit www.mdp.state.md.us/data/mdview.htm or call 410-767-4614 or 410-767-4474. No name searching.

Montgomery County   *Real Property, Land Survey/Plat Records*
www.co.mo.md.us/judicial
Access to clerk records is available via JIS Dialup Access; contact Mary Hutchins 410-260-1031. Also, online search real property data at http://sdatcert3.resiusa.org/rp_rewrite. No name searching. Also, see state introduction for add'l land records online from www.plats.net (use username "Plato" and password "plato#") and MDPropertyview at www.mdp.state.md.us/data/mdview.htm. No name searching.

Statewide Systems Available
Read the text above for descriptions of ceveral statewide systems.

Federal Courts in Maryland...

Standards for Federal Courts: The universal PACER sign-up number is 800-676-6856. Find PACER and the Party/Case Index on the Web at http://pacer.psc.uscourts.gov. PACER dial-up access is $.60 per minute. Also, courts offering internet access via RACER, PACER, Web-PACER or the new CM-ECF charge $.07 per page fee unless noted as free.

US District Court -- Northern District of Maryland
Home Page: www.mdd.uscourts.gov
PACER: Toll-free access: 800-241-2259. Local access phone: 410-962-1812. Case records are available back to October 1990. Records are purged every six months. New records are available online after 1 day. **PACER URL:** http://pacer.mdd.uscourts.gov.
Electronic Filing: Electronic filing information is available online at (CM/ECF available Summer, 2002).
Opinions Online: Court opinions are available online at www.mdd.uscourts.gov.
Baltimore Division counties: Allegany, Anne Arundel, Baltimore, City of Baltimore, Caroline, Carroll, Cecil, Dorchester, Frederick, Garrett, Harford, Howard, Kent, Queen Anne's, Somerset, Talbot, Washington, Wicomico, Worcester.

US Bankruptcy Court -- Northern District of Maryland
Home Page: www.mdb.uscourts.gov
PACER: Toll-free access: 800-927-0474. Local access phone: 410-962-0776. Case records are available back to mid 1991. Records are purged every six months. New civil records are available online after 2 days. **PACER URL:** http://pacer.mdb.uscourts.gov.
Electronic Filing: (Currently in the process of implementing CM/ECF). **Also:** access via phone on VCIS (Voice Case Information System) is available: 800-829-0145, 410-962-0733
Baltimore Division counties: Anne Arundel, Baltimore, City of Baltimore, Caroline, Carroll, Cecil, Dorchester, Harford, Howard, Kent, Queen Anne's, Somerset, Talbot, Wicomico, Worcester.

US District Court -- Southern District of Maryland

Home Page: www.mdd.uscourts.gov

PACER: Toll-free access: 800-241-2259. Local access phone: 410-962-1812. Case records are available back to October 1990. Records are purged every six months. New records are available online after 1 day. **PACER URL:** http://pacer.mdd.uscourts.gov.

Electronic Filing: Electronic filing information is available online at (CM/ECF available Summer, 2002).

Opinions Online: Court opinions are available online at www.mdd.uscourts.gov.

Greenbelt Division counties: Calvert, Charles, Montgomery, Prince George's, St. Mary's.

US Bankruptcy Court -- Southern District of Maryland

Home Page: www.mdb.uscourts.gov

PACER: Toll-free access: 800-927-0474. Local access phone: 410-962-0776. Case records are available back to mid 1991. Records are purged every six months. New civil records are available online after 2 days. **PACER URL:** http://pacer.mdb.uscourts.gov.

Electronic Filing: (Currently in the process of implementing CM/ECF). **Also:** access via phone on VCIS (Voice Case Information System) is available: 800-829-0145, 410-962-0733

Greenbelt Division counties: Allegany, Calvert, Charles, Frederick, Garrett, Montgomery, Prince George's, St. Mary's, Washington.

Editor's Tip: Just because records are maintained in a certain way in your state or county do not assume that any other county or state does things the same way that you are used to.

Massachusetts

Capital:　　　Boston
　　　　　　　Suffolk County

Time Zone:　EST

Number of Counties:　14

Home Page　　　www.state.ma.us

Attorney General　www.ago.state.ma.us

Archives　　　　www.state.ma.us/sec/arc

State Level ... Major Agencies

Corporation Records, Trademarks/Servicemarks, Limited Liability Partnerships, Limited Partnerships, Limited Liability Companys

Secretary of the Commonwealth, Corporation Division, One Ashburton Pl, 17th Floor, Boston, MA 02108; 617-727-9640 (Corporations), 617-727-2850 (Records), 617-727-8329 (Trademarks), 617-727-9440 (Forms request line), 617-742-4538 (Fax), 8:45AM-5PM.

www.state.ma.us/sec/cor/coridx.htm

There is a free Internet lookup at http://corp.sec.state.ma.us/Portal/Functionality/Search.htm. This site also provides UCC information. The agency offers a commercial system called "Direct Access." The annual subscription fee is $149.00 and there is a $.40 a minute access fee. System is available from 8 AM to 10 PM. Call 617-727-7655 for a sign-up packet.

Uniform Commercial Code, State Tax Liens

UCC Division, Secretary of the Commonwealth, One Ashburton Pl, Room 1711, Boston, MA 02108; 617-727-2860, 900-555-4500 (Computer Prints), 900-555-4600 (Copies), 8:45AM-5PM.

www.state.ma.us/sec/

Free access to records is available at http://corp.sec.state.ma.us/Portal/Functionality/Search.htm. "Direct Access" is the commercial systems available for $149 per year plus a $.40 per minute network fee. The system is open from 8 AM to 9:50 PM. Call 617-727-7655 to obtain information packet. **Other options:** Microfiche may be purchased.

Driver Records-Insurance

Merit Rating Board, Attn: Driving Records, PO Box 199100, Boston, MA 02119-9100 (Courier: 630 Washington St, Boston, MA 02108); 617-351-4400, 617-351-9660 (Fax), 8:45AM-5:00PM.

www.state.ma.us/rmv

The Merit Rating Board provides both online and tape inquiry to the insurance industry for rating and issuance of new and renewal automobile insurance policies. Per statute, this method of retrieval is not open to the general public.

Vehicle Ownership, Vehicle Identification

Registry of Motor Vehicles, Document Control, PO Box 199100, Boston, MA 02119-9100; 617-351-9458, 617-351-9524 (Fax), 8AM-4:30PM.

www.state.ma.us/rmv

Searching is limited to Massachusetts based insurance companies and agents for the purpose of issuing or renewing insurance. This system is not open to the public. There is no fee, but line charges will be incurred. **Other options:** The state offers an extensive array of customized bulk record requests to authorzied users. For further information, contact the Production Control Office.

Legislation Records

www.state.ma.us/legis/

The web site has bill information for the current session and the previous session. **Other options:** The state does make available a listing of all bills filed and several bulletins; call 617-722-2860 for more information.

State Level ... Occupational Licensing

Adoption Center	www.qualitychildcare.org/adoption_search_a.asp
Alarm Installer, Burglar/Fire	http://license.reg.state.ma.us/pubLic/licque.asp?color=red&Board=EL
Allied Health Profession	http://license.reg.state.ma.us/pubLic/licque.asp?color=red&Board=AH
Allied Mental Health & Human Svcs Prof.	http://license.reg.state.ma.us/pubLic/licque.asp?query=personal&color=red&board=MH
Amusement Device Inspector	www.state.ma.us/dps/Lic_srch.htm
Architect	http://license.reg.state.ma.us/pubLic/licque.asp?color=red&Board=AR
Athletic Trainer	http://license.reg.state.ma.us/pubLic/licque.asp?color=red&Board=AH
Attorney	www.state.ma.us/obcbbo/bboreg/
Auctioneer School	www.state.ma.us/standards/auc-sch.htm
Bank & Savings Institution	http://db.state.ma.us/dob/in-choose.asp
Barber/Barber Shop	http://license.reg.state.ma.us/pubLic/licque.asp?color=red&Board=BR
Boilers/Pressure Vessels Inspector	www.state.ma.us/dps/Lic_srch.htm
Boxer	www.state.ma.us/mbc/ranking.htm
Building Inspector/Local Inspector	www.state.ma.us/bbrs/bocert.PDF
Building Producer	www.state.ma.us/bbrs/mfg98.pdf
Chiropractor	http://license.reg.state.ma.us/pubLic/licque.asp?color=red&Board=CH
Concrete Technician	www.state.ma.us/bbrs/programs.htm
Concrete Testing Laboratory	www.state.ma.us/bbrs/programs.htm
Construction Supervisor	www.state.ma.us/bbrs/cslsearch.htm
Cosmetologist (& Manicurist, Aesthetician)	http://license.reg.state.ma.us/pubLic/licque.asp?color=red&Board=HD
Credit Union	http://db.state.ma.us/dob/in-choose.asp
Day Care Center	www.qualitychildcare.org/
Dental Hygienist	http://license.reg.state.ma.us/pubLic/licque.asp?color=red&Board=DN
Dentist	http://license.reg.state.ma.us/pubLic/licque.asp?color=red&Board=DN
Educational Psychologist	http://license.reg.state.ma.us/pubLic/licque.asp?query=personal&color=red&board=MH
Electrician	http://license.reg.state.ma.us/pubLic/licque.asp?color=red&Board=EL
Electrologist	http://license.reg.state.ma.us/pubLic/licque.asp?color=red&Board=ET
Embalmer	http://license.reg.state.ma.us/pubLic/licque.asp?color=red&Board=EM
Engineer	http://license.reg.state.ma.us/pubLic/licque.asp?color=red&Board=EN
Family Child Care Provider	www.qualitychildcare.org/
Fire Protect Sprinkler System Contr./Fitter	www.state.ma.us/dps/Lic_srch.htm
Firemen / Engineer	www.state.ma.us/dps/Lic_srch.htm
Foster Care Provider	www.qualitychildcare.org/adoption_search_fc.asp
Funeral Director	http://license.reg.state.ma.us/pubLic/licque.asp?color=red&Board=EM
Gas Fitter	http://license.reg.state.ma.us/pubLic/licque.asp?color=red&Board=PL
Health Officer (Certified)	http://license.reg.state.ma.us/pubLic/licque.asp?color=red&Board=HO
HMO	www.state.ma.us/doi/Consumer/css_health_HMO.html
Hoisting Machinery (Forklift, Hydraulic, Crane) Operator	www.state.ma.us/dps/Lic_srch.htm
Home Improvement Contractor	www.state.ma.us/bbrs/Hicsearch.htm
Insurance, Domestic/Foreign Company	www.state.ma.us/doi/companies/companies_home.html

Land Surveyor .... http://license.reg.state.ma.us/pubLic/licque.asp?color=red&Board=EN
Landscape Architect .... http://license.reg.state.ma.us/pubLic/licque.asp?color=red&Board=LA
Lobbyist/Lobbyist Employer .... http://db.state.ma.us/SEC/PRE/search.asp
Lumber Producer, Native www.state.ma.us/bbrs/lumber99.PDF
Marriage & Family Therapist .... http://license.reg.state.ma.us/pubLic/licque.asp?query=personal&color=red&board=MH
Medical Doctor .... www.docboard.org/ma/df/name.html
Mental Health Counselor .... http://license.reg.state.ma.us/pubLic/licque.asp?query=personal&color=red&board=MH
Nuclear Power Plant Engineer/Operator .... www.state.ma.us/dps/Lic_srch.htm
Nurse, LPN/RN/Midwife .... http://license.reg.state.ma.us/pubLic/licque.asp?color=red&Board=RN
Nursing Home Administrator .... http://license.reg.state.ma.us/pubLic/licque.asp?color=red&Board=NH
Nursing Home/Rest Home .... www.medicare.gov/nhcompare/home.asp
Occupational Therapist/Assistant .... http://license.reg.state.ma.us/pubLic/licque.asp?color=red&Board=AH
Oil Burner Technician/Contractor .... www.state.ma.us/dps/Lic_srch.htm
Optician .... http://license.reg.state.ma.us/pubLic/licque.asp?query=personal&color=red&board=DO
Optician, Dispensing .... http://license.reg.state.ma.us/pubLic/licque.asp?color=red&Board=DO
Optometrist .... http://license.reg.state.ma.us/pubLic/licque.asp?color=red&Board=OP
Pharmacist .... http://license.reg.state.ma.us/pubLic/licque.asp?color=red&Board=PH
Physical Therapist/Assistant .... http://license.reg.state.ma.us/pubLic/licque.asp?color=red&Board=AH
Physician Assistant .... http://license.reg.state.ma.us/pubLic/licque.asp?color=red&Board=AP
Pipefitter .... www.state.ma.us/dps/Lic_srch.htm
Plumber .... http://license.reg.state.ma.us/pubLic/licque.asp?color=red&Board=PL
Podiatrist .... http://license.reg.state.ma.us/pubLic/licque.asp?color=red&Board=PD
Psychologist/Provider .... http://license.reg.state.ma.us/pubLic/licque.asp?color=red&Board=PY
Public Accountant-CPA .... http://license.reg.state.ma.us/pubLic/licque.asp?color=red&Board=PA
Radio & TV Repair Technician .... http://license.reg.state.ma.us/pubLic/licque.asp?color=red&Board=TV
Real Estate Appraiser .... http://license.reg.state.ma.us/pubLic/licque.asp?color=red&Board=RA
Real Estate Broker/Salesperson .... http://license.reg.state.ma.us/pubLic/licque.asp?color=red&Board=RE
Refrigeration Technician/Contractor .... www.state.ma.us/dps/Lic_srch.htm
Rehabilitation Therapist .... http://license.reg.state.ma.us/pubLic/licque.asp?query=personal&color=red&board=MH
Residential Care, Youth .... www.qualitychildcare.org/residential_search.asp
Respiratory Care Therapist .... http://license.reg.state.ma.us/pubLic/licque.asp?color=red&Board=RC
Sanitarian .... http://license.reg.state.ma.us/pubLic/licque.asp?color=red&Board=SA
Social Worker .... http://license.reg.state.ma.us/pubLic/licque.asp?color=red&Board=SW
Speech-Language Pathologist/Audiologist ... http://license.reg.state.ma.us/pubLic/licque.asp?color=red&Board=SP
Veterinarian .... http://license.reg.state.ma.us/pubLic/licque.asp?color=red&Board=VT
Water Supply Facility Operator .... http://license.reg.state.ma.us/pubLic/licque.asp?color=red&Board=DW

County Level ... Courts

Court Administration: Chief Justice for Administration and Management, 2 Center Plaza, Room 540, Boston, MA, 02108; 617-742-8575; www.state.ma.us/courts/admin/index.html

Court Structure: The various court sections are called "Departments." While Superior and District Courts have concurrent jurisdiction in civil cases, the practice is to assign cases less than $25,000 to the District Court and those over $25,000 to Superior Court. In addition to misdemeanors, the District Courts and Boston Municipal Courts have jurisdiction over certain minor felonies. Eviction cases may be filed at a county District Court or at the regional "Housing Court." A case may be moved from a District Court to a Housing Court, but never the reverse. They also hear misdemeanor "Code Violation" cases and prelims for these. There are five Housing Court Regions - Boston (Suffolk County), Worcester (County), Southeast (Plymouth and Bristol Counties), Northeast (Essex County), and Western (Berkshire, Franklin, Hampden and Hampshire Counties). The SE Housing Court has three branches - Brockton, Fall River, and New Bedford.

Online Access Note: Online access to records on the statewide Trial Courts Information Center web site is available to attorneys and law firms at www.ma-trialcourts.org/tcic/welcome.jsp. Contact Peter Nylin by email at nylin_p@jud.state.ma.us. Site is updated daily.

County Level ... Recorders & Assessors

Recording Office Organization: 14 counties, 312 towns, and 39 cities; 21 recording offices and 365 UCC filing offices. Filing locations vary depending upon the type of document, as noted below. Berkshire and Bristol counties each have three recording offices. Essex, Middlesex and Worcester counties each have two recording offices. Cities/towns bearing the same name as a county are Barnstable, Essex, Franklin, Hampden, Nantucket, Norfolk, Plymouth, and Worcester. Some UCC financing statements on personal property collateral were submitted to cities/towns until June 30, 2001, while real estate recording continues to be handled by the counties. The recording officers are Town/City Clerk (UCC), County Register of Deeds (real estate), and Clerk of US District Court (federal tax liens). The entire state is in the Eastern Time Zone (EST). Federal tax liens on personal property were filed with the Town/City Clerks prior to 1970. Since that time federal tax liens on personal property are filed with the US District Court in Boston as well as with the towns/cities.

The federal tax liens are indexed at US District Court, 1 Courthouse Way, Boston, MA 02110 on a computer system. Searches are available by mail or in person, or you can do the search yourself at no charge on their public computer terminal. Do not telephone. The court suggests including the Social Security number and/or address of individual names in your search request in order to narrow the results. A mail search costs $15.00 and will take about two weeks. Copies are included.

State tax liens on personal property are filed with the Town/City Clerk or Tax Collector. All tax liens against real estate are filed with the county Register of Deeds. Some towns file state tax liens on personal property with the UCC index and include tax liens on personal property automatically with a UCC search. Others will perform a separate state tax lien search usually for a fee of $10.00 plus copies.

Online Access Note: A large number of towns and several counties offer online access to assessor records via the Internet for no charge. Also, a private vendor has placed assessor records from a number of towns on the Internet. Visit http://data.visionappraisal.com

> **Editor's Tip:** Towns and cities that offer online access are listed under their county location.

Barnstable County   *Real Estate, Lien Records*

www.bcrd.co.barnstable.ma.us
Access to County records requires a $50 annual fee, plus $.50 per minute of use. Records date back to 1976. Lending agency information is available. For information, contact Janet Hoben at 508-362-7733.

Barnstable Town   *Assessor Records*

www.town.barnstable.ma.us
Town of Barnstable Assessor records are available free online at
http://town.barnstable.ma.us/Information_01/Assessment/asse_online_db.htm. Email questions or comments to webadm@town.barnstable.ma.us or call the Assessing Dept. at 508-862-4022.

Falmouth Town   *Assessor Records*

www.town.falmouth.ma.us
Records on the Town of Falmouth Assessor database are available free by experiment on the Internet at www.town.falmouth.ma.us/propinq.html. Provides owner, address, and valuation only.

Mashpee Town   *Assessor Records*

www.ci.mashpee.ma.us
Records on the Town of Mashpee Assessor database are available free online at www.capecode.com/mashpee/search.asp

Provincetown   *Assessor, Property Sales Records*

www.provincetowngov.org

Records on the Provincetown Assessor database are available free online at www.provincetowngov.org/assessor.html.

Yarmouth Town   *Assessor Records*

www.yarmouthcapecod.org

Records on the Assessor's database are available free online at http://data.visionappraisal.com/yarmouthma. Free registration for full data. Non-registered users can access a limited set of data.

Berkshire County (Middle District)   *Real Estate, Lien Records*

Online search: see Berkshire County Southern District.

Berkshire County (Northern District)   *Real Estate, Lien Records*

www.bcn.net/~nbrd

Online search: see Berkshire County Southern District.

Berkshire County (Southern District)   *Real Estate, Lien Records*

Searching of Titlesearch records requires a one-time $100 signup and $.50 per minute of use. System provides access to all three District Recorder's records; records date back to 1985. Searchable indices: recorded land, plans, registered land. Lending agency information available. For information, contact Sharon Henault at 413-443-7438.

Bristol County (Fall River District)   *Real Estate, Lien Records*

Online search: see Bristol County Southern District.

Bristol County (Northern District)   *Real Estate, Lien Records*

Online search: see Bristol County Southern District.

Bristol County (Southern District)   *Real Estate, Lien Records*

Access to County records requires a $100 set up fee and $.50 per minute of use. All three districts are on this system; the record dates vary by district. Lending agency information is available. For information, contact Rosemary at 508-993-2605.

Attleboro City   *Property Assessor Records*

Search the city assessor data at http://data.visionappraisal.com/attleboroMA. Free registration for full data. Non-registered users can access a limited set of data.

Dartmouth Town   *Assessor Records*

www.town.dartmouth.ma.us/town_hall.htm

Search the town assessor database at http://data.visionappraisal.com/DartmouthMA/. Free registration for full data.

New Bedford City   *Property, Assessor Records*

www.ci.new-bedford.ma.us/Nav3.htm

Access to the assessor's property database is available free at www.ci.new-bedford.ma.us/Assessors/RealPropertyLookup.htm.

North Attleborough Town   *Assessor Records*

Search the town assessor database at http://data.visionappraisal.com/NorthAttleboroMA/. Free registration for full data.

Dukes County

Edgartown   *Real Estate, Property Tax Records*

Search the Town assessor's database at http://data.visionappraisal.com/EdgartownMA. Free registration for full data.

Oak Bluffs Town   *Assessor Records*

Search the town assessor database at http://data.visionappraisal.com/OakBluffsMA/. Free registration for full data.

Tisbury Town   *Assessor Records*

www.ci.tisbury.ma.us

Search the town assessor database at http://data.visionappraisal.com/TisburyMA/. Free registration for full data.

Essex County (Northern District)   *Real Estate, Lien, Grantor/Grantee, Recording Records*
www.lawrencedeeds.com
Search the county recorder database for free at www.lawrencedeeds.com/dsSearch.asp. Also see Andover Town and Essex County Southern District.

Essex County (Southern District)   *Real Estate, Lien, Deed Records*
Access to the Essex County online records requires a $25 deposit, with a $.25 per minute charge for use. Records date back to 1981. Lending agency information is available. For information, contact David Burke at 978-683-2745. Records on the Essex County South Registry of Deeds database are available free on the Internet at www.salemdeeds.com. Click on "Deeds online". Images start 1/1992; records back to 1/1984. Search by grantee/grantor, town & date, street, or book & page.

Andover Town   *Assessor, Land, Grantor/Grantee, Recording Records*
www.town.andover.ma.us
Property tax records on the Assessor's database are available free online at www.town.andover.ma.us/assess/values.htm. Also, search the county recorder database for free at www.lawrencedeeds.com/dsSearch.asp.

Lawrence City   *Land, Grantor/Grantee, Recording Records*
www.cityoflawrence.com/Departments.asp
Search the county recorder database for free at www.lawrencedeeds.com/dsSearch.asp.

Manchester-by-the-Sea Town   *Property Assessor Records*
www.manchester.ma.us
Search the property assessment data at www.patriotproperties.com/manchester.

Methuen City   *Property Assessor, Land, Grantor/Grantee, Recording Records*
www.ci.methuen.ma.us
Search the property assessment data free at http://host229.ci.methuen.ma.us. Also, search the county recorder database for free at www.lawrencedeeds.com/dsSearch.asp.

Newburyport City   *Assessor Records*
Search the city assessor database at http://data.visionappraisal.com/NewBURYPORTMA/. Free registration for full data.

North Andover Town   *Land, Grantor/Grantee, Recording Records*
www.townofnorthandover.com
Search the county recorder database for free at www.lawrencedeeds.com/dsSearch.asp.

Swampscott Town   *Assessor, Real Estate Records*
www.swampscott.org/government.htm
Access to the Assessor's Property Valuation List fy-2002 is available free at www.swampscott.org. Click on "Assessors Valuation Book". Search the name column: Contol+F then enter name information, then "Find Next." Site may be temporarily down.

Hampden County   *Real Estate, Lien Records*
Access to County online records requires a $50 annual fee and $.50 per minute of use. Records date back to 1962. Lending agency information is available. Searchable indexes are bankruptcy (from PACER), unregistered land site and registered land site. For information, contact Donna Brown or Mary Caron at 413-755-1722 x121.

Agawam Town   *Property Assessment Data Records*
Access to Property Assessment Data is available free at www.patriotproperties.com/agawam/Default.asp?br=exp&vr=5

Holyoke City   *Tax Assessor Records*
www.ci.holyoke.ma.us
Access to property valuations on the tax assessor database are available free at www.ci.holyoke.ma.us/Assesment.asp. No name searching.

Longmeadow Town   *Assessor Records*
www.longmeadow.org
Access to tax records is free at http://data.visionappraisal.com/LONGMEADOWMA/. Free registration for full data.

Hampden County *continued*

Southwick Town *Assessor Records*

Search the town assessor database at http://data.visionappraisal.com/SouthwickMA/. Free registration for full data.

West Springfield Town *Assessor Records*

Search the town assessor database at http://data.visionappraisal.com/WestSpringfieldMA/. Free registration for full data.

Westfield City *Assessor Records*

www.ci.westfield.ma.us
Property tax records on the Assessor's database are available free online at www.ci.westfield.ma.us/realest/rea00.htm.

Hampshire County *Real Estate, Lien Records*

Access to County Register of Deeds online records requires a $100 annual fee and $.50 per minute of use, $.60 for out-of-state. Records date back to 9/2/1986. Lending agency information is available. For information, contact MaryAnn Foster at 413-584-3637.

Middlesex County (Northern District) *Real Estate, Lien, Grantor/Grantee Records*

www.lowelldeeds.com
The Telesearch subscription online system with North District records has been replaced with free internet access at http://216.60.44.25/MA25017/namesearch.jsp or the main web site.

Middlesex County (Southern District) *Real Estate, Lien Records*

Access to the LandTrack online system with Southern District records requires a $100 annual fee, plus $.50 per minute of use. Lending agency information is available as is a fax back service for documents. No new customers are being accepted and the system will be replaced by free web access late 2002.

Arlington Town *Assessor Records*

www.town.arlington.ma.us/arthalli.htm
Search the town assessor database for free at http://arlserver.town.arlington.ma.us/property.html.

Cambridge City *Assessor Records*

http://www2.ci.cambridge.ma.us/assessor
Records on the City of Cambridge Assessor database are available free online at www2.ci.cambridge.ma.us/assessor/index.html.

Concord Town *Property Assessor Records*

www.concordnet.org
Visit www.concordnet.org/assessor/fy01value_main.htm.

Dracut Town *Assessor Records*

Search the town assessor database at http://data.visionappraisal.com/DracutMA/. Free registration for full data.

Lowell City *Assessor Records*

Search the Assessor's database at http://data.visionappraisal.com/LowellMA/. Free registration for full data.

Medford City *Property Assessor Records*

www.medford.org
Seach the city assessor database at http://data.visionappraisal.com/MedfordMA/. Free registration for full data.

Natick Town *Assessor, Property Records*

Search town assessments free at www.natickma.org/assess/cama.asp.

Newton City *Assessor Records*

www.ci.newton.ma.us
Records on the City of Newton Fiscal 1998 Assessment database are available free at www.ci.newton.ma.us/GIS/Assessors/Default.asp. Data represents market value as of 1/1/1997.

Reading Town *Assessor Records*
www.ci.reading.ma.us/depts.htm
Records on the Town of Reading Assessor database are available free online at www.ziplink.net/~reading1/assessor.htm.

Somerville City *Assessor Records*
Search the city assessor database at http://data.visionappraisal.com/SomervilleMA/. Free registration for full data.

Waltham City *Assessor Records*
www.city.waltham.ma.us
Records on the City of Waltham Assessor database are available free online at
www.city.waltham.ma.us/assessors/caveat.htm.

Watertown *Assessor Records*
Records on the Watertown Town Online Assessed Values site are available free online at
www.townonline.com/watertown/realestate/assessments/index.html.

Wayland Town *Assessor Records*
www.wayland.ma.us/townadministration.html
Property tax records on the Assessor's database are available free online at www.wayland.ma.us/assess-reval99.htm. Also, the read only tax assessor information is available through a private company's site at
www.mypropertyrecords.com/univers.

Norfolk County *Real Estate, Lien Records*
www.norfolkdeeds.org
Access to county online records requires a $25 set up fee, plus $1 fee for the first minute and $.50 per minute thereafter per session. The system is only accessible in Massachusetts. Lending agency information is available. For info, contact Pam at 781-461-6116.

Brookline Town *Assessor, Property Records*
www.town.brookline.ma.us/Assessors
Records on the Town of Brookline Assessors database are available free online at
www.townofbrooklinemass.com/assessors/propertylookup.asp.

Dedham Town *Assessor Records*
Property records on the Assessor's database are available free online at http://data.visionappraisal.com/dedhamma/. Registration is required for full access; registration is free.

Walpole Town *Property Assessor Records*
www.walpole.ma.us
Search the town assessor database at http://data.visionappraisal.com/WalpoleMA/. Free registration for full data.

Wellesley Town *Assessor Records*
www.ci.wellesley.ma.us/town/index.html
Property tax records on the Assessor's database are available free online at www.ci.wellesley.ma.us/asr/index.html.

Plymouth County *Real Estate, Lien, Judgment Records*
Access to Online Titleview for Plymouth County records requires a usage charge of $.60 per minute of use. Records date back to 1971. Lending agency information is available. A fax back service is $3 plus $1 per page in county, $5. plus $1 per page, outside. For information, call 508-830-9287.

Duxbury Town *Property Assessor Records*
Search the town public documents free at http://duxburyma.virtualtownhall.net/Public_Documents/Search.

Hingham Town *Property Assessor Records*
Search the property rolls for free at www.hingham-ma.com/html/assessment_data.html. Click on "Click here to view data."

Suffolk County *Real Estate, Lien, Deed, Property Assessor Records*
www.suffolkdeeds.com
Searches on the Registry of Deeds site are free; real estate/liens on the county online system is not. Access to the County online system requires a written request submitted to Register of Deeds, POB 9660, Boston MA 02114. Online charges are $.50 per minute.

A fax back service is available. Records on the County Registry of Deeds database are available free on the Internet at www.suffolkdeeds.com/search/default.asp. Search by name, corporation, and grantor/grantee. Recorded land records begin 1979; Registered land, 1983. Also, search the Boston assessor property records for free at www.cityofboston.gov/assessing/search.asp. City property taxes are also available, but no name searching.

Boston City *Assessor Records*

www.ci.boston.ma.us/assessing
Records on the City of Boston Assessor database are available free online at www.ci.boston.ma.us/assessing/search.asp.

Chelsea City *Assessor Records*

Search the city assessor database at http://data.visionappraisal.com/ChelseaMA/. Free registration for full data.

Revere City *Assessor Records*

Search the town assessor database at http://data.visionappraisal.com/RevereMA/. Free registration for full data.

Worcester County (Northern District) *Real Estate, Lien Records*

www.state.ma.us/nwrod
Access to the "Northfield" online service requires $50 annually, plus $.25 per minute of use. Records date back to 1983. Viewable images are available back to 1995. Lending agency information is available. A fax back service is available. For information, contact Ruth Piermarini at 978-342-2637.

Worcester County (Worcester District) *Real Estate, Property Tax Records*

Records on the Town of Holden assessor's database are available free online at http://140.239.211.227/HOLDENMA. Registration is required; sign-up is free.

Dudley Town *Assessor Records*

Search the town assessor database at http://data.visionappraisal.com/DudleyMA/. Free registration for full data.

Holden Town *Real Estate, Property Tax Records*

Search the Town assessor's database free at http://data.visionappraisal.com/HOLDENMA. Registration is required; sign-up is free.

Leominster City *Assessor Records*

Search the assessor's database at http://data.visionappraisal.com/leominsterma. Free registration for full data.

Oxford Town *Property Assessor Records*

www.town.oxford.ma.us
Search the property assessments by street name for free at www.town.oxford.ma.us/Assessor/Assessor.htm.

West Boylston Town *Assessor Records*

www.westboylston.com
Search the town assessor Valuations Listings for free at www.westboylston.com/ASSESS/Assessors1.htm. Files are searchable by street and include owner names.

Worcester City *Real Estate, Lien, Assessor Records*

Data is available online in 2 ways. Online access to the City Assessor Valuation Search database is available free at www.ci.worcester.ma.us/assessing/index.html. And, access to the "Landtrack System" for Worcester District records requires a $50 annual fee plus $.25 per minute of use. Index records date back to 1966. Images are viewable from 1974 onward. Lending agency info is available. Fax back service is available for $.50 per page. For information, contact Joe Ursoleo at 508-798-7713 X233.

Federal Courts in Massachusetts...

Standards for Federal Courts: The universal PACER sign-up number is 800-676-6856. Find PACER and the Party/Case Index on the Web at http://pacer.psc.uscourts.gov. PACER dial-up access is $.60 per minute. Also, courts offering internet access via RACER, PACER, Web-PACER or the new CM-ECF charge $.07 per page fee unless noted as free.

US District Court -- District of Massachusetts

Home Page: www.mad.uscourts.gov

PACER: Toll-free access: 888-399-4639. Local access phone: 617-748-4294. Case records are available back to January 1990. Records are purged every 12 months. New records are available online after 1 day. **PACER URL:** http://pacer.mad.uscourts.gov. Document images available.

Electronic Filing: Electronic filing information is available online at (CM/ECF available Summer, 2002).

Boston Division counties: Barnstable, Bristol, Dukes, Essex, Middlesex, Nantucket, Norfolk, Plymouth, Suffolk.

Springfield Division counties: Berkshire, Franklin, Hampden, Hampshire.

Worcester Division counties: Worcester.

US Bankruptcy Court -- District of Massachusetts

Home Page: www.mab.uscourts.gov

PACER: Toll-free access: 888-201-3571. Local access phone: 617-565-6021. Case records are available back to April 1, 1987. Records are purged every 12 months. New civil records are available online after 1 day. **PACER URL:** http://pacer.mab.uscourts.gov. Document images available.

Electronic Filing: (Currently in the process of implementing CM/ECF). **Also:** access via phone on VCIS (Voice Case Information System) is available: 888-201-3572, 617-565-6025

Boston Division counties: Barnstable, Bristol, Dukes, Essex (except towns assigned to Worcester Division), Nantucket, Norfolk (except towns assigned to Worcester Division), Plymouth, Suffolk, and the following towns in Middlesex: Arlington, Belmont, Burlington, Everett,Lexington, Malden, Medford, Melrose, Newton, North Reading, Reading, Stoneham, Wakefield, Waltham, Watertown, Wilmington, Winchester and Woburn.

Worcester Division counties: Berkshire, Franklin, Hampden, Hampshire, Middlesex (except the towns assigned to the Boston Division), Worcester and the following towns: in Essex-Andover, Haverhill, Lawrence, Methuen and North Andover; in Norfolk-Bellingham, Franklin, Medway,Millis and Norfolk.

Editor's Tip: Just because records are maintained in a certain way in your state or county do not assume that any other county or state does things the same way that you are used to.

Capital:	Lansing Ingham County	Home Page	www.state.mi.us
		Attorney General	
Time Zone:	EST/CST		www.ag.state.mi.us
Number of Counties:	83	Archives	www.sos.state.mi.us /history/archive

State Level ... Major Agencies

Criminal Records

Michigan State Police, Ident. Section, Criminal Justice Information Center, 7150 Harris Dr, Lansing, MI 48913; 517-322-5531, 517-322-0635 (Fax), 8AM-5PM.

www.msp.state.mi.us

Online access is limited to businesses that are ongoing requesters. Access is via the Internet, credit cards are required. To set up an account, call 517-322-5546.

Sexual Offender Registry

The State Police maintain the state sex offender data. One may search online by name or ZIP Code at at www.mipsor.state.mi.us. Local law enforcement agencies also provide access to the database.

Incarceration Records

Information on current and former inmates is available at www.state.mi.us/mdoc. Location, MDOC number, conviction and sentencing information, physical identifiers, and release dates are provided.

Corporation Records, Limited Liability Company Records, Limited Partnership Records, Assumed Name

Department of Consumer & Industry Svcs, bureau of Commercial Services, PO Box 30054, Lansing, MI 48909-7554 (Courier: 6546 Mercantile Way, Lansing, MI 48910); 517-241-6470, 517-241-0538 (Fax), 8AM-noon, 1-5PM.

http://michigan.gov/cis/0,1607,7-154-10557_12901---,00.html

At he web site, search by company name or file number for records of domestic corporations, limited liability companies, and limited partnerships and of foreign corporations, and limited partnerships qualified to transact business in the state. **Other options:** The database is for sale on tape or microfiche.

Trademarks/Servicemarks

Bureua of Commercial Services, Trademarks & Service Marks, PO Box 30054, Lansing, MI 48909-7554 (Courier: 6546 Mercantile Way, Lansing, MI 48910); 517-241-6470, 8AM-5PM (closed at noon for 1 hr).

www.cis.state.mi.us/bcs/corp/forms.htm

Free searching is available at www.cis.state.mi.us/bcs/corp/pdf/markcom.pdf. This is a search of a PDF file of their system. It is very tricky to get to on the web.

Workers' Compensation Records

Department of Consumer & Industry Services, Bureau of Workers & Unemployment Compensation, 7150 Harris Dr, Lansing, MI 48909; 517-322-1884, 888-396-5041, 517-322-1808 (Fax), 8AM-5PM.

www.michigan.gov/cis

Go to the web site and follow the links to see if an employer has coverage. The site does not allow searching by employee name.

Driver Records

Dept. of State Police, Record Look-up Unit, 7064 Crowner Dr, Lansing, MI 48918; 517-322-1624, 517-322-1181 Fax, 8AM-4:45PM.

www.sos.state.mi.us/dv

Online ordering is available on an interactive basis. The system is open 7 days a week. Ordering is by DL or name and DOB. An account must be established and billing is monthly. Access is also available from the Internet. Fee is $6.55 per record. For more information, call 517-322-1591. **Other options:** Magnetic tape inquiry is available. Also, the state offers the license file for bulk purchase. Customized runs are $64 per thousand records; the complete database can be purchased for $16 per thousand. A $10,000 surety bond is required.

Vehicle Ownership, Vehicle Identification, Vessel Ownership, Vessel Registration

Dept. of State Police, Record Look-up Unit, 7064 Crowner Dr, Lansing, MI 48918; 517-322-1624, 517-322-1181 Fax, 8AM-4:45PM.

www.sos.state.mi.us/dv

Online searching is single inquiry and requires a VIN or plate number. A $25,000 surety bond is required. Fee is $6.55 per record. Direct dialup or Internet access is offered. For more information, call 517-322-1591. **Other options:** Michigan offers bulk retrieval from the VIN and plate database. A written request letter, stating purpose, must be submitted and approved. A surety bond is required upon approval. Please call 517-322-3454.

Legislation Records

www.michiganlegislature.org

Access is available from their Internet site. Adobe Acrobat Reader is required. Information available includes status of bills, bill text, joint resolution text, journals, calendars, session and committee schedules, and MI complied laws.

State Level ... Occupational Licensing

Airport Manager	www.michigan.gov/documents/MGRLST_17899_7.pdf
Ambulance Attendant	www.michigan.gov/cis/0,1607,7-154-10557---,00.html
Amusement Ride	http://cis.state.mi.us/verify.htm
Appraiser, Real Estate/General/Residential	http://cis.state.mi.us/verify.htm
Architect	http://cis.state.mi.us/verify.htm
Assessor	www.michigan.gov/documents/CertificationLevel_3022_7.pdf
Athletic Control	http://cis.state.mi.us/verify.htm
Attorney (State Bar)	www.michbar.org/framemaker.cfm?content_dir=member&content=content.html
Aviation Medical Examiner	www.michigan.gov/aero/0,1607,7-145-6775_7027---,00.html
Bank & Trust Company	www.michigan.gov/cis/1,1607,7-154--22352--,00.html
Barber	http://cis.state.mi.us/verify.htm

Boxing/Wrestling Occupation ....http://cis.state.mi.us/verify.htm
Builder, Residential..http://cis.state.mi.us/verify.htm
Camp, Children/Adult Foster Care ....www.michigan.gov/cis/0,1607,7-154-10568_17846_17885---,00.html
Carnival...http://cis.state.mi.us/verify.htm
Cemetery ....http://cis.state.mi.us/verify.htm
Check Seller ....www.michigan.gov/cis/0,1607,7-154-10555_13251_13257---,00.html
Child Caring Institution...www.michigan.gov/cis/0,1607,7-154-10568_17846---,00.html
Child Court Operated Facility ....www.michigan.gov/cis/0,1607,7-154-10568_17846---,00.html
Child Day Care...www.michigan.gov/cis/0,1607,7-154-10568_17949---,00.html
Child Welfare Agency (Child Placing Agency).........www.michigan.gov/cis/0,1607,7-154-10568_17846---,00.html
Chiropractor ....http://cis.state.mi.us/verify.htm
Collection Manager ....http://cis.state.mi.us/verify.htm
Community Planner...http://cis.state.mi.us/verify.htm
Consumer Financial Service......................................www.michigan.gov/cis/0,1607,7-154-10555_13251_13257---,00.html
Contractor, Residential..http://cis.state.mi.us/verify.htm
Cosmetologist...http://cis.state.mi.us/verify.htm
Counselor ....http://cis.state.mi.us/verify.htm
Credit Card Issuer..www.michigan.gov/cis/0,1607,7-154-10555_13251_13257---,00.html
Credit Union...www.michigan.gov/cis/1,1607,7-154--22352--,00.html
Dentist/Dental Assistant ....http://cis.state.mi.us/verify.htm
Emergency Medical Personnel ....http://cis.state.mi.us/verify.htm
EMT Advanced/Specialist/Instructor www.michigan.gov/cis/0,1607,7-154-10557---,00.html
Employment Agency ....http://cis.state.mi.us/verify.htm
Engineer ....http://cis.state.mi.us/verify.htm
Flight School ....www.michigan.gov/aero/0,1607,7-145-6774_6887---,00.html
Forester..http://cis.state.mi.us/verify.htm
Foster Care Facility/Adult Camp...............................www.michigan.gov/emi/1,1303,7-102-117_401_459---CI,00.html
Foster Care Program...www.michigan.gov/cis/0,1607,7-154-10568_17801---,00.html
Foster Care, Child ....www.michigan.gov/cis/0,1607,7-154-10568_17846_17865---,00.html
Foster Family Home ....www.michigan.gov/cis/0,1607,7-154-10568_17801---,00.html
Funeral Home...http://cis.state.mi.us/verify.htm
Funeral Salesperson (Prepaid Funeral Contr. Reg.)...http://cis.state.mi.us/verify.htm
Grain Dealer...www.mda.state.mi.us/prodag/GrainDealers/dealers.html
Health Facilities/Laboratory ....http://cis.state.mi.us/verify.htm
Hearing Aid Dealer...http://cis.state.mi.us/verify.htm
HMO ....www.michigan.gov/cis/0,1607,7-154-10555_13251_13262---,00.html
Hygenist, Dental...http://cis.state.mi.us/verify.htm
Insurance Adjuster..www.michigan.gov/cis/0,1607,7-154-10555_13251_13262---,00.html
Insurance Agent/Counselor/Solicitor/Admin............www.michigan.gov/cis/0,1607,7-154-10555_13251_13262---,00.html
Insurance-related Entity..www.michigan.gov/cis/0,1607,7-154-10555_13251_13262---,00.html
Landscape Architect..http://cis.state.mi.us/verify.htm
Liquor License..www.michigan.gov/cis/0,1607,7-154-10570_12905---,00.html
Living Care Facility..www.michigan.gov/cis/0,1607,7-154-10555_13251---,00.html
Long Term Care Company ....www.michigan.gov/cis/0,1607,7-154-10555_13251_13262---,00.html
Mammography Facility..http://cis.state.mi.us/verify.htm
Marriage & Family Therapist ....http://cis.state.mi.us/verify.htm
Medical Doctor...http://cis.state.mi.us/verify.htm
Medical First Responder www.michigan.gov/cis/0,1607,7-154-10557---,00.html
Mortgage Licensee ....www.michigan.gov/cis/0,1607,7-154-10555_13251_13257---,00.html
Mortuary Science ....http://cis.state.mi.us/verify.htm
Motor Vehicle Installment Seller...............................www.michigan.gov/cis/0,1607,7-154-10555_13251_13257---,00.html
Motor Vehicle Sales Financer ....www.michigan.gov/cis/0,1607,7-154-10555_13251_13257---,00.html
Notary Public ....www.sos.state.mi.us/greatse/notaries/notaries.html
Nurse..http://cis.state.mi.us/verify.htm
Nursery Dealer/Grower...www.mda.state.mi.us/industry/Nursery/license/index.html
Nurses' Aide ....http://cis.state.mi.us/verify.htm
Nursing Home ....http://cis.state.mi.us/verify.htm
Nursing Home Administrator ....http://cis.state.mi.us/verify.htm
Occularist...http://cis.state.mi.us/verify.htm
Optometrist...http://cis.state.mi.us/verify.htm

Osteopathic Physician	http://cis.state.mi.us/verify.htm
Paramedic	www.michigan.gov/cis/0,1607,7-154-10557---,00.html
Pesticide Applicator Company	www.michigan.gov/mda/0,1607,7-125-1569_2459-13075--,00.html
Pharmacist	http://cis.state.mi.us/verify.htm
Physical Therapist	http://cis.state.mi.us/verify.htm
Physician Assistant	http://cis.state.mi.us/verify.htm
Pilot Examiner	www.michigan.gov/aero/0,1607,7-145-6775_7029-30993--,00.html
Podiatrist	http://cis.state.mi.us/verify.htm
Polygraph Examiner	http://cis.state.mi.us/verify.htm
Potato Dealer	www.michigan.gov/mda/0,1607,7-125-1566_1733_2321-11149--,00.html
Psychologist	http://cis.state.mi.us/verify.htm
Public Accountant-CPA	http://cis.state.mi.us/verify.htm
Real Estate Broker/Salesperson	http://cis.state.mi.us/verify.htm
Regulatory Loan Licensee	www.michigan.gov/cis/0,1607,7-154-10555_13251_13257---,00.html
Sanitarian	http://cis.state.mi.us/verify.htm
Savings Bank	www.michigan.gov/cis/1,1607,7-154--22352--,00.html
Social Worker	http://cis.state.mi.us/verify.htm
Surety Company	www.michigan.gov/cis/0,1607,7-154-10555_13251_13262---,00.html
Surplus Line Broker	www.michigan.gov/cis/0,1607,7-154-10555_13251_13262---,00.html
Surveyor, Professional	http://cis.state.mi.us/verify.htm
Third-Party Administrator	www.michigan.gov/cis/0,1607,7-154-10555_13251_13262---,00.html
Veterinarian/Veterinary Technician	http://cis.state.mi.us/verify.htm

County Level ... Courts

Court Administration: State Court Administrator, PO Box 30048 (925 W Ottawa St), Lansing, MI, 48909; 517-373-0130; http://courts.michigan.gov/scao/

Court Structure: The Circuit Court is the court of general jurisdiction. District, Municipal and probate Courts are limited jurisdiction. There is a Court of Claims in Lansing that is a function of the 30th Circuit Court with jurisdiction over claims against the state of Michigan. A Recorder's Court in Detroit was abolished as of October 1, 1997. Mental health and estate cases are handled by the Probate Courts. Seven counties (Barry, Berrien, Iron, Isabella, Lake, and Washtenaw) and the 46th Circuit Court are participating in a "Demonstration" pilot project designed to streamline court services and consolidate case management. These courts may refer to themselves as County Trial Courts.

Online Access Note: There is a wide range of online computerization of the judicial system from "none" to "fairly complete," but there is no statewide court records network. Some Michigan courts provide public access terminals in clerk's offices, and some courts are developing off-site electronic filing and searching capability. A few offer remote online to the public. The Criminal Justice Information Center (CJIC), the repository for MI criminal record info, offers online access, but the requester must be a business. Results are available in seconds; fee is $5.00 per name. For more information, call 517-322-5546.

Crawford County
46th Circuit Court *Civil and Criminal Records*
Probate Court *Probate Records*
www.Circuit46.org
Online access to court case records (open or closed cases for 90 days only) available free at www.circuit46.org/Cases/cases.html. Search by name.

Genesee County
7th Circuit Court *Civil and Criminal Records*
www.co.genesee.mi.us
Online access to court records is available free at the web site; click on "Circuit Court Records."

Kalkaska County
46th Circuit Court *Civil and Criminal Records*
Circuit Trial Court - Probate Division *Probate Records*
www.Circuit46.org
Online access to court case records (open or closed cases for 90 days only) available free at www.circuit46.org/Cases/cases.html.

Otsego County
46th Circuit Court *Civil and Criminal Records*
Probate Court *Probate Records*
www.Circuit46.org
Online access to court case records (closed cases for 90 days only) is free at www.circuit46.org/Cases/cases.html. Search by name.

County Level ... Recorders & Assessors

Recording Office Organization: 83 counties, 83 recording offices. The recording officer is the County Register of Deeds. 79 counties are in the Eastern Time Zone (EST) and 4 are in the Central Time Zone (CST). Federal and state tax liens on personal property of businesses are filed with the Secretary of State. Other federal and state tax liens are filed with the Register of Deeds. Most counties search each tax lien index separately. Some charge one fee to search both, while others charge a separate fee for each one. When combining a UCC and tax lien search, total fee is usually $9.00 for all three searches. Some counties require tax identification number as well as name to do a search.

Online Access Note: There is no statewide online access, but a number of counties, including Wayne, offer free access to assessor and register of deeds records.

Eaton County   *Assessor, Tax Records*
www.co.eaton.mi.us/cntsrv/online.htm
Two levels of service are available on the County Online Data Service site. For free information, click on the Free Limited Public Information on the main page; then, on the Access System Page, at "User" enter PUBLIC. For "password," enter PUBLIC. The more sophisticated, restricted "Enhanced Records Access" requires registration, a password, and an associated fee. Access fees are billable monthly and can be prepaid to cover usage for any length of time. Also,search the Delta Charter Township assessments free at www.township.delta.mi.us/Assessing/BSALink.htm.

Genesee County   *Recording, Property, Deed, Marriage, Death Records*
www.co.genesee.mi.us
Access to Register of Deeds database is available free at www.co.genesee.mi.us/rod/. But to view documents back to 10/2000, there is a fee, and user ID and password required. Also, online access to the county clerk's marriage (back to 1963) and death (back to 1930) indexes are available free at www.co.genesee.mi.us/vitalrec.

Ingham County   *Assumed Business Name Records*
www.ingham.org/rd/rodindex.htm
County DBA and co-partnership listings are available free online at www.ingham.org/CL/dbalists.htm.

Jackson County   *Real Estate, Lien, Deed Records*
www.co.jackson.mi.us
Access to county online records requires pre-payment and $1 per minute of use (this may be revised). Records date back to 1985. Indexes include grantor/grantee, deeds, mortgage information. Lending agency information is available. Vital records will be added to the system when it is upgraded. For information, contact Mindy at 517-768-6682. Also, online access to deeds should be available free at www.co.jackson.mi.us/officials/elected/reilly/deeds.htm.

Kent County   *Assessor, Property Records*
www.co.kent.mi.us/government/departments/
Records on the Walker City Assessing Dept. database are available free online at www.ci.walker.mi.us/Services/Assessor/AssessingData/DataIntro.html. In most cases, sales and permit histories go back to 1993. Database contains residential assessment and structural information. Also, records on the Alpine Charter Township Assessment database are available free online at http://alpine.data-web.net. Search by parcel number or street name.

Livingston County   *Real Estate, Lien, Tax Assessor Records*

Access to county online records is available for occasional users, and a dedicated line is available for $1200 for professional users. Annual fee for occasional use is $400, plus $.000043 per second. Records date back to 1984. Lending agency information is available. For information, contact Judy Epley at 517-546-2530.

Macomb County   *Business Registration, Death Records*

www.co.macomb.mi.us
Business registration information - owner name, address, type and filing date - is available free online at http://macomb.mcntv.com/businessnames. Search by full or partial company name. County death records are available free online at http://macomb.mcntv.com/deathrecords. Search by name or apx. date. Also, County Recorder records are available from a private online source at www.landaccess.com; Fees and registration required. Also, Clinton Township Assessor records are available free online at www.clintontownship.com/assprd.htm. Enter user name: "clintwp" and password "assessor"

Marquette County   *Warrant List Records*

www.co.marquette.mi.us
Access to the sheriff's warrants list is available free at www.co.marquette.mi.us/Sheriff/WARRANTS.htm.

Mecosta County   *Assessor, Property Records*

Search the City of Big Rapids assessing and tax page for free at www.ci.big-rapids.mi.us/Assessing/onlinesearch.htm.

Montcalm County   *Real Estate, Lien Records*

Two sources are available. To view the index, the monthly fee is $250. To view both the index and document image, the monthly fee is $650. Records date back to 1/1/1988. Lending agency information is available. For information, call 989-831-7321.

Oakland County   *Real Estate, Property Tax, Tax Lien Records*

www.co.oakland.mi.us
Access to Access Oakland property information is available by subscription. Available monthly or per use. For information or sign-up, visit www.co.oakland.mi.us (click on "@cess Oakland") or call Information Services at 248-858-0861. Also, County Recorder records are accessible through a private online service at www.landaccess.com; Fees and registration are required.

Saginaw County   *Assessor, Assumed Business Name, Marriage, Death, Elections, Notary Records*

Access to the county clerks database is available free at www.saginawcounty.com/clerk/search/index.html. Records go back to 1995. Also, records on the Saginaw Charter Township Assessor's Property Data Page are available free online at www.sagtwp.org/pt_scripts/search.cfm. Search by address, tax roll number, or owner name.

Wayne County   *Assessor, Recording, Deed, Judgment, Lien, Tax Sales, Assumed Name Records*

Search the recorders land records database for free at http://208.246.137.57/default.asp. A full data on-demand or business service is also available; all 313-967-6857 or visit http://208.246.137.57/RODC/Default.asp. Search the recorders assumed names index at www.waynecounty.com/clerk/default_names.htm. Also, two county property auction listings are available free at www.waynecounty.com/property/default.htm and http://208.246.137.55/wcop/ Records on the City of Dearborn Residential Property Assessment Database are available free online at http://65.186.162.37/dbnassessor/. Search by street name and number.

Federal Courts in Michigan...

Standards for Federal Courts: The universal PACER sign-up number is 800-676-6856. Find PACER and the Party/Case Index on the Web at http://pacer.psc.uscourts.gov. PACER dial-up access is $.60 per minute. Also, courts offering internet access via RACER, PACER, Web-PACER or the new CM-ECF charge $.07 per page fee unless noted as free.

US District Court -- Eastern District of Michigan

Home Page: www.mied.uscourts.gov
PACER: Toll-free access: 800-229-8015. Local access phone: 313-234-5376. Case records are available back to 1988. New records are available online after 2 days. **PACER URL:** http://pacer.mied.uscourts.gov.
Ann Arbor Division counties: Jackson, Lenawee, Monroe, Oakland, Washtenaw, Wayne. Civil cases in these counties are assigned randomly to the Detroit, Flint or Port Huron Divisions. Case files are maintained where the case is assigned.
Bay City Division counties: Alcona, Alpena, Arenac, Bay, Cheboygan, Clare, Crawford, Gladwin, Gratiot, Huron, Iosco, Isabella, Midland, Montmorency, Ogemaw, Oscoda, Otsego, Presque Isle, Roscommon, Saginaw, Tuscola.

Detroit Division counties: Macomb, St. Clair, Sanilac. Civil cases for these counties are assigned randomly among the Flint, Ann Arbor and Detroit divisions. Port Huron cases may also be assigned here. Case files are kept where the case is assigned.
Flint Division counties: Genesee, Lapeer, Livingston, Shiawassee. This office handles all criminal cases for these counties. Civil cases are assigned randomly among the Detroit, Ann Arbor and Flint divisions.

US Bankruptcy Court -- Eastern District of Michigan

Home Page: www.mieb.uscourts.gov
PACER: Toll-free access: 800-498-5061. Local access phone: 313-961-4934. Case records are available back to October 1, 1992. New civil records are available online after 1-2 days. **PACER URL:** http://pacer.mieb.uscourts.gov. **Also:** access via phone on VCIS (Voice Case Information System) is available: 877-422-3066, 313-961-4940
Bay City Division counties: Alcona, Alpena, Arenac, Bay, Cheboygan, Clare, Crawford, Gladwin, Gratiot, Huron, Iosco, Isabella, Midland, Montmorency, Ogemaw, Oscoda, Otsego, Presque Isle, Roscommon, Saginaw, Tuscola.
Detroit Division counties: Jackson, Lenawee, Macomb, Monroe, Oakland, Sanilac, St. Clair, Washtenaw, Wayne.
Flint Division counties: Genesee, Lapeer, Livingston, Shiawassee.

US District Court -- Western District of Michigan

Home Page: www.miwd.uscourts.gov
PACER: Toll-free access: 800-547-6398. Local access phone: 616-732-2765. Case records are available back to September 1989. Records are purged never. New records are available online after 1-2 days. **PACER URL:** http://pacer.miwd.uscourts.gov.
Electronic Filing: Electronic filing information is available online at https://ecf.miwd.uscourts.gov.
Grand Rapids Division counties: Antrim, Barry, Benzie, Charlevoix, Emmet, Grand Traverse, Ionia, Kalkaska, Kent, Lake, Leelanau, Manistee, Mason, Mecosta, Missaukee, Montcalm, Muskegon, Newaygo, Oceana, Osceola, Ottawa, Wexford. The Lansing and Kalamazoo Divisions also handle cases from these counties.
Kalamazoo Division counties: Allegan, Berrien, Calhoun, Cass, Kalamazoo, St. Joseph, Van Buren. Also handle cases from the counties in the Grand Rapids Division.
Lansing Division counties: Branch, Clinton, Eaton, Hillsdale, Ingham. Also handle cases from the counties in the Grand Rapids Division.
Marquette-Northern Division counties: Alger, Baraga, Chippewa, Delta, Dickinson, Gogebic, Houghton, Iron, Keweenaw, Luce, Mackinac, Marquette, Menominee, Ontonagon, Schoolcraft.

US Bankruptcy Court -- Western District of Michigan

Home Page: www.miwb.uscourts.gov
PACER: Toll-free access: 800-526-0342. Local access phone: 616-456-2415. Case records are available back to September 1989. Records are purged six months after case closed. New civil records are available online after 1 day. **PACER URL:** http://pacer.miwb.uscourts.gov.
Electronic Filing: (Currently in the process of implementing CM/ECF). **Also:** access via phone on VCIS (Voice Case Information System) is available: 616-456-2075.
Grand Rapids Division counties: Allegan, Antrim, Barry, Benzie, Berrien, Branch, Calhoun, Cass, Charlevoix, Clinton, Eaton, Emmet, Grand Traverse, Hillsdale, Ingham, Ionia, Kalamazoo, Kalkaska, Kent, Lake, Leelanau, Manistee, Mason, Mecosta, Missaukee, Montcalm, Muskegon, Newaygo, Oceana, Osceola, Ottawa, St. Joseph, Van Buren, Wexford.
Marquette Division counties: Alger, Baraga, Chippewa, Delta, Dickinson, Gogebic, Houghton, Iron, Keweenaw, Luce, Mackinac, Marquette, Menominee, Ontonagon, Schoolcraft.

Minnesota

Capital: St. Paul
                  Ramsey County

Time Zone: CST

Number of Counties: 87

Home Page   www.state.mn.us

Archives   www.mnhs.org

Attorney General   www.ag.state.mn.us

State Level ... Major Agencies

Corporation Records, Limited Liability Company Records, Assumed Name, Trademarks/Servicemarks, Limited Partnerships

Business Records Services, Secretary of State, 180 State Office Bldg, 100 Constitution Ave, St Paul, MN 55155-1299; 651-296-2803 (Information), 651-297-7067 (Fax), 8AM-4:30PM.

www.sos.state.mn.us

The Internet site permits free look-ups of "business" names. Also, a commercial program called Direct Access is available 24 hours. There is an annual subscription fee of $50.00. Records are $1-4, depending on item needed. Please call 651-296-2803 or 877-551-6767 for more information. **Other options:** Information can be purchased in bulk format. Call 651-298-4059 for more information.

Uniform Commercial Code, Federal Tax Liens, State Tax Liens

UCC Division, Sec. of State, 180 State Office Bldg, St Paul, MN 55155-1299; 651-296-2803, 651-215-1009 (Fax), 8AM-4:30PM.

www.sos.state.mn.us

There is a free look-up by filing number available from the web site. A comprehensive commercial program called Direct Access is available 24 hours. There is an annual subscription fee of$50.00 per year, plus $4.00 per debtor name. Call 651-296-2803 for more information. **Other options:** The state will provide information in bulk form on paper, CD or disk. Call 651-296-2803 or 877-551-6767 for more information.

Sexual Offender Registry

The Predatory Offender Registry Unit of the Bureau of Criminal Apprehension maintains the state database of sexual offenders. Search by city or county the Level 3 sexual offenders registry at www.doc.state.mn.us/level3/search.asp.

Driver Records

Driver & Vehicle Services, Records Section, 445 Minnesota St, #180, St Paul, MN 55101; 651-296-6911, 8AM-4:30PM.

www.dps.state.mn.us/dvs/index.html

Online access costs $2.50 per record. Online inquiries can be processed either as interactive or as batch files (overnight) 24 hours a day, 7 days a week. Requesters operate from a "bank." Records are accessed by either DL number or full name and DOB. Call 651-

297-1714 for more information. **Other options:** Minnesota will sell its entire database of driving record information with monthly updates. Customized request sorts are available. Fees vary by type with programming and computer time and are quite reasonable.

Vehicle Ownership, Vehicle Identification

Driver & Vehicle Services, Vehicle Record Requests, 445 Minnesota St, #180, St Paul, MN 55101; 651-296-6911 (General Information), 8AM-4:30PM.

www.dps.state.mn.us/dvs/index.html

Online access costs $2.50 per record. There is an additional monthly charge for dial-in access. The system is the same as described for driving record requests. It is open 24 hours a day, 7 days a week. Lien information is included. Call 651-297-1714 for more information.

Legislation Records

www.leg.state.mn.us

Information available through the Internet site includes full text of bills, status, previous 4 years of bills, and bill tracking.

State Level ... Occupational Licensing

Acupuncturist	www.docboard.org/mn/df/mndf.htm
Alarm & Com. System Contr./Installer	www.electricity.state.mn.us/Elec_lic/index.html
Ambulance Service/Personnel	www.emsrb.state.mn.us/cert.asp?p=s
Athletic Trainer	www.docboard.org/mn/df/mndf.htm
Auditor	www.boa.state.mn.us/
Bingo Operation	www.gcb.state.mn.us/
Building Contractors, Residential	www.commerce.state.mn.us/pages/Contractors/BuilderList.htm
Chiropractor	www.mn-chiroboard.state.mn.us/main-licensing.htm
Consumer Credit/Payday Lender	www.commerce.state.mn.us/pages/FinService/FSLicensees/SL.HTM
Credit Union	www.commerce.state.mn.us/pages/FinService/FSLicensees/CU.HTM
Debt Prorate Company	www.commerce.state.mn.us/pages/FinService/FSLicensees/DP.HTM
Electrician	www.electricity.state.mn.us/Elec_lic/index.html
Emergency Medical Technician	www.emsrb.state.mn.us/cert.asp?p=s
EMS Examiner	www.emsrb.state.mn.us/examiner.asp?p=s
Funeral Establishment	www.health.state.mn.us/divs/hpsc/mortsci/mortsciselect.cfm
Gambling Equipment Dist./Mfg.	www.gcb.state.mn.us/
Gambling, Lawful Organization	www.gcb.state.mn.us/
Grain Licensing	http://www2.mda.state.mn.us/webapp/lis/default.jsp
Industr. Loan/Thrift Company	www.commerce.state.mn.us/pages/FinService/FSLicensees/IL.HTM
Insurance Agent/Salesman	licensing.commerce@state.mn.us
Liquor On-sale Retail	www.dps.state.mn.us/alcgamb/alcenf/liquorlic/liquorlic.html
Liquor Store, On-sale Retail Municipal	www.dps.state.mn.us/alcgamb/alcenf/liquorlic/liquorlic.html
Livestock Dealer/Market	http://www2.mda.state.mn.us/webapp/lis/default.jsp
Livestock Weighing	http://www2.mda.state.mn.us/webapp/lis/default.jsp
Loan Company	www.commerce.state.mn.us/pages/FinService/FSLicensees/RL.HTM
Lobbyist	www.cfboard.state.mn.us/Lobby.htm
Lottery Retailer	www.lottery.state.mn.us/retailer/lookup.html
LPA	www.boa.state.mn.us/
Medical Doctor	www.docboard.org/mn/df/mndf.htm
Midwife	www.docboard.org/mn/df/mndf.htm
Mortgage Originators/Servicers, Residential	www.commerce.state.mn.us/pages/FinService/MOList.htm
Mortician	www.health.state.mn.us/divs/hpsc/mortsci/mortsciselect.cfm
Motor Vehicle Financer	www.commerce.state.mn.us/pages/FinService/FSLicensees/MV.HTM
Notary Public	licensing.commerce@state.mn.us
Optometrist	www.odfinder.org/LicSearch.asp
Pesticide Applicator Company	http://www2.mda.state.mn.us/webapp/lis/pestappdefault.jsp
Pesticide Applicator, Private	www.mda.state.mn.us/privapp/default.asp
Physical Therapist	www.docboard.org/mn/df/mndf.htm

Physician Assistant...www.docboard.org/mn/df/mndf.htm
Political Candidate ....www.cfboard.state.mn.us/legcand.html
Public Accountant-CPA ....www.boa.state.mn.us/
Real Estate Broker/Dealer ....license.commerce@state.mn.us
Respiratory Care Practitioner ....www.docboard.org/mn/df/mndf.htm
Securities/Investment Advisor..securities.commerce@state.mn.us
Surgeon ....www.docboard.org/mn/df/mndf.htm
Teacher...http://cfl.state.mn.us/licen/licinfo.html
Underground Storage Tank Contractro/Supervisor. .....www.pca.state.mn.us/cleanup/ust.html#certification
Weather Modifier http://www2.mda.state.mn.us/webapp/lis/default.jsp

County Level ... Courts

Court Administration: State Court Adminstrator, 135 Minn. Judicial Center, 25 Constitution Ave, St Paul, MN, 55155; 651-296-2474; www.courts.state.mn.us

Court Structure: There are 97 District Courts comprising 10 judicial districts. The 3rd, 5th, 8th and 10th Judicial Districts no longer will perform criminal record searches for the public.

Online Access Note: There is an online system in place that allows internal and external access, but only for government personnel. Some criminal information is available online from St Paul through the Bureau of Criminal Apprehension (BCA), 1246 University Ave, St. Paul, MN 55104. Additional information is available from BCA by calling 651-642-0670.

There are no known courts that independently offer access to their records.

County Level ... Recorders & Assessors

Recording Office Organization: 87 counties, 87 recording offices. The recording officer is the County Recorder. The entire state is in the Central Time Zone (CST). Federal and state tax liens on personal property of businesses are filed with the Secretary of State. Other federal and state tax liens are filed with the County Recorder. Some counties search each tax lien index separately. Some charge one $15.00 fee to search both indexes, but others charge a separate fee for each index searched. Search and copy fees vary widely.

Online Access Note: There is no statewide system, but a number of counties offer web access to assessor data and recorded deeds.

Anoka County   *Real Estate, Tax Assessor Records*
www.co.anoka.mn.us
Access to the County online records requires an annual fee of $35 and a $25 monthly fee and $.25 per transaction. Records date back to 1995. Lending agency information is available. For information, contact Pam LeBlanc at 763-323-5424. Also, you may access property information at https://anoka.mn.ezgov.com/ezproperty/review_search.jsp. No name searching. There is also a dial-up property information system at 763-323-5400.

Carver County   *Property Tax Records*
www.co.carver.mn.us
Records on the County Property Tax Information database are available free online at www.co.carvr.mn.us/Prop_Tax/default.asp. Information is updated bi-monthly.

Clay County   *Real Estate Records*
www.co.clay.mn.us
The county online GIS mapping service provides property record searching, but by parcel number only. County Recorder records may be available at the web site in the near future.

Dakota County   *Real Estate, Assessor Records*
www.co.dakota.mn.us
Records on the County Real Estate Inquiry database are available free online at
www.co.dakota.mn.us/assessor/real_estate_inquiry.htm. Information includes items such as address, estimated value, taxes, last sale price, building details.

Hennepin County   *Real Estate, Lien Records*
www.co.hennepin.mn.us
Three sources available. Access to Hennepin County online records requires a $35 annual fee with a charge of $5 per hour from 7AM-7PM, or $4.15 per hour at other times. Records date back to 1988. Only UCC & lending agency information is available. Property tax info is at the Treasurer office. For information, contact Jerry Erickson at 612-348-3856. Also, records on the County Property Information Search database are available free on the Internet at www2.co.hennepin.mn.us/pins. Search by Property ID #, address, or addition name. An Automated phone system is also available; 612-348-3011.

Martin County   *Property Records*
Access to County property records are available for a fee at https://www.landrecords.net/. Search fee is $3.99 plus $.50 per image.

Ramsey County   *Property Assessor Records*
Search the property assessment rolls free at www.co.ramsey.mn.us/prr/propertytax/index.asp. No name searching.

Rice County   *Property Assessor, Property Sales Records*
Search parcel information and residential/commercial sales data free at www.minnesotaassessors.com/rice/. No name searching.

St. Louis County   *Real Estate, Property Tax Records*
Access to the Auditor and Recorder's tax records for tax professionals database is available by subscription. Fee is $100 quarterly; password provided. For information or sign-up, contact Pam Palen at 218-726-2380 or email to palenp@co.st-louis.mn.us or visit www.co.st-louis.mn.us/auditorsoffice/subscription.pdf. Also, search the City of Duluth property assessor data free at www.ci.duluth.mn.us/city/assessor/index.htm.

Scott County   *Land, Property Tax Records*
www.co.scott.mn.us
Search the county property databases free at
www.co.scott.mn.us/xpedio/groups/public/documents/web_files/scottcountywebframe.hcsp. There is also a free online document subscription service and GIS mapping.

Sherburne County   *Real Estate, Tax Assessor Records*
www.co.sherburne.mn.us
Records from the county tax assessor database are available free online at
www.hometimes.com/Communities/Taxes/TaxSearch/Shurburne/index.html.

Stearns County   *Real Estate, Tax Assessor Records*
Records from the county tax assessor database are available free online at
www.hometimes.com/Communities/Taxes/TaxSearch/index.html.

Washington County   *Real Estate, Lien, Tax Assessor Records*
www.co.washington.mn.us
Access to county online records requires a $250 set up fee; no fees apply to Recorder office information. Records date back 3 years. Lending agency information is available, but UCC information is on a separate system. For information, contact Larry Haseman at 651-430-6423. Also, online access to property tax records is available free at
https://washington.mn.ezgov.com/ezproperty/review_search.jsp; no name searching - property ID or address required.

Federal Courts in Minnesota...

Standards for Federal Courts: The universal PACER sign-up number is 800-676-6856. Find PACER and the Party/Case Index on the Web at http://pacer.psc.uscourts.gov. PACER dial-up access is $.60 per minute. Also, courts offering internet access via RACER, PACER, Web-PACER or the new CM-ECF charge $.07 per page fee unless noted as free.

US District Court -- District of Minnesota

Home Page: www.mnd.uscourts.gov

PACER: Case records are available back to February 1990. New records are available online after 1 day. **PACER URL:** http://pacer.mnd.uscourts.gov.

Duluth Division counties: Aitkin, Becker*, Beltrami*, Benton, Big Stone*, Carlton, Cass, Clay*, Clearwater*, Cook, Crow Wing, Douglas*, Grant*, Hubbard*, Itasca, Kanabec, Kittson*, Koochiching, Lake, Lake of the Woods*, Mahnomen*, Marshall*, Mille Lacs, Morrison, Norman*, Otter Tail,* Pennington*, Pine, Polk*, Pope*, Red Lake*, Roseau*, Stearns*, Stevens*, St. Louis, Todd*, Traverse*, Wadena*, Wilkin*. From March 1, 1995, to 1998, cases from the counties marked with an asterisk (*) were heard here. Before and after that period, cases were and are allocated between St. Paul and Minneapolis.

Minneapolis Division counties: All counties not covered by the Duluth Division. Cases are allocated between Minneapolis and St Paul.

St Paul Division counties: All counties not covered by the Duluth Division. Cases are allocated between Minneapolis and St Paul.

US Bankruptcy Court -- District of Minnesota

Home Page: www.mnb.uscourts.gov

PACER: Case records are available back to January 1993. Records are purged up to April 1996. New civil records are available online after 1 day.

Other Online Access: Search records using the Internet. Searching is currently free. Images go back to 1997. **Also:** access via phone on VCIS (Voice Case Information System) is available: 800-959-9002, 612-664-5302

Duluth Division counties: Aitkin, Benton, Carlton, Cass, Cook, Crow Wing, Itasca, Kanabec, Koochiching, Lake, Mille Lacs, Morrison, Pine, St. Louis. A petition commencing Chapter 11 or 12 proceedings may initially be filed in any of the four divisons, but may be assigned toanother division.

Fergus Falls Division counties: Becker, Beltrami, Big Stone, Clay, Clearwater, Douglas, Grant, Hubbard, Kittson, Lake of the Woods, Mahnomen, Marshall, Norman, Otter Tail, Pennington, Polk, Pope, Red Lake, Roseau, Stearns, Stevens, Todd, Traverse, Wadena, Wilkin. A petition commencing Chapter 11 or 12 proceedings may be filed initially in any of the four divisions, but may then be assigned to another division.

Minneapolis Division counties: Anoka, Carver, Chippewa, Hennepin, Isanti, Kandiyohi, McLeod, Meeker, Renville, Sherburne, Swift, Wright. Initial petitions for Chapter 11 or 12 may be filed initially at any of the four divisions, but may then be assigned to a judge in another division.

St Paul Division counties: Blue Earth, Brown, Chisago, Cottonwood, Dakota, Dodge, Faribault, Fillmore, Freeborn, Goodhue, Houston, Jackson, Lac qui Parle, Le Sueur, Lincoln, Lyon, Martin, Mower, Murray, Nicollet, Nobles, Olmsted, Pipestone, Ramsey, Redwood, Rice, Rock, Scott, Sibley, Steele, Wabasha, Waseca, Washington, Watonwan, Winona, Yellow Medicine. Cases from Benton, Kanabec, Mille Lacs, Morrison and Pine may also be heard here. A petition commencing Chapter 11 or 12 proceedings may be filed initially with any of the four divisions, but may then be assigned to another division.

Mississippi

Capital:	Jackson Hinds County	Home Page	www.state.ms.us
Time Zone:	CST	Archives	www.mdah.state.ms.us
Number of Counties:	82	Attorney General	www.ago.state.ms.us

State Level ... Major Agencies

Corporation Records, Limited Partnership Records, Limited Liability Company Records, Trademarks/Servicemarks

Corporation Commission, Secretary of State, PO Box 136, Jackson, MS 39205-0136 (Courier: 202 N Congress, Suite 601, Jackson, MS 39201); 601-359-1633, 800-256-3494, 601-359-1607 (Fax), 8AM-5PM.

www.sos.state.ms.us

The system is called "CorpSnap" and is available online at www.sos.state.ms.us/busserv/corpsnap/index.html. There is no fee to view records, including officers and registered agents. **Other options:** The Data Division offers bulk release of data on paper or disk.

Uniform Commercial Code, Federal Tax Liens

Business Services Division, Secretary of State, PO Box 136, Jackson, MS 39205-0136 (Courier: 202 N Congress St, Suite 601, Union Planters Bank Bldg, Jackson, MS 39201); 601-359-1633, 800-256-3494, 601-359-1607 (Fax), 8AM-5PM.

www.sos.state.ms.us

Two systems available. Free searching for UCC debtors is at www.sos.state.ms.us/busserv/ucc/soskb/SearchStandardRA9.asp. Also, the commerical system called "Success" is open 24 hours daily. There is a $250 set-up fee and usage fee of $.10 per screen. Users can access via the Internet to avoid any toll charges. Customers are billed quarterly. For more information, call Burrell Brown at 601-359-1633. **Other options:** A monthly list of farm liens is available for purchase.

Sexual Offender Registry

The Department of Public Safety maintians the state Sex Offender Registry. Name and location searching is available at access at www.sor.mdps.state.ms.us

Workers' Compensation Records

Workers Compensation Commission, PO Box 5300, Jackson, MS 39296-5300 (Courier: 1428 Lakeland Dr, Jackson, MS 39216); 601-987-4200, 8AM-5PM.

www.mwcc.state.ms.us

The First Report of Injury is available via the web. There is no fee, but users must register. **Other options:** A first report of injury database is available on CD-ROM for $500.00.

Driver Records

Department of Public Safety, Driver Records, PO Box 958, Jackson, MS 39205 (Courier: 1900 E Woodrow Wilson, Jackson, MS 39216); 601-987-1274, 8AM-5PM.

www.dps.state.ms.us

Both interactive and batch delivery is offer for high volume users only. Billing is monthly. Hook-up is through the Advantis System, fees apply. Lookup is by name only-not by driver license number. Fee is $7.00 per record. For more information, call 601-987-1337. **Other options:** Overnight batch delivery by tape is available.

Legislation Records

www.ls.state.ms.us

The Internet site has an excellent bill status and measure information program. Data includes current and the previous year.

Voter Registration

Secretary of State, Elections Division, PO Box 136, Jackson, MS 39205-0136; 800-829-6786, 601-359-1350, 601-359-5019 (Fax), 8AM-5PM.

www.sos.state.ms.us/elections/elections.asp

County Voter Rolls are available to download free online at www.sos.state.ms.us/elections/Voter_Registration_Downloads/voter_reg_main.asp. Individual county files are in delimited text and may be downloaded to a database program.

State Level...Occupational Licensing

Architect .... www.archbd.state.ms.us/roster_tmp.htm
Attorney .... www.msbar.org/lawyerdirectory.htm
Attorney Firm .... www.msbar.org/lawyerdirectory.htm
Camp, Youth www.msdh.state.ms.us/msdhsite/index.cfm/15,0,81,html
Charity .... www.sos.state.ms.us/regenf/charities/charannrpt/index.asp
Child Care Facility www.msdh.state.ms.us/msdhsite/index.cfm/15,0,81,html
Contractor, General .... www.msboc.state.ms.us/Search.cfm
Dental Hygienist .... www.msbde.state.ms.us
Dental Radiologist .... www.msbde.state.ms.us
Dentist .... www.msbde.state.ms.us
Engineer http://dsitspe01.its.state.ms.us/pepls/EngSurveyors.nsf
Fund Raiser .... www.sos.state.ms.us/regenf/charities/charannrpt/index.asp
HMO .... www.doi.state.ms.us/hmolist.pdf
Insurance Company .... www.doi.state.ms.us/compdir.html
Landscape Architect .... www.archbd.state.ms.us/roster_tmp.htm
Lobbyist .... www.sos.state.ms.us/elections/Lobbying/Lobbyist_Dir.asp
Long Term Care Insurance Company .... www.doi.state.ms.us/ltclist.html
Notary Public .... www.sos.state.ms.us/regenf/notaries/notaries.asp
Optometrist .... www.odfinder.org/LicSearch.asp
Real Estate Appraiser .... www.mrec.state.ms.us/asp/findappraiser.asp
Real Estate Broker .... www.mrec.state.ms.us/asp/findrealtor.asp
Real Estate Salesperson .... www.mrec.state.ms.us/asp/findrealtor.asp
Surveyor, Land http://dsitspe01.its.state.ms.us/pepls/EngSurveyors.nsf

County Level ... Courts

Court Administration: Court Administrator, Supreme Court, Box 117, Jackson, MS, 39205; 601-359-3697; www.mssc.state.ms.us

Court Structure: The court of general jurisdiction is the Circuit Court with 70 courts in 22 districts. Justice Courts were first created in 1984, replacing the Justice of the Peace. Prior to 1984, records were kept separately by each Justice of the Peace court, so the location of such records today is often unknown. Probate is handled by the Chancery Courts, as are property matters.

Online Access Note: A statewide online computer system is in use internally for court personnel. There were plans underway to make this system available to the public, but this was put on hold in 2002. The web site allows the public to search the Mississippi Supreme Court and Court of Appeals Decisions

Jackson County

Circuit Court *Civil and Criminal Records*
www.co.jackson.ms.us/Dept_Pages/Dept_Courts.htm
Online access to current dockets is available free at www.co.jackson.ms.us/Dept_Pages/Dept_Circuit_Court_Docket.htm. Click on "Circuit Court Dockets."

County Level ... Recorders & Assessors

Recording Office Organization: 82 counties, 92 recording offices. The recording officers are the Chancery Clerk and the Clerk of Circuit Court (state tax liens). Ten counties have two separate recording offices - Bolivar, Carroll, Chickasaw, Craighead, Harrison, Hinds, Jasper, Jones, Panola, Tallahatchie, and Yalobusha. The entire state is in the Central Time Zone (CST). Federal tax liens on personal property of businesses are filed with the Secretary of State. Federal tax liens on personal property of individuals are filed with the county Chancery Clerk. State tax liens on personal property are filed with the county Clerk of Circuit Court. State tax liens on real property are filed with the Chancery Clerk. Most Chancery Clerk offices will perform a federal tax lien search for a fee of $5.00 per name.

Online Access Note: A limited number of counties offer online access to records. There is no statewide system except for the Secretary of State's UCC access – see State Agencies section.

Alcorn County   *Property Tax, Appraisal Records*
Access is available free at www.deltacomputersystems.com/MS/MS02/index.html

Harrison County (1st District)   *Property, Deed, Recording, UCC, Tax Sales Records*
Access is available free at www.deltacomputersystems.com/MS/MS24DELTA/DATALINK.html. Also, search the delinquent tax sales list for free at www.co.harrison.ms.us/departments/chancery/delinquent.html

Harrison County (2nd District)   *Property, Deed, Recording, UCC, Tax Sales Records*
Access is available free at www.deltacomputersystems.com/MS/MS24DELTA/DATALINK.html. Also, search the delinquent tax sales list for free at www.co.harrison.ms.us/departments/chancery/delinquent.html

Hinds County (1st District)   *Real Estate, Grantor/Grantee, Judgment, Lien, Assessor, Condominium, Acreage Records*
www.co.hinds.ms.us/pgs/elected/chanceryclerk.asp
Access to the county records databases are available free at www.co.hinds.ms.us/pgs/apps/gindex.asp. Also, search the assessor landrolls for free at www.co.hinds.ms.us/pgs/apps/landroll_query.asp.

Hinds County (2nd District)   *Real Estate, Assessor, Grantor/Grantee, Judgment Records*
www.co.hinds.ms.us
Access to the county clerk database is available free at www.co.hinds.ms.us/pgs/apps/gindex.asp. Chose to search general index, landroll, judgments, acreage, subdivision, condominiums.

Lamar County   *Property Tax, Appraisal Records*
Access is available free at www.deltacomputersystems.com/MS/MS37/INDEX.html

Lauderdale County   *Property Tax, Appraisal Records*
Access is available free at www.deltacomputersystems.com/MS/MS38/INDEX.html

Lee County   *Property Tax, Appraisal Records*
Access is available free at www.deltacomputersystems.com/MS/MS41/INDEX.html.

Madison County   *Real Estate, Tax Assessor Records*
http://mcatax.com
Records from the county Assessor office are available free online. At www.mcatax.com/mcasearch.asp, click on "Search The Database." Records include parcel number, address, legal description, value information, and tax district.

Marshall County   *Property Tax, Appraisal Records*
Access is available free at www.deltacomputersystems.com/MS/MS47/INDEX.html.

Pearl River County   *Property Tax, Appraiser Records*
Access is available free at www.deltacomputersystems.com/MS/MS55/INDEX.html

Rankin County   *Real Estate, Tax Assessor Records*
www.rankincounty.org
Records on the county Land Roll database are available free online at www.rankincounty.org/TA/interact_LandRoll.asp.

Warren County   *Property Tax, Appraisal Records*
www.co.warren.ms.us
Access is available free at www.deltacomputersystems.com/MS/MS75/INDEX.html.

Washington County   *Property Tax, Appraisal Records*
Access is available free at www.deltacomputersystems.com/MS/MS76/INDEX.html.

Federal Courts in Mississippi...

Standards for Federal Courts: The universal PACER sign-up number is 800-676-6856. Find PACER and the Party/Case Index on the Web at http://pacer.psc.uscourts.gov. PACER dial-up access is $.60 per minute. Also, courts offering internet access via RACER, PACER, Web-PACER or the new CM-ECF charge $.07 per page fee unless noted as free.

US District Court -- Northern District of Mississippi

Home Page: www.msnd.uscourts.gov
PACER: Case records are available back to 1990. Records are purged every six months. New records are available online after 1 day.
PACER URL: http://pacer.msnd.uscourts.gov.
Opinions Online: Court opinions are available online at http://sunset.backbone.olemiss.edu/~llibcoll/ndms.
Aberdeen-Eastern Division counties: Alcorn, Attala, Chickasaw, Choctaw, Clay, Itawamba, Lee, Lowndes, Monroe, Oktibbeha, Prentiss, Tishomingo, Winston.
Clarksdale/Delta Division counties: Bolivar, Coahoma, De Soto, Panola, Quitman, Tallahatchie, Tate, Tunica.
Greenville Division counties: Carroll, Humphreys, Leflore, Sunflower, Washington.
Oxford-Northern Division counties: Benton, Calhoun, Grenada, Lafayette, Marshall, Montgomery, Pontotoc, Tippah, Union, Webster, Yalobusha.

US Bankruptcy Court -- Northern District of Mississippi

Home Page: www.msnb.uscourts.gov
PACER: Toll-free access: 888-372-5709. Local access phone: 662-369-9805. Case records are available back to April 1, 1987. Records are purged every 6 months. New civil records are available online after 2 days. **PACER URL:** http://pacer.msnb.uscourts.gov.
Electronic Filing: (Currently in the process of implementing CM/ECF). **Also:** access via phone on VCIS (Voice Case Information System) is available: 800-392-8653, 662-369-8147
Aberdeen Division counties: Alcorn, Attala, Benton, Bolivar, Calhoun, Carroll, Chickasaw, Choctaw, Clay, Coahoma, De Soto, Grenada, Humphreys, Itawamba, Lafayette, Lee, Leflore, Lowndes, Marshall, Monroe, Montgomery, Oktibbeha, Panola, Pontotoc, Prentiss, Quitman, Sunflower, Tallahatchie, Tate, Tippah, Tishomingo, Tunica, Union, Washington, Webster, Winston, Yalobusha.

US District Court -- Southern District of Mississippi

Home Page: www.mssd.uscourts.gov
PACER: Toll-free access: 800-839-6425. Local access phone: 601-965-5141. Case records are available back to 1992. New records are available online after 2 days. **PACER URL:** http://pacer.mssd.uscourts.gov.
Biloxi-Southern Division counties: George, Hancock, Harrison, Jackson, Pearl River, Stone.
Hattiesburg Division counties: Covington, Forrest, Greene, Jefferson Davis, Jones, Lamar, Lawrence, Marion, Perry, Walthall.
Jackson Division counties: Amite, Copiah, Franklin, Hinds, Holmes, Leake, Lincoln, Madison, Pike, Rankin, Scott, Simpson, Smith.
Meridian Division counties: Clarke, Jasper, Kemper, Lauderdale, Neshoba, Newton, Noxubee, Wayne.
Vicksburg Division counties: Adams, Claiborne, Issaquena, Jefferson, Sharkey, Warren, Wilkinson, Yazoo.

US Bankruptcy Court -- Southern District of Mississippi

Home Page: www.mssb.uscourts.gov
PACER: Toll-free access: 800-223-1078. Local access phone: 601-965-6103. Use of PC Anywhere V4.0 recommended. Case records are available back to 1986. New civil records are available online after 1 day. **Also:** access via phone on VCIS (Voice Case Information System) is available: 800-293-2723, 601-435-2905
Biloxi Division counties: Clarke, Covington, Forrest, George, Greene, Hancock, Harrison, Jackson, Jasper, Jefferson Davis, Jones, Kemper, Lamar, Lauderdale, Lawrence, Marion, Neshoba, Newton, Noxubee, Pearl River, Perry, Stone, Walthall, Wayne.
Jackson Division counties: Adams, Amite, Claiborne, Copiah, Franklin, Hinds, Holmes, Issaquena, Jefferson, Leake, Lincoln, Madison, Pike, Rankin, Scott, Sharkey, Simpson, Smith, Warren, Wilkinson, Yazoo.

Missouri

Capital:	Jefferson City	Home Page	
	Cole County	www.state.mo.us	
Time Zone:	CST	Attorney General	www.ago.state.mo.us
Number of Counties:	114	Archives	www.sos.state.mo.us/archives/

State Level ... Major Agencies

Corporation Records, Fictitious Name, Limited Partnership Records, Assumed Name, Trademarks/Servicemarks, Limited Liability Company Records

Secretary of State, Corporation Services, PO Box 778, Jefferson City, MO 65102 (Courier: 600 W Main, Jefferson City, MO 65101); 573-751-4153, 573-751-5841 (Fax), 8AM-5PM.

www.sos.state.mo.us

Search free online at www.sos.state.mo.us/BusinessEntity. The corporate name, the agent name or the charter number is required to search. The site will indicate the currency of the data. Many business entity type searches are available.

Uniform Commercial Code

UCC Division, Secretary of State, PO Box 1159, Jefferson City, MO 65102 (Courier: 600 W Main St, Rm 302, Jefferson City, MO 65101); 573-751-2360, 573-522-2057 (Fax), 8AM-5PM.

www.sos.state.mo.us/ucc/

Free searching for debtor names is available on the Internet. Images are available. **Other options:** The agency will release information for bulk purchase, call for procedures and pricing.

Driver Records

Department of Revenue, Driver and Vehicle Services Bureau, PO Box 200, Jefferson City, MO 65105-0200 (Courier: Harry S Truman Bldg, 301 W High St, Room 470, Jefferson City, MO 65105); 573-751-400, 573-526-4769 (Fax), 7:45AM-4:45PM.

www.dor.state.mo.us/mvdl/drivers

Online access costs $1.25 per record. Online inquiries can be put in Missouri's "mailbox" any time of the day. These inquiries are then picked up at 2 AM the following morning, and the resulting MVR's are sent back to each customer's "mailbox" approximately two hours later. **Other options:** The tape-to-tape process has been replaced by the online system. The entire license file can be purchased, with updates. Call 573-751-5579 for more information.

Legislation Records

www.moga.state.mo.us

The web site offers access to bills and statutes. One can search or track bills by key words, bill number, or sponsors. Request can be made via email to library@mail.state.mo.us

State Level ... Occupational Licensing

Architect...http://riversrun.ded.state.mo.us/cgi-bin/professionalregistration.pl
Athletic Trainer http://showme.ded.state.mo.us/dynded/pronline.form1
Attorney..www.mobar.org/directory/index.htm
Audiologist, Clinical ....http://riversrun.ded.state.mo.us/cgi-bin/professionalregistration.pl
Audiologist/Speech (Combined), Clinical....................http://riversrun.ded.state.mo.us/cgi-bin/professionalregistration.pl
Barber Instructor/School ....http://riversrun.ded.state.mo.us/cgi-bin/professionalregistration.pl
Barber/Barber Shop..http://riversrun.ded.state.mo.us/cgi-bin/professionalregistration.pl
Beauty Shop ....http://riversrun.ded.state.mo.us/cgi-bin/professionalregistration.pl
Boxer/Boxing Professional.............................http://riversrun.ded.state.mo.us/cgi-bin/professionalregistration.pl
Cemetery (Endowed Care Cemetery) ....www.ecodev.state.mo.us/pr/endowed.html
Chiropractor ....http://riversrun.ded.state.mo.us/cgi-bin/professionalregistration.pl
Cosmetologist...http://riversrun.ded.state.mo.us/cgi-bin/professionalregistration.pl
Cosmetology School/Instructor ....http://riversrun.ded.state.mo.us/cgi-bin/professionalregistration.pl
Cosmetology Shop..http://riversrun.ded.state.mo.us/cgi-bin/professionalregistration.pl
Counselor, Professional ....http://riversrun.ded.state.mo.us/cgi-bin/professionalregistration.pl
Dental Hygienist...http://riversrun.ded.state.mo.us/cgi-bin/professionalregistration.pl
Dental Specialist...http://riversrun.ded.state.mo.us/cgi-bin/professionalregistration.pl
Dentist...http://riversrun.ded.state.mo.us/cgi-bin/professionalregistration.pl
Drug Distribution ....http://riversrun.ded.state.mo.us/cgi-bin/professionalregistration.pl
Embalmer ....http://riversrun.ded.state.mo.us/cgi-bin/professionalregistration.pl
Engineer ....http://riversrun.ded.state.mo.us/cgi-bin/professionalregistration.pl
Funeral Director ....http://riversrun.ded.state.mo.us/cgi-bin/professionalregistration.pl
Funeral Establishment ....http://riversrun.ded.state.mo.us/cgi-bin/professionalregistration.pl
Funeral Preneed Provider/Seller ....http://riversrun.ded.state.mo.us/cgi-bin/professionalregistration.pl
Geologist ....http://riversrun.ded.state.mo.us/cgi-bin/professionalregistration.pl
Geologist Registrant in Training ....http://riversrun.ded.state.mo.us/cgi-bin/professionalregistration.pl
Insurance Agent/Broker..................................www.insurance.state.mo.us/industry/agtstatus.htm
Interpreter for the Deaf..................................http://riversrun.ded.state.mo.us/cgi-bin/professionalregistration.pl
Land Surveyor ....http://riversrun.ded.state.mo.us/cgi-bin/professionalregistration.pl
Landfill..www.dnr.state.mo.us/deq/swmp/availpub.htm
Landscape Architect.......................................http://riversrun.ded.state.mo.us/cgi-bin/professionalregistration.pl
Landscape Architect Corp./or/Partnership....................http://riversrun.ded.state.mo.us/cgi-bin/professionalregistration.pl
Manicurist ....http://riversrun.ded.state.mo.us/cgi-bin/professionalregistration.pl
Marital & Family Therapist............................http://riversrun.ded.state.mo.us/cgi-bin/professionalregistration.pl
Martial Artist/Martial Arts Professional......................http://riversrun.ded.state.mo.us/cgi-bin/professionalregistration.pl
Medical Doctor..http://riversrun.ded.state.mo.us/cgi-bin/professionalregistration.pl
Nurse, Advanced Practical ....http://riversrun.ded.state.mo.us/cgi-bin/professionalregistration.pl
Nurse, Registered ....http://riversrun.ded.state.mo.us/cgi-bin/professionalregistration.pl
Nurse-LPN ....http://riversrun.ded.state.mo.us/cgi-bin/professionalregistration.pl
Nursing School..http://riversrun.ded.state.mo.us/cgi-bin/professionalregistration.pl
Occupational Therapist ....http://riversrun.ded.state.mo.us/cgi-bin/professionalregistration.pl
Occupational Therapist Assistant...............................http://riversrun.ded.state.mo.us/cgi-bin/professionalregistration.pl
Optometrist...http://riversrun.ded.state.mo.us/cgi-bin/professionalregistration.pl
Osteopathic Physician ....http://riversrun.ded.state.mo.us/cgi-bin/professionalregistration.pl
Perfusionist...http://riversrun.ded.state.mo.us/cgi-bin/professionalregistration.pl
Pharmacist/Pharmacy Intern...........................http://riversrun.ded.state.mo.us/cgi-bin/professionalregistration.pl
Pharmacy...http://riversrun.ded.state.mo.us/cgi-bin/professionalregistration.pl
Pharmacy Technician ....http://riversrun.ded.state.mo.us/cgi-bin/professionalregistration.pl
Physical Therapist ....http://riversrun.ded.state.mo.us/cgi-bin/professionalregistration.pl
Physician Assistant...http://riversrun.ded.state.mo.us/cgi-bin/professionalregistration.pl

Podiatrist .... http://riversrun.ded.state.mo.us/cgi-bin/professionalregistration.pl
Podiatrist Temporary... http://riversrun.ded.state.mo.us/cgi-bin/professionalregistration.pl
Podiatrist/Ankle.. http://riversrun.ded.state.mo.us/cgi-bin/professionalregistration.pl
Psychologist .... http://riversrun.ded.state.mo.us/cgi-bin/professionalregistration.pl
Public Accountant Partnership .... http://riversrun.ded.state.mo.us/cgi-bin/professionalregistration.pl
Public Accountant-CPA .... http://riversrun.ded.state.mo.us/cgi-bin/professionalregistration.pl
Real Estate Appraiser .... http://riversrun.ded.state.mo.us/cgi-bin/professionalregistration.pl
Real Estate Broker/Partner/Associate.......................... http://riversrun.ded.state.mo.us/cgi-bin/professionalregistration.pl
Real Estate Instructor .... http://riversrun.ded.state.mo.us/cgi-bin/professionalregistration.pl
Real Estate Officer/Corp/Association........................... http://riversrun.ded.state.mo.us/cgi-bin/professionalregistration.pl
Real Estate Sales Agent.. http://riversrun.ded.state.mo.us/cgi-bin/professionalregistration.pl
Respiratory Care Practitioner .... http://riversrun.ded.state.mo.us/cgi-bin/professionalregistration.pl
Social Worker, Clinical .... http://riversrun.ded.state.mo.us/cgi-bin/professionalregistration.pl
Speech-Language Pathologist/Audiologist .... http://riversrun.ded.state.mo.us/cgi-bin/professionalregistration.pl
Transfer Station .... www.dnr.state.mo.us/deq/swmp/tranlist.htm
Veterinarian.. http://riversrun.ded.state.mo.us/cgi-bin/professionalregistration.pl
Veterinary Technician .... http://riversrun.ded.state.mo.us/cgi-bin/professionalregistration.pl
Waste Tire End User .... www.dnr.state.mo.us/deq/swmp/tireend.htm
Waste Tire Hauler... www.dnr.state.mo.us/deq/swmp/tirehaul.htm
Waste Tire Processor/Site... www.dnr.state.mo.us/deq/swmp/tireend.htm
Wrestler/Wrestling Professional .... http://riversrun.ded.state.mo.us/cgi-bin/professionalregistration.pl

County Level ... Courts

Court Administration: State Court Administrator, 2112 Industrial Dr., PO Box 104480, Jefferson City, MO, 65109; 573-751-4377; www.osca.state.mo.us

Court Structure: The Circuit Court is the court of general jurisdiction. There are 45 circuits comprised of 114 county circuit courts and one independent city court. There are also Associate Circuit Courts with limited jurisdiction and some counties have Combined Courts. Municipal Courts only have jurisdiction over traffic and ordinance violations.

Online Access Note: Casenet, a limited but growing online system, is available at http://casenet.osca.state.mo.us/casenet. The system includes 44 counties (with more projected) as well as the Eastern, Western, and Southern Appellate Courts, the Supreme Court, and Fine Collection Center. Cases can be searched case number, filing date, or litigant name.

The following counties participate in the free state online civil and criminal court record system CaseNet at http://casenet.osca.state.mo.us/casenet. Please note that each county may or may not include the Associate Circuit Court and the Circuit Court, or vice versa. (Online access to Probate records is noted)
(Also see bottom of this section for counties offering online access to non-CaseNet courts)

Andrew County
Circuit & Associate Courts Online records go back to 1993.
Barton County
Circuit & Associate Court   Online records go back to 9/20/1999.
Benton County
Circuit & Associate Court
Bollinger County
Circuit and Associate Courts   Online records go back to 7/1/2001; judgments to 8/23/1993.
Boone County
Circuit and Associate Court
Civil records go back to 3/23/79. Probate records back to 2/23/1956 are also available online. Online criminal records go back to 7/7/1953.

Buchanan County
Circuit & Associate Court   Online records go back to 1992.

Callaway County
Circuit and Associate Courts Online public cases go back to 2000; online probate to 1977.

Cape Girardeau County
Circuit & Associate Circuit Courts Online records go back to 7/1/2001. Circuit court judgmentsgo back to 8/23/1993.

Carter County
Circuit and Associate Courts   Online records go back to 4/17/2000.

Cedar County
Circuit and Associate Coruts   Online records go back to 9/20/1999. Online records include Probate Court.

Clay County
This county has its own system; see below.

Cole County
Circuit and Associate Courts   Online records go back to 1/1980. Probate online records go back to 6/2/1972.

Cooper County
Circuit and Associate Courts   Online records go back to 4/2001. Online criminal records go back 1/1990.

Crawford County
Circuit and Associate Courts
Participates in the free state online Banner court record system at http://casenet.osca.state.mo.us/casenet.

Dade County
Circuit and Associate Courts   Online records go back to 9/20/1999. Online records include Probate Court.

Dallas County
Circuit Court

Dunklin County
Circuit Court Division I and Associate Courts   Online records go back to 7/1/2001.

Franklin County
Circuit and Associate Courts
Online civil and criminal records go back to 1/1995. Online probate court records go back to 10/14/1967.

Gasconade County
Circuit and Associate Courts   Online records go back to 7/31/2000.

Greene County
Circuit and Associate Courts
Online access to records at the court's web site www.greenecountymo.org as well as at http://casenet.osca.state.mo.us/casenet/.

Grundy County
Circuit and Associate Courts
Online civil records go back to 9/97. Online criminal records go back to 6/93. Online Associate Court records go back to 3/29/2000.

Harrison County
Circuit and Associate Courts Online records go back to 1995.

Hickory County
Circuit Court

Howard County
Circuit Court

Howell County
Circuit and Associate Courts Online records go back to 8/2000; pending cases back to 1990.

Jackson County
Circuit Court   Jackson Casenet records go back to 1/89. Includes Probate records.

Jasper County
Circuit and Associate Courts   Online records go back to 6/26/2000.

Mercer County
Associate Circuit Court   Online records go back to 3/29/2000.

Lincoln County
Associate Circuit Court   Scheduled to be on the system in Fall, 2002.
Mercer County
Circuit and Associate Courts   Online Circuit records go back to 3/29/2000. Online Associate records go back to 3/2000.
Mississippi County
Circuit & Associate Court   Online records go back to 6/15/2001.
Montgomery County
Circuit and Associate Courts   Online civil records go back to 6/25/1997. Online criminal records go back to 12/10/1996. Online Associate Court criminal records go back to 8/29/1950.
New Madrid County
Circuit and Associate Courts   Online records go back to 2/7/2001.
Oregon County
Circuit and Associate Courts   Online records go back to 1991.
Osage County
Circuit and Associate Courts   Online circuit civil records go back to 6/20/1985. Online circuit criminal records go back to 8/26/1987. Online Associate court civil records go back to 7/14/1994. Online probate records go back to 9/18/2000. Online Associate criminal records go back to 5/30/1990. Also, traffic is available back to 7/4/1997.
Pemiscot County
Circuit and Associate Courts   Online records go back to 2/7/2001.
Perry County
Circuit and Associate Courts   Online records go back to 7/1/2001. Online judgments go back to 8/23/1993.
Pettis County
Circuit and Associate Courts   Online civil records go back to 4/2001. Online circuit criminal records go back to 1/1992. Online access to Associate criminal records go back to 1/1993. Includes Probate records.
Pike County
Circuit Court   Online records go back 4/2002.
Platte County
Circuit and Associate Courts
Polk County
Circuit and Associate Courts
Putnam County
Circuit and Associate Courts   Online records go back to 3/29/2000.
Randolph County
Circuit and Associate Courts
Reynolds County
Circuit and Associate Courts
St. Charles County
Circuit and Associate Courts   Online civil records go back to 1/1994. Online circuit criminal records go back to 10/1992. Associate court criminal online may be limited to criminal traffic and DUI back to 1/1996.
St. Louis County
Associate Circuit - Civil Division
St. Louis City
Circuit & Associate Circuit Courts
In addition to civil and criminal records, online probate records are available (probate records go back to 5/31/2000.)
Saline County
Circuit Court
Scott County
Circuit and Associate Courts   Online records go back to 6/15/2001.
Shannon County
Circuit and Associate Courts   Online records go back to 1992.

Stoddard County
Circuit and Associate Courts Online records go back to 7/1/2001. Includes probate records.

Vernon County
Circuit Court

Online circuit records go back to 9/26/1999. Online records include probate court. Associate court records go back to 9/2000.

Warren County
Circuit and Associate Courts Online records go back to 9/20/1999. Associate court records may be available.

Webster County
Circuit and Associate Courts

The following courts offer online access to court records other than through CaseNet.

Clay County
Circuit and Associate Courts *Civil and Criminal Records*

www.circuit7.net

Online access to records on the circuit database are available free at www.circuit7.net/pages/publicaccess/publicaccess.htm. Includes traffic.

Greene County
Circuit and Associate Courts *Civil and Criminal Records*

Online access to records at the court's web site www.greenecountymo.org as well as at http://casenet.osca.state.mo.us/casenet/.

Jackson County
Circuit Court - Criminal Division *Some Criminal Records*

www.16thcircuit.org

Online access to criminal traffic dockets is available at www.16thcircuit.org/trafficdockets.asp. This includes private process servers, jury verdicts, criminal traffic, and criminal sureties. Search surety bonding agents at www.16thcircuit.org/suretyqualifications.asp. Also participates in the free state online court record system at http://casenet.osca.state.mo.us/casenet.

Circuit Court *Probate Records*

www.16thcircuit.org

Probate records are also available at www.16thcircuit.org/publicaccess.asp. The Court also participates in the Casenet system.

St. Louis City
Circuit & Associate Circuit Courts *Civil Records*

Remote access is through MoBar Net and is open only to attorneys. Call 314-535-1950 for information.

County Level ... Recorders & Assessors

Recording Office Organization: 114 counties and one independent city -- 115 recording offices. The recording officer is the Recorder of Deeds. The City of St. Louis has its own recording office. The entire state is in the Central Time Zone (CST). All federal and state tax liens are filed with the county Recorder of Deeds. They are usually indexed together. Some counties will perform tax lien searches. Search and copy fees vary widely.

Online Access Note: A handful of counties offer online access. UCCs are available from the Sec. of State.

Boone County   *Real Estate, Lien, Vital Statistic, UCC Records*
www.showmeboone.com
Access to the County Recorder database is available free at www.showmeboone.com/recorder.

Cass County   *Real Estate, Lien Records*
www.casscounty.com/cassfr.htm
Access to county online records via modem requires a $250 monthly fee plus $.10 per minute after 90 minutes usage. Records date back to 1990. Images are viewable and can be printed, $1.00 each. Prepaid fax accounts available. For information, contact Sandy Gregory at 816-380-8117

Clay County   *Real Estate, Marriage, Military Discharge, UCC, Recording Records*
http://recorder.co.clay.mo.us
Access to the recorder's database is available free at http://recorder.co.clay.mo.us/online_access.htm. Overall index goes back to 1986; images back to 1998. UCCs are 1986-91 real estate only.

Greene County   *Divorce Records*
www.greenecountymo.org
Records for divorces that occurred 1837 to 1920 in Greene County are available free online at http://userdb.rootsweb.com/divorces.

Jackson County (Kansas City)   *Property, Tax Assessor, Recording, Marriages, Grantor/Grantee, Deed, Lien, Judgment, UCC Records*
www.co.jackson.mo.us
Records from the county tax assessor database are available free at www.jacksongov.org/Tax/Choice.asp. Search the recorder Grantor/Grantee database for fee at http://records.co.jackson.mo.us/search.asp?cabinet=opr. Search Kansas City land information for free at http://kivaweb.kcmo.org/kivanet/2/land/lookup/index.cfm?fa=dslladdr. Search the marriage records for free at http://records.co.jackson.mo.us/search.asp?cabinet=marriage. Search the UCC database at http://records.co.jackson.mo.us/search.asp?cabinet=ucc.

St. Charles County   *Assessor Records*
www.win.org
Records on the county Property Assessment database are available free online at www.win.org/library/library_office/assessment. No name searching; address, street or map ID only.

Federal Courts in Missouri...

Standards for Federal Courts: The universal PACER sign-up number is 800-676-6856. Find PACER and the Party/Case Index on the Web at http://pacer.psc.uscourts.gov. PACER dial-up access is \$.60 per minute. Also, courts offering internet access via RACER, PACER, Web-PACER or the new CM-ECF charge \$.07 per page fee unless noted as free.

US District Court -- Eastern District of Missouri

Home Page: www.moed.uscourts.gov

PACER: Toll-free access: 800-533-8105. Local access phone: 314-244-7775. Case records are available back to 1992. Records are purged never. New records are available online after 4-5 days. **PACER URL:** http://pacer.moed.uscourts.gov.

Cape Girardeau Division counties: Bollinger, Butler, Cape Girardeau, Carter, Dunklin, Madison, Mississippi, New Madrid, Pemiscot, Perry, Reynolds, Ripley, Scott, Shannon, Stoddard, Wayne.

Hannibal Division counties: Adair, Audrain, Chariton, Clark, Knox, Lewis, Linn, Macon, Marion, Monroe, Montgomery, Pike, Ralls, Randolph, Schuyler, Scotland, Shelby.

St Louis Division counties: Crawford, Dent, Franklin, Gasconade, Iron, Jefferson, Lincoln, Maries, Phelps, St. Charles, Ste. Genevieve, St. Francois, St. Louis, Warren, Washington, City of St. Louis.

US Bankruptcy Court -- Eastern District of Missouri

Home Page: www.moeb.uscourts.gov

PACER: Toll-free access: 888-577-1668. Local access phone: 314-244-4998. Case records are available back to January 1991. Records are purged every six months. New civil records are available online after 1 day. **PACER URL:** http://pacer.moeb.uscourts.gov.

Electronic Filing: (Currently in the process of implementing CM/ECF).

Other Online Access: Search records on the Internet using RACER at http://racer.moeb.uscourts.gov/perl/bkplog.html. Access fee is \$.07 per page. **Also:** access via phone on VCIS (Voice Case Information System) is available: 888-223-6431, 314-425-4054

St Louis Division counties: Adair, Audrain, Bollinger, Butler, Cape Girardeau, Carter, Chariton, Clark, Crawford, Dent, Dunklin, Franklin, Gasconade, Iron, Jefferson, Knox, Lewis, Lincoln, Linn, Macon, Madison, Maries, Marion, Mississippi, Monroe, Montgomery, New Madrid, Pemiscot, Perry, Phelps, Pike, Ralls, Randolph, Reynolds, Ripley, Schuyler, Scotland, Scott, Shannon, Shelby, St. Charles, St. Francois, St. Louis, St. Louis City, Ste. Genevieve, Stoddard, Warren, Washington, Wayne.

US District Court -- Western District of Missouri

Home Page: www.mow.uscourts.gov

PACER: Case records are available back to May 1, 1989. Records are purged as deemed necessary. New records are available online after 1 day. **PACER URL:** http://pacer.mowd.uscourts.gov.

Electronic Filing: Electronic filing information is available online at https://ecf.mowd.uscourts.gov/.

Jefferson City-Central Division counties: Benton, Boone, Callaway, Camden, Cole, Cooper, Hickory, Howard, Miller, Moniteau, Morgan, Osage, Pettis.

Joplin-Southwestern Division counties: Barry, Barton, Jasper, Lawrence, McDonald, Newton, Stone, Vernon.

Kansas City-Western Division counties: Bates, Carroll, Cass, Clay, Henry, Jackson, Johnson, Lafayette, Ray, St. Clair, Saline.

Springfield-Southern Division counties: Cedar, Christian, Dade, Dallas, Douglas, Greene, Howell, Laclede, Oregon, Ozark, Polk, Pulaski, Taney, Texas, Webster, Wright.

St Joseph Division counties: Andrew, Atchison, Buchanan, Caldwell, Clinton, Daviess, De Kalb, Gentry, Grundy, Harrison, Holt, Livingston, Mercer, Nodaway, Platte, Putnam, Sullivan, Worth.

US Bankruptcy Court -- Western District of Missouri

Home Page: www.mow.uscourt.gov

PACER: New records are available online after. **PACER URL:** http://pacer.mowb.uscourts.gov/bc/index.html.

Electronic Filing: Electronic filing information is available online at https://ecf.mowb.uscourts.gov. **Also:** access via phone on VCIS (Voice Case Information System) is available: 888-205-2527, 816-426-5822

Kansas City-Western Division counties: Andrew, Atchison, Barry, Barton, Bates, Benton, Boone, Buchanan, Caldwell, Callaway, Camden, Carroll, Cass, Cedar, Christian, Clay, Clinton, Cole, Cooper, Dade, Dallas, Daviess, De Kalb, Douglas, Gentry, Greene, Grundy, Harrison, Henry, Hickory, Holt, Howard, Howell, Jackson, Jasper, Johnson, Laclede, Lafayette, Lawrence, Livingston, McDonald, Mercer, Miller, Moniteau, Morgan, Newton, Nodaway, Oregon, Osage, Ozark, Pettis, Platte, Polk, Pulaski, Putnam, Ray, Saline, St. Clair, Stone, Sullivan, Taney, Texas, Vernon, Webster, Worth, Wright.

Capital: Helena
                  Lews & Clark County

                                          Home Page   www.mt.gov

Time Zone: MST   Attorney General www.doj.state.mt.us/ago

Number of Counties: 56   Archives   www.his.state.mt.us

State Level ... Major Agencies

Corporation Records, Limited Liability Company Records, Fictitious Name, Limited Partnerships, Assumed Name, Trademarks/Servicemarks

Business Services Bureau, Secretary of State, PO Box 202801, Helena, MT 59620-2801 (Courier: State Capitol, Room 225, Helena, MT 59620); 406-444-3665, 406-444-3976 (Fax), 8AM-5PM.

http://sos.state.mt.us/css/index.asp

Visit http://app.discoveringmontana.com/bes/ for free searches of MT business entities. **Other options:** Lists of the new corporations per month are available.

Uniform Commercial Code, Federal Tax Liens

Business Services Bureau, Secretary of State, Rm 260, PO Box 202801, Helena, MT 59620-2801 (Courier: State Capital, 2nd Fl, Helena, MT 59620); 406-444-3665, 406-444-3976 (Fax), 8AM-5PM.

http://sos.state.mt.us/css/index.asp

This web-based subscription service provides information about all active liens filed with the office. (It does not include lapsed and terminated liens.) To use the service, you need to establish a prepaid account with the Secretary of State's Office for a fee of $25 per month. Contact the Business Services Bureau, P.O. Box 202801, Helena MT 59620-2801, 406-444-3665 or visit the web site. **Other options:** The agency offers farm bill filings lists on a monthly basis for $5.00 per product. A CD-Rom for Farm Products is available for $20.00.

Sexual Offender Registry

The state sexual offender list is maintained by the agency listed above and is open to the public. Online access is available at http://svor2.doj.state.mt.us:8010/index.htm.

Driver Records

Motor Vehicle Division, Driver's Services, PO Box 201430, Helena, MT 59620-1430 (Courier: Records Unit, 303 N Roberts, Room 262, Helena, MT 59620); 406-444-4590, 406-444-1631 (Fax), 8AM-5PM.

www.doj.state.mt.us

Both interactive and batch delivery is offered. Fee is $6.00 per record. An Agreement for Driver's License Record Processing must be signed and a $50.00 annual fee is required. For more information, visit http://app.discoveringmontana.com/premium/ **Other options:** Magnetic tape overnight batch retrieval is available for higher volume users.

Legislation Records

www.leg.state.mt.us

Information is available on the Internet. Committee minutes for 1999 forward are available on the Internet. Exhibits from 1999 forward are available on CD-ROM. **Other options:** Current session bills and resolutions are available on CD-ROM for $150; other products include the Montana Code, House and Senate Journals, and Annotations, among others.

State Level ... Occupational Licensing

Acupuncturist...www.discoveringmontana.com/dli/bsd/license/bsd_boards/med_board/board_page.htm
Architect...www.discoveringmontana.com/dli/bsd/license/license.htm
Athletic Event/Event Timekeeper.............www.discoveringmontana.com/dli/bsd/license/license.htm
Audiologist...www.discoveringmontana.com/dli/bsd/license/license.htm
Barber/Barber Instructor............................www.discoveringmontana.com/dli/bsd/license/BSD_boards/BAR_Board/Board_page.htm
Boxer/Boxing Professional........................www.discoveringmontana.com/dli/bsd/license/license.htm
Boxing Manager/Promoter/Judge..............www.discoveringmontana.com/dli/bsd/license/license.htm
Cemetery ....www.discoveringmontana.com/dli/bsd/license/license.htm
Chemical Dependency Counselor..............www.discoveringmontana.com/dli/bsd/license/license.htm
Child Care Provider...................................http://vhsp.dphhs.state.mt.us/dph_r2.htm
Chiropractor ....www.discoveringmontana.com/dli/bsd/license/license.htm
Clinical Social Worker ....www.discoveringmontana.com/dli/bsd/license/license.htm
Construction Blaster...................................www.discoveringmontana.com/dli/bsd/license/license.htm
Contractor, Public ....http://erd.dli.state.mt.us/WorkCompRegs/CRlist.pdf
Cosmetologist/Cosmetology Instr./School.www.discoveringmontana.com/dli/bsd/license/BSD_boards/COS_Board/Board_page.htm
Crematory/Crematory Operator/Techn. ......www.discoveringmontana.com/dli/bsd/license/license.htm
Day Care Center ....http://vhsp.dphhs.state.mt.us/dph_r2.htm
Dental Hygienist..www.discoveringmontana.com/dli/bsd/license/license.htm
Dentist/Dental Assistant ....www.discoveringmontana.com/dli/bsd/license/license.htm
Denturist..www.discoveringmontana.com/dli/bsd/license/license.htm
Drug Wholesaler..www.discoveringmontana.com/dli/bsd/license/license.htm
Drugs, Dangerous......................................www.discoveringmontana.com/dli/bsd/license/license.htm
Electrician ....www.discoveringmontana.com/dli/ele
Electrologist ....www.discoveringmontana.com/dli/bsd/license/BSD_boards/BAR_Board/Board_page.htm
Emergency Medical Technician ....www.discoveringmontana.com/dli/bsd/license/bsd_boards/med_board/board_page.htm
Engineer ....www.discoveringmontana.com/dli/bsd/license/bsd_boards/pel_board/board_page.htm
Esthetician...www.discoveringmontana.com/dli/bsd/license/BSD_boards/BAR_Board/Board_page.htm
Firearms Instructor ....www.discoveringmontana.com/dli/bsd/license/license.htm
Funeral Director ....www.discoveringmontana.com/dli/bsd/license/license.htm
Hairstylist..www.discoveringmontana.com/dli/bsd/license/license.htm
Hearing Aid Dispenser ....www.discoveringmontana.com/dli/bsd/license/license.htm
Insurance Adjuster.....................................http://sao.state.mt.us/Database/findagent.htm
Insurance Producer....................................http://sao.state.mt.us/Database/findagent.htm
Land Surveyor ....www.discoveringmontana.com/dli/bsd/license/bsd_boards/pel_board/board_page.htm
Landscape Architect...................................www.discoveringmontana.com/dli/bsd/license/license.htm
Manicurist..www.discoveringmontana.com/dli/bsd/license/BSD_boards/BAR_Board/Board_page.htm
Medical Doctor..www.discoveringmontana.com/dli/bsd/license/bsd_boards/med_board/board_page.htm
Midwife Nurse...www.discoveringmontana.com/dli/bsd/license/bsd_boards/nur_board/board_page.htm
Midwife, Direct Entry/Apprentice.............www.discoveringmontana.com/dli/ahc
Mortuary/Mortician...................................www.discoveringmontana.com/dli/bsd/license/license.htm
Naturopathic Physician ....www.discoveringmontana.com/dli/ahc
Nurse Anesthetist ....www.discoveringmontana.com/dli/bsd/license/bsd_boards/nur_board/board_page.htm
Nurse-RN/LPN..www.discoveringmontana.com/dli/bsd/license/bsd_boards/nur_board/board_page.htm
Nursing Professional ....www.discoveringmontana.com/dli/bsd/license/bsd_boards/nur_board/board_page.htm

Nutritionist ....www.discoveringmontana.com/dli/bsd/license/bsd_boards/med_board/board_page.htm
Occupational Therapist ....www.discoveringmontana.com/dli/bsd/license/license.htm
Optometrist...www.odfinder.org/LicSearch.asp
Osteopathic Physician ....www.discoveringmontana.com/dli/bsd/license/bsd_boards/med_board/board_page.htm
Outfitter..www.discoveringmontana.com/dli/bsd/license/license.htm
Pharmacist...www.discoveringmontana.com/dli/bsd/license/license.htm
Physical Therapist ....www.discoveringmontana.com/dli/bsd/license/license.htm
Physician Assistant..................................www.discoveringmontana.com/dli/bsd/license/bsd_boards/med_board/board_page.htm
Plumber...www.discoveringmontana.com/dli/plu
Podiatrist ....www.discoveringmontana.com/dli/bsd/license/bsd_boards/med_board/board_page.htm
Prescriptive Authority, Nurse ....www.discoveringmontana.com/dli/bsd/license/bsd_boards/nur_board/board_page.htm
Private Investigator..................................www.discoveringmontana.com/dli/bsd/license/license.htm
Private Security Guard ....www.discoveringmontana.com/dli/bsd/license/license.htm
Process Server ....www.discoveringmontana.com/dli/bsd/license/license.htm
Property Manager.....................................www.discoveringmontana.com/dli/bsd/license/bsd_boards/rre_board/board_page.htm
Psychologist ....www.discoveringmontana.com/dli/bsd/license/license.htm
Public Accountant ....http://app.discoveringmontana.com/bsdinq/index.html
Radiologic Technologist...........................www.discoveringmontana.com/dli/bsd/license/license.htm
Real Estate Appraiser ....www.discoveringmontana.com/dli/bsd/license/license.htm
Real Estate Broker/Salesperson ....www.discoveringmontana.com/dli/bsd/license/bsd_boards/rre_board/board_page.htm
Referee ....www.discoveringmontana.com/dli/bsd/license/license.htm
Respiratory Care Practitioner ....www.discoveringmontana.com/dli/bsd/license/license.htm
Sanitarian ....www.discoveringmontana.com/dli/bsd/license/license.htm
Security Alarm Installer............................www.discoveringmontana.com/dli/bsd/license/license.htm
Security Company/Organization ....www.discoveringmontana.com/dli/bsd/license/license.htm
Security Guard...www.discoveringmontana.com/dli/bsd/license/license.htm
Social Worker, LSW................................www.discoveringmontana.com/dli/bsd/license/license.htm
Speech Pathologist ....www.discoveringmontana.com/dli/bsd/license/license.htm
Surveyor, Land ....www.discoveringmontana.com/dli/bsd/license/bsd_boards/pel_board/board_page.htm
Teacher..http://data.opi.state.mt.us/certification/
Timeshare Broker/Salesperson ....www.discoveringmontana.com/dli/bsd/license/bsd_boards/rre_board/board_page.htm
Veterinarian...www.discoveringmontana.com/dli/bsd/license/license.htm
Wrestler...www.discoveringmontana.com/dli/bsd/license/license.htm

County Level ... Courts

Court Administration: Court Administrator, Justice Building, 215 N Sanders, Room 315 (PO Box 203002), Helena, MT, 59620; 406-444-2621

Court Structure: The District Courts have no maximum amount for civil judgment cases. Most District Courts handle civil over $7,000; there are exceptions that handle a civil minimum as low as $5,000. Limited Jurisdiction Courts, which are also known as Justice Courts, may handle civil actions up to $7,000. The Small Claims limit is $3,000. Many Montana Justices of the Peace maintain case record indexes on their personal PCs, which does speed the retrieval process.

Online Access Note: There is no statewide internal or external online computer system available. No counties offer online access, one offers e-mail requests. Historical information of Supreme Courts decisions may be found at www.state.mt.us/css/govt/state_agencies.asp.

Lewis and Clark County
District Court *Civil and Criminal Records*
www.co.lewis-clark.mt.us
Will accept email record requests to ikallio@co.lewis-clark.mt.us.

County Level ... Recorders & Assessors

Recording Office Organization: 57 counties, 56 recording offices. The recording officer is the County Clerk and Recorder (it is the Clerk of District Court for state tax liens). Yellowstone National Park is considered a county but is not included as a filing location. The entire state is in the Mountain Time Zone (MST). Federal tax liens on personal property of businesses are filed with the Secretary of State. Other federal tax liens are filed with the county Clerk and Recorder. State tax liens are filed with the Clerk of District Court. Usually tax liens on personal property filed with the Clerk and Recorder are in the same index with UCC financing statements.

Online Access Note:
Search for a for a Montana property owner by name and county on the Montana Cadastral Mapping Project GIS mapping database at http://gis.doa.state.mt.us.

Lewis and Clark County   *Real Estate, Lien, Recording Records*
www.co.lewis-clark.mt.us
Currently the Records Department is in the processing of automating their recording and filing procedures. This automation will include document imaging. Available is the GIS map and parcel search at www.co.lewis-clark.mt.us/gis/atlas/index.html.

Missoula County   *Property, Assessor Records*
www.co.missoula.mt.us
Access to the county property information system is available free at www.co.missoula.mt.us/owner/. No name searching at this time.

Yellowstone County   *Assessor, Tax, Grantor/Grantee Records*
www.co.yellowstone.mt.us/clerk
Access to the county clerk & recorder records are available free online at www.co.yellowstone.mt.us/clerk. Also, access to the tax assessor records is available free at www.co.yellowstone.mt.us/gis.

Federal Courts in Montana...

Standards for Federal Courts: The universal PACER sign-up number is 800-676-6856. Find PACER and the Party/Case Index on the Web at http://pacer.psc.uscourts.gov. PACER dial-up access is $.60 per minute. Also, courts offering internet access via RACER, PACER, Web-PACER or the new CM-ECF charge $.07 per page fee unless noted as free.

US District Court -- District of Montana
Home Page: www.mtd.uscourts.gov
PACER: Toll-free access: 800-305-5235. Local access phone: 406-452-9851. Case records are available back to 1992. Records are purged never. New records are available online after 5 days. .
Billings Division counties: Big Horn, Carbon, Carter, Custer, Daniels, Dawson, Fallon, Garfield, Golden Valley, McCone, Musselshell, Park, Petroleum, Powder River, Prairie, Richland, Rosebud, Stillwater, Sweet Grass, Treasure, Wheatland,Wibaux, Yellowstone, Yellowstone National Park.
Butte Division counties: Beaverhead, Deer Lodge, Gallatin, Madison, Silver Bow.
Great Falls Division counties: Blaine, Cascade, Chouteau, Daniels, Fergus, Glacier, Hill, Judith Basin, Liberty, Phillips, Pondera, Roosevelt, Sheridan, Teton, Toole, Valley.
Helena Division counties: Broadwater, Jefferson, Lewis and Clark, Meagher, Powell.
Missoula Division counties: Flathead, Granite, Lake, Lincoln, Mineral, Missoula, Ravalli, Sanders.

US Bankruptcy Court -- District of Montana
Home Page: www.mtb.uscourts.gov
PACER: Toll-free access: 800-716-4305. Local access phone: 406-782-1051. Use of PC Anywhere v4.0 suggested. Case records are available back to 1986. New civil records are available online after 1 day. **PACER URL:** http://pacer.mtb.uscourts.gov.
Electronic Filing: (Currently in the process of implementing CM/ECF).
Other Online Access: Court does not participate in the U.S. party case index. **Also:** access via phone on VCIS (Voice Case Information System) is available: 888-879-0071, 406-782-1060
Butte Division counties: All counties in Montana.

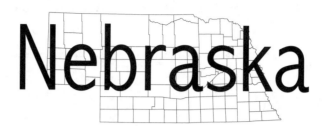

Nebraska

Capital:	Lincoln Lancaster County	Home Page	www.state.ne.us
Time Zone:	CST/MST	Attorney General	www.ago.state.ne.us
Number of Counties:	93	Archives	www.nebraskahistory.org

State Level ... Major Agencies

Corporation Records, Limited Liability Company Records, Limited Partnerships, Trade Names, Trademarks/Servicemarks

Secretary of State, Corporation Commission, 1305 State Capitol Bldg, Lincoln, NE 68509; 402-471-4079, 402-471-3666 (Fax), 8AM-5PM.

www.sos.state.ne.us/htm/corpmenu.htm

The state has designated Nebrask@ Online (800-747-8177) to facilitate online retrieval of records. Access is through both a dial-up system and the Internet; however an account and payment is required. The state Internet site has general information only. **Other options:** Nebrask@ Online has the capability of offering database purchases.

Uniform Commercial Code, Federal Tax Liens, State Tax Liens

UCC Division, Secretary of State, PO Box 95104, Lincoln, NE 68509 (Courier: 1301 State Capitol Bldg, Lincoln, NE 68509); 402-471-4080, 402-471-4429 (Fax), 7:30AM-5PM.

www.sos.state.ne.us/htm/UCCmenu.htm

Access is outsourced to Nebrask@ Online at www.nol.org. The system is available 24 hours daily. There is an annual $50.00 fee but no further charges to view records. Call 800-747-8177 for more information. **Other options:** Check with Nebrask@ Online for bulk purchase programs.

Sexual Offender Registry

The Nebraska State Patrol maintains the sexual offender database for the state. A Level 3 sexual offender registry search is available at www.nsp.state.ne.us/sor/find.cfm.

Incarceration Records

To search online go to www.corrections.state.ne.us.

Sales Tax Registrations

Revenue Department, Taxpayer Assistance, PO Box 94818, Lincoln, NE 68509-4818 (Courier: 301 Centennial Mall South, Lincoln, NE 68509); 402-471-7729, 402-471-5990 (Fax), 8AM-5PM.

www.revenue.state.ne.us

Information is available through Nebrask@ Online (402-471-7810). This is a commercial service with annual fee and monthly download fees.

Birth Certificates

NE Health & Human Services System, Vital Statistics Section, PO Box 95065, Lincoln, NE 68509-5065 (Courier: 301 Centennial Mall S, 3rd Floor, Lincoln, NE 68509); 402-471-2871, 8AM-5PM.

www.hhs.state.ne.us/ced/cedindex.htm

Records may be ordered online from the Internet site.

Workers' Compensation Records

Workers' Compensation Court, PO Box 98908, Lincoln, NE 68509-8908 (Courier: State Capitol, 13th Floor, Lincoln, NE 68509); 402-471-6468, 800-599-5155 (In-state), 402-471-2700 (Fax), 8AM-5PM.

www.nol.org/workcomp

Access to orders and decisions is available from the web site.

Driver Records

Department of Motor Vehicles, Driver & Vehicle Records Division, PO Box 94789, Lincoln, NE 68509-4789 (Courier: 301 Centennial Mall, S, Lincoln, NE 68509); 402-471-3918, 8AM-5PM.

www.nol.org/home/DMV

Nebraska outsources all online and tape record requests through Nebrask@ Online (800-747-8177). The system is interactive and open 24 hours a day, 7 days a week. Fee is $3.00 per record. There is an annual fee of $50.00 and a $.40 per minute connect fee or $.12 if connected through the Internet.

Vehicle Ownership, Vehicle Identification, Vessel Ownership

Department of Motor Vehicles, Driver & Vehicle Records Division, PO Box 94789, Lincoln, NE 68509-4789 (Courier: 301 Centennial Mall, S, Lincoln, NE 68509); 402-471-3918, 8AM-5PM.

www.nol.org/home/DMV

Electronic access is through Nebrask@ Online. There is a start-up fee and line charges are incurred in addition to the $1.00 per record fee. The system is open 24 hours a day, 7 days a week. Call 800-747-8177 for more information. **Other options:** Bulk requesters must be authorized by state officials. Purpose of the request and subsequent usage are reviewed. For more information, call 402-471-3909.

Legislation Records

www.unicam.state.ne.us

The web site features the state statutes, legislative bills for the present session and a legislative journal. You can search by bill number or subject.

State Level ... Occupational Licensing

Alcohol/Drug Testing	www.hhs.state.ne.us/lis/lis.asp
Architect	www.ea.state.ne.us/search/arch.htm
Asbestos-related Occupation	www.hhs.state.ne.us/lis/lis.asp
Assisted Living Facility	www.nlc.state.ne.us/docs/pilot/pubs/h.html
Athletic Trainer	www.hhs.state.ne.us/lis/lis.asp

Attorney	www.nebar.com/directory/dir.asp
Bank	www.ndbf.org/banks.htm
Barber School	www.barbers.state.ne.us/
Chiropractor	www.hhs.state.ne.us/lis/lis.asp
Collection Agency	www.nol.org/home/SOS/Collections/col-agn.htm
Cosmetology Salon/School	www.hhs.state.ne.us/lis/lis.asp
Credit Union	www.ndbf.org/culist.htm
Debt Management Agency	www.nol.org/home/SOS/Collections/debtlist.htm
Delayed Deposit Service	www.ndbf.org/ddslist.htm
Dental Hygienist	www.hhs.state.ne.us/lis/lis.asp
Dentist	www.hhs.state.ne.us/lis/lis.asp
Developmentally Disabled Center	www.nlc.state.ne.us/docs/pilot/pubs/h.html
Emergency Medical Care Facility/Clinic	www.hhs.state.ne.us/lis/lis.asp
Engineer	www.ea.state.ne.us/search
Environmental Health Specialist	www.hhs.state.ne.us/lis/lis.asp
Exterminator	www.kellysolutions.com/ne/
Funeral Establishment	www.hhs.state.ne.us/lis/lis.asp
Health Clinic	www.hhs.state.ne.us/lis/lis.asp
Hearing Aid Dispenser/Fitter	www.hhs.state.ne.us/lis/lis.asp
Home Health Agency	www.nlc.state.ne.us/docs/pilot/pubs/h.html
Hospice	www.nlc.state.ne.us/docs/pilot/pubs/h.html
Hospital	www.nlc.state.ne.us/docs/pilot/pubs/h.html
Insurance Company	www.nol.org/home/NDOI/company_search/index.html
Investigator, Plainclothes	www.nol.org/home/SOS/Privatedetectives/pilist.htm
Investment Advisor/Advisor Rep.	www.nasdr.com/2001.asp
Landscape Architect	www.landarch.state.ne.us/registrants.pdf
Liquor Vendor	www.nol.org/home/NLCC/nlccsearch.html
Massage Therapy School	www.hhs.state.ne.us/lis/lis.asp
Mental Health Center	www.hhs.state.ne.us/lis/lis.asp
Nurse	www.hhs.state.ne.us/lis/lis.asp
Nursing Home	www.hhs.state.ne.us/lis/lis.asp
Nutrition Therapy, Medical	www.hhs.state.ne.us/lis/lis.asp
Occupational Therapist	www.hhs.state.ne.us/lis/lis.asp
Optometrist	www.hhs.state.ne.us/lis/lis.asp
Pesticide Applicator/Dealer	www.kellysolutions.com/ne/
Pharmacist	www.hhs.state.ne.us/lis/lis.asp
Pharmacy	www.hhs.state.ne.us/lis/lis.asp
Physical Therapist	www.hhs.state.ne.us/lis/lis.asp
Physician	www.hhs.state.ne.us/lis/lis.asp
Physician Assistant	www.hhs.state.ne.us/lis/lis.asp
Podiatrist	www.hhs.state.ne.us/lis/lis.asp
Polygraph Examiner, Private	www.nol.org/home/SOS/Polygraph/polypri.htm
Polygraph Examiner, Public	www.nol.org/home/SOS/Polygraph/polypub.htm
Polygraph/Voice Stress Examiner	www.nol.org/home/SOS/Polygraph/voice.htm
Private Detective	www.nol.org/home/SOS/Privatedetectives/pdlist.htm
Psychologist	www.hhs.state.ne.us/lis/lis.asp
Public Accountant-CPA	www.nol.org/home/BPA/license/
Radiographer	www.hhs.state.ne.us/lis/lis.asp
Real Estate Appraiser	http://dbdec.nrc.state.ne.us/appraiser/docs/list.html
Respiratory Care	www.hhs.state.ne.us/lis/lis.asp
Securities Agent	www.nasdr.com/2001.asp
Securities Broker/Dealer	www.nasdr.com/2001.asp
Substance Abuse Treatment Center	www.nlc.state.ne.us/docs/pilot/pubs/h.html
Surveyor, Land	www.sso.state.ne.us/bels/
Swimming Pool Operator	www.hhs.state.ne.us/lis/lis.asp
Veterinarian	www.hhs.state.ne.us/lis/lis.asp
Water Operator	www.hhs.state.ne.us/lis/lis.asp

County Level ... Courts

Court Administration: Court Administrator, PO Box 98910, Lincoln, NE, 68509-8910; 402-471-2643; http://court.nol.org/AOC

Court Structure: The District Court is the court of general jurisdiction. The minimum on civil judgment matters for District Courts is $15,000, however, the State raised the County Court limit on civil matters from $15,000 to $45,000 as of Sept. 1, 2001. As it is less expensive to file civil cases in County Court than in District Court, civil cases in the $15,000 to $45,000 range are more likely to be found in County Court, if after Sept. 1, 2001. Consequently, some District Courts have raised their civil minimum to $45,000. County Courts have juvenile jurisdiction in all but 3 counties. Douglas, Lancaster, and Sarpy counties have separate Juvenile Courts.

Online Access Note: Online access to District and County courts is being tested and may offer statewide access to all 185 Nebraska District and County Courts starting late in 2002. For more information, call John Cariotto at 402-471-2643. Currently, Douglas, Lancaster, and Sarpy county courts offer internet access with registration and password required.

Douglas County
Lancaster County
Sarpy County
County Courts *Civil and Criminal Records*
www.co.douglas.ne.us
Access to the Internet system requires registration and password. Call John at 402-471-3049 for more information. System can be searched by name or case number.

County Level ... Recorders & Assessors

Recording Office Organization: 93 counties, 109 recording offices. The recording officers are County Clerk (UCC and some state tax liens) and Register of Deeds (real estate and most tax liens). Most counties have a combined Clerk/Register office. Sixteen counties have separate offices for County Clerk and for Register of Deeds - Adams, Cass, Dakota, Dawson, Dodge, Douglas, Gage, Hall, Lancaster, Lincoln, Madison, Otoe, Platte, Sarpy, Saunders, and Scotts Bluff. In combined offices, the Register of Deeds is frequently a different person from the County Clerk. 74 counties are in the Central Time Zone (CST) and 19 are in the Mountain Time Zone (MST). All federal and some state tax liens are filed with the County Register of Deeds. Some state tax liens on personal property are filed with the County Clerk. Most counties will perform tax lien searches, some as part of a UCC search, and others for a separate fee, usually $3.50 per name in each index.

Online Access Note: Nebrask@online offers online access to Secretary of State's UCC database; registration and a usage fee is required. For information, visit www.nol.org/subinfo.html. The state treasurer's unclaimed property database is searchable free at www.treasurer.state.ne.us/ie/uphome.asp.

Dodge County Register of Deeds *Real Estate Records*
www.registerofdeeds.com
Access to Register of Deeds mortgages database is available at the web site. Registration is required. The site is under development.

Douglas County Clerk *Assessor Records*
Property tax records on the county assessor database are available free online at www.co.douglas.ne.us/dept.assessor/framevalinfo.htm. There is no name searching.

Lancaster County Clerk *Assessor, Recording, Grantor/Grantee, Deed, Judgment, Dog Tag, Treasurer, Marriage, Accident, Parking Ticket, Building Permit Records*
http://interlinc.ci.lincoln.ne.us
Records on the county Assessor Property Information Search database are available free at www.dcassessor.org/valuation.html. Search parking tickets at www.ci.lincoln.ne.us/city/finance/treas/tickets.htm. Also, search the register of deeds Grantor/Grantee index for free at www.ci.lincoln.ne.us/cnty/deeds/deeds.htm. Search City of Lincoln accident reports at www.ci.lincoln.ne.us/city/police/stats/acc.htm. Also, search treasurer' property info at www.ci.lincoln.ne.us/cnty/treas/property.htm. Search dog tag registrations at www.ci.lincoln.ne.us/city/health/animal/acttag.htm. Search marriages at www.ci.lincoln.ne.us/cnty/clerk/marrsrch.htm

Lancaster County Register of Deeds *Real Estate, Lien, Grantor/Grantee, Assessor, Treasurer Records*
www.ci.lincoln.ne.us/cnty/co_agenc.htm
Access to the county online deeds search is available free at www.ci.lincoln.ne.us/cnty/deeds/deeds.htm. Also, access to the assessor database is available at www.ci.lincoln.ne.us/cnty/assess/property.htm. Treasurer information is also here. Also, search property information free on the map server site at http://ims.ci.lincoln.ne.us/isa/parcel.

Sarpy County Clerk *Real Estate Records*
www.sarpy.com
Records on the county Property Lookup database are available free online at www.sarpy.com/boe/capslookup.htm.

Federal Courts in Nebraska...

US District Court - District of Nebraska
Home Page: www.ned.uscourts.gov
PACER: Sign-up number is 800-676-6856. Access fee is $.60 per minute. Toll-free access: 800-252-9724. Local access: 402-221-4797. Case records are available back to late 1990. Records are purged every year. New records are available online after 2 days.
PACER Internet Access: http://pacer.ned.uscourts.gov.
Lincoln Division Counties: Nebraska cases may be filed in any of the three courts at the option of the attorney, except that filings in the North Platte Division must be during trial session.
North Platte Division Counties: Nebraska cases may be filed in any of the three courts at the option of the attorney, except that filings in the North Platte Division must be during trial session. Some case records may be in the Omaha Division as well as the Lincoln Division.
Omaha Division Counties: Nebraska cases may be filed in any of the three courts at the option of the attorney, except that filings in the North Platte Division must be during trial session.

US Bankruptcy Court - District of Nebraska
PACER: Sign-up number is 800-676-6856. Access fee is $.60 per minute. Toll-free access: 800-788-0656. Local access: 402-221-4882. Case records are available back to September 1989. Records are purged every six months. New civil records are available online after 3 days.
PACER Internet Access: http://pacer.neb.uscourts.gov.
Lincoln Division Counties: Adams, Antelope, Boone, Boyd, Buffalo, Butler, Cass, Clay, Colfax, Fillmore, Franklin, Gage, Greeley, Hall, Hamilton, Harlan, Holt, Howard, Jefferson, Johnson, Kearney, Lancaster, Madison, Merrick, Nance, Nemaha, Nuckolls, Otoe, Pawnee, Phelps, Platte,Polk, Richardson, Saline, Saunders, Seward, Sherman, Thayer, Webster, Wheeler, York. Cases from the North Platte Division may also be assigned here.
North Platte Division Counties: Arthur, Banner, Blaine, Box Butte, Brown, Chase, Cherry, Cheyenne, Custer, Dawes, Dawson, Deuel, Dundy, Frontier, Furnas, Garden, Garfield, Gosper, Grant, Hayes, Hitchcock, Hooker, Keith, Keya Paha, Kimball, Lincoln, Logan, Loup, McPherson, Morrill,Perkins, Red Willow, Rock, Scotts Bluff, Sheridan, Sioux, Thomas, Valley. Cases may be randomly allocated to Omaha or Lincoln.
Omaha Division Counties: Burt, Cedar, Cuming, Dakota, Dixon, Dodge, Douglas, Knox, Pierce, Sarpy, Stanton, Thurston, Washington, Wayne.

Nevada

Capital:	Carson City Carson City County	Home Page	www.silver.state.nv.us
Time Zone:	PST	Attorney General	http://ag.state.nv.us
Number of Counties:	17	Archives	http://dmla.clan.lib.nv.us/docs/nsla

State Level ... Major Agencies

Corporation Records, Limited Partnerships, Limited Liability Company Records, Limited Partnership Records

Secretary of State, Records, 101 N Carson, #3, Carson City, NV 89701-4786; 775-684-5708, 702-486-2880 (Las Vegas Ofc.:), 702-486-2888 (Las Vegas Ofc fax:), 775-684-5725 (Fax), 8AM-5PM.

www.sos.state.nv.us

Online access is offered on the Internet site for no charge. You can search by corporate name, resident agent, corporate officers, or by file number.

Uniform Commercial Code, Federal Tax Liens, State Tax Liens

UCC Division, Secretary of State, 200 N Carson St, Carson City, NV 89701-4069; 775-684-5708, 775-684-5630 (Fax), 8AM-5PM.

www.sos.state.nv.us

This is a PC dial-up system. The fee is $24.50 per hour or $10.75 per hour on an 800 number for unlimited access. There is a $50.00 minimum deposit. The system is up from 7 AM to 5 PM. Call 775-684-5704 and ask for Tom Horgan.

Incarceration Records

Information on current inmates is available at www.ndoc.state.nv.us/ncis/.

Driver Records

Department of Motor Vehicles, Records Section, 555 Wright Way, Carson City, NV 89711-0250; 775-684-4590, 800-992-7945 (In-state), 8AM-5PM.

www.dmvstat.com

The state has an FTP type online system available for high volume users. All files received by 5:30 PM are processed and returned at 6:30 PM. Call 775-684-4742 for details.

Legislation Records

www.leg.state.nv.us

Bills and bill status information is available via this agency's web site. Legislative bills, hearings, journals are searchable online for years 1997, 1999, and 2001.

State Level ... Occupational Licensing

Ambulatory Surgery Centers (Pharm)	http://glsuitewww.glsuite.com/NVBoPWeb/Consumers/default.asp
Architect	http://nsbaidrd.state.nv.us
Carpentry Contractor	http://nscb.tecxprs.com
Chiropractor	www.state.nv.us/chirobd/home.htm
Dental Hygienist	www.nvdentalboard.org/databaseRDH.html
Dentist	www.nvdentalboard.org/databaseDDS.html
Drug Wholesalers/Distributor/Mfg	http://glsuitewww.glsuite.com/NVBoPWeb/Consumers/default.asp
Engineer	http://boe.state.nv.us/ROST_HOME.HTM
Euthanasia Technicians (Animal)	http://glsuitewww.glsuite.com/NVBoPWeb/Consumers/default.asp
Floor & Carpet Layer	http://nscb.tecxprs.com
GCB Most-Wanted & Banned List	http://gaming.state.nv.us/wanted_main.htm
Glazier Contractor	http://nscb.tecxprs.com
Guard Dog Handler	http://ag.state.nv.us/pilb/020802pilb.pdf
Heating & Air Conditioning Mechanic	http://nscb.tecxprs.com
Hospital Pharmacy, Institutional	http://glsuitewww.glsuite.com/NVBoPWeb/Consumers/default.asp
Insulation Installer Contractor	http://nscb.tecxprs.com
Interior Designer	http://nsbaidrd.state.nv.us
Lobbyist	www.leg.state.nv.us/lobbyistdb/index.cfm
Medical Devices, Equipment & Gases	http://glsuitewww.glsuite.com/NVBoPWeb/Consumers/default.asp
Narcotic Treatment Center	http://glsuitewww.glsuite.com/NVBoPWeb/Consumers/default.asp
Nurse, Advanced Practitioner	http://glsuitewww.glsuite.com/NVBoPWeb/Consumers/default.asp
Optometrist	www.odfinder.org/LicSearch.asp
Painter	http://nscb.tecxprs.com
Painter/Paper Hanger	http://nscb.tecxprs.com
Patrol Company/Man, Private	http://ag.state.nv.us/pilb/020802pilb.pdf
Pharmacist/Pharmaceutical Technician	http://glsuitewww.glsuite.com/NVBoPWeb/Consumers/default.asp
Pharmacy	http://glsuitewww.glsuite.com/NVBoPWeb/Consumers/default.asp
Pharmacy Practitioner	http://glsuitewww.glsuite.com/NVBoPWeb/Consumers/default.asp
Physician Assistant (Pharmacy)	http://glsuitewww.glsuite.com/NVBoPWeb/Consumers/default.asp
Plasterer/Drywall Installer	http://nscb.tecxprs.com
Plumber	http://nscb.tecxprs.com
Polygraph Examiner	http://ag.state.nv.us/pilb/020802pilb.pdf
Prison (correctional) Pharmacy	http://glsuitewww.glsuite.com/NVBoPWeb/Consumers/default.asp
Private Investigator	http://ag.state.nv.us/pilb/020802pilb.pdf
Process Server	http://ag.state.nv.us/pilb/020802pilb.pdf
Repossessor	http://ag.state.nv.us/pilb/020802pilb.pdf
Residential Designer	http://nsbaidrd.state.nv.us
Roofer	http://nscb.tecxprs.com
Surveyor, Land	http://boe.state.nv.us/ROST_HOME.HTM
Water Well Driller	http://ndwr.state.nv.us/Engineering/welldrill.htm
Well Driller/Monitor	http://ndwr.state.nv.us/Engineering/welldrill.htm

County Level ... Courts

Court Administration: Supreme Court of Nevada, Administrative Office of the Courts, Capitol Complex, 201 S Carson St, Carson City, NV, 89701; 775-684-1700; http://silver.state.nv.us/elec_judicial.htm

Court Structure: There are 17 District Courts within 9 judicial districts. The 45 Justice Courts are named for the township of jurisdiction. Note that, due to their small populations, some townships no longer have Justice Courts. Probate is handled by the District Courts.

Online Access Note: Some Nevada Courts have internal online computer systems, but only Clark County offers online access to the public. A statewide court automation system is being implemented.

Clark County
8th Judicial District Court *Civil, Probate, and Criminal Records*
www.co.clark.nv.us/district_court/courthome.htm
Records from the court available free online at http://courtgate.coca.co.clark.nv.us:8490. Search by case number or party name. Probate also available.

Las Vegas Township Justice *Civil and Criminal Records*
www.co.clark.nv.us/justicecourt_lv/welcome.htm
Calendars are available online at the web site.

County Level ... Recorders & Assessors

Recording Office Organization: 16 counties and one independent city -- 17 recording offices. The recording officer is the County Recorder. Carson City has a separate filing office. The entire state is in the Pacific Time Zone (PST). Federal tax liens on personal property of businesses are filed with the Secretary of State. Federal tax liens on personal property of individuals are filed with the County Recorder. Although not called state tax liens, employment withholding judgments have the same effect and are filed with the County Recorder. Most counties will provide tax lien searches for a fee of $15.00 per name - $20.00 if the standard UCC request form is not used.

Online Access Note: Clark County has many searchable databases online. A private company, GoverNet, offers online access to Assessor, Treasurer, Recorder and other county databases. Registration is required, sliding monthly and per-hit fees apply. Counties online are Churchill, Clark, Elko, Esmeralda, Eureka, Humboldt, Lander, Lyon, Mineral, Nye, Pershing, Storey, Washoe, and White Pine. Also included is Carson City. System includes access to Secretary of State's Corporation, Partnership, UCC, Fictitious Name, and Federal Tax Lien records. For more information, visit www.governet.net/SurfNV/ or call 208-522-1225.

Clark County   *Real Estate, Lien, Deed, UCC, Vital Statistic, Marriage, Property Assessor, Fictitious Name, Business License Records*
www.co.clark.nv.us/recorder/recindex.htm
Property records, assessor maps, manufactured housing and road documents on the county Assessor database are available free online at www.co.clark.nv.us/assessor/Disclaim.htm. Marriage records available at www.co.clark.nv.us/recorder/mar_srch.htm. Search property owners at GIS site at http://gisgate.co.clark.nv.us:8487/openweb/. Search business licenses at http://sandgate.co.clark.nv.us:8498/businessLicense/blindex.htm. Recorder's real estate, UCC and Vital records are available online at www.co.clark.nv.us/recorder/recindex.htm. UCCs go back to 1986; liens to '84. Search county fictitious names at http://sandgate.co.clark.nv.us:8498/clarkcounty/clerk/clerkSearch.html.

Douglas County   *Assessor, Real Estate, Property Tax Records*
http://recorder.co.douglas.nv.us
Property records on the Assessor's database are available free at www.co.douglas.nv.us/databases/assessors. Also, the clerk/treasurer propety tax database is available free at www.co.douglas.nv.us/databases/treasurers/.

Federal Courts in Nevada...

Standards for Federal Courts: The universal PACER sign-up number is 800-676-6856. Find PACER and the Party/Case Index on the Web at http://pacer.psc.uscourts.gov. PACER dial-up access is $.60 per minute. Also, courts offering internet access via RACER, PACER, Web-PACER or the new CM-ECF charge $.07 per page fee unless noted as free.

US District Court -- District of Nevada

Home Page: www.nvd.uscourts.gov

PACER: Document images are available online. New records are available online after. **PACER URL:** https://pacer.psc.uscourts.gov/cgi-bin/login/login.pl?court_id=nvdc. Document images available.
Las Vegas Division counties: Clark, Esmeralda, Lincoln, Nye.
Reno Division counties: Carson City, Churchill, Douglas, Elko, Eureka, Humboldt, Lander, Lyon, Mineral, Pershing, Storey, Washoe, White Pine.

US Bankruptcy Court -- District of Nevada

Home Page: www.nvb.uscourts.gov

PACER: Case records are available back to September 1993. Records are purged every 16 months. New civil records are available online after 1 day. **PACER URL:** http://pacer.nvb.uscourts.gov. Any cases filed as of 8/1/2002 are found on PACER only.
Electronic Filing: Electronic filing information is available online at https://ecf.nvb.uscourts.gov.
Other Online Access: Search records online using RACER. Currently the system, which is being phased out, is free and requires free registration. Access RACER via the court main web site, above. Allows acces to cases from 1998 through 7/31/2002. **Also:** access via phone on VCIS (Voice Case Information System) is available: 800-314-3436, 702-388-6708
Las Vegas Division counties: Clark, Esmeralda, Lincoln, Nye.
Reno Division counties: Carson City, Churchill, Douglas, Elko, Eureka, Humboldt, Lander, Lyon, Mineral, Pershing, Storey, Washoe, White Pine.

Editor's Note: While several Nevada state agencies have offices in both Las Vegas and in the Carson City area, the agency's online records include the entire state.

New Hampshire

Capital:	Concord		Home Page
	Merrimack County		www.state.nh.us
Time Zone:	EST	Archives	http://webster.state.nh.us/state/
Number of Counties:	10	Attorney General	http://webster.state.nh.us/nhdoj

State Level ... Major Agencies

Driver Records

Department of Motor Vehicles, Driving Records, 10 Hazen Dr, Concord, NH 03305; 603-271-2322, 8:15AM-4:15PM.

http://webster.state.nh.us/dmv/

Online access is offered for approved commercial accounts. The system is open 22 hours a day. Searches are by license number or by name and DOB. Fee is $7.00 per record. For more information, call the Diretcor's Office. **Other options:** Overnight magnetic tape access is available for higher volume users. Minimum order is 50 requests.

Legislation Records

New Hampshire State Library, 20 Part St, Concord, NH 03301; 603-271-2239, 603-271-2205 (Fax), 8AM-4:30PM.

http://gencourt.state.nh.us/ie/

Information can be viewed from the web site.

State Level ... Occupational Licensing

Architect	www.state.nh.us/jtboard/arlist.htm
Bank	http://webster.state.nh.us/banking/banking.html
Credit Union	http://webster.state.nh.us/banking/banking.html
Engineer	www.state.nh.us/jtboard/pe.htm
Forester	www.state.nh.us/jtboard/forlist.htm
Lobbyist	http://webster.state.nh.us/sos/lobbyist information.htm
Marital Mediator	www.state.nh.us/marital/mediators.html
Natural Scientist	www.state.nh.us/jtboard/ns.htm
Nurse, LPN/Practical/Advanced	www.nh.inthe.org/
Nursing Assistant	www.nh.inthe.org/
Optometrist	www.odfinder.org/LicSearch.asp
Pharmacist	www.state.nh.us/pharmacy/database.html
Pharmacy	www.state.nh.us/pharmacy/database.html
Real Estate Appraiser	www.asc.gov/content/category1/appr_by_state.asp
Surveyor, Land	www.state.nh.us/jtboard/lsis.htm

County Level ... Courts

Court Administration: Administrative Office of the Courts, Supreme Court Bldg, Noble Dr, Concord, NH, 03301; 603-271-2521; www.state.nh.us/courts/home.htm

Court Structure: The Superior Court is the court of General Jurisdiction. Felony cases include Class A misdemeanors. The District Court upper civil limit was increased to $25,000 from $10,000 on 1/1/93. Filing a civil case in the monetary "overlap" area between the Superior Court minimum and the District Court maximum is at the discretion of the filer. The municipal courts have been closed as the judges retire. The caseload and records are absorbed by the nearest District Court.

Online Access Note: There is no remote online computer access available.

There are no known courts that independently offer access to their records.

County Level ... Recorders & Assessors

Recording Office Organization: 238 cities/towns and 10 counties, 10 recording offices and 242 UCC filing offices. The recording officers are Town/City Clerk (UCC) and Register of Deeds (real estate only). Be careful to distinguish the following names that are identical for both a town/city and a county - Grafton, Hillsborough, Merrimack, Strafford, and Sullivan. The following unincorporated towns do not have a Town Clerk, so all liens are located at the corresponding county: Cambridge (Coos), Dicksville (Coos), Green's Grant (Coos), Hale's Location (Carroll), Millsfield (Coos), and Wentworth's Location (Coos). The entire state is in the Eastern Time Zone (EST). Federal and state tax liens on personal property of businesses are filed with the Secretary of State. Other federal and state tax liens on personal property are filed with the Town/City Clerk. Federal and state tax liens on real property are filed with the county Register of Deeds. There is wide variation in indexing and searching practices among the recording offices.

Online Access Note: The New Hampshire Counties Registry of Deeds web site allows free searching of real estate-related records for Belknap, Cheshire, Hillsborough and Strafford counties at www.nhdeeds.com. Also, a private vendor has placed on the Internet the assessor records from a number of towns. Visit http://data.visionappraisal.com.

Belknap County *Real Estate, Deed, Mortgage, Lien Records*
Access to county register of deeds data is available free at www.nhdeeds.com/belk/web/agree5.htm. Online records go back to 1960.

Laconia City *Assessor Records*
http://data.visionappraisal.com/LaconiaNH
Property records on the Town assessor database are available online at http://data.visionappraisal.com/LaconiaNH. Free registration is required for full access.

Cheshire County *Real Estate, Deed, Mortgage, Lien Records*
www.nhdeeds.com
Access to county register of deeds data is available free at www.nhdeeds.com/chsr/web/agree2.htm. Online records go back to 1980.

Grafton County *Real Estate, Lien Records*
Access to the County dial-up service requires a $100 set up fee and $40 per month access fee. Two years of data are kept on system; prior years on CD. Lending agency information is available. A fax-back service is available in-state only. For further information, call 603-787-6921.

Bridgewater Town *Property Assessor Records*
Search the town assessor database at http://data.visionappraisal.com/BridgewaterNH/. Free registration required.

Lebanon City   *Assessor Records*
www.lebcity.com
Records from the city assessor database are available free online at http://data.visionappraisal.com/LEBANONNH/. Free registration is required to view full data.

Hillsborough County   *Real Estate, Deed, Mortgage, Lien Records*
Access to county register of deeds data is available free at www.nhdeeds.com/hils/web/argthc.htm. Online records go back to 1966.

Hollis Town   *Property Assessor Records*
Search the town assessor database at http://data.visionappraisal.com/HollisNH/. Free registration required.

Nashua City   *Property Assessor Records*
Search the City Assessor database for free at www.ci.nashua.nh.us/defaulto.asp?url=/welcome.asp.

Merrimack County   *Real Estate Records*
www.nhdeeds.com
Records on the county Registry of Deeds database are available free online at www.nhdeeds.com.

Concord City   *Assessor Records*
Records on the city assessor database are available free online at http://data.visionappraisal.com/ConcordNH/. Registration is required to view full data.

New London Town   *Property Appraiser Records*
Search the town assessor database at http://data.visionappraisal.com/HollisNH/. Free registration required.

Rockingham County   *Most Wanted Records*
The sheriff's most wanted list is available free at www.co.rockingham.nh.us/sheriff/warrants.htm.

Derry Town   *Assessor, Property, Sales Records*
www.derry.nh.us
Records of Derry assessed values are available free at www.derry.nh.us/assessor/default.htm. Lists are by address; names are provided.

Greenland Town   *Assessor, Property Records*
Access via a private company at http://data.visionappraisal.com/GreenlandNH/. Free registration required to view full data.

Newmarket Town   *Assessor, Property Records*
www.visionappraisal.com
Access is via a private company at http://data.visionappraisal.com/NewMarketNH/. You may apply for a free registered user ID (more data) or search anonymously (less data, no name searching).

Portsmouth City   *Assessor Records*
Records from the Portsmouth Assessed Property Values database are available free online at www.portsmouthnh.com/realestate/index.html.

Raymond Town   *Assessor Records*
Free access via a private company to the Town assessor database is available at http://data.visionappraisal.com/RaymondNH. Free registration is required to view full data.

Rye Town   *Assessor, Property Records*
Access is via a private company at http://data.visionappraisal.com/RyeNH. Free registration is required to view full data.

Salem Town   *Assessor, Property Records*
www.ci.salem.nh.us
Records available free online at http://data.visionappraisal.com/SalemNH/. Registration is required, no charge.

Strafford County   *Real Estate, Deed, Mortgage, Lien Records*
Access to county register of deeds data is available free at www.nhdeeds.com/stfd/web/agree3.htm. Online records go back to 1970.

Federal Courts in New Hampshire...

Standards for Federal Courts: The universal PACER sign-up number is 800-676-6856. Find PACER and the Party/Case Index on the Web at http://pacer.psc.uscourts.gov. PACER dial-up access is $.60 per minute. Also, courts offering internet access via RACER, PACER, Web-PACER or the new CM-ECF charge $.07 per page fee unless noted as free.

US District Court -- District of New Hampshire

Home Page: www.nhd.uscourts.gov
PACER: Case records are available back to 1980. Records are purged every two years. New records are available online after 1 day.
PACER URL: http://pacer.nhd.uscourts.gov.
Concord Division counties: Belknap, Carroll, Cheshire, Coos, Grafton, Hillsborough, Merrimack, Rockingham, Strafford, Sullivan.

US Bankruptcy Court -- District of New Hampshire

Home Page: www.nhb.uscourts.gov
PACER: Case records are available back to 1989. Records are purged every six months. New civil records are available online after 2 days. **PACER URL:** http://pacer.nhb.uscourts.gov.
Electronic Filing: Electronic filing information is available online at https://ecf.nhb.uscourts.gov. **Also:** access via phone on VCIS (Voice Case Information System) is available: 800-851-8954, 603-666-7424
Manchester Division counties: Belknap, Carroll, Cheshire, Coos, Grafton, Hillsborough, Merrimack, Rockingham, Strafford, Sullivan.

Editor's Tip: Just because records are maintained in a certain way in your state or county do not assume that any other county or state does things the same way that you are used to.

New Jersey

Capital: Trenton
Mercer County

Time Zone: EST

Number of Counties: 21

Home Page www.state.nj.us

Attorney General www.state.nj.us/lps

Archives www.state.nj.us/state/darm/index.html

State Level ... Major Agencies

Corporation Records, Limited Liability Company Records, Fictitious Name, Limited Partnerships

Division of Revenue, Business Support Services Bureau, PO 308, Trenton, NJ 08625 (Courier: 225 W State St, 3rd Fl, Trenton, NJ 08608); 609-292-9292, 8:30AM-5:00PM.

www.state.nj.us/njbgs

Records are available from the New Jersey Business Gateway Service (NJBGS) web site at www.state.nj.us/njbgs. There is no fee to browse the site to locate a name; however fees are involved for copies or status reports.

Trademarks/Servicemarks

Department of Treasury, Trademark Division, PO Box 453, Trenton, NJ 08625-0453 (Courier: 225 W State St, 3rd Floor, Trenton, NJ 08608); 609-633-8259, 8:30AM-5PM.

www.state.nj.us/njbgs/services.html

Search the trademarks and trade names list for free at www.accessnet.state.nj.us/businesslistsearch.asp.

Uniform Commercial Code

UCC Section, Secretary of State, PO 303, Trenton, NJ 08625 (Courier: 225 West State St, Trenton, NJ 08608); 609-292-9292, 8AM-5PM.

www.state.nj.us/njbgs

Go to www.accessnet.state.nj.us/home.asp to find a business entity, UCC debtor, or other business name without accruing a service charge with the Division of Revenue. However, if you wish to receive status reports or other information services, you will need to pay the applicable statutory fee.

Sexual Offender Registry

The New Jersey State Police maintain the state's sexual offender data. The database can be searched online at www.njsp.org/info/reg_sexoffend.html.

Driver Records

Motor Vehicle Services, Driver History Abstract Unit, PO Box 142, Trenton, NJ 08666; 609-292-6500 (Forms request), 888-486-3339 (In-state only), 609-292-7500 (Suspensions), 8AM-5PM.

www.state.nj.us/mvs

Fee is $8.00 per record. Access is limited to insurance, bus and trucking companies, parking authorities, and approved vendors. There is a minimum of 100 requests per quarter. For more information, call 609-984-7771. **Other options:** High volume requesters can use the magnetic tape method to obtain overnight records (minimum 500 requests) or purchase control cards at (100 purchased at a time, used whenever).

Vehicle Ownership, Vehicle Identification, Vessel Ownership, Vessel Registration

Motor Vehicle Svcs, Certified Information Unit, PO Box 146, Trenton, NJ 08666; 609-292-6500, 888-486-3339 (In-state), 8AM-5PM.

www.state.nj.us/mvs

Limited online access is available for insurance companies, bus and trucking companies, highway/parking authorities, and approved vendors for these businesses. Participation requires a minimum of 100 requests per calendar quarter at $4.00 per request. Call 609-684-7771 for more information. **Other options:** Electronic file transfer is available for volume users at $4.00 per record. There is no program for massive/customized bulk look-ups. Each request is looked at on an individual basis. Records are not sold for commercial or political reasons.

Legislation Records

New Jersey State Legislature, State House Annex, PO Box 068, Room B01, Trenton, NJ 08625-0068; 609-292-4840 (Bill Status Only), 609-292-6395 (Copy Room), 800-792-8630 (In State Only), 609-777-2440 (Fax), 8:30AM-5PM.

www.njleg.state.nj.us

The web site is a good source of information about bills. All statutes are online, also.

State Level ... Occupational Licensing

Acupuncturist .... www.state.nj.us/lps/ca/bme/acupdir.htm
Alcohol/Drug Counselor .... www.state.nj.us/lps/ca/marriage/pcdir.htm
Appraiser, General/Residential .... www.state.nj.us/lps/ca/real/realdir.htm
Architect .... www.state.nj.us/lps/ca/arch/archdir.htm
Audiologist .... www.state.nj.us/lps/ca/aud/auddir.htm
Barber .... www.state.nj.us/lps/ca/cosmetology/bardir.htm
Beautician .... www.state.nj.us/lps/ca/cosmetology/beautdir.htm
Cemetery Salesperson .... www.state.nj.us/lps/ca/cemetery/cemdir.htm
Charities .... www.state.nj.us/lps/ca/charfrm.htm
Chiropractor .... www.state.nj.us/lps/ca/chiro/chirofrm.htm
Cosmetologist/Hairstylist .... www.state.nj.us/lps/ca/cosmetology/cosmodir.htm
Counselor, Social Work .... www.state.nj.us/lps/ca/social/socdir.htm
Court Reporter .... www.state.nj.us/lps/ca/short/shortdir.htm
Dentist .... www.state.nj.us/lps/ca/dentistry/dentdir.htm
Electrical Contractor .... www.state.nj.us/lps/ca/electric/elecdir.htm
Embalmer .... www.state.nj.us/lps/ca/mort/mortdir.htm
Engineer .... www.state.nj.us/lps/ca/pels/engdir.htm
Funeral Practitioner .... www.state.nj.us/lps/ca/mort/mortdir.htm
Hearing Aid Dispenser/Fitter .... www.state.nj.us/lps/ca/hear/heardir.htm
Home Health Aide .... www.state.nj.us/lps/ca/medical.htm#nur6
Lab Director, Bio-Analytical .... www.state.nj.us/lps/ca/bme/labdir.htm
Landscape Architect .... www.state.nj.us/lps/ca/arch/landdir.htm
Manicurist/Manicure Shop .... www.state.nj.us/lps/ca/cosmetology/mandir.htm
Marriage & Family Counselor, Professional .... www.state.nj.us/lps/ca/marriage/pcdir.htm
Marriage & Family Therapist .... www.state.nj.us/lps/ca/marriage/pcdir.htm
Marriage Counselor .... www.state.nj.us/lps/ca/marriage/pcdir.htm

Midwife	www.state.nj.us/lps/ca/bme/middir.htm
Mortician	www.state.nj.us/lps/ca/mort/mortdir.htm
Nurse, Advance Practice	www.state.nj.us/lps/ca/medical.htm#nur6
Nurse-LPN	www.state.nj.us/lps/ca/medical.htm#nur6
Nurse-RN	www.state.nj.us/lps/ca/medical.htm#nur6
Occupational Therapist	www.state.nj.us/lps/ca/occup/otdir.htm
Occupational Therapy Asst.	www.state.nj.us/lps/ca/occup/otadir.htm
Opthalmic Dispenser/Technician	www.state.nj.us/lps/ca/ophth/tddir.htm
Optician/Optician Technician	www.state.nj.us/lps/ca/ophth/ttdir.htm
Optometrist	www.state.nj.us/lps/ca/optometry/optdir.htm
Pharmacist	www.state.nj.us/lps/ca/pharm/pharmdir.htm
Physical Therapist	www.state.nj.us/lps/ca/pt/ptdir.htm
Physical Therapist Assistant	www.state.nj.us/lps/ca/pt/ptdir.htm
Physician	www.state.nj.us/lps/ca/bme/docdir.htm
Planner, Professional	www.state.nj.us/lps/ca/plan/plandir.htm
Plumber/Master Plumber	www.state.nj.us/lps/ca/plumber/plumdir.htm
Podiatrist	www.state.nj.us/lps/ca/bme/poddir.htm
Psychologist	www.state.nj.us/lps/ca/psy/psydir.htm
Public Accountant-CPA	www.state.nj.us/lps/ca/accountancy/accdir.htm
Real Estate Appraiser/Apprentice	www.state.nj.us/lps/ca/real/realdir.htm
Real Estate School/ Instructor	www.state.nj.us/lps/ca/dobi/recskool.htm
Respiratory Therapist	www.state.nj.us/lps/ca/respcare/respdir.htm
Shorthand Reporter	www.state.nj.us/lps/ca/short/shortdir.htm
Skin Care Specialist	www.state.nj.us/lps/ca/cosmetology/skindir.htm
Social Worker	www.state.nj.us/lps/ca/social/socdir.htm
Speech-Language Pathologist	www.state.nj.us/lps/ca/aud/auddir.htm
Surveyor, Land	www.state.nj.us/lps/ca/pels/engdir.htm
Tree Expert	www.state.nj.us/dep/forestry/community/cte.html
Veterinarian	www.state.nj.us/lps/ca/vetmed/vetdir.htm

County Level ... Courts

Court Administration: Administrative Office of the Courts, RJH Justice Complex, Courts Bldg 7th Floor, CN 037, Trenton, NJ, 08625; 609-984-0275; www.judiciary.state.nj.us

Court Structure: Each Superior Court has 2 divisions; one for the Civil Division and another for the Criminal Division. Search requests should be addressed separately to each division. The Special Civil Part of the Superior Court acts like a division of the court, and handles only the smaller civil claims. The small claims limit is $2,000. The Superior Court designation refers to the court where criminal cases and civil claims over $10,000 are heard. Probate is handled by Surrogates.

Online Access Note: Online computer access is available through the ACMS, AMIS, and FACTS.

ACMS (Automated Case Management System) contains data on all active civil cases statewide from the Law Division-Civil Part, Chancery Division-Equity Part, the Special Civil Part statewide, and the Appellate Division.

AMIS (Archival Management Information System) contains closed civil case information. Records go back to the late 1980s.

FACTS (Family Automated Case Tracking System) contains information on dissolutions from all counties.

The fee is $1.00 per minute of use, and a $500 collateral account is required. For further information or an Inquiry System Guidebook containing hardware and software requirements and an enrollment form, write to: Superior Court Clerk's Office, Electronic Access Program, 25 Market St, CN971, Trenton NJ 08625, FAX 609-292-6564, or call 609-292-4987.

The Judiciary's civil motion calendar is searchable online at www.judiciary.state.nj.us/calendars.htm. The database includes all Superior Court Motion Calendars for the Civil Division (Law-Civil Part, Special CivilPart and Chancery-General Equity), and proceeding information for a six-week period (two weeks prior to the current date and four weeks following the current date).

There are no known courts that independently offer access to their records.

County Level ... Recorders & Assessors

Recording Office Organization: 21 counties, 21 recording offices. The recording officer title varies depending upon the county. It is either Register of Deeds or County Clerk. The Clerk of Circuit Court records the equivalent of some state's tax liens. The entire state is in the Eastern Time Zone (EST). All federal tax liens are filed with the County Clerk/Register of Deeds and are indexed separately from all other liens. State tax liens comprise two categories - certificates of debt are filed with the Clerk of Superior Court (some, called docketed judgments are filed specifically with the Trenton court), and warrants of execution are filed with the County Clerk/Register of Deeds. Few counties will provide tax lien searches.

Online Access Note: There is no statewide government database online, but a statewide database of property tax records can be accessed from a private vendor at at http://taxrecords.com.

Atlantic County   *Real Estate Records*
www.atlanticcountyclerk.org
Property records for communities along the Jersey Shore in Atlantic county are available free online at www.philly.com/packages/njshore/lookup.htm. Site is sponsored by the Philadelphia Inquirer. Search by clicking on community name, then search by owner name, owner's city/state, address, or property value range.

Cape May County   *Real Estate, Recording Records*
www.co.cape-may.nj.us
Property records for Cape May county are available to view free online at http://209.201.24.238/ALIS/WW400R.PGM. To print and have full access to documents, registration and login is required. Online documents go back to 1996, images to 2000.

Gloucester County   *Real Estate, Recording Records*
www.co.gloucester.nj.us
County Recorder records are accessible through a private online service at www.landaccess.com; Fees and registration are required.

Monmouth County   *Real Estate, Deed, Mortgage Records*
www.co.monmouth.nj.us
Access to the county clerk database is available free at http://tax0.co.monmouth.nj.us/monmouthnew/monmouth/search.asp. Records from 10/1/96 to present.

Ocean County   *Property Tax, Real Estate Records*
www.oceancountyclerk.com
Land records on the County Clerk database are available free online at www.oceancountyclerk.com/search.htm. Search by parties, document or instrument type, or township. Tax records for Ocean county are also available on the taxrecords.com web site at http://oc.taxrecords.com. Search by name, address or property description.

Somerset County   *Property, Recording Records*
www.co.somerset.nj.us
Access to the County Clerk's recordings database is available free at http://209.92.88.21/. Registration required, or enter as "Guest." Index available back to 1/93; images back to 6/11/01.

Federal Courts in New Jersey...

Standards for Federal Courts: The universal PACER sign-up number is 800-676-6856. Find PACER and the Party/Case Index on the Web at http://pacer.psc.uscourts.gov. PACER dial-up access is $.60 per minute. Also, courts offering internet access via RACER, PACER, Web-PACER or the new CM-ECF charge $.07 per page fee unless noted as free.

US District Court -- District of New Jersey
Home Page: http://pacer.njd.uscourts.gov

PACER: Toll-free access: 888-297-9938. Local access phone: 609-989-0590. Case records are available back to May 1991. Records are purged never. New records are available online after 1 day. **PACER URL:** http://pacer.njd.uscourts.gov.
Opinions Online: Court opinions are available online at http://lawlibrary.rutgers.edu/fed/search.html.
Camden Division counties: Atlantic, Burlington, Camden, Cape May, Cumberland, Gloucester, Salem.
Newark Division counties: Bergen, Essex, Hudson, Middlesex, Monmouth, Morris, Passaic, Sussex, Union. Monmouth County was transferred from Trenton Division in late 1997; closed cases remain in Trenton.
Trenton Division counties: Hunterdon, Mercer, Ocean, Somerset, Warren. Monmouth County was transferred to Newark and Camden Division in late 1997; closed Monmouth cases remain in Trenton.

US Bankruptcy Court -- District of New Jersey
Home Page: www.njb.uscourts.gov

PACER: Document images available. Case records are available back to 1991. Records are purged every 6 months. New civil records are available online after 1 day. **PACER URL:** http://pacer.njb.uscourts.gov. Document images available.
Electronic Filing: Electronic filing information is available online at https://ecf.njb.uscourts.gov.
Other Online Access: Search records on the Internet using RACER at http://racer.njb.uscourts.gov. Access fee is $.07 per page. **Also:** access via phone on VCIS (Voice Case Information System) is available: 877-239-2547, 973-645-6044
Camden Division counties: Atlantic, Burlington (partial), Camden, Cape May, Cumberland, Gloucester, Salem.
Newark Division counties: Bergen, Essex, Hudson, Morris, Passaic, Sussex. Also Elizabeth, Springfield and Hillside townships in Union County.
Trenton Division counties: Burlington (partial), Hunterdon, Mercer, Middlesex, Monmouth, Ocean, Somerset, Warren, Union except the townships of Elizabeth, Hillside and Springfield.

Editor's Tip: In the past, several private companies have provided New Jersey real estate data on their web sites. Often this type of data is not complete or is dated and thus it should not be relied upon as a substitute for official information from the official public record source.

New Mexico

Capital: Santa Fe
             Santa Fe County

Time Zone: MST

Number of Counties: 33

Home Page
www.state.nm.us

Attorney General   www.ago.state.nm.us

Archives   www.nmcpr.state.nm.us

State Level ... Major Agencies

Corporation Records, Limited Liability Company Records

New Mexico Public Regulation Commission, Corporations Bureau, PO Box 1269, Santa Fe, NM 87504-1269 (Courier: 1120 Paseo de Peralta, Pera Bldg 4th Fl, Rm 413, Santa Fe, NM 87501); 505-827-4502 (Main Number), 800-947-4722 (In-state Only), 505-827-4510 (Good Standing), 505-827-4513 (Copy Request), 505-827-4387 (Fax), 8AM-12:00: 1PM-5PM.

www.nmprc.state.nm.us/corporation.htm

There is no charge to view records at the Internet site, www.nmprc.state.nm.us/ftq.htm. Records can be searched by company name or by director name. **Other options:** The state makes the database available on electronic format using a 3480 tape cartridge.

Uniform Commercial Code

UCC Division, Secretary of State, State Capitol North, Santa Fe, NM 87503; 505-827-3610, 505-827-3611 (Fax), 8AM-5PM.

www.sos.state.nm.us/ucc/ucchome.htm

The web site permits searches and provides a form to use to order copies of filings. You can also request records via email.

Sexual Offender Registry

The Department of Public Safety maintains the state sexual offender list. Access is available online at www.nmsexoffender.dps.state.nm.us/.

Driver Records

Motor Vehicle Division, Driver Services Bureau, PO Box 1028, Santa Fe, NM 87504-1028 (Courier: Joseph M. Montoya Bldg, 1100 S St. Francis Dr, 2nd Floor, Santa Fe, NM 87504); 505-827-2234, 505-827-2267 (Fax), 8AM-5PM.

www.state.nm.us/tax/mvd

Records are avilable, for authorized users, from the state's designated vendors - Oso Grande (505-345-655) and Samba (888-94-samba). Subscription fees are $2.50 per record for interactive, $1.50 per record for batch, plus a $.25 per minute network fee. The system is open 24 hours a day, batch requesters must wait 24 hours.

Vehicle Ownership, Vehicle Identification, Vessel Ownership, Vessel Registration

Motor Vehicle Division, Vehicle Services Bureau, PO Box 1028, Santa Fe, NM 87504-1028 (Courier: Joseph M. Montoya Bldg, 1100 S St. Francis Dr, 2nd Floor, Santa Fe, NM 87504); 505-827-4636, 505-827-1004, 505-827-0395 (Fax), 8AM-5PM.

www.state.nm.us/tax/mvd

Records are available, for authorized users, from the state's designated vendors - Oso Grande (505-345-6555) and Samba (888-94-samba). **Other options:** Bulk requests for vehicle or ownership information must be approved by the Director's office. Once a sale is made, further resale is prohibited.

Accident Reports

Department of Public Safety, Records, PO Box 1628, Santa Fe, NM 87504-1628 (Courier: New Mexico State Police Complex, 4491 Cerrillos Rd, Santa Fe, NM 87504); 505-827-9181, 505-827-9189 (Fax), 8AM-5PM.

www.dps.nm.org

Reports are available online at https://www.nmaccidentreports.com. The officer's diagram and narrative is included. There is a $1.00 fee. Credit cards are accepted.

Legislation Records

http://legis.state.nm.us

The Internet site is a complete source of information about bills and legislators. There are also links to other NM state agencies and NM statutes. **Other options:** Subscription purchase for the complete file of current session is available. However, you must request your subscription by mid-session.

State Level ... Occupational Licensing

Acupuncturist	www.rld.state.nm.us/b&c/acupuncture/licensee_search.asp
Alcohol Server	www.rld.state.nm.us/agd/licensee_search_servers.asp
Architect	www.nmbea.org/People/Aroster.htm
Art Therapist	www.rld.state.nm.us/b&c/counseling/licensee_search.asp
Athletic Trainer	www.rld.state.nm.us/b&c/athtrn/licensee_search.asp
Attorney	www.nmbar.org/cgi-bin/QQQ/search.pl
Audiologist	www.rld.state.nm.us/b&c/speech/licensee_search.asp
Bank	www.rld.state.nm.us/fid/licensee_search_index.htm
Barber	www.rld.state.nm.us/b&c/barbcosmo/licensee_search.asp
Barber Shop/School	www.rld.state.nm.us/b&c/barbcosmo/licensee_search.asp
Boiler Operator Journeyman	www.contractorsnm.com/searchlic.html
Chiropractor	www.rld.state.nm.us/b&c/chiro/licensee_search.asp
Clinical Nurse Specialist	www.state.nm.us/nursing/lookup.html
Collection Agency	www.rld.state.nm.us/fid/licensee_search_index.htm
Collection Agency Manager	www.rld.state.nm.us/fid/licensee_search_index.htm
Consumer Credit Grantor	www.rld.state.nm.us/fid/licensee_search_index.htm
Consumer Loan Company	www.rld.state.nm.us/fid/licensee_search_index.htm
Contractor	www.contractorsnm.com/searchlic.html
Cosmetologist	www.rld.state.nm.us/b&c/barbcosmo/licensee_search.asp
Cosmetology Shop/School	www.rld.state.nm.us/b&c/barbcosmo/licensee_search.asp
Credit Union	www.rld.state.nm.us/fid/licensee_search_index.htm
Crematory	www.rld.state.nm.us/b&c/thanato/licensee_search_facilities.asp
Dental Assistant	www.rld.state.nm.us/b&c/dental/
Dental Hygienist	www.rld.state.nm.us/b&c/dental/
Dentist	www.rld.state.nm.us/b&c/dental/
Direct Disposer (Funerary)	www.rld.state.nm.us/b&c/thanato/licensee_search_index.asp
Doctor of Oriental Medicine	www.rld.state.nm.us/b&c/acupuncture/licensee_search.asp

Electrologist	www.rld.state.nm.us/b&c/barbcosmo/licensee_search.asp
Electrophysician	www.rld.state.nm.us/b&c/barbcosmo/licensee_search.asp
Endowed/Perpetual Care Cemetery	www.rld.state.nm.us/fid/licensee_search_endowed_care.asp
Engineer	www.state.nm.us/pepsboard/roster.htm
Escrow Company	www.rld.state.nm.us/fid/licensee_search_index.htm
Esthetician	www.rld.state.nm.us/b&c/barbcosmo/licensee_search.asp
Funeral Director/Practitioner	www.rld.state.nm.us/b&c/thanato/licensee_search_fsp.asp
Funeral Home	www.rld.state.nm.us/b&c/thanato/licensee_search_facilities.asp
Funeral Service Intern	www.rld.state.nm.us/b&c/thanato/licensee_search_index.asp
Hearing Aid Specialist	www.rld.state.nm.us/b&c/speech/licensee_search.asp
Hemodialysis Technician	www.state.nm.us/nursing/lookup.html
Journeyman	www.contractorsnm.com/searchlic.html
Landscape Architect	www.rld.state.nm.us/b&c/landscape/licensee_search.asp
Lobbyist	http://web.state.nm.us/LOBBY/LOB.htm
LPG-Liquefied Petroleum Gas Licensing	www.contractorsnm.com/searchlic.html
Manicurist	www.rld.state.nm.us/b&c/barbcosmo/licensee_search.asp
Marriage & Family Therapist	www.rld.state.nm.us/b&c/counseling/licensee_search.asp
Massage Instructor/Practitioner/School	www.rld.state.nm.us/b&c/massage/licensee_search.asp
Massage Therapist	www.rld.state.nm.us/b&c/massage/licensee_search.asp
Medical Doctor	www.docboard.org/nm/
Medication Aide	www.state.nm.us/nursing/lookup.html
Mental Health Counselor	www.rld.state.nm.us/b&c/counseling/licensee_search.asp
Money Order Agent/Exempt Agent	www.rld.state.nm.us/fid/licensee_search_index.htm
Money Order Company	www.rld.state.nm.us/fid/licensee_search_index.htm
Mortgage Company/Loan Broker/Branch	www.rld.state.nm.us/fid/licensee_search_index.htm
Motor Vehicle Sales Finance Company	www.rld.state.nm.us/fid/licensee_search_index.htm
Nurse	www.state.nm.us/nursing/lookup.html
Nurse Anesthetist	www.state.nm.us/nursing/lookup.html
Nurse-LPN	www.state.nm.us/nursing/lookup.html
Nurse-RN	www.state.nm.us/nursing/lookup.html
Nursing Home Administrator	www.rld.state.nm.us/b&c/nhab/licensee_search.asp
Occupational Therapist	www.rld.state.nm.us/b&c/otb/licensee_search.asp
Occupational Therapist Assistant	www.rld.state.nm.us/b&c/otb/licensee_search.asp
Optometrist	www.rld.state.nm.us/b&c/optometry/licensee_search.asp
Osteopathic Physician	www.rld.state.nm.us/b&c/osteo/licensee_search.asp
Physical Therapist	www.rld.state.nm.us/b&c/ptb/licensee_search.asp
Physical Therapist Assistant	www.rld.state.nm.us/b&c/ptb/licensee_search.asp
Physician Assistant	www.docboard.org/nm/
Podiatrist	www.rld.state.nm.us/b&c/podiatry/licensee_search.asp
Psychologist	www.rld.state.nm.us/b&c/rcb/licensee_search.asp
Public Accountant-CPA	www.rld.state.nm.us/b&c/accountancy/licensee_search.asp
Real Estate Agent/Salesperson	www.rld.state.nm.us/b&c/rec/licensee_search.asp
Real Estate Appraiser	www.rld.state.nm.us/b&c/reappraisers/licensee_search.asp
Real Estate Broker	www.rld.state.nm.us/b&c/rec/licensee_search.asp
Respiratory Care Therapist	www.rld.state.nm.us/b&c/rcb/licensee_search.asp
Savings & Loan	www.rld.state.nm.us/fid/licensee_search_index.htm
Small Loan Company	www.rld.state.nm.us/fid/licensee_search_index.htm
Speech-Language Pathologist	www.rld.state.nm.us/b&c/speech/licensee_search.asp
Substance Abuse Counselor/Intern	www.rld.state.nm.us/b&c/counseling/licensee_search.asp
Surveyor, Land	www.state.nm.us/pepsboard/roster.htm
Trust Company	www.rld.state.nm.us/fid/licensee_search_index.htm

County Level ... Courts

Court Administration: Administrative Office of the Courts, Supreme Court Building Room 25, Santa Fe, NM, 87503; 505-827-4800; www.nmcourts.com/aoc.htm

Court Structure: The 30 District Courts in 13 districts are the courts of general jurisdiction. Starting July 1, 2001, the Magistrate Courts began handling civil cases up to $10,000. Previously, the Magistrate Court limit was $7,500. The Bernalillo Metropolitan Court has jurisdiction in cases up to $5000. There are some "shared" courts in New Mexico, with one county handling cases arising in another. All magistrate courts and the Bernalillo Metropolitan Court have public access terminals to access civil records only.

Online Access Note: The www.nmcourts.com web site offers free access to District and Magistrate Court case information. In general, records are available from June, 1997 forward.

Also, a commercial online service is available for the Metropolitan Court of Bernalillo County. There is a $35.00 set up fee, a connect time fee based on usage. The system is available 24 hours a day. Call 505-345-6555 for more information.

Bernalillo County

2nd Judicial District Court *Civil and Criminal Records*
www.cabq.gov/cjnet/dst2alb
Online access is available free at www.nmcourts.com/disclaim.html. Most data goes back to 6/1997. Online access to criminal records is available free at www.nmcourts.com/disclaim.html. Most data goes back to 6/1997.

Metropolitan Court *Civil and Criminal Records*
www.metrocourt.state.nm.us
Access Metropolitan court civil records online at www.technet.nm.net/newmenu/new-mexico-courts.htm. There is set up fee plus a per minute charge based on usage. For information or to obtain an account call 505-345-6555. Also, Metro Court dockets are available free at www.metrocourt.state.nm.us/docket_help.htm. Online access to criminal records is available free at http://164.64.140.222/metro1/website.nsf/frames?readform. Also, online access to Metro Court criminal dockets is available free at www.metrocourt.state.nm.us/docket_help.htm.

Statewide Access

The www.nmcourts.com web site offers free access to District and Magistrate Court case information. In general, records are available from June, 1997 forward.

County Level ... Recorders & Assessors

Recording Office Organization: 33 counties, 33 recording offices. The recording officer is the County Clerk. Most counties maintain a grantor/grantee index and a miscellaneous index. The entire state is in the Mountain Time Zone (MST). All federal and state tax liens are filed with the County Clerk. Most counties will not provide tax lien searches.

Bernalillo County   *Real Estate, Property Assessor Records*
www.berncotreasurer.com
Records on the county treasurer tax bill page are available free online at
www.berncotreasurer.com/ProcessSearch.asp?cmd=NewSearch. No name searching. Also, search via the assessor records at www.bernco-assessor.com. Also, search property information via the GIS-mapping site at
http://outside.bernco.gov/website/blcas31/viewer.htm. Also, the recorders data and Grantor/Grantee index is available at http://cyclops.bernco.gov/splash.jsp. Free registration and password required. For more information call 505-768-4090.

Dona Ana County   *Assessor, Real Estate, Personal Property, Voter Registration Records*
www.co.dona-ana.nm.us
Records on the Real Property database are available free online at www.co.dona-ana.nm.us/assr/search.html. Also, search the voter registration rolls for free at www.co.dona-ana.nm.us/boe/voter.html.

San Juan County   *Real Estate, Assessor Records*
www.co.san-juan.nm.us
Access to county real estate tax data is available free at www.co.san-juan.nm.us/Empire/CountyTax.htm.

Federal Courts in New Mexico...

Standards for Federal Courts: The universal PACER sign-up number is 800-676-6856. Find PACER and the Party/Case Index on the Web at http://pacer.psc.uscourts.gov. PACER dial-up access is $.60 per minute. Also, courts offering internet access via RACER, PACER, Web-PACER or the new CM-ECF charge $.07 per page fee unless noted as free.

US District Court -- District of New Mexico
Home Page: www.nmcourt.fed.us/dcdocs

Electronic Filing: This utilizes ACE (Advanced Court Engin.), and not the US Courts standard CM/ECF system. Electronic filing information is available online at www.nmcourt.fed.us/dcdocs (Click on Electronic Filing).
Other Online Access: Email alerts for cases or names you select are available; must use yourACE user name and password to set up.
Albuquerque Division counties: All counties in New Mexico. Cases may be assigned to any of its three divisions.

US Bankruptcy Court -- District of New Mexico
Home Page: www.nmcourt.fed.us/bkdocs

PACER: Toll-free access: 888-821-8813. Local access phone: 505-348-2496. Case records are available back to July 1, 1991. New civil records are available online after 1 day.
Electronic Filing: (Currently in the process of implementing CM/ECF). **Also:** access via phone on VCIS (Voice Case Information System) is available: 888-435-7822, 505-248-6536
Albuquerque Division counties: All counties in New Mexico.

Capital:	Albany		Home Page
	Albany County		www.state.ny.us
Time Zone:	EST	Attorney General	www.oag.state.ny.us
Number of Counties:	62	Archives	www.sara.nysed.gov

State Level ... Major Agencies

Corporation Records, Limited Partnership Records, Limited Liability Company Records, Limited Liability Partnerships

Division of Corporations, Department of State, 41 State St, Albany, NY 12231; 518-473-2492 (General Information), 900-835-2677 (Corporate Searches), 518-474-1418 (Fax), 8AM-4:30PM.

www.dos.state.ny.us

A commercial account can be set up for direct access. Fee is \$.75 per transaction through a drawdown account. There is an extensive amount of information available including historical information. Also, the Division's corporate and business entity database may be accessed via the Internet without charge. Historical information is not available, nor is it real time. The Internet files are updated weekly. The web has not for profit corporations, limited partnerships, limited liability companies and limited liability partnerships as well. **Other options:** You may submit an email search request at corporations@dos.state.ny.us.

Sexual Offender Registry

The Department of Criminal Justice maintains the state sexual offender registry. Sex offender registry Level 3 can be searched at www.criminaljustice.state.ny.us/nsor/.

Incarceration Records

Information on current and former inmates is available at www.docs.state.ny.us. Location, DIN number, conviction and sentencing information, and release dates are provided.

Driver Records

Department of Motor Vehicles, MV-15 Processing, 6 Empire State Plaza, Room 430, Albany, NY 12228; 518-473-5595, 800-225-5368 (In-state), 8AM-5PM.

www.nydmv.state.ny.us

NY has implemented a "Dial-In Inquiry" system which enables customers to obtain data online 24 hours a day. The DL# or name, DOB and sex are required to retrieve. If the DOB and sex are not entered, the system defaults to a limited group of 5 records. The fee is \$5.00 per record. For more information, call 518-474-4293. **Other options:** The state offers a program to employers whereby the state will notify the employers when an event is posted to an employee's record. To find out about the "LENS" program, call 518-486-4480.

Vehicle Ownership, Vehicle Identification, Vessel Ownership, Vessel Registration

Department of Motor Vehicles, Customer Service Center, 6 Empire State Plaza, Room 430, Albany, NY 12228; 518-474-0710, 518-474-8510, 8AM-5PM.

www.nydmv.state.ny.us

New York offers plate, VIN and ownership data through the same network discussed in the Driving Records Section. The system is interactive and open 24 hours a day. The fee is $5.00 per record. Call 518-474-4293 for more information.

Legislation Records

Both the Senate - www.senate.state.ny.us - and the Assembly - www.assembly.state.ny.us - have web sites to search for a bill or specific bill text. A much more complete system is the LRS online system. This offers complete state statutes, agency rules and regulations, bill text, bill status, summaries, and more. For more information, call Barbara Lett at 800-356-6566.

State Level ... Occupational Licensing

Accountant, CPA/Public	www.op.nysed.gov/opsearches.htm#nme
Acupuncturist/Acupuncturist Assistant	www.op.nysed.gov/opsearches.htm#nme
Apartment Information Vendor	http://wdb.dos.state.ny.us/lcns_public/lcns_wdb.status_check_lcns.show
Apartment Sharing Manager	http://wdb.dos.state.ny.us/lcns_public/lcns_wdb.status_check_lcns.show
Appearance Enhancement Business	http://wdb.dos.state.ny.us/lcns_public/lcns_wdb.status_check_lcns.show
Architect	www.op.nysed.gov/opsearches.htm#nme
Armored Car/Car Carrier	http://wdb.dos.state.ny.us/lcns_public/lcns_wdb.status_check_lcns.show
Athletic Trainer	www.op.nysed.gov/opsearches.htm#nme
Attorney	www.courts.state.ny.us/webdb/wdbcgi.exe/apps/INTERNETDB.attyreghome.show
Audiologist	www.op.nysed.gov/opsearches.htm#nme
Bail Enforcement Agent	http://wdb.dos.state.ny.us/lcns_public/lcns_wdb.status_check_lcns.show
Barber	http://wdb.dos.state.ny.us/lcns_public/lcns_wdb.status_check_lcns.show
Chiropractor	www.op.nysed.gov/opsearches.htm#nme
Court Reporter	www.op.nysed.gov/opsearches.htm#nme
Dental Hygienist	www.op.nysed.gov/opsearches.htm#nme
Dentist/Dental Assistant	www.op.nysed.gov/opsearches.htm#nme
Dietitian	www.op.nysed.gov/opsearches.htm#nme
Dispatch Facility (Alarm/Security/Fire)	http://wdb.dos.state.ny.us/lcns_public/lcns_wdb.status_check_lcns.show
Engineer	www.op.nysed.gov/opsearches.htm#nme
Guard Dog Agency	http://wdb.dos.state.ny.us/lcns_public/lcns_wdb.status_check_lcns.show
Guard/Patrol Agency	http://wdb.dos.state.ny.us/lcns_public/lcns_wdb.status_check_lcns.show
Hearing Aid Dealer	http://wdb.dos.state.ny.us/lcns_public/lcns_wdb.status_check_lcns.show
HMO	www.ins.state.ny.us/tocol4.htm
Insurance Company	www.ins.state.ny.us/tocol4.htm
Interior Designer	www.op.nysed.gov/opsearches.htm#nme
Landscape Architect	www.op.nysed.gov/opsearches.htm#nme
Lobbyist	www.nylobby.state.ny.us/lobbysearch.html
Massage Therapist	www.op.nysed.gov/opsearches.htm#nme
Medical Doctor	www.op.nysed.gov/opsearches.htm#nme
Midwife	www.op.nysed.gov/opsearches.htm#nme
Notary Public	http://wdb.dos.state.ny.us/lcns_public/lcns_wdb.status_check_lcns.show
Nurse-LPN/RPN	www.op.nysed.gov/opsearches.htm#nme
Nutritionist	www.op.nysed.gov/opsearches.htm#nme
Occupational Therapist/Assistant	www.op.nysed.gov/opsearches.htm#nme
Ophthalmic Dispenser	www.op.nysed.gov/opsearches.htm#nme
Optometrist	www.op.nysed.gov/opsearches.htm#nme
Pharmacist	www.op.nysed.gov/opsearches.htm#nme
Physical Therapist/Assistant	www.op.nysed.gov/opsearches.htm#nme
Physician	www.op.nysed.gov/opsearches.htm#nme
Physician Assistant	www.op.nysed.gov/opsearches.htm#nme

Physicians' Specialist Assistant .... www.op.nysed.gov/opsearches.htm#nme
Podiatrist .... www.op.nysed.gov/opsearches.htm#nme
Private Investigator.. http://wdb.dos.state.ny.us/lcns_public/lcns_wdb.status_check_lcns.show
Psychiatrist .... www.nyspsych.org
Psychologist .... www.op.nysed.gov/opsearches.htm#nme
Public Accountant-CPA .... www.op.nysed.gov/opsearches.htm#nme
Radiologic Technology School............................. www.health.state.ny.us/nysdoh/radtech/schlist2.htm
Radon Testing Lab .... www.wadsworth.org/labcert/elap/radon.html
Real Estate Salesperson/Broker/Appraiser .... http://wdb.dos.state.ny.us/lcns_public/lcns_wdb.status_check_lcns.show
Respiratory Therapist/Therapy Technician............ www.op.nysed.gov/opsearches.htm#nme
Security & Fire Alarm Installer .... http://wdb.dos.state.ny.us/lcns_public/lcns_wdb.status_check_lcns.show
Security Guard.. http://wdb.dos.state.ny.us/lcns_public/lcns_wdb.status_check_lcns.show
Social Worker.. www.op.nysed.gov/opsearches.htm#nme
Speech Pathologist/Audiologist............................. www.op.nysed.gov/opsearches.htm#nme
Surveyor, Land .... www.op.nysed.gov/opsearches.htm#nme
Teacher.. www.highered.nysed.gov/tcert/respublic/ocvs.htm
Telemarketer Business.. http://wdb.dos.state.ny.us/lcns_public/lcns_wdb.status_check_lcns.show
Veterinarian/Veterinary Technician .... www.op.nysed.gov/opsearches.htm#nme

County Level ... Courts

Court Administration: Office of Court Administration, Empire State Plaza, Agency Plaza #4, Suite 2001, Albany, NY, 12223; 518-473-1196; www.courts.state.ny.us

Court Structure: New York State has two sites for Administration; in addition to the Albany address above, there is a New York City office at this address: Office of Administration, 25 Beaver St, New York NY 10004, and telephone: 212-428-2100. "Supreme Courts" are the highest trial courts in the state, equivalent to Circuit or District Courts in other states; they are not appeals courts. Many New York City courts are indexed by plaintiff only. Records for Supreme and County Courts are maintained by County Clerks. In most counties, the address for the clerk is the same as for the court. Exceptions are noted in the court profiles. In at least 20 New York Counties, Misdemeanor records are only available at city, town or village courts.

Online Access Note: Civil Supreme Court case information is available for all 62 New York counties through the court system's web site - http://e.courts.state.ny.us. More limited case information for housing courts and criminal courts, and a directory of all New York State attorneys is also available at that site. There is no charge for this information. The information is also available at all courts.

Also, you may search for future court dates for defendants in these 21 criminal courts: Bronx Criminal Court, Bronx Supreme Court, Dutchess County Court, Buffalo City Court, Erie County Court, Kings Criminal Court, Kings Supreme Court, Nassau County Court, Nassau District Court, New York Criminal Court, New York Supreme Court, Orange County Court, Putnam County, Queens Criminal Court, Queens Supreme Court, Richmond Criminal Court, Richmond Supreme Court, Rockland County Court, Suffolk County Court, Suffolk District Court, Westchester County Court.

The New York State Office of Court Administration will perform an electronic search for criminal history information from a database of criminal case records from the boroughs and counties of Bronx, Dutchess, Erie, Kings, Nassau, New York, Orange, Putnam, Queens, Richmond, Rockland, Suffolk and Westchester. The request must include complete name and date of birth, and, for mail requests, be accompanied by two (2) self addressed stamped return envelopes. The fee, payable by check, is $16.00 per name per county. Mail and in person requests go to: Office of Court Administration, Criminal History Search, 25 Beaver St, 8th Floor, New York, NY 10004, 212-428-2810. You may obtain copies of any case dispositions found from the applicable county court.

Erie County

Supreme & County Court *Civil Records*

www.erie.gov

Online access to the county clerk's database of civil matters is available free at http://ecclerk.erie.gov. Records go back to 2/1994.

Monroe County

Supreme & County Court *Civil and Criminal Records*

www.clerk.co.monroe.ny.us

Online access to felony, civil, and divorce records available free online at www.clerk.co.monroe.ny.us. Records go back to 6/1993, although earlier film images are being added. Also, access to the remote online system requires $.50 per minute usage. Fax back available for $.50 per page. Call Tom Fiorilli 716-428-5151 for more information.

Rockland County

Supreme & County Court *Civil and Criminal Records*

www.rocklandcountyclerk.com

Online access is the county clerk's court records index is available free at www.rocklandcountyclerk.com/court_records.html. Includes criminal, civil judgments, real estate records, tax warrants. Includes criminal index back to 1982. Call Paul Pipearto at 845-638-5221 for more information.

Ulster County

Supreme & County Court *Civil and Criminal Records*

Access to the remote online system requires minimum $33.33 per month fee (over 2500 transactions is $44.50), 12 months required to signup. Search by name or case number. Call Valerie Harris 845-334-5367 for more information.

Several extensive court records systems are available. Please refer to the "Online Access Note" on the previous page for details.

County Level ... Recorders & Assessors

Recording Office Organization: 62 counties, 62 recording offices. The recording officer is the County Clerk (it is the New York City Register in the counties of Bronx, Kings, New York, and Queens). The entire state is in the Eastern Time Zone (EST). Federal tax liens on personal property of businesses are filed with the Secretary of State. Other federal tax liens are filed with the County Clerk. State tax liens are filed with the County Clerk, with a master list - called state tax warrants - available at the Secretary of State's office. Federal tax liens are usually indexed with UCC Records. State tax liens are usually indexed with other miscellaneous liens and judgments. Some counties include federal tax liens as part of a UCC search, and others will search tax liens for a separate fee. Search fees and copy fees vary.

Online Access Note: There are growing number of counties and towns offering free Internet access to assessor records.

Albany County *Naturalization Records*

www.albanycounty.com/departments

Access to the clerk's naturalization records from 1821-1991 are available free online at www.albanycounty.com/online/online.asp. Records are being added by volunteers.

Bronx County *Real Estate, Lien, Deed, UCC, Tax Assessor Records*

Two sources are available. Access to Bronx County online records - including Boroughs of Brooklyn, Queens, Staten Island, Bronx, Manhattan - requires a $250 monthly fee and $5 per transaction fee. Records are kept 3-6 years. For information, contact Richard Reskin at 718-935-6523. Also, they offer daily downloads are available for borough-wide transactions of UCCs, Fed Liens, deeds, real estate. Also, property assessment rolls from NYC's Dept. of Finance are available free at www.ci.nyc.ny.us/html/dof/html/asmt.html. Search by borough, block and lot number. Tax reports are also available, with enrollment required.

Cattaraugus County *Real Estate, Tax Assessor Records*

Records on the City of Olean assessor database are available free online at www.cityofolean.com/Assessor/main.htm.

Erie County   *Recording, Deed, Mortgage, Judgment Records*

http://ecclerk.erie.gov

Access to the county clerk's database is available free at http://ecclerk.erie.gov. Records go back to 2/1994.

Kings County   *Real Estate, Lien, Tax Assessor Records*

Two sources exist: the fee service supports the Boroughs of Brooklyn, Queens, Staten Island, Bronx, and Manhattan. There is a $250 monthly fee and a $5.00 fee per transaction. Records are kept 2-5 years. Search by name, grantor/grantee, and address. For information, contact Richard Reskin at 718-935-6523. Also, property assessment rolls from NYC's Dept. of Finance are available free online at www.ci.nyc.ny.us/html/dof/html/asmt.html. Search by borough, block and lot number. Tax reports are also available, with enrollment required.

Monroe County   *Land, Judgment, UCC, Lien, Court Records*

www.co.monroe.ny.us

Access to the county clerk database are available online at www.clerk.co.monroe.ny.us. Includes mortgages, deeds, court records; free registration. Land records back to 1984. Liens, judgments, UCCS back to 5/1989. Court records - civil, felony, divorce - back to June, 1993. Earlier microfilm images are being added as time permits.

New York County   *Real Estate, Lien, Tax Assessor Records*

Several sources available. Access to NY County online records - including Boroughs of Brooklyn, Queens, Staten Is, Bronx, Manhattan - requires $250 monthly and $5 per transaction. Records are kept 2-5 years. Call Richard Reskin at 718-935-6523. Also, property assessment rolls from NYC's Dept. of Finance are available free online at www.ci.nyc.ny.us/html/dof/html/asmt.html. Search by borough, block and lot number. Tax reports are also available, with enrollment required. Also, online access to assessor's property db is available free at http://nycserv.nyc.gov/nycproperty/nynav/jsp/selectbbl.jsp. Search by address of property description.

Putnam County   *Real Estate, UCC Records*

www.putnamcountyny.com

County Recorder records are accessible through a private online service at www.landaccess.com; Registration is required.

Queens County   *Real Estate, Lien, Tax Assessor Records*

Two sources are available. Access to Queens County online records - including Boroughs of Brooklyn, Queens, Staten Island, Bronx, Manhattan - requires a $250 monthly fee and $5 per transaction fee. Records are kept 2-5 years. For information, contact Richard Reskin at 718-935-6523. Also, property assessment rolls from NYC's Dept. of Finance are available free at www.ci.nyc.ny.us/html/dof/html/asmt.html. Search by borough, block and lot number. Tax reports are also available, with enrollment required.

Richmond County   *Real Estate, Lien, Tax Assessor Records*

Two sources are available. Access to Richmond-Staten Is. online records - including Boroughs of Brooklyn, Queens, Staten Island, Bronx, Manhattan - requires a $250 monthly fee and $5 per transaction fee. Records are kept 2-5 years. For further information, contact Richard Reskin at 718-935-6523. Property assessment rolls from NYC's Dept. of Finance are available free online at www.ci.nyc.ny.us/html/dof/html/asmt.html. Search by borough, block and lot number. Tax reports are also available, with enrollment required.

Rockland County   *Real Estate, Lien, Deed, Court Records*

www.rocklandcountyclerk.com

Access is the county clerk's records index is available free at www.rocklandcountyclerk.com/court_records.html. Includes criminal records back to 1982, civil judgments, real estate records, tax warrants. Images back to 6/96 are viewable, and more are being added. Call Paul Pipearto at 845-638-5221 for more information.

Schenectady County   *Real Estate, Tax Assessor Records*

www.scpl.org

Records for approximately 2/5 of the county property assessments are available free online on the library database at www.scpl.org/assessments.

Steuben County   *Tax Assessor Records*

www.steubencony.org

Search Town of Erwin Real Property Assessment Roll free online at www.pennynet.org/erwin/er95tax.htm.

Tompkins County   *Real Estate, Assessor Records*

www.tompkins-co.org

Access to property records on the ImageMate system at www.tompkins-co.org/assessment/online.html has two levels: basic free and a registration/password fee-based full system. There is no name searching on the free version. The fee service is $20 monthly or $200 per year. For information and registration for the latter, email assessment@tompkins-co.org.

Ulster County *Real Estate, Lien, Property Tax, Voter Registration, Court Records*
www.co.ulster.ny.us
Two sources exist. Access to county online records requires a $33.33 (under 25 transactions) or $44.55 monthly fee; 12 month agreement required. Land Records date back to 1984. Includes county court records back to 7/1987. Lending agency information is available. For information, contact Valerie Harris at 845-334-5367. Also, the County Parcel Viewer at www.maphost.com/ulster provides free access to tax parcel information. Search by GIS map, parcel ID number, street name, or other criteria.

Wyoming County *Real Estate, Recording Records*
County Recorder records are accessible through a private online service at www.landaccess.com; Fees and registration are required.

Federal Courts in New York...

Standards for Federal Courts: The universal PACER sign-up number is 800-676-6856. Find PACER and the Party/Case Index on the Web at http://pacer.psc.uscourts.gov. PACER dial-up access is $.60 per minute. Also, courts offering internet access via RACER, PACER, Web-PACER or the new CM-ECF charge $.07 per page fee unless noted as free.

US District Court -- Eastern District of New York
Home Page: www.nyed.uscourts.gov
PACER: Toll-free access: 888-331-4965. Local access phone: 718-250-4420. Case records are available back to January 1, 1990. Records are purged never. New records are available online after 1 day. **PACER URL:** http://pacer.nyed.uscourts.gov.
Electronic Filing: Only law firms and practitioners may file cases electronically. Anyone can search online. Electronic filing information is available online at https://ecf.nyed.uscourts.gov.
Brooklyn Division counties: Kings, Queens, Richmond. Cases from Nassau and Suffolk may also be heard here.
Central Islip Division counties: Nassau, Suffolk.

US Bankruptcy Court -- Eastern District of New York
Home Page: www.nyeb.uscourts.gov
PACER: Toll-free access: 800-263-7790. Local access phone: 718-488-7012, 718-488-7013. Case records are available back to 1991. Records are purged every year. New civil records are available online after 3 days. **PACER URL:** http://pacer.nyeb.uscourts.gov.
Electronic Filing: Electronic filing information is available online at https://ecf.nyeb.uscourts.gov. **Also:** access via phone on VCIS (Voice Case Information System) is available: 800-252-2537, 718-852-5726
Brooklyn Division counties: Kings, Queens, Richmond. Kings and Queens County Chapter 11 cases may also be assigned to Westbury. Other Queens County cases may be assigned to Westbury Division. Nassau County Chapter 11 cases may be assigned here.
Central Islip Division counties: Suffolk, Nassau.

US District Court -- Northern District of New York
Home Page: www.nynd.uscourts.gov
PACER: Toll-free access: 800-480-7525. Local access phone: 315-234-8663. Case records are available back to June 1991. New records are available online after 2 days. .
Albany Division counties: Albany, Clinton, Columbia, Essex, Greene, Rensselaer, Saratoga, Schenectady, Schoharie, Ulster, Warren, Washington.
Binghamton Division counties: Broome, Chenango, Delaware, Franklin, Jefferson, Lewis, Otsego, St. Lawrence, Tioga.
Syracuse Division counties: Cayuga, Cortland, Fulton, Hamilton, Herkimer, Madison, Montgomery, Onondaga, Oswego, Tompkins.
Utica Division counties: Oneida.

US Bankruptcy Court -- Northern District of New York

Home Page: www.nynb.uscourts.gov

PACER: Toll-free access: 800-390-8432. Local access phone: 518-257-1669. Case records are available back to 1992. New civil records are available online after 48 hours. **PACER URL:** http://pacer.nynb.uscourts.gov.

Electronic Filing: (Currently in the process of implementing CM/ECF). **Also:** access via phone on VCIS (Voice Case Information System) is available: 800-206-1952.

Albany Division counties: Albany, Clinton, Essex, Franklin, Fulton, Jefferson, Montgomery, Rensselaer, Saratoga, Schenectady, Schoharie, St. Lawrence, Warren, Washington.

Utica Division counties: Broome, Cayuga, Chenango, Cortland, Delaware, Hamilton, Herkimer, Lewis, Madison, Oneida, Onondaga, Otsego, Oswego, Tioga, Tompkins.

US District Court -- Southern District of New York

Home Page: www.nysd.uscourts.gov

PACER: Case records are available back to early 1990. Records are purged every six months. New records are available online after 1 day.

Electronic Filing: (Currently in the process of implementing CM/ECF).

Opinions Online: Selected rulings are searchable online using CourtWeb. To download and view copies of rulings you must have Adobe Acrobat Reader. Court opinions are available online at www.nysd.uscourts.gov/courtweb.

New York City Division counties: Bronx, New York. Some cases from the counties in the White Plains Division are also assigned to the New York Division.

White Plains Division counties: Dutchess, Orange, Putnam, Rockland, Sullivan, Westchester. Some cases may be assigned to New York Division.

US Bankruptcy Court -- Southern District of New York

Home Page: www.nysb.uscourts.gov

PACER: Case records are available back to June 1991. Records are purged every six months. New civil records are available online after 2 days. **PACER URL:** https://ecf.nysb.uscourts.gov/cgi-bin/login.pl.

Electronic Filing: Electronic filing information is available online at http://ecf.nysb.uscourts.gov. **Also:** access via phone on VCIS (Voice Case Information System) is available: 212-668-2772.

New York Division counties: Bronx, New York.

Poughkeepsie Division counties: Columbia, Dutchess, Greene, Orange, Putnam, Sullivan, Ulster.

White Plains Division counties: Rockland, Westchester.

US District Court -- Western District of New York

Home Page: www.nywd.uscourts.gov

PACER: Case records are available back to 1992. Records are purged never. New civil records are available online after 1 day. New criminal records are available online after 2 days. **PACER URL:** http://pacer.nywd.uscourts.gov.

Buffalo Division counties: Allegany, Cattaraugus, Chautauqua, Erie, Genesee, Niagara, Orleans, Wyoming. Prior to 1982, this division included what is now the Rochester Division.

Rochester Division counties: Chemung, Livingston, Monroe, Ontario, Schuyler, Seneca, Steuben, Wayne, Yates.

US Bankruptcy Court -- Western District of New York

Home Page: www.nywb.uscourts.gov

PACER: Toll-free access: 800-450-8052. Local access phone: 716-551-3152. Case records are available back to August 1987. Records are purged never. New civil records are available online after 1 day. **PACER URL:** http://pacer.nywb.uscourts.gov.

Electronic Filing: (Currently in the process of implementing CM/ECF). **Also:** access via phone on VCIS (Voice Case Information System) is available: 800-776-9578, 716-551-5311

Buffalo Division counties: Allegany, Cattaraugus, Chautauqua, Erie, Genesee, Niagara, Orleans, Wyoming.

Rochester Division counties: Chemung, Livingston, Monroe, Ontario, Schuyler, Seneca, Steuben, Wayne, Yates.

North Carolina

Capital:	Raleigh Wake County	Home Page	www.ncgov.com
Time Zone:	EST	Attorney General	www.jus.state.nc.us
Number of Counties:	100	Archives	www.ah.dcr.state.nc.us

State Level ... Major Agencies

Corporation Records, Limited Partnerships, Limited Liability Company Records, Trademarks/Servicemarks

Secretary of State, Corporations Section, PO Box 29622, Raleigh, NC 27626-0622 (Courier: 2 S Salisbury, Raleigh, NC 27603); 919-807-2251 (Corporations), 919-807-2164 (Trademarks), 919-807-2039 (Fax), 8AM-5PM.

www.secretary.state.nc.us

The web site offers a free search of status and registered agent by corporation name. The trademark database is not available online. **Other options:** The state makes database information available for purchase via an FTP site. Contact Bonnie Elek at 919-807-2196 for details.

Uniform Commercial Code, Federal Tax Liens

UCC Division, Secretary of State, Raleigh, NC 27626-0622 (Courier: 2 South Salisbury St, Raleigh, NC 27603-5909); 919-807-2111, 919-807-2120 (Fax), 8AM-5PM.

www.secretary.state.nc.us/UCC

Free access is available at www.secretary.state.nc.us/ucc/. Click on "UCC research" or "Tax Liens." Search by ID number or debtor name. **Other options:** The UCC or tax lien database can be purchased on either a weekly or monthly basis vai an FTP site. For more information, call 919-807-2196.

Sales Tax Registrations

Revenue Department, Sales & Use Tax Division, PO Box 25000, Raleigh, NC 27640 (Courier: 501 N Wilmington Street, Raleigh, NC 27604); 919-733-3661, 919-715-6086 (Fax), 8AM-5PM.

www.dor.state.nc.us

Delinquent debtors are shown on the web at www.dor.state.nc.us/collect/delinquent.html.

Sexual Offender Registry

The Division of Criminal Information of the State Bureau of Investigation maintains the state database of sexual offenders. Records are searchable online at http://sbi.jus.state.nc.us/dojhaht/sor/.

Incarceration Records

The online system allows one to search by name or ID number for public information on inmates, probationers or parolees since 1972. Go to www.doc.state.nc.us.

Driver Records

Division of Motor Vehicles, Driver's License Section, 1100 New Bern Ave, Raleigh, NC 27697; 919-715-7000, 8AM-5PM.

www.dmv.dot.state.nc.us

To qualify for online availability, a client must be an insurance agent or insurance company support organization. The mode is interactive and is open from 7 AM to 10 PM. The DL# and name are needed when ordering. Records are $5.00 each. A minimum $500 security deposit is required. **Other options:** Magnetic tape for high volume batch users is available. Requests must be pre-paid.

Legislation Records

www.ncleg.net

The Internet site has copies of bills, status, and state statutes. **Other options:** This agency will mail lists of bills on computer printouts.

Voter Registration

State Board of Elections, PO Box 27255, Raleigh, NC 27611-7255; 919-733-7173, 919-715-0135 (Fax), 8AM-5PM.

www.sboe.state.nc.us

Online access to voter registration records is available free at www.sboe.state.nc.us/voterweb/seimsvot.htm. **Other options:** The records are sold in database format in electronic, magnetic or digital media. The maximum fee is $25.00.

State Level ... Occupational Licensing

Acupuncturist	http://ncaaom.org/directory.php?sort=city
Anesthetist Nurse	https://www.ncbon.com/Lic-verif.asp
Architect	www.member-base.com/ncbarch/public/lic/searchdb.asp
Architectural Firms	www.member-base.com/ncbarch/public/firms/searchdb.asp
Banking Division	www.banking.state.nc.us/banks.htm
Charitable/Sponsor Organization	www.secretary.state.nc.us/csl/index.html
Check Casher	www.banking.state.nc.us/checkcas.htm
Chiropractor	www.ncchiroboard.org/public/licensed_chiros.html
Clinical Nurse Specialist	https://www.ncbon.com/Lic-verif.asp
Consumer Financer	www.banking.state.nc.us/cf.htm
Contractor, General	www.nclbgc.org/lic_fr.html (site may be down)
Dental Hygienist	www.ncdentalboard.org/ncdbe_search.asp
Dentist	www.ncdentalboard.org/ncdbe_search.asp
Electrical Contractor/Inspector	www.ncbeec.org/LicSearch.asp
Engineer	www.member-base.com/ncbels/public/searchdb.asp
Fire Sprinkler Contractor/Inspector	www.nclicensing.org/OnlineReg.htm
Fund Raiser Consultant/Solicitor	www.secretary.state.nc.us/csl/index.html
Geologist	www.ncblg.org/licensees.html
Hearing Aid Dispenser/Fitter	www.nchalb.org/getmembers.cfm
Heating Contractor	www.nclicensing.org/OnlineReg.htm
Landscape Architect	www.ncbola.org/rosternew.html
Lobbyist	www.secretary.state.nc.us/lobbyists/Lsearch.asp
Medical Doctor/Physician	www.ncmedboard.org/find.htm
Midwife Nurse	https://www.ncbon.com/Lic-verif.asp
Mortgage Division	www.banking.state.nc.us/mbb.htm
Nurse Practitioner	www.ncmedboard.org/find.htm
Nurse Practitioner	https://www.ncbon.com/Lic-verif.asp
Nurse-LPN	https://www.ncbon.com/Lic-verif.asp
Nursing Home Administrator	www.ncbenha.org/searchdb.asp

Occupational Therapist	www.ncbot.org/fpdb/otimport.html
Occupational Therapist Assistant	www.ncbot.org/fpdb/otimport.html
Optometrist	www.ncoptometry.org/verify/index.asp
Osteopathic Physician	www.ncmedboard.org/find.htm
Pesticide Applicator	www.ncagr.com/aspzine/Fooddrug/data/advsearch.asp
Pesticide Consultant	www.ncagr.com/aspzine/Fooddrug/data/advsearch.asp
Pesticide Dealer	www.ncagr.com/aspzine/Fooddrug/data/advsearch.asp
Pharmacist	www.ncbop.org/names1.asp
Physician Assistant	www.ncmedboard.org/find.htm
Plumber	www.nclicensing.org/OnlineReg.htm
Podiatrist	www.ncbpe.org/search.php
Psychological Associate	www.ncpsychologyboard.org/search.htm
Psychologist	www.ncpsychologyboard.org/search.htm
Public Accountant-CPA	www.cpaboard.state.nc.us
Real Estate Broker/Dealer	www.memberbase.com/ncrec-new/licdb/indv/searchdb.asp
Real Estate Firm	www.memberbase.com/ncrec-new/licdb/firms/searchdb.asp
Surveyor, Land	www.member-base.com/ncbels/public/searchdb.asp

County Level ... Courts

Court Administration: Administrative Office of the Courts, Justice Bldg, 2 E Morgan St, Raleigh, NC, 27602; 919-733-7107; www.nccourts.org/Courts/

Court Structure: The Superior Court is the court of general jurisdiction, the District Court is limited. The counties combine the courts, thus searching is done through one court, not two, within the county.

Online Access Note: While there is no statewide online access, web access to civil and criminal dockets is available at some individual courts.

Access active District/Superior Court criminal calendars on a county or statewide basis at http://www1.aoc.state.nc.us/www/calendars.html. Historical information is not available.

Also, Civil Court calendars are now available online at http://www1.aoc.state.nc.us/www/calendars/Civil.html for nine counties -- Cateret, Craven, Cumberland, Durham, Mecklenburg, New Hanover, Pender, Pamlico, and Rowan.

Cleveland County
Superior-District Court *Criminal Records*
www.aoc.state.nc.us/www/public/courts/cleveland.html
Search the active Criminal Calendar by defendant name at http://www1.aoc.state.nc.us/www/calendars/CriminalQuery.html. Includes an impaired driving query.

Cumberland County
Superior-District Court *Civil and Criminal Records*
www.aoc.state.nc.us/data/district12
Search active calendars by court date on the web site. The web site presents a list of online vendors to instant record access. Also, online name search dockets at http://www1.aoc.state.nc.us/www/calendars/Civil.html.

These counties offer online name search Civil Court dockets at http://www1.aoc.state.nc.us/www/calendars/Civil.html. (For information on criminal docket searches, see the section introduction, above.)

Cateret	**Durham**	**Pender**
Craven	**Mecklenburg**	**Pamlico**
Cumberland	**New Hanover**	**Rowan**

County Level ... Recorders & Assessors

Recording Office Organization: 100 counties, 100 recording offices. The recording officers are the Register of Deeds and the Clerk of Superior Court (tax liens). The entire state is in the Eastern Time Zone (EST). Federal tax liens on personal property of businesses are filed with the Secretary of State. Other federal and all state tax liens are filed with the county Clerk of Superior Court, not with the Register of Deeds. (Oddly, even tax liens on real property are also filed with the Clerk of Superior Court, not with the Register of Deeds.)

Online Access Note: A growing number of counties offer free access to assessor and real estate records via the web.

Alleghany County   *Real Estate, Grantor/Grantee Records*
www.allcorod.com
Access to the Register of Deeds database are available free at www.allcorod.com/cgi-bin/viewer/date.sh. Records go back to 12/1988. Also, search for property information on a GIS mapping site at www.webgis.net/Alleghany.

Anson County   *Assessor, Real Estate Records*
www.co.anson.nc.us/servicesf0.htm
Records on the county Online Tax Inquiry System are available free online at www.co.anson.nc.us/pubcgi/taxinq.

Ashe County   *Assessor, Real Estate Records*
Access to records on the county Tax Parcel Information System are available free at www.webgis.net/ashe.

Buncombe County   *Assessor, Real Estate Records*
www.buncombecounty.org
Access to property information is available free on the gis mapping site at www.buncombecounty.org/GIS/Default.htm. Click on "Search methods" and search by owner name. Also, records from the county assessor are available free online at www.buncombetax.org. Property records are also available from a private company at www.propex.com/txrecd_ncbun.htm.

Burke County   *Real Estate, Assessor Records*
www.co.burke.nc.us
Access to the property information is available free on the gis mapping site at www.webgis.net/burke.

Cabarrus County   *Assessor, Real Estate Records*
www.co.cabarrus.nc.us
Search the tax assessor database for free online at www.co.cabarrus.nc.us/Pages/Tax/T_Disclaim.html. also, parcel information is available at http://166.82.128.222/ParcelInfo.html.

Caldwell County   *Assessor, Real Estate Records*
www.co.caldwell.nc.us
Records on the county GIS map server site are available free online at http://maps.co.caldwell.nc.us. Click on "Start Spatial-data Explorer" then find query field at bottom of next page.

Catawba County   *Assessor, Real Estate Records*
www.co.catawba.nc.us
Records on the Catawba County Geographic Information System database are available free online at www.gis.catawba.nc.us/. Click on map area; zoom in to find the parcel on the map, or search using query fields.

Cleveland County   *Real Estate, Assessor Records*
www.clevelandcounty.com
Access to property information on a gis mapping site is available free at www.webgis.net/Cleveland. Choose to search by name,address, parcel number, or map.

Craven County   *Assessor, Real Estate Records*
Records on the County Assessor database are available free online at http://gismaps.cravencounty.com/taxinfo.htm.

Cumberland County *Land, Deed, Recording, UCC Records*
www.ccrod.org
Search two systems free at www.logansystems-cumberlandnc.com/welcome.asp. The land records index and images go back to 1984; images go back to 1/21/1975; UCCs are from 1995 tp June 29, 2001.

Currituck County *Property Tax Records*
Access to tax department requires that you download the terminal emulator, then the tax files at www.co.currituck.nc.us/Tax/taxdept.htm.

Dare County *Assessor, Real Estate Records*
www.co.dare.nc.us
Records on the county Property Inquiry database are available free online at www.co.dare.nc.us/interactive/setup.htm.

Davidson County *Assessor, Real Estate Records*
www.co.davidson.nc.us
Records on the county Tax Department database are available free online at www.co.davidson.nc.us/asp/taxsearch.asp.

Durham County *Real Estate, Deed, Judgment, Recording, Voter Registration Records*
www.co.durham.nc.us/rgds
Access to the Register of Deeds database is available free at http://207.4.222.118. Access to the tax accessor data is available free at http://207.4.222.117/tax/index.cfm. Also, search property records from the GIS mapping site free at http://199.72.142.253/. After the disclaimer, click on "Spatial Data Explorer" to search. Also, search voter registration free at www.co.durham.nc.us/departments/elec/votersearch/VoterRecSearch.cfm.

Forsyth County *Real Estate, Land Records*
Access to the county Geo-Data Explorer database is available free online at http://maps.co.forsyth.nc.us. Address and Parcel ID searching only. Includes Board of Adjustment and building permit records. Also, Register of Deed records are available on CD-ROM. Also, search tax liens by name lists for free at www.co.forsyth.nc.us/tax/header.htm. Also, Online access to property and deeds indexes and images is available via a private company at http://auth.titlesearcher.com/ts/ts.asp or support@TitleSearcher.com. Fee/registration required; Monthly and per day available.

Franklin County *Real Property Records*
www.co.franklin.nc.us
Access to the county spatial data explorer database is available free at www.co.franklin.nc.us/docs/frame_tax.htm. Search the gis map or click on "text search" for name searching.

Guilford County *Recorder, Assessor, Property, UCC, Vital Statistic Records*
www.co.guilford.nc.us
Access to the county e-gov databases is available free at www.co.guilford.nc.us/egov/index.html. Site may be down.

Harnett County *Real Estate, Grantor/Grantee, Sheriff Sales, Missing Person, Most Wanted Records*
www.harnett.org/harnett/departments/rod.html
County real estate and property tax information is available free online at http://152.34.178.4/nc32. The sheriff's lists of most wanted, sheriff sales, and missing persons is available at www.harnettsheriff.com

Haywood County *Real Estate Records*
Records on the Land Records Search database are available free online at www.undersys.com/haywood/haywood.html. Search will result in a map showing the parcel and owner, parcel number, and deed book & page information.

Henderson County *Land Records*
Search property records at the GIS site free at www.henderson.lib.nc.us/county/ca/landrecord.html. Click on "4. Online Interactive GIS Web Site" the go to "GIS Online."

Mecklenburg County *Assessor, Real Estate, Grantor/Grantee, Judgment, Lien, Vital Statistic, Personal Property Records*
http://meckrod.hartic.com
Access to biirth, death, marriage, recordings, judgments, liens, and grantor/grantee indices are available free at http://meckrod.hartic.com/default.asp. Also, online access to the assessors records for real estate, personal property, and tax bills are

available free at http://mcmf.co.mecklenburg.nc.us:3007/cics/txar/txar00i/. The sheriff's inmate lookup is available free at http://mcmf.co.mecklenburg.nc.us:3007/cjjl01w/cjjl/webnull. Search warrants free at http://mcmf.co.mecklenburg.nc.us:3007/cjcr01w/cjjl/webnull.

Moore County   *Real Estate, Lien, Grantor/Grantee, Vital Statistic, DD214, Property Tax Records*
www.co.moore.nc.us
Access to the recorder's Online Public Records (OPR) database is available free at http://rod.co.moore.nc.us/nc32. Also, access to county Tax Information System (TIS) data is available free online to registrants and subject to approval at www.co.moore.nc.us/property/TIS/Taxpayer%20Information%20Login.htm. For information, call 910-947-6306.

New Hanover County   *Real Estate, Assessor, Granto/Grantee, Lien, UCC, Judgment Records*
Access to the register of deeds database is available free at http://srvrodweb.nhcgov.com/nc32/RODsearch.asp Also, online access to the real estate tax database is available free at www.nhcgov.com/HostPublisher/Oasinq/Oasinput.jsp Also, you may search for property information on the GIB-mappings site at www.nhcgov.com/GIS/GISservices.asp.

Onslow County   *Real Estate Records*
http://co.onslow.nc.us/register_of_deeds
Access is to property information is available free at www.roktech.net/onslow/. Enter the site and name search using the advanced search in the Parcel Query box.

Orange County   *Property Records*
www.co.orange.nc.us/deeds/
Access to property records on the GIS mapping site is available free at http://gis.co.orange.nc.us/gisdisclaimer.htm

Pitt County   *Property, Tax Sales Records*
www.co.pitt.nc.us/depts/
Access to property information on the GIS-mapping site is available free at http://opis.co.pitt.nc.us/opis/. Also, online access to the county tax sales list is available free at www.co.pitt.nc.us/foreclosure/.

Randolph County   *Real Property Records*
www.co.randolph.nc.us
Access to the county GIS database is available free at www.co.randolph.nc.us/gis.htm. In the "Search functions" on the map page, click on "parcel owner."

Richmond County   *Property Records*
Access to County property records is available via a subscription service; registration and fees are required. For information, call 334-344-3333.

Rockingham County   *Land, Grantor/Grantee, Judgment, Tax Sales Records*
www.rockinghamcorod.org
Access to Register of Deeds database is available free at www.rockinghamcorod.org. Land indexes 1996 to present; and record images 1984 to present; plats 1907 to present. Also, online access to real estate and tax appraiser data is available free at www.co.rockingham.nc.us/taxinfo2.html. Also, online access to the tax sales property is available at www.co.rockingham.nc.us/forecl.htm

Rowan County   *Real Estate, Recording Records*
www.co.rowan.nc.us/rod
Access to the Register of Dees land records database is available free at http://rod.co.rowan.nc.us. Records go back to 1975; financing statements back to 1993; images back to 6/2000.

Stanly County   *Real Estate, Assessor Records*
www.co.stanly.nc.us
Access to the county Property database is available free on the gis mapping site at www.webgis.net/stanly. Provides parcel ID and tax numbers, owner, address, year, land and building values.

Wake County   *Real Estate, Assessor, Deed, Judgment, Lien, Voter Registration Records*
http://web.co.wake.nc.us/rdeeds/
Records from the County Department of Revenue are downloadable by township for free at http://web.co.wake.nc.us/revenue/wcmap.html. Also, a free real estate property search is available at

http://aws1.co.wake.nc.us/realestate/search.asp. Also, online access to the Register of Deeds database is available free at http://rodweb01.co.wake.nc.us/books/genext/genextsearch.asp. Records go back to 10/1991. Registered voters can be found at http://web.co.wake.nc.us/bordelec/Waves/WavesOptions.asp. Also, Online access to Town of Cary property information is available free at a gis mapping site at www.webgis.net/cary.

Watauga County *Grantor/Grantee, Judgment, Deed, UCC, Assessor, Property Records*
www.wataugacounty.org/deeds/index.html
Access to register of deeds database is available free at www.wataugacounty.org/deeds/disclaimer.shtml Also, online access to county tax search data is available free at www.wataugacounty.org/tax/search_tax.shtml.

Wilson County *Assessor, Real Estate, Voter Registration Records*
www.wilson-co.com
Records on the county Tax Administrator database are available free online at www.wilson-co.com/wctax.html. Records on the county registered voter database are available at www.wilson-co.com/wcbe_search.cfm.

Federal Courts in North Carolina...

Standards for Federal Courts: The universal PACER sign-up number is 800-676-6856. Find PACER and the Party/Case Index on the Web at http://pacer.psc.uscourts.gov. PACER dial-up access is $.60 per minute. Also, courts offering internet access via RACER, PACER, Web-PACER or the new CM-ECF charge $.07 per page fee unless noted as free.

US District Court -- Eastern District of North Carolina
Home Page: www.nced.uscourts.gov
PACER: Toll-free access: 800-995-0313. Local access phone: 919-856-4768. Case records are available back to 1989. Records are purged when deemed necessary. New records are available online after 3 days. .
Elizabeth City Division counties: Bertie, Camden, Chowan, Currituck, Dare, Gates, Hertford, Northampton, Pasquotank, Perquimans, Tyrrell, Washington.
Greenville-Eastern Division counties: Beaufort, Carteret, Craven, Edgecombe, Greene, Halifax, Hyde, Jones, Lenoir, Martin, Pamlico, Pitt.
Raleigh Division counties: Cumberland, Franklin, Granville, Harnett, Johnston, Nash, Vance, Wake, Warren, Wayne, Wilson.
Wilmington Division counties: Bladen, Brunswick, Columbus, Duplin, New Hanover, Onslow, Pender, Robeson, Sampson.

US Bankruptcy Court -- Eastern District of North Carolina
Home Page: www.nceb.uscourts.gov
Other Online Access: Search records on the Internet using RACER at http://pacer.nceb.uscourts.gov. There is no fee. **Also:** access via phone on VCIS (Voice Case Information System) is available: 888-847-9138, 252-234-7655
Raleigh Division counties: Franklin, Granville, Harnett, Johnston, Vance, Wake, Warren.
Wilson Division counties: Beaufort, Bertie, Bladen, Brunswick, Camden, Carteret, Chowan, Columbus, Craven, Cumberland, Currituck, Dare, Duplin, Edgecombe, Gates, Greene, Halifax, Hertford, Hyde, Jones, Lenoir, Martin, Nash, New Hanover, Northampton, Onslow, Pamlico, Pasquotank,Pender, Perquimans, Pitt, Robeson, Sampson, Tyrrell, Washington, Wayne, Wilson.

US District Court -- Middle District of North Carolina
Home Page: www.ncmd.uscourts.gov
PACER: Toll-free access: 800-372-8820. Local access phone: 336-332-6010. Case records are available back to September 1991. Records are purged never. New records are available online after 2 days. **PACER URL:** http://pacer.ncmd.uscourts.gov.
Greensboro Division counties: Alamance, Cabarrus, Caswell, Chatham, Davidson, Davie, Durham, Forsyth, Guilford, Hoke, Lee, Montgomery, Moore, Orange, Person, Randolph, Richmond, Rockingham, Rowan, Scotland, Stanly, Stokes, Surry, Yadkin.

US Bankruptcy Court -- Middle District of North Carolina
Home Page: www.ncmb.uscourts.gov
PACER: Toll-free access: 800-417-3571. Local access phone: 336-333-5389. Document images available on Pacer. Case records are available back to 1992. Records are purged every two years. New civil records are available online after 1 day. **PACER URL:** http://pacer.ncmb.uscourts.gov. Document images available.
Electronic Filing: (Currently in the process of implementing CM/ECF). **Also:** access via phone on VCIS (Voice Case Information System) is available: 888-319-0455, 336-333-5532

Greensboro Division counties: Alamance, Cabarrus, Caswell, Chatham, Davidson, Davie, Durham, Guilford, Hoke, Lee, Montgomery, Moore, Orange, Person, Randolph, Richmond, Rockingham, Rowan, Scotland, Stanly.
Winston-Salem Division counties: Forsyth, Stokes, Surry, Yadkin.

US District Court -- Western District of North Carolina

Home Page: www.ncwd.uscourts.gov
PACER: Document images available. Case records are available back to 1991. New records are available online after 2 days.
PACER URL: www.ncwd.uscourts.gov/index.html. Document images available.
Asheville Division counties: Avery, Buncombe, Haywood, Henderson, Madison, Mitchell, Transylvania, Yancey.
Bryson City Division counties: Cherokee, Clay, Graham, Jackson, Macon, Swain.
Charlotte Division counties: Anson, Gaston, Mecklenburg, Union.
Shelby Division counties: Burke, Cleveland, McDowell, Polk, Rutherford.
Statesville Division counties: Alexander, Alleghany, Ashe, Caldwell, Catawba, Iredell, Lincoln, Watauga, Wilkes.

US Bankruptcy Court -- Western District of North Carolina

Home Page: www.ncwb.uscourts.gov
PACER: Case records are available back to 1992. Records are purged every 2 years. New civil records are available online after 1 day.
Electronic Filing: Electronic filing information is available online at https://ecf.ncwb.uscourts.gov. **Also:** access via phone on VCIS (Voice Case Information System) is available: 800-884-9868, 704-350-7505
Charlotte Division counties: Alexander, Alleghany, Anson, Ashe, Avery, Buncombe, Burke, Caldwell, Catawba, Cherokee, Clay, Cleveland, Gaston, Graham, Haywood, Henderson, Iredell, Jackson, Lincoln, Macon, Madison, McDowell, Mecklenburg, Mitchell, Polk, Rutherford, Swain, Transylvania, Union, Watauga, Wilkes, Yancey. There are five offices within this division; records for all may be searched here or at Asheville: 100 Otis St #112, Asheville, NC 28801, 828-771-7300.

Editor's Tip: Just because records are maintained in a certain way in your state or county do not assume that any other county or state does things the same way that you are used to.

North Dakota

Capital:	Bismark	Home Page	www.state.nd.us
	Burleigh County	Attorney General	www.ag.state.nd.us
Time Zone: CST		Archives	www.state.nd.us/hist/sal.htm
Number of Counties: 53			

State Level ... Major Agencies

Corporation Records, Limited Liability Company Records, Limited Partnership Records, Limited Liability Partnership Records, Trademarks/Servicemarks, Fictitious Name, Assumed Name

Secretary of State, Business Information/Registration, 600 E Boulevard Ave, Dept 108, Bismarck, ND 58505-0500; 701-328-4284, 800-352-0867, 701-328-2992 (Fax), 8AM-5PM.

www.state.nd.us/sec

The Secretary of State's registered business database may be viewed at the Internet for no charge. Records include corporations, limited liability companies, limited partnerships, limited liability partnerships, limited liability limited partnerships, partnership fictitious names, trade names, trademarks, and real estate investment trusts. The database includes all active records and those records inactivated within the past twelve months. Access by the first few words of a business name, by any significant word in a business name, or by the System ID number assigned to the record. **Other options:** The state provides a database purchase program. Costs are $35.00 per database and processing fees vary for type of media.

Uniform Commercial Code, Federal Tax Liens, State Tax Liens

UCC Division, Secretary of State, 600 E Boulevard Ave Dept 108, Bismarck, ND 58505-0500; 701-328-3662, 701-328-4214 (Fax), 8AM-5PM.

www.state.nd.us/sec

There is a limited free public search and a commercial system for professionals. Sign-up for access to the Central Indexing System includes an annual subscription $120 fee and a one-time $50.00 registration fee. The $7.00 fee applies, but documents will not be certified. Searches include UCC-11 information listing and farm product searches.

Sexual Offender Registry

The Bureau of Criminal Investigation, which is a part of the State Attorney General's Office, maintains the state database of sexual offenders. You can search online at www.ndsexoffender.com, but only the high offender level names are found

Driver Records

Department of Transportation, Driver License & Traffic Safety Division, 608 E Boulevard Ave, Bismarck, ND 58505-0700; 701-328-2603, 701-328-2435 (Fax), 8AM-5PM.

www.state.nd.us/dot

The system is interactive and is open 24 hours daily. Fee is $3.00 per record, requesters must be approved. There is a minimum of 100 requests per month. For more information, call 701-328-4790. **Other options:** Magnetic tape ordering is available for high volume users.

Vessel Ownership, Vessel Registration

North Dakota Game & Fish Department, 100 N Bismarck Expressway, Bismarck, ND 58501; 701-328-6335, 701-328-6352 (Fax), 8AM-5PM.

www.state.nd.us/gnf

There is a free public inquiry system on the home page. One can also search lottery hunting permit applications. **Other options:** A printed list is available of all registered vessels.

Legislation Records

www.state.nd.us/lr

Their Internet site offers an extensive array of legislative information at no charge, including proposed and enacted legislation since 1997. Also, one may email requests for information.

GED Certificates

Department of Public Instruction, GED Testing, 600 E Blvd Ave, Bismarck, ND 58505-0440; 701-328-2393, 701-328-4770 (Fax), 8AM-4:30PM.

www.dpi.state.nd.us

One may request records via email at JMarcell@mail.dpi.state.nd.us. There is no fee, unless a transcript is ordered.

State Level ... Occupational Licensing

Asbestos Abatement Contr./Worker	www.health.state.nd.us/ndhd/environ/ee/rad/asb/
Asbestos Abatement Insp./Monitor/Supvr.	www.health.state.nd.us/ndhd/environ/ee/rad/asb/
Asbestos Abatement Planner/Designer	www.health.state.nd.us/ndhd/environ/ee/rad/asb/
Attorney	www.court.state.nd.us/court/lawyers/index/frameset.htm
Bank	www.state.nd.us/dfi/Bank List.htm
Charitable Solicitation	www.state.nd.us/sec/charitableorganizationsearch.htm
Collection Agency	www.state.nd.us/dfi/collectionagency.html
Consumer Finance Company	www.state.nd.us/dfi/consumerfinance.html
Contractor/General Contractor	www.state.nd.us/sec/contractorsearch.htm
Credit Union	www.state.nd.us/dfi/Credit Union List.htm
Livestock Agent	www.agdepartment.com/Programs/Livestock/Agents.html
Livestock Auction Market	www.agdepartment.com/Programs/Livestock/markets.html
Livestock Dealer	www.agdepartment.com/Programs/Livestock/Dealers.html
Lobbyist	www.state.nd.us/sec/RegLobbyists/lobbyistregmnu.htm
Medical Doctor	www.docboard.org/nd/
Money Broker Firm	www.state.nd.us/dfi/moneybrokers.html
Optometrist	www.ndsbopt.org/directory.asp
Pesticide Applicator/Dealer	www.ag.ndsu.nodak.edu/aginfo/pesticid/cert_info.htm
Physician Assistant	www.docboard.org/nd/
Public Accountant-CPA	www.state.nd.us/ndsba/database/sbasearch.asp
Public Accounting Firm	www.state.nd.us/ndsba/database/sbasearch.asp
Social Worker	www.ndbswe.com/list/main_pg.htm
Trust Company	www.state.nd.us/dfi/Trust Companies.htm

County Level ... Courts

Court Administration: State Court Administrator, North Dakota Judiciary, 600 E Blvd, 1st Floor Judicial Wing, Dept. 180, Bismarck, ND, 58505-0530; 701-328-4216; www.ndcourts.com or www.court.state.nd.us

Court Structure: In 1995, the County Courts merged with the District Courts statewide. County court records are maintained by the 53 District Court Clerks in the seven judicial districts. in search requests, we recommend stating "include all County Court cases."

There are 76 Municipal Courts that handle traffic cases.

Online Access Note: A statewide computer system for internal purposes is in operation in most counties. You may now search North Dakota Supreme Court dockets and opinions at www.ndcourts.com. Search by docket number, party name, or anything else that may appear in the text. Records are from 1991 forward. Email notification of new opinions is also available.

Nelson County
Northeast Central Judicial District Court *Civil and Criminal Records*
Will accept email record requests at rstevens@pioneer.state.nd.us.

County Level ... Recorders & Assessors

Recording Office Organization: 53 counties, 53 recording offices. The recording officer is the Register of Deeds. The entire state is in the Central Time Zone (CST). Federal tax liens on personal property of businesses are filed with the Secretary of State. Other federal and all state tax liens are filed with the county Register of Deeds. All counties will perform tax lien searches. Some counties automatically include business federal tax liens as part of a UCC search because they appear on the statewide database. (Be careful - federal tax liens on individuals may only be in the county lien books, not on the statewide system.) Separate searches are usually available at $5.00-7.00 per name.

Online Access Note: The North Dakota Recorders Information Network (NDRIN) is a electronic central repository for about one-third of ND counties. Burleigh, Cass, Dunn, McKenzie, McLean, Stark, Ward and Walsh currently offer internet access. There are 12 other counties participating in the system. There is a $200 set-up fee and $50 monthly with $1.00 charge per image printed. Register or request information via the web site at www.ndrin.com.

Burleigh County	**Cass County**
Dunn County	**McKenzie County**
McLean County	**Stark County**
Walsh County	**Ward County**

Editor's Note: Access the recorder's land records for the counties listed above are available by subscription to NDRIN's central repository at www.ndrin.com. See section introduction.

Federal Courts in North Dakota...

Standards for Federal Courts: The universal PACER sign-up number is 800-676-6856. Find PACER and the Party/Case Index on the Web at http://pacer.psc.uscourts.gov. PACER dial-up access is $.60 per minute. Also, courts offering internet access via RACER, PACER, Web-PACER or the new CM-ECF charge $.07 per page fee unless noted as free.

US District Court -- District of North Dakota

Home Page: www.ndd.uscourts.gov

PACER: Toll-free access: 800-407-4453. Local access phone: 701-530-2367. Case records are available back to October 1990. Records are purged never. New records are available online after 1 day. .

Bismarck-Southwestern Division counties: Adams, Billings, Bowman, Burleigh, Dunn, Emmons, Golden Valley, Grant, Hettinger, Kidder, Logan, McIntosh, McLean, Mercer, Morton, Oliver, Sioux, Slope, Stark.

Fargo-Southeastern Division counties: Barnes, Cass, Dickey, Eddy, Foster, Griggs, La Moure, Ransom, Richland, Sargent, Steele, Stutsman. Rolette County cases prior to 1995 may be located here.

Grand Forks-Northeastern Division counties: Benson, Cavalier, Grand Forks, Nelson, Pembina, Ramsey, Towner, Traill, Walsh.

Minot-Northwestern Division counties: Bottineau, Burke, Divide, McHenry, McKenzie, Mountrail, Pierce, Renville, Rolette, Sheridan, Ward, Wells, Williams. Case records from Rolette County prior to 1995 may be located in Fargo-Southeastern Division.

US Bankruptcy Court -- District of North Dakota

Home Page: www.ndb.uscourts.gov

PACER: Toll-free access: 800-810-4092. Local access phone: 701-297-7164. Document images available on Pacer. Case records are available back to 1990. New civil records are available online after 1 day. **PACER URL:** http://pacer.okwd.uscourts.gov.

Other Online Access: Search records on the Internet using RACER at https://racer.ndb.uscourts.gov/perl/bkplog.html. Access fee is $.07 per page. **Also:** access via phone on VCIS (Voice Case Information System) is available: 701-297-7166.

Fargo Division counties: All counties in North Dakota.

Editor's Note: The southwestern area of North Dakota (west and south of the Missouri River) is in Mountain Time Zone. The remainder of the state is in the Central Time Zone.

Capital: Columbus
             Franklin County

Time Zone: EST

Number of Counties: 88

Home Page   www.state.oh.us

Attorney General   www.ag.state.oh.us

Archives   www.ohiohistory.org/ar_tools.html

State Level ... Major Agencies

Corporation Records, Fictitious Name, Limited Partnership Records, Assumed Name, Trademarks/Servicemarks, Limited Liability Company Records

Secretary of State, Corporate Records - Customer Service, PO Box 130, Columbus, OH 43215 (Courier: 180 E Broad Street, 16th Fl, Columbus, OH 43215); 877-767-3453, 614-466-3910, 614-466-3899 (Fax), 8AM-5PM.

www.state.oh.us/sos

The agency provides free Internet searching for business and corporation records, the site also includes UCC and campaign finance. **Other options:** The state makes the database available for purchase, call for details.

Uniform Commercial Code

UCC Records, Secretary of State, PO Box 2795, Columbus, OH 43216 (Courier: 180 E Broad Street, 16th Fl, Columbus, OH 43215); 877-767-3453, 614-466-3126, 614-466-2892 (Fax), 8AM-5PM.

www.state.oh.us/sos

The Internet site offers free online access to records. **Other options:** The complete database is available on electronic media with weekly updates. Call for current pricing.

Incarceration Records

Information on current and former inmates is available at www.drc.state.oh.us. Location, physical identifiers, conviction and sentencing information, and release dates are provided.

Death Records

Ohio Department of Health, Bureau of Vital Statistics, PO Box 15098, Columbus, OH 43215-0098 (Courier: 246 N High Street, 1st Fl, Revenue Room, Columbus, OH 43215); 614-466-2531, 7:45AM-4:30PM.

www.odh.state.oh.us/Birth/birthmain.htm

The Ohio Historical Society Death Certificate Index Searchable Database at www.ohiohistory.org/dindex/search.cfm permits searching by name, county, index. Data is available from 1913 to 1937 only.

Workers' Compensation Records

Bureau of Workers Compensation, Customer Assistance, 30 W Spring St, Fl 10, Columbus, OH 43215-2241; 800-644-6292, 877-520-6446 (Fax), 7:30AM-5:30PM.

www.ohiobwc.com

Injured workers, injured worker designees, representatives and managed care organizations (MCOs) can view a list of all claims associated with a given SSN, but are limited to viewing only the claims with which they are associated. Employers, their representatives or designees, and managed care organizations can view a list of all claims associated to their BWC policy number. Medical providers can view all claims associated with any given SSN. Access is through the web site listed above. **Other options:** Bulk data is released to approved accounts; however, the legal department must approve requesters. The agency has general information available on a web site.

Driver Records

Department of Public Safety, Bureau of Motor Vehicles, 1970 W Broad St, Columbus, OH 43223-1102; 614-752-7600, 8AM-5:30PM M-T-W; 8AM-4:30PM TH-F.

www.ohiobmv.com/

The system is called "Defender System" and is suggested for requesters who order 100 or more motor vehicle reports per day in batch mode. Turnaround is in 4-8 hours. The DL# or SSN and name are needed when ordering. Fee is $2.00 per record. For more information, call 614-752-7692. **Other options:** Overnight magnetic tape service is available for larger accounts.

Vehicle Ownership, Vehicle Identification

Bureau of Motor Vehicles, Motor Vehicle Title Records, 1970 W Broad St, Columbus, OH 43223-1102; 614-752-7671, 614-752-8929 (Fax), 7:30AM-4:45PM.

www.ohiobmv.com/

Ohio offers online access through AAMVAnet. All requesters must comply with a contractual agreement prior to release of data, which complies with DPPA regulations. Fee is $2.00 per record. Call 614-752-7692 for more information.

Legislation Records

www.legislature.state.oh.us

The Internet site offers access to bill text, status, and enactment back to 1997/98. **Other options:** Email requests are accepted.

State Level ... Occupational Licensing

Accounting Firm	www.state.oh.us/acc/search.html
Acupuncturist	www.state.oh.us/med/license/query.stm
Anesthesiologist Assistant	www.state.oh.us/med/license/query.stm
Architect	www.state.oh.us/arc/license/query.asp
Athletic Trainer	www.state.oh.us/scripts/pyt/query.asp
Audiologist/Audiologist Aide	www.state.oh.us/slp/licenses.htm
Barber School	www.state.oh.us/brb/barbsch.htm
Chiropractor	http://156.63.245.111/index.html
Clinical Nurse Specialist	www.state.oh.us/nur/Verification.stm
Coil Cleaner (Liquor/Beverage)	www.state.oh.us/com/liquor/liquor13.htm
Contractor	www.com.state.oh.us/odoc/dic/scripts/ociebqy.htm
Cosmetic Therapist	www.state.oh.us/med/license/query.stm
Counselor	www.state.oh.us/scripts/csw/query.asp
Dental Assistant Radiologist	www.state.oh.us/scripts/den/query.stm
Dental Hygienist	www.state.oh.us/scripts/den/query.stm
Dentist	www.state.oh.us/scripts/den/query.stm
Dialysis Technician	www.state.oh.us/nur/Dialysis.stm
Drug Wholesaler/Distributor	www.ohio.gov/pharmacy/license.htm
Electrician	www.com.state.oh.us/odoc/dic/scripts/ociebqy.htm

Heating/Refrigeration (HVAC)	www.com.state.oh.us/odoc/dic/scripts/ociebqy.htm
Hydronic	www.com.state.oh.us/odoc/dic/scripts/ociebqy.htm
Insurance Agent	www.ohioinsurance.gov/ConsumServ/ocs/agentloc.asp
Landscape Architect	www.state.oh.us/arc/license/query.asp
Legislative Agent/Agent Employer	www.jlec-olig.state.oh.us/agent_search_form.cfm
Liquor Distributor	www.state.oh.us/com/liquor/liquor15.htm
Liquor License	www.state.oh.us/com/liquor/phone.txt
Lobbyist/Lobbyist Employer (Exec. Agency)	www.jlec-olig.state.oh.us/agent_search_form.cfm
Lottery Retailer	www.ohiolottery.com/frameset/games/retailer.html
Massage Therapist	www.state.oh.us/med/license/query.stm
Mechanotherapist	www.state.oh.us/med/license/query.stm
Medical Doctor	www.state.oh.us/med/license/query.stm
Midwife Nurse	www.state.oh.us/nur/Verification.stm
Naprapath	www.state.oh.us/med/license/query.stm
Nurse Anesthetist	www.state.oh.us/nur/Verification.stm
Nurse Practitioner	www.state.oh.us/nur/Verification.stm
Nurse-RN/LPN	www.state.oh.us/nur/Verification.stm
Occupational Therapist/Assistant	www.state.oh.us/scripts/pyt/query.asp
Optometrist	www.state.oh.us/scripts/opt/query.asp
Optometrist, Diagnostic/Therapeutic	www.state.oh.us/scripts/opt/query.asp
Osteopathic Physician	www.state.oh.us/med/license/query.stm
Pharmacist	www.ohio.gov/pharmacy/license.htm
Pharmacy/Pharmacy Dispensary	www.ohio.gov/pharmacy/license.htm
Physical Therapist/Assistant	www.state.oh.us/scripts/pyt/query.asp
Physician Assistant	www.state.oh.us/med/license/query.stm
Plumber	www.com.state.oh.us/odoc/dic/scripts/ociebqy.htm
Podiatrist	www.state.oh.us/med/license/query.stm
Polygraph Examiner	http://polygraph.org/states/oape/directory.htm
Prescriptive Authority	www.state.oh.us/nur/RxAuth.stm
Psychologist	http://www2.state.oh.us/psy/query.asp
Public Accountant-CPA	www.state.oh.us/acc/search.html
Real Estate Appraiser	www.asc.gov/content/category1/appr_by_state.asp
Real Estate Sales Agent	www.ohiorealtors.org/search/locate.html
Respiratory Therapist/Student	www.state.oh.us/scripts/rsp/license/query.asp
School Psychologist	http://www2.state.oh.us/psy/query.asp
Social Worker	www.state.oh.us/scripts/csw/query.asp
Speech Pathologist/Audiologist	www.state.oh.us/slp/licenses.htm
Teacher/Teacher's Aide	https://www.ode.state.oh.us/Teaching-Profession/Teacher/ Certification_Licensure/certifact.asp
Veterinarian	www.state.oh.us/ovmlb/consumers.htm
Veterinary Technician	www.state.oh.us/ovmlb/consumers.htm

County Level ... Courts

Court Administration: Administrative Director, Supreme Court of Ohio, 30 E Broad St, 3rd Fl, Columbus, OH, 43266-0419; 614-466-2653; www.sconet.state.oh.us

Court Structure: The Circuit Court is the highest court of record. Effective 10/1/98, the civil judgment limit increased from $20,000 to $25,000 at the District Court level. Certain categories of minor felonies are handled by the District Courts. However, all misdemeanors and felonies that require a jury trial are handled by Circuit Courts.

Online Access Note: There is no statewide computer system, but a number of Circuits and Municipal courts offer online access.

Athens County

Common Pleas Court *Civil and Criminal Records*
www.athenscountycpcourt.org
Online access to the CP court records is available free at the web site.

Butler County

Common Pleas Court *Civil, Criminal and Probate Records*
www.butlercountyclerk.org/
Online access to County Clerk of Courts records available free at http://24.123.15.5/pa/pa.urd/pamw6500-display. Search by name, dates, or case number and type. Online access to Probate Court records is available free at www.butlercountyohio.org/probate/estate.cfm. Search the Estate or Guardianship databases.

Clark County

Common Pleas Court *Civil and Criminal Records*
www.co.clark.oh.us
Online access to clerk's records are available free at http://64.56.97.140/.

Clark County Municipal Court *Civil and Criminal Records*
www.clerkofcourts.municipal.co.clark.oh.us
Online access to case information available free at www.clerkofcourts.municipal.co.clark.oh.us/cases/courtcases.nsf. Name searching on "New Cases" other types require a case number. Access to criminal records is the same as civil.

Clermont County

Common Pleas Court *Civil and Criminal Records*
Clermont County Municipal Court *Civil and Criminal Records*
www.clermontclerk.org
Online access to court records is available free at www.clermontclerk.org/Case_Access.htm. Online records go back to 1/1998. Includes later Municipal Court records which go back to 5/1/1996.

Columbiana County

Common Pleas Court *Civil and Criminal Records*
Municipal Courts *Civil and Criminal Records*
www.ccclerk.org/
Free online access to all county court records is at www.ccclerk.org/case_access.htm.

Coshocton County

Coshocton Municipal Court *Civil and Criminal Records*
www.coshoctonmunicipalcourt.com
Online access to civil records is available at the web site. Searchcivil records by name, case number, attorney, date. Search criminal records by name, attorney, citation or case number.

Crawford County

Common Pleas Court *Civil and Criminal Records*
www.crawford-co.org/Clerk/default.html
Online access to Common Please court records is available free at www.crawford-co.org/Clerk/default.html and click on "Internet Inquiry."

Cuyahoga County

Common Pleas Court - General Division *Civil and Criminal Records*
www.cuyahoga.oh.us
Online access to Common Please civil courts is available by clicking on Civil Case Dockets at www.cuyahoga.oh.us/home/default.asp. Online access to criminal records is available free at http://198.30.212.17/cpdock/.

Cleveland Heights Municipal Court *Civil and Criminal Records*
www.clevelandheightscourt.com
Civil (to $15,000) or misdemeanor docket records for Municipal Court are available on the web site. Search by name or case number.

Garfield Heights Municipal Court *Civil and Criminal Records*
www.ghmc.org
Online access is limited to current dockets; search by name, date or case number at www.ghmc.org/docket.html.

Delaware County
Common Pleas Court *Civil Records*
www.co.delaware.oh.us/clerk/index.htm
Access to court records is available free at www.delawarecountyclerk.org. Search the sheriff's county database of sex offenders, deadbeat parents, and most wanted list for free at www.delawarecountysheriff.com.

Erie County
Vermilion Municipal Court *Civil and Criminal Records*
www.vermilionmunicipalcourt.org
Online access to municipal court records is available at the web site or directly at http://209.142.158.114/search.html.

Fairfield County
Common Pleas Court *Civil and Criminal Records*
Online access to County Clerk's court records database is available free at www.fairfieldcountyclerk.com/Search/.

Franklin County
Common Pleas Court *Civil, Probate, and Marriage Records*
www.franklincountyclerk.com
Access records via the web site. Java-enable web browser required. Online access to probate court records available free at www.co.franklin.oh.us/probate/ProbateSearch.html; search marriage records at www.co.franklin.oh.us/probate/PBMLSearch.html.

Franklin County Municipal Court *Civil and Criminal Records*
www.fcmcclerk.com
Records from the Clerk's database are available free at the Internet site. Search by name, SSN, dates, ticket, DL or case numbers.

Geauga County
Common Pleas Court *Civil and Criminal Records*
www.co.geauga.oh.us
Online access is available free from the Clerk of Courts at www.co.geauga.oh.us/departments/clerk_of_courts/docket/Courtintro.asp. Online records go back to 1990.

Greene County
Common Pleas Court *Civil and Criminal Records*
www.co.greene.oh.us/clerk.htm
Online access to clerk of court records is available free at http://198.30.12.229/pa/pa.htm. Search by name or case number.

Xenia Municipal Court *Civil and Criminal Records*
http://xmcwa.ci.xenia.oh.us
Online access to Municipal Court records is available free through CourtView at http://xmcwa.ci.xenia.oh.us. Access to criminal records is the same as civil.

Hamilton County
Common Pleas Court *Civil, Probate and Criminal Records*
Hamilton County Municipal Court *Civil Records*
www.courtclerk.org
Records from the court clerk are available free online at the web site. Online civil index goes back to 1991. Online criminal index goes back to 1986. Also, each probate records free online back to 1/2000 at www.probatect.org/case_search/cs-scripts/pimain.html.

Knox County
Common Pleas Court *Civil and Criminal Records*
www.knoxcountyclerk.org
Search court index, dockets, calendars free online at www.knoxcountycpcourt.org. Search by name or case number.

Lake County

Common Pleas Court *Civil and Criminal Records*
www.lakecountyohio.org/clerk
Online access to court records, dockets, and quick index are available free at http://web2.lakecountyohio.org/clerk/search.htm.
Includes domestic and appeals cases.

Painesville Municipal Court *Civil and Criminal Records*
www.painesvillemunicipalcourt.org/
Free online access to records at www.painesvillemunicipalcourt.org/search.html.

Lawrence County

Common Pleas Court *Civil and Criminal Records*
www.lawrencecountyclkofcrt.org
Online access to civil records is available free at the web site.

Licking County

Licking County Municipal Court *Civil and Criminal Records*
Online access to Municipal Court records is available free at http://206.31.219.164.

Lorain County

Common Pleas Court *Civil and Criminal Records*
www.loraincounty.com/clerk
The web site offers free access to indices and dockets for civil and domestic relationship cases.

Elyria Municipal Court *Civil Records*
www.elyriamunicourt.org
Search by email to civil@elyriamunicourt.org. Search by email to crtr@elyriamunicourt.org.

Lorain Municipal Court *Civil and Criminal Records*
www.lorainmunicourt.org
Online access to municipal court records available free at www.lorainmunicourt.org/search.shtml. Search by name, date, case number, driver license number or attorney.

Vermilion Municipal Court *Civil and Criminal Records*
www.vermilionmunicipalcourt.org
Online access to municipal court records is available at the web site or directly at http://209.142.158.114/search.html.

Lucas County

Common Pleas Court *Civil and Criminal Records*
www.co.lucas.oh.us/clerk
Online access to clerk of courts dockets is available free at www.co.lucas.oh.us/Clerk/dockets.asp. Online records go back to 9/1997.

Maumee Municipal Court *Civil and Criminal Records*
www.maumee.org/court/court.htm
Online access to the interactive web court system database is available free at www.maumee.org/court/courtsystem/index.html.

Toledo Municipal Court *Civil and Criminal Records*
www.tmc-clerk.com
The daily docket is available online at the web site. Direct email requests to clerk@tmc-clerk.com.

Medina County

Medina Municipal Court *Civil and Criminal Records*
www.medinamunicipalcourt.org
Access to the online system requires Procomm Plus. There are no fees. Search by name or case number. The computer access number is 330-723-4337. For more information, call Rich Armstrong at ext. 230.

Miami County

Miami County Municipal Court *Civil and Criminal Records*
www.onthesquare.com/mc_muni
Online access to Miami County municipal court records is available free at www.co.miami.oh.us/pa/.

Montgomery County

Common Pleas Court *Civil and Criminal Records*
www.clerk.co.montgomery.oh.us
Online access to the Courts county-wide PRO system is available free at www.clerk.co.montgomery.oh.us/pro/index.cfm. Online access to criminal and traffic records is included.

County Court - Area 1 *Civil and Criminal Records*
County Court - Area 2 *Civil and Criminal Records*
http://areacourts.dnaco.net
Search county-wide records online at www.clerk.co.montgomery.oh.us/clerk/pro/index.cfm. Also, online access to area civil/traffic records is available free at http://areacourts.dnaco.net/areaone. Click on "Public records online."

Dayton Municipal Courts *Civil, Traffic and Criminal Records*
www.daytonmunicipalcourt.org
Online access to municipal court records is available free at www.daytonmunicipalcourt.org/scripts/rgw.dll/Docket; includes traffic and criminal.

Muskingum County

County Court *Civil and Criminal Records*
www.muskingumcountycourt.org
Access to county court records is available free at www.muskingumcountycourt.org/sear.html.

Scioto County

Common Pleas Court *Civil and Criminal Records*
www.sciotocountycpcourt.org
Online access to court records available free at www.sciotocountycpcourt.org/search.htm. Search by court calendar, quick index, general index or docket sheet.

Portsmouth Municipal Court *Civil and Criminal Records*
www.portsmouth-municipal-court.com
Online access is available free at www.portsmouth-municipal-court.com/disc.html.

Stark County

Common Pleas Court *Civil and Criminal Records*
www.starkclerk.org
Online access to the county online case docket database is available free at www.starkclerk.org/docket/index.html. Search by name, case number or SSN.

Summit County

Common Pleas Court *Civil and Criminal Records*
Access to County clerk of courts records is available free at www.cpclerk.co.summit.oh.us/ Click on "Case Search.".

Akron Municipal Court *Civil and Criminal Records*
http://courts.ci.akron.oh.us
Online access to court records is available free at http://courts.ci.akron.oh.us/disclaimer.htm.

Barberton Municipal Court *Civil and Criminal Records*
www.cityofbarberton.com/clerkofcourts
Online records for Barberton, Green, Norton, Franklin, Clinton, Copley and Coventry are available free at http://24.93.200.18/.

Trumbull County

Common Pleas Court *Civil, Probate and Criminal Records*
www.clerk.co.trumbull.oh.us

Online access to court records is available free at www.clerk.co.trumbull.oh.us/search/search.htm. Records go back to May, 1996. Online access access to probate court records is available free at www.trumbullprobate.org/paccessfront.htm.

Union County
Common Pleas Court *Civil and Criminal Records*
www.co.union.oh.us/Clerk_of_Courts/clerk_of_courts.html
Online access to the court clerk's public record and index is available free at http://www2.co.union.oh.us/clerkofcourts/. Records go back to 1/1990, older added as accessed. Images go back to 1/2002.

Washington County
Marietta Municipal Court *Civil and Criminal Records*
www.mariettacourt.com
Online access to 4 weeks of dockets are available free at the web site.

Wood County
Bowling Green Municipal Court *Civil and Criminal Records*
www.bgcourt.org
Online access to be available in the Spring of 2003 at the web site.

Perrysburg Municipal Court *Civil and Criminal Records*
www.perrysburgcourt.com/
Online access to court records is available free at www.perrysburgcourt.com/disc.html.

County Level ... Recorders & Assessors

Recording Office Organization: 88 counties, 88 recording offices. The recording officers are the County Recorder and Clerk of Common Pleas Court (state tax liens). The entire state is in the Eastern Time Zone (EST). All federal tax liens are filed with the County Recorder. All state tax liens are filed with the Clerk of Common Pleas Court. Federal tax liens are filed in the "Official Records" of each county. Most counties will not perform a federal tax lien search.

Online Access Note: A growing number of Ohio counties offer online access via the Internet to assessor and real estate data.

Ashland County   *Real Estate, Auditor Records*
Property records on the county Auditor's database are available free online at www.ashlandcoauditor.org/ashland208/landrover.asp.

Ashtabula County   *Real Estate, Auditor Records*
www.co.ashtabula.oh.us
Property records on the county Auditor's database are available free online at http://216.28.192.48/ashtabula208/LandRover.asp.

Athens County   *Property, Deed, UCC Records*
Access to county land and UCC records is available free at www.landaccess.com. Records go back to 1/1981.

Brown County   *Property, Deed, UCC Records*
Access to recordorings is available free at www.landaccess.com/sites/oh/brown/index.php.

Butler County   *Property, Deed, UCC, Probate, Voter Registration Records*
www.butlercountyohio.org/recorder
County voter records are available at www.butlercountyohio.org/elections. County probate records are available at www.butlercountyohio.org/probate/estate.cfm. Search auditor records at http://propertysearch.butlercountyohio.org/butler/. Also, online access to county land and UCC records is available free at www.landaccess.com. Records go back to 1/1987. Online access to dog license registrations is available at www.butlercountyohio.org/auditor/dl_search.cfm; county available property at www.butlercountyohio.org/edabc/availand_index.html

Clark County   *Property, Deed, UCC Records*

Access to county land and UCC records is available free at www.landaccess.com. Records go back to 1/1988.

Clermont County   *Property, Deed, UCC Records*

www.landaccess.com

Records from the assessor's county property database are available free online at http://clermont.akanda.com. Also, free access to the recorder's property, deed, and UCC records is available at www.landaccess.com/sites/oh/clermont/index.php.

Columbiana County   *Real Estate, Auditor Records*

www.columbianacntyauditor.org

Property records on the county Auditor's database are available free online at www.columbianacntyauditor.org/columbv208/LandRover.asp.

Coshocton County   *Property, Deed, UCC Records*

Access to county land and UCC records is available free at www.landaccess.com. Records go back to 1/1980.

Cuyahoga County   *Auditor/Assessor, Probate, Marriage, Real Estate, Tax Lien, Recording, Dog Tag, Most Wanted, Sexual Predator Records*

www.cuyahoga.oh.us/recorder

Access to the County Auditor Property Information database is available free at http://198.30.214.5/auditor/propinfo/Default.asp. Also, the Recorder's db has all land document records from 1965-2002. Online access to the Recorders database is available free at http://198.30.212.18/presearch.cfm. And, search 22 catagories of Probate records including marriages free online at http://198.30.212.11/pa.urd/pamw6500.display. Also, the sexual predator data and most wanted lists are at www.cuyahoga.oh.us/sheriff/law/sou/sou_disclaimer.htm. Foreclosure sales: www.cuyahoga.oh.us/sheriff/foreclosures/sales.htm. Lost dogs: http://198.30.214.5/auditor/genservices/finddog.asp.

Darke County   *Real Estate, Deed, UCC Records*

Property records on the Darke County database are available free online at www.darkecountyrealestate.org. Also, online access to county land and UCC records is available free at www.landaccess.com. Records go back to 1/1996.

Delaware County   *Real Estate, Auditor, Sheriff Sales Records*

www.co.delaware.oh.us

The Delaware Appraisal Land Information System Project (DALIS) maps with County Auditor records are available free online. At main site, click on "GIS mapping" in the lefthand menu bar, then select a search method. Once parcel is identified on the map, click on "identify" then on parcel map to get parcel information, values, sales, and building information. Also, access to auditor's property information is available free at www.delawarecountyauditor.org/delaware208/LandRover.asp. Sheriff sales information is available free at www.delawarecountysheriff.com.

Fairfield County   *Property, Deed, UCC, Auditor Records*

www.co.fairfield.oh.us

Access to county land and UCC records is available free at www.landaccess.com. Records go back to 8/1996. Also, online access to the Auditor's property database is available free at http://realestate.co.fairfield.oh.us/. Also, access to the sheriff's real estate sale list and sex offenders list is available free at www.sheriff.fairfield.oh.us/

Franklin County   *Property, Auditor, Unclaimed Funds, Marriage Records*

www.co.franklin.oh.us/recorder/

Access to the recordors data is available free at www.co.franklin.oh.us/recorder/documents.html. Free registration required. Search veterans graves at http://mvsp.co.franklin.oh.us:5080/cics/cwba/dfhwbtta/rg11. Search marriage licenses back to 1995 free at www.co.franklin.oh.us/probate/PBMLSearch.html. Also, search unclimed funds at www.co.franklin.oh.us/auditor/fiscal_services/unclaimed%20funds.html. Also, the auditor's property database at http://64.56.97.159/realestate/ and other county/municipal court databases are available free at www.co.franklin.oh.us.

Fulton County   *Property, Deed, UCC Records*

www.fultoncountyoh.com

Access to property, deed, and UCC records is to be available free at www.landaccess.com.

Gallia County   *Property, Real Estate Records*
http://galliaauditor.ddti.net
Property records on the county auditor real estate database are available free online at http://galliaauditor.ddti.net. Click on "attributes" for property information; click on "sales" to search by real estate attributes.

Geauga County   *Delinquent Property Tax Records*
Search the treasurer's delinquent tax list free at www.co.geauga.oh.us/departments/treasurer/rp_tax_delq_lst.htm.

Greene County   *Real Estate, Auditor, Recording, Deed, Mortgage, Grantor/Grantee Records*
www.co.greene.oh.us/recorder.htm
Access to the recorders data is available free at http://198.30.12.229/recdoc.asp. Also, records on the county Internet Map Server are available free online at www.co.greene.oh.us/gismapserver.htm. Click on "Click here to enter. Server Site #1". Data includes owner, address, valuation, taxes, sales data, and parcel ID number.

Hamilton County   *Real Estate, Lien, Recording, Lien, Deed, Mortgage, UCC, Auditor Records*
www.recordersoffice.hamilton-co.org
Access to county recorder records is available free at www.recordersoffice.hamilton-co.org. Also, online access to the auditor's tax records database is available free at www.hamiltoncountyauditor.org./realestate/. Also, search probate records back to 1/2000 at www.probatect.org/case_search/cs-scripts/pimain.html.

Hancock County   *Property Auditor Records*
Search the auditor's property database free at http://hancock.iviewauditor.com. No name searching.

Hardin County   *Property Records*
www.co.hardin.oh.us
Property records from the county database are available at the web site. Click on "Real Estate Internet Inquiry."

Highland County   *Property, Deed, UCC Records*
www.ohiorecorders.com
Access to recordings is available free at www.landaccess.com/sites/oh/highland/index.php.

Knox County   *Property Records*
Records on the county auditor database are available free online at www.knoxcountyauditor.org/knox208/LandRover.asp.

Lake County   *Real Estate, Auditor, Recording, Lien, Deed Records*
www.lakecountyrecorder.org
Access to the Recorder's Document Index database is available free at http://web2.lakecountyohio.org/recorders/search/index.asp. Records go back to 1986. Also, access to the treasurer and auditor's real estate databases is available free at www.lake.iviewauditor.com. Click on "by attribute." Also, online access to Land Bank sales is available at www.lakecountyohio.org/auditor/index.htm and click on "Land Bank Sales". Access warrants and sex offenders lists at www.lakecountyohio.org/sheriff/index.htm.

Lawrence County   *Real Estate, Deed, Mortgage, Lien Records*
www.lawrencecountyohiorecorder.org
Search the recorders data free at www.lawrencecountyohiorecorder.org/record_search.htm. Deeds go back to 1983; mortgages to 1988; liens back to 1981; financing statements to 1989. Documents filed since 1/1997 can be printed.

Licking County   *Real Estate, Tax Lien, Recording, Property Tax Records*
www.lcounty.com/rec/
Access to the county recorders database is available free at www.lcounty.com/recordings/. Records with images go back to 1997. Also, online access to the Auditor's county property database is available free at www.lcounty.com/licking208/.

Logan County   *Real Estate, Auditor Records*
www.co.logan.oh.us/recorder/
Records on the County Auditor's database are available free online at www2.co.logan.oh.us/logan208/LandRover.asp. Also, online access to the recorders database is available free at http://www3.co.logan.oh.us/record30.asp. Click on "Document Search."

Lorain County   *Real Estate, Lien, Auditor Records*

www.loraincounty.com/government/

Access to the county assessor database is available free at www.loraincounty.com/recorder/register. Free registration is required. Also, records on the County Auditor's database are available free at www.loraincountyauditor.org/lorain208/LandRover.asp.

Lucas County   *Real Estate, Auditor, Unclaimed Funds, Sheriff Sale Records*

www.co.lucas.oh.us

Property records on the County Auditor's Real Estate Information System (AREIS) database are available free online at www.co.lucas.oh.us/Areis/areismain.asp. This replaces the old system. Also, online access to the treasurer's unclaimed funds and sheriff sale lists are available free at www.raytkest.com.

Madison County   *Real Estate, Auditor, Deed, UCC Records*

www.co.madison.oh.us/elected.htm

Records on the County Auditor's database are available free online at www.co.madison.oh.us/auditor/iView/iView.asp. Also, online access to county land and UCC records is available free at www.landaccess.com. Records go back to 5/1994.

Mahoning County   *Real Estate, Auditor, Deed, UCC Records*

www.mahoningcountyauditor.org

Property records on the County Auditor's database are available free online at www.mahoningcountyauditor.org/maho208/LandRover.asp. Also, property, deed, and UCC records are to be available free at www.landaccess.com.

Marion County   *Real Estate, Auditor Records*

www.co.marion.oh.us

Access to the county auditor real estate database is available free at www.co.marion.oh.us. Click on "Real Estate Inquiry."

Medina County   *Real Estate, Auditor Records*

www.recorder.co.medina.oh.us

Access to indexes 1983 to present on the County Recorder database is available free at www.recorder.co.medina.oh.us/indexes2.htm. Click on "Indexes" and use "View" as user name and password. Also, online access to property records on the Medina County Auditor database are available free online at www.medinacountyauditor.org - "Public Records." Also, find a lost dog's owner at www.medinacountyauditor.org/finddog.htm. The sheriff's sex offender list is available via www.medinasheriff.com.

Mercer County   *Real Estate, Auditor Records*

www.mercercountyohio.org

Property records on the County Auditor - Real Estate Department database are available free online at www.mercercountyohio.org/auditor/RealEstate/PcardInq/category.htm.

Montgomery County   *Property, Real Estate, Lien, Recording Records*

www.mcrecorder.org

Access to the recorders data is available free at www.mcrecorder.org/search_selection.cfm. Also, property records on the county treasurer real estate tax information database are available free online at www.mctreas.org.

Muskingum County   *Real Estate, Assessor Records*

www.muskingumcountyauditor.org

Records on the county assessor database are available free online at www.muskingumcountyauditor.org/realestate/LandRover.asp

Preble County   *Real Estate, Auditor Records*

Property records on the County Auditor's database are available free online at www.preblecountyauditor.org/preble208/LandRover.asp.

Richland County   *Real Estate, Auditor, Deed, UCC Records*

Property records from the County Auditor database are available free online at www.richlandcountyauditor.org. Also, online access to county land and UCC records is available free at www.landaccess.com. Records go back to 4/1989.

Ross County   *Property, Deed, UCC Records*

Access to county land and UCC records is available free at www.landaccess.com. Records go back to 1/1974.

Stark County   *Real Estate, Deed, Recording Records*
www.recorder.co.stark.oh.us
Access to the recorder's database is available free at www.recorder.co.stark.oh.us/DTS/. Chose from simple, advanced or instrument search. Also, the elected officials list is available free at www.stark.lib.oh.us/officials.html. Also, online access to the sheriff sales lists are available free at www.sheriff.co.stark.oh.us/RealEstate.htm. Sex offenders list is at www.sheriff.co.stark.oh.us/OffenderLinks.htm.

Summit County   *Real Estate, Auditor, Property Tax, Recording Records*
www.co.summit.oh.us
Tax map information from the county auditor is available free online at http://scids.summitoh.net/taxmapsinternet, also property appraisal and tax information at www.summitoh.net. Access to the full document images database requires registration, password and one-time $150.00 fee. Call Summit County Data Center, Help Desk at 330-643-2687 for information and sign-up. Images are available from the recorder division at www.summitoh.net/rec/html/rcd4.html. The Sheriff's sex offenders list is available at www.co.summit.oh.us/sheriff/sexoffenders01.htm.

Trumbull County   *Auditor, Property Tax, Recording, Deed, Mortgage, Lien Records*
Access to the recorder's database requires free registration and password at http://tcrecorder.co.trumbull.oh.us/index.cfm. Dog registration is at www.dogtagsplus.com/Start.asp?CountyID=2. Also, real estate records from the County Auditor available free at www.co.auditor.trumbull.oh.us/propertymax/LandRover.asp. Also, unclaimed funds list is available from probate court at www.trumbullprobate.org/UnclaimedFunds.htm. The Sheriff's warrants list is at www.sheriff.co.trumbull.oh.us/warrants.htm.

Tuscarawas County   *Real Estate, Unclaimed Funds Records*
www.co.tuscarawas.oh.us
County real estate records are available free online at www.co.tuscarawas.oh.us/Auditor/realsearch.htm. The auditor's deliquent tax list is available in September. Also, the countyauditor's list of Unclaimed Funds may be searched at www.co.tuscarawas.oh.us/Auditor/Unclaimed%20Funds.htm. Also, the clerk of court's page (see county main web site) can be searched free for unclaimed funds and outstanding checks.

Union County   *Auditor, Property Tax, Real Estate, Recording, Delinquent Taxpayers Records*
Access to the Auditors tax assessment/property records database and the appriaser property information database is available free at http://www2.co.union.oh.us/PropInfoGuide.htm. You may also search for property information via the online GIS map. Search the treasurers list of delinquent taxpayers at www.co.union.oh.us/Treasurer/List_of_Delinquent_Taxpayers/list_of_delinquent_taxpayers.html.

Van Wert County   *Property, Deed, UCC Records*
Access to county land and UCC records is available free at www.landaccess.com. Records go back to 1/1994.

Warren County   *Real Estate, Auditor Records*
www.co.warren.oh.us
Access to the county auditor database is available free at www.co.warren.oh.us/auditor/index.htm. Click on Warren County Property Information Search at the bottom of web page.

Washington County   *Property, Auditor, Deed, UCC Records*
www.ohiorecorders.com
Access to the county auditor's Property search database is available free at www.washingtoncountyauditor.org/washington208/LandRover.asp. Also, access to property, deed, and UCC records is available free at www.landaccess.com/sites/oh/washington/index.php

Wyandot County   *Real Estate, Auditor Records*
Access to the Auditor's real estate database is available free at www.co.wyandot.oh.us/auditor/default.html. Click on "Real estate Internet Inquiry." Site may be down.

Federal Courts in Ohio...

Standards for Federal Courts: The universal PACER sign-up number is 800-676-6856. Find PACER and the Party/Case Index on the Web at http://pacer.psc.uscourts.gov. PACER dial-up access is $.60 per minute. Also, courts offering internet access via RACER, PACER, Web-PACER or the new CM-ECF charge $.07 per page fee unless noted as free.

US District Court -- Northern District of Ohio

Home Page: www.ohnd.uscourts.gov
PACER: Toll-free access: 800-673-4409. Local access phone: 216-522-3669. Many cases prior to the indicated dates are also online. Case records are available back to January 1, 1990. Records are purged never. New records are available online after 1 day. **PACER URL:** http://pacer.ohnd.uscourts.gov. Use the CM/ECF system (below) when PACER is phased out.
Electronic Filing: Electronic filing information is available online at http://ecf.ohnd.uscourts.gov.
Akron Division counties: Carroll, Holmes, Portage, Stark, Summit, Tuscarawas, Wayne. Cases filed prior to 1995 for counties in the Youngstown Division may be located here.
Cleveland Division counties: Ashland, Ashtabula, Crawford, Cuyahoga, Geauga, Lake, Lorain, Medina, Richland. Cases prior to July 1995 for the counties of Ashland, Crawford, Medina and Richland are located in the Akron Division. Cases filed prior to 1995 from the counties in the Youngstown Division may be located here.
Toledo Division counties: Allen, Auglaize, Defiance, Erie, Fulton, Hancock, Hardin, Henry, Huron, Lucas, Marion, Mercer, Ottawa, Paulding, Putnam, Sandusky, Seneca, Van Wert, Williams, Wood, Wyandot.
Youngstown Division counties: Columbiana, Mahoning, Trumbull. This division was reactivated in the middle of 1995. Older cases will be found in Akron or Cleveland.

US Bankruptcy Court -- Northern District of Ohio

Home Page: www.ohnb.uscourts.gov
PACER: Case records are available back to January 1985. Records are purged only up to September 1990. New civil records are available online after 2 days. **PACER URL:** http://pacer.ohnb.uscourts.gov.
Electronic Filing: Electronic filing information is available online at https://ecf.ohnb.uscourts.gov. **Also:** access via phone on VCIS (Voice Case Information System) is available: 800-898-6899, 330-489-4731
Akron Division counties: Medina, Portage, Summit.
Canton Division counties: Ashland, Carroll, Crawford, Holmes, Richland, Stark, Tuscarawas, Wayne.
Cleveland Division counties: Cuyahoga, Geauga, Lake, Lorain.
Toledo Division counties: Allen, Auglaize, Defiance, Erie, Fulton, Hancock, Hardin, Henry, Huron, Lucas, Marion, Mercer, Ottawa, Paulding, Putnam, Sandusky, Seneca, Van Wert, Williams, Wood, Wyandot.
Youngstown Division counties: Ashtabula, Columbiana, Mahoning, Trumbull.

US District Court -- Southern District of Ohio

Home Page: www.ohsd.uscourts.gov
PACER: Toll-free access: 800-710-4939. Local access phone: 614-469-6990. Case records are available back to 1994. Records are purged never. New records are available online after 1 day. **PACER URL:** http://pacer.ohsd.uscourts.gov.
Cincinnati Division counties: Adams, Brown, Butler, Clermont, Clinton, Hamilton, Highland, Lawrence, Scioto, Warren.
Columbus Division counties: Athens, Belmont, Coshocton, Delaware, Fairfield, Fayette, Franklin, Gallia, Guernsey, Harrison, Hocking, Jackson, Jefferson, Knox, Licking, Logan, Madison, Meigs, Monroe, Morgan, Morrow, Muskingum, Noble, Perry, Pickaway, Pike, Ross, Union, Vinton, Washington.
Dayton Division counties: Champaign, Clark, Darke, Greene, Miami, Montgomery, Preble, Shelby.

US Bankruptcy Court -- Southern District of Ohio

Home Page: www.ohsb.uscourts.gov
PACER: Toll-free access: 800-793-7003. Local access phone: 937-225-7561. Case records are available back to 1990. Records are purged every six months. New civil records are available online after 1 day. **PACER URL:** http://pacer.ohsb.uscourts.gov.
Electronic Filing: (Currently in the process of implementing CM/ECF). **Also:** access via phone on VCIS (Voice Case Information System) is available: 800-726-1004, 937-225-2544
Cincinnati Division counties: Adams, Brown, Clermont, Hamilton, Highland, Lawrence, Scioto and a part of Butler.
Columbus Division counties: Athens, Belmont, Coshocton, Delaware, Fairfield, Fayette, Franklin, Gallia, Guernsey, Harrison, Hocking, Jackson, Jefferson, Knox, Licking, Logan, Madison, Meigs, Monroe, Morgan, Morrow, Muskingum, Noble, Perry, Pickaway, Pike, Ross, Union, Vinton, Washington.
Dayton Division counties: Butler, Champaign, Clark, Clinton, Darke, Greene, Miami, Montgomery, Preble, Shelby, Warren; parts of Butler County are handled by Cincinnati Division.

Oklahoma

Capital:	Oklahoma City Oklahoma County	Home Page	www.state.ok.us
Time Zone:	CST	Attorney General	www.oag.state.ok.us
Number of Counties:	77	Archives	www.odl.state.ok.us

State Level ... Major Agencies

Uniform Commercial Code

UCC Recorder, Oklahoma County Clerk, 320 R.S. Kerr Ave, County Office Bldg, Rm 105, Oklahoma City, OK 73102; 405-713-1521, 405-713-1810 (Fax), 8AM-5PM.

www.oklahomacounty.org/countyclerk

Records of all UCC financing statements may be viewed free on the Internet at www.oklahomacounty.org/coclerk/default.htm. Neither certified searches nor record requests are accepted at the web. **Other options:** The entire database is available on microfilm or computer tapes, prices start at $500.

Incarceration Records

Information on current and former inmates is available at www.doc.state.ok.us. Location, physical identifiers, conviction and sentencing information, and release dates are provided.

Sexual Offender Records

Sexual offeser records are availabler at www.doc.state.ok.us/DOCS/offender_info.htm

Legislation Records

www.lsb.state.ok.us

The web page provides a variety of legislative information including searching by topic or bill number.

State Level ... Occupational Licensing

Accounting Firm	www.state.ok.us/~oab/firms.html
Architect	www.state.ok.us/~architects/architects.html
Audiologist	www.obespa.state.ok.us/License%20Data.htm
Bank	www.state.ok.us/~osbd/
Consumer Finance Company	www.okdocc.state.ok.us/introSL.htm
Credit Services Organization	www.okdocc.state.ok.us/introCSO.htm
Credit Union	www.state.ok.us/~osbd/
Dental Hygienist	www.dentist.state.ok.us/lists/index.htm
Dental Laboratory	www.dentist.state.ok.us/lists/index.htm
Dentist/Dental Assistant	www.dentist.state.ok.us/lists/index.htm
Dietitian/Provisional Licensed Dietitian	www.okmedicalboard.org/medboard/index.php
Electrologist	www.okmedicalboard.org/medboard/index.php
Engineer	www.okpels.org/rosters.htm
Funeral Home	www.okfuneral.com/funeralhomedirectory/index.htm
Health Spa	www.okdocc.state.ok.us/introSpa.htm
Investment Company	www.securities.state.ok.us/_private/DB_Query/Corp_Fin_Search.htm
Landscape Architect	www.state.ok.us/~architects/landscape.html
Lobbyist	www.state.ok.us/~ethics/lobbyist.html
Medical Doctor	www.okmedicalboard.org/medboard/index.php
Midwife Nurse	www.youroklahoma.com/nursing/verify/
Money Order Agent	www.state.ok.us/~osbd/
Mortgage Banker	www.okdocc.state.ok.us/introMB.htm
Nurse Anesthetist	www.youroklahoma.com/nursing/verify/
Nurse Specialist, Clinical	www.youroklahoma.com/nursing/verify/
Nurse-RN/LPN	www.youroklahoma.com/nursing/verify/
Occupational Therapist/Assistant	www.okmedicalboard.org/medboard/index.php
Optometrist	www.odfinder.org/LicSearch.asp
Orthotist/Prosthetist	www.okmedicalboard.org/medboard/index.php
Osteopathic Physician	www.docboard.org/ok/df/oksearch.htm
Pawnbroker	www.okdocc.state.ok.us/introPB.htm
Perdorthist	www.okmedicalboard.org/medboard/index.php
Perfusionist	www.okmedicalboard.org/medboard/index.php
Physical Therapist/Assistant	www.okmedicalboard.org/medboard/index.php
Physician Assistant	www.okmedicalboard.org/medboard/index.php
Precious Metals & Gem Dealer	www.okdocc.state.ok.us/introPMD.htm
Private Investigator/Agency	www.opia.com/searches/search.html
Public Accountant-CPA	www.state.ok.us/~oab/twotier.html
Real Estate Appraiser	www.asc.gov/content/category1/appr_by_state.asp
Real Estate Broker/Salesperson/Corp./Partnership	www.orec.state.ok.us/agents2.html
Rent to Own Dealer	www.okdocc.state.ok.us/introRTO.htm
Respiratory Care Practitioner	www.okmedicalboard.org/medboard/index.php
Savings & Loan Association	www.state.ok.us/~osbd/
Speech Pathologist	www.obespa.state.ok.us/License%20Data.htm
Surveyor, Land	www.okpels.org/rosters.htm
Trust Company	www.state.ok.us/~osbd/

County Level ... Courts

Court Administration: Administrative Director of Courts, 1915 N Stiles #305, Oklahoma City, OK, 73105; 405-521-2450; www.oscn.net

Court Structure: There are 80 District Courts in 26 judicial districts. Cities with populations in excess of 200,000 (Oklahoma City and Tulsa) have municipal criminal courts of record. Cities with less than 200,000 do not have such courts. The small claims limit was raised from $3000 to $4500 in 1998.

Online Access Note: Free Internet access is available for eight District Courts and all Appellate courts at www.oscn.net. Both civil and criminal docket information is available. The counties are Canadian, Cleveland, Comanche, Garfield, Oklahoma, Payne, Rogers, and Tulsa.

Also, launched in 2002 is the Oklahoma District Court Records free web site at www.odcr.com where you may search twelve District Courts databases - Bryan, Craig, Creek, Garvin, Haskell, Hughes, Kay, Lincoln, Mayes, Noble, Pawnee, and Pottawatomie Counties. More counties are being added as they are readied; they hope to eventually feature all Okla. District courts.

Also, one can search the Oklahoma Supreme Court Network by single cite or multiple cite (no name searches) from the www.oscn.net Internet site. Case information is available in bulk form for downloading to computer. For information, call the Administrative Director of Courts, 405-521-2450.

Access to the Oklahoma District Court Records site is available free at www.odcr.com and includes the District Courts in the following counties:

Bryan County	**Kay County**
Craig County	**Lincoln County**
Creek County	**Mayes County**
Garvin County	**Noble County**
Haskell County	**Pawnee County**
Hughes County	**Pottawatamie County**

Canadian County
26th Judicial District Court *Civil and Criminal Records*
Online access to court dockets available free online at www.oscn.net/applications/oscn/casesearch.asp. Dockets go back to 3/1983.

Carter County
20th Judicial District Court *Criminal Records*
www.brightok.net/chickasaw/ardmore/county/crtclerk.html
Only current week dockets are available online at clerk's web site. Only current week dockets and bench warrants are available online at clerk's web site.

Cleveland County
21st Judicial District Court *Civil and Criminal Records*
Online access to court dockets available free online at www.oscn.net/applications/oscn/casesearch.asp. Dockets go back to 1/1989..

Comanche County
5th Judicial District Court *Civil and Criminal Records*
Online access to court dockets available free online at www.oscn.net/applications/oscn/casesearch.asp. Dockets go back to 8/1988.

Garfield County
4th Judicial District Court *Civil and Criminal Records*
Online access to court dockets available free online at www.oscn.net/applications/oscn/casesearch.asp. Dockets go back to 3/1989.

Garvin County

21st Judicial District Court *Civil and Criminal Records*
Online access to court dockets available free online at www.oscn.net/applications/oscn/casesearch.asp. Also, access to the OK Dist. Ct. Records site is available free at www.odcr.com.

McCurtain County

17th Judicial District Court *Civil and Criminal Records*
Online access to court records via the statewide OSCN system is pending.

Oklahoma County

District Court *Civil and Criminal Records*
Online access to court dockets available free online at www.oscn.net/applications/oscn/casesearch.asp. Civil dockets go back to 12/1984. Criminal dockets go back to 9/1988. The sheriff's current inmates and warrants list is available free at www.oklahomacounty.org/cosheriff/.

Payne County

9th Judicial District Court *Civil and Criminal Records*
Online access to court dockets available free online at www.oscn.net/applications/oscn/casesearch.asp. Dockets go back to 1/1994.

Rogers County

12th Judicial District Court *Civil and Criminal Records*
Online access to court dockets available free online at www.oscn.net/applications/oscn/casesearch.asp. Dockets go back to 7/1997.

Tulsa County

14th Judicial District Court *Civil and Criminal Records*
Online access to court dockets available free online at www.oscn.net/applications/oscn/casesearch.asp. Civil dockets go back to 10/1984. Criminal dockets go back to 1/1988.

County Level ... Recorders & Assessors

Recording Office Organization: 77 counties, 77 recording offices. The recording officer is the County Clerk. The state is in the Central Time Zone (CST). Federal tax liens on personal property of businesses are filed with the County Clerk of Oklahoma County, which is the central filing office for the state. Other federal and all state tax liens are filed with the County Clerk. Usually state and federal tax liens on personal property are filed in separate indexes. Some counties will perform tax lien searches. Search fees vary.

Online Access Note: Very little is available online.

Carter County   *Assessor, Unsolved Case Records*

www.brightok.net/chickasaw/ardmore/county/coclerk.html
The sheriff's unsolved mysteries page is available free at www.brightok.net/chickasaw/ardmore/county/unsolved.html. Search the county assessor database for free at www.cartercountyassessor.org/disclaim.htm.

Oklahoma County   *Real Estate, Assessor, Grantor/Grantee, UCC Records*

www.oklahomacounty.org
Assessor and property information on the county assessor database are available free online at www.oklahomacounty.org/assessor/disclaim.htm. Real estate, UCC, grantor/grantee records on the county clerk database are available free online at www.oklahomacounty.org/coclerk.

Washington County   *Land, Deed, Mortgage, Lien, Sex Offender Records*

www.countycourthouse.org
Access to the recorders database is available free at www.countycourthouse.org/countyclerk/disclaimer.htm. Also, access to the sex offenders registry is available free at www.countycourthouse.org/registry/index.htm.

Federal Courts in Oklahoma...

Standards for Federal Courts: The universal PACER sign-up number is 800-676-6856. Find PACER and the Party/Case Index on the Web at http://pacer.psc.uscourts.gov. PACER dial-up access is $.60 per minute. Also, courts offering internet access via RACER, PACER, Web-PACER or the new CM-ECF charge $.07 per page fee unless noted as free.

US District Court -- Eastern District of Oklahoma
Home Page: www.oked.uscourts.gov

PACER: Toll-free access: 866-863-3767. Local access phone: 918-687-2625. Case records are available back to 1996. Records are purged never. New records are available online after 1 day. .

Muskogee Division counties: Adair, Atoka, Bryan, Carter, Cherokee, Choctaw, Coal, Haskell, Hughes, Johnston, Latimer, Le Flore, Love, McCurtain, McIntosh, Marshall, Murray, Muskogee, Okfuskee, Pittsburg, Pontotoc, Pushmataha, Seminole, Sequoyah, Wagoner.

US Bankruptcy Court -- Eastern District of Oklahoma
Home Page: www.okeb.uscourts.gov

PACER: Toll-free access: 866-863-3767. Local access phone: 918-756-4812. Case records are available back to 1986. Records are purged every six months. New civil records are available online after 1 day. **PACER URL:** http://pacer.okeb.uscourts.gov. Document images available.

Electronic Filing: (Currently in the process of implementing CM/ECF). **Also:** access via phone on VCIS (Voice Case Information System) is available: 877-377-1221, 918-756-8617

Okmulgee Division counties: Adair, Atoka, Bryan, Carter, Cherokee, Choctaw, Coal, Haskell, Hughes, Johnston, Latimer, Le Flore, Love, Marshall, McCurtain, McIntosh, Murray, Muskogee, Okfuskee, Okmulgee, Pittsburg, Pontotoc, Pushmataha, Seminole, Sequoyah, Wagoner.

US District Court -- Northern District of Oklahoma
Home Page: www.oknd.uscourts.gov

PACER: Toll-free access: 888-881-0574. Local access phone: 918-699-4742. Document images available. Case records are available back to 1992. New records are available after 1 day. **PACER URL:** http://pacer.oknd.uscourts.gov. Document images available.

Other Online Access: Search records on the Internet using RACER at www.oknd.uscourts.gov/perl/bkplog.html.

Tulsa Division counties: Craig, Creek, Delaware, Mayes, Nowata, Okmulgee, Osage, Ottawa, Pawnee, Rogers, Tulsa, Washington.

US Bankruptcy Court -- Northern District of Oklahoma
Home Page: www.oknb.uscourts.gov

PACER: Toll-free access: 800-790-0860. Local access phone: 918-699-4033. Case records are available back to 1990. Records are purged never. New civil records are available online after 1 day.

Other Online Access: Search records on the Internet using RACER at www.oknb.uscourts.gov/perl/bkplog.html. Access fee is $.07 per page. **Also:** access via phone on VCIS (Voice Case Information System) is available: 888-501-6977, 918-699-4001

Tulsa Division counties: Craig, Creek, Delaware, Mayes, Nowata, Osage, Ottawa, Pawnee, Rogers, Tulsa, Washington.

US District Court -- Western District of Oklahoma
Home Page: www.okwd.uscourts.gov

PACER: Toll-free access: 888-699-7068. Local access phone: 405-231-4531. Case records are available back to 1991. Records are purged never. New records are available online after 2 days. **PACER URL:** http://pacer.okwd.uscourts.gov.

Oklahoma City Division counties: Alfalfa, Beaver, Beckham, Blaine, Caddo, Canadian, Cimarron, Cleveland, Comanche, Cotton, Custer, Dewey, Ellis, Garfield, Garvin, Grady, Grant, Greer, Harmon, Harper, Jackson, Jefferson, Kay, Kingfisher, Kiowa, Lincoln, Logan, McClain, Major, Noble,Oklahoma, Payne, Pottawatomie, Roger Mills, Stephens, Texas, Tillman, Washita, Woods, Woodward.

US Bankruptcy Court -- Western District of Oklahoma
PACER: Case records are available back to May 1, 1992. Records are purged every six months. New civil records are available online after 1 day. **Also:** access via phone on VCIS (Voice Case Information System) is available: 800-872-1348, 405-231-4768

Oklahoma City Division counties: Alfalfa, Beaver, Beckham, Blaine, Caddo, Canadian, Cimarron, Cleveland, Comanche, Cotton, Custer, Dewey, Ellis, Garfield, Garvin, Grady, Grant, Greer, Harmon, Harper, Jackson, Jefferson, Kay, Kingfisher, Kiowa, Lincoln, Logan, Major, McClain, Noble,Oklahoma, Payne, Pottawatomie, Roger Mills, Stephens, Texas, Tillman, Washita, Woods, Woodward.

Capital:	Salem	Home Page
	Marion County	www.state.or.us
Time Zone:	PST	Attorney General www.doj.state.or.us
Number of Counties:	36	Archives http://arcweb.sos.state.or.us

State Level ... Major Agencies

Criminal Records

Oregon State Police, Unit 11, Identification Services Section, PO Box 4395, Portland, OR 97208-4395 (Courier: 3772 Portland Rd NE, Bldg C, Salem, OR 97303); 503-378-3070, 503-378-2121 (Fax), 8AM-5PM.

www.osp.state.or.us

A web based site is available for requesting and receiving criminal records. Web site is ONLY for high-volume requesters who must be pre-approved. Results are posted as "No Record" or "In Process" ("In Process" means a record will be mailed in 14 days). Use the "open records" link to get into the proper site. Fee is $12.00 per record. Call 503-373-1808, ext 230 to receive the application, or visit the web site.

Corporation Records, Limited Partnership Records, Trademarks/Servicemarks, Fictitious Name, Assumed Name, Limited Liability Company Records

Corporation Division, Public Service Building, 255 Capital St NE, #151, Salem, OR 97310-1327; 503-986-2200, 503-378-4381 (Fax), 8AM-5PM.

www.filinginoregon.com

There is free, limited access at the web site for business registry information. A commercial dial-up system is also available. Call 503-229-5133 for details. In addition, the complete database can be purchased with monthly updates via email, call 503-986-2343. **Other options:** A subscription service for new business lists and tapes of the database are available for $15.00 per month or $150.00 for an annual subscription. Call 503-986-2343 for more information.

Uniform Commercial Code, Federal Tax Liens, State Tax Liens

UCC Division, Sec. of State, 255 Capitol St NE, Suite 151, Salem, OR 97310-1327; 503-986-2200, 503-373-1166 (Fax), 8AM-5PM.

www.sos.state.or.us/corporation/

UCC index information can be obtained for free from the web site. You can search by debtor name or by lien number. You can also download forms from here. **Other options:** Monthly UCC information is released via email or diskette. Prices start at $15.00 per month or $150.00 annually for new filings, or $200 per month for all active filings. For more information, call Program Services at 503-986-2212.

Legislation Records

Oregon Legislative Assembly, Legislative Publications, 900 Court St, #49, Salem, OR 97310; 503-986-1180 (Current Bill Information), 503-373-0701 (Archives), 503-373-1527 (Fax), 8AM-5PM.

www.leg.state.or.us

Text and histories of measures can be found at the Internet site for no charge.

State Level ... Occupational Licensing

Acupuncturist	www.bme.state.or.us/search.html
Animal Feed (Livestock)	www.oda.state.or.us/dbs/licenses/search.lasso?&division=commercial_feed
Animal Food Processor	www.oda.state.or.us/dbs/licenses/search.lasso?&division=ahid
Architect	www.architect-board.state.or.us/A-B.htm
Architectural Firm	www.architect-board.state.or.us/ARFirms.htm
Attorney	www.osbcle.org/members/start.asp
Audiologist	http://bspa.ohd.hr.state.or.us
Bakery	www.oda.state.or.us/dbs/licenses/search.lasso?&division=fsd
Bank	www.cbs.state.or.us/external/dfcs/banking/regagent.htm
Brand (Livestock - Available)	www.oda.state.or.us/dbs/search.lasso
Brand Inspector	www.oda.state.or.us/dbs/brandinspector/search.lasso
Building Official	www.cbs.state.or.us/external/imd/database/bcd/licensing/index.html
Check & Money Order Seller	www.oregondfcs.org/e_commerce/m_tran/m_tran.htm
Chiropractor/Chiropractic Assistant	www.obce.state.or.us
Christmas Tree Grower	www.oda.state.or.us/dbs/licenses/search.lasso?&division=nursery
Collection Agency	www.oregondfcs.org/ca/ca.htm
Construction Contractor/Subcontractor	www.ccb.state.or.us/newq_start.htm
Consumer Finance Company	www.cbs.state.or.us/external/dfcs/cf/cfdatabase/search_main.htm
Credit Service Organization	www.oregondfcs.org/cso/cso.htm
Credit Union	www.cbs.state.or.us/external/dfcs/cu/cuagents.htm
Dairy Industries	www.oda.state.or.us/dbs/licenses/search.lasso?&division=fsd
Debt Consolidation Agency	www.cbs.state.or.us/external/dfcs/dca/lic_dca.htm
Dentist	www.oregondentistry.org/
Egg Handler/Breaker	www.oda.state.or.us/dbs/licenses/search.lasso?&division=fsd
Electrical Installation	www.cbs.state.or.us/external/imd/database/bcd/licensing/index.html
Fertilizer/Mineral/Lime Registrants	www.oda.state.or.us/dbs/search.lasso
Florist	www.oda.state.or.us/dbs/licenses/search.lasso?&division=nursery
Food Establishment, Retail	www.oda.state.or.us/dbs/licenses/search.lasso?&division=fsd
Food Exporter/ Processing Facility/ Producer/Dist.	www.oda.state.or.us/dbs/licenses/search.lasso?&division=fsd
Food Storage Facility	www.oda.state.or.us/dbs/licenses/search.lasso?&division=fsd
Frozen Desert Industry	www.oda.state.or.us/dbs/licenses/search.lasso?&division=fsd
Geologist	www.open.org/~osbge/registrants.htm
Geologist, Engineering	www.open.org/~osbge/registrants.htm
Greenhouse Grower of Herbaceous Plants	www.oda.state.or.us/dbs/licenses/search.lasso?&division=nursery
Inspector	www.cbs.state.or.us/external/imd/database/bcd/licensing/index.html
Inspector, Structural/Mechanical	www.cbs.state.or.us/external/imd/database/bcd/licensing/index.html
Insurance Adjuster/Consultant	www.cbs.state.or.us/external/imd/database/inslic/main.htm
Insurance Agency	www.cbs.state.or.us/external/imd/database/inslic/agency_main.htm
Insurance Agent	www.cbs.state.or.us/external/imd/database/inslic/main.htm
Insurance Company	www.cbs.state.or.us/external/imd/database/inslic/comp_main.htm
Investment Advisor	www.cbs.state.or.us/external/imd/database/lear/adviser_search_main.htm
Landscape Business	www.ccb.state.or.us/lcbmenu.htm
Landscaper	www.oda.state.or.us/dbs/licenses/search.lasso?&division=nursery
Livestock Industry (Feedlot, Transport, etc.)	www.oda.state.or.us/dbs/licenses/search.lasso?&division=ahid
LPG Meter	www.oda.state.or.us/dbs/licenses/search.lasso?&division=msd
Manufactured Housing Construction	www.cbs.state.or.us/external/imd/database/bcd/licensing/index.html
Medical Doctor/Surgeon	www.bme.state.or.us/search.html

Milk Hauler/Milk Stabilization/Handler	www.oda.state.or.us/dbs/licenses/search.lasso?&division=fsd
Money Transmitter	www.oregondfcs.org/e_commerce/m_tran/m_tran.htm
Mortgage Banker/Broker/Lender	www.cbs.state.or.us/external/imd/database/lear/search_main.htm
Non-Alcoholic Beverage Plant	www.oda.state.or.us/dbs/licenses/search.lasso?&division=fsd
Nursery Dealer	www.oda.state.or.us/dbs/licenses/search.lasso?&division=nursery
Nursery Stock/Native Plants Collector	www.oda.state.or.us/dbs/licenses/search.lasso?&division=nursery
Occupational Therapist/ Therapist Assistant	www.otlb.state.or.us/licensees.htm
Optometrist	www.obo.state.or.us/doctorinfo.htm
Oregon Product	www.oda.state.or.us/dbs/oregon_products/search.lasso
Osteopathic Physician/Surgeon	www.bme.state.or.us/search.html
Pawnbroker	www.cbs.state.or.us/external/dfcs/pawn/pawnshop.htm
Pesticide Applicator/Trainee	www.oda.state.or.us/dbs/licenses/search.lasso?&division=pest
Pesticide Dealer/Company./Consultant/Product	www.oda.state.or.us/dbs/licenses/search.lasso?&division=pest
Physician Assistant	www.bme.state.or.us/search.html
Plans Examiner	www.cbs.state.or.us/external/imd/database/bcd/licensing/index.html
Plumber	www.cbs.state.or.us/external/imd/database/bcd/licensing/index.html
Podiatrist	www.bme.state.or.us/search.html
Police Chief	www.oregonvos.net/dpsst/downloads/misc/Address.txt
Psychologist	www.obpe.state.or.us/licensee_applicant.htm
Psychologist Associate	www.obpe.state.or.us/licensee_applicant.htm
Public Accountant-CPA	http://boahost.forest.net/licsearch.lasso
Pump Installation Contractor (Limited)	www.cbs.state.or.us/external/imd/database/bcd/licensing/index.html
Real Estate Appraiser	http://oregonaclb.org/app_search.lasso
Refrigerated Plant	www.oda.state.or.us/dbs/licenses/search.lasso?&division=fsd
Scales/Weigher	www.oda.state.or.us/dbs/licenses/search.lasso?&division=msd
Shellfish Industries	www.oda.state.or.us/dbs/licenses/search.lasso?&division=fsd
Sign Contractor (Limited)	www.cbs.state.or.us/external/imd/database/bcd/licensing/index.html
Slaughterhouse	www.oda.state.or.us/dbs/licenses/search.lasso?&division=fsd
Speech Language Pathologist	http://bspa.ohd.hr.state.or.us
Teacher	www.tspc.state.or.us/lookup_query.asp
Trust Company	www.cbs.state.or.us/external/dfcs/banking/regagent.htm
Veterinary Clinic, Livestock	www.oda.state.or.us/dbs/clinics/search.lasso
Veterinary Product, Livestock	www.oda.state.or.us/dbs/licenses/search.lasso?&division=vet_products

County Level ... Courts

Court Administration: Court Administrator, Supreme Court Building, 1163 State St, Salem, OR, 97310; 503-986-5500; www.ojd.state.or.us

Court Structure: Effective January 15, 1998, the District and Circuit Courts were combined into "Circuit Courts." At the same time, three new judicial districts were created by splitting existing ones. The Circuit Court is the highest court of record. Most Circuit Courts that have records on computer do have a public access terminal that will speed up in-person or retriever searches. Most records offices close from Noon to 1PM Oregon time for lunch. No staff is available during that period.

Online Access Note: Online computer access is available through the Oregon Judicial Information Network (OJIN). OJIN Online includes almost all cases filed in the Oregon state courts. Generally, the OJIN database contains criminal, civil, small claims, probate, and some but not all juvenile records. However, it does not contain any records from municipal nor county courts. There is a one-time setup fee of $295.00, plus a monthly usage charge (minimum $10.00) based on transaction type, type of job, shift, and number of units/pages (which averages $10-13 per hour). For further information and/or a registration packet, write to: Oregon Judicial System, Information Systems Division, ATTN: Technical Support, 1163 State Street, Salem OR 97310, or call 800-858-9658, or visit www.ojd.state.or.us/ojin.

Deschutes County
Deschutes County Courts *Civil and Criminal Records*
www.deschutescircuitcourt.org
Index available remotely online on the statewide OJIN system, call 800-858-9658 for information. Also, current calendars are available free at www.ojd.state.or.us/des/calendar.nsf/.

Marion County
Circuit Court *Civil and Criminal Records*
http://marion-court.ojd.state.or.us
Index available remotely online on the statewide OJIN system, call 800-858-9658 for information. Online access to the County sexual offenders registry is available free at www.open.org/~msheriff/sexnotif.htm.

Statewide Access
The www.ojd.state.or.us/ojin web site offers commercial access to almost all cases filed in the Oregon state courts. See the state introduction for details.

County Level ... Recorders & Assessors

Recording Office Organization: 36 counties, 36 recording offices. The recording officer is the County Clerk. 35 counties are in the Pacific Time Zone (PST) and one is in the Mountain Time Zone (MST). All federal and state tax liens on personal property are filed with the Secretary of State. Other federal and state tax liens are filed with the County Clerk. Most counties will perform tax lien searches and include both with a UCC search for an extra $7.50 per name. Search fees vary widely.

Online Access Note: A few counties offer Internet access to assessor records. There is no statewide system available.

Benton County *Real Estate Records*
www.co.benton.or.us
The County is developing a Geographic Information System Internet site for viewing property information at www.co.benton.or.us/irm/gis/GISpage.htm. Search fee is $3.75 per record found. A law enforcement case system may soon offer open case data.

Deschutes County *Real Estate, Tax Assessor Records*
http://recordings.co.deschutes.or.us
To access records on the Deshutes County "Assessor Inquiry System" web site, click on DIAL on the menu bar. Tax information, assessment, appraisal details, ownership, sales information, transaction histories, account histories, land use records, and lot numbers are available for no fee.

Lane County *Assessor, Real Estate Records*
Property records on the County Tax Map site are available at www.co.lane.or.us/taxmap/TaxMapSelect.asp.

Linn County *Assessor, Real Estate Records*
www.co.linn.or.us
Records on the County Property Records database are available free online at the web site.

Multnomah County *Real Property Records*
www.co.multnomah.or.us/dss/at/index.html
Records on the County Metromap database are available free online at http://metromap.metro-region.org/public. No name searching.

Tillamook County *Assessor, Real Estate Records*
www.co.tillamook.or.us/gov/clerk/default.htm
Assessment and taxation records on the County Property database are available free online at www.co.tillamook.or.us/Documents/Search/query.asp. Search by property ID number or by name in the general query. Also, search for property info on the GIS-mapping service site at http://gisweb.co.tillamook.or.us.

Washington County *Real Estate Records*

www.co.washington.or.us

Records on County GIS Intermap database are available free online at www.co.washington.or.us/gisaps/cfdocs/gisweb/par_2.htm. General Recording Office information is available at www.co.washington.or.us/deptmts/at/recordng/record.htm.

Federal Courts in Oregon...

Standards for Federal Courts: The universal PACER sign-up number is 800-676-6856. Find PACER and the Party/Case Index on the Web at http://pacer.psc.uscourts.gov. PACER dial-up access is $.60 per minute. Also, courts offering internet access via RACER, PACER, Web-PACER or the new CM-ECF charge $.07 per page fee unless noted as free.

US District Court -- District of Oregon

Home Page: www.ord.uscourts.gov

PACER: Case records are available back to September 1988. Records are purged never. New records are available online after 1 day.
PACER URL: http://pacer.ord.uscourts.gov.
Electronic Filing: Electronic filing information is available online at https://ecf.ord.uscourts.gov.
Other Online Access: Logon to ECF/PACER at https://ecf.ord.uscourts.gov/cgi-bin/login.pl. Access fee is $.07 per page.
Eugene Division counties: Benton, Coos, Deschutes, Douglas, Lane, Lincoln, Linn, Marion.
Medford Division counties: Curry, Jackson, Josephine, Klamath, Lake. Court set up in April 1994; Cases prior to that time were tried in Eugene.
Portland Division counties: Baker, Clackamas, Clatsop, Columbia, Crook, Gilliam, Grant, Harney, Hood River, Jefferson, Malheur, Morrow, Multnomah, Polk, Sherman, Tillamook, Umatilla, Union, Wallowa, Wasco, Washinton, Wheeler, Yamhill.

US Bankruptcy Court -- District of Oregon

Home Page: www.orb.uscourts.gov

PACER: Toll-free access: 800-610-9315. Local access phone: 503-326-5650. Case records are available back to 1989. Records are purged every six months. New civil records are available online after 1 day. **PACER URL:** http://pacer.orb.uscourts.gov.
Electronic Filing: (Currently in the process of implementing CM/ECF). **Also:** access via phone on VCIS (Voice Case Information System) is available: 800-726-2227, 503-326-2249
Eugene Division counties: Benton, Coos, Curry, Deschutes, Douglas, Jackson, Josephine, Klamath, Lake, Lane, Lincoln, Linn, Marion.
Portland Division counties: Baker, Clackamas, Clatsop, Columbia, Crook, Gilliam, Grant, Harney, Hood River, Jefferson, Malheur, Morrow, Multnomah, Polk, Sherman, Tillamook, Umatilla, Union, Wallowa, Wasco, Washington, Wheeler, Yamhill.

Editor's Tip: Just because records are maintained in a certain way in your state or county do not assume that any other county or state does things the same way that you are used to.

Capital:	Harrisburg Dauphin County	Home Page	www.state.pa.us
Time Zone:	EST	Attorney General	www.attorneygeneral.gov
Number of Counties:	67	Archives	www.phmc.state.pa.us

State Level ... Major Agencies

Criminal Records

State Police Central Repository, 1800 Elmerton Ave, Harrisburg, PA 17110-9758; 717-783-5494, 717-783-9973, 717-705-8840 (Fax), 8:15AM-4:15PM.

www.psp.state.pa.us/psp/site/default.asp

Record checks are available for approved agencies through the Internet on the Pennsylvania Access to Criminal Histories (PATCH). This is a commercial system, a $10.00 fee per name applies. Go to http://patch.state.pa.us or call 717-705-1768.

Incarceration Records

The online system is available at www.cor.state.pa.us, it provides the physical identifiers and the facility location.

Corporation Records, Limited Partnership Records, Trademarks/Servicemarks, Fictitious Name, Assumed Name, Limited Liability Company Records, Limited Liability Partnerships

Corporation Bureau, Department of State, PO Box 8722, Harrisburg, PA 17105-8722 (Courier: 206 North Office Bldg, Harrisburg, PA 17120); 717-787-1057, 717-783-2244 (Fax), 8AM-5PM.

http://corps.state.pa.us/corps.htm

There is free general searching by entity name or number from the web site. Searching by name provides a list of entities whose name starts with the search name entered.Users can click on any one entity in the list displayed to get more detailed information regarding that entity. **Other options:** Business lists, UCC on microfilm, and financing statements are available in bulk for $.25 per name.

Uniform Commercial Code

UCC Division, Department of State, PO Box 8721, Harrisburg, PA 17105-8721 (Courier: North Office Bldg, Rm 206, Harrisburg, PA 17120); 717-787-1057 x2, 717-783-2244 (Fax), 8AM-5PM.

www.dos.state.pa.us/corps/site/default.asp

The web site allows a search of UCC-1 financing statements filed with the Corporation Bureau by debtor name, which displays a list of financing statements. Users can refine the search further by entering a city and/or state for the search. The site also allows a search of financing statement records filed with the Corporation Bureau by financing statement number. **Other options:** Daily computer tapes and copies of microfilm are available. Call the number above for details.

Driver Records

Department of Transportation, Driver Record Services, PO Box 68695, Harrisburg, PA 17106-8695 (Courier: 1101 S Front Street, Harrisburg, PA 17104); 717-391-6190, 800-932-4600 (In-state only), 7:30AM-4:30PM.

www.dmv.state.pa.us

The online system is available to high volume requesters only. Fee is $5.00 per record. Call 717-787-7154 for more information. The sale of records over the Internet is strictly forbidden.

Legislation Records

www.legis.state.pa.us

Free access to bill text is available at the Electronic Bill Room found at the web page by selecting "Session Information."

State Level ... Occupational Licensing

Acupuncturist	http://licensepa.state.pa.us/default.asp
Amphetamine Program	http://licensepa.state.pa.us/default.asp
Animal Health Technician	http://licensepa.state.pa.us/default.asp
Appraiser, Residential	http://licensepa.state.pa.us/default.asp
Architect	http://licensepa.state.pa.us/default.asp
Athletic Agent	http://web.dos.state.pa.us/sac/cgi-bin/aalist.cgi
Auctioneer	http://licensepa.state.pa.us/default.asp
Auctioneer, Real Estate	http://licensepa.state.pa.us/default.asp
Audiologist	http://licensepa.state.pa.us/default.asp
Bank	www.banking.state.pa.us/PA_Exec/Banking/organiz.htm#exambureau
Barber	http://licensepa.state.pa.us/default.asp
Boxer	www.dos.state.pa.us/sac/cwp/view.asp?a=1090&q=436810&sacNav=|
Chiropractor	http://licensepa.state.pa.us/default.asp
Cosmetologist/Cosmetician	http://licensepa.state.pa.us/default.asp
Counselor, Professional	http://licensepa.state.pa.us/default.asp
Credit Union	www.banking.state.pa.us/PA_Exec/Banking/resource/cufrm.pdf
Dental Assistant, Expanded Function	www.licensepa.state.pa.us/default.asp
Dental Hygienist	www.licensepa.state.pa.us/default.asp
Dentist	www.licensepa.state.pa.us/default.asp
Engineer	http://licensepa.state.pa.us/default.asp
Funeral Director	http://licensepa.state.pa.us/default.asp
Geologist	http://licensepa.state.pa.us/default.asp
Hearing Examiners	http://licensepa.state.pa.us/default.asp
Insurance Company	www.insurance.state.pa.us/html/licensed.html
Landscape Architect	http://licensepa.state.pa.us/default.asp
Manicurist	http://licensepa.state.pa.us/default.asp
Marriage & Family Therapist	http://licensepa.state.pa.us/default.asp
Medical Doctor	http://licensepa.state.pa.us/default.asp
Midwife	http://licensepa.state.pa.us/default.asp
Nuclear Medicine Technologist	http://licensepa.state.pa.us/default.asp
Nurse	http://licensepa.state.pa.us/default.asp
Nursing Home Administrator	http://licensepa.state.pa.us/default.asp
Occupational Therapist/Assistant	http://licensepa.state.pa.us/default.asp
Optometrist	http://licensepa.state.pa.us/default.asp
Osteopathic Physician/ Physician Assistant	http://licensepa.state.pa.us/default.asp
Pharmacist	http://licensepa.state.pa.us/default.asp
Physical Therapist/Assistant	http://licensepa.state.pa.us/default.asp

Physician Assistant..http://licensepa.state.pa.us/default.asp
Podiatrist ....http://licensepa.state.pa.us/default.asp
Psychologist ....http://licensepa.state.pa.us/default.asp
Public Accountant-CPA, Individual or Corporation.....http://licensepa.state.pa.us/default.asp
Public Accounting Partnership....................................http://licensepa.state.pa.us/default.asp
Radiation Therapy Technician ....http://licensepa.state.pa.us/default.asp
Radiologic Technologist..http://licensepa.state.pa.us/default.asp
Real Estate Appraiser..http://licensepa.state.pa.us/default.asp
Real Estate Broker/Salesperson..................................http://licensepa.state.pa.us/default.asp
Respiratory Care Practitioner ....http://licensepa.state.pa.us/default.asp
Savings Association ....www.banking.state.pa.us/PA_Exec/Banking/organiz.htm#exambureau
Social Worker..http://licensepa.state.pa.us/default.asp
Speech-Language Pathologist......................................http://licensepa.state.pa.us/default.asp
Surveyor, Land..http://licensepa.state.pa.us/default.asp
Teacher..https://www.tcs.ed.state.pa.us/validchk.asp
Trust Company...www.banking.state.pa.us/PA_Exec/Banking/organiz.htm#exambureau
Veterinarian/ Veterinary Technician ....http://licensepa.state.pa.us/default.asp

County Level ... Courts

Court Administration:　　Administrative Office of Pennsylvania Courts, PO Box 719, Mechanicsburg, PA, 17055; 717-795-2000; www.courts.state.pa.us

Court Structure:　　Effective January 15, 1998, the District and Circuit Courts were combined into "Circuit Courts." At the same time, three new judicial districts were created by splitting existing ones. The Circuit Court is the highest court of record. Most Circuit Courts that have records on computer do have a public access terminal that will speed up in-person or retriever searches. Most records offices close from Noon to 1PM Oregon time for lunch. No staff is available during that period.

Online Access Note:　　The state's 550 Magisterial District Courts are served by a statewide, automated case management system; online access to the case management system is not available. However, public access to statutorily authorized information is available from the Special Courts, filing offices of Appellate Courts, and from the AOPC. The courts are considering ways to implement a unified, statewide system in the Criminal Division of the Courts of Common Pleas.

The Infocon County Access System provides direct dial-up access to court record information for 15 counties - Armstrong, Bedford, Blair, Butler, Clarion, Clinton, Erie, Franklin, Huntingdon, Juaniata, Lawrence, Mercer, Mifflin, Pike, and Potter. Set up entails a $25.00 base set-up fee plus $25.00 per county. The monthly usage fee minimum is $25.00, plus time charges. For Information, call Infocon at 814-472-6066.

Allegheny County
Court of Common Pleas　*Civil and Criminal Records*
www.county.allegheny.pa.us
Online access to prothonotary civil records available free at http://prothonotary.county.allegheny.pa.us/allegheny/welcome.htm. Registration required; search by case number. Also, the Techi provides court records services for those with PA Bar ID at www.techi.org/login.CFM.

Armstrong County
Court of Common Pleas　*Civil and Criminal Records*
www.geocities.com/acprothonotary
Online access is available through a private company. For information, call Infocon at 814-472-6066.

Bedford County
Court of Common Pleas, Register of Wills *Civil, Probate and Criminal Records*
Online access is available through a private company. For information, call Infocon at 814-472-6066.

Berks County
Court of Common Pleas *Civil Records*
The Registry of Wills has a free searchable web site at www.berksregofwills.com including marriage, estate, birth and death records for the county. The estate and marriage records are current. Also, the Prothontary has a remote dial-up system that allows users to access archived record indexes back to 1/1996 via the telephone. Fee is $95 for the first 5 users, plus phone per minute charges. For info, call 610-478-6968.

Blair County
Court of Common Pleas, Register of Wills *Civil, Probate and Criminal Records*
Online access is available through a private company. For information, call Infocon at 814-472-6066.

Bucks County
Court of Common Pleas *Civil and Criminal Records*
www.buckscounty.org
Access to the criminal online system requires Sprint ID ($25). The per minute fee is $.60 with a 2 minute minimum. Search by name or case number. Contact John Morris at 215-348-6579 for more information or visit www.buckscounty.org/departments/public_access/.

Butler County
Court of Common Pleas *Civil and Criminal Records*
www.co.butler.pa.us/CoC.htm
Online access is available through a private company. For information, call Infocon at 814-472-6066.

Carbon County
Court of Common Pleas, Register of Wills *Civil, Probate and Criminal Records*
Online access to the clerk of courts docket records is available free at www.carboncourts.com/pubacc.htm. Registration required. Probate docket information is available.

Chester County
Court of Common Pleas *Civil and Criminal Records*
www.chesco.org
Internet access to county records including court records requires a sign-up and credit card payment. Application fee: $50. There is a $10.00 per month minimum (no charge for no activity); and $.10 each transaction beyond 100. Sign-up and/or logon at http://epin.chesco.org.

Clarion County
Court of Common Pleas *Civil and Criminal Records*
Online access is available through a private company. For information, call Infocon at 814-472-6066.

Clinton County
Court of Common Pleas *Civil and Criminal Records*
Online access is available through a private company. For information, call Infocon at 814-472-6066.

Delaware County
Court of Common Pleas *Civil Records*
www.co.delaware.pa.us
Online access to court civil records available free at www2.co.delaware.pa.us/pa/default.htm. For more information, call 610-891-4675. Search online by name or document type. No online access to criminal records.

Erie County
Court of Common Pleas *Civil and CriminalRecords*
www.eriecountygov.org
Online access is available through a private company. For information, call Infocon at 814-472-6066.

Franklin County
Register of Wills *Probate Records*
Access to probate records is available through a private company. For information, call Infocon at 814-472-6066.

Huntingdon County

Court of Common Pleas, Register of Wills *Civil, Probate and Criminal Records*
Register of Wills *Probate Records*
Online access is available through a private company. For information, call Infocon at 814-472-6066.

Lancaster County

Court of Common Pleas *Civil Records*
www.co.lancaster.pa.us/courts/site/default.asp
Access to remote online records requires a $25.00 monthly fee plus $.18 per minute. Search by name or case number. Call Kathy
Harris at 717-299-8252 for more information. Also, search the Prothonotary "Protection from Abuse" list for free at
www.co.lancaster.pa.us/scripts/PFAWebQuery.exe. Also, historic court case schedules are available free at www.co.lancaster.pa.us
(click on "Court Schedules").

Court of Common Pleas *Criminal Records*
Search the Prothonotary "Protection from Abuse" list for free at www.co.lancaster.pa.us/scripts/PFAWebQuery.exe. Also, historic
court case schedules are available free at www.co.lancaster.pa.us (click on "Court Schedules").

Lawrence County

Court of Common Pleas, Register of Wills *Civil, Probate and Criminal Records*
www.co.lawrence.pa.us   Online access is available through a private company. For information, call Infocon at 814-472-6066.

Lehigh County

Court of Common Pleas *Civil and Criminal Records*
www.lccpa.org
 Access to the countywide online system requires monthly usage fee. Search by name or case number. Call Lehigh Cty Computer Svcs
Dept at 610-782-3286 for more information. Also, free online access is under development; currently calendars and bench warrants
are available online at www.lehighcountycourt.org under "Calendars & Schedules."

Mercer County

Court of Common Pleas *Civil and Criminal Records*
www.mcc.co.mercer.pa.us/LOCRULES.htm
Online access is available through a private company. For information, call Infocon at 814-472-6066.

Mifflin County

Court of Common Pleas *Civil, Probate Opinion, and Criminal Records*
http://mifflincounty.lcworkshop.com/
Online access is available through a private company. For information, call Infocon at 814-472-6066. Online opinions are available at
http://mifflincounty.lcworkshop.com/rowoffices/court_of_common_pleas/default.asp. Includes probate court opinions and tax sales.

Monroe County

Register of Wills *Civil Records, Wills*
Online access to wills is available through a private company at www.landex.com/remote/. Fee is $.20 per minute and $.50 per fax
page. Wills go back to 11/1836.

Montgomery County

Court of Common Pleas *Civil Records*
www.montcopa.org   Court and other records are available free online at www1.montcopa.org. System is experimental and may or may
not be adapted full time. A pay service, offering remote dial-up, is also available.

Court of Common Pleas *Civil, Probate and Criminal Records*
www.montcopa.org
Online access to the county civil and probate active and purged records is available free at www.montcopa.org/mway/index.html.
Criminal court and other records are available free online at www.montcopa.org/mway/index.html. Includes purged cases.

Philadelphia County

Court of Common Pleas - *Civil Records*
Access to 1st Judicial District Civil Trial records available free online at http://dns2.phila.gov:8080. Search by name, judgment and
docket information.

Pike County
Court of Common Pleas *Civil and Criminal Records*
Online access to criminal records is available through a private company. For information, call Infocon at 814-472-6066.

Potter County
Register of Wills *Probate Records*
Access to probate records is available through a private company. For information, call Infocon at 814-472-6066.

Tioga County
Register of Wills *Probate Records*
Online access to wills is available through a private company at www.landex.com/remote/. Fee is $.20 per minute and $.50 per fax page. Images and wills go back to 2/1999.

Washington County
Court of Common Pleas *Civil Records*
www.co.washington.pa.us
Civil records online access to be available in 2003. See the web site.

Westmoreland County
Court of Common Pleas *Civil and Criminal Records*
Access to the remote online system requires $100 setup (no set-up if accessed via Internet) plus $20 monthly minimum fee. System includes civil, criminal, prothonotary indexes, and recorder information. For information, call 724-830-3874.

York County
Court of Common Pleas *Civil Records*
www.york-county.org/departments/courts/crtf1.htm
Access to the remote online system is set-up through Information Services and requires $.75 per minute plus a $200.00 setup fee. For more information, call 717-771-9235. Criminal records go back to mid-1988.

Register of Wills *Probate Records*
Online access to wills is available through a private company at www.landex.com/remote/. Fee is $.20 per minute and $.50 per fax page. Images and wills go back to 2/1999.

County Level ... Recorders & Assessors

Recording Office Organization: 67 counties, 67 recording offices and 134 UCC filing offices. Each county has two different recording offices: the Prothonotary - their term for "Clerk" - who accepted UCC and tax lien filings until 07/01/2001, and the Recorder of Deeds who maintains real estate records. The entire state is in the Eastern Time Zone (EST). All federal and state tax liens on personal property and on real property are filed with the Prothonotary. Usually, tax liens on personal property are filed in the judgment index of the Prothonotary. Some Prothonotaries will perform tax lien searches.

Online Access Note: A number of counties provide web access to assessor data. The Infocon County Access System provides Internet and direct dial-up access to recorded record information for 15 Penn. counties - Armstrong, Bedford, Blair, Butler, Clarion, Clinton, Erie, Franklin, Huntingdon, Juaniata, Lawrence, Mercer, Mifflin, Pike, and Potter. Fees are involved. Document images are available. For information, call Infocon at 814-472-6066 or visit www.ic-access.com.

Allegheny County Prothonotary   *Civil Court, UCC, Tax Lien, Real Estate, Assessor Records*
http://www2.county.allegheny.pa.us/realestate/
Access to Comon Pleas Civil records is available free at http://prothonotary.county.allegheny.pa.us/allegheny/welcome.htm. Registration is required. UCC records are pre-7-1-2001. Online access to the certified values database is available free at the web site. Also, online access to Allegheny County real estate database is available free at http://www2.county.allegheny.pa.us/realestate/Search.asp.

Armstrong County   *Tax Lien, Real Estate, Marriage, Probate Records*

Access is available through a private company. For information, call Infocon at 814-472-6066.

Beaver County Recorder   *Real Estate, Deed, Mortgage Records*

www.co.beaver.pa.us

Access to the Recorder's database is to be available free at http://co.beaver.pa.us/RecorderofDeeds/Disclaimer.htm. Registration is required. Deed records go back to 1957; Mortgages to 7/1974; images to 6/1998.

Bedford County   *Tax Lien, Real Estate, Assessor, Probate, Marriage Records*

www.bedford.net/regrec/home.html

Access is available through a private company. For information, call Infocon at 814-472-6066.

Berks County Prothonotary   *Judgment, Lien, UCC, Civil Court Records*

www.berksprothy.com

The Prothontary has a remote dial-up system that allows users to access archived record indexes back to 1/1996 via the telephone. Fee is $95 for the first 5 users, plus phone per minute charges. For info, call 610-478-6968. Also, a web site is being developed where you can access document images.

Berks County Recorder   *Vital Statistic, Probate Records*

www.berksrecofdeeds.com

Access to the Registry of Wills' databases are available free at www.berksregofwills.com including county marriage, estate, birth and death records. Estate and marriage records are current.

Blair County   *Tax Lien, Real Estate, Marriage, Probate Records*

Access is available through a private company. For information, call Infocon at 814-472-6066.

Bucks County Prothonotary
Recording, Judgment, Courts, Sheriff Sales, Assessor, Voter Registration Records

www.buckscounty.org/courts/

Access to County records requires a Sprint ID number and payment of $25 annual Sprint fee, plus $.60 per minute of use. Records go back to 1980. Lending agency, Register of Wills, liens, sheriff sales, voter registration, criminal also available. For information, contact Jack Morris at 215-348-6579 or visit www.buckscounty.org/departments/public_access/

Bucks County Recorder   *Assessor, Real Estate, Tax Lien, Probate Records*

www.buckscounty.org/departments/registerofwills/index.html

Access to County records requires a Sprint ID number and payment of $25 annual Sprint fee, plus $.60 per minute of use. Records go back to 1980. Lending agency, Register of Wills, liens, sheriff sales, voter registration, courts, prothonotary available. For information, contact Jack Morris at 215-348-6579 or visit www.buckscounty.org/departments/public_access/.

Butler County   *Tax Lien, Marriage, Probate Records*

www.butlercounty.com/court/index.htm

Marriage and probate records are available through a private company. For information, call Infocon at 814-472-6066.

Carbon County   *Tax Lien, UCC, Real Estate, Probate, Grantor/Grantee Records*

Access to information on the county's remote public access dial-up database is available free; 570-325-3288; instructions and registration are at www.carboncourts.com/pubacc.htm.

Chester County Prothonotary   *Court Dockets, Property Tax, Warrant, Lien, Assessor Records*

www.chesco.org/prothy.html

Access to the prothonotary database is available at www.chesco.org/prothy.html. Click on "SEARCH:~." There is a $50 set up fee and $10 each month of use (if over 100 transcation per/mo, $.10 per document). Registration/password at 610-344-6884. Prothonotary records go back to 1990.

Chester County Recorder   *Recording, Deed, Court, Vital Statistic Records*

www.chesco.org/recorder

Searching countywide records including court records requires a sign-up and credit card payment. Application fee is $50. with $10.00 per month minimum (no charge for no activity); and $.10 each transaction beyond 100. Sign-up and/or logon at http://epin.chesco.org/. County data is also available as reports, labels, magnetic tape, and diskette. Also, genealogical and older vital statistics are available free at www.chesco.org/archives. All Recorder of Deeds records will shortly be on Internet; no fee planned.

Clarion County   *Tax Lien, Assessor, Real Estate, Voter Registration Records*

Clinton County   *Tax Lien, Real Estate, Probate Records*

Access is available through a private company. For information, call Infocon at 814-472-6066.

Delaware County Recorder   *Assessor, Deed, Real Estate Records*

http://www2.co.delaware.pa.us/pa/default.htm
Access to the public access system is available free - temporarily - at the web site. Records go back to 1982. Also, property tax records are available free on the Internet at http://taxrecords.com.

Erie County   *Tax Lien, Real Estate, Marriage, Probate Records*

Access is available through a private company. For information, call Infocon at 814-472-6066. Also, online access to property records data is available free at www.mypropertyrecords.com/eriecountypa/.

Fayette County Recorder   *Property, Assessor Records*

Access to property assessments is available free at www.fayetteproperty.org/assessor.

Franklin County   *Tax Lien, Real Estate, Probate Records*

Huntingdon County   *Tax Lien, Real Estate, Marriage, Probate Records*

Juniata County   *Real Estate, Marriage, Probate Records*

Access is available through a private company. For information, call Infocon at 814-472-6066.

Lancaster County Prothonotary   *Real Estate, Recording, UCC, Tax Lien, PFA, Termination List Records*

www.co.lancaster.pa.us
See Register of Deeds. The PFA (protection from abuse) records data kept by the Prothonotary is searchable for free at www.co.lancaster.pa.us/scripts/PFAWebQuery.exe. Also, search the court case termination list (argument report) for the prior year from the Prothonotary's web page.

Lancaster County Recorder   *Assessor, Real Estate, Recording, Tax Lien Records*

www.co.lancaster.pa.us
Access to deeds, UCCs and other recordings is available free at http://198.51.78.24/splash.jsp.

Lawrence County   *Tax Lien, Real Estate, Assessor, Marriage, Probate Records*

Access is available through a private company. For information, call Infocon at 814-472-6066.

Lehigh County Recorder   *Assessor, Real Estate, Tax Lien, Marriage Records*

The system is open 24 hours daily; there are set-up and usage fees. Records go back to 1984. Lending agency information is available. Court records are also available. Call Lehigh City Computer Svcs Dept at 610-782-3286 for more information.

Mercer County   *Tax Lien, Real Estate, Assessor Records*

Access is available through a private company. For information, call Infocon at 814-472-6066.

Mifflin County   *Tax Lien, Real Estate, Assessor, Probate Records*

http://mifflincounty.lcworkshop.com/rowoffices/register_and_recorder/default.asp
Access is available through a private company. For information, call Infocon at 814-472-6066. Also, property assessment and occupational tax records are available free online at http://mifflincounty.lcworkshop.com/departments/assessment/. Also available is a advanced fee-based system with greater land and property records; fee is $99 per year. Sign up is available online.

Monroe County Recorder   *Real Estate, Wills Records*

Access is available through a private company at www.landex.com/remote/. Fee is $.20 per minute and $.50 per fax page. Land Index goes back to 1/1979; wills go back to 11/1836; images go back to 8/1997.

Montgomery County Recorder   *Assessor, Real Estate, Tax Lien Records*

www.montcopa.org
Two sources are available. Access to County online records requires a $10 sign up fee plus $.15 per minute of use. Records date back to 1990. Lending agency and prothonotary information are available on the system. For information or to sign up, contact Berkheimer Assoc. at 800-360-8989. Also, records on the County PIR database are available free on the Internet at www.montcopa.org/reassessment/boahome0.htm. Click on "Instructions" to learn how to use the search features, then search by parcel number, name, address, or municipality.

Northampton County Recorder   *Deed, Mortgage, Misc. Recording, Property, Assessor Records*

Two sources are available. One is a private company at www.landex.com/remote/. Fee is $.20 per minute and $.50 per fax page. Deeds data goes back to 11/85; mortgages to 2/88; faxable images go back to 5/94. Also, online access to assessor's property records data is available free at www.ncpub.org.

Philadelphia County Recorder   *Death Records*

Search the Philadelphia area obituaries for free at www.legacy.com/philly/LegacyHome.asp

Pike County   *Tax Lien, Probate Records*

Potter County   *Tax Lien, Real Estate, Assessor, Probate Records*

Access is available through a private company. For information, call Infocon at 814-472-6066.

Tioga County Recorder   *Real Estate, Recording, Wills Records*

Access is available through a private company at www.landex.com/remote/. Fee is $.20 per minute and $.50 per fax page. Recorders data goes back to 1977; images and wills go back to 2/1999.

Washington County Recorder   *Assessor, Real Estate Records*

www.co.washington.pa.us
Records are available on the county online system. Records date back to 1952. Register of Wills information and lending agency information is also available. For information, call 724-228-6766.

Westmoreland County Recorder   *Real Estate, Tax Lien Records*

www.co.westmoreland.pa.us
The online system costs $100 setup plus $20 per month minimum fee, and a per minute charge of $.50 after 40 minutes. The system also includes civil, criminal, prothonotary indexes. Recorder information dates back to 1957. No tax lien information is available, only UCC liens. For information, call 724-830-3874.

York County Recorder   *Assessor, Real Estate Records*

www.york-county.org/departments/deeds/deeds.htm
Two sources are available. Online access to the assessors database is available free at www.york-county.org/test/manager.htm. Also, online access is available through Landex at www.landex.com/remote. Some records are free, others on a pay per time usage. Records go back to 1990; images to 1994. Also, parcel numbers are available to the public at www.york-county.org/departments/assessment/tx_asmnt.htm.

Federal Courts in Pennsylvania...

Standards for Federal Courts: The universal PACER sign-up number is 800-676-6856. Find PACER and the Party/Case Index on the Web at http://pacer.psc.uscourts.gov. PACER dial-up access is $.60 per minute. Also, courts offering internet access via RACER, PACER, Web-PACER or the new CM-ECF charge $.07 per page fee unless noted as free.

US District Court -- Eastern District of Pennsylvania

Home Page: www.paed.uscourts.gov
PACER: Sign-up number is 215-597-5710. Toll-free access: 800-458-2993. Local access phone: 215-597-0258. Case records are available back to July 1, 1990. Records are purged never. New records are available online after 1 day. **PACER URL:** http://pacer.paed.uscourts.gov.
Electronic Filing: Electronic filing information is available online at https://ecf.paed.uscourts.gov.
Opinions Online: Court opinions are available online at www.paed.uscourts.gov/contents.shtml.

Other Online Access: Online access is available free at www.paed.uscourts.gov/us04000.shtml. No fee to search; select document type and enter name as search string.
Allentown/Reading Division counties: Berks, Lancaster, Lehigh, Northampton, Schuylkill.
Philadelphia Division counties: Bucks, Chester, Delaware, Montgomery, Philadelphia.

US Bankruptcy Court -- Eastern District of Pennsylvania

Home Page: www.paeb.uscourts.gov

PACER: Toll-free access: 888-381-2921. Local access phone: 215-597-3501. Case records are available back to 1988. Records are purged every 6 months. New civil records are available online after 1 day. **PACER URL:** http://pacer.paeb.uscourts.gov.
Electronic Filing: (Currently in the process of implementing CM/ECF). **Also:** access via phone on VCIS (Voice Case Information System) is available: 215-597-2244.
Philadelphia Division counties: Bucks, Chester, Delaware, Montgomery, Philadelphia.
Reading Division counties: Berks, Lancaster, Lehigh, Northampton, Schuylkill.

US District Court -- Middle District of Pennsylvania

Home Page: www.pamd.uscourts.gov

PACER: Toll-free access: 800-658-8381. Local access phone: 570-347-8286. Document images available. Case records are available back to May 1989. Records are purged never. New records are available online after 1 day. **PACER URL:** http://pacer.pamd.uscourts.gov. Document images available.
Electronic Filing: Electronic filing information is available online at (CM/ECF available late 2002).
Other Online Access: Search records on the Internet using RACER at https://racer.pamd.uscourts.gov/perl/bkplog.html. Access fee is $.07 per page.
Harrisburg Division counties: Adams, Cumberland, Dauphin, Franklin, Fulton, Huntingdon, Juniata, Lebanon, Mifflin, York.
Scranton Division counties: Bradford, Carbon, Lackawanna, Luzerne, Monroe, Pike, Susquehanna, Wayne, Wyoming.
Williamsport Division counties: Cameron, Centre, Clinton, Columbia, Lycoming, Montour, Northumberland, Perry, Potter, Snyder, Sullivan, Tioga, Union.

US Bankruptcy Court -- Middle District of Pennsylvania

Home Page: www.pamd.uscourts.gov

PACER: Toll-free access: 800-882-6899. Local access phone: 570-901-2835. Case records are available back to August 1986. Records are purged never. New civil records are available online after 1 day. **PACER URL:** http://pacer.pamb.uscourts.gov. Document images available.
Electronic Filing: (Currently in the process of implementing CM/ECF). **Also:** access via phone on VCIS (Voice Case Information System) is available: 877-440-2699.
Harrisburg Division counties: Adams, Centre, Cumberland, Dauphin, Franklin, Fulton, Huntingdon, Juniata, Lebanon, Mifflin, Montour, Northumberland, Perry, Schuylkill, Snyder, Union, York.
Wilkes-Barre Division counties: Bradford, Cameron, Carbon, Clinton, Columbia, Lackawanna, Luzerne, Lycoming, Monroe, Pike, Potter, Schuylkill, Sullivan, Susquehanna, Tioga, Wayne, Wyoming.

US District Court -- Western District of Pennsylvania

Home Page: www.pawd.uscourts.gov

PACER: Toll-free access: 800-770-4745. Local access phone: 412-208-7588. Case records are available back to 1989. Records are purged never. New records are available online after 1 day. **PACER URL:** http://pacer.pawd.uscourts.gov.
Erie Division counties: Crawford, Elk, Erie, Forest, McKean, Venango, Warren.
Johnstown Division counties: Bedford, Blair, Cambria, Clearfield, Somerset.
Pittsburgh Division counties: Allegheny, Armstrong, Beaver, Butler, Clarion, Fayette, Greene, Indiana, Jefferson, Lawrence, Mercer, Washington, Westmoreland.

US Bankruptcy Court -- Western District of Pennsylvania

Home Page: www.pawb.uscourts.gov

PACER: Toll-free access: 800-795-2829. Local access phone: 412-355-2588. Case records are available back to 1991. Records are purged every six months. New civil records are available online after 1 day. **PACER URL:** http://pacer.pawb.uscourts.gov.
Electronic Filing: (Currently in the process of implementing CM/ECF). **Also:** access via phone on VCIS (Voice Case Information System) is available: 412-355-3210.
Erie Division counties: Clarion, Crawford, Elk, Erie, Forest, Jefferson, McKean, Mercer, Venango, Warren.
Pittsburgh Division counties: Allegheny, Armstrong, Beaver, Bedford, Blair, Butler, Cambria, Clearfield, Fayette, Greene, Indiana, Lawrence, Somerset, Washington, Westmoreland.

Capital:	Providence Providence County	Home Page	www.state.ri.us
Time Zone:	EST	Attorney General	www.riag.state.ri.us
Number of Counties:	5	Archives	www.state.ri.us/archives

State Level ... Major Agencies

Criminal Records

Department of Attorney General, Bureau of Criminal Identification, 150 S Main Street, Providence, RI 02903; 401-274-4400 x2353, 8:30AM-4;30PM.

This agency does not have online access, but the state court system does. The Adult Criminal Information Database is available at http://courtconnect.courts.state.ri.us/pls/ri_adult/ck_public_qry_main.cp_main_idx. Search by name or case number.

Corporation Records, Fictitious Name, Limited Partnerships, Limited Liability Companys, Limited Liability Partnerships, Not For Profit Entities

Secretary of State, Corporations Division, 100 N Main St, Providence, RI 02903-1335; 401-222-3040, 401-222-1309 (Fax), 8:30AM-4:30PM.

http://155.212.254.78/corporations.htm

At the web, search filings for active and inactive Rhode Island and foreign business corporations, non-profit corporations, limited partnerships, limited liability companies, and limited liability partnerships. Weekly listing of new corporations are also available. There is no fee. **Other options:** The corporation database may be purchased on CD.

Driver Records

Division of Motor Vehicles, Driving Record Clerk, Operator Control, 286 Main Street, Pawtucket, RI 02860; 401-588-3010, 8:30AM-4:30PM.

www.dmv.state.ri.us

Driving records are available online for permissible users from the state's web portal. The fee is $18.00 per record. All users must be approved by the DMV's Administrator's Office. For details, please call Ms. Elaine Phillips.

Legislation Records

www.rilin.state.ri.us

The web site provides excellent means to search enactments and measures by keywords or bill numbers.

State Level ... Occupational Licensing

Acupuncturist	http://63.72.31.182/
Ambulatory Care Facility	http://63.72.31.182/
Asbestos Abatement Worker	http://63.72.31.182/
Athletic Trainer	http://63.72.31.182/
Audiologist	http://63.72.31.182/
Barber Shop	http://63.72.31.182/
Barber/Barber Instructor	http://63.72.31.182/
Birth Center	http://63.72.31.182/
Blood Test Screener	http://63.72.31.182/
Cable Installer	www.crb.state.ri.us/search.asp
Charter School	www.ridoe.net/charterschools/list.htm
Chimney Sweep	www.crb.state.ri.us/search.asp
Chiropractor	http://63.72.31.182/
Clinical Lab Scientist, Cytogenetic	http://63.72.31.182
Clinical Lab Scientist/Technician	http://63.72.31.182
Contractor, Residential Building	www.crb.state.ri.us/search.asp
Cytotechnologist	http://63.72.31.182
Day Care, Children	www.dcyf.state.ri.us/cgi-bin/dcyf.cgi
Dental Hygienist	http://63.72.31.182/
Dentist	http://63.72.31.182/
Dietitian/Nutritionist	http://63.72.31.182/
Electrologist	http://63.72.31.182/
Electron Microscopy, Clinical Lab Scientist	http://63.72.31.182
Embalmer	http://63.72.31.182/
Emergency Care Facility	http://63.72.31.182/
Emergency Medical Technician/Services	http://63.72.31.182/
Esthetician	http://63.72.31.182/
Funeral Director	http://63.72.31.182/
Group Home	http://63.72.31.182/
Hairdresser/Hairdresser Instructor	http://63.72.31.182/
Hazardous Waste Transporter	www.state.ri.us/dem/programs/benviron/waste/transpor/index.htm
Hearing Aid Dispenser	http://63.72.31.182/
Histologic Technician, Clinical	http://63.72.31.182
Home Care Providers	http://63.72.31.182/
Home Nursing Care	http://63.72.31.182/
Hospice Provider	http://63.72.31.182/
Hospital	http://63.72.31.182/
Interpreter for the Deaf	http://63.72.31.182/
Laboratory, Medical	http://63.72.31.182/
Lobbyist	www.corps.state.ri.us/lobby/default.asp
Manicurist	http://63.72.31.182/
Manicurist Shop	http://63.72.31.182/
Marriage & Family Therapist	http://63.72.31.182/
Massage Therapist	http://63.72.31.182/
Medical Doctor	www.docboard.org/ri/df/search.htm
Medical Waste Transporter	www.state.ri.us/dem/programs/benviron/waste/transpor/index.htm
Mental Health Counselor	http://63.72.31.182/
Midwife	http://63.72.31.182/
Notary Public	www.corps.state.ri.us/notaries/notaries.htm
Nuclear Medicine Technologist	http://63.72.31.182/
Nurse	http://63.72.31.182/
Nurse-LPN	http://63.72.31.182/
Nursing Assistant	http://63.72.31.182/
Nursing Home Administrator	http://63.72.31.182/
Nursing Service	http://63.72.31.182/
Occupational Therapist	http://63.72.31.182/

Office Operatories (Medical).. http://63.72.31.182/
Optician... http://63.72.31.182/
Optometrist.. http://63.72.31.182/
Osteopathic Physician .... www.docboard.org/ri/df/search.htm
Outpatient Rehabilitation http://63.72.31.182/
Pharmacist/Pharmacy Technician http://63.72.31.182/
Pharmacy, Residential/Non-Resi................................. http://63.72.31.182/
Phlebotomy Station http://63.72.31.182/
Physical Therapist http://63.72.31.182/
Physical Therapist Assistant....................................... http://63.72.31.182/
Physician... http://63.72.31.182/
Physician Assistant.. http://63.72.31.182/
Podiatrist http://63.72.31.182/
Portable X-ray http://63.72.31.182/
Prevention Specialist/Spvr./Advanced http://63.72.31.182
Prosthetist... http://63.72.31.182/
Psychologist http://63.72.31.182/
Radiation Therapist http://63.72.31.182/
Radiographer.. http://63.72.31.182/
Real Estate Appraiser .... www.asc.gov/content/category1/appr_by_state.asp
Res. Care/Assisted Living Facility http://63.72.31.182/
Respiratory Care Practitioner http://63.72.31.182/
Sanitarian http://63.72.31.182/
Security Alarm Installer... www.crb.state.ri.us/search.asp
Septic Transporter .... www.state.ri.us/dem/programs/benviron/waste/transpor/index.htm
Social Worker... http://63.72.31.182/
Speech/Language Pathologist...................................... http://63.72.31.182/
Surgery Center, Freestanding http://63.72.31.182/
Tanning Facility http://63.72.31.182/
Tattoo Artist http://63.72.31.182/
Underground Sprinkler Installer .... www.crb.state.ri.us/search.asp
Veterinarian... http://63.72.31.182/
X-ray Facility http://63.72.31.182/

County Level ... Courts

Court Administration:　　Court Administrator, Supreme Court, 250 Benefit St, Providence, RI, 02903; 401-222-3272; www.courts.state.ri.us

Court Structure:　　Rhode Island has five counties, but only four Superior/District Court Locations (2nd-Newport, 3rd-Kent, 4th-Washignton, and 6th-Pridivence/Bristol Districts). Bristol and Providence counties are completely merged at the Providence location. Civil claims between $5000 and $10,000 may be filed in either Superior or District Court at the discretion of the filer.

Online Access Note:　　The Rhode Island Judiciary offers free Internet access to court criminal records statewide at http://courtconnect.courts.state.ri.us. A word of caution, this website is provided as an informational service only and should not be relied upon as an official record of the court.

The Superior (civil, family) and Appellate courts are online internally for court personnel only.

There are no known courts that independently offer access to their records.

County Level ... Recorders & Assessors

Recording Office Organization: 5 counties and 39 towns, 39 recording offices. The recording officer is the Town/City Clerk (Recorder of Deeds). The Town/City Clerk usually also serves as the Recorder of Deeds. There is no county administration in Rhode Island that handles recording. The entire state is in the Eastern Time Zone (EST). Do not confuse the counties of Bristol, Newport, and Providence with the towns of Bristol, Newport, and Providence. Towns will not perform real estate searches. All federal and state tax liens on personal property and on real property are filed with the Recorder of Deeds. Towns will not perform tax lien searches.

Online Access Note: A number of towns have property records available. A private vendor has placed on the Internet the assessor records from several towns. Visit http://data.visionappraisal.com.

Editor's Tip: Towns and cities that offer online access are listed under their county location.

Kent County

Coventry Town *Assessor, Property Records*
Access is to be available in 2002 at www.town.coventry.ri.us/assess.htm.

East Greenwich Town *Property Records*
www.eastgreenwichri.com
Limited Finance Dept. property sales information is listed at www.eastgreenwichri.com/finance.htm. See bottom of web page.

Newport County

Middletown *Assessor, Property Records*
Records on the Town of Middletown assessor database are available online at http://data.visionappraisal.com/MiddletownRI/. Free registration is required for full data.

Newport City *Assessor, Property Records*
www.cityofnewport.com
Access is available via a private company at http://data.visionappraisal.com/NewportRI/. Free registration is required for full data.

Portsmouth Town *Assessor, Property Records*
Records on the Town of Portsmouth assessor database are available online at http://data.visionappraisal.com/PortsmouthRI/. Free registration is required to view full data.

Providence County

North Smithfield Town *Assessor, Property Records*
Access is available via a private company at http://data.visionappraisal.com/NorthsmithfieldRI/. Free registration is required to view full data.

Washington County

Exeter Town *Assessor, Property Records*
www.town.exeter.ri.us
Access is may be available from a private company at http://data.visionappraisal.com/ExeterRI/. Free registration is required to view full data.

Narragansett Town *Assessor Records*
Access may soon be available via a private company, see www.narragansettri.com/townhall/assessor.htm

North Kingstown *Assessor, Property Records*
www.northkingstown.org
Access is available via a private company at http://data.visionappraisal.com/NorthkingstownRI/. Free registration is required for full data.

South Kingstown *Real Estate, Assessor Records*
www.southkingstownri.com
Access to the property values database is available free at www.southkingstownri.com/code/propvalues_search.cfm.

Federal Courts in Rhode Island...

Standards for Federal Courts: The universal PACER sign-up number is 800-676-6856. Find PACER and the Party/Case Index on the Web at http://pacer.psc.uscourts.gov. PACER dial-up access is $.60 per minute. Also, courts offering internet access via RACER, PACER, Web-PACER or the new CM-ECF charge $.07 per page fee unless noted as free.

US District Court -- District of Rhode Island
Home Page: www.rid.uscourts.gov
PACER: Toll-free access: 888-421-6861. Local access phone: 401-752-7262. Case records are available back to December 1988. Records are purged never. New records are available online after 2 days. **PACER URL:** http://pacer.rid.uscourts.gov.
Providence Division counties: All counties in Rhode Island.

US Bankruptcy Court -- District of Rhode Island
Home Page: www.rib.uscourts.gov
PACER: Toll-free access: 800-610-9310. Local access phone: 401-528-4062. Case records are available back to 1990. Records are purged every three years. New civil records are available online after 1 day. **PACER URL:** http://pacer.rib.uscourts.gov. Document images available.
Electronic Filing: (Currently in the process of implementing CM/ECF). **Also:** access via phone on VCIS (Voice Case Information System) is available: 800-843-2841, 401-528-4476
Providence Division counties: All counties in Rhode Island.

South Carolina

Capital: Columbia
Richland County

Time Zone: EST

Number of Counties: 46

Home Page www.state.sc.us

Attorney General www.scattorneygeneral.org

Archives www.state.sc.us/scdah

State Level ... Major Agencies

Criminal Records

South Carolina Law Enforcement Division (SLED), Criminal Records Section, PO Box 21398, Columbia, SC 29221 (Courier: 4400 Broad River Rd, Columbia, SC 29210); 803-896-7043, 803-896-7022 (Fax), 8:30AM-5PM.

www.sled.state.sc.us

SLED offers commercial access to criminal record history from 1960 forward on the web site. Fees are $25.00 per screening or $8.00 if for a charitable organization. Credit card ordering accepted. Visit the web site or call 803-896-7219 for details.

Sexual Offender Registry

Sex offender data is available online at www.scattorneygeneral.com (click on "Sex Offender Registry"). Searches are available by name, city, county or ZIP Code.

Corporation Records, Trademarks/Servicemarks, Limited Partnerships, Limited Liability Companys, Limited Liability Partnerships

Corporation Division, Capitol Complex, PO Box 11350, Columbia, SC 29211 (Courier: Edgar A. Brown Bldg, Room 525, Columbia, SC 29201); 803-734-2158, 803-734-2164 (Fax), 8:30PM-5PM.

www.scsos.com/

This free web-based program is called the Online Business Filings search page at www.scsos.com/corp_search.htm. The database provides access to basic filing information about any entity filed with the office. Registered agents' names and addresses, dates of business filings and types of filings are all available. The database is updated every 48 hours.

Uniform Commercial Code

UCC Division, Secretary of State, PO Box 11350, Columbia, SC 29211 (Courier: Edgar Brown Bldg, 1205 Pendelton St #525, Columbia, SC 29201); 803-734-1961, 803-734-2164 (Fax), 8:30AM-5PM.

www.scsos.com/Uniform_Commercial_Code.htm

"Direct Access" is open 24 hours daily, there are no fees. Inquiry is by debtor name. The system provides for copies to be faxed automatically. Call 803-734-2345 for registration information.

Driver License Information, Driver Records

Division of Motor Vehicles, Driver Records Section, PO Box 1498, Columbia, SC 29216-0035 (Courier: 955 Park St, Columbia, SC 29201); 803-737-4000, 803-737-1077 (Fax), 8:30AM-5PM.

www.scdps.org/dmv

The online system offers basic driver data, for a 3 year or a 10 year record. This is a single inquiry process. Network charges will be incurred as well as initial set-up and a security deposit. The system is up between 8 AM and 7 PM. Fee is $6.00 per record. Access is through the AAMVAnet (IBMIN), which requesters much "join." Call Wanda DeLeon at 803-737-1546 for further information. **Other options:** Magnetic tape and cassette batch processing is available.

Legislation Records

www.scstatehouse.net

At the web site, search by bill number, subject, or sponser. The site has a myriad of data including state codes, laws and regulations.

State Level...Occupational Licensing

Accounting Practitioner-AP	http://lookup.llronline.com/index.asp
Acupuncturist	http://lookup.llronline.com/Lookup/Medical.asp
Airport Contact	www.scaeronautics.com/directorysearch.asp
Alcoholic Beverage Sunday Sales	www.sctax.org/DOR/Tax+Information/tax/sundaysales.html
Animal Health Technician	http://lookup.llronline.com/Lookup/Mh.asp
Architect	http://lookup.llronline.com/Lookup/Architects.asp
Architectural Partnership/Corp	http://lookup.llronline.com/Lookup/Architects.asp
Attorney	http://gandalf.scbar.org/lawyer_directory/default.asp
Auction Company	http://lookup.llronline.com/Lookup/Auctioneers.asp
Auctioneer/Auctioneer Apprentice	http://lookup.llronline.com/Lookup/Auctioneers.asp
Aviation Facility	www.scaeronautics.com/AirportSearch.asp
Barber Instructor/School	http://lookup.llronline.com/lookup/barbers.asp
Barber/Barber Apprentice	http://lookup.llronline.com/lookup/barbers.asp
Bodywork Therapist	http://lookup.llronline.com/Lookup/Massage.asp
Building Inspector/Official	http://lookup.llronline.com/Lookup/BuildingCodes.asp
Burglar Alarm Contractor	http://lookup.llronline.com/index.asp
Chiropractor	http://lookup.llronline.com/lookup/Chiropractic.asp
Contractor, General & Mechanical	http://lookup.llronline.com/Lookup/Contractors.asp
Cosmetologist	http://lookup.llronline.com/lookup/cosmetology.asp
Counselor, Professional	http://lookup.llronline.com/lookup/Counselors.asp
Dentist	http://lookup.llronline.com/Lookup/Dentistry.asp
Embalmer	http://lookup.llronline.com/Lookup/Funeral.asp
Emergency Medical Svc. (Ambulance Co)	www.scems.com/emsassn/members.html
Engineer	http://lookup.llronline.com/lookup/Engineers.asp
Forester	http://lookup.llronline.com/Lookup/Foresters.asp
Funeral Director	http://lookup.llronline.com/Lookup/Funeral.asp
Funeral Home	http://lookup.llronline.com/Lookup/Funeral.asp
Geologist	http://lookup.llronline.com/Lookup/Geologists.asp
Hair Care Master Specialist	http://lookup.llronline.com/lookup/barbers.asp
Hearing Aid Dispenser/Fitter	http://lookup.llronline.com/Lookup/Speech.asp
Home Builder, Residential	http://lookup.llronline.com/Lookup/ResidentialBuilders.asp
Housing Inspector	http://lookup.llronline.com/Lookup/BuildingCodes.asp
Inspector, Mech./Elec./Plumb./Prov.	http://lookup.llronline.com/Lookup/BuildingCodes.asp
Insurance Agency/Company/Filing	www.doi.state.sc.us/Eng/Public/Static/DBSearch.asp
Insurance Agent	www.doi.state.sc.us/Eng/Public/Static/DBSearch.asp
Landscape Architect	www.dnr.state.sc.us/water/envaff/prolicense/prolicense.html
Lobbyist	www.lpitr.state.sc.us/reports/ethrpt.htm
Manicure Assistant	http://lookup.llronline.com/lookup/barbers.asp
Manufactured House Mfg/Dealer/Rep	http://lookup.llronline.com/Lookup/Mh.asp
Manufactured House Sales/Install/Repair	http://lookup.llronline.com/Lookup/Mh.asp

Marriage & Family Therapist .... http://lookup.llronline.com/lookup/Counselors.asp
Massage Therapist .... http://lookup.llronline.com/Lookup/Massage.asp
Medical Doctor .... http://lookup.llronline.com/Lookup/Medical.asp
Nurse .... http://lookup.llronline.com/lookup/nurses.asp
Nurse-LPN .... http://lookup.llronline.com/lookup/nurses.asp
Nursing Home Administrator .... http://lookup.llronline.com/Lookup/LTC.asp
Occupational Therapist/Assistant .... http://lookup.llronline.com/Lookup/OT.asp
Optician .... http://lookup.llronline.com/Lookup/Opticians.asp
Optometrist .... http://lookup.llronline.com/Lookup/Optometry.asp
Osteopathic Physician .... http://lookup.llronline.com/Lookup/Medical.asp
Percolation Test Technician .... http://lookup.llronline.com/Lookup/Environmental.asp
Pharmacist/Pharmacy Technician .... http://lookup.llronline.com/lookup/pharmacy.asp
Pharmacy/Drug Outlet .... http://lookup.llronline.com/lookup/pharmacy.asp
Physical Therapist/Therapist Asst .... http://lookup.llronline.com/Lookup/PT.asp
Physician Assistant .... http://lookup.llronline.com/Lookup/Medical.asp
Plans Examiner .... http://lookup.llronline.com/Lookup/BuildingCodes.asp
Podiatrist .... http://lookup.llronline.com/Lookup/Podiatry.asp
Psycho-Educational Specialist .... http://lookup.llronline.com/lookup/Counselors.asp
Psychologist .... http://lookup.llronline.com/Lookup/Psychology.asp
Public Accountant-CPA .... http://lookup.llronline.com/index.asp
Real Estate Appraiser .... www.asc.gov/content/category1/appr_by_state.asp
Residential Care, Community .... http://lookup.llronline.com/Lookup/LTC.asp
Respiratory Care Practitioner .... http://lookup.llronline.com/Lookup/Medical.asp
Roadside Market www.scda.state.sc.us/Consinfo/rsmktdir00.html
Shampoo Assistant .... http://lookup.llronline.com/lookup/barbers.asp
Social Worker .... http://lookup.llronline.com/Lookup/SW.asp
Soil Classifier .... www.dnr.state.sc.us/water/envaff/prolicense/prolicense.html
Solid Waste Landfill .... www.scdhec.net/lwm/html/min.html
Specialty Contractor, Residential .... http://lookup.llronline.com/Lookup/RhbSpecialty.asp
Specialty Food Producer www.scda.state.sc.us/Consinfo/scsfp00mem.html
Speech-Language Pathologist .... http://lookup.llronline.com/Lookup/Speech.asp
Sprinkler Systems Contractor .... http://lookup.llronline.com/index.asp
Surveyor, Land .... http://lookup.llronline.com/lookup/Engineers.asp
Swimming Pool/Spa Operator .... http://lookup.llronline.com/Lookup/Environmental.asp
Veterinarian .... http://lookup.llronline.com/Lookup/Mh.asp
Waste Water Treatment Plant Operator .... http://lookup.llronline.com/Lookup/Environmental.asp
Water Treatment Registration .... http://lookup.llronline.com/Lookup/Environmental.asp
Well Driller .... http://lookup.llronline.com/Lookup/Environmental.asp
Wholesaler/Shipper (Food) .... www.scda.state.sc.us/Ship/wholeandship.htm

County Level ... Courts

Court Administration: Court Administration, 1015 Sumter St, 2nd Floor, Columbia, SC, 29201; 803-734-1800; www.judicial.state.sc.us

Court Structure: The 46 SC counties are divided among sixteen judicial circuits. The circuit courts are in operation at the county level and consist of a court of general sessions (criminal) and a court of common pleas (civil). A family court is also in operation at the county level. The over 300 Magistrate and Municipal Courts (often referred to as "Summary Courts") only handle misdemeanor cases involving a $500.00 fine and/or 30 days or less jail time.

Online Access Note: The judicial Department is developing a statewide court case management system. At present only Charleston County offers Internet access to Circuit Court records and Sumter County to Family Court records.

Charleston County
Circuit Court *Civil and Criminal Records*
http://www3.charlestoncounty.org
Access to civil records (1988 forward), judgments and lis pendens are available free online at www3.charlestoncounty.org/connect. Online document images go back to 1/1/1999. The Internet offers access to criminal records from 04/92 forward. Search by name or case number. There is no fee.

Search these ounty magistrate courts records from 1998 forward at www3.charlestoncounty.org/connect?ref=Magistrates. Charleston Magistrate Courts -- East Cooper Magistrate Court -- Edisto Island Magistrate Court -- James Island Magistrate Court -- Johns Island Magistrate Court -- McClellanville Magistrate Court -- North Charleston Magistrate Courts -- Ravenel Magistrate Court

Sumter County
Circuit Court *Civil and Family Records*
www.sumtercountysc.org
Family court records are available online at the web site.

County Level ... Recorders & Assessors

Recording Office Organization: 46 counties, 46 recording offices. The recording officer is the Register of Mesne Conveyances or Clerk of Court (the title varies by county). The entire state is in the Eastern Time Zone (EST). All federal and state tax liens on personal property and on real property are filed with the Register of Mesne Conveyances (Clerk of Court). Some counties will perform tax lien searches. Search fees and copy fees vary.

Online Access Note: There is no statewide system but several counties have placed free record data on their web sites.

Beaufort County *Property, Assessor Records*
www.co.beaufort.sc.us
Access to the public records search database is available free online at http://rodweb.co.beaufort.sc.us. Also, search county property information at the GIS mapping database at http://maps.co.beaufort.sc.us/Search.htm. A fuller records subscription service requiring registration, fees, and logon is under development.

Charleston County *Real Estate, Property Tax Records*
www.charlestoncounty.org
Access to the county's GIS mapping database of property records is available free at http://gisweb.charlestoncounty.org. Also, online access the the auditor & tresurer's tax system database is available free at http://taxweb.charlestoncounty.org.

Greenville County *Real Property Records*
www.greenvillecounty.org
Search the Register of Deeds database free online at www.greenvillecounty.org

Greenwood County *Property Records*
www.co.greenwood.sc.us
Records on the County Parcel Search database are available free online at http://165.166.39.5/website/gis/viewer.htm. Click on search and choose to search by owner name. An interactive map is included.

Lexington County *Tax Assessor Records*
www.lex-co.com/my_lex.html
Access to county Reassessment Information is available free at www.lex-co.com/my_lex.html. Click on "Assessment Information."

Sumter County *Real Estate, Recording, Deed, Property Tax Records*
Search county e-gov data free at www.sumtercountysc.org/disclaim.htm.

Federal Courts in South Carolina...

Standards for Federal Courts: The universal PACER sign-up number is 800-676-6856. Find PACER and the Party/Case Index on the Web at http://pacer.psc.uscourts.gov. PACER dial-up access is $.60 per minute. Also, courts offering internet access via RACER, PACER, Web-PACER or the new CM-ECF charge $.07 per page fee unless noted as free.

US District Court -- District of South Carolina

Home Page: www.scd.uscourts.gov

PACER: Toll-free access: 800-831-6162. Local access phone: 803-765-5871. Case records are available back to January 1990. Records are purged never. New records are available online after 1 day. **PACER URL:** http://pacer.scd.uscourts.gov.

Opinions Online: Court opinions are available online at www.law.sc.edu/dsc/dsc.htm.

Anderson Division counties: Anderson, Oconee, Pickens.

Beaufort Division counties: Beaufort, Hampton, Jasper.

Charleston Division counties: Berkeley, Charleston, Clarendon, Colleton, Dorchester, Georgetown.

Columbia Division counties: Kershaw, Lee, Lexington, Richland, Sumter.

Florence Division counties: Chesterfield, Darlington, Dillon, Florence, Horry, Marion, Marlboro, Williamsburg.

Greenville Division counties: Greenville, Laurens.

Greenwood Division counties: Abbeville, Aiken, Allendale, Bamberg, Barnwell, Calhoun, Edgefield, Fairfield, Greenwood, Lancaster, McCormick, Newberry, Orangeburg, Saluda.

Spartanburg Division counties: Cherokee, Chester, Spartanburg, Union, York.

US Bankruptcy Court -- District of South Carolina

Home Page: www.scb.uscourts.gov

PACER: Toll-free access: 800-410-2988. Local access phone: 803-765-5965. Case records are available back to November 1988. Records are purged never. New civil records are available online after 1 day. **PACER URL:** http://pacer.scb.uscourts.gov. Document images available.

Electronic Filing: (Currently in the process of implementing CM/ECF). **Also:** access via phone on VCIS (Voice Case Information System) is available: 800-669-8767, 803-765-5211

Columbia Division counties: All counties in South Carolina.

Editor's Tip: Just because records are maintained in a certain way in your state or county do not assume that any other county or state does things the same way that you are used to.

Capital: Pierre
                Hughes County

                                          Home Page   www.state.sd.us

Time Zone: CST/MST   Attorney General   www.state.sd.us/attorney/index.htm

Number of Counties: 66   Archives   www.sdhistory.org/archives.htm

State Level ... Major Agencies

Corporation Records, Limited Partnerships, Limited Liability Company Records, Trademarks/Servicemarks

Corporation Division, Secretary of State, 500 E Capitol Ave, Suite B-05, Pierre, SD 57501-5070; 605-773-4845, 605-773-5666 (Trademarks), 605-773-4550 (Fax), 8AM-5PM.

www.state.sd.us/sos/sos.htm

Search the Secretary of State Corporations Div. Database free at www.state.sd.us/applications/st02corplook/corpfile.asp

Uniform Commercial Code, Federal Tax Liens

UCC Division, Secretary of State, 500 East Capitol, Pierre, SD 57501-5077; 605-773-4422, 605-773-4550 (Fax), 8AM-5PM.

www.state.sd.us/sos/sos.htm

Dakota Fast File is the filing and searching service available from the web site. This is a commercial service that requires registration and a $120-360 fee per year. A certified search is also available.

Sexual Offender Registry

A search of the sexual offender registry is available online at www.sddci.com/administration/id/sexoffender/index.htm. Note, however, this is not a statewide database, and one must search by county.

Birth Certificates

South Dakota Dept. of Health, Vital Records, 600 E Capitol, Pierre, SD 57501-2536; 605-773-4961, 605-773-5683 (Fax), 8AM-5PM.

www.state.sd.us/doh/VitalRec/index.htm

You can search free at the web site for birth records over 100 years old. You can order recent (less than 100 years) birth records at the web site, for a fee. Note that Death, Marriage and Divorce records may be ordered online at the web site, but results are not retruned online.

Driver Records

Dept of Commerce & Regulation, Office of Driver Licensing, 118 W Capitol, Pierre, SD 57501; 605-773-6883, 605-773-3018 (Fax), 8AM-5PM.

www.state.sd.us/dcr/dl/sddriver.htm

The system is open for batch requests 24 hours a day. There is a minimum of 250 requests daily. It generally takes 10 minutes to process a batch. The current fee is $4.00 per record and there are some start-up costs. For more information, call 605-773-6883. **Other options:** Lists are available to the insurance industry.

Legislation Records

http://legis.state.sd.us

Information is available at their web site at no charge. The site is very thorough and has enrolled version of bills.

State Level ... Occupational Licensing

Abstractor Business	www.state.sd.us/dcr/abstractors/roster.htm
Ambulance Service	www.state.sd.us/doh/ems/direct.pdf
Animal Remedy (medicine/drug for animals)	www.state.sd.us/doa/das/hp-af-ar.htm
Architect	www.state.sd.us/dcr/engineer/Roster/index.cfm
Assessor	www.state.sd.us/dcr/engineer/Roster/index.cfm
Auctioneer	www.state.sd.us/dcr/realestate/roster/index.cfm
Bank	www.state.sd.us/dcr/bank
Barber Shop	www.state.sd.us/dcr/barber/roster.htm
Counselor	www.state.sd.us/dcr/counselor/roster.htm
Engineer	www.state.sd.us/dcr/engineer/Roster/index.cfm
Engineer, Petroleum Environmental	www.state.sd.us/dcr/engineer/Roster/index.cfm
Fertilizer	www.state.sd.us/doa/das/hp-fert.htm
Home Inspector	www.state.sd.us/dcr/realestate/roster/index.cfm
Landscape Architect	www.state.sd.us/dcr/engineer/Roster/index.cfm
Lobbyist	www.state.sd.us/sos/lobbyist/lobbyist.htm
Marriage & Family Therapist	www.state.sd.us/dcr/counselor/roster.htm
Mortgage Broker	www.state.sd.us/dcr/bank
Mortgage Lender	www.state.sd.us/dcr/bank
Nurse	https://www.state.sd.us/applications/bn99/secure/Entry.asp
Nurse-RN	https://www.state.sd.us/applications/bn99/secure/Entry.asp
Optometrist	www.odfinder.org/LicSearch.asp
Pesticide Applicator/Dealer	www.state.sd.us/doa/das/
Petroleum Release Remediator	www.state.sd.us/dcr/engineer/Roster/index.cfm
Podiatrist	www.state.sd.us/dcr/podiatry/pod-home.htm
Property Manager	www.state.sd.us/dcr/realestate/roster/index.cfm
Public Accountant-CPA	www.state.sd.us/dcr/accountancy/annreg.pdf
Real Estate Broker	www.state.sd.us/dcr/realestate/roster/index.cfm
Real Estate Salesperson	www.state.sd.us/dcr/realestate/roster/index.cfm
Remediator	www.state.sd.us/dcr/engineer/Roster/index.cfm
Surveyor, Land	www.state.sd.us/dcr/engineer/Roster/index.cfm
Timeshare Real Estate	www.state.sd.us/dcr/realestate/roster/index.cfm
Waste Water Collection System Operator	www.state.sd.us/denr/databases/operator/index.cfm
Waste Water Treatment Plant Operator	www.state.sd.us/denr/databases/operator/index.cfm
Water Distributor	www.state.sd.us/denr/databases/operator/index.cfm
Water Treatment Operator	www.state.sd.us/denr/enviro/wastewtr.htm
Water Treatment Plant Operator	www.state.sd.us/denr/databases/operator/index.cfm
Well Driller	www.state.sd.us/denr/des/waterrights/drillers.htm

County Level ... Courts

Court Administration: State Court Administrator, State Capitol Building, 500 E Capitol Av, Pierre, SD, 57501; 605-773-3474; www.sdjudicial.com

Court Structure: The state re-aligned their circuits from 8 to 7 effective June 2000. South Dakota has a statewide criminal record search database, administered by the State Court Administrator's Office in Pierre. All criminal record information from July 1, 1989 forward, statewide, is contained in the database. To facilitate quicker access for the public, the state has designated 10 county record centers to process all mail or ongoing commercial accounts' criminal record requests. All mail requests are forwarded to, and commercial account requests are assigned to one of 10 specific county court clerks for processing a statewide search. For quicker service on mail requests, use Hanson or Miner counties.

Online Access Note: There is no statewide online access computer system currently available. Larger courts are being placed on computer systems at a rate of 4 to 5 courts per year. Access is intended for internal use only. Smaller courts place their information on computer cards that are later sent to Pierre for input by the state office.

There are no known courts that independently offer online access to their records.

County Level ... Recorders & Assessors

Recording Office Organization: 66 counties, 66 recording offices. The recording officer is the Register of Deeds. 48 counties are in the Central Time Zone (CST) and 18 are in the Mountain Time Zone (MST). Federal and state tax liens on personal property of businesses are filed with the Secretary of State. Other federal and state tax liens are filed with the county Register of Deeds. Most counties will perform tax lien searches. Search fees and copy fees vary.

Online Access Note: Access to UCC records is available online through the SOS's Fast File Internet Access System at https://www.state.sd.us/sos/ucc.htm. Registration and annual fee is required. A certified search is also available. A new system named "Expa" is soon to be available for the occasional user.

There are no known recorder offices that independently offer online access to their records.

Federal Courts in South Dakota...

Standards for Federal Courts: The universal PACER sign-up number is 800-676-6856. Find PACER and the Party/Case Index on the Web at http://pacer.psc.uscourts.gov. PACER dial-up access is $.60 per minute. Also, courts offering internet access via RACER, PACER, Web-PACER or the new CM-ECF charge $.07 per page fee unless noted as free.

US District Court -- District of South Dakota

Home Page: www.sdd.uscourts.gov

Note: Criminal record information is NOT available from PACER in the South Dakota US District Court system.

PACER: Case records are available back to 1991. Records are purged every six months. New records are available online after 1 day. **PACER URL:** http://pacer.sdd.uscourts.gov. Court does not allow electronic access to criminal cases. Civil document images available.

Other Online Access: Access is also available through Racer at http://racer.sdd.uscourts.gov/perl/bkplog.html; $.07 per page fees charged; includes document images.

Aberdeen Division counties: Brown, Butte, Campbell, Clark, Codington, Corson, Day, Deuel, Edmunds, Grant, Hamlin, McPherson, Marshall, Roberts, Spink, Walworth. Judge Battey's closed case records are located at the Rapid City Division.

Pierre Division counties: Buffalo, Dewey, Faulk, Gregory, Haakon, Hand, Hughes, Hyde, Jackson, Jerauld, Jones, Lyman, Mellette, Potter, Stanley, Sully, Todd, Tripp, Ziebach.

Rapid City Division counties: Bennett, Custer, Fall River, Harding, Lawrence, Meade, Pennington, Perkins, Shannon. Judge Battey's closed cases are located here.

Sioux Falls Division counties: Aurora, Beadle, Bon Homme, Brookings, Brule, Charles Mix, Clay, Davison, Douglas, Hanson, Hutchinson, Kingsbury, Lake, Lincoln, McCook, Miner, Minnehaha, Moody, Sanborn, Turner, Union, Yankton.

US Bankruptcy Court -- District of South Dakota

Home Page: www.sdb.uscourts.gov

PACER: Toll-free access: 800-410-2988. Local access phone: 803-765-5965. Case records are available back to October 1, 1991. Records are purged never. New civil records are available online after 1 day. **PACER URL:** http://pacer.sdb.uscourts.gov. Document images available.

Electronic Filing: Electronic filing information is available online at https://ecf.sdb.uscourts.gov. **Also:** access via phone on VCIS (Voice Case Information System) is available: 800-768-6218, 605-330-4559

Pierre Division counties: Bennett, Brown, Buffalo, Butte, Campbell, Clark, Codington, Corson, Custer, Day, Deuel, Dewey, Edmunds, Fall River, Faulk, Grant, Gregory, Haakon, Hamlin, Hand, Harding, Hughes, Hyde, Jackson, Jerauld, Jones, Lawrence, Lyman, Marshall, McPherson, Meade,Mellette, Pennington, Perkins, Potter, Roberts, Shannon, Spink, Stanley, Sully, Todd, Tripp, Walworth, Ziebach.

Sioux Falls Division counties: Aurora, Beadle, Bon Homme, Brookings, Brule, Charles Mix, Clay, Davison, Douglas, Hanson, Hutchinson, Kingsbury, Lake, Lincoln, McCook, Miner, Minnehaha, Moody, Sanborn, Turner, Union, Yankton.

| Capital: | Nashville | | Home Page | www.state.tn.us |
| | Davidson County | | | |

Time Zone: CST/EST   Attorney General   www.attorneygeneral.state.tn.us

Number of Counties: 95   Archives   www.state.tn.us/sos/statelib/tslahome.htm

State Level ... Major Agencies

Corporation Records, Limited Partnership Records, Fictitious Name, Assumed Name, Limited Liability Company Records

Division of Business Svcs; Corporations, Department of State, 312 Eighth Ave. N, 6th Fl, Nashville, TN 37243; 615-741-2286, 615-741-7310 (Fax), 8AM-4:30PM.

www.state.tn.us/sos/service.htm

There is a free online search at www.tennesseeanytime.org/sosname/. While this is intended for business name availability, details are given on existing entities. **Other options:** Some data can be purchased in bulk or list format. Call 615-532-9007 for more details.

Trademarks/Servicemarks, Trade Names

Secretary of State, Trademarks/Tradenames Division, 312 8th Ave North, 6th Fl, Nashville, TN 37243-0306; 615-741-0531, 615-741-7310 (Fax), 8AM-4:30PM.

www.state.tn.us/sos/service.htm

The Internet provides a record search of TN Trademarks, newest records are 3 days old. **Other options:** The agency will provide a file update every three months for $1.00 per page. Requests must be in writing.

Uniform Commercial Code

Division 0f Business Services, Secretary of State, 312 Eighth Ave N, 6th Fl, Nashville, TN 37243; 615-741-3276, 615-741-7310 (Fax), 8AM-4:30PM.

www.state.tn.us/sos

Free access at http://ndweb.state.tn.us/cgi-bin/nd_CGI_50/ietm/PgUCCSearch.

Sexual Offender Registry

The Tennessee Bureau of Investigation maintains a web site at www.ticic.state.tn.us/ that permits searching of sexual offenders, missing children, and people placed on parole from another state but who reside in TN.

Death Records

Tennessee Department of Health, Office of Vital Records, 421 5th Ave North, 1st floor, Nashville, TN 37247; 615-741-1763, 615-741-0778 (Credit card order), 615-726-2559 (Fax), 8AM-4PM.

www.state.tn.us/health/vr

The Cleveland (Tennessee) Public Library staff and volunteers have published the 1914-1925 death records of thirty-three counties at www.state.tn.us/sos/statelib/pubsvs/death.htm#index. It should be noted that the records of children under two years of age have been omitted from this project. Note that all vital record (birth, death, marrige, divorce) records may be ordered online at the web site, but are returned by mail.

Driver Records

Dept. of Safety, Financial Responsibility Section, Attn: Driving Records, 1150 Foster Ave, Nashville, TN 37210; 615-741-3954, 8AM-4:30PM.

www.state.tn.us/safety

Driving records are available to subscribers, signup at www.tennesseeanytime.org. There is a $75 registration fee. Records are available 24 hours daily on an interactive basis. Records are $5.00 each. Suggested only for ongoing users. Call 1-866-886-3468 for more information. **Other options:** Magnetic tape retrieval is available for high volume users. Purchase of the DL file is available for approved requesters.

Legislation Records

www.legislature.state.tn.us

Bill information can be viewed at the Internet site. The Tennessee Code is also available from the web page.

State Level ... Occupational Licensing

Accounting Firm	www.state.tn.us/cgi-bin/commerce/roster2.pl
Alarm Contractor	www.state.tn.us/cgi-bin/commerce/roster2.pl
Alcohol & Drug Abuse Counselor	http://www2.state.tn.us/health/licensure/index.htm
Animal Euthanasia Technician	http://www2.state.tn.us/health/licensure/index.htm
Architect	www.state.tn.us/cgi-bin/commerce/roster2.pl
Athletic Trainer	http://www2.state.tn.us/health/licensure/index.htm
Auction Company	www.state.tn.us/cgi-bin/commerce/roster2.pl
Auctioneer	www.state.tn.us/cgi-bin/commerce/roster2.pl
Audiologist	http://www2.state.tn.us/health/licensure/index.htm
Barber School/Barber Shop	www.state.tn.us/cgi-bin/commerce/roster2.pl
Barber/Barber Technician	www.state.tn.us/cgi-bin/commerce/roster2.pl
Boxing/Racing Personnel	www.state.tn.us/cgi-bin/commerce/roster2.pl
Chiropractor/Chiropractic Therapy Assist	http://www2.state.tn.us/health/licensure/index.htm
Clinical Lab Technician/Personnel	http://www2.state.tn.us/health/licensure/index.htm
Collection Agent/Manager	www.state.tn.us/cgi-bin/commerce/roster2.pl
Contractor	www.state.tn.us/cgi-bin/commerce/roster2.pl
Cosmetologist/Cosmetology Shop	www.state.tn.us/cgi-bin/commerce/roster2.pl
Cosmetology School	www.state.tn.us/cgi-bin/commerce/roster2.pl
Counselor, Associate/Professional	http://www2.state.tn.us/health/licensure/index.htm
Dental Hygienist	http://www2.state.tn.us/health/licensure/index.htm
Dentist/Dental Assistant	http://www2.state.tn.us/health/licensure/index.htm
Dietitian/Nutritionist	http://www2.state.tn.us/health/licensure/index.htm
Electrologist	http://www2.state.tn.us/health/licensure/index.htm
Electrology Instructor/School	http://www2.state.tn.us/health/licensure/index.htm
Embalmer	www.state.tn.us/cgi-bin/commerce/roster2.pl
Emergency Medical Personnel/Dispatcher	http://www2.state.tn.us/health/licensure/index.htm
Emergency Medical Service	http://www2.state.tn.us/health/licensure/index.htm
Engineer	www.state.tn.us/cgi-bin/commerce/roster2.pl
First Responder EMS	http://www2.state.tn.us/health/licensure/index.htm

Funeral & Burial Director/Apprentice	www.state.tn.us/cgi-bin/commerce/roster2.pl
Funeral & Burial Est./Cemetery	www.state.tn.us/cgi-bin/commerce/roster2.pl
Geologist	www.state.tn.us/cgi-bin/commerce/roster2.pl
Hearing Aid Dispenser	http://www2.state.tn.us/health/licensure/index.htm
Home Improvement	www.state.tn.us/cgi-bin/commerce/roster2.pl
Insurance Agent	www.state.tn.us/cgi-bin/commerce/roster2.pl
Insurance Firm	www.state.tn.us/cgi-bin/commerce/roster2.pl
Interior Designer	www.state.tn.us/cgi-bin/commerce/roster2.pl
Landscape Architect	www.state.tn.us/cgi-bin/commerce/roster2.pl
Landscape Architect Firm	www.state.tn.us/cgi-bin/commerce/roster2.pl
Lobbyist	www.state.tn.us/tref/lobbyists/lobbyists.htm
Marriage & Family Therapist	http://www2.state.tn.us/health/licensure/index.htm
Massage Therapist/Establishment	http://www2.state.tn.us/health/licensure/index.htm
Med. Disciplinary Tracking (Abuse Registry)	http://www2.state.tn.us/health/abuseregistry/index.html
Medical Doctor	http://www2.state.tn.us/health/licensure/index.htm
Medical Laboratory Personnel	http://www2.state.tn.us/health/licensure/index.htm
Midwife	http://www2.state.tn.us/health/licensure/index.htm
Motor Vehicle Auction	www.state.tn.us/cgi-bin/commerce/roster2.pl
Motor Vehicle Dealer/Salesperson	www.state.tn.us/cgi-bin/commerce/roster2.pl
Nurse-RN/LPN	http://www2.state.tn.us/health/licensure/index.htm
Nurses' Aide	http://www2.state.tn.us/health/licensure/index.htm
Nursing Home Administrator	http://www2.state.tn.us/health/licensure/index.htm
Occupational Therapist/Assistant	http://www2.state.tn.us/health/licensure/index.htm
Optician, Dispensing	http://www2.state.tn.us/health/licensure/index.htm
Optometrist	http://www2.state.tn.us/health/licensure/index.htm
Orthopedic Physician Assistant	http://www2.state.tn.us/health/licensure/index.htm
Osteopathic Physician	http://www2.state.tn.us/health/licensure/index.htm
Pastoral Therapist, Clinical	http://www2.state.tn.us/health/licensure/index.htm
Personnel Leasing	www.state.tn.us/cgi-bin/commerce/roster2.pl
Pharmacist	www.state.tn.us/cgi-bin/commerce/roster2.pl
Pharmacy	www.state.tn.us/cgi-bin/commerce/roster2.pl
Pharmacy Researcher	www.state.tn.us/cgi-bin/commerce/roster2.pl
Physical Therapist/Assistant	http://www2.state.tn.us/health/licensure/index.htm
Physician Assistant	http://www2.state.tn.us/health/licensure/index.htm
Podiatrist	http://www2.state.tn.us/health/licensure/index.htm
Polygraph Examiner	www.state.tn.us/cgi-bin/commerce/roster2.pl
Private Investigative Company	www.state.tn.us/cgi-bin/commerce/roster2.pl
Private Investigator	www.state.tn.us/cgi-bin/commerce/roster2.pl
Psychological Examiner	http://www2.state.tn.us/health/licensure/index.htm
Psychologist	http://www2.state.tn.us/health/licensure/index.htm
Public Accountant-CPA	www.state.tn.us/cgi-bin/commerce/roster2.pl
Racetrack	www.state.tn.us/cgi-bin/commerce/roster2.pl
Real Estate Appraiser	www.state.tn.us/cgi-bin/commerce/roster2.pl
Real Estate Broker	www.state.tn.us/cgi-bin/commerce/roster2.pl
Real Estate Firm	www.state.tn.us/cgi-bin/commerce/roster2.pl
Real Estate Sales Agent	www.state.tn.us/cgi-bin/commerce/roster2.pl
Respiratory Care Therapist/Tech./Assist.	http://www2.state.tn.us/health/licensure/index.htm
Security Company	www.state.tn.us/cgi-bin/commerce/roster2.pl
Security Guard	www.state.tn.us/cgi-bin/commerce/roster2.pl
Security Trainer	www.state.tn.us/cgi-bin/commerce/roster2.pl
Social Worker, Master/Clinical	http://www2.state.tn.us/health/licensure/index.htm
Speech Pathologist	http://www2.state.tn.us/health/licensure/index.htm
Teacher	https://www.k-12.state.tn.us/tcertinf/Search.asp
Timeshare Agent	www.state.tn.us/cgi-bin/commerce/roster2.pl
Veterinarian	http://www2.state.tn.us/health/licensure/index.htm
X-ray Operator	http://www2.state.tn.us/health/licensure/index.htm
X-ray Technologist, Podiatry	http://www2.state.tn.us/health/licensure/index.htm

County Level ... Courts

Court Administration: Administrative Office of the Courts, 511 Union St (Nashville City Center) #600, Nashville, TN, 37219; 615-741-2687; www.tsc.state.tn.us

Court Structure: Criminal cases are handled by the Circuit Courts and General Sessions Courts. All General Sessions Courts have raised the maximum civil case limit to $15,000 from $10,000. Generally, misdemeanor cases are heard by General Sessions, but in Circuit Court if connected to a felony. The Chancery Courts, in addition to handling probate, also hear certain types of equitable civil cases. Combined courts vary by county. Davidson, Hamilton, Knox, and Shelby Counties have separate Criminal Courts.

Online Access Note: The Administrative Office of Courts provides access to Appellate Court opinions at the web site www.tsc.state.tn.us. Several counties offer online access to court records.

Davidson County
20th District Criminal Court *Criminal Records*
www.nashville.org/ccrt/
Records from Metropolitan Nashville and Davidson County Criminal Court database are available free online at www.nashville.org/ccrt. Search the criminal court dockets by date. Also, the City of Nashville sponsors an Internet site at www.police.nashville.org/justice/default.asp.

Hamilton County
11th District Civil Court *Civil Records*
www.hamiltontn.gov/courts/
Online access to current court dockets are available free at www.hamiltontn.gov/courts/CircuitClerk/dockets/default.htm.

11th District General Sessions Court *Civil Records*
www.hamiltontn.gov/courts/sessions/default.htm
Online access to current court dockets is available free at www.hamiltontn.gov/Courts/Sessions/dockets/default.htm.

11th District Criminal Court *Criminal Records*
www.hamiltontn.gov/courts/
Online access to current court dockets are available free at www.hamiltontn.gov/Courts/CriminalClerk/dockets/default.htm.

Chancery Court *Civil Records*
www.hamiltontn.gov/Courts/ClerkMaster/default.htm
Chancery dockets are available online at www.hamiltontn.gov/Courts/Chancery/dockets/default.htm.

Shelby County
Circuit Court *Civil Records*
Search the clerk's circuit court records for free at http://jssi.co.shelby.tn.us/.

30th District Criminal Court *Criminal Records*
www.co.shelby.tn.us/county_gov/court_clerks/criminal_court/index.html
Search the criminal court records for free at http://jssi.co.shelby.tn.us/.

Chancery Court *Civil Records*
Search the court records for free at http://chancerydata.co.shelby.tn.us/chwebplsql/ck_public_qry_main.cp_main_idx.

General Sessions *Civil and Criminal Records*
http://generalsessionscourt.co.shelby.tn.us
Search the court records for free at http://jssi.co.shelby.tn.us/.

County Level ... Recorders & Assessors

Recording Office Organization: 95 counties, 96 recording offices. The recording officer is the Register of Deeds. Sullivan County has two offices. 66 counties are in the Central Time Zone (CST) and 29 are in the Eastern Time Zone (EST). All federal tax liens are filed with the county Register of Deeds. State tax liens are filed with the Secretary of State or the Register of Deeds. Counties will not perform tax lien searches.

Online Access Note: The State Comptroller of the Treasury Real Estate Assessment Database can be searched free at http://170.142.31.248/. Select a county then search by name for real property infromation. Counties not on the system are Davidson, Hamilton, Knox, Shelby, and Unicoi.

Online access to over 40 counties' property and deeds indexes and images is available via a private company at http://auth.titlesearcher.com/ts/ts.asp or email support@TitleSearcher.com. Registration, login, and monthly $35 fee per county required, plus $20. set up. A $5 per day plan is also available.

Also, online access to 22 counties' property, deeds, judgment, liens, and UCCs is available via a private company at www.ustitlesearch.com or call 615-223-5420. Registration, login, and monthly $25 fee required, plus $50 set up. Use DEMO username to try system.

Also, www.tnrealestate.com offers free and fee services for real estate information from all Tennessee counties.

Davidson County *Property Records*
www.nashville.org
Property records on the Metropolitan Planning Commission City of Nashville database are available free online at www.nashville.org/mpc/maps/index.html. Click on "Go straight to maps." There is also a commercial online service that allows subscribers to download information via an FTP site.

Dickson County *Real Estate, Deed, Judgment, Lien, UCC Records*
Access to indexes and images is available via a private company at www.ustitlesearch.com. Registration and monthly fee required; see state introduction. Also, a second private company offers access to online access to property and deeds indexes and images at http://auth.titlesearcher.com/ts/ts.asp. Fee/registration required; see state introduction.

Dyer County *Real Estate, Deed, Judgment, Lien, UCC, Property Tax Records*
www.co.dyer.tn.us
Access to indexes and images is available via a private company at www.ustitlesearch.com. Registration and monthly fee required; see state introduction. Also, property tax information is available free online at https://dyer.tn.ezgov.com/property/review_search.jsp however, no name searching.

Franklin County *Land Records*
www.titlesearcher.com
Access is through a private company at www.titlesearcher.com. Registration and password required; signup at web site. Per day usage available; see state introduction. Also, online access to property and deeds indexes and images is available via a private company at http://auth.titlesearcher.com/ts/ts.asp. Fee/registration required; see state introduction.

Hamilton County *Real Estate, Recording, Deeds, Property Assessor, Delinquent Tax Records*
www.hamiltontn.gov/register
The County Register of Deeds subscription service is available online for $50 per month and $1.00 per fax page. Search by name, address, or book & page. For further information, call 423-209-6560. Also, property assessor records are available free online at www.hamiltontn.gov/DataServices/default.htm. Click on "Assessor of Property Inquiry." Also, search the county trustees back taxes list at www.hamiltontn.gov/Trustee/backtax.htm

Knox County *Real Estate, Property Tax Records*
www.knoxcounty.org/rod/default.asp
Search the property tax rolls for free at www.knoxcounty.org/tax_search.

Shelby County *Real Estate, Lien, UCC, Recording, Property Tax Records*

http://register.shelby.tn.us

Access to the register database is available free online at http://auth.titlesearcher.com/shelby/menu.asp. Images go back to 12/3/01; indexes to 1986 Also, online access to the assessor property appraisal database is available free at www.assessor.shelby.tn.us/. Also, a commercial site at http://64.132.246.16/default.asp allows for 20 public record database searches. Most records go back to 1990. Low monthly fee; apply at web site.

Sumner County *Property, Recording Records*

www.deeds.sumnertn.org

Access to the Register of Deeds website requires a $25.00 set-up fee and $50.00 monthly user fee. For information, call the Registrar at 615-452-3892 or download the User Agreement from the website.

Williamson County *Deed, Property, Tax Assessor Records*

www.rod.williamson-tn.org

Access to the Professional Access database is available for a $50 per month fee. Information and sign-up at http://williamson-tn.org/co_gov/profacc.htm.

Wilson County *Real Estate, Lien, Recording Records*

www.register.co.wilson.tn.us

Access to the Register of Deeds database requires a $10 registration fee then $25.00 per month usage fee. Includes indexes and images back to 11/1999, expanding to include 1994. Also, Online access to property and deeds indexes and images is available via a private company at http://auth.titlesearcher.com/ts/ts.asp. A per day only fee/registration required; see state introduction.

Access to property and deeds indexes and images is available via a private company at http://auth.titlesearcher.com/ts/ts.asp for these counties:

Anderson -- Bedford -- Bradley -- Clay -- Coffee -- Cumberland -- Decatur -- Fayette -- Fentress -- Giles -- Grainger -- Green -- Grundy -- Hamblen -- Hickman -- Humphreys -- Jackson -- Jefferson -- Lawrence -- Lincoln -- Macon -- Madison -- Marion -- Marshall -- Maury -- Monroe -- Perry -- Sequatchie -- Sevier -- Smith -- Van Buren -- Wayne -- Weakley -- White

Access to indexes and images is available via a private company at www.ustitlesearch.com for these counties:

Benton -- Cannon -- Carroll -- Carter -- Cheatham -- Chester -- Claiborne -- Cocke -- Gibson -- Hardeman -- Hardin -- Henderson -- Henry -- Lake -- Lauderdale -- Lewis -- McMinn -- McNairy -- Robertson -- Tipton -- Warren.

Federal Courts in Tennessee...

Standards for Federal Courts: The universal PACER sign-up number is 800-676-6856. Find PACER and the Party/Case Index on the Web at http://pacer.psc.uscourts.gov. PACER dial-up access is $.60 per minute. Also, courts offering internet access via RACER, PACER, Web-PACER or the new CM-ECF charge $.07 per page fee unless noted as free.

US District Court -- Eastern District of Tennessee

Home Page: www.tned.uscourts.gov

PACER: Toll-free access: 800-869-1265. Local access phone: 865-545-4647. Case records are available back to 1994. Records are purged never. New records are available online after 1 day. **PACER URL:** http://pacer.tned.uscourts.gov.

Chattanooga Division counties: Bledsoe, Bradley, Hamilton, McMinn, Marion, Meigs, Polk, Rhea, Sequatchie.

Greeneville Division counties: Carter, Cocke, Greene, Hamblen, Hancock, Hawkins, Johnson, Sullivan, Unicoi, Washington.

Knoxville Division counties: Anderson, Blount, Campbell, Claiborne, Grainger, Jefferson, Knox, Loudon, Monroe, Morgan, Roane, Scott, Sevier, Union.

Winchester Division counties: Bedford, Coffee, Franklin, Grundy, Lincoln, Moore, Van Buren, Warren.

US Bankruptcy Court -- Eastern District of Tennessee

Home Page: www.tneb.uscourts.gov

PACER: Toll-free access: 888-833-9512. Local access phone: 423-752-5136. Case records are available back to January 1986. Records are purged as deemed necessary. New civil records are available online after 1 day. **PACER URL:** http://pacer.tneb.uscourts.gov. **Also:** access via phone on VCIS (Voice Case Information System) is available: 800-767-1512, 423-752-5272

Chattanooga Division counties: Bedford, Bledsoe, Bradley, Coffee, Franklin, Grundy, Hamilton, Lincoln, Marion, McMinn, Meigs, Moore, Polk, Rhea, Sequatchie, Van Buren, Warren.

Knoxville Division counties: Anderson, Blount, Campbell, Carter, Claiborne, Cocke, Grainger, Greene, Hamblen, Hancock, Hawkins, Jefferson, Johnson, Knox, Loudon, Monroe, Morgan, Roane, Scott, Sevier, Sullivan, Unicoi, Union, Washington.

US District Court -- Middle District of Tennessee

Home Page: www.tnmd.uscourts.gov

PACER: Toll-free access: 800-458-2994. Local access phone: 615-736-7164. Case records are available back three years. Records are purged every year. New records are available online after 1 day. **PACER URL:** http://pacer.tnmd.uscourts.gov.

Columbia Division counties: Giles, Hickman, Lawrence, Lewis, Marshall, Maury, Wayne.

Cookeville Division counties: Clay, Cumberland, De Kalb, Fentress, Jackson, Macon, Overton, Pickett, Putnam, Smith, White.

Nashville Division counties: Cannon, Cheatham, Davidson, Dickson, Houston, Humphreys, Montgomery, Robertson, Rutherford, Stewart, Sumner, Trousdale, Williamson, Wilson.

US Bankruptcy Court -- Middle District of Tennessee

Home Page: www.tnmb.uscourts.gov

PACER: Sign-up number is 615-736-5577. Case records are available back to September 1989. Records are purged never. New civil records are available online after 1 day. **PACER URL:** http://pacer.tnmb.uscourts.gov. To search for free you may request an exemption by downloading a registration form from: http://pacer.psc.uscourts.gov/faxform.html. Fax the form to (210) 301-6441.

Electronic Filing: (Currently in the process of implementing CM/ECF).

Other Online Access: Search "mega cases" at the web site main page; in the database selection box choose "Mega Cases" and follow prompts. Court calendars are also available. Court does not participate in the U.S. party case index.

Nashville Division counties: Cannon, Cheatham, Clay, Cumberland, Davidson, De Kalb, Dickson, Fentress, Giles, Hickman, Houston, Humphreys, Jackson, Lawrence, Lewis, Macon, Marshall, Maury, Montgomery, Overton, Pickett, Putnam, Robertson, Rutherford, Smith, Stewart, Sumner, Trousdale, Wayne, White, Williamson, Wilson.

US District Court -- Western District of Tennessee

Home Page: www.tnwd.uscourts.gov

PACER: Toll-free access: 800-407-4456. Local access phone: 901-495-1259. Case records are available back to 1993. Records are purged as deemed necessary. New records are available online after 2 days. .

Jackson Division counties: Benton, Carroll, Chester, Crockett, Decatur, Gibson, Hardeman, Hardin, Haywood, Henderson, Henry, Lake, McNairy, Madison, Obion, Perry, Weakley.

Memphis Division counties: Dyer, Fayette, Lauderdale, Shelby, Tipton.

US Bankruptcy Court -- Western District of Tennessee

Home Page: www.tnwb.uscourts.gov

PACER: Toll-free access: 800-406-0190. Local access phone: 901-328-3617. Case records are available back to 1989. Records are purged never. New civil records are available online after 2 days. **Also:** access via phone on VCIS (Voice Case Information System) is available: 888-381-4961.

Jackson Division counties: Benton, Carroll, Chester, Crockett, Decatur, Gibson, Hardeman, Hardin, Haywood, Henderson, Henry, Lake, Madison, McNairy, Obion, Perry, Weakley.

Memphis Division counties: Dyer, Fayette, Lauderdale, Shelby, Tipton.

Capital:	Austin Travis County	Home Page	www.state.tx.us
Time Zone:	CST/MST	Archives	www.tsl.state.tx.us
Number of Counties:	254	Attorney General	www.oag.state.tx.us

State Level ... Major Agencies

Criminal Records

Dept of Public Safety, Correspondence Section, Crime Records Service, PO Box 15999, Austin, TX 78761-5999 (Courier: 5805 N Lamar, Bldg G, Austin, TX 78752); 512-424-2474, 8AM-5PM.

http://records.txdps.state.tx.us

Records can be pulled from the web site. Requesters may use a credit card or must establish an account and have a pre-paid bank to work from. The fee established by the Department (Sec. 411.135(b)) is $3.15 per request plus a $.57 handling fee.

Sexual Offender Registry

Sex offender data is available online at http://records.txdps.state.tx.us/soSearch/soSearch.cfm, you can search by name or local area. There is no charge.

Corporation Records, Fictitious Name, Limited Partnership Records, Limited Liability Company Records, Assumed Name, Trademarks/Servicemarks

Secretary of State, Corporation Section, PO Box 13697, Austin, TX 78711-3697 (Courier: J Earl Rudder Bldg, 1019 Brazos, B-13, Austin, TX 78701); 512-463-5555 (Information), 512-463-5578 (Copies), 512-463-5709 (Fax), 8AM-5PM.

www.sos.state.tx.us

There are several online methods available. Web access is available 24 hours daily. There is a $1.00 fee for each record searched. Filing procedures and forms are available from the web site or from 900-263-0060 ($1.00 per minute). Also, Corporate and other TX Sec of State data is available via SOSDirect on the Web; visit www.sos.state.tx.us/corp/sosda/index.shtml. SOSDA accounts are converted to SOSDirect. Printing and certifying capabilities. Also, general corporation information is available at no fee at http://ecpa.cpa.state.tx.us/coa/coaStart.html from the State Comptroller office. **Other options:** The agency makes portions of its database available for purchase. Call 512-475-2755 for more information.

Uniform Commercial Code, Federal Tax Liens

UCC Section, Secretary of State, PO Box 13193, Austin, TX 78711-3193 (Courier: 1019 Brazos St, Rm B-13, Austin, TX 78701); 512-475-2705, 512-475-2812 (Fax), 8AM-5PM.

www.sos.state.tx.us/ucc/index.shtml

There are two systems. Direct dial-up is open from 7 AM to 6 PM. The fee is $3.00 per search, $10.00 for a secured party search. Also, UCC and other TX Sec of State data is available via SOSDirect on the Web; visit www.sos.state.tx.us/corp/sosda/index.shtml. UCC records are $1.00 per search, with printing ($1.00 per page) and certifying ($10.00), also. General information and forms can be found at the web site. **Other options:** The state offers the database for sale, contact the Information Services Dept at 512-463-5609 for further details.

Sales Tax Registrations

Comptroller of Public Accounts, PO Box 13528, Austin, TX 78711-3528 (Courier: LBJ Office Bldg, 111 E 17th St, Austin, TX 78774); 800-252-5555, 800-252-1386 (Searches), 512-475-1610 (Fax), 8AM-5PM.

www.window.state.tx.us

Go to http://aixtcp.cpa.state.tx.us/star/ to search 16,000+ documents by index or collection. This office makes general corporation information available at http://ecpa.cpa.state.tx.us/coa/coaStart.html. There is no fee.

Vehicle Ownership, Vehicle Identification

Department of Transportation, Vehicle Titles and Registration Division, 40th and Jackson Ave, Austin, TX 78779-0001; 512-465-7611, 512-465-7736 (Fax), 8AM-5PM.

www.dot.state.tx.us

Online access is available for pre-approved accounts. A $200 deposit is required, there is a $23.00 charge per month and $.12 fee per inquiry. Searching by name is not permitted. For more information, contact Production Data Control. **Other options:** The state offers tape cartridge retrieval for customized searches or based on the entire database, to eligible organizations. Weekly updates are available. There are approximately 26,000,000 records in the database.

> **Editor's Note:** The Texas Department of Public Safety recently completed a pilot project for online access to driving records. This service is available to high volume, ongoing requester s but it is not open to the general public or pre-employment screeners.

Legislation Records

www.lrl.state.tx.us

The web is a thorough searching site of bills and status.

State Level ... Occupational Licensing

Air Conditioning/Refrigeration Contractor	www.license.state.tx.us/LicenseSearch/
Architectural Barrier	www.license.state.tx.us/LicenseSearch/
Athletic Trainer	www.tdh.state.tx.us/hcqs/plc/at_rost.txt
Attorney	www.texasbar.com/members/onlinetools/qrymbr.asp
Auctioneer	www.license.state.tx.us/LicenseSearch/
Audiologist	www.tdh.state.tx.us/hcqs/plc/speech.htm
Bank Agency, Foreign	www.banking.state.tx.us/asp/fba/lookup.asp
Bank, State Chartered	www.banking.state.tx.us/asp/bank/lookup.asp
Barber School	www.tsbbe.state.tx.us/schoolr.htm
Boiler Inspector/Installer	www.license.state.tx.us/LicenseSearch/
Boxing/Combative Sports Event	www.license.state.tx.us/LicenseSearch/
Career Counselor	www.license.state.tx.us/LicenseSearch/
Check Seller	www.banking.state.tx.us/asp/soc/lookup.asp
Chiropractor	www.tbce.state.tx.us
Counselor, Professional	www.tdh.state.tx.us/hcqs/plc/lpcrost.txt
Currency Exchange	www.banking.state.tx.us/asp/cex/lookup.asp
Dental Hygienist	www.tsbde.state.tx.us/dbsearch/
Dental Laboratory	www.tsbde.state.tx.us/dbsearch/
Dentist	www.tsbde.state.tx.us/dbsearch/
Dietitian	www.tdh.state.tx.us/hcqs/plc/dtrost.txt
ECA	http://160.42.108.3/ems_web/blh_html_page1.htm

Elevator/Escalator .... www.license.state.tx.us/LicenseSearch/
Emergency Medical Technician .... http://160.42.108.3/ems_web/blh_html_page1.htm
Engineer/Engineering Firm .... www.tbpe.state.tx.us/downloads.htm
Funeral Establishment/Preneed Funeral Home.............. www.banking.state.tx.us/asp/pfc/lookup.asp
Funeral Prepaid Permit Holder .... www.banking.state.tx.us/asp/pfc/lookup.asp
Health Facility, Occupational/Physical Therapy .... www.ecptote.state.tx.us/license/ftverif.php
Hearing Instrument Dispenser/Fitter .... www.tdh.state.tx.us/hcqs/plc/fdhi.htm
Industrialized Housing .... www.license.state.tx.us/LicenseSearch/
Insurance Adjuster/Agency .... www.tdi.state.tx.us/general/forms/colists.html
Insurance Agent... www.tdi.state.tx.us/general/forms/agentlists.html
Insurance Company... www.tdi.state.tx.us/general/forms/colists.html
Lead Training Program Providers................................ www.tdh.state.tx.us/beh/lead/TRnlist.htm
Lobbyist.. www.ethics.state.tx.us/php/index.html
Marriage & Family Therapist .... www.tdh.state.tx.us/hcqs/plc/mft.htm#rosters
Massage Therapist.. www.tdh.state.tx.us/hcqs/plc/mtrost.txt
Massage Therapist, Temporary .... www.tdh.state.tx.us/hcqs/plc/mtrostt.txt
Massage Therapy Establishment .... www.tdh.state.tx.us/hcqs/plc/mtroste.txt
Massage Therapy School... www.tdh.state.tx.us/hcqs/plc/mtrosts.txt
Massage Therapy School Instructor............................ www.tdh.state.tx.us/hcqs/plc/mtrosti.txt
Medical Doctor... http://204.65.101.19/OnLineVerif/Phys_SearchVerif.asp
Medical Specialty (Doctor) .... http://204.65.101.19/OnLineVerif/Phys_SearchVerif.asp
Occupational Therapist/Assistant............................... www.ecptote.state.tx.us/license/otverif.php
Optometrist... www.odfinder.org/LicSearch.asp
Orthotics & Prosthetics Facility .... www.tdh.state.tx.us/hcqs/plc/op_fac.htm
Orthotist/Prosthetist... www.tdh.state.tx.us/hcqs/plc/op.htm
PAC List... www.ethics.state.tx.us/dfs/paclists.htm
Paramedic... http://160.42.108.3/ems_web/blh_html_page1.htm
Perfusionist... www.tdh.state.tx.us/hcqs/plc/perfusn.htm
Perpetual Care Cemetery .... www.banking.state.tx.us/asp/pcc/lookup.asp
Personal Employment Service .... www.license.state.tx.us/LicenseSearch/
Pharmacist/Pharmacist Intern..................................... www.tsbp.state.tx.us/dbsearch/Default.htm
Pharmacy.. www.tsbp.state.tx.us/dbsearch/Default.htm
Physical Therapist/Assistant....................................... www.ecptote.state.tx.us/license/ptverif.php
Physicist, Medical .... www.tdh.state.tx.us/hcqs/plc/mprost.txt
Podiatrist .... www.foot.state.tx.us/verifications.htm
Political Contributor... http://txprod.ethics.state.tx.us/tx00/
Polygraph Examiner .... http://polygraph.org/states/tape/members_roster.htm
Polygraph Examiner of Sex Offenders .... www.tdh.state.tx.us/hcqs/plc/csp.htm
Property Tax Consultant.. www.license.state.tx.us/LicenseSearch/
Public Accountant-CPA .... www.tsbpa.state.tx.us
Radiologic Technologist.. www.tdh.state.tx.us/hcqs/plc/mrtrost.txt
Radiology Technician.. www.tdh.state.tx.us/hcqs/plc/mrtrost.txt
Real Estate Appraiser .... www.talcb.state.tx.us
Real Estate Broker/Salesperson/Inspector .... www.trec.state.tx.us/publicinfo/
Representative Offices (Banking) .... www.banking.state.tx.us/asp/rep/lookup.asp
Respiratory Care Practitioner .... www.tdh.state.tx.us/hcqs/plc/rcrost.txt
Service Contract Provider... www.license.state.tx.us/LicenseSearch/
Sex Offender Treatment Provider .... www.tdh.state.tx.us/hcqs/plc/csotrost.txt
Social Worker... www.tdh.state.tx.us/hcqs/plc/lsw/lsw_default.htm#roster
Speech-Language Pathologist...................................... www.tdh.state.tx.us/hcqs/plc/speech.htm
Staff Leasing .... www.license.state.tx.us/LicenseSearch/
STAP Vendor .... www.puc.state.tx.us/relay/stap/vendors.cfm
Talent Agency .... www.license.state.tx.us/LicenseSearch/
Temporary Common Worker....................................... www.license.state.tx.us/LicenseSearch/
Transportation Service Provider .... www.license.state.tx.us/LicenseSearch/
Trust Company.. www.banking.state.tx.us/asp/trustco/lookup.asp
Underground Storage Tank Installer............................ www.tnrcc.state.tx.us/enforcement/csd/ics/ustlicense.html
Vehicle Protection Provider.. www.license.state.tx.us/LicenseSearch/
Water Well & Pump Installer .... www.license.state.tx.us/LicenseSearch/
Weather Modification Service...................................... www.license.state.tx.us/LicenseSearch/

County Level ... Courts

Court Administration: Office of Court Administration, PO Box 12066, Austin, TX, 78711; 512-463-1625; www.courts.state.tx.us

Court Structure: The legal court structure for Texas takes up 30 pages in the "Texas Judicial Annual Report." Generally, Texas District Courts have general civil jurisdiction and exclusive felony jurisdiction, along with typical variations such as contested probate, contested elections, and divorce. District Courts handle felonies. County Courts handle misdemeanors and general civil cases.

The County Court structure includes two forms of courts - "Constitutional" and "at Law" - which come in various configurations depending upon the county. County Courts' upper claim limits vary from $5,000 to $100,000. For civil matters up to $5000, we recommend searchers start at the Constitutional County Court as they, generally, offer a shorter waiting time for cases in urban areas. In addition, keep in mind that the Municipal Courts have, per the Texas manual, "limited civil penalties in cases involving dangerous dogs." In some counties the District Court or County Court handles evictions.

Online Access Note: Statewide appellate court case information is searchable for free on the Internet at www.info.courts.state.tx.us/appindex/appindex.exe. A growing number of individual county courts also offer online access to their records.

Bailey County
District and County Courts *Civil and Criminal Records*
Online access is through www.idocket.com; registration and password required. Records go back to 12/31/1995.

Bandera County
District Court *Civil and Criminal Records*
Civil case information is available free online at www.idocket.com. Free searching is limited. Records go back to 12/31/1990. Criminal records require registration and password.

Bexar County
District and County Courts - Central Records *Civil and Criminal Records*
www.co.bexar.tx.us/dclerk
Access to the remote online system requires $100 setup fee, plus a $25 monthly fee, plus inquiry fees. Call Jennifer Mann at 210-335-0212 for more information. Also, free online access to records is being implemented. Check www.co.bexar.tx.us/dclerk/e-Services/e-services.htm for updates.

Brooks County
District Court *Civil and Criminal Records*
Civil case information is available online at www.idocket.com. Free searching is limited. Records go back to 12/31/1993. Criminal records requires registration and password. Records go back to 12/31/1993.

Cameron County
District Court *Civil and Criminal Records*
Online access is available 24 hours daily. $125 setup fee includes software, there is a $30 monthly access fee also. For more information, call Eric at 956-544-0838 X475. Also, online access is through www.idocket.com; registration and password required. Records go back to 12/31/1988. Criminal records requires registration and password.

Cochran County
District & County Court *Civil and Criminal Records*
Email address for search requests is cclerk@door.net.

Collin County

District and County Courts *Civil and Criminal Records*

Online is available 7am to 7pm M-Sat, 6 to 6 on Sun. Access fee is $.12 a minute, there is a monthly minimum of $31.13. Procomm Plus is suggested. Subscribers also receive fax call-back service. Call Patty Ostrom at 972-548-4503 for subscription information.

Comal County

District and County Courts *Civil and Criminal Records*

www.co.comal.tx.us

Online access to county judicial records is available free at www.co.comal.tx.us/Search/judsrch.htm. Search civil records by either party name. Search criminal records by defendant name.

Dallas County

District Court *Civil Records*

Criminal District Courts 1-5 *Criminal Records*

County Court *Civil and Misdemeanor Records*

www.dallascounty.org

Public Access System allows remote access at $1.00 per minute to these and other court/public records. Will invoice to your telephone bill. Dial-in access number is 900-263-INFO. ProComm Plus is recommended. The system is open 8am to 4:30pm. Searching is by name or case number. Call the Public Access Administrator at 214-653-6807 for more information.
www.dallascounty.org

Denton County

District Court *Civil and Criminal Records*

http://dentoncounty.com/dept/main.asp?Dept=26

Searching is available at http://justice.dentoncounty.com at no charge. Search by name or cause number. Criminal records available from 1994 forward. Access also includes sheriff bond and jail records.

County Court *Civil and Criminal Records*

www.dentoncounty.com/dept/ccl.htm

Online access to civil court records is available free online at http://justice.dentoncounty.com/CivilSearch/civfrmd.htm. Online access to county criminal records available free at http://justice.dentoncounty.com/CrimSearch/crimfrmd.htm. Jail, bond, and parole records are also available at http://justice.dentoncounty.com. Search for registered sex offenders by zip code at http://sherrif.dentoncounty.com/sex_offenders/default.htm.

Eastland County

District Court *Civil and Criminal Records*

Civil case information is available online at www.idocket.com. Free searching is limited. Records go back to 12/31/1940. Criminal records require registration and password. Records go back to 12/31/1966.

El Paso County

District Court *Civil and Criminal Records*

Online access to court records is available free at www.co.el-paso.tx.us/search.htm (pending cases only) Online access to criminal records is available at free at www.co.el-paso.tx.us/search.htm. Also, online access is through www.idocket.com; registration and password required; records go back to 6/1/2002.

County Court *Civil and Criminal Records*

Online access to civil court records is available free at www.co.el-paso.tx.us/search.htm.

Fort Bend County

District Court *Civil and Criminal Records*

www.co.fort-bend.tx.us/Admin_of_justice/district_clerk/district_courts.htm

Online searching available through a 900 number service. Access fee is $.55 per minute plus a deposit. Call 281-341-4522 for information. Criminal records from 1987 are available on the same online system as civil records.

County Court *Civil, Probate and Criminal Records*

www.co.fort-bend.tx.us

Online access to the records index is available free at www.co.fort-bend.tx.us/Admin_of_Justice/County_Clerk/index_info_research.htm. Includes Probate records index online.

Galveston County
County Court *Civil and Criminal Records*
www.co.galveston.tx.us/County_Courts/
Access to the GCNET remote online service has been suspended. For more information, call 409-770-5115.

Grayson County
County Court *Civil and Criminal Records*
www.co.grayson.tx.us
Online access to records is available free online at http://209.151.115.130:3004/judsrch.asp. Also includes sheriffs' bail, and sheriff's jail searching.

Gregg County
District Court *Civil and Criminal Records*
www.co.gregg.tx.us/government/courts.asp
County Court *Civil and Criminal Records*
www.co.gregg.tx.us/government/commissionersCourt/county_judge.asp
Online access to county judicial records is available free at www.co.gregg.tx.us/judsrch.htm. Search by name, cause number, status. Also includes jail and bond search.

Guadalupe County
District Court *Civil and Criminal Records*
www.co.guadalupe.tx.us/districtclerk.htm
Online access is available at www.idocket.com; one free search per day; subscription required for more. Online records go back to 12/31/1991. Criminal records requires registration and password.

Harris County
District Court *Civil and Criminal Records*
www.hcdistrictclerk.com
The online subscriber fee site is now replaced by the free-to-view e-docs service at https://e-docs.hcdistrictclerk.com/FormsLogin.asp?/. There is a $1 per pg charge (credit cards accepted) for documents and you may choose the delivery method. Online records go back to 10/1989. Also, civil court general information is available on the Internet at www.ccl.co.harris.tx.us/civil/default.htm; online access to criminal records is the same as civil. Also, Internet access to criminal records available to qualified JIMs subscribers at www.co.harris.tx.us/subscriber/cb/submenu.htm. Records include felonies and A & B class misdemeanors.

County Court *Civil Records*
www.cclerk.hctx.net
Online access is free at the web site. System includes civil data search and county civil settings inquiry and other county clerk functions. For further information, visit the web site, send email request to dcsa@dco.co.harris.tx.us, or call 713-755-6421.

Probate Court *Probate Records*
Probate dockets are available through the Harris County online system. Call (713) 755-7815 for information. Also, dockets are available free at www.cclerk.hctx.net/coolice/default.asp?Category=ProbateCourt&Service=pc_inquiry. Records go back to 1837.

Hays County
District and County Courts *Civil, Probate and Criminal Records*
www.co.hays.tx.us
Access is through www.idocket.com; registration and password required. Records go back to 12/31/1986. Includes probate records

Hidalgo County
District and County Courts *Civil and Criminal Records*
Online access is through www.idocket.com; registration and password required. Civil records go back to 12/31/1986. Criminal records go back to 12/31/1991.

Hill County
District Court *Civil and Criminal Records*
Online access to court records is available through idocket.com. One search a day is free; subcription required for more. Civil records go back to 12/31/1990. Criminal records access requires registration and password required.

Jefferson County

District Court *Civil and Criminal Records*

www.co.jefferson.tx.us

Online access to the civil records index available at www.co.jefferson.tx.us/dclerk/civil_index/main.htm. Search by defendant or plaintiff by year 1985 to present. Online access to the criminal records index is available at www.co.jefferson.tx.us/dclerk/criminal_index/main.htm. Search by name by year 1981 to present.

McCulloch County

District Court *Civil, Probate, and Criminal Records*

Civil case information is available free online at www.idocket.com. Free searching is limited. Records go back to 12/31/1995. Criminal records access requires registration and password. County court and Probate records go back to 12/31/1996.

Midland County

District and County Courts *Civil and Criminal Records*

www.co.midland.tx.us/DC/default.asp

Online access to the district Clerk database is available at www.co.midland.tx.us/DC/Database/search.asp. Registration and password is required; contact the clerk for access restrictions.

Navarro County

District Court *Civil and Criminal Records*

Civil case information is available online at www.idocket.com. Free searching is limited. Records go back to 12/31/1990. Criminal records requires registration and password.

Nueces County

District and County Courts *Civil and Criminal Records*

www.co.nueces.tx.us/districtclerk/

Online access to civil District Court records are available free online at the web site. Search criminal District Court records by name, SID number, or cause number.

Parmer County

District Court *Civil and Criminal Records*

Online access is through www.idocket.com; registration and password required. Records go back to 12/31/1995.

Potter County

District Court *Civil and Criminal Records*

www.co.potter.tx.us/districtclerk

Civil case information from 1988 forward is available online at www.idocket.com. Free case searching is limited.

Randall County

District Courts *Civil and Criminal Records*

www.randallcounty.org

Civil case information is available free online at www.idocket.com. Free searching is limited.

County Court *Civil, Probate, and Criminal Records*

www.randallcounty.org/cclerk/default.htm

Civil case information is available online from idocket at http://idocket.com/counties.htm. Free searching is limited. Civil records go back to 12/31/1999; probate back to 12/31/1969. Criminal case information goes back to 12/31/1991.

Tarrant County

District and County Courts *Civil and Criminal Records*

www.tarrantcounty.com

Access to the remote online system requires $50 setup that includes software. The per minute fee is $.05 plus $25 per month. Call Mr. Hinojosa at 817-884-1419 for more information.

Tom Green County

District and County Courts *Civil and Criminal Records*

http://justice.co.tom-green.tx.us

Online access to civil case records back to 1994 is available online at the web site. Search by name, case number, DOB. Web site also includes Sheriff jail and bond records.

Webb County
District and County Courts *Civil and Criminal Records*
www.webbcounty.com
Online access is through www.idocket.com; registration and password required. Records go back to 12/31/1988. County Court criminal records access requires registration and password; records go back to 12/31/1989.

County Level ... Recorders & Assessors

Recording Office Organization: 254 counties, 254 recording offices. The recording officer is the County Clerk. 252 counties are in the Central Time Zone (CST) and 2 are in the Mountain Time Zone (MST). Federal tax liens on personal property of businesses are filed with the Secretary of State. Other federal and all state tax liens are filed with the County Clerk. All counties will perform tax lien searches. Search fees and copy fees can vary, but records are usually provided as part of the UCC search.

Online Access Note: Numerous Texas counties offer online access to assessor and recorded document data. Also, listed below are two private companies offer access via the web to multiple counties' tax assessor data. Some counties can be accessed from either company site.

www.txcountydata.com - Assessor and property information records for over fifty Texas counties on the TXCOUNTYDATA site are available for no fee. At this site click on "County Search" then use the pull down menu in the county field to select the county to search. The County Info page for each county lists the Appraiser, mailing address, phone, fax, web site, e-mail. Generally, you can search any county account, owner name, address, or property ID number. Search allows you to access owner address, property address, legal description, taxing entities, exemptions, deed, account number, abstract/subdivision, neighborhood, valuation info, and more.

Counties with Assessor/tax records online **no fee:**

Anderson	Angelina	Aransas	Atascosa
Austin	Bastrop	Blanco	Brazoria
Brazos	Brown	Burleson	Burnet
Caldwell	Calhoun	Coleman	Comanche
Fannin	Ft. Bend	Gillespie	Hays
Hunt	Kendall	Kerr	Kimble
Lamb	Liberty	Limestone	Llano
Lubbock	Madison	Maverick	Milam
Montgomery	Newton	Nueces	Rockwall
San Jacinto	Somervell	Swisher	Upshur
Victoria	Waller	Washington Wharton	
Wilson	Wood		

ALSO...

www.taxnetusa.com - TaxNetUSA offers free appraisal district and property information records for a growing number of Texas counties as well as a few counties in other states. The site also offers advanced and subscriptions services for many of the counties.

At the TaxNetUSA site, user chooses "advanced search subscribers login" (fee service) or "Appraisal Districts Online Basic Search" (no fee). For a basic search, use the pull down menu in the county field to select the county to search. Select county and click go. At the county Assessor/Tax site, follow the directions for that county. Generally, but in varying degrees from county to county, the basic search allows you to access general property information: name, address, valuation, etc., and you may search by parcel number, owner name, or address. Depending on the county, more "detailed" information may be available.

TaxNetUSA's Advanced Search Information (fee) allows most counties to be searched by any combination of criteria. Fees vary and can range from a simple $25 search to multiple county subscriptions as high as $1,500.

TaxNetUSA Texas counties with appraisal district information online **no fee:**

Archer	Bandera	Bastrop	Brazoria	
Bee	Brazos	Caldwell	Cameron	*continued next page*

continued next page

Chambers	Clay	Collin	Dallas
Denton	Ellis	ElPaso	Erath
Fannin	Franklin	Galveston	Grayson
Gregg	Guadalupe	Hardin*	Harrison
Hays	Henderson	Hidalgo	Hill
Hood	Jack	Jefferson	Johnson
Kaufman	Kleberg	Limestone	Lubbock
McLennan*	Montgomery	Nacogdoches	Nueces
Rockwall	Rusk	San Patricio	Smith*
Swisher*	Tarrant	Taylor	Travis
Van Zandt	Victoria	Webb	Wichita*
Wilbarger	Williamson	Wise	Zapata

* Counties that do NOT offer **Advanced**

TaxNetUSA Texas counties with Assessor/tax records **Advanced (fee) only:**

| Fort Bend | Harris | Hunt |
| Navarro | Parker | Potter-Randall |

TaxNetUSA Texas counties that offer **Assessor/Collector information:**

| Hidalgo | Johnson | Kaufman | Lubbock | Taylor | Travis |

Anderson County *Assessor, Property Tax, Land, Judgment, Lien Records*

The recording database is available at www.titlex.com. Login required. Select Anderson from the county list. Also, see note at beginning of section.

Aransas County *Recording, Birth, Death, Assessor, Property Tax Records*

Access to recordings, land records, births, deaths is available free at http://apolloplus.com then click on member counties to access Washington Co. Also, assessor and property tax information is available at www.aransascad.org, also see note at beginning of section.

Austin County *Assessor, Property Tax, Land, Judgment, Lien Records*

The recording database is available at www.titlex.com. Login required. Select Austin from the county list. Also, see note at beginning of section.

Bastrop County *Assessor, Property Tax, Land, Judgment, Lien Records*

The recording database is available at www.titlex.com. Login required. Select Bastrop from the county list. Also, see note at beginning of section.

Bell County *Assessor, Property Tax Records*

TexasTax provides two methods of access to county records. Access to "Advanced Search" records requires a login and subscription fee. Subs are allowed in monthly increments. Advanced Search includes full data, maps, and Excel spreadsheet. For information, see www.texastax.com/bell/subscriptioninfo.asp. Records on "Quick Search - FREE" at www.texastax.com/bell/index/asp allows access to these County records: tax ID number, owner, parcel address, land value data. Search FREE by tax ID number, address, name, city or value. View details.

Bexar County *Grantor/Grantee, Marriage, UCC, Assumed Name, Recording, Property Tax, Assessor Records*

www.bexar.org
Access to the County Clerk database is available free at www.countyclerk.bexar.landata.com. Also, Online access to the county Central Appraisal District database is available free at www.bcad.org/property.htm.

Brazoria County *Assessor, Property Tax, Land, Grantor/Grantee Records*

www.brazoria-county.com
Access to the county Central Appraisal District database is available free at www.brazoriacad.org. Click on "appraisal roll." Also, the recording database is available at www.titlex.com. Login required. Select Brazoria from the county list.

Burnet County *Assessor, Property Tax, Land, Grantor/Grantee Records*

The recording database is available at www.titlex.com. Login required. Select Burnet from the county list.

Caldwell County   *Assessor, Property Tax, Personal Property Records*
www.caldwellcad.org
Access to the county Appraisal database is available free at www.caldwellcad.org/search.htm. Also, see notes at beginning of section.

Calhoun County   *Land, Grantor/Grantee, Judgment, Lien Records*
The recording database is available at www.titlex.com. Login required. Select Calhoun from the county list.

Chambers County   *Property Tax, Appraiser Records*
Search the appraiser property tax database for free at www.chamberscad.org.

Cherokee County   *Land, Grantor/Grantee, Judgment, Lien Records*
The recording database is available at www.titlex.com. Login required. Select Cherokee from the county list.

Collin County   *Property Tax, Assessor, Business Personal Property Records*
www.co.collin.tx.us
Search the assessor's property tax and business property database for free at www.collincad.org/search.cfm.

Colorado County   *Land, Grantor/Grantee, Judgment, Lien Records*
The recording database is available at www.titlex.com. Login required. Select Colorado from the county list.

Coryell County   *Recording, Land Records*
Access may be available at http://apolloplus.com in late 2002.

Dallas County   *Property Tax, Personal Property, Voter Registration, Marriage, UCC,*
    Assumed Name, Probate Records
www.dallascounty.org/html/citizen-serv/county-clerk/
Access to the County Voter Registration Records is available free online at www.openrecords.org/records/voting/dallas_voting.
Search by name or partial name. Also, online access to the Central Appraisal District database is available free at
www.dallascad.org/search.htm. Business personal property searches are available. Also, search marriages, assumed names, UCCs
back to 1977 on the online records search system, either per item or $75 annual fee. Credit cards accepted; see
www.dallascounty.org/applications/english/record-search/intro.html. Probate/court records also.

Denton County   *Real Estate, Property, Recording, Voter Registration, Most Wanted, Parollee, Sex Offender,*
    Bond, Jail, Conviction Records
www.dentoncounty.com/dept/ccl.htm
Access to the county property database indices is available free for name/instrument searches. There is for fee for access, but to print
is $1.00 per page. Visit www.texaslandrecords.com/Denton/index.jsp. And, with a full subscription, you can search full indices and
download images. Also, search the voter registration rolls for free at http://elections.dentoncounty.com/VRSearch/default.asp. Search
the "justice" database for free at http://justice.dentoncounty.com. Includes Parollees, sex offenders, most wanted lists, bond, jail,
convictions and court records databases.

Ector County   *Real Estate, Appraiser, Personal Property Records*
Search the county appraisal district database for free at www.ectorcad.org/real_name.html.

Ellis County   *Appraiser, Property Tax Records*
Search the property appraiser database for free at www.elliscad.org.

El Paso County   *Assumed Name, Property Tax, Real Estate, Vital Statistic Records*
Search vital statistics (birth, death, marriage), assumed names, and property (land) records free at www.co.el-paso.tx.us/search.htm.
Also, search property tax data at www.elpasocad.org.

Fayette County   *Recording, Land, Grantor/Grantee Records*
The recording database is available at www.titlex.com. Login required. Select Fayette from the county list. Also, access may be
available at http://apolloplus.com in late 2002.

Fort Bend County   *Real Estate, Lien, Assessor, UCC, Marriage, Death, Birth, Probate Records*
www.co.fort-bend.tx.us

Access to the county clerk database is available free at www.co.fort-bend.tx.us/admin_of_justice/County_Clerk/index_info_research.htm. Search the property index by name, or the plat index. And, search county UCCs, probate and court records. Also, for full records, their fee remote system is available, including images. Access fee is $.25 per minute plus set-up. For information, contact Diane Shepard at 281-341-8664.

Freestone County *Assessor, Property Tax Records*
Search the assessor's property tax database for free at www.freestonecad.org/search.html.

Galveston County *Real Estate, Lien, Assessor, Grantor/Grantee Records*
www.galvestoncad.org
Several sources exist. Access to County online records requires $200 escrow deposit, $25 monthly fee, plus $.25 per minute. Index records date back to 1965; image documents to 1/95. Lending agency information and fax back services are available. For information, contact Robert Dickinson at 409-770-5115. Also, access to the Central Appraisal District database is available free at www.galvestoncad.org/search.htm. Also, online access to sheriff sales is available free at www.co.galveston.tx.us/sheriff/sheriff.htm. A Grantor/Grantee index is available at www.titlex.com; Login and select Galveston County.

Goliad County *Land, Grantor/Grantee, Judgment, Lien Records*
The recording database is available at www.titlex.com. Login required. Select Goliad from the county list.

Gregg County *Property Tax, Land, Grantor/Grantee Records*
www.co.gregg.tx.us
The recording database is available at www.titlex.com. Login required. Select Gregg from the county list.

Guadalupe County *Property Tax, Assessor Records*
www.guadalupecad.org
Access to the county Appraisal District database is available free at at www.guadalupecad.org/gadname.html. Name search here, but other methods are allowed at the web site above.

Harris County
Real Estate, Lien, Assessor, Voter, UCC, Assumed Name, Grantor/Grantee, Vital Statistic Records
www.co.harris.tx.us/cclerk
Two sources for County Clerk information exist. Access to the County online subscription service requires a $300 deposit and $40 per hour of use. For info, call Ken Peabody at 713-755-7151. Also, free access to records is available free on the web. Assumed Name records, UCC filings, vital statistic, and Real Property are at www.cclerk.hctx.net/coolice/default.asp?Category=RealProperty&Service=mastermenu. Assessor records are at www.hcad.org/Records. County Court Civil, marriage and informal marriage records are also available there. Also, search the Assessor-Collector database free at www.tax.co.harris.tx.us/dbsearch.htm.

Harrison County *Property Tax Records*
Search the appraiser database for free at www.harrisoncad.org.

Hood County *Assessor, Property Tax Records*
Search the county appraisal roll for free at www.hoodcad.org.

Jackson County *Land, Grantor/Grantee, Judgment, Lien Records*
The recording database is available at www.titlex.com. Login required. Select Jackson from the county list.

Jefferson County *Property Tax Records*
www.co.jefferson.tx.us
Search the appraiser database for free at www.jcad.org/search2.asp.

Johnson County *Assessor, Property Tax Records*
www.johnsoncad.com/search.htm
Records from the County Appraiser are available fee online at the web site.

Knox County *Land, Grantor/Grantee Records*
The recording database is available at www.titlex.com. Login required. Select Knox from the county list.

Lamar County   *Death Records*
Cemetery records in Lamar County are available free online at http://userdb.rootsweb.com/cemeteries/TX/Lamar.

Lubbock County   *Elections, Appraiser, Property Tax Records*
www.co.lubbock.tx.us
Access to the county clerks records is limited to election results at www.co.lubbock.tx.us/CClerk/county_clerk.htm. Also, search the property appraiser database for free at www.lubbockcad.org/search.cfm.

McLennan County   *Property Tax, Land, Grantor/Grantee Records*
The recording database is available at www.titlex.com. Login required. Select McLennan from the county list.

Midland County   *Property Assessor, Voter Registration Records*
Access to the property tax database is available free at www.co.midland.tx.us/Tax/Property/Database/search.asp. Also, search property data on the mapping page at www.midcad.org/Search/index.htm. Online access to the voter registration database is available free at www.co.midland.tx.us/Elections/VoterDatabase/input.asp.

Milam County   *Assessor, Property Tax, Land, Grantor/Grantee, Judgment, Lien Records*
The recording database is available at www.titlex.com. Login required. Select Milam from the county list.

Montgomery County   *Assessor, Property Tax, Land, Grantor/Grantee, Judgment, Lien Records*
www.co.montgomery.tx.us
The recording database is available at www.titlex.com. Login required. Select Montgomery from the county list.

Nacogdoches County   *Property Tax Records*
Access to the county Central Appraisal District Appraisal Roll from TaxNetUSA is available free at www.taxnetusa.com/nacogdoches.

Newton County   *Assessor, Property Tax, Death Records*
For assessor/property tax: see note at beginning of section. Death records in this county may be accessed over the Internet at www.jas.net/jas.htm (site may be temporarily down).

Nueces County   *Assessor, Property Tax Records*
www.co.nueces.tx.us
Records from the County Appraiser are available fee online at www.nuecescad.org/nueces3.html.

Potter County   *Assessor, Property Tax Records*
www.prad.org
Two sources exist. Records on the Potter-Randall Appraisal District database are available free online at www.prad.org/search.html. Records periodically updated; for current tax information call Potter (806-342-2600) or Randall (806-665-6287).

Randall County   *Assessor, Property Tax Records*
www.prad.org
Two sources exist. Randall County records are combined online with Potter County; see Potter County for access information.

Rusk County   *Property Tax, Land, Grantor/Grantee, Judgment, Lien Records*
The recording database is available at www.titlex.com. Login required. Select Rush from the county list.

San Patricio County   *Assessor, Property Tax, Personal Property Records*
Searh the assessor data for free at www.sanpatriciocad.org/sanpatsearch.htm.

Swisher County   *Assessor, Property Tax Records*
Search the appraisal tax rolls for free at www.txcountydata.com/county.asp?County=219.

Tarrant County   *Property Tax, Assessor, Real Estate, Grantor/Grantee Records*
www.tarrantcounty.com/tc_countyclerk/site/default.asp
Access to the county Appraisal District Property data is available free at www.tad.org/Datasearch/datasearch.htm. Also, online access to the county clerk's real estate and grantor/grantee index is available free at www.tarrantcounty.com/tc_countyclerk/lib/tc_county clerk/search.asp. Also, online access to property tax data is available free at www.tad.org/Datasearch/datasearch.htm.

Taylor County   *Assessor, Property Tax, Personal Property, Unclaimed Property Records*
www.taylorcad.org
Access to the county Central Appraisal District database is available free at www.taylorcad.org/tayname.html. Search is by name, but other methods are available via the web site listed above. Search business personal property at www.taylorcad.org/tayppname.html. Also, search the treasurer's database of unclaimed property free at www.taylorcountytexas.org/unclaime.html.

Travis County   *Assessor, Property Tax, Business Property, Voter Registration Records*
www.traviscad.org
Access to the Central Appraisal District database is available free at www.traviscad.org/search.htm. Also search business personal property. Also, search the voter registration rolls free at www.texasonline.com/travisco/voter/home.htm.

Van Zandt County   *Property Appraisal, Land, Grantor/Grantee, Judgment, Lien Records*
Search the county appraisal rolls for free at www.vanzandtcad.org. Also includes plat maps online. Also, the recording database is available at www.titlex.com. Login required. Select Van Zandt from the county list.

Victoria County   *Assessor, Property Tax, Land, Grantor/Grantee, Judgment, Lien Records*
The recording database is available at www.titlex.com. Login required. Select Victoria from the county list.

Washington County   *Recording, Land, Marriage, Death, Birth, Military Discharge, Grantor/Grantee, Judgment, Lien Records*
Access is available free at http://apolloplus.com then click on member counties to access Washington Co. Also, the recording database is available at www.titlex.com. Login required. Select Washington from the county list.

Webb County   *Appraiser, Property Tax Records*
www.webbcad.org
Search the county Central Appraisal District database available at www.webbcad.org/search1.htm.

Wharton County   *Assessor, Property Tax, Land, Grantor/Grantee, Judgment, Lien Records*
The recording database is available at www.titlex.com. Login required. Select Wharton from the county list.

Wilbarger County   *Property Tax, Personal Property Records*
Search the appraisal rolls for free at www.taxnetusa.com/wilbarger.

Willacy County   *Land, Grantor/Grantee Records*
The recording database is available at www.titlex.com. Login required. Select Willacy from the county list.

Williamson County   *Assessor, Property Tax, Tax Sales, Land, Grantor/Grantee, Judgment, Lien Records*
www.wilco.org
The recording database is available at www.titlex.com. Login required. Select Williamson from the county list. Also, online access to the appraiser database is available free at www.wcad.org/Search/Quicksearch.asp. Also, online access to the monthly delinquent tax sale list is available free at www.williamson-county.org/Assessor/Tax.html.

Wood County   *Assessor, Property Tax, Land, Grantor/Grantee, Judgment, Lien Records*
The recording database is available at www.titlex.com. Login required. Select Wood from the county list.

Federal Courts in Texas...

Standards for Federal Courts: The universal PACER sign-up number is 800-676-6856. Find PACER and the Party/Case Index on the Web at http://pacer.psc.uscourts.gov. PACER dial-up access is $.60 per minute. Also, courts offering internet access via RACER, PACER, Web-PACER or the new CM-ECF charge $.07 per page fee unless noted as free.

US District Court -- Eastern District of Texas
Home Page: www.txed.uscourts.gov
PACER: Case records are available back to 1992. Records are purged once per year. New records are available online after 1 day.
PACER URL: http://pacer.txed.uscourts.gov.
Beaumont Division counties: Delta*, Fannin*, Hardin, Hopkins*, Jasper, Jefferson, Lamar*, Liberty, Newton, Orange, Red River. Counties marked with an asterisk are called the Paris Division, whose case records are maintained here.

Lufkin Division counties: Angelina, Houston, Nacogdoches, Polk, Sabine, San Augustine, Shelby, Trinity, Tyler.
Marshall Division counties: Camp, Cass, Harrison, Marion, Morris, Upshur.
Sherman Division counties: Collin, Cooke, Denton, Grayson.
Texarkana Division counties: Bowie, Franklin, Titus.
Tyler Division counties: Anderson, Cherokee, Gregg, Henderson, Panola, Rains, Rusk, Smith, Van Zandt, Wood.

US Bankruptcy Court -- Eastern District of Texas

Home Page: www.txeb.uscourts.gov
PACER: Toll-free access: 800-466-1681. Local access phone: 903-590-1220. Case records are available back to 1989. Records are purged every six months. New civil records are available online after 1 day. **PACER URL:** http://pacer.txeb.uscourts.gov. Document images available.
Electronic Filing: Electronic filing information is available online at https://ecf.txeb.uscourts.gov. **Also:** access via phone on VCIS (Voice Case Information System) is available: 800-466-1694, 903-590-1217
Beaumont Division counties: Angelina, Hardin, Houston, Jasper, Jefferson, Liberty, Nacogdoches, Newton, Orange, Polk, Sabine, San Augustine, Shelby, Trinity, Tyler.
Marshall Division counties: Camp, Cass, Harrison, Marion, Morris, Upshur.
Plano Division counties: Collin, Cooke, Delta, Denton, Fannin, Grayson, Hopkins, Lamar, Red River.
Texarkana Division counties: Bowie, Franklin, Titus.
Tyler Division counties: Anderson, Cherokee, Gregg, Henderson, Panola, Rains, Rusk, Smith, Van Zandt, Wood.

US District Court -- Northern District of Texas

Home Page: www.txnd.uscourts.gov
PACER: Toll-free access: 800-684-2393. Local access phone: 214-753-2449. Case records are available back to June 1991. Records are purged once per year. New records are available online after 1 day. **PACER URL:** http://pacer.txnd.uscourts.gov. Document images available.
Electronic Filing: (Currently in the process of implementing CM/ECF).
Abilene Division counties: Callahan, Eastland, Fisher, Haskell, Howard, Jones, Mitchell, Nolan, Shackelford, Stephens, Stonewall, Taylor, Throckmorton.
Amarillo Division counties: Armstrong, Briscoe, Carson, Castro, Childress, Collingsworth, Dallam, Deaf Smith, Donley, Gray, Hall, Hansford, Hartley, Hemphill, Hutchinson, Lipscomb, Moore, Ochiltree, Oldham, Parmer, Potter, Randall, Roberts, Sherman, Swisher, Wheeler.
Dallas Division counties: Dallas, Ellis, Hunt, Johnson, Kaufman, Navarro, Rockwall.
Fort Worth Division counties: Comanche, Erath, Hood, Jack, Palo Pinto, Parker, Tarrant, Wise.
Lubbock Division counties: Bailey, Borden, Cochran, Crosby, Dawson, Dickens, Floyd, Gaines, Garza, Hale, Hockley, Kent, Lamb, Lubbock, Lynn, Motley, Scurry, Terry, Yoakum.
San Angelo Division counties: Brown, Coke, Coleman, Concho, Crockett, Glasscock, Irion, Menard, Mills, Reagan, Runnels, Schleicher, Sterling, Sutton, Tom Green.
Wichita Falls Division counties: Archer, Baylor, Clay, Cottle, Foard, Hardeman, King, Knox, Montague, Wichita, Wilbarger, Young.

US Bankruptcy Court -- Northern District of Texas

Home Page: www.txnb.uscourts.gov
PACER: Toll-free access: 888-225-1738. Local access phone: 214-753-2134. Case records are available back to 1994. Records are purged every six months. New civil records are available online after 1 day. **PACER URL:** https://pacer.txnb.uscourts.gov. Document images available.
Electronic Filing: (Currently in the process of implementing CM/ECF). **Also:** access via phone on VCIS (Voice Case Information System) is available: 800-886-9008, 214-753-2128
Amarillo Division counties: Armstrong, Briscoe, Carson, Castro, Childress, Collingsworth, Dallam, Deaf Smith, Donley, Gray, Hall, Hansford, Hartley, Hemphill, Hutchinson, Lipscomb, Moore, Ochiltree, Oldham, Parmer, Potter, Randall, Roberts, Sherman, Swisher, Wheeler.
Dallas Division counties: Dallas, Ellis, Hunt, Johnson, Kaufman, Navarro, Rockwall.
Fort Worth Division counties: Comanche, Erath, Hood, Jack, Palo Pinto, Parker, Tarrant, Wise.
Lubbock Division counties: Bailey, Borden, Brown, Callahan, Cochran, Cooke, Coleman, Concho, Crockett, Crosby, Dawson, Dickens, Eastland, Fisher, Floyd, Gaines, Garza, Glasscock, Hale, Haskell, Hockley, Howard, Irion, Jones, Kent, Lamb, Lubbock, Lynn, Menard, Mills, Mitchell, Motley, Nolan, Reagan, Runnels, Schleicher, Scurry, Shackelford, Stephens, Sterling, Stonewall, Sutton, Taylor, Terry, Throckmorton, Tom Green, Yoakum.
Wichita Falls Division counties: Archer, Baylor, Clay, Cottle, Foard, Hardeman, King, Knox, Montague, Wichita, Wilbarger, Young.

US District Court -- Southern District of Texas

Home Page: www.txsd.uscourts.gov

PACER: Toll-free access: 800-998-9037. Local access phone: 713-250-5000. Case records are available back to June 1990. Records are purged every six months. New records are available online after 1 day. **PACER URL:** http://pacer.txs.uscourts.gov. Document images available.

Brownsville Division counties: Cameron, Willacy.

Corpus Christi Division counties: Aransas, Bee, Brooks, Duval, Jim Wells, Kenedy, Kleberg, Live Oak, Nueces, San Patricio.

Galveston Division counties: Brazoria, Chambers, Galveston, Matagorda.

Houston Division counties: Austin, Brazos, Colorado, Fayette, Fort Bend, Grimes, Harris, Madison, Montgomery, San Jacinto, Walker, Waller, Wharton.

Laredo Division counties: Jim Hogg, La Salle, McMullen, Webb, Zapata.

McAllen Division counties: Hidalgo, Starr.

Victoria Division counties: Calhoun, De Witt, Goliad, Jackson, Lavaca, Refugio, Victoria.

US Bankruptcy Court -- Southern District of Texas

Home Page: www.txsd.uscourts.gov

PACER: Toll-free access: 800-998-9037. Local access phone: 713-250-5000. Case records are available back to June 1, 1991. Records are purged every six months. New civil records are available online after 1-3 days. **PACER URL:** http://pacer.txs.uscourts.gov. Document images available.

Electronic Filing: Electronic filing information is available online at https://ecf.txsb.uscourts.gov. **Also:** access via phone on VCIS (Voice Case Information System) is available: 800-745-4459, 713-250-5049

Corpus Christi Division counties: Aransas, Bee, Brooks, Calhoun, Cameron, Duval, Goliad, Hidalgo, Jackson, Jim Wells, Kenedy, Kleberg, Lavaca, Live Oak, Nueces, Refugio, San Patricio, Starr, Victoria, Willacy. Files from Brownsville, Corpus Christi, and McAllen are maintained here.

Houston Division counties: Austin, Brazoria, Brazos, Chambers, Colorado, De Witt, Fayette, Fort Bend, Galveston, Grimes, Harris, Jim Hogg*, La Salle*, Madison, Matagorda, McMullen*, Montgomery, San Jacinto, Walker,Waller, Wharton, Webb* Zapata*. Open case records for the counties marked with an asterisk are being moved to the Laredo Division.

US District Court -- Western District of Texas

Home Page: www.txwd.uscourts.gov

PACER: Toll-free access: 888-869-6365. Local access phone: 210-472-5256. Case records are available back to 1994. Records are purged every six months. New records are available online after 1 day. **PACER URL:** http://pacer.txwd.uscourts.gov.

Austin Division counties: Bastrop, Blanco, Burleson, Burnet, Caldwell, Gillespie, Hays, Kimble, Lampasas, Lee, Llano, McCulloch, Mason, San Saba, Travis, Washington, Williamson.

Del Rio Division counties: Edwards, Kinney, Maverick, Terrell, Uvalde, Val Verde, Zavala.

El Paso Division counties: El Paso.

Midland Division counties: Andrews, Crane, Ector, Martin, Midland, Upton.

Pecos Division counties: Brewster, Culberson, Hudspeth, Jeff Davis, Loving, Pecos, Presidio, Reeves, Ward, Winkler.

San Antonio Division counties: Atascosa, Bandera, Bexar, Comal, Dimmit, Frio, Gonzales, Guadalupe, Karnes, Kendall, Kerr, Medina, Real, Wilson.

Waco Division: Bell, Bosque, Coryell, Falls, Freestone, Hamilton, Hill, Leon, Limestone, McLennan, Milam, Robertson, Somervell.

US Bankruptcy Court -- Western District of Texas

Home Page: www.txwb.uscourts.gov

PACER: Toll-free access: 888-372-5708. Local access phone: 210-472-6262. Case records are available back to May 1, 1987. Records are purged every 6-8 months. New civil records are available online after 1 day. **PACER URL:** http://pacer.txwb.uscourts.gov.

Electronic Filing: Electronic filing information is available online at http://ecf.txwb.uscourts.gov. **Also:** access via phone on VCIS (Voice Case Information System) is available: 888-436-7477, 210-472-4023

Austin Division counties: Bastrop, Blanco, Burleson, Burnet, Caldwell, Gillespie, Hays, Kimble, Lampasas, Lee, Llano, Mason, McCulloch, San Saba, Travis, Washington, Williamson.

El Paso Division counties: El Paso.

Midland/Odessa Division counties: Andrews, Brewster, Crane, Culberson, Ector, Hudspeth, Jeff Davis, Loving, Martin, Midland, Pecos, Presidio, Reeves, Upton, Ward, Winkler.

San Antonio Division counties: Atascosa, Bandera, Bexar, Comal, Dimmit, Edwards, Frio, Gonzales, Guadalupe, Karnes, Kendall, Kerr, Kinney, Maverick, Medina, Real, Terrell, Uvalde, Val Verde, Wilson, Zavala.

Waco Division: Bell, Bosque, Coryell, Falls, Freestone, Hamilton, Hill, Leon, Limestone, McLennan, Milam, Robertson, Somervell.

Capital: Salt Lake City
            Salt Lake County

Time Zone: MST

Number of Counties: 29

Home Page   www.state.ut.us

Archives
            www.archives.state.ut.us

Attorney General   http://attorneygeneral.utah.gov

State Level ... Major Agencies

Corporation Records, Limited Liability Company Records, Fictitious Name, Limited Partnership Records, Assumed Name, Trademarks/Servicemarks

Commerce Department, Corporate Division, PO Box 146705, Salt Lake City, UT 84114-6705 (Courier: 160 E 300 S, 2nd fl, Salt Lake City, UT 84111); 801-530-4849 (Call Center), 801-530-6111 (Fax), 8AM-5PM.

www.commerce.utah.gov

A business entity/principle search service is available at www.utah.gov/government/onlineservices.html. Basic information (name, address, agent) is free, detailed data is a available for minimal fees, but registration is required. The web site also offers an Unclaimed Property search page. **Other options:** State allows email access for orders of Certification of Existence at orders@br.state.ut.us.

Uniform Commercial Code

Department of Commerce, UCC Division, Box 146705, Salt Lake City, UT 84114-6705 (Courier: 160 E 300 South, Heber M Wells Bldg, 2nd Floor, Salt Lake City, UT 84111); 801-530-4849, 801-530-6438 (Fax), 8AM-5PM.

www.commerce.utah.gov/cor/index.html

UCC records are available free online at www.utah.gov/uccsearch/searchby.html. Search by debtor individual name or organization, or by filing number. There is also a pay system and it is the same system used for corporation records. User fee is $10.00 per month. There is no additional fee at this time; however, the state is considering a certification fee. Open 24 hours daily. Email requests are accepted at orders@br.state.ut.us. **Other options:** Records are available on CD-ROM. Call 801-530-2267 for details.

Sexual Offender Registry

Requests of sex offender data are available online from the Utah Department of Corrections athttp://corrections.utah.gov/asp-bin/sexoffendersearchform.asp. The online search permits access by name or by ZIP Code.

Driver Records

Department of Public Safety, Driver License Division, Customer Service Section, PO Box 30560, Salt Lake City, UT 84130-0560 (Courier: 4501 South 2700 West, 3rd Floor South, Salt Lake City, UT 84119); 801-965-4437, 801-965-4496 (Fax), 8AM-5PM.

http://driverlicense.utah.gov

Driving records are available to eligible organizations through the eUtah. The system is available 24 hours daily. The fee per driving record is $5.75, there is an annual $50.00 subscription fee, also. For more information, visit the website at www.utah.gov/government/onlineservices.html. **Other options:** Magnetic tape inquiry is available for high volume users. The state will not sell its DL file to commercial vendors.

Vehicle Ownership, Vehicle Identification, Vessel Ownership, Vessel Registration

State Tax Commission, Motor Vehicle Records Section, 210 North 1950 West, Salt Lake City, UT 84134; 801-297-3507, 801-297-3578 (Fax), 8AM-5PM.

www.dmv-utah.com

Motor Vehicle Dept. titles, liens, and registration searches are available at www.utah.gov/government/onlineservices.html; registration is required. Records are usually $2.00 each. **Other options:** Utah offers a bulk or batch format for obtaining registration information on magnetic tape or paper. A written request stating the purpose of the usage is required. Call 801-297-2700 for further information.

Legislation Records

http://le.utah.gov

Web site contains bill information, the Utah Code, floor debates (house only; limited years), interim committee histories, committee notices, agendas and minutes, votes on bills, bill summaries, and drafting and research. You may search by name, committee, subject, year, bill number, keyword, or legislator. Records go back to 1990.

State Level ... Occupational Licensing

Accounting Firm	https://secure.e-utah.org/llv
Acupuncturist	https://secure.e-utah.org/llv
Alarm Company/Agent/Response Runner	https://secure.e-utah.org/llv
Animal Euthanasia Agency	https://secure.e-utah.org/llv
Arbitrator, Alternate Dispute Resolution	https://secure.e-utah.org/llv
Architect	https://secure.e-utah.org/llv
Athletic Judge	https://secure.e-utah.org/llv
Attorney	www.utahbar.org/html/find_a_lawyer.html
Bank	www.dfi.state.ut.us/Banks.htm (site may be down)
Boxer	https://secure.e-utah.org/llv
Building Inspector/Trainee	https://secure.e-utah.org/llv
Building Trades, General	https://secure.e-utah.org/llv
Burglar Alarm Agent	https://secure.e-utah.org/llv
Chiropractor	https://secure.e-utah.org/llv
Consumer Lender	www.dfi.state.ut.us/consumer.htm (site may be down)
Contractor	https://secure.e-utah.org/llv
Controlled Substance Precursor Distributor	https://secure.e-utah.org/llv
Cosmetologist	https://secure.e-utah.org/llv
Cosmetology School/Instructor	https://secure.e-utah.org/llv
Counselor Trainee, Professional	https://secure.e-utah.org/llv
Counselor, Professional	https://secure.e-utah.org/llv
Credit Union	www.dfi.state.ut.us/CreditUn.htm (site may be down)
Deception Detection Examiner/Intern	https://secure.e-utah.org/llv
Dental Hygienist/ Dental Hygienist-Local Anesthesia	https://secure.e-utah.org/llv
Dentist	https://secure.e-utah.org/llv
Dietitian	https://secure.e-utah.org/llv
Electrician (Residential) Trainee/Journeyman/Master	https://secure.e-utah.org/llv
Electrician, Apprentice/Journeyman/Master	https://secure.e-utah.org/llv
Electrologist	https://secure.e-utah.org/llv
Employee Leasing Company	https://secure.e-utah.org/llv
Employment Provider, Professional	https://secure.e-utah.org/llv
Engineer	https://secure.e-utah.org/llv

Engineer, Structural Professional	https://secure.e-utah.org/llv
Environmental Health Specialist/Spec.-In-Training	https://secure.e-utah.org/llv
Escrow Agent	www.dfi.state.ut.us/OtherInt.htm (site may be down)
Funeral Service Establishment	https://secure.e-utah.org/llv
Genetic Counselor	https://secure.e-utah.org/llv
Health Care Assistant	https://secure.e-utah.org/llv
Health Facility Administrator	https://secure.e-utah.org/llv
Hearing Aid Specialist	https://secure.e-utah.org/llv
Hearing Instrument Professional/Intern	https://secure.e-utah.org/llv
Industrial Loan	www.dfi.state.ut.us/IndustLn.htm (site may be down)
Insurance Agent	www.insurance.state.ut.us/companies.html
Insurance Establishment	www.insurance.state.ut.us/companies.html
Laboratory, Analytical	https://secure.e-utah.org/llv
Landscape Architect	https://secure.e-utah.org/llv
Lien Recovery Fund Member	https://secure.e-utah.org/llv
Manufactured Housing Dealer/Salesman	https://secure.e-utah.org/llv
Marriage & Family Therapist/Trainee	https://secure.e-utah.org/llv
Massage Technician/Apprentice	https://secure.e-utah.org/llv
Mediator, Alternate Dispute Resolution	https://secure.e-utah.org/llv
Medical Doctor/Surgeon	https://secure.e-utah.org/llv
Midwife Nurse	https://secure.e-utah.org/llv
Mortgage Broker, Residential	www.commerce.state.ut.us/dre/database.html
Mortgage Lender	www.dfi.state.ut.us/mortgage.htm (site may be down)
Naturopath	https://secure.e-utah.org/llv
Naturopathic Physician	https://secure.e-utah.org/llv
Negotiator, Alternate Dispute Resolution	https://secure.e-utah.org/llv
Nuclear Pharmacy	https://secure.e-utah.org/llv
Nurse/Nurse-LPN	https://secure.e-utah.org/llv
Occupational Therapist/Assistant	https://secure.e-utah.org/llv
Optometrist	https://secure.e-utah.org/llv
Osteopathic Physician	https://secure.e-utah.org/llv
Pharmaceutical Admin. Facility	https://secure.e-utah.org/llv
Pharmaceutical Dog Trainer/ Teaching Organization	https://secure.e-utah.org/llv
Pharmaceutical Researcher	https://secure.e-utah.org/llv
Pharmaceutical Whse./Dist./Mfg.	https://secure.e-utah.org/llv
Pharmacist/Pharmacist Intern	https://secure.e-utah.org/llv
Pharmacy Out-of-State Mail Svc	https://secure.e-utah.org/llv
Pharmacy Retail/Branch/ Institutional/Hospital	https://secure.e-utah.org/llv
Pharmacy Technician	https://secure.e-utah.org/llv
Physical Therapist	https://secure.e-utah.org/llv
Physician Assistant	https://secure.e-utah.org/llv
Plumber (Residential) Journeyman/Appren.	https://secure.e-utah.org/llv
Plumber Apprentice/Journeyman	https://secure.e-utah.org/llv
Podiatrist	https://secure.e-utah.org/llv
Preneed Provider/Sales Agent	https://secure.e-utah.org/llv
Probation Provider, Private	https://secure.e-utah.org/llv
Psychologist	https://secure.e-utah.org/llv
Public Accountant-CPA	https://secure.e-utah.org/llv
Radiology Practical Technician	https://secure.e-utah.org/llv
Radiology Technologist	https://secure.e-utah.org/llv
Real Estate Appraiser/ Broker/Agent	www.commerce.state.ut.us/dre/database.html
Real Estate Establishment	https://secure.e-utah.org/llv
Recreational Therapist	https://secure.e-utah.org/llv
Recreational Vehicle Dealer	https://secure.e-utah.org/llv
Respiratory Care Practitioner	https://secure.e-utah.org/llv
Sanitarian	https://secure.e-utah.org/llv
Security Company/ Security Officer, Armed/Unarmed	https://secure.e-utah.org/llv
Security Officer, Armed/Unarmed Private	https://secure.e-utah.org/llv
Shorthand Reporter	https://secure.e-utah.org/llv
Social Service Aide/Worker/Trainee	https://secure.e-utah.org/llv

Social Worker/ Social Worker, Clinical .... https://secure.e-utah.org/llv
Speech Pathologist/Audiologist.................................. https://secure.e-utah.org/llv
Substance Abuse Counselor .... https://secure.e-utah.org/llv
Surveyor, Land .... https://secure.e-utah.org/llv
Trade Instructor.. https://secure.e-utah.org/llv
Veterinarian/Veterinary Intern.................................... https://secure.e-utah.org/llv
Veterinary Pharmaceutical Outlet............................... https://secure.e-utah.org/llv

County Level ... Courts

Court Administration: Court Administrator, 450 S State Street, Salt Lake City, UT, 84114; 801-578-3800; http://courtlink.utcourts.gov

Court Structure: 41 District Courts are arranged in eight judicial districts. Effective July 1, 1996, each Circuit Court (the lower court) was combined with District Court (the higher court) in each county. It is reported that branch courts in larger counties such as Salt Lake which were formerly Circuit Courts have been elevated to District Courts, with full jurisdiction over felony as well as misdemeanor cases. Many misdemeanors are handled at Justice Courts, which are limited jurisdiction.

Online Access Note: Case information from all Utah District Court locations is available through XChange. Fees include $25.00 registration and $30.00 per month plus $.10 per minute for usage over 120 minutes. Records go back 7 to 10 years. Information about XChange and the subscription agreement can be found at http://courtlink.utcourts.gov/howto/access or call 801-238-7877.

Salt Lake County
3rd District Court *Civil and Criminal Records*
Online access available through Xchange, see http://courtlink.utcourts.gov. An automated court information line allows phone access to court dates, fine balances, and judgment/divorce decrees (case or citation number required) at 801-238-7830.

Weber County
2nd District Court *Civil and Criminal Records*
Online access available through Xchange, see http://courtlink.utcourts.gov. An automated court information line allows phone access to court dates, fine balances, and judgment/divorce decrees (case or citation number required) at 801-395-1111.

Statewide Access -- See beginning of this section.

County Level ... Recorders & Assessors

Recording Office Organization: 29 counties 29 recording offices. The recording officers are the County Recorder and the Clerk of District Court (state tax liens). The entire state is in the Mountain Time Zone (MST). All federal tax liens are filed with the County Recorder. All state tax liens are filed with Clerk of District Court.

Online Access Note: A number of counties offer online access, some are fee-based.

Davis County   *Real Estate, Lien Records*
www.co.davis.ut.us
Access to the county land records database requires written registration and $15.00 per month fee plus $.10 per transaction. Records go back to 1981. For information and sign-up, contact Janet at 801-451-3347.

Salt Lake County *Assessor, Property Tax, Land Records*

www.co.slc.ut.us
Two sources are available. Records on the county Truth-In-Tax Information web site are available free online at
www.slpropertyinfo.org. Also, Assessor, real estate, appraisal, abstracts, and GIS mapping are available for $150.00 fee on the online
system at http://rec.co.slc.ut.us/polaris/default.cfm. Search by GIS, name, or property data. Register online or call 801-468-3013.

Tooele County *Property Tax Records*

www.co.tooele.ut.us
Access to the property information database may be operational at www.co.tooele.ut.us/taxinfo.html.

Uintah County *Property Records*

www.co.uintah.ut.us
Access to the county recorder's land records is available free at www.co.uintah.ut.us/recorder/landinfo.html.

Utah County *Real Estate, Lien, Assessor Records*

www.co.utah.ut.us
Access to the land records database and also map searching is available free at www.co.utah.ut.us/omninet/land. Indexes go back to
1978; parcel indexes back to 1981. Document images go back to 1994. Building and GIS information is also available online.

Wasatch County *Real Property Records*

www.co.wasatch.ut.us/d/
The county GIS Dept. plans to have "metadata" (property information) available free online from its GIS mapping site at
www.co.wasatch.ut.us/d/dpgis.html.

Weber County *Real Estate Records*

www.co.weber.ut.us
Property records on the County Parcel Search site are available free online at www.co.weber.ut.us/netapps/Parcel/main.htm.

Federal Courts in Utah...

Standards for Federal Courts: The universal PACER sign-up number is 800-676-6856. Find PACER and the Party/Case Index on
the Web at http://pacer.psc.uscourts.gov. PACER dial-up access is $.60 per minute. Also, courts offering internet access via RACER,
PACER, Web-PACER or the new CM-ECF charge $.07 per page fee unless noted as free.

US District Court -- District of Utah

Home Page: www.utd.uscourts.gov
All counties in Utah. Although all cases are heard here, the district is divided into Northern and Central Divisions. The Northern
Division includes the counties of Box Elder, Cache, Rich, Davis, Morgan and Weber, and the Central Division includes all other
counties.
PACER: Case records are available back to July 1, 1989. Records are purged never. New records are available online after 1 day.
PACER URL: http://pacer.utd.uscourts.gov. Document images available.

US Bankruptcy Court -- District of Utah

Home Page: www.utb.uscourts.gov
Although all cases are handled here, the court divides itself into two divisions. The Northern Division includes the counties of Box
Elder, Cache, Rich, Davis, Morgan and Weber, and the Central Division includes the remainingcounties. Court is held once per week
in Ogden for Northern cases.
PACER: Case records are available back to January 1985. Records are purged after 12 months. New civil records are available online
after 2 days or more. **PACER URL:** http://pacer.utb.uscourts.gov. Document images available.
Electronic Filing: Recent case filings reports are free. Electronic filing information is available online at https://ecf.utb.uscourts.gov.
Opinions Online: Court opinions are available online at www.utb.uscourts.gov/OPINIONS/opin.htm. **Also:** access via phone on
VCIS (Voice Case Information System) is available: 800-733-6740, 801-524-3107

Vermont

Capital:	Montpelier Washington County	Home Page	www.state.vt.us
Time Zone:	EST	Attorney General	www.state.vt.us/atg
Number of Counties:	14	Archives	http://vermont-archives.org

State Level ... Major Agencies

Corporation Records, Limited Liability Company Records, Limited Liability Partnerships, Limited Partnerships, Trademarks/Servicemarks

Secretary of State, Corporation Division, 81 River St, Drawer 9, Montpelier, VT 05609-1101; 802-828-2386, 802-828-2853 (Fax), 7:45AM-4:30PM.

www.sec.state.vt.us/soshome.htm

Corporate and trademark records can be accessed from the Internet for no fee. All records are available. Also, the web site offers a "Trade Name Finder." **Other options:** There is an option on the Internet to download the entire corporation (and tradename) database.

Uniform Commercial Code

UCC Division, Secretary of State, 81 River St, Drawer 4, Montpelier, VT 05609-1101; 802-828-2386, 802-828-2853 (Fax), 7:45AM-4:30PM.

www.sec.state.vt.us/corps/corpindex.htm

Searches are available from the Internet site. You can search by debtor or business name, there is no fee.

Incarceration Records

Go to www.doc.state.vt.us/ and click on "Incarcerated Offender Locator."

Driver Records, Driver License Information

Department of Motor Vehicles, DI - Records Unit, 120 State St, Montpelier, VT 05603-0001; 802-828-2050, 802-828-2098 (Fax), 7:45AM-4:30PM.

www.aot.state.vt.us/dmv/dmvhp.htm

Online access costs $8.00 per 3 year record. The system is called "GovNet." Two methods are offered-single inquiry and batch mode. The system is open 24 hours a day, 7 days a week (except for file maintenance periods). Only the license number is needed when ordering, but it is suggested to submit the name and DOB also. **Other options:** The state will sell its license file to approved requesters, but customization is not available.

Legislation Records

www.leg.state.vt.us

The web site offers access to bill information. **Other options:** A subscription service is available for bill text.

State Level ... Occupational Licensing

Accounting Firm	www.sec.state.vt.us/seek/lrspseek.htm
Acupuncturist	www.sec.state.vt.us/seek/lrspseek.htm
Architect	www.sec.state.vt.us/seek/lrspseek.htm
Auctioneer	www.sec.state.vt.us/seek/lrspseek.htm
Bank	www.bishca.state.vt.us/consumpubs/Bankpubs/AnnReport/banks.htm
Barber	www.sec.state.vt.us/seek/lrspseek.htm
Boxing Manager/Promoter	www.sec.state.vt.us/seek/lrspseek.htm
Chiropractor	www.sec.state.vt.us/seek/lrspseek.htm
Cosmetologist	www.sec.state.vt.us/seek/lrspseek.htm
Credit Union	www.bishca.state.vt.us/consumpubs/Bankpubs/AnnReport/credunions.htm
Dental Assistant	www.sec.state.vt.us/seek/lrspseek.htm
Dental Hygienist	www.sec.state.vt.us/seek/lrspseek.htm
Dentist	www.sec.state.vt.us/seek/lrspseek.htm
Dietitian	www.sec.state.vt.us/seek/lrspseek.htm
Embalmer	www.sec.state.vt.us/seek/lrspseek.htm
Engineer	www.sec.state.vt.us/seek/lrspseek.htm
Esthetician	www.sec.state.vt.us/seek/lrspseek.htm
Funeral Director	www.sec.state.vt.us/seek/lrspseek.htm
Hearing Aid Dispenser	www.sec.state.vt.us/seek/lrspseek.htm
Lobbyist	www.sec.state.vt.us/seek/lbylseek.htm
Manicurist	www.sec.state.vt.us/seek/lrspseek.htm
Marriage & Family Therapist	www.sec.state.vt.us/seek/lrspseek.htm
Medical Doctor/Surgeon	www.docboard.org/vt/df/vtsearch.htm
Mental Health Counselor, Clinical	www.sec.state.vt.us/seek/lrspseek.htm
Naturopathic Physician	www.sec.state.vt.us/seek/lrspseek.htm
Notary Public	www.sec.state.vt.us/seek/not_seek.htm
Nurse/Nurse Practitioner/LNA	www.sec.state.vt.us/seek/lrspseek.htm
Nursing Home Administrator	www.sec.state.vt.us/seek/lrspseek.htm
Occupational Therapist	www.sec.state.vt.us/seek/lrspseek.htm
Optician	www.sec.state.vt.us/seek/lrspseek.htm
Optometrist	www.sec.state.vt.us/seek/lrspseek.htm
Osteopathic Physician	www.sec.state.vt.us/seek/lrspseek.htm
Pharmacist	www.sec.state.vt.us/seek/lrspseek.htm
Pharmacy	www.sec.state.vt.us/seek/lrspseek.htm
Physical Therapist/Assistant	www.sec.state.vt.us/seek/lrspseek.htm
Physician Assistant	www.docboard.org/vt/df/vtsearch.htm
Podiatrist	www.docboard.org/vt/df/vtsearch.htm
Private Investigator	www.sec.state.vt.us/seek/lrspseek.htm
Psychoanalyst	www.sec.state.vt.us/seek/lrspseek.htm
Psychologist	www.sec.state.vt.us/seek/lrspseek.htm
Psychotherapist	www.sec.state.vt.us/seek/lrspseek.htm
Public Accountant-CPA	www.sec.state.vt.us/seek/lrspseek.htm
Racing Promoter	www.sec.state.vt.us/seek/lrspseek.htm
Radiologic Technologist	www.sec.state.vt.us/seek/lrspseek.htm
Real Estate Appraiser	www.sec.state.vt.us/seek/lrspseek.htm
Real Estate Broker/Agent	www.sec.state.vt.us/seek/lrspseek.htm
Real Estate Salesperson	www.sec.state.vt.us/seek/lrspseek.htm
Security Guard	www.sec.state.vt.us/seek/lrspseek.htm
Social Worker, Clinical	www.sec.state.vt.us/seek/lrspseek.htm
Surveyor, Land	www.sec.state.vt.us/seek/lrspseek.htm
Tattoo Artist	www.sec.state.vt.us/seek/lrspseek.htm
Veterinarian	www.sec.state.vt.us/seek/lrspseek.htm

County Level ... Courts

Court Administration: Administrative Office of Courts, Court Administrator, 109 State St, Montpelier, VT, 05609-0701; 802-828-3278; www.vermontjudiciary.org

Court Structure: As of September, 1996, all small claims came under the jurisdiction of Superior Court, the court of general jurisdiction. All counties have a diversion program in which first offenders go through a process that includes a letter of apology, community service, etc. and, after 2 years, the record is expunged. These records are never released. The Vermont Judicial Bureau has jurisdiction over Traffic, Municipal Ordinance, and Fish and Game, Minors in Possession, and hazing.

Online Access Note: There is no online computer access to the public; however, some courts offer calendar data over the Internet. Supreme Court opinions are maintained by the Vermont Department of Libraries at http://dol.state.vt.us.

There are no known courts that independently offer online access to their records.

County Level ... Recorders & Assessors

Recording Office Organization: 14 counties and 246 towns/cities -- recording offices. The recording officer is the Town/City Clerk. There is no county administration in Vermont. The entire state is in the Eastern Time Zone (EST). All federal and state tax liens on personal property and on real property are filed with the Town/City Clerk in the lien/attachment book and indexed in real estate records. Most towns/cities will not perform tax lien searches.

Online Access Note: There is virtually no online access to county recorded documents. State recorded UCC data is available online from the Vermont Secretary of State.

Bennington Town *Property, Assessor Records*
www.bennington.com/local.html
Access to the Grand List search program is available free at www.bennington.com/government/grandlist/index.html. No name searching at this time; site is under construction and data is incomplete.

Federal Courts in Vermont...

US District Court -- District of Vermont
Home Page: www.vtd.uscourts.gov **PACER:** Toll-free access: 800-263-9396. Local access phone: 802-951-6623. Case records are available back to January 1991. Records are purged never. New records are available online after 1 day.

Other Online Access: Search records on the Internet using the RACER link at www.vtd.uscourts.gov. Access fee is $.07 per page.
Burlington Division counties: Caledonia, Chittenden, Essex, Franklin, Grand Isle, Lamoille, Orleans, Washington. However, cases from all counties in the state are assigned randomly to either Burlington or Brattleboro. Brattleboro is a hearing location only, not listed here.
Rutland Division counties: Addison, Bennington, Orange, Rutland, Windsor, Windham. However, cases from all counties in the state are randomly assigned to either Burlington or Brattleboro. Rutland is a hearing location only, not listed here.

US Bankruptcy Court -- District of Vermont
Home Page: www.vtb.uscourts.gov **PACER:** Case records are available back to 1992 (limited information prior). Records are purged never. New civil records are available online after 1 day. **PACER URL:** http://pacer.vtb.uscourts.gov. Document images available.

Electronic Filing: Electronic filing information is available online at https://ecf.vtb.uscourts.gov. **Also:** access via phone on VCIS (Voice Case Information System) is available: 800-260-9956, 802-776-2007
Rutland Division counties: All counties in Vermont.

Capital:	Richmond	Home Page	www.state.va.us
	Richmond City County		
Time Zone:	EST	Attorney General	www.oag.state.va.us
Number of Counties:	95	Archives	www.lva.lib.va.us

State Level ... Major Agencies

Criminal Records

Virginia State Police, CCRE, PO Box 85076, Richmond, VA 23261-5076 (Courier: 7700 Midlothian Turnpike, Richmond, VA 23235); 804-674-2084, 8AM-5PM.

www.vsp.state.va.us

Certain entities, including screening companies, are entitled to online access. The system is ONLY available to IN-STATE accounts. Fees are same as manual submission with exception of required software package purchase. The system is windows oriented, but will not handle networks. The PC user must be a stand alone system. There is a minimum usage requirement of 25 requests per month. Turnaround time is 24-72 hours. Fee is $15.00 per record.

Sexual Offender Registry

The State Police maintain the state's sexual offender registry, but the data is divided into two separate searchable databases. The "Violent Sex Offender" database is available online at at http://sex-offender.vsp.state.va.us/cool-ICE/.

Corporation Records, Limited Liability Company Records, Fictitious Name, Limited Partnerships, Uniform Commercial Code, Federal Tax Liens

State Corporation Commission, Clerks Office, PO Box 1197, Richmond, VA 23218-1197 (Courier: Tyler Bldg, 1st Floor, 1300 E Main St, Richmond, VA 23219); 804-371-9733, 804-371-9133 (Fax), 8:15AM-5PM.

www.state.va.us/scc/division/clk/index.htm

Their system is called Clerk's Information System and is available at www.state.va.us/scc/division/clk/diracc.htm. There are no fees. A wealth of information is available on this system. **Other options:** Magnetic tape purchase is offered to those who wish the entire database.

Driver, Vehicle and Vessel Records

Motorist Records Services, Attn: Records Request Work Center, PO Box 27412, Richmond, VA 23269; 804-367-0538, 8:30AM-5:30PM M-F; 8:30AM-12:30PM S.

www.dmv.state.va.us

Online service is provided by the Virginia Information Providers Network (VIPNet). Online reports are provided via the Internet on an interactive basis 24 hours daily. There is a $75 annual administrative fee and records are $5.00 each. Go to www.vipnet.org for more information or call 804-786-4718. **Other options:** Magnetic tape ordering for batch requests is available from VIPnet. No records are sold for marketing purposes.

Also, the VA boat registration database may be searched on the web at www.vipnet.org. There is both a free service and a more advanced pay service, but both require a subscription which is $75.00 a year.

Legislation Records

http://legis.state.va.us/

Information can be found on the web site. There is no fee. Lists of General Assembly members, information on General Assembly, documents summarizing bills introduced and enacted are all available through this office.

State Level ... Occupational Licensing

Accountant/Accounting Firm/Sponsor .... www.boa.state.va.us/
Acupuncturist .... www.vipnet.org/dhp/cgi-bin/search_publicdb.cgi
Air Conditioning Contractor .... www.dpor.state.va.us/regulantlookup/
Architect .... www.dpor.state.va.us/regulantlookup/
Asbestos-Related Occupation .... www.dpor.state.va.us/regulantlookup/
Auctioneer/Auction Company .... www.dpor.state.va.us/regulantlookup/
Barber/Barber School/Business .... www.dpor.state.va.us/regulantlookup/
Boxer .... www.dpor.state.va.us/regulantlookup/
Carpenter .... www.dpor.state.va.us/regulantlookup/
Cemetery/ Cemetery Company/ Cemetery Seller .... www.dpor.state.va.us/regulantlookup/
Chiropractor .... www.vipnet.org/dhp/cgi-bin/search_publicdb.cgi
Clinical Nurse Specialist .... www.vipnet.org/dhp/cgi-bin/search_publicdb.cgi
Contractor .... www.dpor.state.va.us/regulantlookup/
Cosmetologist/Cosmetology School/Business .... www.dpor.state.va.us/regulantlookup/
Dental Hygienist .... www.vipnet.org/dhp/cgi-bin/search_publicdb.cgi
Dentist .... www.vipnet.org/dhp/cgi-bin/search_publicdb.cgi
Electrical Contractor .... www.dpor.state.va.us/regulantlookup/
Embalmer .... www.vipnet.org/dhp/cgi-bin/search_publicdb.cgi
Engineer .... www.dpor.state.va.us/regulantlookup/
Funeral Director .... www.vipnet.org/dhp/cgi-bin/search_publicdb.cgi
Gas Fitter .... www.dpor.state.va.us/regulantlookup/
Geologist .... www.dpor.state.va.us/regulantlookup/
Hearing Aid Specialist .... www.dpor.state.va.us/regulantlookup/
Heating & Air Conditioning Mechanic .... www.dpor.state.va.us/regulantlookup/
Heating Contractor .... www.dpor.state.va.us/regulantlookup/
Interior Designer .... www.dpor.state.va.us/regulantlookup/
Landscape Architect .... www.dpor.state.va.us/regulantlookup/
Lead-Related Occupation .... www.dpor.state.va.us/regulantlookup/
Lobbyist .... www.soc.state.va.us/databa.htm
Marriage & Family Therapist .... www.vipnet.org/dhp/cgi-bin/search_publicdb.cgi
Medical Doctor .... www.vipnet.org/dhp/cgi-bin/search_publicdb.cgi
Medical Equipment Supplier .... www.vipnet.org/dhp/cgi-bin/search_publicdb.cgi
Nail Technician .... www.dpor.state.va.us/regulantlookup/
Nurse/Nurse's Aide .... www.vipnet.org/dhp/cgi-bin/search_publicdb.cgi
Nurse-LPN / Nurse-RN .... www.vipnet.org/dhp/cgi-bin/search_publicdb.cgi
Nursing Home Administrator/Preceptor .... www.vipnet.org/dhp/cgi-bin/search_publicdb.cgi
Occupational Therapist .... www.vipnet.org/dhp/cgi-bin/search_publicdb.cgi
Optician .... www.dpor.state.va.us/regulantlookup/
Optometrist .... www.odfinder.org/LicSearch.asp
Osteopathic Physician .... www.vipnet.org/dhp/cgi-bin/search_publicdb.cgi
Pharmacist/Pharmacy .... www.vipnet.org/dhp/cgi-bin/search_publicdb.cgi
Physical Therapist .... www.vipnet.org/dhp/cgi-bin/search_publicdb.cgi

Physician .... www.vipnet.org/dhp/cgi-bin/search_publicdb.cgi
Pilot, Branch.. www.dpor.state.va.us/regulantlookup/
Plumber .... www.dpor.state.va.us/regulantlookup/
Podiatrist .... www.vipnet.org/dhp/cgi-bin/search_publicdb.cgi
Polygraph Examiner .... www.dpor.state.va.us/regulantlookup/
Property Association .... www.dpor.state.va.us/regulantlookup/
Psychologist, Clinical/Applied .... www.vipnet.org/dhp/cgi-bin/search_publicdb.cgi
Psychology School .... www.vipnet.org/dhp/cgi-bin/search_publicdb.cgi
Public Accountant-CPA .... www.dpor.state.va.us/regulantlookup/
Real Estate Agent/Business/School.............................. www.dpor.state.va.us/regulantlookup/
Real Estate Appraiser/Appraiser Business .... www.dpor.state.va.us/regulantlookup/
Respiratory Care Practitioner .... www.vipnet.org/dhp/cgi-bin/search_publicdb.cgi
Social Worker, Clinical .... www.vipnet.org/dhp/cgi-bin/search_publicdb.cgi
Soil Scientist .... www.dpor.state.va.us/regulantlookup/
Speech Pathologist/Audiologist................................... www.vipnet.org/dhp/cgi-bin/search_publicdb.cgi
Substance Abuse Treatment Practitioner..................... www.vipnet.org/dhp/cgi-bin/search_publicdb.cgi
Surveyor, Land .... www.dpor.state.va.us/regulantlookup/
Tradesman.. www.dpor.state.va.us/regulantlookup/
Veterinarian/Veterinary Technician .... www.vipnet.org/dhp/cgi-bin/search_publicdb.cgi
Waste Mgmt./Waste Water Facility Operator.............. www.dpor.state.va.us/regulantlookup/
Wrestler... www.dpor.state.va.us/regulantlookup/

County Level ... Courts

Court Administration: Executive Secretary, Administrative Office of Courts, 100 N 9th St 3rd Fl, Supreme Court Bldg, Richmond, VA, 23219; 804-786-6455; www.courts.state.va.us

Court Structure: 123 Circuit Courts in 31 districts are the courts of general jurisdiction. There are 123 District Courts of limited jurisdiction. Please note that a district can comprise a county or a city. Records of civil action from $3000 to $15,000 can be at either the Circuit or District Court as either can have jurisdiction. It is necessary to check both record locations as there is no concurrent database nor index.

Online Access Note: 130 General District Courts (many are combined courts) may be searched free at http://208.210.219.132/courtinfo/vadistrict/select.jsp?court=. Here you will have to search both active and inactive cases.

Also, Virginia has the growing "Circuit Court Case Information Pilot Project" with free access to Circuit Court records. Also, you may select among 80 courts at http://208.210.219.132/courtinfo/vacircuit/select.jsp?court=.

Another option is the statewide public access computer system: the Law Office Public Access System (LOPAS). The LOPAS system allows remote access to the court case indexes and abstracts from most of the state's courts. Searching is by specific court (there is no combined index) as well as criminal and civil case information from Circuit and District Courts. There are no sign-up or other fees to use LOPAS. Access is granted on a request-by-request basis. Anyone wishing to establish an account or receive information on LOPAS must contact the CIO, Supreme Court of Virginia, 100 N 9th St, Richmond VA 23219 or by phone at 804-786-6455 or Fax at 804-786-4542.

The www.courts.state.va.us site offers access to Supreme Court and Appellate opinions.

Virginia Counties (Virginia Independent Cities are listed following this County Section)
Accomack County
2nd Circuit Court *Civil and Criminal Records*
Remote online access to court case indexes is via LOPAS; call 804-786-6455 to apply.

2A General District Court *Civil and Criminal Records*
Select and search District Courts at http://208.210.219.132/courtinfo/vadistrict/select.jsp?court=.

Albemarle County

16th Circuit & District Court *Civil and Criminal Records*
Remote online access to court case indexes is via LOPAS; call 804-786-6455 to apply.

Alleghany County

25th Circuit Court *Civil and Criminal Records*
www.alleghanycountyclerk.com
Select and search Circuit Courts online at http://208.210.219.132/courtinfo/vacircuit/select.jsp?court=.

25th General District Court *Civil and Criminal Records*
Select and search District Courts at http://208.210.219.132/courtinfo/vadistrict/select.jsp?court=.

Amelia County

11th Circuit Court *Civil and Criminal Records*
www.governdata.com/amelia.htm
Select and search Circuit Courts online at http://208.210.219.132/courtinfo/vacircuit/select.jsp?court=.

11th General District Court *Civil and Criminal Records*
Select and search District Courts at http://208.210.219.132/courtinfo/vadistrict/select.jsp?court=.

Amherst County

24th Circuit Court *Civil and Criminal Records*
Remote online access to court case indexes is via LOPAS; call 804-786-6455 to apply.

24th General District Court *Civil and Criminal Records*
Select and search District Courts at http://208.210.219.132/courtinfo/vadistrict/select.jsp?court=.

Appomattox County

10th Circuit Court *Civil and Criminal Records*
Select and search Circuit Courts online at http://208.210.219.132/courtinfo/vacircuit/select.jsp?court=.

10th General District Court *Civil and Criminal Records*
Select and search District Courts at http://208.210.219.132/courtinfo/vadistrict/select.jsp?court=.

Arlington County

17th Circuit Court *Civil and Criminal Records*
http://158.59.15.115/arlington/
Online access available free at http://208.210.219.132/courtinfo/vacircuit/select.jsp?court=.

17th General District Court *Civil and Criminal Records*
Select and search District Courts at http://208.210.219.132/courtinfo/vadistrict/select.jsp?court=.

Augusta County

25th Circuit Court *Civil and Criminal Records*
Online access available free at http://208.210.219.132/courtinfo/vacircuit/select.jsp?court=.

25th General District Court *Civil and Criminal Records*
Select and search District Courts at http://208.210.219.132/courtinfo/vadistrict/select.jsp?court=.

Bath County

25th Circuit Court *Civil and Criminal Records*
Remote online access to court case indexes is via LOPAS; call 804-786-6455 to apply.

25th General District Court *Civil and Criminal Records*
Select and search District Courts at http://208.210.219.132/courtinfo/vadistrict/select.jsp?court=.

Bedford County

County Circuit Court *Civil and Criminal Records*

Online access available free at http://208.210.219.132/courtinfo/vacircuit/select.jsp?court=. Also, remote online access to court case indexes is via LOPAS; call 804-786-6455 to apply.

24th General District Court *Civil and Criminal Records*
Select and search District Courts at http://208.210.219.132/courtinfo/vadistrict/select.jsp?court=.

Bland County
27th Circuit Court *Civil and Criminal Records*
Select and search Circuit Courts online at http://208.210.219.132/courtinfo/vacircuit/select.jsp?court=.

27th General District Court *Civil and Criminal Records*
Select and search District Courts at http://208.210.219.132/courtinfo/vadistrict/select.jsp?court=.

Botetourt County
25th Circuit Court *Civil and Criminal Records*
Select and search Circuit Courts online at http://208.210.219.132/courtinfo/vacircuit/select.jsp?court=.

25th General District Court *Civil and Criminal Records*
Select and search District Courts at http://208.210.219.132/courtinfo/vadistrict/select.jsp?court=.

Brunswick County
6th Circuit Court *Civil and Criminal Records*
Select and search Circuit Courts online at http://208.210.219.132/courtinfo/vacircuit/select.jsp?court=.

6th General District Court *Civil and Criminal Records*
Select and search District Courts at http://208.210.219.132/courtinfo/vadistrict/select.jsp?court=.

Buchanan County
29th Circuit Court *Civil and Criminal Records*
Remote online access to court case indexes is via LOPAS; call 804-786-6455 to apply.

29th Judicial District Court *Civil Records*
Select and search District Courts at http://208.210.219.132/courtinfo/vadistrict/select.jsp?court=.

Buckingham County
10th Circuit Court *Civil and Criminal Records*
Remote online access to court case indexes is via LOPAS; call 804-786-6455 to apply.

Buckingham General District Court *Civil and Criminal Records*
Select and search District Courts at http://208.210.219.132/courtinfo/vadistrict/select.jsp?court=.

Campbell County
24th Circuit Court *Civil and Criminal Records*
Remote online access to court case indexes is via LOPAS; call 804-786-6455 to apply.

24th General District Court *Civil and Criminal Records*
Select and search District Courts at http://208.210.219.132/courtinfo/vadistrict/select.jsp?court=.

Caroline County
15th Circuit Court *Civil and Criminal Records*
Remote online access to court case indexes is via LOPAS; call 804-786-6455 to apply.

15th General District Court *Civil and Criminal Records*
Select and search District Courts at http://208.210.219.132/courtinfo/vadistrict/select.jsp?court=.

Carroll County
27th Circuit Court *Civil and Criminal Records*
Select and search Circuit Courts online at http://208.210.219.132/courtinfo/vacircuit/select.jsp?court=.

Carroll Combined District Court *Civil and Criminal Records*
Select and search District Courts at http://208.210.219.132/courtinfo/vadistrict/select.jsp?court=.

Charles City County
9th Circuit Court *Civil and Criminal Records*
Select and search Circuit Courts online at http://208.210.219.132/courtinfo/vacircuit/select.jsp?court=.

9th General District Court *Civil and Criminal Records*
Select and search District Courts at http://208.210.219.132/courtinfo/vadistrict/select.jsp?court=.

Charlotte County
Charlotte General District Court *Civil and Criminal Records*
Select and search District Courts at http://208.210.219.132/courtinfo/vadistrict/select.jsp?court=.

Chesterfield County
12th General District Court *Civil and Criminal Records*
Select and search District Courts at http://208.210.219.132/courtinfo/vadistrict/select.jsp?court=.

Clarke County
26th Circuit Court *Civil and Criminal Records*
Remote online access to court case indexes is via LOPAS; call 804-786-6455 to apply.

General District Court *Civil and Criminal Records*
www.co.clarke.va.us
Select and search District Courts at http://208.210.219.132/courtinfo/vadistrict/select.jsp?court=.

Craig County
25th Circuit Court *Civil and Criminal Records*
Remote online access to court case indexes is via LOPAS; call 804-786-6455 to apply.

25th General District Court *Civil and Criminal Records*
Select and search District Courts at http://208.210.219.132/courtinfo/vadistrict/select.jsp?court=.

Culpeper County
16th Circuit Court *Civil and Criminal Records*
Remote online access to court case indexes is via LOPAS; call 804-786-6455 to apply.

16th General District Court *Civil and Criminal Records*
Select and search District Courts at http://208.210.219.132/courtinfo/vadistrict/select.jsp?court=.

Cumberland County
10th Circuit Court *Civil and Criminal Records*
Select and search Circuit Courts online at http://208.210.219.132/courtinfo/vacircuit/select.jsp?court=.

10th General District Court *Civil and Criminal Records*
Select and search District Courts at http://208.210.219.132/courtinfo/vadistrict/select.jsp?court=.

Dickenson County
29th Circuit Court *Civil and Criminal Records*
Online access available free at http://208.210.219.132/courtinfo/vacircuit/select.jsp?court=.

29th General District Court *Civil and Criminal Records*
Select and search District Courts at http://208.210.219.132/courtinfo/vadistrict/select.jsp?court=.

Dinwiddie County
11th Circuit Court *Civil and Criminal Records*
Select and search Circuit Courts online at http://208.210.219.132/courtinfo/vadistrict/select.jsp?court=.

11th General District Court *Civil and Criminal Records*
Select and search District Courts at http://208.210.219.132/courtinfo/vadistrict/select.jsp?court=.

Essex County
15th General District Court *Civil and Criminal Records*
Select and search District Courts at http://208.210.219.132/courtinfo/vadistrict/select.jsp?court=.

Fairfax County
19th Circuit Court *Civil and Criminal Records*
www.co.fairfax.va.us/courts
Remote online access to court case indexes is via LOPAS; call 804-786-6455 to apply.

19th General District Court *Civil and Criminal Records*
www.co.fairfax.va.us/courts
Select and search District Courts at http://208.210.219.132/courtinfo/vadistrict/select.jsp?court=.

Fauquier County
20th Circuit Court *Civil and Criminal Records*
http://co.fauquier.va.us/services/ccc/index.html
Online access available free at http://208.210.219.132/courtinfo/vacircuit/select.jsp?court=.

20th General District Court *Civil and Criminal Records*
Select and search District Courts at http://208.210.219.132/courtinfo/vadistrict/select.jsp?court=.

Floyd County
27th Circuit Court *Civil and Criminal Records*
Select and search Circuit Courts online at http://208.210.219.132/courtinfo/vacircuit/select.jsp?court=.

27th General District Court *Civil and Criminal Records*
Select and search District Courts at http://208.210.219.132/courtinfo/vadistrict/select.jsp?court=. Also, remote online access to court case indexes is via LOPAS; call 804-786-6455 to apply.

Fluvanna County
16th Circuit Court *Civil and Criminal Records*
Select and search Circuit Courts online at http://208.210.219.132/courtinfo/vacircuit/select.jsp?court=.

16th General District Court *Civil and Criminal Records*
Select and search District Courts at http://208.210.219.132/courtinfo/vadistrict/select.jsp?court=.

Frederick County
Circuit Court *Civil and Criminal Records*
www.winfredclerk.com
Select and search Circuit Courts online at http://208.210.219.132/courtinfo/vacircuit/select.jsp?court=.

26th District Court *Civil and Criminal Records*
Select and search District Courts at http://208.210.219.132/courtinfo/vadistrict/select.jsp?court=.

Giles County
27th General District Court *Civil and Criminal Records*
Select and search District Courts at http://208.210.219.132/courtinfo/vadistrict/select.jsp?court=.

Gloucester County
9th Circuit Court *Civil and Criminal Records*
www.co.gloucester.va.us
Online access available free at http://208.210.219.132/courtinfo/vacircuit/select.jsp?court=.

9th General District Court *Civil and Criminal Records*
Select and search District Courts at http://208.210.219.132/courtinfo/vadistrict/select.jsp?court=.

Goochland County

16th Circuit Court *Civil and Criminal Records*
Remote online access to court case indexes is via LOPAS; call 804-786-6455 to apply.

General District Court *Civil and Criminal Records*
Select and search District Courts at http://208.210.219.132/courtinfo/vadistrict/select.jsp?court=.

Grayson County

27th Circuit Court *Civil and Criminal Records*
Select and search Circuit Courts online at http://208.210.219.132/courtinfo/vacircuitselect.jsp?court=.

27th General District Court *Civil and Criminal Records*
Select and search District Courts at http://208.210.219.132/courtinfo/vadistrict/select.jsp?court=.

Greene County

16th Circuit Court *Civil and Criminal Records*
Remote online access to court case indexes is via LOPAS; call 804-786-6455 to apply.

16th General District Court *Civil and Criminal Records*
Select and search District Courts at http://208.210.219.132/courtinfo/vadistrict/select.jsp?court=.

Greensville County

6th Circuit Court *Civil and Criminal Records*
Select and search Circuit Courts online at http://208.210.219.132/courtinfo/vacircuit/select.jsp?court=.

Greenville/Emporia Combined Court *Civil and Criminal Records*
Select and search District Courts at http://208.210.219.132/courtinfo/vadistrict/select.jsp?court=.

Halifax County

10th Circuit Court *Civil and Criminal Records*
Remote online access to court case indexes is via LOPAS; call 804-786-6455 to apply.

10th General District Court *Civil and Criminal Records*
Select and search District Courts at http://208.210.219.132/courtinfo/vadistrict/select.jsp?court=.

Hanover County

15th Circuit Court *Civil and Criminal Records*
Remote online access to court case indexes is via LOPAS; call 804-786-6455 to apply.

15th General District Court *Civil and Criminal Records*
Select and search District Courts at http://208.210.219.132/courtinfo/vadistrict/select.jsp?court=.

Henrico County

14th Circuit Court *Civil and Criminal Records*
Remote online access to court case indexes is via LOPAS; call 804-786-6455 to apply.

14th General District Court *Civil and Criminal Records*
Select and search District Courts at http://208.210.219.132/courtinfo/vadistrict/select.jsp?court=.

Henry County

21st Circuit Court *Civil and Criminal Records*
www.courts.state.va.us   Online access available free at http://208.210.219.132/courtinfo/vacircuit/select.jsp?court=.

21st General District Court *Civil and Criminal Records*
www.courts.state.va.us   Select and search District Courts at http://208.210.219.132/courtinfo/vadistrict/select.jsp?court=.

Highland County

25th Circuit Court *Civil and Criminal Records*
Remote online access to court case indexes is via LOPAS; call 804-786-6455 to apply.

25th General District Court *Civil and Criminal Records*
Select and search District Courts at http://208.210.219.132/courtinfo/vadistrict/select.jsp?court=.

Isle of Wight County
5th Circuit Court *Civil and Criminal Records*
Online access available free at http://208.210.219.132/courtinfo/vacircuit/select.jsp?court=.

5th General District Court *Civil and Criminal Records*
Select and search District Courts at http://208.210.219.132/courtinfo/vadistrict/select.jsp?court=.

James City County
Williamsburg-James City Circuit Court *Civil and Criminal Records*
Online access available free at http://208.210.219.132/courtinfo/vacircuit/select.jsp?court=.

9th General District Court *Civil and Criminal Records*
Select and search District Courts at http://208.210.219.132/courtinfo/vadistrict/select.jsp?court=.

King and Queen County
9th Circuit Court *Civil and Criminal Records*
Remote online access to court case indexes is via LOPAS; call 804-786-6455 to apply.

King & Queen General District Court *Civil and Criminal Records*
Select and search District Courts at http://208.210.219.132/courtinfo/vadistrict/select.jsp?court=.

King George County
15th Circuit Court *Civil and Criminal Records*
Select and search Circuit Courts online at http://208.210.219.132/courtinfo/vacircuit/select.jsp?court=.

15th Judicial District King George Combined Court *Civil and Criminal Records*
Select and search District Courts at http://208.210.219.132/courtinfo/vadistrict/select.jsp?court=.

King William County
9th Circuit Court *Civil and Criminal Records*
Select and search Circuit Courts online at http://208.210.219.132/courtinfo/vacircuit/select.jsp?court=.

King William General District Court *Civil and Criminal Records*
Select and search District Courts at http://208.210.219.132/courtinfo/vadistrict/select.jsp?court=.

Lancaster County
15th Circuit Court *Civil and Criminal Records*
Select and search Circuit Courts online at http://208.210.219.132/courtinfo/vacircuit/select.jsp?court=.

15th General District Court *Civil and Criminal Records*
Select and search District Courts at http://208.210.219.132/courtinfo/vadistrict/select.jsp?court=.

Lee County
30th Circuit Court *Civil and Criminal Records*
Select and search Circuit Courts online at http://208.210.219.132/courtinfo/vacircuit/select.jsp?court=.

30th General District Court *Civil and Criminal Records*
Select and search District Courts at http://208.210.219.132/courtinfo/vadistrict/select.jsp?court=.

Loudoun County
20th Circuit Court *Civil and Criminal Records*
Remote online access to court case indexes is via LOPAS; call 804-786-6455 to apply. Also, docket lists are available online for free at www.loudoun.gov/clerk/docs/dockets_/index.htm.

20th General District Court *Civil and Criminal Records*
Select and search District Courts at http://208.210.219.132/courtinfo/vadistrict/select.jsp?court=.

Louisa County
16th Circuit Court *Civil and Criminal Records*
Select and search Circuit Courts online at http://208.210.219.132/courtinfo/vacircuit/select.jsp?court=.

16th General District Court *Civil and Criminal Records*
Select and search District Courts at http://208.210.219.132/courtinfo/vadistrict/select.jsp?court=.

Lunenburg County
10th Circuit Court *Civil and Criminal Records*
Select and search Circuit Courts online at http://208.210.219.132/courtinfo/vacircuit/select.jsp?court=.

10th General District Court *Civil and Criminal Records*
Select and search District Courts at http://208.210.219.132/courtinfo/vadistrict/select.jsp?court=.

Madison County
16th Circuit Court *Civil and Criminal Records*
Select and search Combined Courts online at http://208.210.219.132/courtinfo/vacircuit/select.jsp?court=.

16th General District Court *Civil and Criminal Records*
Select and search District Courts at http://208.210.219.132/courtinfo/vadistrict/select.jsp?court=.

Mathews County
9th Circuit Court *Civil and Criminal Records*
www.courts.state.va.us/courts/circuit/Mathews/home.html Remote online access to court case indexes is via LOPAS; call 804-786-6455.

9th General District Court *Civil and Criminal Records*
Select and search District Courts at http://208.210.219.132/courtinfo/vadistrict/select.jsp?court=.

Mecklenburg County
10th Circuit Court *Civil and Criminal Records*
Remote online access to court case indexes is via LOPAS; call 804-786-6455 to apply.

10th General District Court *Civil and Criminal Records*
Select and search District Courts at http://208.210.219.132/courtinfo/vadistrict/select.jsp?court=.

Middlesex County
9th Circuit Court *Civil and Criminal Records*
Online access available free at http://208.210.219.132/courtinfo/vacircuit/select.jsp?court=.

9th General District Court *Civil and Criminal Records*
Select and search District Courts at http://208.210.219.132/courtinfo/vadistrict/select.jsp?court=.

Montgomery County
27th Circuit Court *Civil and Criminal Records*
Online access available free at http://208.210.219.132/courtinfo/vacircuit/select.jsp?court=.

27th General District Court *Civil and Criminal Records*
Select and search District Courts at http://208.210.219.132/courtinfo/vadistrict/select.jsp?court=.

Nelson County
24th Circuit Court *Civil and Criminal Records*
Online access available free at http://208.210.219.132/courtinfo/vacircuit/select.jsp?court=.

24th General District Court *Civil and Criminal Records*
Select and search District Courts at http://208.210.219.132/courtinfo/vadistrict/select.jsp?court=.

New Kent County
9th Circuit Court *Civil and Criminal Records*
Online access available free at http://208.210.219.132/courtinfo/vacircuit/select.jsp?court=.

9th General District Court *Civil and Criminal Records*
Select and search District Courts at http://208.210.219.132/courtinfo/vadistrict/select.jsp?court=.

Northampton County
2nd Circuit Court *Civil and Criminal Records*
Select and search Circuit Courts online at http://208.210.219.132/courtinfo/vacircuit/select.jsp?court=.

Northampton General District Court *Civil and Criminal Records*
Select and search District Courts at http://208.210.219.132/courtinfo/vadistrict/select.jsp?court=.

Northumberland County
15th Circuit Court *Civil and Criminal Records*
Online access available free at http://208.210.219.132/courtinfo/vacircuit/select.jsp?court=.

15th General District Court *Civil and Criminal Records*
Select and search District Courts at http://208.210.219.132/courtinfo/vadistrict/select.jsp?court=.

Nottoway County
11th Circuit Court *Civil and Criminal Records*
Select and search Circuit Courts online at http://208.210.219.132/courtinfo/vacircuit/select.jsp?court=.

11th General District Court *Civil and Criminal Records*
Select and search District Courts at http://208.210.219.132/courtinfo/vadistrict/select.jsp?court=.

Orange County
16th Circuit Court *Civil and Criminal Records*
Select and search Circuit Courts online at http://208.210.219.132/courtinfo/vacircuit/select.jsp?court=.

16th General District Court *Civil and Criminal Records*
Select and search District Courts at http://208.210.219.132/courtinfo/vadistrict/select.jsp?court=.

Page County
26th Circuit Court *Civil and Criminal Records*
Online access available free at http://208.210.219.132/courtinfo/vacircuit/select.jsp?court=.

26th General District Court *Civil and Criminal Records*
Select and search District Courts at http://208.210.219.132/courtinfo/vadistrict/select.jsp?court=.

Patrick County
21st Circuit Court *Civil and Criminal Records*
Online access available free at http://208.210.219.132/courtinfo/vacircuit/select.jsp?court=.

21st General District Court *Civil and Criminal Records*
Select and search District Courts at http://208.210.219.132/courtinfo/vadistrict/select.jsp?court=.

Pittsylvania County
22nd Circuit Court *Civil and Criminal Records*
Remote online access to court case indexes is via LOPAS; call 804-786-6455 to apply.

22nd General District Court *Civil and Criminal Records*
www.courts.state.va.us/courts/gd/Pittsylvania/home.html
Select and search District Courts at http://208.210.219.132/courtinfo/vadistrict/select.jsp?court=.

Powhatan County
11th Circuit Court *Civil and Criminal Records*
Remote online access to court case indexes is via LOPAS; call 804-786-6455 to apply.

11th Judicial District Court *Civil and Criminal Records*
Select and search District Courts at http://208.210.219.132/courtinfo/vadistrict/select.jsp?court=.

Prince Edward County

Circuit Court *Civil and Criminal Records*
Remote online access to court case indexes is via LOPAS; call 804-786-6455 to apply.

General District Court *Civil and Criminal Records*
Select and search District Courts at http://208.210.219.132/courtinfo/vadistrict/select.jsp?court=.

Prince George County

6th Circuit Court *Civil and Criminal Records*
Select and search Circuit Courts online at http://208.210.219.132/courtinfo/vacircuit/select.jsp?court=.

6th General District Court *Civil and Criminal Records*
Select and search District Courts at http://208.210.219.132/courtinfo/vadistrict/select.jsp?court=.

Prince William County

31st General District Court *Civil and Criminal Records*
www.courts.state.va.us/courts/gd/Prince_William/home.html
Select and search District Courts at http://208.210.219.132/courtinfo/vadistrict/select.jsp?court=.

Pulaski County

27th Circuit Court *Civil and Criminal Records*
www.pulaskicircuitcourt.com
Online access to court records available free at http://records.pulaskicircuitcourt.com/splash.jsp. Registration required; search by name, document type or number. Also, online access is available free at http://208.210.219.132/courtinfo/vacircuit/select.jsp?court=.

27th General District Court *Civil and Criminal Records*
Select and search District Courts at http://208.210.219.132/courtinfo/vadistrict/select.jsp?court=.

Rappahannock County

20th Circuit Court *Civil and Criminal Records*
Select and search Circuit Courts online at http://208.210.219.132/courtinfo/vacircuit/select.jsp?court=.

20th Combined District Court *Civil and Criminal Records*
Select and search District Courts at http://208.210.219.132/courtinfo/vadistrict/select.jsp?court=.

Richmond County

15th Circuit Court *Civil and Criminal Records*
Select and search Circuit Courts online at http://208.210.219.132/courtinfo/vacircuit/select.jsp?court=.

15th Judicial District Court *Civil and Criminal Records*
Select and search District Courts at http://208.210.219.132/courtinfo/vadistrict/select.jsp?court=.

Roanoke County

23rd Circuit Court *Civil and Criminal Records*
www.co.roanoke.va.us   Online access available free at http://208.210.219.132/courtinfo/vacircuit/select.jsp?court=.

23rd General District Court *Civil and Criminal Records*
www.co.roanoke.va.us   Select and search District Courts at http://208.210.219.132/courtinfo/vadistrict/select.jsp?court=.

Rockbridge County

25th Circuit Court *Civil and Criminal Records*
Select and search Circuit Courts online at http://208.210.219.132/courtinfo/vacircuit/select.jsp?court=.

District Court *Civil and Criminal Records*
Select and search District Courts at http://208.210.219.132/courtinfo/vadistrict/select.jsp?court=.

Rockingham County

26th Circuit Court *Civil and Criminal Records*
Online access available free at http://208.210.219.132/courtinfo/vacircuit/select.jsp?court=.

26th General District Court *Civil and Criminal Records*
Select and search District Courts at http://208.210.219.132/courtinfo/vadistrict/select.jsp?court=.

Russell County
29th Circuit Court *Civil and Criminal Records*
Select and search Circuit Courts online at http://208.210.219.132/courtinfo/vacircuit/select.jsp?court=.

29th General District Court *Civil and Criminal Records*
Select and search District Courts at http://208.210.219.132/courtinfo/vadistrict/select.jsp?court=.

Scott County
30th Circuit Court *Civil and Criminal Records*
Select and search Circuit Courts online at http://208.210.219.132/courtinfo/vacircuit/select.jsp?court=.

30th General District Court *Civil and Criminal Records*
Select and search District Courts at http://208.210.219.132/courtinfo/vadistrict/select.jsp?court=.

Shenandoah County
26th Circuit Court *Civil and Criminal Records*
Select and search Circuit Courts online at http://208.210.219.132/courtinfo/vacircuit/select.jsp?court=.

26th General District Court *Civil and Criminal Records*
Select and search District Courts at http://208.210.219.132/courtinfo/vadistrict/select.jsp?court=.

Smyth County
28th Circuit Court *Civil and Criminal Records*
Select and search Circuit Courts online at http://208.210.219.132/courtinfo/vacircuit/select.jsp?court=.

28th General District Court *Civil and Criminal Records*
Select and search District Courts at http://208.210.219.132/courtinfo/vadistrict/select.jsp?court=.

Southampton County
5th Circuit Court *Civil and Criminal Records*
Select and search Circuit Courts online at http://208.210.219.132/courtinfo/vacircuit/select.jsp?court=.

5th General District Court *Civil and Criminal Records*
Select and search District Courts at http://208.210.219.132/courtinfo/vadistrict/select.jsp?court=.

Spotsylvania County
15th Circuit Court *Civil and Criminal Records*
Remote online access to court case indexes is via LOPAS; call 804-786-6455 to apply.

15th General District Court *Civil and Criminal Records*
Select and search District Courts at http://208.210.219.132/courtinfo/vadistrict/select.jsp?court=.

Stafford County
15th Circuit Court *Civil and Criminal Records*
Select and search Circuit Courts online at http://208.210.219.132/courtinfo/vacircuit/select.jsp?court=.

15th General District Court *Civil and Criminal Records*
Select and search District Courts at http://208.210.219.132/courtinfo/vadistrict/select.jsp?court=.

Surry County
6th Circuit Court *Civil and Criminal Records*
Remote online access to court case indexes is via LOPAS; call 804-786-6455 to apply.

6th General District Court *Civil and Criminal Records*
Select and search District Courts at http://208.210.219.132/courtinfo/vadistrict/select.jsp?court=.

Sussex County
6th Circuit Court *Civil and Criminal Records*
Remote online access to court case indexes is via LOPAS; call 804-786-6455 to apply.

6th Judicial District Court *Civil and Criminal Records*
Select and search District Courts at http://208.210.219.132/courtinfo/vadistrict/select.jsp?court=.

Tazewell County
29th Circuit Court *Civil and Criminal Records*
Online access available free at http://208.210.219.132/courtinfo/vacircuit/select.jsp?court=.

29th General District Court *Civil and Criminal Records*
Select and search District Courts at http://208.210.219.132/courtinfo/vadistrict/select.jsp?court=.

Warren County
Circuit Court *Civil and Criminal Records*
www.courts.state.va.us/courts/circuit/warren/home.html
Online access available free at http://208.210.219.132/courtinfo/vacircuit/select.jsp?court=.

26th General District Court *Civil and Criminal Records*
Select and search District Courts at http://208.210.219.132/courtinfo/vadistrict/select.jsp?court=.

Washington County
Circuit Court *Civil and Criminal Records*
Remote online access to court case indexes is via LOPAS; call 804-786-6455 to apply.

28th General District Court *Civil and Criminal Records*
Select and search District Courts at http://208.210.219.132/courtinfo/vadistrict/select.jsp?court=.

Westmoreland County
15th General District Court *Civil and Criminal Records*
Select and search District Courts at http://208.210.219.132/courtinfo/vadistrict/select.jsp?court=.

Wise County
30th Circuit Court *Civil and Criminal Records*
Online access available free at http://208.210.219.132/courtinfo/vacircuit/select.jsp?court=. Also, court indexes are available at www.courtbar.org. Registration and a fee is required. Records go back to June, 2000.

30th General District Court *Civil and Criminal Records*
Select and search District Courts at http://208.210.219.132/courtinfo/vadistrict/select.jsp?court=.

Wythe County
27th Circuit Court *Civil and Criminal Records*
Remote online access to court case indexes is via LOPAS; call 804-786-6455 to apply.

Wythe General District Court *Civil and Criminal Records*
Select and search District Courts at http://208.210.219.132/courtinfo/vadistrict/select.jsp?court=.

York County
9th Circuit Court *Civil and Criminal Records*
Online access available free at http://208.210.219.132/courtinfo/vacircuit/select.jsp?court=.

9th Judicial District Court *Civil and Criminal Records*
www.yorkcounty.gov
Select and search District Courts at http://208.210.219.132/courtinfo/vadistrict/select.jsp?court=.

Virginia Independent Cities -- Courts

Alexandria City County
18th District Court *Civil and Criminal Records*
Select and search District Courts at http://208.210.219.132/courtinfo/vadistrict/select.jsp?court=.

Bristol City
28th Circuit Court *Civil and Criminal Records*
Select and search Circuit Courts online at http://208.210.219.132/courtinfo/vacircuit/select.jsp?court=.

28th General District Court *Civil and Criminal Records*
Select and search District Courts at http://208.210.219.132/courtinfo/vadistrict/select.jsp?court=.

Buena Vista City
25th Circuit & District Court *Civil and Criminal Records*
Select and search Circuit Courts online at http://208.210.219.132/courtinfo/vacircuit/select.jsp?court=. Search District courts at http://208.210.219.132/courtinfo/vadistrict/select.jsp?court=

Charles City is listed as Charles City County

Charlottesville City
16th Circuit Court *Civil and Criminal Records*
Remote online access to court case indexes is via LOPAS; call 804-786-6455 to apply.

Charlottesville General District Court *Civil and Criminal Records*
Select and search District Courts at http://208.210.219.132/courtinfo/vadistrict/select.jsp?court=.

Chesapeake City
1st Circuit Court *Civil and Criminal Records*
Online access available free at http://208.210.219.132/courtinfo/vacircuit/select.jsp?court=.

1st General District Court *Civil and Criminal Records*
Select and search District Courts at http://208.210.219.132/courtinfo/vadistrict/select.jsp?court=.

Clifton Forge City
25th Circuit Court *Civil and Criminal Records*
Remote online access to court case indexes is via LOPAS; call 804-786-6455 to apply.

25th General District Court *Civil and Criminal Records*
Select and search District Courts at http://208.210.219.132/courtinfo/vadistrict/select.jsp?court=.

Colonial Heights City
12th Circuit Court *Civil and Criminal Records*
Remote online access to court case indexes is via LOPAS; call 804-786-6455 to apply.

12th General District Court *Civil and Criminal Records*
Select and search District Courts at http://208.210.219.132/courtinfo/vadistrict/select.jsp?court=.

Danville City County
22nd Circuit Court *Civil and Criminal Records*
Online access available free at http://208.210.219.132/courtinfo/vacircuit/select.jsp?court=.

22nd General District Court *Civil and Criminal Records*
Select and search District Courts at http://208.210.219.132/courtinfo/vadistrict/select.jsp?court=.

Emporia City
6th General District Court *Civil and Criminal Records*
Select and search District Courts at http://208.210.219.132/courtinfo/vadistrict/select.jsp?court=.

Falls Church City
17th District Courts Combined *Civil and Criminal Records*
www.ci.falls-church.va.us
Select and search District Courts at http://208.210.219.132/courtinfo/vadistrict/select.jsp?court=.

Franklin City
5th Circuit Court *Civil and Criminal Records*
Select and search Circuit Courts online at http://208.210.219.132/courtinfo/vacircuit/select.jsp?court=.

22nd General District Court *Civil and Criminal Records*
Select and search District Courts at http://208.210.219.132/courtinfo/vadistrict/select.jsp?court=.

Fredericksburg City
15th Circuit Court *Civil and Criminal Records*
Online access available free at http://208.210.219.132/courtinfo/vacircuit/select.jsp?court=.

15th General District Court *Civil and Criminal Records*
Select and search District Courts at http://208.210.219.132/courtinfo/vadistrict/select.jsp?court=.

Galax City County
27th General District Court *Civil and Criminal Records*
Select and search District Courts at http://208.210.219.132/courtinfo/vadistrict/select.jsp?court=.

Hampton City
8th Circuit Court *Civil and Criminal Records*
Online access available free at http://208.210.219.132/courtinfo/vacircuit/select.jsp?court=.

8th General District Court *Civil and Criminal Records*
Select and search District Courts at http://208.210.219.132/courtinfo/vadistrict/select.jsp?court=.

Hopewell City
6th Circuit Court *Civil and Criminal Records*
Select and search Circuit Courts online at http://208.210.219.132/courtinfo/vacircuit/select.jsp?court=.

Hopewell District Court *Civil and Criminal Records*
Select and search District Courts at http://208.210.219.132/courtinfo/vadistrict/select.jsp?court=.

Lynchburg City
24th Circuit Court *Civil and Criminal Records*
Select and search Circuit Courts online at http://208.210.219.132/courtinfo/vacircuit/select.jsp?court=.

24th General District Court *Civil Records*
Select and search District Courts at http://208.210.219.132/courtinfo/vadistrict/select.jsp?court=.

24th General District Court *Criminal Records*
Select and search General District Courts at http://208.210.219.132/courtinfo/vadistrict/select.jsp?court=.

Martinsville City
21st Circuit Court *Civil and Criminal Records*
www.ci.martinsville.va.us/crms/
Online access available free at http://208.210.219.132/courtinfo/vacircuit/select.jsp?court=. For information about the statewide online systems, see the state introduction. Also, judgments are available free online at www.ci.martinsville.va.us/crms/.

21st General District Court *Civil and Criminal Records*
www.courts.state.va.us   Select and search District Courts at http://208.210.219.132/courtinfo/vadistrict/select.jsp?court=.

Newport News City County
7th Circuit Court *Civil and Criminal Records*
Online access available free at http://208.210.219.132/courtinfo/vacircuit/select.jsp?court=.

7th General District Court *Civil and Criminal Records*
Select and search District Courts at http://208.210.219.132/courtinfo/vadistrict/select.jsp?court=.

Norfolk City

4th Circuit Court *Civil and Criminal Records*
Access available free at http://208.210.219.132/courtinfo/vacircuit/select.jsp?court=. Online access to criminal dockets also available.

4th General District Court *Civil and Criminal Records*
Select and search District Courts at http://208.210.219.132/courtinfo/vadistrict/select.jsp?court=.

Petersburg City

11th Circuit Court *Civil and Criminal Records*
Online access available free at http://208.210.219.132/courtinfo/vacircuit/select.jsp?court=.

11th Judicial District Court *Civil and Criminal Records*
Select and search District Courts at http://208.210.219.132/courtinfo/vadistrict/select.jsp?court=.

Portsmouth City

Circuit Court *Civil and Criminal Records*
Online access available free at http://208.210.219.132/courtinfo/vacircuit/select.jsp?court=.

General District Court *Civil and Criminal Records*
Select and search District Courts at http://208.210.219.132/courtinfo/vadistrict/select.jsp?court=.

Radford City

27th Circuit Court *Civil and Criminal Records*
Select and search Circuit Courts online at http://208.210.219.132/courtinfo/vacircuit/select.jsp?court=.

27th General District Court *Civil and Criminal Records*
Select and search District Courts at http://208.210.219.132/courtinfo/vadistrict/select.jsp?court=.

Richmond City

13th Circuit Court - Division I *Civil and Criminal Records*
www.courts.state.va.us/courts/circuit/Richmond/home.html
A second web site is www.vipnet.org/vipnet/clerks/richmondjohnmarshall.html. Online access available free at http://208.210.219.132/courtinfo/vacircuit/select.jsp?court=.

13th General District Court *Civil and Criminal Records*
Select and search District Courts at http://208.210.219.132/courtinfo/vadistrict/select.jsp?court=.

13th General District Court - Division II *Criminal Records*
Select and search General District Courts at http://208.210.219.132/courtinfo/vadistrict/select.jsp?court=.

Richmond City - Manchester County

13th Circuit Court *Civil and Criminal Records*
www.vipnet.org/vipnet/clerks/richmondmanchester.html
Online access available free at http://208.210.219.132/courtinfo/vacircuit/select.jsp?court=.

Roanoke City

23rd Circuit Court *Civil and Criminal Records*
www.co.roanoke.va.us
Online access available free at http://208.210.219.132/courtinfo/vacircuit/select.jsp?court=.

General District Court *Civil and Criminal Records*
Select and search District Courts at http://208.210.219.132/courtinfo/vadistrict/select.jsp?court=.

Salem City

23rd Circuit Court *Civil and Criminal Records*
Select and search Circuit Courts online at http://208.210.219.132/courtinfo/vacircuit/select.jsp?court=.

23rd General District Court *Civil and Criminal Records*
Select and search District Courts at http://208.210.219.132/courtinfo/vadistrict/select.jsp?court=.

Staunton City
25th Circuit Court *Civil and Criminal Records*
Select and search Circuit Courts online at http://208.210.219.132/courtinfo/vacircuit/select.jsp?court=.

Staunton General District Court *Civil and Criminal Records*
Select and search District Courts at http://208.210.219.132/courtinfo/vadistrict/select.jsp?court=.

Suffolk City
Suffolk Circuit Court *Civil and Criminal Records*
Select and search Circuit Courts online at http://208.210.219.132/courtinfo/vacircuit/select.jsp?court=.

5th General District Court *Civil and Criminal Records*
Select and search District Courts at http://208.210.219.132/courtinfo/vadistrict/select.jsp?court=.

Virginia Beach City
2nd Circuit Court *Civil and Criminal Records*
www.virginia-beach.va.us/courts
Online access available free at http://208.210.219.132/courtinfo/vacircuit/select.jsp?court=.

2nd General District Court *Civil and Criminal Records*
www.vbgov.com
Select and search District Courts at http://208.210.219.132/courtinfo/vadistrict/select.jsp?court=.

Waynesboro City
25th Circuit Court *Civil and Criminal Records*
Online access available free at http://208.210.219.132/courtinfo/vacircuit/select.jsp?court=.

25th General District Court - Waynesboro *Civil and Criminal Records*
Select and search District Courts at http://208.210.219.132/courtinfo/vadistrict/select.jsp?court=.

Winchester City
26th Circuit Court *Civil and Criminal Records*
www.winfredclerk.com
Online access available free at http://208.210.219.132/courtinfo/vacircuit/select.jsp?court=.

26th General District Court *Civil and Criminal Records*
Select and search District Courts at http://208.210.219.132/courtinfo/vadistrict/select.jsp?court=.

County Level ... Recorders & Assessors

Recording Office Organization: 95 counties and 41 independent cities -- 123 recording offices. The recording officer is the Clerk of Circuit Court. Fifteen independent cities share the Clerk of Circuit Court with the county - Bedford, Covington (Alleghany County), Emporia (Greenville County), Fairfax, Falls Church (Arlington or Fairfax County), Franklin (Southhampton County), Galax (Carroll County), Harrisonburg (Rockingham County), Lexington (Rockbridge County), Manassas and Manassas Park (Prince William County), Norton (Wise County), Poquoson (York County), South Boston (Halifax County), and Williamsburg (James City County). Charles City and James City are counties, not cities. The City of Franklin is not in Franklin County, the City of Richmond is not in Richmond County, and the City of Roanoke is not in Roanoke County. The entire state is in the Eastern Time Zone (EST). Federal tax liens on personal property of businesses are filed with the State Corporation Commission. Other federal and all state tax liens are filed with the county Clerk of Circuit Court. They are usually filed in a "Judgment Lien Book." Most counties will not perform tax lien searches.

Online Access Note:

A growing number of Virginia counties and cities provide free access to real estate-related information via the Internet. A limited but growing private company network named VamaNet provides free residential, commercial and vacant property and tax records for nine Virginia jurisdictions at www.vamanet.com/cgi-bin/LOCS - at the web site, click on the county name at left.

Virginia Counties (Virginia Independent Cities are listed following this County Section)

Arlington County   *Real Estate, Assessor, Trade Name Records*
Property records on the County assessor database are available free at www.co.arlington.va.us/REAssessments/Scripts/DreaDefault.asp.

Augusta County   *Property, Appraisal, Most Wanted Records*
Click on Augusta County to search property data for free at www.vamanet.com/cgi-bin/LOCS. Search the sheriff's most wanted list for free at www.augustacountyvirginia.com/sheriff/wanted.htm.

Bedford County   *Property Tax Records*
County real estate records on the Bedford County Commissioner of the Revenue site are available free online at http://208.206.84.33/realestate2/. Records on the City of Bedford (www.ci.bedford.va.us) Property Tax database are available free online at www.ci.bedford.va.us/taxf.shtml. Search by name, address or tax map reference number.

Caroline County   *Appraiser, Property Records*
Click on Caroline County to search property records for free at www.vamanet.com/cgi-bin/LOCS.

Carroll County   *Real Estate Records*
Access to Carroll county property information is available free on the gis mapping site at http://arcims.webgis.net/webgis/carroll_grayson. No name searching at this time. Access to Town of Hillsville property information is available on the gis mapping site at http://arcims.webgis.net/webgis/hillsville.

Chesterfield County   *Assessor, Property Tax, Property Sales Records*
Search the real estate assessment data for free at www.co.chesterfield.va.us/ManagementServices/RealEstateAssessments/Rea_Search_Home.asp.

Clarke County   *Property, Appraiser Records*
Click on Clarke County to search property data for free at www.vamanet.com/cgi-bin/LOCS.

Fairfax County   *Real Estate, Property Tax, Tax Sales Records*
www.co.fairfax.va.us
Records on the Dept. of Tax Administration Real Estate Assessment database are available free online at www.co.fairfax.va.us/dta/re/. Also, the Automated Information System operates Monday-Saturday 7AM-7PM at 703-222-6740. Hear about property descriptions, assessed values and sales prices. Fax-back service is available. Also, the list of properties to be auctioned is available free at www.co.fairfax.va.us/dta/auction.htm.

Floyd County   *Real Estate Records*
Access to county property information is available free at the gis mapping site at http://arcims.webgis.net/webgis/floyd/default.asp. No name searching at this time.

Fluvanna County   *Appraiser, Property Records*
Click on Fluvanna County to serach property data for free at www.vamanet.com/cgi-bin/LOCS.

Giles County   *Appraiser, Property Records*
Click on Fluvanna County to search for property records for free at www.vamanet.com/cgi-bin/LOCS.

Gloucester County   *Judgment Records*
www.courts.state.va.us
Access to Law and Chancery cases is available free at http://208.210.219.132/courtinfo/vacircuit/select.jsp?court=.

Grayson County   *Real Estate Records*

Access to Grayson county property information is available free on the gis mapping site at http://arcims.webgis.net/webgis/carroll_grayson. No name searching at this time.

Greensville County   *Appraiser, Property Records*

Click on Grennsville County to search property data for free at www.vamanet.com/cgi-bin/LOCS.

Henry County   *Real Estate, Assessor Records*

http://henrycounty.neocom.net
Access to county property information is available free at the GIS mapping site at www.webgis.net/henry.

Isle of Wight County   *Judgment Records*

Access to Law and Chancery case judgments is available free at http://208.210.219.132/courtinfo/vacircuit/select2.jsp.

James City County   *Real Estate Records*

www.regis.state.va.us/jcc/
Records on the James City County Property Information database are available free online at www.regis.state.va.us/jcc/public/disclaimer.htm. Also, search the City of Williamsburg property assessor data for free at www.ci.williamsburg.va.us/realestate/disclaimer.html.

King William County   *Land Records*

Access to property and deeds indexes and images is available via a private company at http://auth.titlesearcher.com/ts/ts.asp or support@TitleSearcher.com. Fee/registration required; Monthly and per day available.

Loudoun County   *Property, Assessor Records*

www.loudoun.gov/government/
Search the proeprty assessor data for free at http://inter1.loudoun.gov/webpdbs/. No name searching; search by address, number or ID.

Montgomery County   *Real Estate, Property Tax Records*

www.montva.com
Access to the county Tax Parcel Information System database is available free online at www.webgis.net/montgomery/index.htm. Select what to search and click next. Records on the Town of Blacksburg GIS site are available free online at www.webgis.net/blacksburg. Use map or enter an owner name. Find owner name, address, land or building value.

Pittsylvania County   *Real Estate Records*

See Danville City for Real Estate and Lien records online for Danville City

Powhatan County   *Appraiser, Property Records*

Click on Powhatan County to search property data for free at www.vamanet.com/cgi-bin/LOCS.

Prince William County   *Property Records*

www.pwcgov.org/ccourt
Records on the county Property Information database are available free online at www.pwcgov.org/realestate/LandRover.asp.

Rockbridge County   *Appraiser, Property Records*

Click on City of Lexington to search the city property data for free at www.vamanet.com/cgi-bin/LOCS.

Scott County   *Deed, Property, Recording Records*

Access to Circuit Court records is available for a fifteen day trial demo. After, a username, password, and monthly fee is required. For information and sign-up, see http://auth.titlesearcher.com/ts/ts.asp or support@titlesearcher.com.

Washington County   *Real Estate, Assessor Records*

Search the county GIS-mapping site for free at http://arcims2.webgis.net/washington/default.asp. No name searching, but property and address information is available.

Wise County   *Assessor, Real Estate, Lien, Probate, Marriage Records*

www.courtbar.org
Includes City of Norton. Premium User fee is $395 annually or $39 per month. Genealogists have two plans: the 150-year marriage and probate database is $99 annually or $10 per month. Database index and images include the Court's orders, land documents from

1970 including links to real estate tax assessments, fifty-year real estate transfer histories, tax maps, plat maps, delinquent taxes, and permit images. Probate and marriage records, with recent document images from probate. Access the judgment lien index for the past 20 years; UCC-1 indices for the past five years. Also, property information is available free at http://arcims.webgis.net/webgis/wise.

York County *Property Records*
www.yorkcounty.gov/circuitcourt
Property records from the County GIS site are available free online at http://206.246.204.37.

Virginia Independent Cities -- Recorder Offices

Alexandria City *Assessor, Prooperty Records*
www.ci.alexandria.va.us
Acccss to city real estate assessments is available free at www.ci.alexandria.va.us/city/reasearch/. No name searching.

Danville City *Real Estate, Lien Records*
www.ci.danville.va.us/clerk
Access to Danville City online records is free; signup is required. Records date back to 1993. Lending agency information is available. For information, contact Leigh Ann Thomas at 804-799-5168.

Martinsville City *Property, Deed, Judgment, Wills, Marriage Records*
www.ci.martinsville.va.us/crms/
Access to the Martinsville Circuit Court records is available free at www.ci.martinsville.va.us/crms/. You may also search the tax map and for personal property.

Newport News City *Assessor, Real Estate Records*
www.newport-news.va.us
Access to the City's "Real Estate on the Web" database is available free at http://216.54.20.244/reisweb1. Search by address or parcel number; new "advanced search" may include name searching.

Norfolk City *Real Estate, Assessor Records*
http://norfolkgov.com/home.asp   Records on the City of Norfolk Real Estate Property Assessment database are available free online at www.norfolkgov.com/RealEstate/index.html.

Richmond City *Property, Assessor Records*
Search the city's Accessing Property & Real Estate Assessment Information for free at www.ci.richmond.va.us/accessingGIS.asp. Follow direction; name searching is available.

Roanoke City *Property Records*
Access to Roanoke City property records are available free at www.webgis.net/RoanokeCity.

Virginia Beach City *Real Estate Assessor Records*
www.vbgov.com
Search the assessor database for free at www.vbgov.com/dept/realestate/. No name searching.

Federal Courts in Virginia...

Standards for Federal Courts: The universal PACER sign-up number is 800-676-6856. Find PACER and the Party/Case Index on the Web at http://pacer.psc.uscourts.gov. PACER dial-up access is $.60 per minute. Also, courts offering internet access via RACER, PACER, Web-PACER or the new CM-ECF charge $.07 per page fee unless noted as free.

US District Court -- Eastern District of Virginia
Home Page: www.vaed.uscourts.gov **PACER:** Toll-free access: 800-852-5186. Local access phone: 703-299-2158. Case records are available back to June 1990. New records are available online after 1 day. **PACER URL:** http://pacer.vaed.uscourts.gov.

Alexandria Division counties: Arlington, Fairfax, Fauquier, Loudoun, Prince William, Stafford, City of Alexandria, City of Fairfax, City of Falls Church, City of Manassas, City of Manassas Park.

Newport News Division counties: Gloucester, James City, Mathews, York, City of Hampton, City of Newport News, City of Poquoson, City of Williamsburg.

Norfolk Division counties: Accomack, City of Chesapeake, City of Franklin, Isle of Wight, City of Norfolk, Northampton, City of Portsmouth, City of Suffolk, Southampton, City of Virginia Beach.

Richmond Division counties: Amelia, Brunswick, Caroline, Charles City, Chesterfield, Dinwiddie, Essex, Goochland, Greensville, Hanover, Henrico, King and Queen, King George, King William, Lancaster, Lunenburg, Mecklenburg, Middlesex, New Kent, Northumberland, Nottoway, City of Petersburg, Powhatan, Prince Edward, Prince George, Richmond, City of Richmond, Spotsylvania, Surry, Sussex, Westmoreland, City of Colonial Heights, City of Emporia, City of Fredericksburg, City of Hopewell.

US Bankruptcy Court -- Eastern District of Virginia

Home Page: www.vaeb.uscourts.gov

PACER: Toll-free access: 800-890-2858. Local access phone: 703-258-1234. Use of PC Anywhere v4.0 suggested. Case records are available back to mid 1989. Records are purged never. New civil records are available online after 1 day. PACER access is available online through CM/ECF at the web site. This replaces the free NIBS system.

Electronic Filing: Electronic filing information is available online at http://ecf.vaeb.uscourts.gov.

Other Online Access: Free online searching discontinued 8/1/2002. Court does not participate in the U.S. party case index. **Also:** access via phone on VCIS (Voice Case Information System) is available: 800-326-5879, 804-771-2736

Alexandria Division counties: City of Alexandria, Arlington, Fairfax, City of Fairfax, City of Falls Church, Fauquier, Loudoun, City of Manassas, City of Manassas Park, Prince William, Stafford.

Newport News Division counties: Newport News City. Records are at the Norfolk Bankruptcy Court.

Norfolk Division counties: Accomack, City of Cape Charles, City of Chesapeake, City of Franklin, Gloucester, City of Hampton, Isle of Wight, James City, Matthews, City of Norfolk, Northampton, City of Poquoson, City of Portsmouth, Southampton, City of Suffolk, City of Virginia Beach, City of Williamsburg, York.

Richmond Division counties: Amelia, Brunswick, Caroline, Charles City, Chesterfield, City of Colonial Heights, Dinwiddie, City of Emporia, Essex, City of Fredericksburg, Goochland, Greensville, Hanover, Henrico, City of Hopewell, King and Queen, King George, King William, Lancaster, Lunenburg, Mecklenburg, Middlesex, New Kent, Northumberland, Nottoway, City of Petersburg, Powhatan, Prince Edward, Prince George, Richmond, City of Richmond, Spotsylvania, Surry, Sussex, Westmoreland.

US District Court -- Western District of Virginia

Home Page: www.vawd.uscourts.gov

PACER: Toll-free access: 888-279-7848. Local access phone: 540-857-5140. Case records are available back to Mid 1990. Records are purged never. New records are available online after 1 day. **PACER URL:** http://pacer.vawd.uscourts.gov.

Abingdon Division counties: Buchanan, City of Bristol, Russell, Smyth, Tazewell, Washington.

Big Stone Gap Division counties: Dickenson, Lee, Scott, Wise, City of Norton.

Charlottesville Division counties: Albemarle, Culpeper, Fluvanna, Greene, Louisa, Madison, Nelson, Orange, Rappahannock, City of Charlottesville.

Danville Division: Charlotte, Halifax, Henry, Patrick, Pittsylvania, City of Danville, City of Martinsville, City of South Boston.

Harrisonburg Division counties: Augusta, Bath, Clarke, Frederick, Highland, Page, Rockingham, Shenandoah, Warren, City of Harrisonburg, City of Staunton, City of Waynesboro, City of Winchester.

Lynchburg Division counties: Amherst, Appomattox, Bedford, Buckingham, Campbell, Cumberland, Rockbridge, City of Bedford, City of Buena Vista, City of Lexington, City of Lynchburg.

Roanoke Division counties: Alleghany, Bland, Botetourt, Carroll, Craig, Floyd, Franklin, Giles, Grayson, Montgomery, Pulaski, Roanoke, Wythe, City of Covington, City of Clifton Forge, City of Galax, City of Radford, City of Roanoke, City of Salem.

US Bankruptcy Court -- Western District of Virginia

Home Page: www.vawb.uscourts.gov

PACER: Toll-free access: 800-248-0329. Local access phone: 540-434-8373. Case records are available back to March 1986. Records are purged never. New civil records are available online after 1 day. **PACER URL:** https://pacer.vawb.uscourts.gov.

Harrisonburg Division counties: Alleghany, Augusta, Bath, City of Buena Vista, Clarke, City of Clifton Forge, City of Covington, Frederick, City of Harrisonburg, Highland, City of Lexington, Page, Rappahannock, Rockbridge, Rockingham, Shenandoah, City of Staunton, Warren, City of Waynesboro, City of Winchester.

Lynchburg Division counties: Albemarle, Amherst, Appomattox, Bedford, City of Bedford, Buckingham, Campbell, Charlotte, City of Charlottesville, Culpeper, Cumberland, City of Danville, Fluvanna, Greene, Halifax, Henry, Louisa, City of Lynchburg, Madison, City of Martinsville, Nelson, Orange, Patrick, Pittsylvania, City of South Boston.

Roanoke Division counties: Bland, Botetourt, City of Bristol, Buchanan, Carroll, Craig, Dickenson, Floyd, Franklin, City of Galax, Giles, Grayson, Lee, Montgomery, City of Norton, Pulaski, City of Radford, Roanoke, City of Roanoke, Russell, City of Salem, Scott, Smyth, Tazewell, Washington, Wise, Wythe.

Capital: Olympia
                Thurston County

Time Zone: PST

Number of Counties: 39

Home Page   http://access.wa.gov

Attorney General   www.wa.gov/ago

Archives   www.secstate.wa.gov/archives

State Level ... Major Agencies

Criminal Records

Washington State Patrol, Identification Section, PO Box 42633, Olympia, WA 98504-2633 (Courier: 3000 Pacific Ave. SE #204, Olympia, WA 98501); 360-705-5100, 360-570-5275 (Fax), 8AM-5PM.

www.wa.gov/wsp/wsphome.htm

WSP offers access through a system called WATCH, which can be accessed from their web site. The fee per search is $10.00. The exact DOB and exact spelling of the name is required. Credit cards are accepted online. To set up a WATCH account, call 360-705-5100 or email watch.help@wsp.wa.gov. **Other options:** The State Court Administrator's office maintains a criminal records database (JIS-Link). There is a $100.00 set-up fee and a $25.00 per hour access charge. Call 360-357-2407 for a packet or visit www.courts.wa.gov.

Corporation Records, Trademarks/Servicemarks, Limited Partnerships, Limited Liability Company Records

Secretary of State, Corporations Division, PO Box 40234, Olympia, WA 98504-0234 (Courier: Dolliver Bldg, 801 Capitol Way South, Olympia, WA 98501); 360-753-7115, 360-664-8781 (Fax), 8AM-5PM.

www.secstate.wa.gov/corps/

Free searching of corporation registrations is at www.secstate.wa.gov/corps/search.aspx. Information is updated weekly.

Trade Names

Master License Service, Business & Professions Div, PO Box 9034, Olympia, WA 98507-9034 (Courier: 405 Black Lake Blvd, Olympia, WA 98507); 360-664-1400, 900-463-6000 (Trade Name Search), 360-570-7875 (Fax), 8AM-5PM.

www.wa.gov/dol

Search options: A trade name search can be done by phone at the 900 number above. Records can be purchased on cartridges or 9 track tapes. Information includes date of registration, owner name, state ID numbers, and cancel date if cancelled. Call main number (area code 360) and ask for Jody Miller.

Uniform Commercial Code, Federal Tax Liens

Department of Licensing, UCC Records, PO Box 9660, Olympia, WA 98507-9660 (Courier: 405 Black Lake Blvd, Olympia, WA 98502); 360-664-1530, 360-586-4414 (Fax), 8AM-5PM.

https://wws2.wa.gov/dol/ucc/

For online access, go to https://wws2.wa.gov/dol/ucc/. There is a $15.00 search fee. **Other options:** The database may be purchased on magnetic tape or microfilm.

Sales Tax Registrations

Department fo Revenue, Taxpayer Services, PO Box 47498, Olympia, WA 98504-7478 (Courier: 415 Gen Admin Bldg, Olympia, WA 98501); 360-486-2345, 800-647-7706, 360-486-2159 (Fax), 8AM-5PM.

www.dor.wa.gov

The agency provides a state business records database with free access on the Internet. Lookups are by owner names, DBAs, and tax reporting numbers. Results show a myriad of data.

Vehicle Ownership, Vehicle Identification, Vessel Ownership, Vessel Registration

Department of Licensing, Vehicle Records, PO Box 2957, Olympia, WA 98507-2957 (Courier: 1125 S Washington MS-48001, Olympia, WA 98504); 360-902-3780, 360-902-3827 (Fax), 8AM-5PM.

www.dol.wa.gov

This is a commercial subscription service and all accounts must be pre-approved. Access is via the Internet. Known as IVIPS, the system processes requests much the phone search. A $25.00 deposit is required and there is a $.04 fee per hit. For more information, call 360-902-3760. **Other options:** Large bulk lists cannot be released for any commercial purposes. Lists are released to non-profit entities and for statistical purposes. For more information, call 360-902-3760.

Legislation Records

www.leg.wa.gov

The web site offers bill text and status look-up.

State Level ... Occupational Licensing

Acupuncturist	www.doh.wa.gov/A-Z.htm
Adult Family Home	www.aasa.dshs.wa.gov/Lookup/AFHRequestv2.asp
Animal Technician	www.doh.wa.gov/A-Z.htm
Announcer, Athletic Event (Ring)	https://wws2.wa.gov/dol/profquery
Architect/ Architect Corporation	https://wws2.wa.gov/dol/profquery/
Athlete, Professional	https://wws2.wa.gov/dol/profquery
Athletic Inspector	https://wws2.wa.gov/dol/profquery
Athletic Judge/Timekeeper/Physician/Manager	https://wws2.wa.gov/dol/profquery
Athletic Promoter/Matchmaker	https://wws2.wa.gov/dol/profquery
Attorney	www.wsba.org/directory/default.htm
Auction Company/ Auctioneer	https://wws2.wa.gov/dol/profquery
Bail Bond Agent/Agency	https://wws2.wa.gov/dol/profquery
Barber	https://wws2.wa.gov/dol/profquery
Barber Instructor/School	https://wws2.wa.gov/dol/profquery
Barber Shop/Mobile/Booth	https://wws2.wa.gov/dol/profquery
Beauty Shop/Salon/Mobile	https://wws2.wa.gov/dol/profquery
Boarding Homes	www.aasa.dshs.wa.gov/Lookup/BHRequestv2.asp
Boxer	https://wws2.wa.gov/dol/profquery
Bulk Hauler	https://wws2.wa.gov/dol/profquery
Cemetery	https://wws2.wa.gov/dol/profquery
Chiropractor	www.doh.wa.gov/A-Z.htm

Collection Agency	https://wws2.wa.gov/dol/profquery
Contractor, General, Company	https://wws2.wa.gov/lni/bbip/contractor.asp
Cosmetologist	https://wws2.wa.gov/dol/profquery
Cosmetology Instructor/School	https://wws2.wa.gov/dol/profquery
Counselor	www.doh.wa.gov/A-Z.htm
Court Reporter	https://wws2.wa.gov/dol/profquery
Crematory	https://wws2.wa.gov/dol/profquery
Dental Hygienist	www.doh.wa.gov/A-Z.htm
Dentist	www.doh.wa.gov/A-Z.htm
Dietitian	www.doh.wa.gov/A-Z.htm
Electrical Contractor/Admin.	https://wws2.wa.gov/lni/bbip/contractor.asp
Electrician	https://wws2.wa.gov/lni/bbip/contractor.asp
Embalmer	https://wws2.wa.gov/dol/profquery
Emergency Medical Technician	www.doh.wa.gov/A-Z.htm
Employment Agency	https://wws2.wa.gov/dol/profquery
Engineer	https://wws2.wa.gov/dol/profquery/LicenseeSearch.asp
Engineering Geologist	https://wws2.wa.gov/dol/profquery
Engineering/Land Surveying Company	https://wws2.wa.gov/dol/profquery/LicenseeSearch.asp
Esthetician Shop/Salon/Booth/Mobile	https://wws2.wa.gov/dol/profquery
Esthetician/Esthetician Instructor	https://wws2.wa.gov/dol/profquery
Feedlot	www.wa.gov/agr/FoodAnimal/Livestock/CertifiedFeedlots.htm
Funeral Director	https://wws2.wa.gov/dol/profquery
Funeral Establishment	https://wws2.wa.gov/dol/profquery
Gaming Occupation	www.wsgc.wa.gov/LicSearch.asp
Gaming Operation	www.wsgc.wa.gov/LicSearch.asp
Geologist	https://wws2.wa.gov/dol/profquery
Health Care Assistant	www.doh.wa.gov/A-Z.htm
Home Health Care Agency	www.doh.wa.gov/Licensing.htm
Hospital	www.doh.wa.gov/Licensing.htm
Hydrogeologist	https://wws2.wa.gov/dol/profquery
Insurance Company	www.insurance.wa.gov/tableofcontents/annualreptins.htm
Kick Boxer	https://wws2.wa.gov/dol/profquery
Land Development Rep	https://wws2.wa.gov/dol/profquery
Land Surveyor/Surveyor-in-Training	https://wws2.wa.gov/dol/profquery/LicenseeSearch.asp
Landscape Architect	https://wws2.wa.gov/dol/profquery/
Limousine Carrier	https://wws2.wa.gov/dol/profquery
Liquor Store	www.liq.wa.gov/services/storesearch.asp
Livestock Market	www.wa.gov/agr/FoodAnimal/Livestock/PublicMarkets.htm
Manicure Shop/Mobile/Booth	https://wws2.wa.gov/dol/profquery
Manicurist/Manicurist Instructor	https://wws2.wa.gov/dol/profquery
Manufactured Home Dealer	https://wws2.wa.gov/dol/profquery
Marriage & Family Therapist	www.doh.wa.gov/A-Z.htm
Mental Health Counselor	www.doh.wa.gov/A-Z.htm
Mobile Home/Travel Trailer Dealer	https://wws2.wa.gov/dol/profquery
Notary Public	https://wws2.wa.gov/dol/profquery/
Nursing Homes	www.aasa.dshs.wa.gov/Professional/NFDir/directory.asp
Optometrist	www.odfinder.org/LicSearch.asp
Pharmacist	www.doh.wa.gov/A-Z.htm
Pharmacy Technician	www.doh.wa.gov/A-Z.htm
Plumber	https://wws2.wa.gov/lni/bbip/contractor.asp
Private Investigative Agency	https://wws2.wa.gov/dol/profquery
Private Investigative Trainer	https://wws2.wa.gov/dol/profquery
Private Investigator, Armed/Unarmed	https://wws2.wa.gov/dol/profquery
Real Estate Appraiser, Cert./Licensed	https://wws2.wa.gov/dol/profquery
Real Estate Broker/ LLC, LLP, Corp./Partnership	https://wws2.wa.gov/dol/profquery
Real Estate Sales Occupation	https://wws2.wa.gov/dol/profquery
Referee	https://wws2.wa.gov/dol/profquery
Scrap Processor	https://wws2.wa.gov/dol/profquery
Security Guard, Private Armed/Unarmed	https://wws2.wa.gov/dol/profquery
Security Guard/Agency	https://wws2.wa.gov/dol/profquery

Snowmobile Dealer	https://wws2.wa.gov/dol/profquery
Social Worker	www.doh.wa.gov/A-Z.htm
Timeshare Seller/Company/Project	https://wws2.wa.gov/dol/profquery
Tow Truck Operator	https://wws2.wa.gov/dol/profquery
Travel Agency	https://wws2.wa.gov/dol/profquery
Travel Seller	https://wws2.wa.gov/dol/profquery
Vehicle Dealer, Miscellaneous/ Mfg./Transporter	https://wws2.wa.gov/dol/profquery
Vessel Dealer	https://wws2.wa.gov/dol/profquery
Veterinarian	www.doh.wa.gov/A-Z.htm
Veterinary Medical Clerk	www.doh.wa.gov/A-Z.htm
Wastewater System Designer/Inspector, On-Site	https://wws2.wa.gov/dol/profquery/LicenseeSearch.asp
Whitewater River Outfitter	https://wws2.wa.gov/dol/profquery
Wrecker	https://wws2.wa.gov/dol/profquery
Wrestler	https://wws2.wa.gov/dol/profquery

County Level ... Courts

Court Administration: Court Administrator, Temple of Justice, PO Box 41174, Olympia, WA, 98504; 360-357-2121; www.courts.wa.gov

Court Structure: District Courts retain civil records for ten years from date of final disposition, then the records are destroyed. District Courts retain criminal records forever. Washington has a mandatory arbitration requirement for civil disputes for $35,000 or less. However, either party may request a trial in Superior Court if dissatisfied with the arbitrator's decision. The limit for civil actions in District Court has been increased from $35,000 to $50,000.

Online Access Note: Appellate, Superior, and District Court records are available online. The Superior Court Management Information System (SCOMIS), the Appellate Records System (ACORDS) and the District/Municipal Court Information System (DISCIS) are on the Judicial Information System's JIS-Link. Case records available through JIS-Link from 1977 include criminal, civil, domestic, probate, and judgments. JIS-Link is generally available 24-hours daily. Minimum browser requirement is Internet Explorer 5.5 or Netscape 6.0. There is a one-time installation fee of $100.00 per site, and a connect time charge of $25.00 per hour (approximately $.42 per minute), plus a surcharge of $.85 per session. For information or a registration packet, contact: JISLink Coordinator, Office of the Admin. for the Courts, 1206 S Quince St., PO Box 41170, Olympia WA 98504-1170, 360-357-3365 or visit www.courts.wa.gov/jislink.

Chelan County
Superior Court *Civil and Criminal Records*
www.co.chelan.wa.us
Index available online from JIS-Link; see www.courts.wa.gov/jislink (see state introduction). Clerk records may also be available at www.co.chelan.wa.us/scc/scc4.htm.

Pierce County
Superior Court *Civil and Criminal Records*
www.co.pierce.wa.us/abtus/ourorg/supct/abtussup.htm
Online Superior Court case information, inmates, attorneys, and scheduled proceedings available free at www.co.pierce.wa.us/cfapps/linx/headerindex.cfm?source=search.cfm&activeTab=search. Also, a statewide index is available remotely online (see state introduction).

Statewide Access
Appellate, Superior, and District Court records are available online. See the "Online Access Note" above for details.

County Level ... Recorders & Assessors

Recording Office Organization: 39 counties, 39 recording offices. The recording officer is the County Auditor. County records are usually combined in a Grantor/Grantee index. The entire state is in the Pacific Time Zone (PST). All federal tax liens on personal property are filed with the Department of Licensing. Other federal and all state tax liens are filed with the County Auditor. Most counties will perform tax lien searches. Search fees are usually $8.00 or $10.00 per hour.

Online Access Note: A number of counties including the larger population counties offer onlice access to assessor or real estate records.

Chelan County *Grantor/Grantee, Property, Marriage Records*
www.co.chelan.wa.us
Access to the Auditor's iCRIS database is available free at www.co.chelan.wa.us/ad/ad5da.htm. Click on the "key" to get to free registration page. Images go back to 1997; marriage images to 1990; earlier online records show indexing information only.

Clark County *Real Estate, Lien, Vital Statistic, Recording Records*
www.co.clark.wa.us/auditor/
Access to County Auditor's database is available at http://auditor.co.clark.wa.us/auditor_new/index.cfm. Court documents are excluded from this index. Also, search maps online for property data at www.rtc.wa.gov/ccgis/mol/property.htm. No name searching.

Cowlitz County *Most Wanted, Missing Person Records*
www.co.cowlitz.wa.us/auditor/
Access to sheriff's most wanted and missing persons lists is available free at www.co.cowlitz.wa.us/sheriff/

Franklin County *Assessor, Property, Sex Offender Records*
Search for property information by address or parcel number at www.co.franklin.wa.us/assessor. Also, search for residential sales data. Also, search the level 2 sex offenders at www.co.franklin.wa.us/sheriff/?p=14&v=2. Level 3 sex offenders are at www.co.franklin.wa.us/sheriff/?p=14&v=3.

Island County *Sex Offender Records*
www.islandcounty.net/auditor/index.htm
Search the sexual offenders and kidnappers list for free at www.islandcounty.net/sheriff/rsolist.htm.

Jefferson County *Assessor, Real Estate Records*
www.co.jefferson.wa.us/departments.htm
Access to the "Recorded Document Search" database is available at www.co.jefferson.wa.us/_hidden/disclaimer.htm. Records on the County Property (Tax Parcel) Database Tool are also available as well as plats & survey images.

King County *Real Estate, Lien, Marriage Records*
www.metrokc.gov
Access to the county recorder's database is available free at www.metrokc.gov/recelec/records. Also, property records on Dept. of Developmental and Environmental Resources database are available free online at www.metrokc.gov/ddes/gis/parcel. After the disclaimer page, search by parcel number, address, street intersection, or map.

Pierce County *Assessor, Real Estate, Recording, Deed, Lien, Vital Statistic, Judgment Records*
Search the auditor's recording database for free at www.co.pierce.wa.us/cfapps/auditor/documentsearch.cfm. Also, property records on County Assessor-Treasurer database are available free online at www.co.pierce.wa.us/CFApps/atr/TIMSNet/index.htm. After the disclaimer page, search by parcel number or site address. Also, the county sexual offrende/kidnappers list is available for free at http://pso.co.pierce.wa.us.

Snohomish County *Real Estate, Assessor, Recording, Marriage Records*
Access to the Auditor's database is available free at http://198.238.192.100/default1.htm. Search on the OPR, map, or marriage page.

Thurston County *Assessor, Real Estate Records*
www.co.thurston.wa.us/auditor

Assessor and property information on Thurston GeoData database are available free online at www.geodata.org/scripts/esrimap.dll?name=TGCMAP&Cmd=Map.

Whatcom County   *Assessor, Real Estate Records*
www.co.whatcom.wa.us/auditor
Search the assessor parcel database information system free at www.co.whatcom.wa.us/cgibin/db2www/assessor/search/RPSearch.ndt/disclaimer. Also, voter registration lists are available for political purposes only; information and requests to www.co.whatcom.wa.us/auditor/elections/elections.htm.

Yakima County   *Assessor, Real Estate Records*
www.pan.co.yakima.wa.us
Assessor and property information on County Assessor database are available free online at www.co.yakima.wa.us/assessor/propinfo/asr_info.asp.

Federal Courts in Washington...

Standards for Federal Courts: The universal PACER sign-up number is 800-676-6856. Find PACER and the Party/Case Index on the Web at http://pacer.psc.uscourts.gov. PACER dial-up access is $.60 per minute. Also, courts offering internet access via RACER, PACER, Web-PACER or the new CM-ECF charge $.07 per page fee unless noted as free.

US District Court -- Eastern District of Washington
Home Page: www.waed.uscourts.gov
PACER: Toll-free access: 888-372-5706. Local access phone: 509-353-2395. Case records are available back to July 1989. Records are purged every six months. New records are available online after 2-3 days. **PACER URL:** http://pacer.waed.uscourts.gov.
Spokane Division counties: Adams, Asotin, Benton, Chelan, Columbia, Douglas, Ferry, Franklin, Garfield, Grant, Lincoln, Okanogan, Pend Oreille, Spokane, Stevens, Walla Walla, Whitman. Also, some cases from Kittitas, Klickitat and Yakima are heard here.
Yakima Division counties: Kittitas, Klickitat, Yakima. Cases assigned primarily to Judge McDonald are here. Some cases from Kittitas, Klickitat and Yakima are heard in Spokane.

US Bankruptcy Court -- Eastern District of Washington
Home Page: www.waeb.uscourts.gov
PACER: New records are available online after. **PACER URL:** http://pacer.waeb.uscourts.gov.
Other Online Access: Search records on the Internet free using RACER at is http://204.227.177.194. Records go back to 1997. Access fee of $.07 per page is planned. **Also:** access via phone on VCIS (Voice Case Information System) is available: 509-353-2404.
Spokane Division counties: Adams, Asotin, Benton, Chelan, Columbia, Douglas, Ferry, Franklin, Garfield, Grant, Kittitas, Klickitat, Lincoln, Okanogan, Pend Oreille, Spokane, Stevens, Walla Walla, Whitman, Yakima.

US District Court -- Western District of Washington
Home Page: www.wawd.uscourts.gov
PACER: Toll-free access: 800-520-8604. Local access phone: 206-553-2288. Case records are available back to 1988. Records are purged never. New civil records are available online after 4 days. New criminal records are available online after 2 days. **PACER URL:** http://pacer.wawd.uscourts.gov. Document images available.
Seattle Division counties: Island, King, San Juan, Skagit, Snohomish, Whatcom.
Tacoma Division counties: Clallam, Clark, Cowlitz, Grays Harbor, Jefferson, Kitsap, Lewis, Mason, Pacific, Pierce, Skamania, Thurston, Wahkiakum.

US Bankruptcy Court -- Western District of Washington
Home Page: www.wawb.uscourts.gov
PACER: Toll-free access: 800-704-4492. Local access phone: 206-553-0060. Case records are available back to June 1995. Records are purged never. New civil records are available online after 2 days. **PACER URL:** http://pacer.wawb.uscourts.gov.
Electronic Filing: Electronic filing information is available online at https://ecf.wawb.uscourts.gov. **Also:** access via phone on VCIS (Voice Case Information System) is available: 888-436-7477, 206-553-8543
Seattle Division counties: Clallam, Island, Jefferson, King, Kitsap, San Juan, Skagit, Snohomish, Whatcom.
Tacoma Division counties: Clark, Cowlitz, Grays Harbor, Lewis, Mason, Pacific, Pierce, Skamania, Thurston, Wahkiakum.

West Virginia

Capital: Charleston
             Kanawha County

Time Zone: EST

Number of Counties: 55

Home Page   www.state.wv.us

Attorney General   www.state.wv.us/wvag

Archives   www.wvculture.org/history/wvsamenu.html

State Level ... Major Agencies

Corporation Records, Limited Liability Company Records, Limited Partnerships, Trademarks/Servicemarks, Limited Liability Partnerships

Secretary of State, Corporation Division, State Capitol Bldg, Room W139, Charleston, WV 25305-0776; 304-558-8000, 304-558-0900 (Fax), 8:30AM-4:30PM.

www.wvsos.com/common/information.htm

Corporation and business types records on the Secretary of State Business Organization Information System are available free online at www.state.wv.us/wvcorporations/verifylogon.asp. Search by organization name. Certified copies may be ordered online or via email to business@wvsos.com.

Sexual Offender Registry

The West Virginia State Police maintains the state's sex offender data. Access is available online at www.wvstatepolice.com/sexoff/ with both a name and county search available. Less serious offenders are not found on the online search, but local law enforcement agencies have extensive localized lists available.

Driver License Information, Driver Records

Division of Motor Vehicles, 1800 Kanawha Blvd, Building 3, Rm 118, State Capitol Complex, Charleston, WV 25317; 304-558-0238, 304-558-5362, 304-558-0037 (Fax), 8:30AM-4:30PM.

www.wvdot.com/6_motorists/dmv/6G_DMV.HTM

Online access is available in either interactive or batch mode. The system is open 24 hours a day. Batch requesters receive return transmission about 3 AM. Users must access through AAMVAnet. A contract is required and accounts must pre-pay. Fee is $5.00 per record. For more information, call Lacy Morgan at (304) 558-3915. **Other options:** The state will sell its DL file to commercial vendors, but records cannot be re-sold.

Legislation Records

www.legis.state.wv.us

The Internet site allows one to search for status and/or text of bills.

State Level ... Occupational Licensing

Aesthetician..www.state.wv.us/wvbc/licensees.cfm
Architect..http://wvbrdarch.org/cgi-wvbrdarch/wvbrdarch_licdb/wvbrdarch/architects/query_form
Attorney..www.wvbar.org/barinfo/mdirectory/
Barber...www.state.wv.us/wvbc/licensees.cfm
Barber/Beauty Culture School...................www.state.wv.us/wvbc/schools.htm
Cosmetologist...www.state.wv.us/wvbc/licensees.cfm
Lobbyist...www.state.wv.us/ethics/lobby.htm
Manicurist ....www.state.wv.us/wvbc/licensees.cfm
Nurse-LPN ....www.state.wv.us/lpnboard/
Optometrist..www.odfinder.org/LicSearch.asp
Public Accountant-CPA ....www.state.wv.us/scripts/wvboa/default.cfm
Radiologic Technologist............................www.state.wv.us/rtboe/RTLIST.pdf
Real Estate Appraiser ....www.asc.gov/content/category1/appr_by_state.asp

County Level ... Courts

Court Administration: Administrative Office, Supreme Court of Appeals, 1900 Kanawha Blvd, 1 E 100 State Capitol, Charleston, WV, 25305; 304-558-0145; www.state.wv.us/wvsca

Court Structure: The 55 Circuit Courts are the courts of general jurisdiction. Probate is handled by the Circuit Court. Records are held at the County Commissioner's Office. Family Courts were created by constitutional amendment and were formed as of 01/01/02. Family Courts hear cases involving such matters as divorce, annulment, separate maintenance, family support, paternity, child custody, and visitation. Family court judges also conduct final hearings in domestic violence cases.

Online Access Note: The state is working towards a statewide system that will allow access to public records, but one is not yet available. Magistrate Courts are on a private system; see www.swcg-inc.com/courts.htm or call 800-795-8543 for information. There is a $125 set-up fee plus a $38.00 or $120 monthly fee plan. This same provider offers access to six Circuit Courts: Kanawha, Putnam, Hancock, Ohio, Nicholas and Mineral.

The following counties have online access to Circuit Court civl and criminal records available via the pay service:

Hancock County	**Nicholas County**	**Mineral County**
Kanawha County	**Ohio County**	**Putnam County**

County Level ... Recorders & Assessors

Recording Office Organization: 55 counties, 55 recording offices. The recording officer is the County Clerk. The entire state is in the Eastern Time Zone (EST). All federal and state tax liens are filed with the County Clerk. Most counties will not perform tax lien searches.

Online Access Note: There is no statewide system open to public.

Monongalia County *Assessor, Real Estate Records*
Records on the County Parcel Search database are available free online at www.assessor.org/parcelweb. Search by a wide variety of criteria including owner name and address.

Wood County *Recording, Deed, Wills, Death, Birth Records*
www.woodcountywv.com
Access is by dial-up modem; visit www.woodcountywv.com/modem.htm for instructions for free connection. Records go back to early 1990s.

Federal Courts in West Virginia...

Standards for Federal Courts: The universal PACER sign-up number is 800-676-6856. Find PACER and the Party/Case Index on the Web at http://pacer.psc.uscourts.gov. PACER dial-up access is $.60 per minute. Also, courts offering internet access via RACER, PACER, Web-PACER or the new CM-ECF charge $.07 per page fee unless noted as free.

US District Court -- Northern District of West Virginia

Home Page: www.wvnd.uscourts.gov

PACER: Toll-free access: 888-513-7959. Local access phone: 304-233-7424. Case records are available back to October 1994. Records are purged every 5 years. New records are available online after 1 day. **PACER URL:** http://pacer.wvnd.uscourts.gov.

Clarksburg Division counties: Braxton, Calhoun, Doddridge, Gilmer, Harrison, Lewis, Marion, Monongalia, Pleasants, Ritchie, Taylor, Tyler.

Elkins Division counties: Barbour, Grant, Hardy, Mineral, Pendleton, Pocahontas, Preston, Randolph, Tucker, Upshur, Webster.

Martinsburg Division counties: Berkeley, Hampshire, Jefferson, Morgan.

Wheeling Division counties: Brooke, Hancock, Marshall, Ohio, Wetzel.

US Bankruptcy Court -- Northern District of West Virginia

Home Page: www.wvnb.uscourts.gov

PACER: Toll-free access: 800-809-3016. Local access phone: 304-233-2871. Case records are available back to early 1990. Records are purged never. New civil records are available online after 1 day. **PACER URL:** http://pacer.wvnb.uscourts.gov. Document images available.

Electronic Filing: (Currently in the process of implementing CM/ECF). **Also:** access via phone on VCIS (Voice Case Information System) is available: 800-809-3028, 304-233-7318

Wheeling Division counties: Barbour, Berkeley, Braxton, Brooke, Calhoun, Doddridge, Gilmer, Grant, Hampshire, Hancock, Hardy, Harrison, Jefferson, Lewis, Marion, Marshall, Mineral, Monongalia, Morgan, Ohio, Pendleton, Pleasants, Pocahontas, Preston, Randolph, Ritchie, Taylor, Tucker, Tyler, Upshur, Webster, Wetzel.

US District Court -- Southern District of West Virginia

Home Page: www.wvsd.uscourts.gov

PACER: Case records are available back to 1991. New records are available online after 1 day. **PACER URL:** http://pacer.wvsd.uscourts.gov. Document images available.

Beckley Division counties: Fayette, Greenbrier, Raleigh, Sumners, Wyoming.

Bluefield Division counties: McDowell, Mercer, Monroe.

Charleston Division counties: Boone, Clay, Jackson, Kanawha, Lincoln, Logan, Mingo, Nicholas, Putnam, Roane.

Huntington Division counties: Cabell, Mason, Wayne.

Parkersburg Division counties: Wirt, Wood.

US Bankruptcy Court -- Southern District of West Virginia

Home Page: www.wvsd.uscourts.gov

PACER: Case records are available back to 1988. Records are purged every 6 months. New civil records are available online after 1 day. **PACER URL:** http://pacer.wvsb.uscourts.gov. Document images available.

Electronic Filing: (Currently in the process of implementing CM/ECF). **Also:** access via phone on VCIS (Voice Case Information System) is available: 304-347-5337.

Charleston Division counties: Boone, Cabell, Clay, Fayette, Greenbrier, Jackson, Kanawha, Lincoln, Logan, Mason, McDowell, Mercer, Mingo, Monroe, Nicholas, Putnam, Raleigh, Roane, Summers, Wayne, Wirt, Wood, Wyoming.

Capital:	Madison	Home Page	www.state.wi.us
	Dane County	Attorney General	
Time Zone:	CST		www.doj.state.wi.us
Number of Counties:	72	Archives	www.shsw.wisc.edu/archives

State Level...Major Agencies

Criminal Records

Wisconsin Department of Justice, Crime Information Bureau, Record Check Unit, PO Box 2688, Madison, WI 53701-2688 (Courier: 17 W Main St, Madison, WI 53703); 608-266-5764, 608-266-7780 (Online Questions), 608-267-4558 (Fax), 8AM-4:30PM.

www.doj.state.wi.us

The agency offers Internet access at http://wi-recordcheck.org. An account is required. Also, there is a free Internet service for access to the state's Circuit Courts' records. However, not all counties participate. Visit http://ccap.courts.state.wi.us.

Sexual Offender Registry

The Department of Corrections offers online access to the sexual offender database online at http://widocoffenders.org. Also, requests for information can be e-mailed to bopadmin@doc.state.wi.us.

Corporation Records, Limited Partnership Records, Limited Liability Company Records, Limited Liability Partnerships

Department of Financial Institutions, Division of Corporate & Consumer Services, PO Box 7846, Madison, WI 53707-7846 (Courier: 345 W Washington Ave, 3rd Floor, Madison, WI 53703); 608-261-7577, 608-267-6813 (Fax), 7:45AM-4:30PM.

www.wdfi.org

Selected elements of the database ("CRIS" Corporate Registration System) are available online on the department's website at www.wdfi.org/corporations/crispix. **Other options:** Some data is released in database format and is available for purchase in print form, cartridge or diskette.

Uniform Commercial Code, Federal Tax Liens, State Tax Liens

Department of Financial Institutions, CCS/UCC, PO Box 7847, Madison, WI 53707-7847 (Courier: 345 W Washington Ave 3rd Fl, Madison, WI 53703); 608-261-9548, 608-264-7965 (Fax), 7:45AM-4:30PM.

www.wdfi.org

There is free Internet access for most records. Some records may require a $1.00 fee. You may do a free debtor name search at www.wdfi.org/ucc/search/. Instant filings are available immediately.

Driver Records

Division of Motor Vehicles, Records & Licensing Info. Section, PO Box 7995, Madison, WI 53707-7995 (Courier: 4802 Sheboygan Ave, Room 350, Madison, WI 53707); 608-266-2353, 608-267-3636 (Fax), 7:30AM-5:15PM.

www.dot.state.wi.us

Commercial online access is available for high volume users only, fee is $5.00 per record. Call 608-266-2353 for more information. **Other options:** Wisconsin offers a magnetic tape retrieval system for high volume users. The state will, also, sell its license file without histories to qualified entities. For more information, call 608-266-1951.

Legislation Records

www.legis.state.wi.us

Information on current bills is available over the Internet. There is a Folio Program to search text of previous session bills.

State Level...Occupational Licensing

Accounting Firm .... http://drlchq.state.wi.us/plsql/chq/cred_holder_query
Acupuncturist.. http://165.189.238.43/plsql/plsql/Search_Ind_Health
Adjustment Service Company .... www.wdfi.org/fi/lfs/licensee_lists
Aesthetics Establ./Specialty School............ http://drlchq.state.wi.us/plsql/chq/cred_holder_query
Aesthetics Instructor.................................. http://165.189.238.43/plsql/plsql/Search_Ind_Bdp
Ambulance Service Provider .... www.dhfs.state.wi.us/reg_licens/dohprog/ems/provider/wicounties.htm
Appraiser, General...................................... http://165.189.238.43/plsql/plsql/Search_Ind_Bdp
Appraiser, Residential .... http://165.189.238.43/plsql/plsql/Search_Ind_Bdp
Architect.. http://165.189.238.43/plsql/plsql/Search_Ind_Bdp
Architectural Corporation............................ http://drlchq.state.wi.us/plsql/chq/cred_holder_query
Art Therapist .... http://165.189.238.43/plsql/plsql/Search_Ind_Health
Attorney... www.wisbar.org
Auction Company .... http://drlchq.state.wi.us/plsql/chq/cred_holder_query
Auctioneer... http://165.189.238.43/plsql/plsql/Search_Ind_Bdp
Audiologist.. http://165.189.238.43/plsql/plsql/Search_Ind_Health
Bank.. www.wdfi.org/fi/savings_institutions/licensee_lists/
Barber.. http://165.189.238.43/plsql/plsql/Search_Ind_Bdp
Barber School.. http://drlchq.state.wi.us/plsql/chq/cred_holder_query
Barber/Apprentice/Instructor/Manager........ http://165.189.238.43/plsql/plsql/Search_Ind_Bdp
Boxer... http://165.189.238.43/plsql/plsql/Search_Ind_Bdp
Boxing Club (Amateur or Professional) ...... http://drlchq.state.wi.us/plsql/chq/cred_holder_query
Boxing Show Permit .... http://drlchq.state.wi.us/plsql/chq/cred_holder_query
Cemetery Authority/Warehouse .... http://drlchq.state.wi.us/plsql/chq/cred_holder_query
Cemetery Preneed Seller............................. http://165.189.238.43/plsql/plsql/Search_Ind_Bdp
Cemetery Salesperson................................. http://165.189.238.43/plsql/plsql/Search_Ind_Bdp
Charitable Organization .... http://drlchq.state.wi.us/plsql/chq/cred_holder_query
Check Seller .... www.wdfi.org/fi/lfs/licensee_lists
Chiropractor .... http://165.189.238.43/plsql/plsql/Search_Ind_Health
Collection Agency .... www.wdfi.org/fi/lfs/licensee_lists
Cosmetologist.. http://165.189.238.43/plsql/plsql/Search_Ind_Bdp
Cosmetology Instructor/Mgr./Apprentice .... http://165.189.238.43/plsql/plsql/Search_Ind_Bdp
Cosmetology School................................... http://drlchq.state.wi.us/plsql/chq/cred_holder_query
Counselor, Professional.............................. http://165.189.238.43/plsql/plsql/Search_Ind_Health
Credit Service Organization .... www.wdfi.org/fi/cu/chartered_lists/default.asp
Credit Union.. www.wdfi.org/fi/cu/chartered_lists/default.asp
Currency Exchange .... www.wdfi.org/fi/lfs/licensee_lists
Dance Therapist .... http://165.189.238.43/plsql/plsql/Search_Ind_Health
Debt Collector .... www.wdfi.org/fi/lfs/licensee_lists
Dental Hygienist... http://165.189.238.43/plsql/plsql/Search_Ind_Health
Dentist... http://165.189.238.43/plsql/plsql/Search_Ind_Health
Designer of Engineering Systems................ http://165.189.238.43/plsql/plsql/Search_Ind_Bdp

Dietitian.. http://165.189.238.43/plsql/plsql/Search_Ind_Health
Drug Distributor/Manufacturer .... http://drlchq.state.wi.us/plsql/chq/cred_holder_query
Electrologist .... http://165.189.238.43/plsql/plsql/Search_Ind_Bdp
Electrology Establ./School .... http://drlchq.state.wi.us/plsql/chq/cred_holder_query
Electrology Instructor .... http://165.189.238.43/plsql/plsql/Search_Ind_Bdp
Engineer/Engineer in Training .... http://165.189.238.43/plsql/plsql/Search_Ind_Bdp
Engineering Corporation .... http://drlchq.state.wi.us/plsql/chq/cred_holder_query
Firearms Permit .... http://drlchq.state.wi.us/plsql/chq/cred_holder_query
Fund Raiser, Professional.. http://165.189.238.43/plsql/plsql/Search_Ind_Bdp
Fund Raising Counsel .... http://drlchq.state.wi.us/plsql/chq/cred_holder_query
Funeral Director/Director Apprentice........................... http://165.189.238.43/plsql/plsql/Search_Ind_Bdp
Funeral Establishment .... http://drlchq.state.wi.us/plsql/chq/cred_holder_query
Funeral Preneed Seller .... http://165.189.238.43/plsql/plsql/Search_Ind_Bdp
Geologist .... http://165.189.238.43/plsql/plsql/Search_Ind_Bdp
Geology Firm.. http://drlchq.state.wi.us/plsql/chq/cred_holder_query
Hearing Instrument Specialist .... http://165.189.238.43/plsql/plsql/Search_Ind_Health
Home Inspector .... http://165.189.238.43/plsql/plsql/Search_Ind_Bdp
Hydrologist... http://165.189.238.43/plsql/plsql/Search_Ind_Bdp
Hydrology Firm .... http://drlchq.state.wi.us/plsql/chq/cred_holder_query
Insurance Company.. http://badger.state.wi.us/agencies/oci/dir_ins.htm
Insurance Premium Finance Company....................... www.wdfi.org/fi/lfs/licensee_lists
Interior Designer... http://165.189.238.43/plsql/plsql/Search_Ind_Bdp
Investment Advisor/Advisor Rep .... www.wdfi.org/fi/securities/licensing/licensee_lists/default.asp
Land Surveyor... http://165.189.238.43/plsql/plsql/Search_Ind_Bdp
Landfill... www.dnr.state.wi.us/org/aw/wm/solid/landfill/licensed.htm
Landfill Operator... www.dnr.state.wi.us/org/aw/wm/solid/landfill/licensed.htm
Landscape Architect.. http://165.189.238.43/plsql/plsql/Search_Ind_Bdp
Loan Company .... www.wdfi.org/fi/lfs/licensee_lists
Loan Solicitor/Originator .... www.wdfi.org/fi/mortbank/licensee_lists/default.asp
Lobbying Organization, Principal http://ethics.state.wi.us/Scripts/OEL2000.asp
Lobbyist.. http://ethics.state.wi.us/Scripts/Lobbyists2000.asp
Manicurist Establ./Specialty School............................ http://drlchq.state.wi.us/plsql/chq/cred_holder_query
Manicurist/Manicurist Instructor................................. http://165.189.238.43/plsql/plsql/Search_Ind_Bdp
Marriage & Family Therapist .... http://165.189.238.43/plsql/plsql/Search_Ind_Health
Massage Therapist/Bodyworker .... http://165.189.238.43/plsql/plsql/Search_Ind_Health
Medical Doctor/Surgeon .... http://165.189.238.43/plsql/plsql/Search_Ind_Health
Midwife Nurse.. http://165.189.238.43/plsql/plsql/Search_Ind_Health
Mobile Home & RV Dealer... www.wdfi.org/fi/lfs/licensee_lists
Mortgage Banker/Broker... www.wdfi.org/fi/mortbank/licensee_lists/default.asp
Motorcycle Dealer .... www.wdfi.org/fi/lfs/licensee_lists
Music Therapist.. http://165.189.238.43/plsql/plsql/Search_Ind_Health
Nurse-RN/LPN.. http://165.189.238.43/plsql/plsql/Search_Ind_Health
Nursing Home Administrator .... http://165.189.238.43/plsql/plsql/Search_Ind_Bdp
Occupational Therapist/Assistant................................. http://165.189.238.43/plsql/plsql/Search_Ind_Health
Optometrist.. http://165.189.238.43/plsql/plsql/Search_Ind_Health
Payday Lender... www.wdfi.org/fi/lfs/licensee_lists
Pesticide Applicator/Application Business................... http://datcp.state.wi.us/arm/agriculture/pest-fert/pesticides/data/
Pesticide Dealer.. http://datcp.state.wi.us/arm/agriculture/pest-fert/pesticides/data/
Pharmacist... http://165.189.238.43/plsql/plsql/Search_Ind_Health
Pharmacy... http://165.189.238.43/plsql/plsql/Search_Ind_Health
Physical Therapist .... http://165.189.238.43/plsql/plsql/Search_Ind_Health
Physician Assistant.. http://165.189.238.43/plsql/plsql/Search_Ind_Health
Podiatrist... http://165.189.238.43/plsql/plsql/Search_Ind_Health
Private Detective .... http://165.189.238.43/plsql/plsql/Search_Ind_Bdp
Private Detective Agency .... http://drlchq.state.wi.us/plsql/chq/cred_holder_query
Psychologist .... http://165.189.238.43/plsql/plsql/Search_Ind_Health
Public Accountant .... http://165.189.238.43/plsql/plsql/Search_Ind_Bdp
Real Estate Appraiser .... http://165.189.238.43/plsql/plsql/Search_Ind_Bdp
Real Estate Broker/Salesperson................................... http://165.189.238.43/plsql/plsql/Search_Ind_Bdp
Real Estate Business Entity.. http://drlchq.state.wi.us/plsql/chq/cred_holder_query

Respiratory Care Practitioner .... http://165.189.238.43/plsql/plsql/Search_Ind_Health
Sales Finance/Loan Company .... www.wdfi.org/fi/lfs/licensee_lists
Savings & Loan Sales Finance Company..................... www.wdfi.org/fi/lfs/licensee_lists
Savings Institution.. www.wdfi.org/fi/savings_institutions/licensee_lists/
School Librarian/Media Specialist .... www.dpi.state.wi.us/dpi/dlsis/tel/lisearch.html
School Psychology Private Practice............................. http://165.189.238.43/plsql/plsql/Search_Ind_Health
Securities Broker/Dealer/Agent.................................. www.wdfi.org/fi/securities/licensing/licensee_lists/default.asp
Security Guard.. http://165.189.238.43/plsql/plsql/Search_Ind_Bdp
Social Worker... http://165.189.238.43/plsql/plsql/Search_Ind_Health
Soil Science Firm .... http://drlchq.state.wi.us/plsql/chq/cred_holder_query
Soil Scientist .... http://165.189.238.43/plsql/plsql/Search_Ind_Bdp
Speech Pathologist/Audiologist................................... http://165.189.238.43/plsql/plsql/Search_Ind_Health
Teacher.. www.dpi.state.wi.us/dpi/dlsis/tel/lisearch.html
Timeshare Salesperson .... http://165.189.238.43/plsql/plsql/Search_Ind_Bdp
Veterinarian/Veterinary Technician .... http://165.189.238.43/plsql/plsql/Search_Ind_Health

County Level ... Courts

Court Administration:		Director of State Courts, Supreme Court, PO Box 1688, Madison, WI, 53701; 608-266-6828; www.courts.state.wi.us

Court Structure:		The Circuit Court is the court of general jurisdiction. The Register in Probate maintains guardianship and mental health records, most of which are sealed but may be opened for cause with a court order. In some counties, the Register also maintains termination and adoption records, but practices vary widely across the state. Most Registers in Probate are putting pre-1950 records on microfilm and destroying the hard copies. This is done as "time and workloads permit," so microfilm archiving is not uniform across the state.

Online Access Note:		Wisconsin Circuit Court Access (WCCA) allows users to view circuit court case information at http://ccap.courts.state.wi.us/internetcourtaccess which is the Wisconsin court system web site. Data is available from all counties except Outagamie and Walworth. Searches can be conducted statewide or county by county. WCCA provides detailed information about circuit cases, and for civil cases the program displays judgment and judgment party information. WCCA also offers the ability to generate reports. In addition, public access terminals are available at each court. Due to statutory requirements WCCA users will not be able to view restricted cases. There are probate records for all counties except Outagamie, Milwaukee and Walworth. Portage County offers probate records only online.

Milwaukee County
Circuit Court *Civil and Criminal Records*
http://204.194.250.11/Service/organizationDetail.asp?id=2830
Civil court records available free online at http://ccap.courts.state.wi.us/internetcourtaccess/. Criminal court records are available free on the Internet at http://ccap.courts.state.wi.us/internetcourtaccess/. Also, criminal case records on Milwaukee Municipal Court Case Information System database are available free online at www.court.ci.mil.wi.us/home.asp. Search by Case Number, by Citation Number, or by Name.

Statewide Access – Civil, Criminal and Probate
See the "Online Access Note" above for details.

County Level ... Recorders & Assessors

Recording Office Organization: 72 counties, 72 recording offices. The recording officers are the Register of Deeds and the Clerk of Court (state tax liens). The entire state is in the Central Time Zone (CST). Federal tax liens on personal property of businesses are filed with the Secretary of State. Other federal tax liens are filed with the county Register of Deeds. State tax liens are filed with the Clerk of Court. Most but not all Registers will perform federal tax lien searches. Search fees and copy fees vary.

Brown County *Real Estate, Recording Records*
www.co.brown.wi.us/rod

Access to Register of Deeds real estate records is available by subscription at www.co.brown.wi.us/rod/LaredoTapestry/main.html. Registration and usage fees are required. Images are available for $.50. A more sophisticated subscription system, named Laredo, offers full access to land records for firms operating in Wisconsin. Alos, Brown County land records can be downloaded from their ftp site; contact the Land Information office at 920-448-6295 to register and user information.

Columbia County *Property Tax, Land, Tax Sales Records*
Search the land records system for free at www.co.columbia.wi.us/landrecords. Also, search the treasurers property/tax sale list at www.co.columbia.wi.us/dept/treasurer/landsale.asp.

Dane County *Assessor, Real Estate Records*
www.co.dane.wi.us/regdeeds/rdhome.htm

Records on the geographic & land database are available free online at http://dc-web.co.dane.wi.us/dane. For fuller access, a subscription service is available. Also, parcel information is available free at http://dc-web.co.dane.wi.us/dane/html/parcelsearch.asp. Professional companies may register to use assessor/land record services at http://dc-web.co.dane.wi.us/dane/html/community.asp. Registration & login. Also, the City of Madison tax assessor database is accessible at www.ci.madison.wi.us/assessor/property.html. Also, search property info for Towns of Cross Plains, Mazomanie, Berry, Medina at www.wendorffassessing.com/municipalities.htm.

Kenosha County *Real Estate, Lien, Vital Statistic, Assessor Records*
The set-up fee is $500, plus $6.00 per hour usage fee. The system operates 24 hours daily; records date back to 5/1986. Federal tax liens are listed. Lending agency information is available. For further information, contact Joellyn Storz at 262-653-2511. Also, search the Kenosha City Assessor's property database for free at www.kenosha.org/departments/assessor/search.html. No name searching.

Manitowoc County *Assessor, Real Estate Records*
www.manitowoc-county.com

Records on the City of Manitowoc Assessor database are available free online at http://assessor.manitowoc.org/default.htm. No name searching. Also, search property data for the Villages of Mishicot and Valders as well as Town of Manitowoc at www.wendorffassessing.com/municipalities.htm.

Milwaukee County *Assessor, Real Estate, Property Sale Records*
www.co.milwaukee.wi.us

Ownership, property and assessment data as well as sales data by year on the Milwaukee City (not county) Assessor Office database are available free online at www.ci.mil.wi.us/citygov/assessor/assessor.htm. No name searching. Also, search the City of Cudahy assessor;s property data for free at http://exch02.ci.cudahy.wi.us/Scripts/GVSWeb.dll/Search. No name searching. Also, search City of Franklin assessor data at www.ci.franklin.wi.us/dynamic/pagetemplate.cfm?template=assessmentSearch.cfm.

Rock County *Assessor, Real Estate Records*
www.co.rock.wi.us/departments/reg_deeds.htm

Records on the City of Janesville Assessor database are available free online at http://assessor.ci.janesville.wi.us/Government/Assessor/PropertySearch/query.asp. No name searching. Also, search Evanville property assessor records for free at www.wendorffassessing.com/municipalities.htm. No name searching.

Sauk County *Property, Assessor Records*
Village of Spring Green property data free at www.wendorffassessing.com/Spring%20Green%20options.htm. No name searching.

Trempealeau County *Real Estate, Assessor Records*
www.tremplocounty.com

Access to the county assessor's database is available free at www.tremplocounty.com/Search.

Walworth County   *Property Tax, Recording, Grantor/Grantee, Deed Records*

www.co.walworth.wi.us
Search the Register of Deeds index for free on the county e-government web page at www.co.walworth.wi.us. Click on "Public Records." Online records go as far back as 1976. Also, search the treasurer's tax roll list under "Tax Roll Documents" on the county e-government web page. Also search the Village of Walworth property data for free at www.wendorffassessing.com/Walworth%20options.htm.

Waukesha County   *Property, Assessor Records*

www.waukeshacounty.gov/departments/register
Search the City of Waukesha assessor property databse or sales lists for free at www.ci.waukesha.wi.us/dept/assessor/index.htm. Property information may be temporarily down.

Winnebago County   *Assessor, Real Estate Records*

Records on the City of Menasha Tax Roll Information database are available free online at www.cityofmenasha.com/finance.htm. Property records on the City of Oshkosh assessor database are available free at www.ci.oshkosh.wi.us/assessor/ProcessSearch.asp?cmd=NewSearch.

Federal Courts in Wisconsin...

US District Court - Eastern District of Wisconsin

Home Page: www.wied.uscourts.gov **PACER:** Sign-up number is 800-676-6856. Access fee is. Toll-free access: 877-253-4862. Local access: 414-297-3361. http://pacer.wied.uscourts.gov. Case records go back to 1991. Records are purged never. New records are available online after 1 day. **PACER Internet Access:** http://pacer.wied.uscourts.gov.
Milwaukee Division Counties: Brown, Calumet, Dodge, Door, Florence, Fond du Lac, Forest, Green Lake, Kenosha, Kewaunee, Langlade, Manitowoc, Marinette, Marquette, Menominee, Milwaukee, Oconto, Outagamie, Ozaukee, Racine, Shawano, Sheboygan, Walworth, Washington, Waukesha, Waupaca,Waushara, Winnebago.

US Bankruptcy Court - Eastern District of Wisconsin

Home Page: www.wieb.uscourts.gov **PACER:** Sign-up number is 800-676-6856. Access fee is $.60 per minute. Toll-free access: 877-467-5537. Local access: 414-297-1400. Case records go back to 1991. Records are purged aafter case is closed. New civil records are available online after 1-2 days. **PACER Internet Access:** http://pacer.wieb.uscourts.gov.
Milwaukee Division Counties: Brown, Calumet, Dodge, Door, Florence, Fond du Lac, Forest, Green Lake, Kenosha, Kewaunee, Langlade, Manitowoc, Marinette, Marquette, Menominee, Milwaukee, Oconto, Outagamie, Ozaukee, Racine, Shawano, Sheboygan, Walworth, Washington, Waukesha, Waupaca,Waushara, Winnebago.

US District Court - Western District of Wisconsin

Home Page: www.wiw.uscourts.gov
PACER: Sign-up number is 800-676-6856. Access fee is $.60 per minute. Toll-free access: 800-372-8791. Local access: 608-264-5914. Case records are available back to 1990. Records are purged never. New records are available online after 1 day.
PACER Internet Access: http://pacer.wiwd.uscourts.gov.
Madison Division Counties: Adams, Ashland, Barron, Bayfield, Buffalo, Burnett, Chippewa, Clark, Columbia, Crawford, Dane, Douglas, Dunn, Eau Claire, Grant, Green, Iowa, Iron, Jackson, Jefferson, Juneau, La Crosse, Lafayette, Lincoln, Marathon, Monroe, Oneida, Pepin, Pierce, Polk,Portage, Price, Richland, Rock, Rusk, Sauk, Sawyer, St. Croix, Taylor, Trempealeau, Vernon, Vilas, Washburn, Wood.

US Bankruptcy Court - Western District of Wisconsin

Home Page: www.wiw.uscourts.gov/bankruptcy
PACER: Sign-up number is 800-676-6856. Access fee is $.60 per minute. Toll-free access: 800-373-8708. Local access: 608-264-5630. Case records are available back to April 1991. New civil records are available online after 1 day.
Eau Claire Division Counties: Ashland, Barron, Bayfield, Buffalo, Burnett, Chippewa, Clark, Douglas, Dunn, Eau Claire, Iron, Jackson, Juneau, La Crosse, Lincoln, Marathon, Monroe, Oneida, Pepin, Pierce, Polk, Portage, Price, Rusk, Sawyer, St. Croix, Taylor, Trempealeau, Vernon,Vilas, Washburn, Wood. Division has satellite offices in LaCrosse and Wausau.
Madison Division Counties: Adams, Columbia, Crawford, Dane, Grant, Green, Iowa, Jefferson, Lafayette, Richland, Rock, Sauk.

Capital: Cheyenne
             Laramie County

Time Zone: MST

Number of Counties: 23

Home Page
www.state.wy.us

Attorney General   http://attorneygeneral.state.wy.us

Archives   http://wyoarchives.state.wy.us

State Level ... Major Agencies

Corporation Records, Limited Liability Company Records, Limited Partnership Records, Fictitious Name, Trademarks/Servicemarks

Corporations Division, Secretary of State, State Capitol, Cheyenne, WY 82002; 307-777-7311, 307-777-5339 (Fax), 8AM-5PM.

http://soswy.state.wy.us

Information is available through the Internet site listed above. You can search by corporate name or even download the whole file. Also, they have 2 pages of excellent searching tips.

Uniform Commercial Code, Federal Tax Liens

UCC Division, Secretary of State, The Capitol, Cheyenne, WY 82002-0020 (Courier: Capitol Bldg, RM 110, Cheyenne, WY 82002); 307-777-5372, 307-777-5988 (Fax), 8AM-5PM.

http://soswy.state.wy.us

There is a $50.00 annual registration, a $20.00 monthly fee, and long distant access fees of between $3.00 and $6.00 per hour. A word of caution, if user fails to log off the "clock" still keeps ticking and user is billed! The system is open 24 hours daily except 1:30AM to 5AM Mon. through Sun., and 4PM to 6PM on Sunday.

Sexual Offender Registry

State law limits disclosure of registered sex offenders to the criminal justice system unless the County or District Attorney petitions the court to disclose registered sex offender information to the public. If a registered sex offender is classified as a high risk of re-offense, information regarding the sex offender can be released to the public via the Internet. This information includes name, address, date and place of birth, date and place of conviction, crime for which convicted, photograph and physical description. Access is at http://attorneygeneral.state.wy.us/dci/so/so_registration.html. Records are maintained by the Division of Criminal Investigation, 307-777-7181.

Driver License Information, Driver Records

Wyoming Department of Transportation, Driver Services, 5300 Bishop Blvd, Cheyenne, WY 82009-3340; 307-777-4800, 307-777-4773 (Fax), 8AM-5PM.

http://wydotweb.state.wy.us

This method is available using FTP or RJE technology. Only approved vendors and permissible users are supported. Call Mark Briggs in Support Services at 307-777-3864 for details. **Other options:** Magnetic tape retrieval is available at $3.00 per record. The entire driver license file may be purchased for $2,500. Call Support Services for more information.

Legislation Records

http://legisweb.state.wy.us

The Internet site contains a wealth of information regarding the legislature and bills.

State Level ... Occupational Licensing

Attorney	www.wyomingbar.org/lawyer_directory.asp
Bank	http://audit.state.wy.us/banking/banks.htm
Collection Agency	http://audit.state.wy.us/banking/CAB.htm
Engineer	www.wrds.uwyo.edu/wrds/borpe/roster/roster.html
Funeral Preneed Agent	http://insurance.state.wy.us/search/search.asp
Geologist	http://wbpgweb.uwyo.edu/roster_search.htm (site may be down)
Insurance Agent	http://insurance.state.wy.us/search/search.asp
Insurance Broker, Resident	http://insurance.state.wy.us/search/search.asp
Insurance Claims Adjuster	http://insurance.state.wy.us/search/search.asp
Insurance Consultant	http://insurance.state.wy.us/search/search.asp
Insurance Service Reps	http://insurance.state.wy.us/search/search.asp
Insurance Solicitor	http://insurance.state.wy.us/search/search.asp
Lobbyist	http://soswy.state.wy.us/election/lob-list.htm
Medical Doctor	http://wyomedboard.state.wy.us/roster.asp
Motor Club Agent	http://insurance.state.wy.us/search/search.asp
Optometrist	www.odfinder.org/LicSearch.asp
Outfitter & Guide	http://outfitte.state.wy.us/directory.html
Pharmacist	http://pharmacyboard.state.wy.us/search.asp
Pharmacy Technician	http://pharmacyboard.state.wy.us/search.asp
Physician Assistant	http://wyomedboard.state.wy.us/PARoster.asp
Public Accountant-CPA	http://cpaboard.state.wy.us/search.cfm
Public Accountant-CPA Firm	http://cpaboard.state.wy.us/search.cfm
Real Estate Appraiser	www.asc.gov/content/category1/appr_by_state.asp
Savings & Loan Association	http://audit.state.wy.us/banking/fsb.htm
Surplus Line Broker, Resident	http://insurance.state.wy.us/search/search.asp
Surveyor, Land	www.wrds.uwyo.edu/wrds/borpe/roster/roster.html

County Level ... Courts

Court Administration: Court Administrator, 2301 Capitol Av, Supreme Court Bldg, Cheyenne, WY, 82002; 307-777-7480; www.courts.state.wy.us

Court Structure: Prior to 2003, for their "lower" jurisdiction court some counties have Circuit Courts and others have Justice Courts. Thus each county has a District Court ("higher" jurisdiction) and either a Circuit or Justice Court. Circuit Courts handle civil claims up to $7,000 while Justice Courts handle civil claims up to $3,000. The District Courts take cases over the applicable limit in each county. Effective January 1, 2003 all Justice Courts become Circuit Courts and follow Circuit Court rules. Probate is handled by the District Court.

Online Access Note: Wyoming's statewide case management system is for internal use only. Planning is underway for a new case management system that will ultimately allow public access. We have listed one county that accepts email requests.

Teton County
9th Judicial District Court *Civil and Criminal Records*
Email record search requests are accepted at clerk-of-district-court@tetonwyo.org.

County Level ... Recorders & Assessors

Recording Office Organization: 23 counties, 23 recording offices. The recording officer is the County Clerk. The entire state is in the Mountain Time Zone (MST). Federal tax liens on personal property of businesses are filed with the Secretary of State. Other federal and all state tax liens are filed with the County Clerk. Most counties will perform tax lien searches. Search fees are usually $10.00 per name.

Teton County   *Real Estate, Lien, Recording Records*
www.tetonwyo.org/clerk/
Access to the Clerk's database of scanned images is available free at www.tetonwyo.org/clerk/query. Search for complete documents back to 7/1996; partial documents back to 4/1991.

Federal Courts in Wyoming...

Standards for Federal Courts: The universal PACER sign-up number is 800-676-6856. Find PACER and the Party/Case Index on the Web at http://pacer.psc.uscourts.gov. PACER dial-up access is $.60 per minute.

US District Court -- District of Wyoming
Home Page: www.ck10.uscourts.gov/wyoming/district
PACER: Toll-free access: 888-417-3560. Local access phone: 307-772-2808. Case records are available back to 1988. Records are purged once per year. New civil records are available online after 1-2 days. New criminal records are available online after 1 day. **PACER URL:** http://pacer.wyd.uscourts.gov.
Cheyenne Division counties: All counties in Wyoming. Some criminal records are held in Casper.

US Bankruptcy Court -- District of Wyoming
Home Page: www.wyb.uscourts.gov
PACER: Case records are available back one year. Records are purged annually. New civil records are available online after 1 day.
PACER URL: http://pacer.wyb.uscourts.gov. Document images available.
Electronic Filing: Electronic filing information is available online at https://ecf.wyb.uscourts.gov.
Opinions Online: Court opinions are available online at www.wyb.uscourts.gov/opinion_search.htm. **Also:** access via phone on VCIS (Voice Case Information System) is available: 888-804-5537, 307-772-2191

Section III

Private Database Vendors

This Section Includes—

- Vendor Information Index
- Vendor Profiles

Why These Vendors Appear in the Book

Obviously, there are many more public record vendors than the 220+ firms appearing in this book. The reason these particular companies were chosen is because they provide either a **Proprietary Database** or offer a non-intervention **Gateway**. We call these vendors "**Distributor**s." There are plenty of excellent record vendors not listed in this book who most likely use these companies or government agencies as their primary source. We call these companies "**Search Firms**" (see page 69). For information about 1500 vendors of all categories, go to www.publicrecordsources.com.

A Few Words About
Database Distributors and Gateways

Distributors are automated public record firms who combine public sources of bulk data and/or online access to develop their own database product(s). Primary Distributors include companies that collect or buy public record information from its original source and reformat the information in some useful way. They tend to focus on one or a limited number of types of information, although a few firms have branched into multiple information categories.

Gateways are companies that either compile data from or provide an automated gateway to Primary Distributors. Gateways thus provide "one-stop shopping" for multiple geographic areas and/or categories of information. A gateway company serves as a middleman for data, allowing you to link directly to the information through them - as one electronic transaction.

Companies can be both Primary Distributors and Gateways. For example, a number of online database companies are both primary distributors of corporate information and also gateways to real estate information from other Primary Distributors

Vendor Information Index

The Information Index is designed to quickly and accurately direct you to the public record information category you need.

This index consists of 28 Information Categories. The vendors are listed alphabetically within each category. Each listing includes geographic coverage area and the name of proprietary databases or gateways offered. Note that CD = Canada. Itl = International.

After finding a potential company, we anticipate that you will usually refer to that company's individual profile for contact information, etc., in the Vendor Profiles Section.

The information categories are listed below.

Companies that report that they will sell their database(s) are listed on page 431.

Record Information Categories

Addresses/Telephone Numbers	Litigation/Judgments/Tax Liens
Associations/Trade Groups	Military Svc
Aviation	News/Current Events
Bankruptcy	Patents
Corporate/Trade Name Data	Real Estate/Assessor
Credit Information	SEC/Other Financial
Criminal Information	Software/Training
Driver and/or Vehicle	Trademarks
Education/Employment	Uniform Commercial Code
Environmental	Vessels
Foreign Country Information	Vital Records
Genealogical Information	Voter Registration
Legislation/Regulation	Wills/Probate
Licenses/Registrations/Permits	Workers Compensation

Address/Telephone Numbers

Address/Telephone Number Records Companies	Product Name	Region
555-1212.com	555-1212.com	US
Accurint	Person	US
American Business Information	Consumer Sales Leads	US
American Business Information	Business Sales Leads	US
Ameridex Information Systems	Live Index	US
ARISTOTLE	ARISTOTLE	US
Avantex Inc	FAA Data	US
ChoicePoint Inc	Consumer Services	US
ChoicePoint, formerly CDB Infotek	Address Inspector	US
ChoicePoint, formerly DBT Online Inc	AutoTrackXP	US
CompactData Solutions	EMarQit	TX
Daily Report, The	The Daily Report (Kern County Only)	CA
Data Downlink xls.com	xls.com	US, FR, GB, CD, Itl
Data-Trac.com, USCrimsearch.com	Profile Reports	US
DCS Information Systems	AmeriFind	TX,US
Dun & Bradstreet	D & B Public Record Search	US
Equifax Credit Services	Investigation System	US
Everton Publishers	Everton's Online Search	US
Experian Information Solutions	File 1	US
Experian Online	Experian Online	US
First American Real Estate Solutions East	PaceNet, MetroScan	KY, MI, OH, MO, PA, IL, TN
FlatRateInfo.com	QI National People Locator	US
Gale Group Inc, The	GaleNet	US
Hoover's Inc	Hoover's Company Profiles	US
Informus Corporation	IntroScan	US
Investigators Anywhere Resource Line	Resource Line	US
IQ Data Systems	IQ Data	US
KnowX	KnowX	US
Kompass USA Inc	Kompass.com	US, Itl
Law Bulletin Information Network	Access Plus	IL
LEXIS-NEXIS	B-Find, P-Find, P-Seek	US
Martindale-Hubbell	Martindale-Hubbell Law Directory	US, Itl
Merlin Information Services	Nat'l People Finder, Nat'l Criminal/Nat'l Credit/~FlatRate/Nat'l Phone File/QuickInfo.net & others	US
Merlin Information Services	CA Superior Civil Indexes, Nat'l Fictitious Business Names, Merlin Cross Directory	CA, US

Address/Telephone Number Records Companies	Product Name	Region
MetroNet	MetroNet, Cole's Directory	US
National Background Data	AIM (Address Information Mgr)	US, FL
National Credit Information Network NCI	NCI Network	US
Northwest Location Services	People Finder	WA
OPENonline (Online Prof. Elect. Network)	OPEN	US
Pallorium Inc	Skiptrace America, People Finder CDs	US
Plat System Services Inc	PropertyInfoNet™ (Minneapolis, St. Paul)	MN
Property Data Center Inc	Owner Phone Numbers	CO
PROTEC	Consta-Trac	US
Public Record Research Library	PRRS	US
Research Archives.com Legal Docs. Library	Legal Documents Library	US
San Diego Daily Transcript/SD Source	Home Sales, Com. Real Estate, Leases	CA
Search Company of North Dakota LLC	North Dakota Records	ND
Southeastern Public Records Inc.	Michigan/Georgia Public Records	MI, GA
Superior Information Services LLC	People Finder	US
Tax Analysts	The Tax Directory	US
Telebase	Dun & Bradstreet@AOL, Brainwave, I-Quest	US
Tenstar Business Services Group	ACB-1	LA, MS
Trans Union Employment Screening Services Inc	TRUSST (Tracking Residences using SSN Trace)	US
United State Mutual Association	National Theft Database	US
US SEARCH.com	US Search	US
USADATA.com	Marketing Portal	US
Utah.gov	Business Entity List	UT
Westlaw Public Records	Business Finder/People Finder	US

Associations/Trade Groups

Associations/Trade Group Records Companies	Product Name	Region
Gale Group Inc, The	GaleNet	US
Virginia Information Providers Network	Health Professionals (free)	VA

Aviation

Aviation Public Records Companies	Product Name	Region
Accurint	FAA	US
Accu-Source Inc.	National Pilot Registration	US
Avantex Inc	FAA Data	US
Commercial Information Systems Inc	Aircraft Registrations	US
FlatRateInfo.com	US Aircraft	US
KnowX	KnowX	US

Aviation Public Records Companies	Product Name	Region
Landings.com	Aviation Databases	US
Merlin Information Services	National FlatRate, Collector's FlatRate	US
Motznik Computer Services Inc	Alaska Public Information Access System	AK
OPENonline (Online Prof. Elect. Network)	OPEN	US
Pallorium Inc	Skiptrace America, People Finder CDs	US
UCC Direct Services	Public Records Portal	US
US SEARCH.com	US Search	US
Westlaw Public Records	Aircraft Locator	US

Bankruptcy

Bankruptcy Public Records Companies	Product Name	Region
Accurint	Bankruptcy	US
Accu-Source Inc.	Federal Bankruptcy Courts	AK, AR, AZ, CA, CO, FL, GA, HI, IA, ID, IL, IN, KS, KY, LA, MN, MO, NC, ND, NE, NM, NV, OK, OH, OR, SC, SD, TN, TX, UT, WA, WI, WY
Banko	BANKO; ACOLLAID	US
Banko Document Retrieval (BDR)	BANKO	US
CaseClerk.com	CourtClerk.com/Caseclerk.com	TN, US
CCH Washington Service Bureau	SECnet	US
ChoicePoint Inc	Legal Information	US
ChoicePoint, formerly CDB Infotek	Legal Information	US
Conrad Grundlehner Inc	Conrad Grundlehner	DC, MD, NC, VA, WV
CourtExpress.com (RIS Legal Svcs)	US Court Records	US
CourtLink	Courtlink Classic, CaseStream	US
Daily Report, The	The Daily Report (Kern County Only)	CA
Diligenz Inc	Diligenz	US
Dolan Information, Data Services Div	Hogan Online	US
Dun & Bradstreet	D & B Public Record Search	US
Equifax Credit Services	Investigation System	US
Experian Online	Experian Online Busi. Record Reports	US
FlatRateInfo.com	QI	US
IQ Data Systems	IQ Data	US
KnowX	KnowX	US
LEXIS-NEXIS	ALLBKT	US
Merlin Information Services	National Bankruptcies/Judgments/Tax Liens, ~FlatRate(s)	US
Motznik Computer Services Inc	Alaska Public Info. Access System	AK
OPENonline (Online Prof. Elect. Network)	OPEN	US

Bankruptcy Public Records Companies	Product Name	Region
Oso Grande Technologies	NM Fed Courts/LegalNet	NM
Realty Data Corp	RDC Database (www.realtydata.com)	NY
Record Information Services Inc	Bankruptcies	IL
Research Archives.com Legal Docs. Library	Legal Documents Library	US
San Diego Daily Transcript/SD Source	Filings	US
Search Company of North Dakota LLC	North Dakota Records	ND
Southeastern Public Records Inc.	Michigan/Georgia Public Records	MI, GA
Superior Information Services LLC	Superior Online	CT, DC, DE, MD, MA, ME, NC, NH, NJ, NY, PA, RI, VA, VT
Tenstar Business Services Group	ACB-1	LA, MS
UCC Direct Services - AccuSearch Inc	AccuSearch	CA, IL, TX
US SEARCH.com	US Search	US
Westlaw Public Records	Bankruptcy Records	US

Corporate/Trade Name Data

Corporate/Trade Name Public Records Companies	Product Name	Region
Access Indiana Information Network	Premium Services	IN
Access Louisiana Inc	LA Corporate Data	LA
Accurint	Business	US
Accutrend Data Corporation	New Business Database	US
Background Information Services Inc	Filings	CO
Better Business Bureau	Business Report	US
BNA, Inc (Bureau of National Affairs)	Corporate Law Daily	US
ChoicePoint Inc	Legal Information	US
ChoicePoint, formerly CDB Infotek	Corporate & Limited Partnerships	US
ChoicePoint, formerly DBT Online Inc	AutoTrackXP	US
Commercial Information Systems Inc	Corporations & Limited Partnerships	CA,ID,OR,WA
Companies Online - Lycos	companiesonline.com	US
CorporateInformation.com	Corporate/Trade Name Data	US
CourtH.com	Courthouse Research	TX
Data Downlink xls.com	xls.com	US, FR, GB, CD, Itl
Derwent Information	World Patents Index, Patent Explorer	US
Dialog	DIALOG Web; DataStar; Profound; Intelliscope; Insite; IntraScope	US
Diligenz Inc	Diligenz.com	US
Discovering Montana	Discoveringmontana	MT
Dun & Bradstreet	D & B Public Record Search	US
e-InfoData.com	QuickInfo.net	AZ, AR, GA, ID, NV, NM, OR, TX, UT, WY

Corporate/Trade Name Public Records Companies	Product Name	Region
Experian Online	Experian Online Busi. Records Reports	US
Fairchild Record Search Ltd	Washington	US, AK, ID, OR, WA
FlatRateInfo.com	QI	US
Gale Group Inc, The	GaleNet	US
GoverNet	SurfNV	NV
GuideStar	Charity Search	US
Hoover's Inc	Hoover's Company Profiles	US
Household Drivers Reports Inc (HDR Inc)	Corp Data	TX
Idealogic	Dynis-Cor:	CD
Information Network of Arkansas	Secretary of State	AR
Information Network of Kansas	Premium Services	KS
Interstate Data Corporation	CA Corporate Records	CA
IQ Data Systems	IQ Data	US
KnowX	KnowX	US
Kompass USA Inc	Kompass.com	US, Itl
KY Direct	Secretary of State	KY
LEXIS-NEXIS	ALLSOS	US
LLC Reporter	LLC Reporter	US
Merlin Information Services	Nat'l FlatRate, Collector's FlatRate, QuikInfo.net	US
Merlin Information Services	CA Corps & Ltd Partnerships, CA Statewide/Nat'l Fictitious Busi. Names	CA, US
Motznik Computer Services Inc	Alaska Public Info. Access System	AK
National Service Information	NSI Online	IN, OH, WI, US
Nebrask@ Online	Nebrask@ Online	NE
Northwest Location Services	Business	CA
OPENonline (Online Prof. Elect. Network)	OPEN	US
Oso Grande Technologies	Oso Grande	NM
Pallorium Inc	BusinessFinder America	US
Research Archives.com Legal Docs. Library	Legal Documents Library	US
Superior Information Services LLC	Corporate Files	NY, PA
Tax Analysts	Exempt Organization Master List	US
Telebase	Brainwave, I-Quest	US
Tennessee Anytime	Free Services	TN
Tenstar Business Services Group	ACB-1	LA, MS
Thomson & Thomson	US Title Availability Search, The deForest Report	US
UCC Direct Services - AccuSearch Inc	AccuSearch	TX, CA, PA, IL, WA, OH, OR, MO
UCC Direct Services	Public Records Portal	US
US Corporate Services	MN Secretary of State Records	MN

Corporate/Trade Name Public Records Companies	Product Name	Region
US SEARCH.com	US Search	US
USADATA.com	Marketing Portal	US
Utah.gov	Business Entity List	UT
West Group	Westlaw	US
Westlaw Public Records	Corporations and Partnerships	US

Credit Information

Credit Information Companies	Product Name	Region
ADP Screening and Selection Services	Credit & Name Link	US
American Business Information	Consumer Sales Leads	US
American Business Information	Business Sales Leads	US
Background Information Services Inc	Criminal DB	US, CO, OK
ConsumerInfo.com	Qspace, Consumer info	US
Contemporary Information Corp.	Continfo/Experian/Equifax	US, CA
Dun & Bradstreet	Business Credit Information	US
Dun & Bradstreet	D & B Public Record Search	US
Equifax Credit Services	Credit Profile	US
Experian Information Solutions	File 1	US
Fidelifacts	Fidelfacts	US, NY
IQ Data Systems	IQ Data	US
Merchants Security Exchange	Credit Reports	FL, US
Merlin Information Services	Merlin Super Header, Collector FlatRate, Link to America, Nat'l Credit Header Search, Nat'l FlatRate	US
Merlin Information Services	Merlin Cross Directory	US
National Credit Information Network NCI	NCI Network	US
NIB Ltd	BACAS, BcomM, Courier	US
OneCreditSource.com	Consumer/Employment Credit	US
OPENonline (Online Prof. Elect. Network)	OPEN	US
Owens OnLine Inc	Owens OnLine	US
Rental Research Inc	Equifax, Trans Union	US, WA
SEAFAX Inc	Business Reports	US
Telebase	Dun & Bradstreet@ AOL, I Brainwave, -Quest	US
Tenstar Business Services Group	ACB-2	LA, US
The Official Providers Source	Transportation Employment/Security Guard History	US
Trans Union	Trans Union	US
Trans Union Employment Screening Svcs	Credit	US

Criminal Information

Criminal Information Companies	Product Name	Region
Agency Records	ARI, MN Court Convictions (15 yrs)	CT, MN
Alacourt.com	Alacourt.com	AL
Arizona Drug Screening & Inv.	AZDSI Criminal Database	AZ, UT, NV
Background Information Services Inc	Criminal DB	CO, OK, US
CaseClerk.com	CourtClerk.com/Caseclerk.com	TN, US
ChoicePoint Inc	Legal Information	US
Circuit Express	Circuit Express, Magistrate Express	WV
CoCourts.com	Colorado Courts Information	CO
Commercial Information Systems Inc	Criminal Records	ID,OR,WA,CA
Confi-Chek	Confi-Chek Online-14 Counties	CA
Contemporary Information Corp.	Criminal Scan	CA, US
Court PC of Connecticut	Superior Index	CT
CourtSearch.com	NC Records	NC
Criminal Information Services Inc	CRIS	AZ,AR,CT,FL,GA,HI,ID,IL,IN ,KY,MI,MN,MS,MO,NC,ND, NJ,NY,OH,OK,OR,SC,TX, UT,WA
Daily Report, The	Daily Report (Kern County Only)	CA
Data-Trac.com, USCrimsearch.com	Profile Reports	NY
DCS Information Systems	AmeriFind	TX,US
Felonies R Us	AR Felonies	AR
Household Drivers Reports Inc (HDR Inc)	Criminal Record Data	TX
iDocket.com	iDockets	TX
Infocon Corporation	INFOCON County Access System-15 counties	PA
Information Inc	Arrest Database (Nashville)	TN
Information Network of Kansas	Sedgwick, Shawnee, Wyandotte Cty	KS
Innovative Enterprises Inc	Virginia Criminal Records Database	VA
Intellicorp Ltd	Court, Inmate, & Booking Records	IN, IL IA, MN, OH
Interstate Data Corporation	Criminal	CA
Investigative & Background Solutions Inc	Colorado Court Records	CO
Judici	CourtLook, Multi-Search	IL
Juritas.com	Juritas	CA, DE, FL, IL, NJ, WA
LEXIS-NEXIS	LEXIS	US
Merchants Security Exchange	Crime Online Database	US, FL
Merlin Information Services	Collector's FlatRate, Nat'l FlatRate, QuickInfo.net	US
Merlin Information Services	CA Criminal Indexes LA Muni. Index	CA
MidSouth Information Services	Carolina Information Inc	NC
Motznik Computer Services Inc	Alaska Public Info. Access System	AK

Criminal Information Companies	Product Name	Region
National Background Data	Let's Check America, Nat'l Background Directory	US, FL
National Fraud Center	Cellular Fraud Database	US
National Fraud Center	Bank Fraud/Insurance Fraud/Organized Crime/The Fraud Bulletin	US, Itl
NC Recordsonline.com	ncrecordsonline.com	NC
OneCreditSource.com	OJIN, JIS	OR, WA
OPENonline (Online Prof. Elect. Network)	Arrest Records	OH,IN,MI
OPENonline (Online Prof. Elect. Network)	National Corrections Records	AZ, AR, CT, FL, GA, ID, IL, IN, KY, ME, MI, MN, MS, NE MO, NJ, NY, NC, OH, OK, OR, SC, TN, TX, UT, WA
Oso Grande Technologies	NM Fed Courts/LegalNet	NM
Rapsheets.com	rapsheets.com	AL, AZ, AR, CO, CT, FL, GA, IL, IN, ID. KS, KY, MI, MN, MS, MO, NC, NV, NJ, NY, OH, OK, OR, SC, TN, TX, UT, VA, WA
Rental Research Inc	COIN	AZ, ID, OR, WA
Search Company of North Dakota LLC	North Dakota Records	ND
Software Computer Group Inc	Circuit Express	WV
Tenstar Business Services Group	ACB-1	LA, MS
The Official Providers Source	20/20 Insight	US, CD, Itl, VI, PR
United State Mutual Association	National Theft Database	US
USAScreening.com	Statewide Criminal Records	AK, AZ, AR, CO, CT, FL, GA, HI, ID, IL, IN, KY, MI, MS, NC, NY, OH, OK, SC, TN, TX, UT, VA, WA
Verifacts	Statewide Criminal Records	AK,AL,AZ,AR,CA,CO,CT,FL ,GA,IA,ID,IL,IN,KS,KY,LA,M D,ME,MI,MN,MO,MS,NC,N H,ND,NJ,NM, NY,OH,OK,OR,PA,RI,SC,S D,TN,TX,UT,VA,WA,WI
Verifacts	Registered Sex Offenders	AK, AZ, CT, FL, GA, HI, ID, IL, IN, KS, KY, MI, MS, NC, NY, OH, OK, SC, TN, TX, UT, VA, WA

Driver and/or Vehicle

Driver and/or Vehicle Records Companies	Product Name	Region
Access Indiana Information Network	Premium Services	IN
Accurint	Florida DL Search	FL
ADP Screening and Selection Services	Driving Records	US
ADREM Profiles Inc	ADREM	US

Driver and/or Vehicle Records Companies	Product Name	Region
Agency Records	ARI	US
American Business Information	Consumer Sales Leads	US
American Driving Records	ADR	US
AutoDataDirect, Inc	ADD123	FL
Carfax	Vehicle History, Motor Vehicle Title Information	US
ChoicePoint Inc	Insurance Services	US
ChoicePoint, formerly DBT Online Inc	AutoTrackXP	US
Commercial Information Systems Inc	Driver's License & Registration	ID,OR
CompactData Solutions	QuikList	TX, FL, OH
Datalink Services Inc	Driving, Vehicle & Dealer Records	CA
DCS Information Systems	Texas Systems	TX
Discovering Montana	Discoveringmontana	MT
e-InfoData.com	QuickInfo.net	FL, ID, IA, LA, ME, MN, MS, MO, NC, OR, SD, TX, UT, WV, WI, WY
Experian Online	Experian Online	US
Explore Information Services	EARS and RiskAlert	AL, AZ, CA, CO, CT, DE, FL, ID, IA, KS, KY, MA, MD, ME, MI, MN, MO, MT, NE, NH, NV, NY, OH, OR, SC, TN, TX, UT, WI, WV, WY
Household Drivers Reports Inc (HDR Inc)	Driver & Vehicle	TX
iiX (Insurance Information Exchange)	Motor Vehicle Reports	US
iiX (Insurance Information Exchange)	UDI-Undisclosed Drivers, VIN	US
Information Network of Arkansas	INA	AR
Information Network of Kansas	Premium Services	KS
InforME - Information Resource of Maine	Bureau of MV Driver's Records	ME
IQ Data Systems	IQ Data	US
KY Direct	Driving Records	KY
Logan Registration Service Inc	Logan	CA, US
MDR/Minnesota Driving Records	MDR	US
Merlin Information Services	Merlin Cross Directory	US
Merlin Information Services	Collector's FlatRate, Link to America, QuikInfo.net	US
Motznik Computer Services Inc	Alaska Public Info. Access System	AK
National Credit Information Network NCI	NCI Network	US
Nebrask@ Online	Nebrask@ Online	NE
Northwest Location Services	Driver and/or Vehicle	OR,ID
OPENonline (Online Prof. Elect. Network)	OPEN	US
Oso Grande Technologies	Oso Grande	NM
Pallorium Inc	Skiptrace Amer., People Finder CDs	US

Driver and/or Vehicle Records Companies	Product Name	Region
Records Research Inc	RRI MVRs	CA,US
Softech International Inc	MVRs	AL, AR, FL, GA, ID, IL, IN, NJ MS, NY, NC, OH, TN, TX, UT
Tennessee Anytime	Premium Services	TN
Tenstar Business Services Group	ACB-2	LA, US
Texas Driving Record Express Service	Certified MVRs	TX
The Official Providers Source	Driving Records	US
TML Information Services Inc	Title File	AL, FL, SD
TML Information Services Inc	Auto-Search (Immediate MVR)	AL, AZ, AR, CT, DC, DE, FL, ID, IL, IN, KS, KY, LA, MA, MD, ME, MI, MN, MS, NC, ND, NE, NH, NJ, NY, OH, RI, SC, TN, TX, VA, VT, WI, WV
TML Information Services Inc	Driving Records	US
TML Information Services Inc	Driver Check	AL, AZ, CA, CT, FL, ID, KS, LA, MD, MI, MN, NE, NH, NY, NC, OH, PA, SC, VA, WV
Trans Union Employment Screening Svcs	TransUnion	US
Utah.gov	TLRIS/MVR	UT
Virginia Information Providers Network	VIPNet	VA
Westlaw Public Records	Motor Vehicle Records	AK, AL, CO, CT, DC, DE, FL, IA, ID, IL, KY, LA, MA, MD, ME, MI, MN, MO, MS, MT, ND, NE, NH, NM, NY, OH, SC, TN, UT, WI, WV, WY

Education/Employment

Education/Employment Records Companies	Product Name	Region
Campus Direct	Campus Direct	US
Credentials Inc	Degreechk	US
EdVerify Inc	EdVerify.com	US
Equifax Credit Services	Investigation System	US
National Student Clearinghouse	EnrollmentVerify, DegreeVerify	US
Tenstar Business Services Group	ACB-1	LA, MS
Virginia Information Providers Network	State Employment Verification	VA

Environmental

Environmental Records Companies	Product Name	Region
BNA, Inc (Bureau of National Affairs)	Environment & Safety Library on the Web	US
Commercial Information Systems Inc	Hazardous Materials	OR,WA
Environmental Data Resources, Inc. (EDR)	NEDIS, Sanborn Maps	US
Loren Data Corp	Commerce Business Daily	US

Environmental Records Companies	Product Name	Region
OSHA DATA	OSHA Data Gateway	US
Public Data Corporation	Public Data	NY
Realty Data Corp	RDC Database (www.realtydata.com)	NY
West Group	Westlaw	US

Foreign Country Information

Foreign Country Information Companies	Product Name	Region
A.M. Best Company	Best's Insight Global	GB, Itl, CD
Ancestry	Ancestry.com	
BNA, Inc (Bureau of National Affairs)	International Trade Daily, WTO Reporter	Itl
Burrelles Information Services	BIO	
CorporateInformation.com	Corporate/Trade Name Data	Itl
CountryWatch Inc.	Countrywatch.com db	Itl (191)
Derwent Information	World Patents Index, Patent Explorer	Itl
Dialog	DIALOG Web; DataStar; Profound; Intelliscope; Insite; IntraScope	
Gale Group Inc, The	GaleNet	Itl
Global Securities Information, Inc	International Prospectuses	Itl
Hoover's Inc	Foreign Country Information	
Investigators Anywhere Resource Line	Resource Line	
Kompass USA Inc	Kompass.com	Itl
Offshore Business News & Research	Courts and Businesses	Bermuda, Cayman Is., Caribbean,
Owens OnLine Inc	Owens OnLine	
Tax Analysts	TAXBASE, The Ratx Directory	
Telebase	Brainwave, I-Quest	
Thomson & Thomson	Worldwide Domain	Itl
Vital Records Information	vitalrec.com	

Genealogical Information

Genealogical Information Companies	Product Name	Region
American Business Information	Consumer Sales Leads	US
Vital Records Information	vitalrec.com	US

Legislation/Regulation

Legislation/Regulation Records Companies	Product Name	Region
Access Indiana Information Network	Free Services	IN
Avantex Inc	FAA Data	US

Legislation/Regulation Records Companies	Product Name	Region
BNA, Inc (Bureau of National Affairs)	Intl Trade Daily, WTO Reporter	US, Itl
Cal Info	Guide to State Statutes	US
Cal Info	Administrative Guide to State Regulations	US
Canadian Law Book Inc	Canada Statute Service	CD
CaseClerk.com	Caseclerk.com	US
Dialog	DIALOG Web; DataStar; Profound; Intelliscope; Insite; IntraScope	US
Information Network of Kansas	Premium Services	KS
KY Direct	Legislature Searching Service	KY
LEXIS-NEXIS	Congressional Information Service	US
Loren Data Corp	Commerce Business Daily	US
OSHA DATA	OSHA Data Gateway	US
Oso Grande Technologies	Oso Grande	NM
Public Record Research Library	PRRS	US
State Net	State Net	US
Tax Analysts	The OneDisc, TAXBASE	US
Thomas Legislative Information	Thomas	US
Virginia Information Providers Network	VIPNet (free)	VA
West Group	West CD-ROM Libraries	US
West Group	Westlaw	US

Licenses/Registrations/Permits

Licenses/Registrations/Permits Companies	Product Name	Region
Access Indiana Information Network	Premium Services	IN
Accutrend Data Corporation	New Business Database	US
ChoicePoint Inc	Information Services	US
Commercial Information Systems Inc	Prof. Licenses, Fish & Wildlife Records	ID,OR,WA
Daily Report, The	The Daily Report (Kern County Only)	CA
e-InfoData.com	QuickInfo.net	FL, ID, IA, LA, MN, MS, MO, NV, NC, OR, TX, UT, WI, WY
E-Merges.com	Hunting/Fishing Licenses	AK,AR,CT,DE,FL,GA, KS,MS,MO,NV,NJ,NC, ND,OH,SC,UT,VA,WA
Environmental Data Resources, Inc. (EDR)	NEDIS, Sanborn Maps	US
GoverNet	eregistry	NV
Information Network of Arkansas	Secretary of State	AR
Interstate Data Corporation	CA Professional Licenses	CA
Investigators Anywhere Resource Line	Resource Line	US
KnowX	KnowX	US

Licenses/Registrations/Permits Companies	Product Name	Region
LEXIS-NEXIS	Professional Licensing Boards	CA, CT, FL, GE, IL, MA,MI,NE,NJ,NC,OG,PA,TX,VA,WI
Merlin Information Services	Collector's FlatRate, Nat'l FlatRate, QuickInfo.net	US
Merlin Information Services	CA Sales/Use Tax, Prof. Licenses	CA
Motznik Computer Services Inc	Alaska Public Info. Access System	AK
Northwest Location Services	Business Licenses	WA
Record Information Services Inc	Business Licenses, News Incorporations	IL
Search Company of North Dakota LLC	North Dakota Records	ND
Thomson & Thomson	US Full Copyright Search	US
Utah.gov	License Data	UT
Westlaw Public Records	Professional Licenses	AZ, CA, CO, CT, FL, GA, IL, IN, LA, MA, MD, MI, NJ, OH, PA, SC, TN, TX, VA, WI

Litigation/Judgments/Tax Liens

Litigation/Judgment/Tax Liens Records Company	Product Name	Region
Access Indiana Information Network	Premium Services	IN
Accurint	Tax Liens & Judgments	US
Alacourt.com	Alacourt.com	AL
Attorneys Title Insurance Fund	Online Data Service	FL
Banko	BANKO	US
BNA, Inc (Bureau of National Affairs)	Class Action Litigation Report	US
Canadian Law Book Inc	Caselaw on Call	CD
Case Record Info Services	Judgment Lists	CA
CaseClerk.com	CourtClerk.com/Caseclerk.com	TN, US
ChoicePoint Inc	Legal Information	US
ChoicePoint, formerly CDB Infotek	Legal Information	US
Circuit Express	Circuit Express, Magistrate Express	WV
CoCourts.com	Colorado Courts Information	CO
Commercial Information Systems Inc	Civil Records	ID, OR, WA, CA
Conrad Grundlehner Inc	Conrad Grundlehner	DC, MD, NC, VA, WV
Contemporary Information Corp.	Lexidate	AZ, CA, NV, OR, WA
Court PC of Connecticut	Superior Index	CT
CourtExpress.com (RIS Legal Svcs)	US Court Records	AZ,CA,CT,FL,IA,MO,VA
CourtH.com	Courthouse Research	TX
CourthouseDirect.com	Real Property Documents	AZ, CA, FL, HI, IL, NY, OK, PA, TX, UT, WA
CourtLink	Courtlink Classic, CaseStream	US

Litigation/Judgment/Tax Liens Records Company	Product Name	Region
CourtSearch.com	NC Records	NC
Daily Report, The	The Daily Report (Kern County Only)	CA
Diligenz Inc	Diligenz	US
Dolan Information, Data Services Div	Hogan Online	US
Dun & Bradstreet	D & B Public Record Search	US
Electronic Property Information Corp (EPIC)	OPRA-Erie, Monroe Counties	NY
Equifax Credit Services	Investigation System	US
Fairchild Record Search Ltd	Courtlink; Motznicks	US, AK, ID, OR, WA
FlatRateInfo.com	QI	US
GoverNet	SurfNV	NV
Hollingsworth Court Reporting Inc	Tenant Eviction/Public Record Report	AL, AR, FL, GA, IL, LA, MS, TN
iDocket.com	iDockets	TX
Infocon Corporation	INFOCON County Access System-15 counties	PA
Information Network of Kansas	-Johnson, Sedgwick, Shawnee, Wyandotte	KS
IQ Data Systems	IQ Data	US
Judici	CourtLook, Multi-Search	IL
Juritas.com	Juritas	CA, DE, FL, IL, NJ, WA
KnowX	KnowX	US
Law Bulletin Information Network	Access Plus-Central, North Counties	IL
LEXIS-NEXIS	LEXIS Law Publishing, Shepard's	US
LIDA Credit Agency Inc	Litigation Report	DE, NJ, NY, PA
Merchants Security Exchange	Public Record	US, FL
Merlin Information Services	CA Civil Superior Indexes	CA
Merlin Information Services	Nat'l FlatRate, Collector's FlatRate, QuikInfo.net, Nat'l Property	US
MidSouth Information Services	Carolina Information Inc	NC
Motznik Computer Services Inc	Alaska Public Info. Access System	AK
MyFloridaCounty.com	Official Records Search	FL
Northwest Location Services	Superior Courts	WA
OPENonline (Online Prof. Elect. Network)	OPEN	US
Oso Grande Technologies	Oso Grande	NM
Public Data Corporation	Public Data	NY
Realty Data Corp	RDC Database (www.realtydata.com)	NY
Richland County Abstract Co	Judgment & Tax Liens	MN, ND
San Diego Daily Transcript/SD Source	San Diego Source	CA
Search Company of North Dakota LLC	North Dakota Records	ND
Software Computer Group Inc	Circuit Express	WV
Software Management Inc - eCCLIX	CCLIX-OptiMA and CCLIX System	KY

Litigation/Judgment/Tax Liens Records Company	Product Name	Region
Southeastern Public Records Inc.	Michigan/Georgia Public Records	MI, GA
Superior Information Services LLC	Superior Online	CT, DC, DE, MD, MA, ME, NC, NH, NJ, NY, PA, RI, VA, VT
Telebase	LEXIS-NEXIS Caselow @AOL	US
Tenstar Business Services Group	ACB-1	LA, MS
TitleSearcher.com		TN
UCC Direct Services	Public Records Portal	US
Unisearch Inc	WALDO	CA, WA
US Title Search Network		TN
Verifacts	Eviction/Unlawful Detainers	AK, AZ, CA, CO, ID, KY, NC, NV, OR, PA, TX, VA, WA
Westlaw Public Records	Lawsuits, Judgments, Liens	US

Military Service

Military Service Records Companies	Product Name	Region
Ameridex Information Systems	Military DB	US
KnowX	KnowX	US
Military Information Enterprises Inc	Nationwide Locator Online	US

News/Current Events

News/Current Events Public Records Companies	Product Name	Region
American Business Information	Business Sales Leads	US
Burrelles Information Services	BIO	US
Dialog	NewsEdge	US
Hoover's Inc	Hoover's Company Profiles	US
Loren Data Corp	Commerce Business Daily	US
Telebase	Brainwave, I-Quest	US

Patents

Patent Information Provider Companies	Product Name	Region
Aurigin Systems Inc.	Aurigin	US, Itl
Canadian Law Book Inc	Canadian Patent Reporter	CD
Derwent Information	World Patents Index, Patent Explorer	US
MicroPatent USA	WPS	US, Itl
Questel Orbit	QPAT-WW	US, Itl
Telebase	Brainwave, I-Quest	US
Thomson & Thomson	Site Comber	US

Real Estate/Assessor

Real Estate/Assessor Records Companies	Product Name	Region
Accurint	Property Assessment	US
ACS Inc	BRC	IL,NJ,NY
American Business Information	Consumer Sales Leads	US
ARCountyData.com - Apprentice Info. Sys.	Arkansas County Assessor Records	AR
Attorneys Title Insurance Fund	Online Data Service	FL
ChoicePoint Inc	Real Property	US
ChoicePoint, formerly CDB Infotek	Real Property Ownership & Transfers	US
Commercial Information Systems Inc	Real Estate Records	ID,NV,OR,WA
CompactData Solutions	EMarQit	TX
ConsumerInfo.com	e-neighborhoods, iplace	US
CourtH.com	Courthouse Research	TX
CourthouseDirect.com	Real Estate/Assessor	AZ, CA, FL, HI, IL, NY, OK, PA, TX, UT, WA
Courthouse Retrieval System Inc.	CRSdata.net; ids™	AL, NC, TN
Daily Report, The	The Daily Report (Kern County Only)	CA
DataQuick	DataQuick	US
DCS Information Systems	AmeriFind	TX,US
Diversified Information Services Corp	Real Property Records-Maricopa Cty	AZ
e-InfoData.com	QuickInfo.net	FL, ID, IA, LA, MN, MS, MO, NV, NC, OR, TX, UT, WI, WY
Electronic Property Information Corp (EPIC)	OPRA-Erie, Monroe Counties	NY
Environmental Data Resources, Inc. (EDR)	NEDIS, Sanborn Maps	US
Ernst Publishing Co, LLC	Real Estate Recording Guide	US
Experian Online	Experian Online	US
First American Corporation, The	Real Estate Information	US
First American Real Estate Solutions East	PaceNet, Prospect Services	KY, MI, OH
First American Real Estate Solutions West	Real Property Database	LA, AZ, CA, CO, DC, DE, FL, GA, HI, IL, IN, LA, MA, MD, MI, MN, MS, NC, NJ, NM, NY, NV, OH, OK, OR, PA, SC, TN, TX, UT, VA, VI, WA, WI
FlatRateInfo.com	QI	US
GoverNet	SurfNV	NV
IDM Corporation	Tax, Assessor and Recorders	US
Infocon Corporation	County Access System-15 counties	PA
Information Network of Kansas	Premium Services	KS
IQ Data Systems	IQ Data	US
KnowX	KnowX	US
Landaccess.com - ACS Gov. Land Records	Landaccess.com	OH

Real Estate/Assessor Records Companies	Product Name	Region
Law Bulletin Information Network	Access Plus-Cook County	IL
LEXIS-NEXIS	ALLOWN	US
Merlin Information Services	CA Statewide Property	CA
Merlin Information Services	Nat'l FlatRate, Collector's FlatRate, Link to America, National Property, QuikInfo.net	US
Metro Market Trends Inc	Real Estate Activity Reporting Sys.	FL, AL
MetroNet	MetroNet, Cole's Directory	US
Motznik Computer Services Inc	Alaska Public Info. Access System	AK
MyFloridaCounty.com	Official Records Search	FL
NETR Real Estate Research and Information	Property Data Store	AL,AZ,CA,DC,FL,HI,IL,IN,MD,MS,MI,MN,MO,NV,NY,OH,PA,TN,TX,UT,WA,WI
OPENonline (Online Prof. Elect. Network)	OPEN	US
Plat System Services Inc	PropertyInfoNet (Minneapolis/St. Paul)	MN
Property Data Center Inc	Real Property Assessments, Taxes	CO
Public Data Corporation	Public Data	NY
Realty Data Corp	RDC Database (www.realtydata.com)	NY
Record Information Services Inc	New Homeowners, Mortgages, Foreclosures	IL
San Diego Daily Transcript/SD Source	Home Sales, Com. Real Estate, Leases	CA
SKLD Information Services LLC	New Homeowners List, Deeds, Loan Activity, Notice of Demand (13 Counties)	CO
Software Management Inc - eCCLIX	CCLIX-OptiMA and CCLIX System	KY
Superior Information Services LLC	Real Property	US
Tennessee Anytime	Free Services	TN
Tenstar Business Services Group	ACB-1	LA, MS
The Search Company Inc	Property Ownership & Tenant Data	CD
TitleSearcher.com		TN
TitleX.com	titleX.com	TX
tnrealestate.com	www.tnrealestate.com	TN
UCC Direct Services	Public Records Portal	US
US SEARCH.com	US Search	US
US Title Search Network		TN
USADATA.com	Marketing Portal	US
Vision Appraisal Technology	various New England Municipalities	CT, ME, MA, NH, RI
Western Regional Data Inc	WRDI's Lead Focus, Property Search	NV
Westlaw Public Records	Real Estate, Liens & Judgments	US
Courthouse Retrieval System Inc.	CRSdata.net; ids™	AL, NC, TN

SEC/Other Financial

SEC/Other Financial Records Companies	Product Name	Region
A.M. Best Company	Best Database Services	US
American Business Information	Business Sales Leads	US
CCH Washington Service Bureau	SECnet	US
CountryWatch Inc.	Countywatch Forecast	Itl (193)
Data Downlink xls.com	xls.com	US, CD, Itl
Dialog	DIALOG Web; DataStar; Profound; Intelliscope; Insite; IntraScope	US
Global Securities Information, Inc	Live Edgar	DC
Hoover's Inc	Real-Time SEC Documents	US
Silver Plume	Insurance Industry Rates, Forms and Manuals, Reference & Research Material	US
Telebase	Brainwave, I-Quest	US
Thomson Research Services	Global Access & Thomas Research	US

Software/Training

Public Records Software/Training Companies	Product Name	Region
Carfax	VINde (VIN Validity Check Program)	US
Corporate Screening	CSS EASE	US
FOIA Group Inc	FOIA-Ware	US
National Fraud Center	NFC Online	US

Trademarks

Trademark Records Companies	Product Name	Region
Access Louisiana Inc	LA Corporate Data	LA
ChoicePoint, formerly DBT Online Inc	AutoTrackXP	US
Dialog	DIALOG Web; DataStar; Profound; Intelliscope; Insite; IntraScope	US
Idealogic	Dynis-Trademarks	CD
MicroPatent USA	TradeMark Checker, Mark Search Plus	US, Itl
Telebase	Brainwave, I-Quest	US
Tennessee Anytime	Free Services	TN
Thomson & Thomson	US Full Trademark Search, Site Comber	US
Trademark Register, The	The Trademark Register	US

Uniform Commercial Code

Uniform Commercial Code Records Companies	Product Name	Region
Access Indiana Information Network	Premium Services	IN
Access Louisiana Inc	LA UCC	LA
Accurint	UCC	US
ACS Inc	BRC	IL,NJ,NY
Background Information Services Inc	UCC	CO
Capitol Lien Records & Research Inc	UCC	WI,US
ChoicePoint Inc	Legal Information	US
ChoicePoint, formerly CDB Infotek	UCC	US
Commercial Information Systems Inc	UCCs	CA,ID,OR,WA
CompactData Solutions	NationsData.com	TX
Daily Report, The	The Daily Report (Kern County Only)	CA
Diligenz Inc	Diligenz.com	US
Dun & Bradstreet	D & B Public Record Search	US
Electronic Property Information Corp (EPIC)	OPRA-Erie, Monroe Counties	NY
Ernst Publishing Co, LLC	UCC Filing Guide	US
Experian Online	Experian Online Busi. Record Reports	US
Fairchild Record Search Ltd	UCC	US, AK, ID, OR, WA
GoverNet	SurfNV	NV
Information Network of Kansas	Premium Services	KS
IQ Data Systems	IQ Data	US
KnowX	KnowX	US
KY Direct	UCC Index Search	KY
Landaccess.com - ACS Gov. Land Records	Landaccess.com	OH
Law Bulletin Information Network	Access Plus-Cook County	IL
LEXIS-NEXIS	ALLUCC	US
Merlin Information Services	Collector's FlatRate, Nat'l Criminal, QuickInfo.net	US
Merlin Information Services	CA UCC Index	CA
Motznik Computer Services Inc	Alaska Public Info. Access System	AK
National Service Information	NSI Online	IN, OH, WI
Nebrask@ Online	Nebrask@ Online	NE
OPENonline (Online Prof. Elect. Network)	OPEN	US
Oso Grande Technologies	Oso Grande	NM
Paragon Document Research, Inc.	Pdrlog - termination database	MN, US
Public Data Corporation	Public Data	NY
Realty Data Corp	RDC Database (www.realtydata.com)	NY
San Diego Daily Transcript/SD Source	San Diego Source	CA
Search Company of North Dakota LLC	ND UCC	ND

Uniform Commercial Code Records Companies	Product Name	Region
Search Network Ltd	Search Network	IA,KS
Software Management Inc - eCCLIX	CCLIX-OptiMA and CCLIX System	KY
Superior Information Services LLC	UCC Files	PA, NJ
Tennessee Anytime	Free Services	TN
Tenstar Business Services Group	ACB-1	LA, MS
UCC Direct Services	Public Records Portal	US
UCC Direct Services - AccuSearch Inc	AccuSearch	TX, CA, PA, IL, WA, OH, OR, MO
Unisearch Inc	WALDO	CA, WA
US Corporate Services	UCCs	MN, WI
Utah.gov	UCC Filing Data	UT
West Group	Westlaw	US

Vessels

Vessel Records Companies	Product Name	Region
AutoDataDirect, Inc	ADD123	FL
E-Merges.com	Boater Database (mix state & federal)	US
FlatRateInfo.com	US Merchant Vessels	US
KnowX	KnowX	US
LEXIS-NEXIS	USBoat	AL, AZ, AR, CO,CT,FL, GE, IA,ME,MD,MA,MS, MO,MN,MT,NE,NV,NH, NC,ND,OH,OR,SC,UT,VA, WV,WI
Merlin Information Services	National FlatRate, Collector's FlatRate	US
Motznik Computer Services Inc	Alaska Public Info. Access System	AK
National Marine Fisheries Service	Vessel Documentation Data	US
OPENonline (Online Prof. Elect. Network)	OPEN	US
Pallorium Inc	Skiptrace Amer., People Finder CDs	US
Research Archives.com Legal Docs. Library	Legal Documents Library	US
UCC Direct Services	Public Records Portal	US
US SEARCH.com	US Search	US
Virginia Information Providers Network	VIPNet	VA
Westlaw Public Records	Watercraft Locator	US

Vital Records

Vital Records Companies	Product Name	Region
Ameridex Information Systems	Death Index	US
Ancestry	SSN Death Index	US
Ancestry	Ancestry.com	US, Itl
Cambridge Statistical Research Associates	Death Master File	US
Daily Report, The	The Daily Report (Kern County Only)	CA
DCS Information Systems	Texas Systems (marriage/divorce)	TX
e-InfoData.com	QuickInfo.net	CO, NV, TX
Infocon Corporation	INFOCON County Access System-15 counties	PA
KnowX	KnoxX	US
KY Direct	Vital Statistics	KY
Merlin Information Services	Merlin Super Header, Collector's FlatRate, DOB File, Link to Amer., Nat'l FlatRate. QuikInfo.net	US
Merlin Information Services	CA Brides/Grooms, CA Birth/Death Indexes, Merlin Cross Directory	CA, US
MyFloridaCounty.com	Official Records Search	FL
Vital Records Information	vitalrec.com	US
VitalChek Network	VitalChek	US

Voter Registration

Voter Registration Records Companies	Product Name	Region
Accu-Source Inc.	Texas Voter Regisitration	TX
ARISTOTLE	GovernmentRecords.com	US
e-InfoData.com	QuickInfo.net	AK, AR, CO, DE, GA, KS, MI, NV, OH, OK, TX, UT
E-Merges.com	US Registered Voter File	AK,AR,CO,CT,DE,DC,FL, GA,IL,IN,IA,KS,LA,MA,MI, MN,MO,NV,NJ,NY,NC,OH, OK,RI,SC,TX,UT,VA,WI
Infocon Corporation	INFOCON County Access System-15 counties	PA
Merlin Information Services	Collector's FlatRate, Link to America, QuikInfo.net, Merlin Cross Directory	US
Motznik Computer Services Inc	Alaska Public Information Access System	AK
National Credit Information Network NCI	NCI Network	US
Pallorium Inc	Skiptrace Amer., People Finder CDs	US

Wills/Probate

Wills/Probate Records Companies	Product Name	Region
Daily Report, The	The Daily Report (Kern County Only)	CA
Electronic Property Information Corp (EPIC)	OPRA-Erie, Monroe Counties	NY

Workers Compensation

Workers Compensation Records Companies	Product Name	Region
ADP Screening and Selection Services	Workers Compensation History	IA, MD, MI, MS
Agency Records	20 yrs of Claims	FL
Industrial Foundation of America	Standard IFA Database	TX, OK, LA, NM
Information Network of Arkansas	INA	AR
Informus Corporation	Informus	MS
Tenstar Business Services Group	ACB-1	LA, MS
The Official Providers Source	Claims and Injury Reports	AR, FL, IA, IL, KS, MA, MD, ME, MI, MS, ND, NE, OH, OK, OR, TX
Trans Union Employment Screening Svcs	TransUnion	US

Companies Who Will Sell Their Database

Accutrend Data Corporation	www.accutrend.com
American Business Information	www.infousa.com
CompactData Solutions	www.emarqit.com
Conrad Grundlehner Inc	
CountryWatch Inc.	www.countrywatch.com
Dolan Information, Data Services Div	www.dolaninfo.com/
E-Merges.com	www.e-merges.com
Ernst Publishing Co, LLC	www.ernst.cc
Kompass USA Inc	www.kompass-intl.com
Merchants Security Exchange	www.merchants-fla.com
Metro Market Trends Inc	www.mmtinfo.com
Paragon Document Research, Inc.	www.banc.com/pdrstore
Plat System Services Inc	www.platsystems.com
Public Record Research Library	www.brbpub.com
Record Information Services Inc	www.public-record.com
San Diego Daily Transcript/San Diego Source	www.sddt.com
SKLD Information Services LLC	www.skld.com
Southeastern Public Records Inc.	www.publicrex.com
Utah.gov	www.utah.gov/

Vendor Profiles

Why These Vendors Appear in the Book

Obviously, there are many more public record vendors than the 200 firms appearing in this book. The reason these particular companies were chosen is because they provide either a **Proprietary Database** or offer a non-intervention **Gateway**. We call these vendors "**Distributor**s." There are plenty of excellent record vendors not listed in this book who most likely use these companies or government agencies as their primary source. We call these companies "**Search Firms**" (see page 69).

A Few Words About
Database Distributors and Gateways

Distributors are automated public record firms who combine public sources of bulk data and/or online access to develop their own database product(s). Primary Distributors include companies that collect or buy public record information from its original source and reformat the information in some useful way. They tend to focus on one or a limited number of types of information, although a few firms have branched into multiple information categories.

Gateways are companies that either compile data from or provide an automated gateway to Primary Distributors. Gateways thus provide "one-stop shopping" for multiple geographic areas and/or categories of information. A gateway company serves as a middleman for data, allowing you to link directly to the information through them - as one electronic transaction.

Companies can be both Primary Distributors and Gateways. For example, a number of online database companies are both primary distributors of corporate information and also gateways to real estate information from other Primary Distributors

How to Read & Use the Profiles

You can get a good sense a company's orientation by reviewing its profile.
Here are some tips:

- What are the Proprietary Products or Gateways provided by the company? Each entry for a company lists the name of the product; the information type according to the categories defined in the Information Index; and the geographic area in which the product is available.

- Are There Any Special Distribution Methods? We have indicated whether a company will sell its databases, offers CD-ROMs, sell its products via the Internet, etc. We have NOT indicated if the company will provide its services through traditional methods (by phone, mail or fax) as that is common practice for most firms.

- What are the Clientele Restrictions? Does the company permit casual (non-recurring) requesters? Is a signed agreement or contract required?

- What National Organizations does the company belong to? The organizations that the company belongs to, listed under Memberships, may indicate the nature and focus of their services and products.

- You should note that some products cover very specific geography (e.g., Motznick in Alaska) or specific information types (e.g., ARISTOTLE International) while others are sometimes vast conglomerations of various information types (e.g., ChoicePoint). You may want to use the same information in one or the other of these products depending upon the breadth or depth of your search requirements.

- Are there any other special characteristics of the company? Each company was invited to submit a short description of special capabilities. This Statement of Capabilities may mention a service or other detail that you are looking for, including for example the availability of an online ordering system.

> **Editor's Tip:** Visit www.publicrecordsources.com for updated information about these and other companies.

Also, additional companies that provide online record services exclusively from government entities are listed among the Government Online Sources by state in Section II pages 77-405.

Keep in Mind...

These profiles were developed from a questionnaire sent to each company. When necessary we completed the information about companies from our own knowledge where they failed to provide adequate details. We have tried to be as accurate as possible. We do not of course guarantee the complete accuracy of every profile. Companies can and do change products, and change coverage areas.

To help you determine which vendor is best suited to your needs, we recommend reviewing "10 Questions to Ask an Online Vendor" on pages 72-74 in the Public Records Primer Section.

555-1212.com

One Sarisome St, 39th Fl, San Francisco, Ca 94104
Phone: 415-288-2453; Fax: 415-288-2465
Web site: www.555-1212.com   **Email:** support@555-1212.com
Clientele Restrictions: None reported

Proprietary Databases or Gateways:
Gateway Name: **555-1212.com**
   Addresses/Telephone Numbers (US)

Special Distribution Methods to Client: Internet

A powerful, free access, web site. Search the white pages, yellow pages, phone reverse look-up, email reverse look-up, and the web site finder. This site ranks among the top 1000 sites on the web, visit-wise.

A.M. Best Company

Ambest Rd, Oldwick, NJ 08858-9988
Phone: 908-439-2200; Fax: 908-439-3296
Web site: www.ambest.com   **Email:** sales@ambest.com
Founded: 1899
Clientele Restrictions: Casual requesters permitted

Proprietary Databases or Gateways:
Database Name: **Best Database Services**
   SEC/Other Financial (US)

Database Name: **Best's Insight Global**
   Foreign Country Information (GB, International, Canada)

Special Distribution Methods to Client: CD-ROM, Disk, Magnetic Tape, Software

A.M. Best Company, known worldwide as The Insurance Information Source, was the first company to report on the financial condition of insurance companies. A.M. Best strives to perform a constructive and objective role in the insurance industry toward the prevention and detection of insurer solvency. The company's exclusive Best's Ratings are the original and most recognized insurer financial strength ratings. A.M. Best provides quantitative and qualitative evaluations, and offers information through more than 50 reference publications and services. Since its inception a century ago, A.M. Best has provided financial services to professionals with timely, accurate and comprehensive insurance information. A.M. Best's London office can be reached at 011-44-171-264-2260. A.M. Best International, also based in London, can be reached at 011-44-181-579-1091.

Access Indiana Information Network

10 W Market St #600, Indianapolis, IN 46204-2497
Toll-free phone: 800-236-5446; Phone: 317-233-2010; Fax: 317-233-2011
Web site: www.ai.org   **Email:** dnsadmin@ai.org
Founded: 1995   **Memberships:** NASIRE
Clientele Restrictions: Subscription required

Proprietary Databases or Gateways:
Gateway Name: **Premium Services**
   Driver and/or Vehicle, Corporate/Trade Name Data, Licenses/Registrations/Permits, Uniform Commercial Code,
      Litigation/Judgments/Tax Liens (IN)

Gateway Name: **Free Services**
   Legislation/Regulation (IN)

Special Distribution Methods to Client: Email, Internet

AIIN (or AccessIndiana) is a comprehensive, one-stop source for electronic access to State of Indiana government information. This network is owned by the state of Indiana. Access to the public records listed here requires a subscription fee and per-use fee. Specialties include drivers records, vehicle title and lien information, vehicle registration records, physician and nurse license verification, Secretary of State records (including UCC, lobbyist, and corporation information) and information on the Indiana General Assembly. See the Internet site for more information.

Access Louisiana Inc

400 Travis St #504, Shreveport, LA 71101
Toll-free phone: 800-489-5620; Phone: 318-227-9730; Fax: 318-222-3053   **Email:** debois41@aol.com
Founded: 1981   **Memberships:** NPRRA, NFPA, PRRN
Clientele Restrictions: None reported

Proprietary Databases or Gateways:
Gateway Name: **LA UCC**
  Uniform Commercial Code (LA)

Gateway Name: **LA Corporate Data**
  Corporate/Trade Name Data, Trademarks/Patents and Addresses/Telephone Numbers (LA)

Special Distribution Methods to Client:
Access Louisiana is a statewide legal research company with a physical presence in every Louisiana parish. Services include: public records (UCC, accounts, receivable, state/federal tax liens, suits, chattel mortgages, bankruptcy records), corporate filing/retrieval, court records and registered agent services. They have extensive knowledge of where information is recorded and how to effectively retrieve Louisiana public records.

Accurint

6601 Park of Commerce Blvd, Boca Raton, FL 33487
Toll-free phone: 888-332-8244; Phone: 561-999-4400; Fax: 561-893-8090
Web site: www.accurint.com/   **Email:** sales@accurint.com   **Parent Company:** Seisint, Inc.
Clientele Restrictions: Subscription required.

Proprietary Databases or Gateways:
Database Name: **Florida DL Search**
  Driver and/or Vehicle (FL)

Gateway Name: **FAA**
  Aviation (US)

Database Name: **UCC**
  Uniform Commercial Code (US)

Database Name: **Bankruptcy**
  Bankruptcy (US)

Database Name: **Business**
  Corporate/Trade Name Data (US)

Database Name: **Property Assessment**
  Real Estate/Assessor (US)

Database Name: **Tax Liens & Judgments**
  Litigation/Judgments/Tax Liens (US)
Database Name: **Persons**
  Addresses/Telephone Numbers (US)

Special Distribution Methods to Client: Internet
Accurint is a leading information management and technology company providing its customers with the accurate and complete information. Accurint's data stores contain billions of records that are searched, analyzed, and compiled in seconds. Because of our cutting-edge technology, we can conduct searches in an extremely cost-effective manner - batch and API services are also available. Accurint has access to over 20 billion records compiled from over 400 sources. Accurint can locate almost anyone, find deep background and historical information, and shorten research time and costs. Accurint provides aliases, historical addresses, relatives, associates, neighbors, assets, and more. Accurint is focused on helping collection agencies, companies with internal collections departments, lawyers, insurance professionals, law enforcement agencies, and corporations locate debtors, witnesses, suspects, and other persons critical to their work.

Accu-Source Inc.

8585 Stemmons #M26, Dallas, TX 75247
Phone: 214-231-2238; Fax: 214-637-1443
Web site: www.accu-source.com　　**Email:** as-sales@accu-source.com
Founded: 1990
Clientele Restrictions: Agreement required.
Proprietary Databases or Gateways:
Gateway Name: **Federal Bankruptcy Courts**
　Bankruptcy (AK, AR, AZ, CA, CO, FL, GA, HI, IA, ID, IL, IN, KS, KY, LA, MN, MO, NC, ND, NE, NM, NV, OK, OH, OR, SC, SD, TN, TX, UT, WA, WI, WY)
Gateway Name: **National Pilot Registration**
　Aviation (US)
Gateway Name: **Texas Voter Regisitration**
　Voter Registration (TX)
Special Distribution Methods to Client: Dial-Up (Other than Internet)
Accu-Source provides a wide variety of searches, both locally and nationally, including fast return of criminal records in key Texas, California, and Kansas counties. They provide online access to a variety of DMV, aviation, bankruptcy records, some real time. It's suggested to visit their web site for a listing of records and services.

Accutrend Data Corporation

6021 S Syracuse Wy #111, Denver, CO 80111
Phone: 303-488-0011; Fax: 303-488-0133
Web site: www.accutrend.com　　**Email:** info@accutrend.com
Founded: 1989　　**Memberships:** DMA
Clientele Restrictions: None reported
Proprietary Databases or Gateways:
Database Name: **New Business Database**
　Licenses/Registrations/Permits and Corporate/Trade Name Data (US)
Special Distribution Methods to Client: CD-ROM, Database, Disk, Email, FTP, Internet, Magnetic Tape
Accutrend Data compiles a new business database which each month adds 165,000 new business registrations, licenses and incorporations. Data is collected from all levels of government and is enhanced with demographic overlays.

ACS Inc

PO Box 4889, Syracuse, NY 13221
Phone: 315-437-1283; Fax: 315-437-3223
Web site: www.landaccess.com
Clientele Restrictions: Signed agreement required, must be ongoing account
Proprietary Databases or Gateways:
Gateway Name: **BRC**
　Real Estate/Assessor, Uniform Commercial Code (IL,NJ,NY)
Special Distribution Methods to Client: Dial-Up (Other than Internet)
ACS specializes in online access to Recorders, County Clerks and Registers across the country. Online access capabilities include OH counties, and also NJ, NY under landaccess.com. Fees are involved, except Ohio. Will be expanding to MI and PA in the near future.

ADP Screening and Selection Services

301 Remington St, Fort Collins, CO 80524
Toll-free phone: 800-367-5933; Phone: 970-484-7722; Fax: 970-221-1526
Web site: www.avert.com　　**Email:** avert-info@avert.com
Founded: 1986
Clientele Restrictions: Casual requesters permitted

Proprietary Databases or Gateways:

Database Name: **Workers Compensation History**
  Workers Compensation (IA, MD, MI, MS)

Gateway Name: **Credit & Name Link**
  Credit Information (US)

Gateway Name: **Driving Records**
  Driver Histories (US)

Special Distribution Methods to Client: Dial-Up (Other than Internet), Email

Formerly Avert Inc, ADP Screening and Selection Services provides pre-employment screening, job fit assessments and human resource solutions to clients nationwide. Combining innovative Internet technology and more than a decade of experience, ADP offers fast turnaround, current data and competitive pricing on background checking products including criminal court records, driving records, reference checks and more.

ADREM Profiles Inc

5461 W Waters Ave #900, Tampa, FL 33634
Toll-free phone: 800-281-1250; Phone: 813-890-0334
Web site: www.adpro.com   **Email:** adrem-sales@adpro.com
Founded: 1992   **Memberships:** SHRM, AIIP, PRRN, NPRRA, ASIS
Clientele Restrictions: Signed agreement required, must be ongoing account

Proprietary Databases or Gateways:

Gateway Name: **ADREM**
  Driver and/or Vehicle (US)

Special Distribution Methods to Client: Automated Telephone Look-Up, Dial-Up (Other than Internet), Email, FTP, Gateway via Another Online Service

ADREM Profiles is an international, full service public records research and retrieval company. Their comprehensive retrieval network allows access to information repositories within the 3,347 counties and independent cities throughout the United States. A staff of over 1,500 field researchers provides access to all counties within the US as well as to the Bahamas, Bermuda, Canada, the Caribbean and Europe. Utilizing ADREM's information ordering system, ADREM Advantage, research requests may be sent and retrieved securely and swiftly via the Net 24 hours a day, 7 days a week.

Agency Records

PO Box 310175, Newington, CT 06131
Toll-free phone: 800-777-6655; Phone: 860-667-1617; Fax: 860-666-4247
Web site: www.agencyrecords.com
Founded: 1972   **Memberships:** ARCO
Clientele Restrictions: Signed Agreement Required; Infrequent requesters permitted.

Proprietary Databases or Gateways:

Database Name: **CT Criminal Records, MN Court Convictions**
  Criminal Information (CT, MN)

Gateway Name: **ARI**
  Driver and/or Vehicle (US)

Database Name: **FL Workers Compensation Claims (20 years)**
  Workers Compensation (FL)

Special Distribution Methods to Client: Dial-Up (Other than Internet), Disk, Email, FTP, Gateway via Another Online Service, Internet, Magnetic Tape

Agency Records or ARI is a business to business provider of public record information. They offer nationwide retrieval of driving records with instant access to MVRs for FL, AL, SC, NC, WV, NJ, NY, CT, VA, MS, NH, and ME. They also provide instant access to court convictions for Connecticut and Minnesota. They offer computer, fax and phone ordering as well as volume discounts. Public companies may be invoiced.

Alacourt.com

PO Box 8173, Mobile, AL 36689
Toll-free phone: 877-799-9898; Phone: 334-633-5484
Web site: www.alacourt.com   **Email:** info@alacourt.com
Founded: 1990   **Parent Company:** On-Line Information Services, Inc
Clientele Restrictions: Subscription required

Proprietary Databases or Gateways:
Gateway Name: **Alacourt.com**
  Litigation/Judgments/Tax Liens, Criminal Information (AL)

Special Distribution Methods to Client: Email, Internet

Alacourt.com is an Internet-browser driven way to access the Alabama Trial Court records. All currently active cases are maintained in the system as are disposed cases, some going back as far as the late 1970's. The courts included are civil circuit and district courts, criminal cases in circuit and district courts, domestic relations & child support, traffic, and small claims. The system includes outstanding alias warrants, trial court dockets, attorney case information, and other features. Search results include case summaries, party & attorney names, dockets, judgments, claims, creditors, and charges.

American Business Information

PO Box 27347, Omaha, NE 68127
Toll-free phone: 800-555-5335; Phone: 402-930-3500; Fax: 402-331-0176
Web site: www.infousa.com   **Parent Company:** InfoUSA Inc   **Memberships:** ALA, DMA, SIIA, NACM, SLA
Clientele Restrictions: Casual requesters permitted

Proprietary Databases or Gateways:
Database Name: **Business Sales Leads**
  Addresses/Telephone Numbers, Credit Information, Foreign Country Information, News/Current Events and
     SEC/Other Financial (US)
Database Name: **Consumer Sales Leads**
  Addresses/Telephone Numbers, Credit Information, Driver and/or Vehicle, Genealogical Information and Real
     Estate/Assessor (US)

Special Distribution Methods to Client: CD-ROM, Database, Dial-Up (Other than Internet), Disk, Gateway via Another Online Service, Internet, Lists/Labels, Magnetic Tape, Publication/Directory, Software

American Business Information, a division of InfoUSA, compiles business information from telephone directories and other public sources. Over the past 20+ years, they have provided services to over 2 million customers. They telephone verify every name in their database before they offer it for sale. They phone-verify address changes from the USPS NCOA. In addition, the provide business credit reports. Their info is available in a variety of ways including online (SalesLeadsUSA.com), CD-ROM, and by telephone (Directory Assistance Plus). A division produces the Pro-CD Disk and another operates Digital Directory Assistance. For business leads call 800-555-5335. For SalesLeads USA call 402-592-9000.

American Driving Records

PO Box 1970, Rancho Cordova, CA 95741-1970
Toll-free phone: 800-766-6877; Phone: 916-456-3200; Fax: 916-456-3332
Web site: www.mvrs.com   **Email:** sales@mvrs.com
Founded: 1986
Clientele Restrictions: Signed agreement required, must be ongoing account

Proprietary Databases or Gateways:
Gateway Name: **ADR**
  Driver and/or Vehicle (US)

Special Distribution Methods to Client: Dial-Up (Other than Internet), Internet

American Driving Record (ADR) services include accessing driving records and registration information. Also, they provide special processing for the insurance industry with such products as automatic checking (ACH), calculating underwriting points, and ZapApp(tm) - an automated insurance application from the agency to the carrier. Driving records can be instant, same day or overnight, depending on the state.

Ameridex Information Systems

PO Box 51314, Irvine, CA 92619-1314
Phone: 714-731-2546; Fax: 714-731-1320
Web site: www.ameridex.com   **Email:** info@ameridex.com
Founded: 1988
Clientele Restrictions: Registration required, must be ongoing account
Proprietary Databases or Gateways:
Database Name: **Live Index**
  Addresses/Telephone Numbers (US)
Database Name: **Military**
  Military Service (US)
Database Name: **Death Index**
  Vital Records, DOB/DEATH/SSN (US)
Special Distribution Methods to Client: Dial-Up (Other than Internet)
Ameridex presents several unique databases for people tracing on the Internet. Over 260 million names and 230 million with a date of birth are compiled from multiple public record sources. Speciality databases include a nationwide death index with supplements, active military personnel database, & vital records (birth, marriage, divorce) for several states.

Ancestry

266 W Center St, Orem, UT 84057
Phone: 801-431-5220
Web site: http://ancestry.com   **Parent Company:** MyFamily.com
Clientele Restrictions: Premium services require subscription
Proprietary Databases or Gateways:
Database Name: **Ancestry.com**
  Vital Records, Foreign Country Information (US, International)
Database Name: **SSN Death Index**
  Vital Records (US)
Special Distribution Methods to Client: Internet
Ancestry.com is one of the leading Family History genealogy web sites. Over 600 million records can be searched from literally thousands of databases. One may search by record type, or locality. Many free searches are available, to access the entrie system, a subscription is required. An editor's choice site.

ARCountyData.com - Apprentice Information Systems

900 N Dixieland, #102, Rogers, AR 72756
Phone: 501-631-8054; Fax: 501-631-9291
Web site: www.arcountydata.com   **Email:** support@apprenticeis.com
Founded: 1989
Clientele Restrictions: Subscription-based service.
Proprietary Databases or Gateways:
Gateway Name: **Arkansas County Assessor Records**
Arkansas County Assessor Records
  Real Estate/Assessor (AR)
Special Distribution Methods to Client: Internet
ARCountyData.com provides access to county assessor records in 16 Arkansas counties, with more scheduled to come online in the future. Access is charged by the minute; online registration and credit cards accepted.

ARISTOTLE International

205 Pennsylvania Ave SE, Washington, DC 20003
Toll-free phone: 800-296-2747; Phone: 202-543-8345; Fax: 202-543-6407
Web site: www.aristotle.com   **Email:** sales@aristotle.org
Branch Offices: San Francisco, CA, 415-440-1012; Fax: 415-440-2162; **Atlanta**, GA, 404-352-9917; Fax: 404-352-5757
Founded: 1983
Clientele Restrictions: Access to government records.com databases is restricted to law enforcement and news agencies

Proprietary Databases or Gateways:
Database Name: **ARISTOTLE**
  Addresses/Telephone Numbers (US)

Database Name: **GovernmentRecords.com**
  Voter Registration (US)

Special Distribution Methods to Client: CD-ROM, Internet, Magnetic Tape

Their GovernmentRecords.com is a comprehensive file of registered voters, licenses drivers or government identification card holders residing in 38 nations, including the United States. Information is obtained directly from government agencies at the federal, state or municipal level at 3,400 locations. The US information is standardized and enhanced with listed phone number, postal correction and national change of address, census geography, and age and is subject to laws governing access and use of driver license information (DPPA) or registered voter information. Access to the GovernmentRecords.com databases is restricted to government, law enforcement and accredited news orgs only.

Attorneys Title Insurance Fund

PO Box 628600, Orlando, FL 32862
Toll-free phone: 800-336-3863; Phone: 407-240-3863; Fax: 407-888-2592
Web site: www.thefund.com
Founded: 1948   **Memberships:** ALTA, REIPA
Clientele Restrictions: Signed agreement required, must be ongoing account; however, certain products are released to one-time clients

Proprietary Databases or Gateways:
Database Name: **Online Data Service**
  Real Estate/Assessor, Litigation/Judgments/Tax Liens (FL-40 counties)

Special Distribution Methods to Client: Dial-Up (Other than Internet), Disk, Email, FTP, Magnetic Tape

Although the primary business of The Fund (as they are called) is to issue title insurance, they offer access to over 100 million real estate records from 40 major counties in FL. The Fund has 15 branch offices as well as operations in SC and IL. Online users can access public records including mortgages, deeds, liens, assessments, right-of-way data, and even judgment and divorce proceedings.

Aurigin Systems Inc.

10710 N Tantau Ave, Cupertino, CA 95014
Phone: 408-873-8400; Fax: 408-257-9133
Web site: www.aurigin.com   **Email:** jross@aurigin.com
Branch Offices: Princeton, NJ, 609-734-4300; Fax: 609-734-4352
Founded: 1992   **Memberships:** AIPLA, ABA, LES
Clientele Restrictions: None reported

Proprietary Databases or Gateways:
Database Name: **Aurigin**
  Patents (US, International)

Special Distribution Methods to Client: Dial-Up (Other than Internet), Software

Aurigin, formally known as SmartPatents Inc, offers the Aurigin Aureka® System to manage a company's intellectual and innovation assets. Other important products are Aurigin Electronic Patents, indexed patents from the US Patent and Trademark Office, and the Aurigin Workbench, a desktop software application.

AutoDataDirect, Inc

2940 E. Park Ave #B, Tallahassee, FL 32301-3427
Phone: 850-877-8804
Web site: www.add123.com   **Email:** jtaylor@add123.com
Founded: 1999
Clientele Restrictions: Signed agreement required

Proprietary Databases or Gateways:
Gateway Name: **ADD123**
  Driver and/or Vehicle, Vessels (FL)

Special Distribution Methods to Client: Internet

AutoDataDirect provides real time access to Florida motor vehicle, vessel and driver's license records. ADD's services are not available to individuals, but companies with a permissible use of personal information as described in the Federal Driver's Privacy Protection Act of 1994 are eligible for ADD's service. To determine if you are eligible to receive the vehicle records, please read the Federal Driver's Privacy Protection Act of 1994 which can be found at their web site.

Avantex Inc

340 Morgantown Road, Reading, PA 19611
Toll-free phone: 800-998-8857; Phone: 610-796-2385; Fax: 610-796-2392
Web site: www.avantext.com   **Email:** dara@avantex.com
Founded: 1992
Clientele Restrictions: None reported

Proprietary Databases or Gateways:
Database Name: **FAA Data**
  Aviation, Addresses/Telephone Numbers, Legislation/Regulations (US)

Special Distribution Methods to Client: CD-ROM, Internet

Avantext product line includes a line of powerful CDs for the aviation industry. The Aircraft and Airman CD includes a full listing of pilots and aircraft owners, schools, technicians, dealers and much more.

Background Information Services Inc

1800 30th St #213, Boulder, CO 80301
Toll-free phone: 800-433-6010; Phone: 303-442-3960; Fax: 303-442-1004
Web site: www.bisi.com   **Email:** dawn@bisi.com
Founded: 1988   **Memberships:** ASIS, NHRA
Clientele Restrictions: Agreement required

Proprietary Databases or Gateways:
Database Name: **Criminal**
  Criminal Information, Credit Information (CO, OK, US)

Gateway Name: **Filings**
  Corporation/Trade Name Data (CO)

Gateway Name: **UCC**
  Uniform Commercial Code (CO)

Special Distribution Methods to Client: Dial-Up (Other than Internet), Email, Internet

Background Information Services (BIS) is a nationwide public records provider specializing in pre-employment and tenant screening. BIS owns and maintains databases containing criminal and civil records, especially for Colorado and Oklahoma. Also serves as a gateway for Colorado Secretary of State, Department of Revenue and UCC Filings. Created in cooperation with state agencies, database information is received electronically from the courts. BIS allows online access to this information with instantaneous results. Nationwide services that BIS offers include civil, criminal, motor vehicle driving reports, Workers compensation claims, credit histories, federal records and UCC filings. BIS is a technologically advanced company offering dial-up or telnet access to database information and ordering screens. Orders can be placed on a secured Internet site that can be tailored to the company's needs.

Banko

100 S. 5th St #300, Minneapolis, MN 55402
Toll-free phone: 800-533-8897; Phone: 612-332-2427; Fax: 612-215-7498
Web site: www.banko.com   **Email:** sales@dolaninformaion.com
Branch Offices: San Diego, CA
Founded: 1987   **Parent Company:** Dolan Information   **Memberships:** ACA, ICA, MBA, DBA
Clientele Restrictions: Casual requesters not permitted; subscription for online searches is available
Proprietary Databases or Gateways:
Database Name: **BANKO**
   Bankruptcy, Litigation/Judgments/Tax Liens (US)

Database Name: **ACOLLAID**
   Addresses/Telephone Numbers (US)

Special Distribution Methods to Client: CD-ROM, Dial-Up (Other than Internet), Disk, Internet, Lists/Labels, Magnetic Tape
Dolan Information is a leading provider of public record information and record retrieval services for bankruptcies, civil judgments, tax liens, and deceased information. Receive electronic notification for bankruptcy and deceased through BANKO's batch process or login to www.banko.com for individual searches and nationwide access to bankruptcy dockets/documents. For more information call 800-533-8897 or email them at sales@dolaninformation.com

Banko Document Retrieval (BDR)

350 W. Ash St #602, San Diego, CA 92101
Toll-free phone: 800-969-2377; Phone: 619-232-9999; Fax: 619-232-9998
Web site: www.bkauthority.com/   **Email:** pat.cline@dolaninformation.com
Branch Offices: Minneapolis, MN, 612-332-2427
Founded: 1989   **Parent Company:** Dolan Media Inc   **Memberships:** MBA, USFN, ABI
Clientele Restrictions: Casual requesters permitted
Proprietary Databases or Gateways:
Database Name: **BANKO**
   Bankruptcy (US)

Special Distribution Methods to Client: Dial-Up (Other than Internet), Disk, Internet, Lists/Labels
Banko Document Retrieval provides a single resource in obtaining copies of documents from bankruptcy files nationwide. They cover both federal courts and federal record centers. BDR has an online ordering system and a customized case monitoring system.

Better Business Bureau

4200 Wilson Blvd # 800, Arlington, VA 22203-1838
Phone: 703-276-0100; Fax: 703-525-8277
Web site: www.bbb.org
Clientele Restrictions: Agreement Required to Join
Proprietary Databases or Gateways:
Gateway Name: **Business Report**
   Corporate/Trade Name Data (US)

Special Distribution Methods to Client: Dial-Up (Other than Internet), Email, Internet
Business Reports are created and maintained by the BBB office where the business is located. Information reported includes time in business, complaint history, and information obtained through special Bureau investigations. Bureaus also have the option of reporting whether companies are Bureau members, or participate in any special Bureau programs, such as Alternative Dispute Resolution or BBBOnLine®. For additional information about the BBB reporting process, visit the BBB Help Desk online. If you desire a report from a BBB office that does not appear online, contact the office directly and request a verbal or printed copy of the report.

BNA, Inc (Bureau of National Affairs)

1231 25th Street, NW, Washington, MD 20037
Toll-free phone: 800-372-1033; Phone: 202-452-4200
Web site: http://web.bna.com   **Email:** icustrel@bna.com
Branch Offices: Rockville, MD, 800-372-1033; Fax: 800-253-0332
Founded: 1929
Clientele Restrictions: Must be ongoing account

Proprietary Databases or Gateways:
Gateway Name: **Intl Trade Daily, WTO Reporter**
  Legislation/Regulation, Foreign Country Information (International)
Gateway Name: **Environment & Safety Library on the Web**
Environment & Safety Library on the Web
  Environmental (US)
Gateway Name: **Class Action Litigation Report**
  Litigation/Judgments/Tax Liens (US)
Gateway Name: **Corporate Law Daily**
  Corporate/Trade Name Data (US)
Special Distribution Methods to Client: Email, Internet, Publication/Directory

BNA is a leading publisher of print and electronic news and information, reporting on developments in health care, business, labor relations, law, economics, taxation, environmental protection, safety, and other public policy and regulatory issues. Its Class Action Litigation Report covers the most important developments in class action and multiparty litigation, in all subject areas. It monitors hard-to-find, significant litigation news acress all subject areas, including antitrust, consumer, employment, health care, mass torts, products and securities. The Report's timely notification is supplemented by analysis and practice pointers by outside experts and attorneys. Visit www.bna.com/new/ for additional products.

Burrelles Information Services

75 East Northfield Rd, Livingston, NJ 07039
Toll-free phone: 800-631-1160; Phone: 973-992-6600
Web site: www.burrelles.com   **Email:** info@burrelles.com
Clientele Restrictions: None reported

Proprietary Databases or Gateways:
Database Name: **BIO**
  News/Current Events (US, International)
Special Distribution Methods to Client: CD-ROM, Dial-Up (Other than Internet), Publication/Directory

For over 100 years Burrelle's has been monitoring, organizing, and delivering media data to clients. Products include Press Clipping, NewsExpress, NewsAlert, Media Direcories, Broadcast Transcripts, and Web Clips. The BIO - Burrelle's Information Office - is software to receive and use information from Burrelle's.

Cal Info

316 W 2nd St #102, Los Angeles, CA 90012
Phone: 213-687-8710; Fax: 213-687-8778
Web site: www.calinfo.net   **Email:** admin@calinfo.net
Branch Offices: Washington, DC, 202-667-9679; Fax: 202-967-9605
Founded: 1986   **Memberships:** AIIP, AALL
Clientele Restrictions: None reported

Proprietary Databases or Gateways:
Database Name: **Guide to State Statutes; Administrative Guide to State Regulations**
  Legislation/Regulation (State Statutes) (US)
Special Distribution Methods to Client: Email, Publication/Directory

Cal Info offers an information research and retrieval service that finds answers to questions that affect law firms and businesses every day. Their personnel are trained to search computerized databases as well as the more traditional information sources, including libraries, publishers, government agencies, courts, trade unions and associations. They provide company reports, financial data, product information, people information, journals and news stories, real estate information, legal research, public records research, government information and document retrieval.

Cambridge Statistical Research Associates

53 Wellesley, Irvine, CA 92612
Toll-free phone: 800-327-2772; Phone: 949-250-8579; Fax: 949-250-8591
Web site: www.csrainc.com/ **Email:** csrainc@csrainc.com
Founded: 1988
Clientele Restrictions: Must be ongoing account
Proprietary Databases or Gateways:
Database Name: **Death Master File**
 Vital Records (US)
Special Distribution Methods to Client: CD-ROM, Dial-Up (Other than Internet)
CSRA traces its origin to an actuarial and programming service established in 1979. In recent years, its efforts moved toward bringing large mainframe databases to the desktop computing platform, including CD-ROM. CSRA specializes in nationwide death index by name and Social Security Number, death auditing service, database consulting, genealogical and probate research, and address trace service.

Campus Direct

One Plymouth Meeting, #610, Plymought Meeting, PA 19462
Toll-free phone: 800-889-4249
Web site: www.campusdirect.com **Email:** sales@campusdirect.com
Founded: 1990 **Parent Company:** Student Advantage Inc
Clientele Restrictions: Registration required.
Proprietary Databases or Gateways:
Database Name: **Campus Direct**
 Education/Employment (US)
Special Distribution Methods to Client: Internet
Student Advantage's Campus Direct® division is one of the nation's premier outsource provider of student information services to colleges and universities. Search the client schools list at the web site. Client schools utilize Campus Direct® as a means by which to provide particular services or as a coexisting backup system where services such as transcript fulfillment are already provided in-house. Campus Direct's knowledgeable staff and state-of-the-art Internet and telephone technologies enable colleges and universities to provide superior service for students and information requesters.

Canadian Law Book Inc

240 Edward St, Aurora, Ontario, CD L4G 3S9
Toll-free phone: 800-263-3269; Phone: 905-841-6472; Fax: 905-841-5085
Web site: www.canadalawbook.ca/ **Email:** bloney@canadalawbook.ca
Branch Offices: Vancouver, BC, 604-844-7855; Fax: 604-844-7813
Founded: 1855
Proprietary Databases or Gateways:
Gateway Name: **Canada Statute Service**
 Legislation/Regulation (Canada)
Gateway Name: **Canadian Patent Reporter**
 Patents (Canada)
Gateway Name: **Caselaw on Call**
 Litigation/Judgments/Tax Liens (Canada)
Special Distribution Methods to Client: Automated Telephone Look-Up, CD-ROM, Internet, Publication/Directory, Software

In Canada, dial 800-263-2037. Canada Law Book resources have expanded to encompass a broad collection of material from leading experts in the legal profession. They're empowered with the latest technological tools to enhance the delivery of the content. Get exactly the information you need, in the manner that suits you best.

Capitol Lien Records & Research Inc

1010 N Dale, St Paul, MN 55117
Toll-free phone: 800-845-4077; Phone: 651-488-0100; Fax: 651-488-0200
Web site: www.capitollien.com/clrridefault.asp   **Email:** tony@capitollien.com
Founded: 1990   **Memberships:** PRRN, NPRRA
Clientele Restrictions: Casual requesters permitted

Proprietary Databases or Gateways:
Gateway Name: **UCC**
   Uniform Commercial Code (MN)

Special Distribution Methods to Client: CD-ROM, Disk, Email, Internet, Magnetic Tape, Software

Capitol Lien Records & Research provides UCC, federal and state tax lien searches, real estate searches, document retrievals, bankruptcy searches, judgment searches, corporate documents, a weekly tax lien report, environmental lien searches, Phase 1, 2 and 3 environmental searches, watercraft, and aircraft and vessel searches. An online ordering system accepting credit cards is provided to clients. They offer online UCC filing for all 50 states.

Carfax

10304 Eaton Place, #500, Fairfax, VA 22030
Phone: 703-934-2664; Fax: 703-218-2465
Web site: www.carfaxonline.com   **Email:** subscribe@carfax.com
Founded: 1986   **Parent Company:** R.L. Polk   **Memberships:** AAMVA, DMA
Clientele Restrictions: Casual requesters permitted

Proprietary Databases or Gateways:
Database Name: **Vehicle History Service, Motor Vehicle Title Information**
   Driver and/or Vehicle (US)

Database Name: **VINde (VIN Validity Check Program)**
   Software/Training (US)

Special Distribution Methods to Client: Dial-Up (Other than Internet), Disk, Internet

With the largest online vehicle history database (over one billion records), Carfax can generate a Vehicle History Report based on a VIN in less than one second. They collect data from a variety of sources including state DMVs and salvage pools. Reports include details from previous titles, city and state, odometer rollbacks, junk and flood damage, etc, reducing the risk of handling used vehicles with hidden problems that affect their value. Reports do not contain personal information on current or previous owners.

Case Record Info Services

33895 Cape Cove, Dana Point, CA 92629
Phone: 949-248-5860 **Email:** jeancris@aol.com
Founded: 1994
Clientele Restrictions: Casual requesters permitted

Proprietary Databases or Gateways:
Database Name: **Judgment Lists**
   Litigation/Judgments/Tax Liens (CA)

Special Distribution Methods to Client: Dial-Up (Other than Internet), Disk, Internet, Lists/Labels

Case Record Info Services provides judgment lists in California. Their data is used by bulk data providers, collection and mediation companies. They are also members of the American Arbitration Association. Note: The telephone number is to the residence of the principal.

CaseClerk.com

PO Box 1519, Dandridge, TN 37725
Phone: 865-387-7900; Fax: 865-397-5900
Web site: www.caseclerk.com/search/default.htm　　**Email:** sales@caseclerk.com
Founded: 1999
Clientele Restrictions: None reported
Proprietary Databases or Gateways:
Gateway Name: **Courtclerk.com**
  Bankruptcy, Criminal Information, Litigation/Judgments/Tax Liens (TN)

Gateway Name: **Caseclerk.com**
  Legislation/Regulation, Bankruptcy, Criminal Information, Litigation/Judgments/Tax Liens (US)

Special Distribution Methods to Client: Internet

By offering case law and legal research (nationwide), Bankruptcy, Criminal Information, Litigation/Judgments/Tax Liens (TN) CaseClerk.com serves as a gateway for case law and legal research. Cases back to 1900, cases, codes, statutes, local and federal rules, local and federal forms, court calendars, and contact information. Access is by subscription on a daily, monthly, or yearly basis.

CaseStream.com

See Courtlink

CaseStream products include; Alert! which notifies you each day of activity in federal civil cases of interest to you; Historical which gives legal research on similar cases before the same federal judge; Docket Direct provides a fast and efficient means to retrieve federal civil or criminal docket on demand; and Delaware Chancery which provides a fully searchable database of the dockets in the Delaware Court of Chancery.

CCH Washington Service Bureau

1015 15th St NW, #1000, Washington, DC 20005
Toll-free phone: 800-955-5219; Phone: 202-312-6602; Fax: 202-962-0152
Web site: www.wsb.com　　**Email:** custserv@wsb.com
Founded: 1967　　**Parent Company:** Wolters Klower US
Clientele Restrictions: Casual requesters permitted.
Proprietary Databases or Gateways:
Database Name: **SECnet**
  SEC/Other Financial, Bankrupcy (US)

Special Distribution Methods to Client: Internet, Microfilm/Microfiche, Publication/Directory

CCH Washington Service Bureau, has been serving the information needs of lawyers, corporate executives, brokers, accountants, and government officials since its inception in 1967. The company offers a number of products and services in a variety of practice areas to the legal and business professional. CCH Washington Service Bureau provides expedited information retrieval on filings made with the Securities and Exchange Commission. A pioneer in the area of "sample" securities research, our experienced research staff uses in-house proprietary databases and a library of SEC filings dating back to 1979 to fulfill the most difficult research request. CCH Washington Service Bureau offers watch services which are tailored by the individual needs of each client. We also offer "filex" services, enabling clients to file documents with federal regulatory agencies.

ChoicePoint Inc

1000 Alderman Dr, Alpharetta, GA 30005
Phone: 770-752-6000; Fax: 770-752-6005
Web site: www.choicepointinc.com
Founded: 1997　　**Memberships:** AALL, ABI, ASIS
Clientele Restrictions: Signed agreement required, must be ongoing account

Proprietary Databases or Gateways:

Database Name: **Legal Information**
   Bankruptcy, Corporation/Trade Name Data, Criminal Information, Litigation/Judgments/Tax Liens, Uniform
      Commercial Code (US)

Database Name: **Real Property**
   Real Estate/Assessor (US)

Database Name: **Consumer Services**
   Addresses/Telephone Numbers ()

Database Name: **Insurance Services**
   Driver and/or Vehicle (US)

Database Name: **Information Services**
   Licenses/Registrations/Permits (Physicians) (US)

Special Distribution Methods to Client: Dial-Up (Other than Internet)

ChoicePoint is a leading provider of intelligence information to help businesses, governments, and individuals to better understand with whom they do business. ChoicePoint services the risk management information needs of the property and casualty insurance market, the life and health insurance market, and business and government, including asset-based lenders and professional service providers. The company, with many branch offices nationwide, was spun off from Equifax in 1997. They offer a variety of useful online products.

ChoicePoint, formerly CDB Infotek

6 Hutton Centre Dr #600, Santa Ana, CA 92707
Toll-free phone: 800-427-3747; Phone: 714-708-2000; Fax: 714-708-1000
Web site: www.choicepointonline.com/cdb/   **Email:** tony.mears@choicepointinc.com
Founded: 1997   **Memberships:** SIIA, NALV, NPRRA, ASIS, ACA, IRSG
Clientele Restrictions: Signed agreement required, must be ongoing account

Proprietary Databases or Gateways:

Database Name: **Real Property Ownership & Transfers**
   Real Estate/Assessor (US)

Database Name: **Corporate & Limited Partnerships**
   Corporate/Trade Name Data (US)

Database Name: **Uniform Commercial Code**
   Uniform Commerical Code (US)

Database Name: **Legal Information**
   Bankruptcy and Litigation/Judgments/Tax Liens (US)

Database Name: **Address Inspector**
   Addresses/Telephone Numbers (US)

Special Distribution Methods to Client: Dial-Up (Other than Internet), Internet

ChoicePoint (CDB Infotek) offers nationwide public records information, including instant access to more than 4 billion records and 1,600 targeted databases to efficiently locate people or businesses, conduct background research, identify assets, control fraud, conduct due diligence, etc. Subscribers learn search strategies at free, year-round seminars and have toll-free access to customer service representatives for help. ChoicePoint also offers direct marketing lists, monitoring services, hard copy document retrieval and high-volume processing services.

ChoicePoint, formerly DBT Online Inc

4530 Blue Lake Dr, Boca Raton, FL 33431
Toll-free phone: 800-279-7710; Phone: 561-982-5000; Fax: 561-982-5872
Web site: www.dbtonline.com
Founded: 1992   **Parent Company:** DBT Online Inc
Clientele Restrictions: License required, must be ongoing account

Proprietary Databases or Gateways:
Database Name: **AutoTrackXP**

Addresses/Telephone Numbers, Real Estate/Assessor, Corporate/Trade Name Data (US)

Gateway Name: **AutoTrackXP**
   Driver and/or Vehicle (US)

Special Distribution Methods to Client: Dial-Up (Other than Internet), Internet

ChoicePoint (DBT Online) offers nationwide public records information, including instant access to more than 4 billion records and 1,600 targeted databases to efficiently locate people or businesses, conduct background research, identify assets, control fraud, conduct due diligence, etc. Subscribers learn search strategies at free, year-round seminars and have toll-free access to customer service representatives for help. ChoicePoint also offers direct marketing lists, monitoring services, hard copy document retrieval and high-volume processing services.

Circuit Express

1200 Bigley Ave., Charleston, WV 25302
Toll-free phone: 800-795-8543; Phone: 304-343-6480; Fax: 304-343-6489
Web site: www.swcg-inc.com   **Email:** info@swcg-inc.com
Founded: 1975   **Parent Company:** Software Computer Group Inc.
Clientele Restrictions: Registration required.

Proprietary Databases or Gateways:
Database Name: **Circuit Express, Magistrate Express**
   Criminal Information, Litigation/Judgments/Tax Liens (WV)

Special Distribution Methods to Client: Internet

Circuit Express is the contract computer access provider of civil and criminal courts records for the West Virginia counties of Kanawha, Putnam, Hancock, Ohio and Mineral, also Nicholas County, Ohio. They also offer Magistrate Court records for 6 circuits, however this is limited to government agency use only.

CoCourts.com

1033 Walnut St #300, Boulder, CO 80302
Toll-free phone: 866-262-6878; Phone: 303-381-2273; Fax: 303-381-2279
Web site: www.cocourts.com   **Email:** info@cocourts.com
Founded: 2000
Clientele Restrictions: Casual requesters permitted

Proprietary Databases or Gateways:
Database Name: **Colorado Courts Information**
   Criminal Information, Litigation/Judgments/Tax Lien (CO)

Special Distribution Methods to Client: Internet

CoCourts.com is a real-time statewide court records site built specifically for the web. It is the official public-access site for records maintained by the Colorado Judicial Department. In addition to those listed above, other applications include collections, employment screening, and tenant screening.

Commercial Information Systems Inc

PO Box 69174, (4747 SW Kelly #110), Portland, OR 97201-0174
Toll-free phone: 800-454-6575; Phone: 503-222-7422; Fax: 503-222-7405
Web site: www.cis-usa.com   **Email:** cis@cis-usa.com
Founded: 1991   **Parent Company:** Openonline LLC   **Memberships:** SIIA, NACM, NALI
Clientele Restrictions: Casual requesters permitted

Proprietary Databases or Gateways:
Database Name: **Aircraft Registrations**
   Aviation (US)

Database Name: **UCCs**
   Uniform Commercial Code (CA, ID, OR, WA)

Database Name: **Corporations & Limited Partnerships**
   Corporate/Trade Name Data (CA, ID, OR, WA)

Database Name: **Professional Licenses**
  Licenses/Registrations/Permits (ID, OR, WA)

Database Name: **Real Estate Records**
  Real Estate/Assessor (ID, NV, OR, WA)

Gateway Name: **Criminal & Civil Records**
  Criminal Information,Litigation/Judgments/Tax Liens (ID, OR, WA, CA)

Database Name: **Fish & Wildlife Records**
  Licenses/Registrations/Permits (ID, OR, NV)

Gateway Name: **Driver's License & Registration**
  Driver and/or Vehicle (ID, OR)

Database Name: **Hazardous Materials**
  Environmental (OR, WA)

Special Distribution Methods to Client: Dial-Up (Other than Internet), Internet

Commercial Information Systems (CIS) is an online/on-site database of public records serving business and government entities. They provide direct access to selected public and private database records on a national level through special gateway relationships - for example, gateway access to OJIN (Oregon) and JIS (Washington) court records. The CIS integrated regional database aggregates, commingles and cross-matches records at the state level by name, address, city, state, ZIP Code, birth date, driver's license, vehicle plates and other identifiers with a search engine that allows a subscriber to return all related records on a common identifier. CIS also provides information on a manual retrieval basis, including credit bureau products and services as well as special data mining capabilities tailored to a clients' specific research or volume searching needs.

CompactData Solutions

2800 W Mockingbird, Dallas, TX 75235
Toll-free phone: 800-935-9093; Phone: 214-956-6300; Fax: 214-956-6350
Web site: www.emarqit.com   **Email:** sales@nationsdata.com
Founded: 1993
Clientele Restrictions: Agreement is required.

Proprietary Databases or Gateways:
DB Name: **EMarQit**
  Addresses/Telephone Numbers, Real Estate/Assessor (TX)

DB Name: **QuikList**
  Driver and/or Vehicle (TX, FL, OH)

GT Name: **NationsData.com**
  Uniform Commercial Code (TX)

Special Distribution Methods to Client: CD-ROM, Database, Gateway via Another Online Service, Internet

First created in 1993 as a CD-rom product, CompactData Solutions now offers Internet access to its data, which is based on appraisal district, and enhanced with address standardization, telephone numbers, historical values of property, owner birthdates, geocoding, US Census Data. Available on a subscription or charge-per-record basis as downloadable file in popular formats, display or Word format mailing labels. CASS Certification and other value-added features also available.

Companies Online - Lycos

400-2 Totten Pond Road, Waltham, MA 02451
Phone: 781-370-2700; Fax: 781-370-3412
Web site: www.companiesonline.com
Founded: 1995   **Parent Company:** Lycos, Inc.

Proprietary Databases or Gateways:
Gateway Name: **companiesonline.com**
  Corporate/Trade Name Data (US)

Special Distribution Methods to Client: Internet

Excellent Internet site with free searching on over 900,000 public and private companies. This is a partnership of Lycos and Dun & Bradstreet, using information from the latter.

Confi-Chek

1816 19th St, Sacramento, CA 95814
Toll-free phone: 800-821-7404; Phone: 916-443-4822; Fax: 916-443-7420
Web site: www.confi-chek.com   **Email:** support@confi-chek.com
Founded: 1988
Clientele Restrictions: Must be ongoing account

Proprietary Databases or Gateways:
Database Name: **Confi-Chek Online**
   Criminal History (CA-14 counties)

Special Distribution Methods to Client: Dial-Up (Other than Internet), Internet
Confi-Check provides instant access to national and local records throughout the US. They also offer asset services. Their web site offers access to almost all state records. Dial-up, and, fax call-in services are also available.

Conrad Grundlehner Inc

8605 Brook Rd, McLean, VA 22102-1504
Phone: 703-506-9648; Fax: 703-506-9580
Founded: 1984   **Memberships:** SIIA, NPRRA
Clientele Restrictions: License required

Proprietary Databases or Gateways:
Database Name: **Conrad Grundlehner**
   Bankruptcy, Litigation/Judgments/Tax Liens (DC, MD, NC, VA, WV)

Special Distribution Methods to Client: Database, Dial-Up (Other than Internet), FTP, Magnetic Tape
Conrad Grundlehner Inc (CGI) was among the first companies to use portable computers to collect legal data at courts and recording offices. The use of notebook computers combined with electronic transmission of data to the customer reduces the time between data collection and its availability to the customer. CGI's information processing expertise also allows it to provide a high degree of customized service to its customers. Data is available online from www.superiorinfo.com.

ConsumerInfo.com

1 City Blvd West #401, Orange, CA 92868
Fax: 215-785-3200
Web site: www.iplace.com   **Email:** producer@creditmatters.com
Branch Offices: San Francisco, CA
Founded: 2000
Clientele Restrictions: Registration required.

Proprietary Databases or Gateways:
DB Name: **Qspace, Consumer info**
   Credit Information (US)
DB Name: **e-neighborhoods, iplace**
   Real Estate/Assessor (US)

Special Distribution Methods to Client: Internet
Formerly iplace.com, they are a provider of personally relevant information about credit, home, neighborhood and other personal assets. The company's services, data, and technologies provide compelling information solutions, relationship building tools and transaction facilitation for more than 100,000 online and offline businesses. With its newly launched iPlace.com, the company introduced its proprietary infoStructure Technology™, enabling businesses to capture and deliver vital customer information while strengthening customer relationships via individually targeted communications.

Contemporary Information Corp.

25044 Peachland Ave #209, Santa Clarita, CA 91321
Toll-free phone: 800-754-0009; Phone: 661-284-2731; Fax: 661-284-2737
Web site: www.continfo.com　　**Email:** wbower@continfo.com
Founded: 1986
Clientele Restrictions: none reported.

Proprietary Databases or Gateways:
Database Name: **Lexidate**
　Litigation/Judgments/Tax Liens (AZ, CA, NV, OR, WA)

Gateway Name: **Continfo/Experiean/Equifax**
　Credit Information (US, CA)

Database Name: **Criminal Scan**
　Criminal Information (US, CA)

Database Name: **Continfo**
　Tenant History (US, CA)

Special Distribution Methods to Client: Dial-Up (Other than Internet), FTP, Gateway via Another Online Service
CIC offers tenant screening and employment background checks including credit, evictions (public records), criminal history, drug testing, bad check search, driving records, and reference verifications. In addition to the applications mentioned above, their services are also of use in fraud prevention, collections, legal compliance, and risk management. CIC is an authorized agent of Experian Business Credit; CIC sells a complete line of business credit reporting solutions. The CA Eviction database is searchable by defendant. CIC offers wholesale prices to other credit reporting agencies. Other public record databases are available.

Corporate Screening

16530 Commerce Court, Cleveland, OH 44130-6305
Toll-free phone: 800-229-8606; Phone: 440-816-0500; Fax: 440-243-4204
Web site: www.corporatescreening.com　　**Email:** screen@corporatescreening.com
Founded: 1986　　**Memberships:** NCISS, AMA, ASIS, WAD, PRRN
Clientele Restrictions: Signed agreement required

Proprietary Databases or Gateways:
Gateway Name: **CSS EASE**
　Software/Training (US)

Special Distribution Methods to Client: Email, Gateway via Another Online Service, Internet
Corporate Screening utilizes a national network of resources for public record search and retrieval services. They offer complete pre-employment and business background investigative packages; can customize to fit needs. Complies with FCRA. Their applicant Screening Engine (CSS EASE) allows registered users to access complete investigative results and updates over the Internet. This has recently expanded to include online public record search ordering.

CorporateInformation.com

440 Wheelers Farms Road, Milford, CT 06460
Toll-free phone: 800-232-0013; Phone: 203-783-4366

Web site: http://www.corporateinformation.com　　**Email:** regnery@wisi.com
Parent Company: The Winthrop Corporation
Clientele Restrictions: None Reported

Proprietary Databases or Gateways:
Database Name: **Corporate/Trade Name Data**
　Corporate/Trade Name Data, Foreign Country Information (US, International)

Special Distribution Methods to Client: Internet
Features include: research a company; research a company's industry; research by country; and research by state among others. A very informative web site with much information available at no charge.

CountryWatch Inc.

Three Riverway #710, Houston, TX 77056
Toll-free phone: 800-879-3885; Phone: 713-355-6500; Fax: 713-355-2008
Web site: www.countrywatch.com   **Email:** subscribe@countrywatch.com
Founded: 1997
Clientele Restrictions: Casual requesters permitted, but subscription required for ongoing customers

Proprietary Databases or Gateways:
Database Name: **Countrywatch.com db**
   Foreign Country Information (International (191))

Special Distribution Methods to Client: CD-ROM, Database, Internet
Countrywatch.com is a growing online publisher providing original content and aggregated news to customers needing real-time, quality, formatted political, economic, cultural/demographic and environmental information and data on each country of the world. In addition, Countrywatch Inc provides a global forecast product that covers 193 countries. The product, which is updated monthly, is based on a standardized economic model that projects key economic variables in a consistent manner across every country in the world. This product is interactive, integrated and visually oriented. Users can agree with the default output or make their own assumptions by varying the chosen parameters in a user friendly Excel environment.

Court PC of Connecticut

PO Box 11081, Greenwich, CT 06831-1081
Phone: 203-531-7866; Fax: 203-531-6899
Web site: http://courtpcofct.com   **Email:** jel@courtpcofct.com
Founded: 1992   **Memberships:** NPRRA
Clientele Restrictions: Casual requesters occasionally permitted

Proprietary Databases or Gateways:
Database Name: **Superior Index**
   Litigation/Judgments/Tax Liens, Criminal Information (CT)

Special Distribution Methods to Client:
Court PC is Connecticut's comprehensive source of docket search information from Superior Court and US District Court cases. Their Connecticut Superior Court database contains records of civil filings since 1985, family/divorce filings since 1989, and discloseable criminal convictions since 1991. Microfiche indexes supplement PACER data to provide complete USDC/CT civil and criminal searches from 1970 forward. Court PC also provides current corporation (also LPs and LLCs) and tax lien data from the Connecticut Secretary of State database.

CourtExpress.com (RIS Legal Svcs)

701 Pennsylvania Avenue NW, Washington, DC 20004-2608
Toll-free phone: 800-542-3320; Phone: 202-737-7111; Fax: 202-737-3324
Web site: http://courtexpress.com   **Email:** info@courtexpress.com
Founded: 2000   **Parent Company:** RIS Legal Services
Clientele Restrictions: Registration required

Proprietary Databases or Gateways:
Gateway Name: **US Court Records**
   Bankruptcy (US)

Gateway Name: **State Court Records**
   Litigation/Judgments/Tax Liens (AZ,CA,CT,FL,IA,MO,VA)

Special Distribution Methods to Client: Email, Internet
CourtEXPRESS.com delivers powerful U.S. Court searching and document delivery features to your desktop. They cover most of the U.S. Federal District and Bankruptcy Courts, also providing searching from the U.S. Party Case Index from three files: civil, criminal and bankruptcy, which they call the National Locator Service or "NLS." Every step is easier and more productive than all other traditional searching methods. Rather than waiting online for results, CourtEXPRESS.com will alert you via Email when your search is done. Each member has access to their last 100

searches, including Due Diligence for Federal cases and Case Tracker for current cases. Other searches can be set up to repeat daily or weekly. Document ordering takes only seconds. Try a Guest Quick Search or a Private Guest Account.

CourtH.com

PO Box 70558, Houston, TX 77270-0558
Toll-free phone: 800-925-4225; Phone: 713-683-0491; Fax: 713-683-0493
Web site: http://courthousedirect.com/courth **Email:** orders@courth.com
Branch Offices: Richmond, TX, 281-342-1777
Founded: 1982 **Parent Company:** Right-of-Way Acquisition Services Inc **Memberships:** NACM
Clientele Restrictions: Casual requesters permitted
Proprietary Databases or Gateways:
Database Name: **Courthouse Research**
   Corporate/Trade Name Data, Real Estate/Assessor, Litigation/judgments/Tax Liens (TX)
Special Distribution Methods to Client: Dial-Up (Other than Internet), Email, Internet

Our Internet service provides access to 30 databases of public information from marriage records to property records to bankruptcies. Our proprietary database consists of public records from Harris, Montgomery, and Fort Bend counties. These records are easily searched on our web site.

Courthouse Retrieval System Inc.

6700 Baum Dr #12, Knoxville, TN 37919
Toll-free phone: 800-374-7488; Phone: 865-584-8017; Fax: 865-584-8047
Web site: www.crsdata.net **Email:** efinger@crsdata.net
Founded: 1985
Clientele Restrictions: Most requesters must sign agreement, but some casual, one-time requesters accepted,
Proprietary Databases or Gateways:
Database Name: **CRSdata.net; ids™**
   Real Estate/Assessor/Mortgage (AL, NC, TN)
Special Distribution Methods to Client: CD-ROM, Disk, Internet, Lists/Labels

CR System Inc provides real estate information (including tax records and mortgage information, but not limited to) on a subscription basis via the internet to realtors, real estate appraisers, mortgage companies, etc. Specializes in AL, NC & TN, and limited counties in SC & VA. Various Internet and CD products available.

CourthouseDirect.com

9800 Northwest Fwy #400, Houston, TX 77092
Phone: 713-683-0314; Fax: 713-683-0493
Web site: http://courthousedirect.com **Email:** info@courthousedirect.com
Branch Offices: Dallas, TX, 214-443-9355; Fax: 214-443-9207; **Richmond**, TX, 281-342-1777; Fax: 281-342-4485;
Bryan/College Station, TX, 979-695-6504; Fax: 979-492-9664
Founded: 1982 **Memberships:** NAR, NPRRA, IRWA
Clientele Restrictions: Subscription preferred; credit card requestors accepted for casual requesters
Proprietary Databases or Gateways:
Gateway Name: **Real Estate/Assessor**
   Real Estate/Assessor (AZ, CA, FL, HI, IL, NY, OK, PA, TX, UT, WA)
Gateway Name: **Real Property Documents**
   Litigation/Judgments/Tax Liens (AZ, CA, FL, HI, IL, NY, OK, PA, TX, UT, WA)
Special Distribution Methods to Client: Internet

CourthouseDirect.com, a specialized Internet portal based in Houston, provides electronic document images of Deeds, Mortgages, Releases, IRS Liens, Assignments, and other county Real Property and Official Record filings via the Internet. CourthouseDirect.com currently provides images for major counties in California, Florida, Arizona, Illinois, Michigan, New York, Oklahoma, and Texas. The current database contains 12 counties in Texas and 138 counties nationwide. CourthouseDirect.com expects to have images for 85% of the U. S. population online by the end of the year 2003. In addition to those listed above, other applications includes collections, geneology research, and litigation.

CourtLink

13427 NE 16th St, #100, Bellevue, WA 98005-2307
Toll-free phone: 800-774-7317; Phone: 425-974-5000; Fax: 425-974-1419
Web site: www.courtlink.com   **Email:** support@courtlink.com
Founded: 1986   **Parent Company:** Lexis-Nexis   **Memberships:** AALL, ABI, NACM, NAFE, SLA
Clientele Restrictions: Casual requesters permitted

Proprietary Databases or Gateways:
Gateway Name: **CourtLink®eAccess**
   Bankruptcy, Litigation/Judgments/Tax Liens (US)

Special Distribution Methods to Client: Dial-Up (Other than Internet), Disk, Email, FTP, Internet, Lists/Labels

CourtLink® has been developing, providing and refining online solutions for accessing court records and filing and processing court documents and case information. With a single online platform for both electronic access and filing, LexisNexis CourtLink is delivering on its mission to improve the speed, quality and overall effectiveness of connecting the legal and business communities to our nation's courts. We offer online access to more than 200 million court records. Our client base represents over 50,000 individual users in all 50 states, including 230 of the 250 largest law firms in the U.S. Our customers also include the largest banks, insurance companies and title insurance companies in the country.

CourtSearch.com

1434 Farrington Rd, Apex, NC 27502
Phone: 910-815-3880; Fax: 919-363-8400
Web site: www.courtsearch.com   **Email:** info@courtsearch.com
Founded: 1998   **Parent Company:** Castle Branch, Inc
Clientele Restrictions: Registration required.

Proprietary Databases or Gateways:
Database Name: **NC Records**
   Criminal Information, Litigation/Judgments/Tax Liens (NC)

Special Distribution Methods to Client: Internet

They offer a subsciption plan or pay as you go for searching court records in North Carolina. They also perform out-of-state civil, criminal, and federal court searches, also NC DMVs. They also offer North Carolina Court Calendar Index by Name search, no fee.

Credentials Inc

550 Frontage Road #3500, Northfield, IL 60093
Phone: 847-446-7422; Fax: 847-446-7424
Web site: www.degreechk.com   **Email:** tmckechney@degreechk.com
Founded: 1997
Clientele Restrictions: Casual requesters permitted

Proprietary Databases or Gateways:
Database Name: **Degreechk**
   Education/Employment (US)

Special Distribution Methods to Client: Email, Internet

Credentials Inc offers 24 hour, 365 day Internet access to degree verification from participating colleges and universities. All verification transactions are uniquely audit-trailed and confirmed to the user via fax or email, often within the hour. In addition to online databases provided by participating schools, the system includes an off-line, archival search capability for degrees that are not included in the online database. This feature is important since most school databases only date back to the early or mid-1980s. All interactions with degreechk.com are fully encrypted. Growth in the number of school listed is expected; will broadcast email notifications of new school additions to the Degreechk.com menu.

Criminal Information Services Inc

PO Box 7235, Aloha, OR 97007-7235
Toll-free phone: 800-973-5500; Phone: 503-591-1355; Fax: 503-642-7730
Web site: www.criminalinfo.com   **Email:** crim@earthlink.net
Founded: 1993
Clientele Restrictions: Casual requesters permitted

Proprietary Databases or Gateways:
Database Name: **CRIS**
  Criminal Information
    (AZ,AR,CT,FL,GA,HI,ID,IL,IN,KY,MI,MN,MS,MO,NC,ND,NJ,NY,OH,OK,OR,SC,TX,UT,WA)
Database Name: **CRIS**
  Tenant History (AZ,CA,ID,NV,OR,WA
  AZ,CA,ID,NV,OR,WA)

Special Distribution Methods to Client: Email, Internet
Criminal Information Services Inc (CRIS) offers Internet access to state-wide Department of Corrections conviction history databases from a growing number of states. More states will be added in the near future. Owned and operated by former criminal-justice professionals, CRIS provides real-time access to these databases, by alpha search and birthdate comparisons, with "hits" providing conviction date, county of offense, offense description and sentencing information. Reports, including "No Record Found" reports are easy to print. Prices, based on a name check basis and monthly volume, are very inexpensive and affordable.

Daily Report, The

310 H Street, Bakersfield, CA 93304-2914
Phone: 661-322-3226; Fax: 661-322-9084
Web site: www.thedailyreport.com   **Email:** staff@thedailyreport.com   **Memberships:** PRRN
Clientele Restrictions: Casual requesters permitted

Proprietary Databases or Gateways:
Database Name: **The Daily Report**
  Addresses/Telephone Numbers, Licenses/Registrations/Permits, Litigation/Judgments/Tax Liens (CA-Kern County ONLY)
Database Name: **The Daily Report**
  Bankruptcy, Real Estate/Assessor, Tenant History, Uniform Commercial Code, Vital Records, Wills/Probate (CA-Kern County ONLY)

Special Distribution Methods to Client: Internet, Publication/Directory
The Daily Report is a legal newspaper, published continuously since 1907. Since publication began, the volume of information filed with the Courts and Hall of Records in Kern County has increased significantly. This web site was developed in response to a growing need expressed by our subscribers to easily search for information filed in the Courts and Hall of Records pertinent to their specific needs. With The Daily Report, online subscribers can now browse for information filed with the Courts such as New Suits or Judgments and the Hall of Records, featuring most all recorded documents, including Notices of Default, Deeds, Maps, Liens and Oil and Gas leases. Other information such as building permits and business Licenses are also available through our specially designed search engine.

Data Downlink xls.com

c/o Alacra (and/or Angle Software), 88 Pine St, 3rd Fl, New York, NY 10005
Phone: 212-363-9620
Web site: www.xls.com   **Email:** info@xls.com
Branch Offices: London, GB, 44.(0)20.7398.1300; **New York**, NY, 888-333-0820; **Paris**, FR, 33 (0)1 44 71 36 72
Founded: 1996   **Parent Company:** Alacra
Clientele Restrictions: Subscription required.

Proprietary Databases or Gateways:
DB Name: **xls.com**

Addresses/Telephone Numbers (US, FR, GB, International)

DB Name: **xls.com**

Corporate/Trade Name Data (US, FR, GB, International)

DB Name: **xls.com**

SEC/Other Financial (US, International)

Special Distribution Methods to Client: Internet, Publication/Directory

Data Dowlink, xls.com offers a wide range of company information, much for investing purposes. They deliver precise, current and reliable business information to the corporate desktop via the Internet or a firm's Intranet. Their Internet technology and sophisticated relational databases (60) are tailored to meet business research needs. Their diverse portfolio of products and services (Portal B is a business search engine) is designed specifically for the business information market.

Datalink Services Inc

PO Box 188416, Sacramento, CA 95818
Phone: 916-451-2600; Fax: 916-916-451-2623
Web site: www.imvrs.com   **Email:** tohare@imvrs.com
Founded: 1983
Clientele Restrictions: Casual requesters not permitted

Proprietary Databases or Gateways:
Gateway Name: **Driving, Vehicle & Dealer Records**
  Driver and/or Vehicle (CA)

Special Distribution Methods to Client: Email, Internet

Datalink specializes in processing and providing instant California DMV records with speed and accuracy, offering one of the industry's most innovative website for California DMV data. Also, the web site processes driving records from all states nationwide. For over nineteen years, Datalink has been at the forefront of technological advances, letting them ensure the quality and reliability of their service. The mission of the highly-trained staff is always to assist with the best and most efficient service possible through loyalty and honesty, principles on which their business is built.

DataQuick

9620 Towne Centre Dr, San Diego, CA 92121
Toll-free phone: 888-604-3282; Phone: 858-597-3100; Fax: 858-455-7406
Web site: www.dataquick.com   **Email:** smorga@dataquick.com
Founded: 1978   **Parent Company:** MacDonald Detwiler   **Memberships:** REIPA
Clientele Restrictions: Casual requesters permitted

Proprietary Databases or Gateways:
Database Name: **DataQuick**
  Real Estate/Assessor (US)

Special Distribution Methods to Client: Dial-Up (Other than Internet), Disk, Lists/Labels, Magnetic Tape

A leading name in real property information products, DataQuick services the title, mortgage, real estate and insurance industries. They provide property details such as: ownership and address information; sale and loan details; characteristics such as sq footage etc.; and historical sales and data such as previous transactions for marketing and research purposes. They cover household development demographics and market trend data.

Data-Trac.com, USCrimsearch.com

PO Box 324, Moriches, NY 11955
Phone: 212-656-1341
Web site: www.data-trac.com   **Email:** support@data-trac.com
Founded: 1988   **Parent Company:** also under the name Criminalcourtsearch.com.
Clientele Restrictions: Access permitted only to the Investigative and Security And Human Resources Communities
an application and signed release with all confirmed documentation
as to professional status is required before access can be obtained.

Proprietary Databases or Gateways:
Database Name: **Profile Reports**
   Addresses/Telephone Numbers (US), Criminal Information (NY)
Special Distribution Methods to Client: Internet
Formerly Data-Trac Network Inc, Data-Trac.com is an online investigative network providing instant access to public records. They also offer customized pre-employment services and hundreds of public records searches. They maintain a database and are a public record manufacturer.

DCS Information Systems

500 N Central Expressway #280, Plano, TX 75074
Toll-free phone: 800-394-3274; Phone: 972-422-3600; Fax: 972-422-3621
Web site: www.dcs-amerifind.com   **Email:** carroll@dcs-amerifind.com
Founded: 1967
Clientele Restrictions: signed agreement required; business or government agencies only
Proprietary Databases or Gateways:
Database Name: **AmeriFind**
   Addresses/Telephone Numbers, Real Estate/Assessor, County Court Records (US)
Database Name: **Texas Systems**
   Driver and/or Vehicle, Real Estate/Assessor, Vital Records (marriage & divorce) (TX)
Special Distribution Methods to Client: Dial-Up (Other than Internet), Internet
DCS' national product, AmeriFind, is a very effective and comprehensive skip tracing, locating, fraud prevention and investigation tools. Access to credit headers is provided for GLB exception purposes. County courthouse criminal history searches and online telephone directory assistance is also available via DCS' products. The Texas product provides comprehensive, up-to-date information on Texas drivers and vehicle owners, with up to 13 years of history. These systems provide the users with search capabilities not available from other suppliers. DCS offers customized information solutions for large volume users.

Derwent Information

1725 Duke Street #250, Alexandria, VA 22314
Toll-free phone: 800-337-9368; Phone: 703-706-4220; Fax: 703-838-5240
Web site: www.derwent.com   **Email:** custserv@derwentus.com
Founded: 1952   **Parent Company:** The Thompson Corporation
Clientele Restrictions: None reported
Proprietary Databases or Gateways:
Database Name: **Derwent World Patents Index, Patent Explorer**
Derwent World Patent Index
   Trademarks/Patents, Corporate/Trade Name Data (US)
Special Distribution Methods to Client: Dial-Up (Other than Internet), Email, Internet, Publication/Directory
With offices in London, Japan, and Alexandria, Derwent provides access to the over 200,000 patents filed each year in the US alone while the European Patent office files around 80,000 patents a year. Derwent makes this information easily accessible by combining the world's patents on one searchable database. During our editorial process, a team of more than 350 specialist editors assess, classify and index patent documents to provide concise English language abstracts which are readily searched and easily understood. With a wide range of delivery options, Derwent ensures that companies are kept fully aware of the latest developments in today's fast moving markets.

Dialog

11000 Regency Parkway, Cary, NC 27511
Toll-free phone: 800-334-2564; Phone: 919-462-8600; Fax: 919-461-7252
Web site: www.dialog.com
Branch Offices: London, 44-20-7940-6900; Fax: 44-20-7940-6800; **Hong Kong**, 852-2530-5778; Fax: 852-2530-5885
Founded: 1972
Clientele Restrictions: Casual Requesters Permitted

Proprietary Databases or Gateways:
Gateway Name: **DIALOG Web; DataStar; Profound; Intelliscope; Insite; IntraScope**
   Foreign Country Information, Corporate/Trade Name Data, Trademarks, Legislation/Regulation, SEC/Other
      Financial (US,International)

Gateway Name: **NewsEdge**
   News/Current Events (US)

Special Distribution Methods to Client: CD-ROM, Dial-Up (Other than Internet), Internet, Software

Dialog, a Thompson company, is a worldwide pioneer and leader in providing online information services to organizations seeking competitive advantages in business, finance and law, among others. With over 15 terabytes of data, Dialog's collection of 900 databases handles more than 700,000 searches and delivers over 17 million document page views per month. Dialog offers 35 products and services, including the Dialog, DataStar and Profound product lines and recent additions NewsEdge and Intelligence Data's Intelliscope. Content areas include intellectual property, government regulations, social sciences, food and agriculture, news and media, business and finance, reference, energy and environment, chemicals, pharmaceuticals, science and technology, and medicine. With operations in 32 countries, Dialog's global knowledge centers provide the highest levels of customer service to an international audience of 100,00+ professional researchers in over 103 countries.

Diligenz Inc

4629 168th St SE, #E, Lynnwood, WA 98037
Toll-free phone: 800-858-5294; Phone: 425-741-0990; Fax: 425-741-0987
Web site: www.diligenz.com   **Email:** sales@diligenz.com   **Memberships:** NPPRA, PRRN, UAEL, CFA
Clientele Restrictions: Sign-up required.

Proprietary Databases or Gateways:
Database Name: **Diligenz.com**
   Uniform Commercial Code, Corporate/Trade Name Data (US)

Gateway Name: **Diligenz**
   Bankruptcy, Litigation/Judgments/Tax Liens (US)

Special Distribution Methods to Client: Email, FTP, Internet

Diligenz is a one-stop source for due dilligence needs from UCC and corporate searches to the management and tracking of filings, plus complete support services. They provide databases of public records, especially to the search and retrieval of Uniform Commercial Code and Corporate information. Financial statements, continuations, amendments are also here, also records pertaining to corporate status, ownership interests, business credit and business licensing information. Their web site offers rapid response and total reliability. The online search interface allows you to order and retrieve searches, and view and print documents online.

Discovering Montana

111 North Last Chance Gulch #3J, Helena, MT 59601
Phone: 406-449-3448
Web site: www.discoveringmontana.com   **Email:** rich@discoveringmontana.com
Founded: 2000
Clientele Restrictions: None, except for premium services which requires membership

Proprietary Databases or Gateways:
Gateway Name: **Discoveringmontana**
   Driver and/or Vehicle, Corporate/Trade Name Data, Legislation/Regulation (MT)

Special Distribution Methods to Client: Internet

DiscoveringMontana.com, the official website of the State of Montana, is a gateway to a myriad of state information and services. Many free services are available, as well as "premium services' which require fees and registration. Online certificates (app.discoveringmontana.com/bes) app allows you to search all businesses registered in the state of Montana then print Certificates of Existence, Authorization, and fact. Registered Principal Search permits look up of officers and directors by name and by organization. This site also gives pre-approved clients access to access driving records in both interatcive and batch modes. In the summer of 2002, Discovering Montana plans to introduce online UCC filing and searching services.

Diversified Information Services Corp

67 East Weldon #220, Phoenix, AZ 85012
Phone: 602-532-0111; Fax: 602-532-0393
Web site: www.discaz.com   **Email:** info@discaz.com
Founded: 1970   **Memberships:** ALTA
Clientele Restrictions: Must be ongoing account
Proprietary Databases or Gateways:
Database Name: **Real Property Records**
  Real Estate/Assessor (AZ-Maricopa)

Special Distribution Methods to Client: CD-ROM, Dial-Up (Other than Internet), Disk, Email, Gateway via Another Online Service

Diversified Information Services is owned by North American Title Agency, Old Republic Title Insurance Agency, Transnation Title, Lawyers Title of Arizona, Fidelity National Title Agency, Stewart Title & Trust of Phoenix, and Nations Title Agency.

Dolan Information, Data Services Div.

1900 NW Expressway #1600, Oklahoma City, OK 73118
Phone: 405-302-6954; Fax: 405-302-6902
Web site: www.dolaninfo.com/   **Email:** Dolan.data@Dolaninfo.com
Founded: 1990   **Parent Company:** Dolan Media
Clientele Restrictions: Signed agreement required, must be ongoing account
Proprietary Databases or Gateways:
Database Name: **Hogan Online**
  Bankruptcy, Litigation/Judgments/Tax Liens (US)

Special Distribution Methods to Client: Database, Dial-Up (Other than Internet), Disk, Lists/Labels, Magnetic Tape

Formally known as Hogan Information Services, Dolan offers one of the most complete, comprehensive, and current public record reporting in the country with a database of more than 100 million bankruptcies, tax liens, civil judgments, evictions, real estate deeds, and more. Hogan collects data in over 8,000 courthouses nationwide. Our collection processes combine court expertise with the latest technology to provide the most timely and accurate public record information in the US. Our extensive public record data is used by credit bureaus, tenant-screening agencies, mail houses, and other businesses to make smarter decisions and manage risk.

Dun & Bradstreet

1 Diamond Hill Rd, Murray Hill, NJ 07974
Toll-free phone: 800-234-3867; Phone: 908-665-5000
Web site: www.dnb.com
Branch Offices: Murry Hill, NJ, 800-234-3867   **Memberships:** NPRRA
Clientele Restrictions: Casual requesters permitted
Proprietary Databases or Gateways:
Database Name: **D & B Public Record Search**
  Addresses/Telephone Numbers, Bankruptcy, Corporate/Trade Name Data, Credit Information,
    Litigation/Judgments/Tax Liens and Uniform Commercial Code (US)
Database Name: **Business Credit Information**
  Credit Information (US)

Special Distribution Methods to Client: Dial-Up (Other than Internet), Disk, Internet, Software

D&B is a leading provider of business information for credit, marketing, purchasing, and receivables management decisions worldwide. More than 100,000 companies rely on D&B to provide the insight they need to help build profitable, quality business relationships with their customers, suppliers and business partners. Dun & Bradstreet's Public Records Search database is one of the most extensive commercial public record information sites available. It is probably the only online database of corporate, UCC, litigation and tax lien information about businesses that covers all

50 states, the Virgin Islands, Puerto Rico and the District of Columbia. The 800 number listed above is for business credit information.

EdVerify Inc

2240 W Woodbright Rd #412, Boynton Beach, FL 33426
Toll-free phone: 877-338-3743;; Fax: 516-746-9023
Web site: www.edverify.com
Founded: 1998
Clientele Restrictions: Signed agreement required, must be ongoing account

Proprietary Databases or Gateways:
Database Name: **EdVerify.com**
  Education/Employment (US)

Special Distribution Methods to Client: Email, Internet

EdVerify has an automated system of education and enrollment verifications for every accredited post secondary school in the nation, and quickly responds to verification requests via the Internet. The company offers the exchange of data to high volume clients through an FTP "batch" transfer protocol or by an HTTPS real time, server-to-server protocol; and offers attractive pricing discounts to large accounts. EdVerify acts as the agent for educational institutions by consolidating Directory Information as defined by FERPA.

e-InfoData.com

1033 Walnut #200, Boulder, CO 80302
Toll-free phone: 888-259-6173; Phone: 303-381-2260; Fax: 303-381-2279
Web site: http://e-infodata.com   **Email:** info@einfodata.com
Founded: 1996
Clientele Restrictions: Signed Agreement Required

Proprietary Databases or Gateways:
Database Name: **QuickInfo.net**
  Voter Registration (AK, AR, CO, DE, GA, KS, MI, NV, OH, OK, TX, UT)

Database Name: **QuickInfo.net**
  Corporate/Trade Name Data (AZ, AR, GA, ID, NV, NM, OR, TX, UT, WY)

Database Name: **QuickInfo.net**
  Driver and/or Vehicle (FL, ID, IA, LA, ME, MN, MS, MO, NC, OR, SD, TX, UT, WV, WI, WY)

Database Name: **QuickInfo.net**
  Real Estate/Assessor (FL, ID, IA, LA, MN, MS, MO, NV, NC, OR, TX, UT, WI, WY)

Database Name: **QuickInfo.net**
  Licenses/Registrations/Permits (FL, ID, IA, LA, MN, MS, MO, NV, NC, OR, TX, UT, WI, WY)

Database Name: **QuickInfo.net**
  Vital Records (CO, NV, TX)

Special Distribution Methods to Client: CD-ROM

Formerly QuickInfo.net Information Services, e-InfoData.com is a governmental and business network for licensed professionals with a need for highly searchable access to critical public and proprietary information. The password-protected network takes you to county courthouses, state agencies and federal archives. Your agency or company will have easy, affordable and expert access to millions of public records. Also, e-InfoData.com is a leader in expanding the number of databases available to the public. Their databases are word-indexed to assure that you receive the best information. Gateway and batching opportunities are also available.

Electronic Property Information Corp (EPIC)

227 Alexander St #206, Rochester, NY 14607
Phone: 585-454-7390; Fax: 585-486-0098
Founded: 1987
Clientele Restrictions: None reported

Proprietary Databases or Gateways:
Database Name: **OPRA-Erie, Monroe Counties**
  Real Estate/Assessor, Uniform Commerical Code, Litigation/Judgments/Tax Liens and Wills/Probate (NY-Erie, Monroe Counties)
Database Name: **OPRA**
  Bankruptcy (NY)

Special Distribution Methods to Client: Dial-Up (Other than Internet), Internet

EPIC provides online access to their proprietary database of all public records affecting real property in Erie and Monroe Counties, NY and bankruptcy records for New York's Western and Northern Districts. In addition to helping create abstracts and write title insurance, the database has been used for collections, asset search, and individual and business screening applications.

E-Merges.com

1756 Ebling Tl #2000, Annapolis, MD 21401-6614
Phone: 410-353-6894; Fax: 801-437-3555
Web site: www.e-merges.com   **Email:** info@e-merges.com
Clientele Restrictions: None reported

Proprietary Databases or Gateways:
Database Name: **US Registered Voter File**
  Voter Registration
  (AK,AR,CO,CT,DE,DC,FL,GA,IL,IN,IA,KS,LA,MA,MI,MN,MO,NV,NJ,NY,NC,OH,OK,RI,SC,TX,UT,VA,WI)
Database Name: **Hunting/Fishing Licenses**
  Licenses/Registrations/Permits (AK,AR,CT,DE,FL,GA,KS,MS,MO,NV,NJ,NC,ND,OH,SC,UT,VA,WA
  AK,AR,CT,DE,FL,GA,KS,MS,MO,NV,NJ,NC,ND,OH,SC,UT,VA,WA)
Database Name: **The Boater Database (mix of state & federal data)**
  Vessels (US)

Special Distribution Methods to Client: CD-ROM, Database, Disk, Magnetic Tape

E-Merges provides voter registration records with date of birth for unrestricted use from AK, AR CO, CT, DE, DC, LA, MA, MI, NV, NY, NC, OH, OK, RI, SC, UT, and WI (and other states with restrictions). They will sell by county, state, or entire file, which is updated annually and is internally compiled from 3600 towns and counties across the USA. They also track Hunting/Fishing data in 17 states; also organ donors and boat ownership for most states.

Environmental Data Resources, Inc. (EDR)

3530 Post Rd, Southport, CT 06490
Toll-free phone: 800-352-0050; Phone: 203-255-6606; Fax: 203-255-1976
Web site: www.edrnet.com
Founded: 1991
Clientele Restrictions: Casual requesters permitted

Proprietary Databases or Gateways:
Database Name: **NEDIS, Sanborn Maps**
  Environmental, Licenses/Registratoins/Permits, and Real Estate/Assessor (US)

Special Distribution Methods to Client:

Environmental Data Resources, Inc. (EDR) is an information company specializing in providing data on environmental liabilities associated with companies and properties. EDR provides this data to environmental consulting firms, banks, insurance companies, law firms, corporations and accounting firms. EDR has compiled and organized more than 600 separate government databases, obtained at the federal, state and local levels, into an environmental database referred to as NEDIS, the National Environmental Data Information System. On March 25, 2002, Environmental Data Resources, Inc. acquired certain assets of Fidelity National Information Solutions' (FNIS) environmental information operations including assets previously owned by VISTAinfo and EcoSearch. FNIS' environmental information businesses were also transitioned to EDR as of this date.

Equifax Credit Services

1600 Peachtree St NW, Atlanta, GA 30309
Toll-free phone: 888-202-4025; Phone: 404-885-8000
Web site: www.equifax.com **Email:** customer.care@equifax.com
Founded: 1899 **Parent Company:** Equifax Inc **Memberships:** AAMVA
Clientele Restrictions: Signed agreement
Proprietary Databases or Gateways:
Database Name: **Credit Profile**
  Credit Information (US)

Database Name: **Investigation System**
  Addresses/Telephone Numbers, Education/Employment, Bankruptcy, Litigation/Judgments/Tax Liens (US)

Special Distribution Methods to Client: Dial-Up (Other than Internet), Internet
Equifax is a leading provider of consumer and commercial financial information worldwide. The database includes information on almost 400 million consumers and businesses around the world.

Ernst Publishing Co, LLC

2280 Grass Valley Hwy #215, Auburn, CA 9603
Toll-free phone: 800-345-3822
Web site: www.ernst.cc **Email:** lrcanier@ernst.cc
Founded: 1992 **Parent Company:** Ernst Publishing Company, LLC **Memberships:** AIIP, SIIA, NPRRA, PRRN
Clientele Restrictions: None reported
Proprietary Databases or Gateways:
Database Name: **Uniform Commercial Code Filing Guide**
  Uniform Commercial Code Filing Guide (US)

Database Name: **Real Estate Recording Guide**
  Real Estate/Assessor (US)

Special Distribution Methods to Client: Database, Internet, Publication/Directory
The Uniform Comemrcial Code Filing Guide™ is a practical "How To" reference for the preparation, filing and searching of Article 9 Financing Statements nationwide. This Guide provides information re: fees, forms, facts for all 4,316 filing jurisidictions and is designed for the high-volume multi-juridiction filer. Included are sections hosting the Model Act, Filing Fundamentals, Purchase Money Secured Interest snd Definitions. Subscription is annual with quarterly updates; a newsletter is provided in non-updating months. The new Revised Article 9 Alert assists filers and searchers to function in the new Revision environment. They publish the Real Estate Recording Guide and National Release Guide and offer a database and web-based product, Nat. Online Mortgage Assistance Database Program.

Everton Publishers

PO Box 368, Logan, UT 84323
Toll-free phone: 800-443-6325; Phone: 801-752-6022
Web site: www.everton.com **Email:** leverton@everton.com
Founded: 1947
Clientele Restrictions: None reported
Proprietary Databases or Gateways:
Database Name: **Everton's Online Search**
  Addresses/Telephone Numbers (US)

Special Distribution Methods to Client: Dial-Up (Other than Internet), Internet
Everton has offered online access since 1990. The company publishes the Everton's Genealogical Helper magazine and The Handbook For Genealogists.

Experian Information Solutions

500 City Parkway West #205, Orange, CA 92868
Toll-free phone: 888-397-3742
Web site: www.experian.com   **Parent Company:** GUS, plc
Clientele Restrictions: Casual requesters permitted

Proprietary Databases or Gateways:
Database Name: **File 1**
Consumer File
   Credit Information, Addresses/Telephone Numbers (US)

Special Distribution Methods to Client: Dial-Up (Other than Internet), Internet

As the consumer credit arm of Experian, data from Experian Information Solutions (formerly Experian Consumer Credit) may be used for a variety of purposes related to individuals, subject to permissible purposes. Individuals who need assistance with reports should call 888-397-3742.

Experian Online

505 City Parkway, Orange, CA 92868
Toll-free phone: 800-831-5614
Web site: www.experian.com   **Parent Company:** GUS, plc
Clientele Restrictions: None reported

Proprietary Databases or Gateways:
Database Name: **Experian Online**
Various Experian Databases
   Addresses/Telephone Numbers, Driver and/or Vehicle, Real Estate/Assessor (US)

Database Name: **Experian Online Business Records Reports**
   Uniform Commercial Code, Corporate/Trade Name Data, Bankruptcy (US)

Special Distribution Methods to Client: Dial-Up (Other than Internet), Disk, Internet, Magnetic Tape

Experian is an information solutions company. We help organizations to use information to reach new customers and to develop successful and long lasting customer relationships. We have built our business on the simple premise that commercial success is about getting close to customers. The more an organisation understands them, the more able it is to respond to their very individual needs and circumstances. This is the approach that we adopt in our own client relationships. It is also the underlying motivation behind everything we do as a company.

Explore Information Services

2945 Lone Oak Dr, #150, Eagan, MN 55121
Toll-free phone: 800-531-9125; Phone: 651-385-2284; Fax: 651-385-2281
Web site: www.exploredata.com   **Email:** explore.info@exploredata.com
Clientele Restrictions: Signed agreement required, must be ongoing account

Proprietary Databases or Gateways:
Database Name: **EARS and RiskAlert**
   Driver and/or Vehicle (AL, AZ, CA, CO, CT, DE, FL, ID, IA, KS, KY, MA, MD, ME, MI, MN, MO, MT, NE, NH, NV, NY, OH, OR, SC, TN, TX, UT, WI, WV, WY)

Special Distribution Methods to Client: Dial-Up (Other than Internet), Disk, FTP, Internet, Magnetic Tape

E.A.R.S. (Electronically Accessed Reunderwriting Service) monitors insured drivers for "moving violations" activity and notifies insurers prior to policy renewal. RiskAlert provides notification of newly licensed youthful drivers.

Fairchild Record Search Ltd

PO Box 1368, Olympia, WA 98507
Toll-free phone: 800-547-7007; Phone: 360-786-8775; Fax: 360-943-6656
Web site: www.recordsearch.com
Founded: 1980   **Memberships:** NPRRA, NFIB, PRRN
Clientele Restrictions: Casual requesters permitted

Proprietary Databases or Gateways:
Gateway Name: **UCC**
  Uniform Commercial Code (US)

Gateway Name: **Washington**
  Corporate/Trade Name Data (WA)

Gateway Name: **Courtlink; Motznicks**
  Litigation/Judgments/Tax Liens (AK, WA)

Special Distribution Methods to Client: Email

Fairchild has specialized in public record retrieval service - emphasize "service" - in the US Northwest and in Alaska for more than 15 years. Primary capabilities include UCC/corporate document filing, retrieval and wildcard searching. Due to their long presence in the area they have established experience in filing and retrieval of virtually any public record documents in those states.

Felonies R Us

1423 W 3rd #21, Little Rock, AR 72201
Phone: 501-376-4719; Fax: 501-376-4619
Founded: 1998
Clientele Restrictions: Must be ongoing account
Proprietary Databases or Gateways:
Database Name: **AR Felonies**
  Criminal Information (AR)

Special Distribution Methods to Client: Lists/Labels

Felonies 'R' Us maintains an updated criminal database obtained from the Arkansas Administrative Office of the Courts. Able to run statewide searches, they retrieve documents desired by the client.

Fidelifacts

42 Broadway, New York, NY 10004
Toll-free phone: 800-678-0007; Phone: 212-425-1520; Fax: 212-248-5619
Web site: www.fidelifacts.com   **Email:** norton@fidelifacts.com
Founded: 1956   **Memberships:** EMA, SHRM, NCISS, ASIS, PRRN
Clientele Restrictions: Casual requesters permitted
Proprietary Databases or Gateways:
Gateway Name: **Fidelifacts**
  Credit Information (US, NY)

Special Distribution Methods to Client:

Among the oldest companies engaged in the business of providing background reports on individuals for employment purposes and on companies, Fidelifacts has a network of investigators in offices around the country, and local personnel who examine public records in less populated areas. Fidelifacts specialty is conducting background investigations, reference checks, screening checks of job applicants and due diligence investigations. They also provide asset location services, skip tracing and other services on legal matters. Their in-house database lists 1,500,000 names of persons arrested, indicted, convicted, and otherwise had problems with the law. Data is primarily for metro New York area, but also includes SEC/NASD filings where unlawful activity may be a question. They are located near the NY Office of Court Admin., and pickup criminal record checks at the OCA daily. They offer 24-hour service to these NY Counties: New York, Queens, Kings, Bronx, Richmond, Nassau, Suffolk, Rockland, Westchester, Dutchess, Orange, Putnam, Erie.

First American Corporation, The

1 First American Way, Santa Ana, CA 92707
Toll-free phone: 800-854-3643; Phone: 714-800-3000
Web site: http://firstam.com   **Email:** jbandy@firstam.com
Branch Offices: 900+ offices in USA & abroad,

Proprietary Databases or Gateways:
Database Name: **Real Estate Information**
  Real Estate/Assessor (US)

Special Distribution Methods to Client: Automated Telephone Look-Up, CD-ROM, Gateway via Another Online Service, Internet
First American Corp. is a leading provider of business information and related products and services. Their 3 primary business segments include: title insurance & services; real estate information & services, which includes mortgage and database information and services; and consumer information & services which provides automotive, subprime and direct-to-consumer credit reporting; residence and pre-employment screening, auto insurance tracking, property & casualty insurance, home warranties, investment advisory, and trust & banking services. Visit www.firstam.com for further information.

First American Real Estate Solutions East

8160 Corporate Park Dr #200, Cincinnati, OH 45242
Toll-free phone: 800-582-7300; Phone: 513-489-7300; Fax: 513-489-4409
Web site: www.firstamres.com   **Email:** sales.res.ca@firstam.com
Branch Offices: Columbus, OH, 614-277-9688; Fax: 614-277-9689; **Detroit**, MI, 248-348-8112; Fax: 248-348-8101; **Cleveland**, OH, 440-974-7863; Fax: 440-974-7935
Founded: 1980   **Memberships:** MBAA, NAR, REIPA
Clientele Restrictions: Casual requesters permitted

Proprietary Databases or Gateways:
Database Name: **PaceNet, MetroScan, Win2Data**
  Mortgage Data and Addresses/Telephone Numbers (KY, MI, OH, MO, PA, IL, TN)
Database Name: **PaceNet, Prospect Services**
  Real Estate/Assessor (KY, MI, OH)

Special Distribution Methods to Client: CD-ROM, Dial-Up (Other than Internet), Disk, Lists/Labels, Magnetic Tape
First Am. Real Estate Solutions maintains databases of existing real estate ownership and gathers and verifies data from courthouse public records and other sources on all real estate sales. They collect most information manually, assuring accuracy, completeness and timely information. Property addresses are standardized and updated quarterly to current CASS standards required by the USPS.

First American Real Estate Solutions West

5601 E. La Palma Ave, Anaheim, CA 92807
Toll-free phone: 800-345-7334; Phone: 714-701-2150; Fax: 714-701-9231
Web site: www.firstamres.com   **Email:** sales.res.ca@firstam.com   **Parent Company:** First American Financial Corporation
Clientele Restrictions: Casual requesters permitted

Proprietary Databases or Gateways:
Database Name: **Real Property Database**
  Real Estate/Assessor (AL, AZ, CA, CO, DC, DE, FL, GA, HI, IL, IN, LA, MA, MD, MI, MN, MS, NC, NJ, NM, NY, NV, OH, OK, OR, PA, SC, TN, TX, UT, VA, VI, WA, WI)

Special Distribution Methods to Client: CD-ROM, Microfilm/Microfiche
First American Real Estate Solutions is now part of the First American Financial Corporation. They are a leading provider of real estate information from major counties in most US states. Call for specific coverage and access via online database, CD-ROM and microfiche information.

FlatRateInfo.com

1033 Walnut #200, Boulder, CO 80302
Toll-free phone: 888-259-6173;; Fax: 303-381-2279
Web site: www.flatrateinfo.com/fri/public/
Founded: 1996   **Parent Company:** e-InfoData.com Inc.
Clientele Restrictions: Signed Agreement Required

Proprietary Databases or Gateways:
Database Name: **QI National People Locator**
  Addresses/Telephone Numbers (US)

Database Name: **QI**
  Bankruptcy, Litigation/Judgments/Tax Liens, Real Estate/Assessor, Fictious Business Names (US)

Database Name: **US Merchant Vessels**
  Vessels (US)

Database Name: **US Aircraft**
  Aviation (US)

Special Distribution Methods to Client: Internet

FlatRateInfo.com provides on-line access to nationwide databases to licensed professionals and qualified businesses with legitimate need for the information. FlatRateInfo.com is the source for accurate, up-to-date and highly searchable information for the investigative and collection industries. As the name implies, most of our databases are available at a flat rate, meaning no per-search fees. Available databases on FlatRateInfo.com include two national people locators; national bankruptcies, judgments and liens; national property; national fictitious business names; the Social Security death index, and others. At the heart of the FlatRateInfo.com system is the QI National People Locator, a powerful searching tool containing over 600 million records from most U.S residents, including SSN, current and previous addresses, date of birth and aliases. Unlimited searching subscriptions. Retrieve valuable and up-to-date information from all states. Call for a free demo.

FOIA Group Inc

1090 Vermont Ave NW # 800, Washington, DC 20005
Phone: 202-408-7028; Fax: 202-347-8419
Web site: www.foia.com   **Email:** foia@foia.com
Founded: 1988   **Memberships:** ABA, SCIP
Clientele Restrictions: Casual requesters permitted

Proprietary Databases or Gateways:
Database Name: **FOIA-Ware**
  Software/Training (US)

Special Distribution Methods to Client: Dial-Up (Other than Internet), Disk, Email, Internet, Software

FOIA specializes in the Freedom of Information Act and State Open Records Act protocols. They help prepare and file FOIA requests, monitor and review documents, and service the legal profession and others seeking information through the Act. They also offer agency and customer competitive research and surveys. FOIA Group attorneys provide whistleblower assistance.

Gale Group Inc, The

27500 Drake Rd, Framington Hills, MI 48331-3535
Toll-free phone: 800-877-4253; Phone: 248-699-4253
Web site: www.gale.com   **Email:** galeord@gale.com
Branch Offices: Cambridge, MA; **Woodbridge**, CT; **Foster City**, CA
Founded: 1998   **Parent Company:** Thomson Corporation
Clientele Restrictions: Casual requesters permitted

Proprietary Databases or Gateways:
Database Name: **GaleNet**
  Associations/Trade Groups, Addresses/Telephone Numbers, Foreign Country Information, Corporate/Trade Name
    Data (US, International)

Special Distribution Methods to Client: CD-ROM, Dial-Up (Other than Internet), Microfilm/Microfiche

As a major publisher of academic, educational, and business research companies serving libraries, educational institutions, and businesses in all major international markets, The Gale Group provides much of its material online through products such as Associations Unlimited, Biography and Genealogy Master Index, Brands and Their Companies, Gale Business Resources, and Peterson's Publications. It was formed Sept. '98 with the merger of Gale Research, Information Access Co., and Primary Source Material.

Global Securities Information, Inc

419 7th St NW, #300, Washignton, DC 20004
Toll-free phone: 800-669-1154; Phone: 202-628-1155; Fax: 202-628-1133
Web site: www.gsionline.com/   **Email:** info@gsionline.com
Founded: 1988
Clientele Restrictions: Casual requesters permitted.
Proprietary Databases or Gateways:
Gateway Name: **Live Edgar**
  SEC/Other Financial (DC)

Database Name: **International Prospectuses**
  Foreign Country Information (Intl)

Special Distribution Methods to Client: Email, Internet

Global Securities will scan and email documents to eliminate delay of overnight delivery. The SEC database contains searchable filings for both electronically filed documents and scanned paper images.

GoverNet

101 Technology Dr, Idaho Falls, ID 83401
Toll-free phone: 208-522-2896; Phone: 208-522-1225
Web site: www.governet.net   **Email:** pgy@governet.net
Founded: 2000
Clientele Restrictions: Approved registration required.
Proprietary Databases or Gateways:
Gateway Name: **surfNV**
  Corporate/Trade Name Data,Litigation/Judgments/Tax Liens, Uniform Commercial Code, Real Estate/Assessor (NV)

Gateway Name: **eregistry**
  Licenses/Registrations/Permits, (NV)

Special Distribution Methods to Client: Internet

GoverNet has packaged together Nevada state online resources including Secretary of State and county assessor/treasurer/recorders for Carson City, Churchill, Clark (licenses), Elko, Esmeralda, Eureka, Humboldt, Lander, Lyon, Mineral, Nye, Pershing, Storey, Washoe, and White Pine. Also availabe is building permits, contractors, licensees, and unsecured property. Register online with credit card. Also includes agency links for AZ and ID.

GuideStar

427 Scotland Street, Williamsburg, VA 23185
Phone: 757-229-4631
Web site: www.guidestar.org   **Email:** administrator@guidestar.org   **Parent Company:** Philanthropic Research Inc
Clientele Restrictions: None
Proprietary Databases or Gateways:
Database Name: **Charity Search**
  Corporate/Trade Name Data (US)

Special Distribution Methods to Client: Internet

GuideStar is a searchable database of more than 640,000 non-profit organizations in the United States. Type a name in the Charity Search box to find your favorite charity, or use the Advanced Search to find a charity by subject, state, zip code, or other criteria.

Haines & Company Inc

8050 Freedom Ave, North Canton, OH 44720
Toll-free phone: 800-843-8452; Phone: 330-494-9111; Fax: 330-494-3862
Web site: www.haines.com   **Email:** criscros@haines.com
Branch Offices: Atlanta, GA, 770-936-9308; Fax: 770-455-1799; **San Francisco**, CA, 510-471-6181; Fax: 510-471-4910; **Chicago**, IL, 847-352-8696; Fax: 847-352-8698

Founded: 1932 **Memberships:** NAR, REIPA, DMA
Clientele Restrictions: Casual requesters permitted

Proprietary Databases or Gateways:
Database Name: **Criss+Cross Plus, Directory**
  Address/Telephone Numbers (US)

Database Name: **Criss+Cross Plus**
  Real Estate/Assessor (US)

Special Distribution Methods to Client: CD-ROM, Dial-Up (Other than Internet), Disk, Lists/Labels, Magnetic Tape, Publication/Directory, Software

Varied products and full-service capabilities allow Haines & Company to satisfy the marketing and research needs of most industries. County Real Estate on CD-ROM has been noted for its ease of use, speed and marketing power. They also offer cross-reference directories in book form or on CD-ROM in 71 major markets, also business and residential lists on labels, manuscripts, CD-ROM, off the Internet or bulletin boards (24-hour turnaround time available). Using their target list or a customer-provided list, they can provide complete direct marketing services, graphic design, printing and database maintenance -- all in-house. In addition to the branches listed above, they have offices in St. Louis, MO (800-922-3846, fax 314-429-2121), Cincinnati, OH (800-582-1734, fax 513-831-4286), Los Angeles, CA (800-562-8262, fax 714-870-4651) and in Washington, DC (877-889-1027, fax 301-780-3673).

Hollingsworth Court Reporting Inc

10761 Perkins Rd #A, Baton Rouge, LA 70810
Phone: 225-769-3386; Fax: 225-769-1814
Web site: www.public-records.com **Email:** Nora@hcrinc.com
Founded: 1983 **Memberships:** NPRRA
Clientele Restrictions: None reported

Proprietary Databases or Gateways:
Database Name: **Tenant Eviction/Public Record Report**
  Litigation/Judgments/Tax Liens, Tenant History (AL, AR, FL, GA, IL, LA, MS, TN)

Special Distribution Methods to Client: Dial-Up (Other than Internet), Email, FTP, Internet

HCR offers regional public record information including access to 25 million records. They have judgment, lien & eviction information. They also process criminal record searches with a 48 hour turnaround time.

Hoover's Inc

5800 Airport Blvd, Austin, TX 78752
Toll-free phone: 800-486-8666; Phone: 512-374-4500; Fax: 512-374-4505
Web site: www.hoovers.com **Email:** info@hoovers.com
Branch Offices: New York, NY, 212-632-1700; Fax: 212-246-6967/73; **San Francisco**, CA, 415-227-2512; Fax: 415-227-2501
Clientele Restrictions: Casual requesters permitted

Proprietary Databases or Gateways:
Database Name: **Hoover's Company Profiles**
  Addresses/Telephone Numbers, Corporate/Trade Name Data, News/Current Events (US)

Database Name: **Real-Time SEC Documents**
  SEC/Other Financial (US)

Database Name: **Foreign Country Information**
  Foreign Country Information (International)

Special Distribution Methods to Client: CD-ROM, Dial-Up (Other than Internet), FTP, Gateway via Another Online Service, Internet, Publication/Directory, Software

Hoover's, is a leading provider of business information. Hoover's publishes authoritative information on public and private companies worldwide, and provides industry and market intelligence. This information, along with advanced searching tools, is available through Hoover's Online (www.hoovers.com), the company's premier online service that helps sales, marketing, recruiting and business development professionals and senor-level executives get the global intelligence they need to grow their business. Hoover's business information is also available through corporate intranets and distribution agreements with licensees, as well as via print and CD-ROM products form Hoover's Business Press.

Household Drivers Reports Inc (HDR Inc)

902 S Friendswood Dr Suite F, Friendswood, TX 77546
Toll-free phone: 800-899-4437; Phone: 281-996-5509; Fax: 281-996-1947
Web site: www.hdr.com   **Email:** sthomas@hdr.com
Founded: 1989
Clientele Restrictions: Signed agreement required, must be ongoing account; business or government agencies only.

Proprietary Databases or Gateways:
Database Name: **Corp Data**
  Corporation/Trade Name Data (TX)

Database Name: **Criminal Record Data**
  Criminal Information (TX)

Database Name: **Driver & Vehicle**
  Driver and/or Vehicle (TX)

Special Distribution Methods to Client: Dial-Up (Other than Internet), Internet

Household Drivers Report Inc has been in the information business since 1989, pioneering its first online database. Subscribers can access the information available through HDR's online system with the slightest amount of information. The HDR system offers the unique capability of wildcard searches. With only a partial last name, plate, VIN or address, HDR can locate that person or business and identify a wealth of information. Information is updated weekly. An online, real time database system, they offer a "no-hit, no-charge" feature on their online searches as well as a competitive pricing structure. The system is available to qualified professionals in law enforcement, private investigation, insurance fraud investigation, business professionals and security investigations. HDR offers customize information solutions for large volume users. They operate strictly in compliance with state and federal laws. HDR allows access to the following: Texas driver license records, vehicle registration records, business records, vehicle by manufacturer, automatic driver update report, criminal conviction records, sex offender records; also, moving violation reports from Texas. New databases are added periodically.

Idealogic

505 University Ave #1603, Toronto, Ontario, CD M5G 1X3
Toll-free phone: 866-506-9900; Phone: 416-506-9900; Fax: 416-506-0700
Web site: www.idealogic.com   **Email:** ideal@idealogic.com
Founded: 1980   **Memberships:** NPRRA, OAPSOR, PRRN
Clientele Restrictions: Casual requesters permitted

Proprietary Databases or Gateways:
Database Name: **Dynis-Cor:**
  Corporate/Trade Name Data (Canada)

Database Name: **Dynis-Trademarks**
  Trademarks (Canada)

Special Distribution Methods to Client:
Idealogic is a full-service provider of public information from all jurisdictions in Canada. Corporate, personal property, UCC, real estate, motor vehicle and other registry information is available, including bankruptcy, civil and probate courts. Idealogic has knowledge about how to translate public information available in the US to its Canadian counterpart. One day turnarounds are common; credit cards accepted. Can perform service of process.

IDM Corporation

3550 W Temple St, Los Angeles, CA 90004
Toll-free phone: 877-436-3282; Phone: 213-389-2793; Fax: 213-389-9569
Web site: www.idmcorp.com

Founded: 1989   **Parent Company:** Fidelity National Information Solutions   **Memberships:** REIPA
Clientele Restrictions: License required, must be ongoing account
Proprietary Databases or Gateways:
Database Name: **Tax, Assessor and Recorders**
   Real Estate/Assessor (US)

Special Distribution Methods to Client: CD-ROM, Dial-Up (Other than Internet), Disk, Magnetic Tape
IDM Corporation is one of the largest source providers of real estate public records. They convert 900 tax/assessor counties and 500 recorder's counties to a uniform format. Their assessment files are updated once per year, and recorder's are updated weekly. Their business-to-business site is www.sitexdata.com, and their consumer site is www.smarthomebuy.com.

iDocket.com

P.O. Box 30514, Amarillo, TX 79120
Toll-free phone: 800-566-7164; Phone: 806-351-0202; Fax: 806-351-2329
Web site: www.idocket.com   **Email:** armandob@SIMAS.COM
Founded: 1999   **Parent Company:** Solutions, Inc
Clientele Restrictions: None reported.
Proprietary Databases or Gateways:
Database Name: **iDockets**
   Criminal Information, Litigation/Judgments/Tax Liens (TX-20 counties)
Special Distribution Methods to Client: Internet
iDockets gathers civil and criminal court case information from participating TX and OK counties each evening and posts it online for the Courts/Circuits. Basic information - name searching - is free; deeper case history information requires registration and fees. TX counties include: Bailey, Bandera, Brooks, Cameron, Eastland, El Paso, Guadalupe, Hays, Harris, Hidalgo, Hill, McCollough, Parmer, Potter, Brooks, Navarro, Randall.

iiX (Insurance Information Exchange)

PO Box 30001, College Station, TX 77842-3001
Toll-free phone: 800-683-8553;; Fax: 979-696-5584
Web site: www.iix.com
Founded: 1966   **Parent Company:** ISO
Clientele Restrictions: Must be ongoing account
Proprietary Databases or Gateways:
Database Name: **UDI-Undisclosed Drivers, VIN**
   Driver and/or Vehicle (US)

Gateway Name: **Motor Vehicle Reports**
   Driver and/or Vehicle (US)

Special Distribution Methods to Client: Dial-Up (Other than Internet), Internet, Software
iiX is an established provider of information systems to the insurance industry. Their services and products include MVR, claims, undisclosed driver, and other underwriting services. The Undisclosed Driver Information (UDI) and VIN are only available on Expressnet, the Internet ordering system. A new program offered by iiX is ExpressFill. Start with a phone number, and ExpressFill prefills information for that address for drivers, VINs and gives the option to order an MVR.

Industrial Foundation of America

16420 Park Ten Pl #520, Houston, TX 77084
Toll-free phone: 800-592-1433; Phone: 281-398-0082
Web site: www.ifa-america.com   **Email:** ifa@ifa-america.com
Founded: 1960   **Memberships:** NHRA, SHRM, BBB
Clientele Restrictions: Restricted to employers only

Proprietary Databases or Gateways:
Database Name: **Member Records & Court Records**
  Workers Compensation (TX, OK, LA, NM)

Special Distribution Methods to Client:
The Industrial Foundation specializes as a database and clearinghouse of industrial accident histories on individuals, whether or not Workers' Comp is involved. Data is acquired from member employers' records and from state and federal records where litigated. No medical information is included. The Industrial Foundation provides free legal services for members, also professional safety and human reserve information for members from its library and key staff members.

Infocon Corporation

PO Box 568, Ebensburg, PA 15931-0568
Phone: 814-472-6066; Fax: 814-472-5019
Web site: www.ic-access.com
Clientele Restrictions: Casual requesters permitted

Proprietary Databases or Gateways:
Gateway Name: **INFOCON County Access System**
  Criminal Information, Vital Records, Voter Registration, Litigation/Judgments/Tax Liens, Real Estate/Assessor (PA-15 counties)

Special Distribution Methods to Client: Dial-Up (Other than Internet), Internet
The Infocon County Access System offers online access to civil, criminal, real estate, and vital record information in Pennsylvania counties of Armstrong, Bedford, Blair, Butler, Clarion, Clinton, Erie, Huntingdon, Lawrence, Mifflin, Potter, and Pike. Fees are involved, access is through a remote 800 number (internet access may be available).

Information Inc

PO Box 382, Hermitage, TN 37076
Toll-free phone: 877-484-4636; Phone: 615-884-8000; Fax: 615-889-6492
Web site: http://hometown.aol.com/publicrecordstn   **Email:** infomantn@aol.com
Founded: 1991   **Memberships:** PRRN, FOP
Clientele Restrictions: Casual requesters permitted

Proprietary Databases or Gateways:
Database Name: **Arrest Database (Nashville)**
  Criminal Information (TN-Nashville)

Special Distribution Methods to Client: Dial-Up (Other than Internet), Email
Information Inc provides a real time criminal arrest database for Davidson County, TN. This includes all agencies in the 20th Judicial District of Tennessee. The database, updated weekly allows you to obtain results 24/7. Instant results let you know if there is more research to be done at the courthouse level, and often allows for the compilation of additional information such as former residences and license information. Free demos and audits are welcomed.

Information Network of Arkansas

425 West Capitol Ave #3565, Little Rock, AR 72201
Toll-free phone: 800-392-6069; Phone: 501-324-8900
Web site: www.state.ar.us/ina.html   **Email:** info@ark.org
Founded: 1998
Clientele Restrictions: Signed agreement required, must be ongoing account

Proprietary Databases or Gateways:
Gateway Name: **INA**
  Driver and/or Vehicle, Workers' Compensation (AR)
Gateway Name: **Secretary of State**
  Corporate/Trade Name Data,Licenses/Registrations/Permits (AR)

Special Distribution Methods to Client: Internet

The Information Network of Arkansas was created by the Arkansas Legislature with the responsibility of assisting the state in permitting citizens to access public records. There is a fee for driving records, Nursing Registry, Lobbyist, and Workers' Comp record access, but none for Secretary of State Trademarks, Corporations, Banking and notaries. There may be fees for new record categories.

Information Network of Kansas

534 S Kansas Ave #1210, Topeka, KS 66603
Toll-free phone: 800-452-6727; Phone: 785-296-5059; Fax: 785-296-5563
Web site: www.ink.org
Founded: 1991
Clientele Restrictions: Signed agreement required, must be ongoing account

Proprietary Databases or Gateways:
Gateway Name: **Premium Services**
   Driver and/or Vehicle, Uniform Commercial Code, Corporate/Trade Name Data, Legislation/Regulations, Real Estate/Assessor (KS)

Gateway Name: **Premium Services**
   Litigation/Judgments/Tax Liens (KS-Johnson, Sedgwick, Shawnee, Wyandotte)

Gateway Name: **Premium Services**
   Criminal Information (KS- Sedgwick, Shawnee, Wyandotte)

Special Distribution Methods to Client: Dial-Up (Other than Internet), Internet
INK is the official source for electronic access to the State of Kansas government information. Access to public record information is a premium service and requires a subscription. Now includes Johnson, Shawnee, and Wyandotte Counties.

InforME - Information Resource of Maine

One Market Square #101, Augusta, ME 04330
Toll-free phone: 877-463-3468; Phone: 207-621-2600
Web site: www.informe.org/subscribe/egovservices.html   **Email:** info@informe.org

Proprietary Databases or Gateways:
Gateway Name: **Bureau of Motor Vehicles Driver's Records**
   Driver and/or Vehicle (ME)

Special Distribution Methods to Client: Internet
InforME provides access to Maine's Bureau of Motor Vehicles Driver's Records on a subscription basis.

Informus Corporation

2001 Airport Rd #201, Jackson, MS 39208
Toll-free phone: 800-364-8380; Phone: 601-664-1900
Web site: www.informus.com   **Email:** info@informus.com
Founded: 1990   **Parent Company:** ChoicePoint
Clientele Restrictions: Signed agreement required, must be ongoing account

Proprietary Databases or Gateways:
Database Name: **Informus**
   Workers Compensation (MS, US)

Gateway Name: **IntroScan**
   Addresses/Telephone Numbers (US)

Special Distribution Methods to Client: Dial-Up (Other than Internet), Internet
Informus provides an online pre-employment screening and public record retrieval service. Online access is available through the Internet. Some searches provide instant information, depending on state and category.

Innovative Enterprises Inc

PO Box 22506, Newport News, VA 23609
Toll-free phone: 888-777-9435; Phone: 757-875-9500; Fax: 757-877-4242
Web site: www.knowthefacts.com   **Email:** innovate@knowthefacts.com
Founded: 1996   **Memberships:** PRRN
Clientele Restrictions: Casual requesters permitted

Proprietary Databases or Gateways:
Database Name: **Virginia Criminal Records Database**
    Criminal Information (VA)

Special Distribution Methods to Client: Email, Internet

Innovative Enterprises' staff brings forward more than 55 years of combined Virginia judicial, law enforcement, and military experience, making them qualified to service client's background research needs. MVR's retrieved from thirty states. Their proprietary VA Criminal Records Database includes millions of disposed court cases from every VA county.

Intellicorp Ltd

3659 Green Road #116, Beachwood, OH 44122
Toll-free phone: 888-946-8355; Phone: 216-591-9032; Fax: 216-591-9578
Web site: www.intellicorp.net   **Email:** info@intellicorp.net   **Founded:** 1996   **Memberships:** ASIS, SHRM
Clientele Restrictions: Signed agreement required, must be ongoing account

Proprietary Databases or Gateways:
Database Name: **Court, Inmate, & Booking Records**
    Criminal Information (IN, IL IA, MN, OH)

Special Distribution Methods to Client: Dial-Up (Other than Internet), Email, Gateway via Another Online Service

Intellicorp is an Ohio-based company providing online access to public records and other information. Their online systems are being used by law enforcement agencies, businesses, and professional organizations throughout the country. Their customers and markets include human resources, health care, insurance companies, investigators, financial, attorneys, government and general business needs for the information. All approved subscribers have been carefully screened and qualified under the company's enrollment process. By utilizing the latest technologies, Intellicorp can provide access to an array of information in a fast and cost efficient manner. Intellicorp is one of a select group of companies licensed to provide access to Arrest and Booking records from OH, MI, IN, MN and IL county sheriff's offices. Information products are made available through its secured online system, accessible via the Internet or by dial-up. With over 700 million records available immediately online and access to millions of other records from other sources, Intellicorp services provide access to the right information to make more informed decisions.

Interstate Data Corporation

113 Latigo Lane, Canon City, CO 81212
Toll-free phone: 800-332-7999
Web site: www.cdrominvestigations.com   **Founded:** 1987   **Clientele Restrictions:** Must be ongoing account
Proprietary Databases or Gateways:
Gateway Name: **CA Criminal**
    Criminal Information (CA)
Database Name: **CA Professional Licenses**
    Licenses/Registration/Permits (CA)
Database Name: **CA Corporate Records**
    Corporate/Trade Name Data (CA)

Special Distribution Methods to Client: CD-ROM, Dial-Up (Other than Internet)

Intertstate Data Corporation provides primary access to over 50 databases for the California area. Databases include professional licenses, Board of Equalization, fictitious business names, criminal and civil courts, and others. Features online and CD-ROM technology at competitive prices.

Investigative & Background Solutions Inc

4155 E Jewell Ave #901, Denver, CO 80222
Toll-free phone: 800-580-0474; Phone: 303-692-8050; Fax: 303-692-8511
Web site: www.ibs-denver.com   **Email:** info@ibs-denver.com
Founded: 1993
Clientele Restrictions: Casual requesters permitted

Proprietary Databases or Gateways:

Gateway Name: **Colorado Court Records**
  Criminal Information (CO)

Special Distribution Methods to Client: Dial-Up (Other than Internet), Software

With almost a decade of experience, IBS can tailor a solution to any circumstance which will effectively ease the applicant screening process in Colorado or nationally.

Investigators Anywhere Resource Line

PO Box 40970, Mesa, AZ 85274-0970
Toll-free phone: 800-338-3463; Phone: 480-730-8088; Fax: 480-730-8103
Web site: www.investigatorsanywhere.com/   **Email:** IONPRRN@IONINC.com
Founded: 1987   **Parent Company:** ION Incorporated   **Memberships:** ASIS, CII, ION, NALI, NAPPS, NCISS
Clientele Restrictions: Casual requesters permitted

Proprietary Databases or Gateways:

Database Name: **Resource Line**
  Addresses/Telephone Numbers, Licenses/Registrations/Permits, Foreign Country Information (US, International)

Special Distribution Methods to Client: Automated Telephone Look-Up, Dial-Up (Other than Internet), Internet

Investigators Anywhere Resources' Resource Line service provides access to over 30,000 investigators, prescreened for excellence of service levels. Connect direct to the web page for 24 hour service. Callers are matched to appropriate investigators. No fee to the callers except for international and non-commercial projects.

IQ Data Systems

1401 El Camino Ave, 5th Fl, Sacramento, CA 95815
Toll-free phone: 800-264-6517; Phone: 916-418-9000; Fax: 916-418-9001
Web site: www.iqdata.com   **Email:** ballas@iqdata.com
Founded: 1996   **Memberships:** NPRRA
Clientele Restrictions: Must be ongoing account

Proprietary Databases or Gateways:

Database Name: **IQ Data**
  Uniform Commercial Code, Bankruptcy, Real Estate/Assessor, Litigation/Judgments/Tax Liens,
    Addresses/Telephone Numbers, Corporate/Trade Name Data (US)

Gateway Name: **IQ Data**
  Driver and/or Vehicle, Credit Information (US)

Special Distribution Methods to Client: Internet

IQ Data Systems is a leading nationwide online public record information provider. Accurate, up-to-date cost effective and instant easy-to-access national data to verify information and identities, conduct background checks, locate people/business/assets, detect fraud, find criminal/civil/financial records, assist law enforcement and more. Empowering corporations, government agencies and individuals to maximize the use and value of public record information. IQ Data's cutting edge technology and proprietary databases direct its customers to make better, timely and more informed decisions.

Judici

1809 W Main, PMB #104, Carbondale, IL 62901
Fax: 618-549-0675
Web site: www.judici.com   **Email:** info@judici.com   **Founded:** 2001
Clientele Restrictions: Subscription agreement required.
Proprietary Databases or Gateways:
Database Name: **CourtLook, Multi-Search**
  Criminal Information, Litigation/Judgments (IL)
Special Distribution Methods to Client: Internet
Judici is a vendor neutral XML/Java based publishing solution for consolidating case information from multiple court sources; i.e., they support Illinois courts' online efforts and provide access for subscribers. Products include Multi-Court (searches and reports), Courtlook (individuals involved in cases) and CaseWatch monitoring service. Several IL courts can be searched for free from the Judici web site.

Juritas.com

247 S State St. #6, Chicago, IL 60604-1901
Toll-free phone: 888-877-9695; Phone: 312-424-0800; Fax: 312-424-0700
Web site: www.juritas.com   **Email:** jparkman@juritas.com   **Founded:** 2000
Clientele Restrictions: Registration required.
Proprietary Databases or Gateways:
Database Name: **Juritas**
  Criminal Information (CA, DE, FL, IL, NJ, WA)
Database Name: **Juritas**
  Litigation/Judgments/Tax Liens (CA, DE, FL, IL, NJ, WA)
Special Distribution Methods to Client: Internet
The documents found on Juritas.com come directly from state and federal trial courts across the United States, and cover the 14 most litigated practice areas, including Antitrust, Personal Injury, Securities, Medical Malpractice, Tax, Insurance, Labor & Employment, Products Liability, White Collar Criminal, Environmental, Civil Rights, Intellectual Property and more.

KnowX

730 Peachtree St. #700, Atlanta, GA 30308
Toll-free phone: 888-975-6699;; Fax: 404-541-0260
Web site: www.knowx.com   **Email:** support@knowx.com   **Parent Company:** ChoicePoint
Clientele Restrictions: Casual requesters permitted
Proprietary Databases or Gateways:
Database Name: **KnowX**
  Addresses/Telephone Numbers, Vital Records, Real Estate/Assessor, Bankruptcy, Licenses/Registrations/Permits, Corporate/Trade Name Data, Military Svc, Aviation, Vessels, Litigation/Judgments/Tax Liens, Uniform Commercial Code (US (with limited Canadian))
Special Distribution Methods to Client: Dial-Up (Other than Internet), Internet
KnowX is one of the most comprehensive sources of public records available on the Internet, and as a subsidiary of ChoicePoint, they have 40 offices nationwide. KnowX provides public records on aircraft ownership, bankruptcies, business directories, partnerships, DBAs, DEAs, death records, Duns, judgments, liens, lawsuits, licensing, residencies, real property foreclosures, tax records, property transfers, sales permits, stock ownership, UCC and watercraft records. Often, they run promotions that offer free services.

Kompass USA Inc

1255 Route 70, #25s, Parkway 70 Plaza, Lakewood, NJ 08701
Phone: 732-730-0340; Fax: 732-730-0342
Web site: www.kompass-intl.com
Clientele Restrictions: Casual Requesters Accepted

Proprietary Databases or Gateways:
Database Name: **Kompass.com**
  Addresses/Telephone Numbers, Corporate/Trade Name Data (US)

Database Name: **Kompass.com**
  Foreign Country Information (International)
Special Distribution Methods to Client: CD-ROM, Database, Email, Internet, Lists/Labels, Publication/Directory
The Kompass Worldwide Database contains access to 1.5 million companies, 23 million product and service references, 600,000 trade and brand names, and 2.9 million executives' names. Many searches are free over the Net.

KY Direct

101 Cold Harbor Dr, Dept.of Info. Systems, Frankfort, KY 40601
Phone: 502-564-7284; Fax: 502-564-1598
Web site: http://more.kydirect.net/OnlineServices.asp/   **Email:** bpuckett@mail.state.ky.us
Founded: 2000   **Parent Company:** Commonwealth of Kentucky

Proprietary Databases or Gateways:
Gateway Name: **Secretary of State**
  Corporate/Trade Name Data (KY)

Gateway Name: **Vital Statistics**
  Vital Records (KY)

Gateway Name: **Legislature Searching Service**
  Legislation/Regulation (KY)

Gateway Name: **UCC Index Search**
  Uniform Commerical Code (KY)

Gateway Name: **Driving Records**
  Driving Records (KY)

Special Distribution Methods to Client: Internet, Lists/Labels, Publication/Directory
KY Direct is the Commonwealth of Kentucky's clearinghouse web site or the dissemination of state agency, Secretary of State information, and vital statistics. Site is a portal for the purchase of online records and online and print directories such as state agencies lists, resource directory, sex offenders lists, nuring registry, state agency telephone directory, agency forms, maps, and more.

Landaccess.com - ACS Government Land Records

PO Box 4889, Syracuse, NY 13221
Toll-free phone: 800-800-7009
Web site: www.landaccess.com   **Email:** registration@landaccess.com
Founded: 2000   **Parent Company:** ACS' Government Records Management Div.
Clientele Restrictions: Registration may be required to access certain states.

Proprietary Databases or Gateways:
Database Name: **Landaccess.com**
  Real Estate/Assessor, UCC (OH)

Special Distribution Methods to Client:
In addition to providing free access to recording information for more than 15 Ohio counties, they offer access to a small number of counties in IA, IL, MI, NJ, and NY, though these may require free registration.

Landings.com

6280 S Valley View Blvd, #314, Las Vegas, NV 89118
Phone: 702-920-8298; Fax: 702-920-8298
Web site: www.landings.com/   **Email:** landings@landings.com
Founded: 1966
Clientele Restrictions: None

Proprietary Databases or Gateways:
Database Name: **Landings.com, Aviation databases**
  Aviation (US)

Special Distribution Methods to Client: Internet

Landings.com is the the Internet's most somprehensive collection of uniquely searchable Aviation Database's including: N-Numbers, Pilots, Mediacl Examiners, Designated Examiners, World Tail Number Registration, A & P, detailed World Airport information and free flight planning service, FAA regulations, NOTAMs, ADs, STCs, TSOs, and TCDs. Also, NTSB accident reports and SDRs, aircraft performance, flight related calculators, and 16,000+ external aviation links are all available free of charge.

Law Bulletin Information Network

415 N State, Chicago, IL 60610-4674
Phone: 312-644-7800; Fax: 312-644-1215
Web site: www.lawbulletin.com
Founded: 1854   **Memberships:** NALFM, NPRRA, NFPA
Clientele Restrictions: Casual requesters permitted

Proprietary Databases or Gateways:
Database Name: **Access Plus**
  Real Estate/Assessor, Court Dockets, Uniform Commercial Code (IL-Cook County)

Database Name: **Access Plus**
  Litigation/Judgments/Tax Liens (IL-Central, North Counties)

Database Name: **Access Plus**
  Addresses/Telephone Numbers (IL)

Special Distribution Methods to Client: Dial-Up (Other than Internet), Email, Internet, Publication/Directory

The Law Bulletin Publishing Company's Information Network's primary product, AccessPlus, provides both online and access to Illinois Courts, vital public record information, UCCs, corporate documents, court dockets, realty sales, etc. They offer other document retrieval services including licensed investigative services through an affiliated licensed, private investigation agency. These services can be requested online through the DocuServices product at www.lawbulletin.com.

LEXIS-NEXIS

PO Box 933, Dayton, OH 45401-0933
Toll-free phone: 800-227-9597; Phone: 937-865-6800
Web site: www.lexis-nexis.com   **Email:** Greg.Noble@lexis-nexis.com
Founded: 1973   **Parent Company:** Reed Elsevier Inc   **Memberships:** AALL, ATLA, NALA, ABI, NPRRA, SCIP
Clientele Restrictions: Signed Agreement Required

Proprietary Databases or Gateways:
Database Name: **LEXIS Law Publishing, Shepard's**
  Litigation/Judgments/Tax Liens (US)

Database Name: **USBoat**
  Vessels
       (AL,AZ,AR,CO,CT,FL,GE,IA,ME,MD,MA,MS,MO,MN,MT,NE,NV,NH,NC,ND,OH,OR,SC,UT,VA,WV,WI)

Database Name: **Congressional Information Service**
  Legislation/Regulation (US)

Database Name: **ALLBKT**
  Bankruptcy (US)
Database Name: **ALLOWN**
  Real Estate/Assessor (US)
Database Name: **ALLUCC**
  Uniform Commercial Code (US)
Database Name: **ALLSOS**
  Corporate/Trade Name Data (US)
Database Name: **B-Find, P-Find, P-Seek**
  Addresses/Telephone Numbers (US)
Database Name: **Professional Licensing Boards**
  Licenses/Registrations/Permits (CA, CT, FL, GE, IL, MA,MI,NE,NJ,NC,OG,PA,TX,VA,WI)

Special Distribution Methods to Client: Dial-Up (Other than Internet), Gateway via Another Online Service, Publication/Directory
The LEXIS-NEXIS services offer one of the most comprehensive aggregations of public records available anywhere. They compile and categorize these records so that you find the information you need faster and easier. With minimal effort, you can search one of the largest and faster growing public records collections in the United States. They offer industry-leading access to critical information such as real and personal property records; business and person locators; civil and criminal filings; Secretary of State records; liens, judgments, and UCC filings; jury verdicts and settlements; professional license, bankruptcy filings; and much more.

LIDA Credit Agency Inc

450 Sunrise Hwy, Rockville Centre, NY 11570
Phone: 516-678-4600; Fax: 516-678-4611
Founded: 1929   **Email:** lcainc@qwest.net
Clientele Restrictions: Casual requesters permitted

Proprietary Databases or Gateways:
Database Name: **Litigation Report**
  Litigation/Judgments/Tax Liens (DE, NJ, NY, PA)

Special Distribution Methods to Client: Email
LIDA's management averages more than 35 years in public record research, investigations and credit/financial reporting. Among their 17 member staff are five licensed and bonded private investigators. They specialize in Metro New York City, including the five boroughs and surrounding counties.

LLC Reporter

Frontier Law Center, 1107 W 6th Ave, Cheyenne, WY 82001
Phone: 307-634-0446; Fax: 307-637-7445
Web site: www.llc-reporter.com   **Email:** WDBagley@LLC-REPORTER.com
Founded: 1993
Clientele Restrictions: Casual Requesters Permitted

Proprietary Databases or Gateways:
Database Name: **LLC Reporter**
  Corporate/Trade Name Data (US)

Special Distribution Methods to Client: Internet, Publication/Directory
The Limited Liability Company Reporter is a national newsletter committed to assisting Lawyers, CPA's and Business Planners who need to stay current in a fast changing field. The Reporter Archive contains all issues of the Reporter from January 1, 1993 to present, accessible by a topic index and author index. The most recent events are found under Current LLC News. The authors are a coast-to-coast network of limited liability company entity practitioners and administrators who contribute their expertise.

Logan Registration Service Inc

PO Box 161644, Sacramento, CA 95816
Phone: 916-457-5787; Fax: 916-457-5789
Web site: www.loganreg.com   **Email:** contact@loganreg.com
Founded: 1976   **Memberships:** NFIB
Clientele Restrictions: Signed agreement required, must be ongoing account

Proprietary Databases or Gateways:
Gateway Name: **Logan**
   Driver and/or Vehicle (CA,US)

Special Distribution Methods to Client: Dial-Up (Other than Internet), Email

Logan has more than 25 years experience working with California driver and vehicle records. They are an online vendor that allows their DMV authorized clients to retrieve driver and vehicle registration records in seconds with a computer software program that is available free of charge. Clients are able to access needed records via phone or fax.

Loren Data Corp

4640 Admiralty Way #430, Marina Del Rey, CA 90292
Toll-free phone: 800-745-6736; Phone: 310-827-7400
Web site: www.LD.com   **Email:** info@LD.com
Founded: 1987
Clientele Restrictions: Casual requesters permitted

Proprietary Databases or Gateways:
Gateway Name: **Commerce Business Daily**
   Environmental, Military Svc, News/Current Events, Legislation/Regulation (US)

Special Distribution Methods to Client: Email

Loren Data Corp provides customers with access to government business, helping make bids and gain government contracts. They offer free access and email based subscriptions to their publication Commerce Business Daily, CBD.

Martindale-Hubbell

121 Chanlon Road, Providence, NJ 07974
Toll-free phone: 800-526-4902; Phone: 908-464-6800; Fax: 908-464-3553
Web site: www.martindale.com   **Email:** ccooper@martindale.com
Branch Offices: London, GB, 44 20 7868 4885; Fax: 44 20 7868 4886
Founded: 1868   **Parent Company:** Reed Elsevier PLC Group
Clientele Restrictions: Casual requesters permitted

Proprietary Databases or Gateways:
Database Name: **Martindale-Hubbell Law Directory (Attorneys and Law Firms)**
   Addresses/Telephone Numbers, Education/Employment (US, International)

Special Distribution Methods to Client: CD-ROM, Lists/Labels, Publication/Directory

Martindale-Hubbell's database is now regarded as the primary source for attorney and law firm information around the world. Their flagship product, Martindale-Hubbell Law Directory consists of more the 900,000 listings, organized by city, state, county, and province with extensive cross-references and indexes. Products are available in four media: hardbound print, CR-ROM, via LEXIS/NEXIS (a sister company) and Internet via the Martindale-Hubbell Lawyer Locator. Data includes corporate law departments, legal-related services for P.I.s, title search companies, law digests.

MDR/Minnesota Driving Records

1710 Douglas Dr. N #103, Golden Valley, MN 55422-4313
Toll-free phone: 800-644-6877; Phone: 612-755-1164; Fax: 612-595-8079
Clientele Restrictions: Signed agreement required, must be ongoing account

Proprietary Databases or Gateways:
Database Name: **MDR**
   Driver and/or Vehicle (MN)

Special Distribution Methods to Client: Lists/Labels

MDR provides an automated touch-tone call-in service for driver information in Minnesota, letting clients retrieve a record with a verbal response in less than one minute, followed by a fax hard copy within minutes. Service available 24 hours a day every day. The service is endorsed by the Minnesota Insurance Agents Assoc.

Merchants Security Exchange

20401 NW 2nd Ave #310, Miami, FL 33169
Toll-free phone: 800-226-4483; Phone: 305-654-6670; Fax: 305-654-6680
Web site: www.merchants-fla.com   **Email:** adobles@merchants-fla.com
Branch Offices: Tampa, FL, 800-226-7757; **Orlando**, FL, 800-226-7757
Founded: 1916   **Parent Company:** Merchants Association of Florida   **Memberships:** ACA, ASIS, MBAA
Clientele Restrictions: Permissable users; agreement required.
Proprietary Databases or Gateways:
Gateway Name: **Credit Reports**
  Credit Information (FL, US)

Database Name: **Crime Online Database**
  Criminal Information (FL)

Database Name: **Eviction**
  Tenant History (FL)

Gateway Name: **Public Record**
  Litigation/Judgments/Tax Liens (FL, US)

Special Distribution Methods to Client: Database, Dial-Up (Other than Internet), FTP

Merchants Security Exchange conducts various pre/post employment verifications, such as criminal, MVR, credit, etc. Since they are a credit bureau, they can produce a credit report and SSN verification instantaneously. They have gathered criminal information - felony & misdemeanor - for the entire state of Florida, providing that data instantaneously. They recently began tenant screening and now provide eviction, credit, and criminal searches to any business, per compliance with DPPA and FCRA. The company holds a private investigation firm license.

Merlin Information Services

215 S Complex Dr, Kalispell, MT 59901
Toll-free phone: 800-367-6646; Phone: 406-755-8550; Fax: 406-755-8568
Web site: www.merlindata.com   **Email:** Support@merlindata.com
Founded: 1991   **Memberships:** ACA, CAC, CAPPS, NARM, SCRIA, NCSEA
Clientele Restrictions: Casual requesters permitted

Proprietary Databases or Gateways:
Database Name: **Merlin Cross Directory**
  Addresses/Telephone #s, Credit Data, Driver and/or Vehicle, Vital Records, Voter Registration (US)

Gateway Name: **National FlatRate, Collector's FlatRate**
  Civil/Criminal Indexes, UCC, Aviation/Vessels, MVRs, Real Estate/Assessor, Litigation/Judgments/Tax Liens,
    Addresses/Telephone #s, Corp./Trade Name Data, SSN, Bankruptcy, Credit Information,
    Licenses/Registration/Permits, Vital Records, Voter Regis. (US)

Gateway Name: **Merlin Super Header**
  Addresses/Telephone #s, SSNs, Credit Information, Vital Statistics (US)

Gateway Name: **QuikInfo.net FlatRate**
  Civil/Criminal (CA), UCC, Aviation/Vessels, Real Estate/Assessor, Criminal Data, Driver and/orVehicle, Wrokers'
    Comp, Addresses/Telephone Numbers, Corporation/Trade Name Data, SSN, Bankruptcy,
    Licenses/Registration/Permits, Vital Records, Voter Regis. (US)

Database Name: **Nat'l Fictitious Business Names**
  Corporation/Trade Names, Addresses/Telephone Numbers (CA, US)

Database Name: **CA Criminal Indexes, CA Brides/Grooms, CA Birth/Death Indexes, many other CA databases**
  UCC (Filing Index), Civil/Criminal Indexes, Vital Records, Licenses/Reg./Permits, Real Estate/Assessor,
    Litigation/Judgments/Tax Liens, Wills/Probate (CA)
Gateway Name: **Link to America, DOB File**
  Addresss/Phone #s, Credit Data, Driver and/or Vehicle, Real Estate/Assessor, Vital Statistics, Voter Registration
    (US)
Database Name: **Nat'l People Finder/Credit Headers/Criminal/Property**
  Addresses/Phone #s, Real Estate/Assessor, Litigation/Judgments/Tax Liens, Criminal Data, Credit Data, Vital
    Statistics (US)
Special Distribution Methods to Client: CD-ROM, Dial-Up (Other than Internet), Internet, Magnetic Tape
Merlin Information Services provides access to public records on the Internet. Their search and retrieval site and their
software assists in obtaining results not found through traditional access. Merlin's extensive California databases are the
most current and complete available. Their wide selection of national databases such as The Merlin Cross-Directory,
Link to America, and Nat'l FlatRate rounds out their extensive skiptracing and investigative tools, helping you locate
people, assets, neighbors, and associates.

Metro Market Trends Inc

PO Box 30042, Pensacola, FL 32503-1042
Toll-free phone: 800-239-1668; Phone: 850-474-1398; Fax: 850-478-6249
Web site: www.mmtinfo.com   **Email:** mmt@mmtinfo.com
Founded: 1990   **Memberships:** REIPA
Clientele Restrictions: Casual requesters permitted

Proprietary Databases or Gateways:
Database Name: **Real Estate Activity Reporting System**
  Real Estate/Assessor (FL, AL)
Special Distribution Methods to Client: CD-ROM, Database, Disk, Email, Lists/Labels, Magnetic Tape, Software
MMTinfo is a leading provider of real estate related information products and software for Florida and south Alabama.
Real estate information products include tax roll databases, updated real estate sales information systems, market share
reports, comparable sales reports, property owner mailing lists, and custom data runs for economic and financial
analysis. Real estate software products include tax roll programs and real estate sales information programs that are
licensed to other real estate information providers.

MetroNet

500 City Parkway West #205, (Attn.: Pat Young), Orange, CA 92868
Toll-free phone: 888-217-6064 ext 1183
Web site: www.experian.com/products/metronet.html
Founded: 1941   **Parent Company:** Experian   **Memberships:** DMA, ACA, ALA
Clientele Restrictions: Casual requesters permitted

Proprietary Databases or Gateways:
Database Name: **MetroNet, Cole's Directory**
  Addresses/Telephone Numbers, Real Estate/Assessor (US)

Special Distribution Methods to Client: Automated Telephone Look-Up, CD-ROM, Dial-Up (Other than Internet), Gateway via
Another Online Service, Publication/Directory
MetroNet includes direct access to the electronic directory assistance databases of the Regional Bells (RBOC's).
Regional editions of the MetroSearch CD-ROM products and call-in services are featured. At the US Experian web
site, select "Subscriber" and click MetroNet.

MicroPatent USA

250 Dodge Ave, East Haven, CT 06512
Toll-free phone: 800-648-6787; Phone: 203-466-5055; Fax: 203-466-5054
Web site: www.micropat.com   **Email:** info@micropat.com
Branch Offices: London, UK

Founded: 1989   **Parent Company:** Information Holdings Inc
Memberships: AALL, ATLA, AIPLA, INTA, NALA, NLG
Clientele Restrictions: Casual requesters permitted

Proprietary Databases or Gateways:
Database Name: **WPS, TradeMark Checker, Mark Search Plus**
   Patents, Trademarks (US, International)

Special Distribution Methods to Client: CD-ROM, Dial-Up (Other than Internet), Disk, Email, Internet, Software

MicroPatent is a global leader in the production and distribution of patent and trademark information. MicroPatent is committed to developing intellectual property systems with its sophisticated and talented programming staff. MicroPatent Europe is located in London, England.

MidSouth Information Services

116 Lakeview Drive, Greenville, NC 27858
Phone: 252-757-2772; Fax: 252-757-3184
Web site: www.midsouthinfo.com   **Email:** ron@midsouthinfo.com
Founded: 1998   **Memberships:** ASIS, SHRM
Clientele Restrictions: Casual requesters permitted

Proprietary Databases or Gateways:
Gateway Name: **Carolina Information Inc**
   Criminal Information, Litigation/Judgments/Tax Liens (NC)

Special Distribution Methods to Client: Dial-Up (Other than Internet), Email, Gateway via Another Online Service

MidSouth provides county criminal record checks for all 50 states and statewide criminal searches. They also provide consumer credit reports, DMV reports, education and prior employment reports, 24-48 hours for credit reports and up to a week for DMV reports. They also provide access to North Carolina's criminal and civil indexes through their sister company Carolina Information, Inc.

Military Information Enterprises Inc

PO Box 17118, Spartanburg, SC 29301
Toll-free phone: 800-937-2133; Phone: 864-595-0981; Fax: 864-595-0813
Web site: www.militaryusa.com   **Email:** thelocator@aol.com
Founded: 1988   **Memberships:** SCALI
Clientele Restrictions: Casual requesters permitted

Proprietary Databases or Gateways:
Database Name: **Nationwide Locator Online**
   Military Svc (US)

Special Distribution Methods to Client: Email, Internet, Publication/Directory

Military Information Enterprises specializes in current and former military locates and background checks, also military reunions and service verifications. They also publish books on locating people. The owner is a South Carolina licensed private investigator.

Motznik Computer Services Inc

8301 Briarwood St #100, Anchorage, AK 99518-3332
Phone: 907-344-6254; Fax: 907-344-1759
Web site: www.motznik.com   **Email:** sales@motznik.com
Founded: 1974   **Memberships:** NFIB
Clientele Restrictions: Casual requesters permitted

Proprietary Databases or Gateways:
Database Name: **Alaska Public Information Access System**
   Aviation, Vessels, Bankruptcy, Licenses/Registrations/Permits, Litigation/Judgments/Tax Liens, Criminal
     Information, Corporate/Trade Name Data, Uniform Commercial Code, Real Estate/Assessor, Voter Registration
     and Driver and/or Vehicle (AK)

Special Distribution Methods to Client: Dial-Up (Other than Internet)

Motznik Computer Services' product is a comprehensive online information research system that provides access to a wide selection of Alaska public files. Information that can be researched includes: tax liens, UCC, address, real property, Anchorage civil suits, commercial fishing vessels, judgments, motor vehicles, partnerships, bankruptcies, aircraft, permanent fund filing, businesses, Anchorage criminal cases and commercial fishing permits. MV data does not include driver's personal information.

MyFloridaCounty.com

400 N. Ashley Dr, Suite 1925, Tampa, FL 33602
Phone: 877-326-8689; Fax: 813-387-2983
Web site: www.myfloridacounty.com   **Email:** Webmaster@MyFloridaCounty.com
Founded: 2001   **Parent Company:** Florida Local Government Internet Consortium
Clientele Restrictions: Casual requesters permitted.

Proprietary Databases or Gateways:
Database Name: **myfloridacounty.com Official Records Search**
   Litigation/Judgments/Tax Liens, Real Estate/Assessor, Vital Records (FL)

Special Distribution Methods to Client: Internet

A coalition of local government officials have teamed to deliver a variety of ecommerce services through www.MyFloridaCounty.com, Florida's new official website for local government information and services. The service enables citizens and businesses to order copies of Official Records, including civil judgments, marriage certificates, and property records from Clerks of the Court throughout Florida via a consolidated website. Ordering a record takes mere moments and constituents can choose to receive either certified or non-certified documents. No criminal records. Most Florida counties participate.

National Background Data

303 SW 8th St, Ocala, FL 34474
Phone: 352-629-9730
Web site: www.nationalbackgrounddata.com   Email: Info@nationalbackgrounddata.com
Clientele Restrictions: Agreement required

Proprietary Databases or Gateways:
Database Name: **Let's Check America, Nat'l Background Directory**
   Criminal Information (US, FL)
Database Name: **AIM (Address Information Mgr)**
   Addresses/Telephone Numbers (US, FL)

Special Distribution Methods to Client: Internet

NBD compiles The National Background Directory(TM) on line to fill emerging needs for criminal background searches across the nation. Currently provides criminal record information from 37 states and more than 87 million criminal records. Records include court records, incarcerations, and sexual offender records. In the coming year, NBD anticipates having more than 100 statewide databases online from as many as 45 states and the District of Columbia that cover about 95% of the US population. Their AIM product provides information on individuals' past addresses and movement patterns.

National Credit Information Network NCI

PO Box 53247, Cincinnati, OH 45253
Toll-free phone: 800-374-1400; Phone: 513-522-3832; Fax: 513-522-1702
Web site: www.wdia.com
Founded: 1983   **Parent Company:** WDIA Corporation
Clientele Restrictions: Signed agreement required; some searches available to non-members

Proprietary Databases or Gateways:
Database Name: **NCI Network**
   Tenant History (IN, KY, OH)
Gateway Name: **NCI Network**
   Credit Information, Addresses/Telephone Numbers, Voter Registration, Driver and/or Vehicle (US)

Special Distribution Methods to Client: Dial-Up (Other than Internet), Email, Internet

National Credit Information Network (NCI) specializes in interfacing with credit and public record databases for online searches with immediate response time. Online ordering is available for setup and for searches using a credit card. Access is available through their Internet site. Various packages include applicant identity, SSNs, DMVs, education, reference and credential verification, criminal history, bankruptcy and civil history, workers comp claims, and more.

National Fraud Center

Four Horsham Business Center, 300 Welsh Road Bldg. 4 Ste 200, Horsham, PA 19044
Toll-free phone: 800-999-5658; Phone: 215-657-0800; Fax: 215-657-7071
Web site: www.nationalfraud.com   **Email:** email@nationalfraud.com
Branch Offices: Dallas, TX; **Minneapolis**, MN; **San Francisco**, CA
Founded: 1981   **Parent Company:** LEXIS-NEXIS   **Memberships:** ASIS, IAAI, CII, IFS
Clientele Restrictions: Casual requesters permitted

Proprietary Databases or Gateways:
Database Name: **NFC Online**
   Software/Training, Publication/Directory (US, International)
Database Name: **Bank Fraud/Insurance Fraud/Organized Crime/The Fraud Bulletin**
   Criminal Information (US, International)
Gateway Name: **Cellular Fraud Database**
   Criminal Information (US)
Special Distribution Methods to Client: CD-ROM, Dial-Up (Other than Internet), Disk

The Center combines its diverse databases into a system: NFConline. They utilize a fraud prevention, an interdiction program, and risk management tools to discover and prevent fraud and risk. They also specialize in pro-active measures such as security policies, training, and installation of security devices to protect corporations from future losses.

National Marine Fisheries Service

Statistics & Economic Division (F/ST1), 1315 East-West Highway, Silver Spring, MD 20910
Web site: www.st.nmfs.gov/st1/commercial/index.html

Proprietary Databases or Gateways:
Database Name: **Vessel Documentation Data**
   Vessels (US)
Special Distribution Methods to Client: Internet

This organization provides free searches to the US Coast Guard vessel database. Data is updated every quarter. Search by vessel number or name.

National Service Information

145 Baker St, Marion, OH 43301
Toll-free phone: 800-235-0337; Phone: 740-387-6806; Fax: 740-382-1256
Web site: www.nsii.net
Branch Offices: Indianpolis, IN, 317-266-0040; Fax: 317-266-8453
Founded: 1989   **Memberships:** NPRRA, REIPA
Clientele Restrictions: Casual requesters permitted

Proprietary Databases or Gateways:
Database Name: **NSI - Online**
   Corporate/Trade Name Data, Uniform Commercial Code (IN, OH, WI, US)
Special Distribution Methods to Client: Internet

National Service Information is engaged in the search, filing and document retrieval of public record information. Having offices in Marion, OH and Indianapolis, IN, they consider Ohio, Indiana and Kentucky their local market in addition to 4300 different jurisdictions they search nationwide. They recently unveiled a comprehensive database to allow clients to perform public record searches via the Web. Their web site allows you to perform state level UCC lien and corporate detail searches for Ohio, and state level UCCs for Indiana. NSI also provides the option of requesting copies of microfilmed UCC lien images.

National Student Clearinghouse

2191 Fox Mill Rd #300, Herndon, VA 20171-3019
Phone: 703-742-7791; Fax: 703-742-7792
Web site: www.studentclearinghouse.com   **Email:** service@studentclearinghouse.org
Clientele Restrictions: Registration required.

Proprietary Databases or Gateways:
Database Name: **EnrollmentVerify, DegreeVerify**
  Education/Employment (US)

Special Distribution Methods to Client: FTP, Internet

They conveniently provide attendance, degree, and financial information about students of a wide number (2400+ or up to 80% of all students) of colleges and universities in the USA. Does not include addresses, SSN verification, or records "on hold" or "blocked."

NC Recordsonline.com

18125 W Catawba Ave, Cornelius, NC 28031
Toll-free phone: 877-442-9600; Phone: 704-439-3900; Fax: 704-439-3901
Web site: www.ncrecordsonline.com   **Parent Company:** RSM Group LLC
Clientele Restrictions: Signed Agreement Required

Proprietary Databases or Gateways:
Gateway Name: **ncrecordsonline.com**
  Criminal Information (NC)

Special Distribution Methods to Client: Gateway via Another Online Service, Internet, Software

NCRecordsonline.com offers a reliable link to the North Carolina Administrative Office of the Courts criminal and civil mainframe. This allows high volume users, research firms, employment screeners, attorneys, PI's, bondsmen, paralegals, etc to log on from any computer and access the same criminal and civil index system that is used by the NC Clerk of Court, 24-hours a day, 7 days a week. NCRecordsonline.com lets its users bypass all state required set-up costs, long distance charges, and equipment fees associated with a direct connection.

Nebrask@ Online

301 South 13th #301, Lincoln, NE 68508
Toll-free phone: 800-747-8177; Phone: 402-471-7810; Fax: 402-471-7817
Web site: www.nol.org   **Email:** info@nol.org
Founded: 1992
Clientele Restrictions: Signed Agreement Required

Proprietary Databases or Gateways:
Gateway Name: **Nebrask@ Online**
  Driver and/or Vehicle, Corporate/Trade Name Data and Uniform Commercial Code (NE)

Special Distribution Methods to Client: CD-ROM, Email, FTP

Nebrask@ Online is a State of Nebraska information system that provides electronic access to state, county, local, association and other public information. Some agency and association data is updated daily, weekly or monthly, Subscribers connect via 800 #, local #s, or the Internet 24-hours per day. There are sign-up and connect fees if not accessing via the Internet. Interactive access to premium services (those with a statutory fee) requires an annual subscription.

NETR Real Estate Research and Information

2055 East Rio Salado Parkway, Suite 201, Tempe, AZ 85281
Phone: 480-967-6752; Fax: 480-966-9422
Web site: www.netronline.com   **Email:** brett@netronline.com   **Founded:** 1993

Proprietary Databases or Gateways:
Database Name: **Property Data Store**
   Real Estate/Assessor (AL,AZ,CA,DC,FL,HI,IL,IN,MD,MS,MI,MN,MO,NV,NY,OH,PA,TN,TX,UT,WA,WI)

Special Distribution Methods to Client:
NETR Real Estate Research and Information (NETR), LLC provides real estate research and information services nationwide. Headquartered in Tempe, Arizona, NETR provides title services beyond that of conventional title insurance companies, without the costly addition of a title insurance policy or guarantee. Most common services are historical chain-of title-reports, images of recorded documents, and condition of title reports. Database completeness of the list above varies by state and county/city. They maintain an excellent list of web links to recorder's offices and tax assessors.

NIB Ltd

100 Canal Pointe Vlvd #114, Princeton, NJ 08540-7063
Toll-free phone: 800-537-5528; Phone: 609-936-2937; Fax: 609-936-2859
Web site: www.nib.com   **Email:** Info@nib.com
Founded: 1993   **Parent Company:** Bristol Investments LTD   **Memberships:** SIIA
Clientele Restrictions: Signed agreement required, must be ongoing account

Proprietary Databases or Gateways:
Gateway Name: **BACAS, BcomM, Courier**
   Credit Information (US)

Special Distribution Methods to Client: Dial-Up (Other than Internet), Software
NIB has been providing credit processing information to businesses for over 10 years. Courier is a combination of the 5 accessible credit reporting agencies. Other state-of-the-art products include BACAS and BcomM.

Northwest Location Services

PO Box 1345, Puyallup, WA 98371
Phone: 253-848-7767; Fax: 253-848-4414
Web site: http://legallocate.com
Founded: 1990
Clientele Restrictions: Agreement required, no casual requesters permitted

Proprietary Databases or Gateways:
Database Name: **Superior Courts Northwest Online**
   Statewide Court Filings (WA)

Database Name: **Business Licenses**
   Licenses/Registration/Permits (WA)

Database Name: **People Finder**
   Name/Address/SSN/DOB (WA)

Database Name: **Corporations**
   Corporations and Fictious Names (CA)

Database Name: **Driver License and Vehicles**
   Driver and/or Vehicle (ID, OR)

Special Distribution Methods to Client: Dial-Up (Other than Internet), Email, Internet
Serving investigative, legal and business professionals, Northwest Location Services specializes in witness location, skip tracing, asset research and other information services, with an eye on protecting privacy and the public safety. Licensed and bonded in Washington, they are allied with Northwest Online and Digital Research Company who produces CD-ROM database products for investigators, attorneys and collection agencies.

Offshore Business News & Research

123 SE 3rd Ave #173, Miami, FL 33131
Phone: 305-372-6267; Fax: 305-372-8724
Web site: www.offshorebusiness.com

Founded: 1996   **Parent Company:** Offshore Business News & Research Inc
Clientele Restrictions: Casual requesters permitted
Proprietary Databases or Gateways:
Database Name: **Courts and Businesses**
  Addresses/Telephone Numbers. Litigations (International (Bermuda & Cayman Is))
Special Distribution Methods to Client: Internet
OBNR supplies information on businesses and individuals involved in offshore finance and insurance. OBNR owns litigation databases covering Bermuda and the Cayman Islands. They offer 24 hour daily access, year around via the Internet. They publish investigative newsletters covering Bermuda and the Caribbean.

OneCreditSource.com

PO Box 2228, Lake Oswego, OR 97035
Toll-free phone: 800-955-1356; Phone: 503-639-6000; Fax: 503-639-0160
Web site: www.onecreditsource.com   **Email:** support@biinc.com
Founded: 1992   **Parent Company:** Background Investigations
Clientele Restrictions: Agreement required, must have permissible purpose
Proprietary Databases or Gateways:
Gateway Name: **OJIN, JIS**
  Criminal Information (OR,WA)

Gateway Name: **Consumer/Employment Credit**
  Credit Information (US)

Special Distribution Methods to Client: Gateway via Another Online Service, Internet
Through Background Investigation's online service, OneCreditSource.com, users enjoy access to the three national credit bureaus (Trans Union, Equifax, Experian) with reports returned online in seconds. Plus, OneCreditSource.com online has OJIN and JIS online for up to the minute criminal information in OR & WA. Finally, the company provides industry leading customer service that allows all users to benefit from the myriad of quality products.

OPENonline (Online Prof. Electronic Network)

PO Box 549, (1650 Lake Shore Dr #350), Columbus, OH 43216-0549
Toll-free phone: 888-381-5656; Phone: 614-481-6999; Fax: 614-481-6980
Web site: www.openonline.com
Founded: 1992   **Memberships:** ASIS, NCISS, NSA, SHRM
Clientele Restrictions: Signed agreement required; can be cancelled with 30-days notice.
Proprietary Databases or Gateways:
Database Name: **OPEN**
  Real Estate/Assessor, Bankruptcy, Uniform Commercial Code, Corporate/Trade Name Data, Addresses/Telephone
    Numbers, Credit Information, Driver and/or Vehicle, Criminal Information, Aviation/Vessels, SSN Trace, Death
    Records, Litigation/Judgments/Tax Liens (US)
Gateway Name: **Arrest Records**
  Criminal Information (OH,IN,MI)
Database Name: **National Corrections Records**
  Criminal Information (AZ, AR, CT, FL, GA, ID, IL, IN, KY, ME, MI, MN, MS, MO, NE, NJ, NY, NC, OH, OK,
    OR, SC, TN, TX, UT, WA)
Database Name: **State Public Records**
  Indexed Statewide Public Records (CA, ID, NV, OH, OR, WA)
Special Distribution Methods to Client: Dial-Up (Other than Internet), Internet
OPENonline provides real-time, direct access to an ever-growing range of nationwide court and criminal records, public records and background check information, including driving records, criminal arrest & conviction records, statewide court records, commercial & consumer credit reports, bankruptcies, liens and judgments. The service is available to businesses for a variety of applications including employment screenings, background checks, skip-traces, verification of information such as addresses, phone numbers, SSNs, previous employment, educational background

and professional licenses. OPENonline is accessible via the Internet and provides free customer support with no monthly minimum. Offers two types of billing accounts – standard and variable (for infrequent users) plans.

OSHA DATA

12 Hoffman St, Maplewood, NJ 07040-1114
Phone: 973-378-8011
Web site: www.oshadata.com   **Email:** mcarmel@oshadata.com
Founded: 1991   **Memberships:** ASSE, AIHA
Clientele Restrictions: Casual requesters permitted

Proprietary Databases or Gateways:
Gateway Name: **OSHA Data Gateway**
  Legislation/Regulation,, Environmental (US)

Special Distribution Methods to Client: CD-ROM, Dial-Up (Other than Internet), Disk, Lists/Labels, Publication/Directory, Software

OSHA DATA's database contains corporate regulator violation records for every business inspected since July 1972. Information includes not only OSHA data, but also wage and hour, EEOC, insurance, NLRB asbestos and other regulatory types. The database is updated quarterly. Consultation and software for the utilization of the data available.

Oso Grande Technologies

5921 Jefferson NE, Albuquerque, NM 87109
Phone: 505-345-6555; Fax: 505-345-6559
Web site: www.technet.nm.org   **Email:** info@nm.net
Founded: 1984   **Parent Company:** New Mexico Technet
Clientele Restrictions: None reported

Proprietary Databases or Gateways:
Gateway Name: **Oso Grande**
  Driver, Vehicle, Litigation/Judgments/Tax Liens, Corporate/Trade Name Data, UCC, Legislation/Regulation (NM)
Gateway Name: **NM Fed Courts/LegalNet**
  Bankruptcy, Criminal Information (NM)

Special Distribution Methods to Client: Dial-Up (Other than Internet), Internet

Oso Grande Technologie is the for-profit portion of a self-supporting, non-profit corporation operating to provide management of a statewide computer network serving New Mexico, its state universities and statewide research, educational and economic-development interests. OGT serves as the primary connection point to the Internet for other Internet Service Providers, business, government and private users. OGT offers a full range of Internet services from dial-up to direct connections and web page services, to co-located services and New Mexico MVR requests. LegalNet provides legal resources; Oso Grande provides premium services.

Owens OnLine Inc

6501 N Himes Ave #104, Tampa, FL 33614
Toll-free phone: 800-745-4656; Phone: 813-877-2008; Fax: 813-877-1826
Web site: www.owens.com   **Email:** email@owens.com
Founded: 1992
Clientele Restrictions: Casual requesters permitted

Proprietary Databases or Gateways:
Gateway Name: **Owens OnLine**
  Credit Information (US, International)
Gateway Name: **Owens OnLine**
  Foreign Country Information (International)

Special Distribution Methods to Client: Email, Internet

Owens OnLine specializes in international background checks and credit reports on businesses and individuals, and in international criminal checks. They provide worldwide coverage and also offer FreeDirectories.com where over 1 billion people, companies, and public records can be found free of charge.

Pallorium Inc

PO Box 155-Midwood Station, Brooklyn, NY 11230
Phone: 212-969-0286; Fax: 212-858-5720
Web site: www.pallorium.com   **Email:** pallorium@pallorium.com
Founded: 1979   **Memberships:** ION, WAD, NAIS, BOMP, ASIS, NCISS
Clientele Restrictions: Casual requesters permitted
Proprietary Databases or Gateways:
Database Name: **Skiptrace America**
  Addresses/Telephone Numbers, Driver and/or Vehicle, Vital Records and Voter Registration (US)
Database Name: **People Finder**
  Aviation, Vessels, Driver and/or Vehicle, Vital Records and Voter Registration (US)
Database Name: **Business Finder America**
  Corporate/Trade Name Data (US)
Special Distribution Methods to Client: Dial-Up (Other than Internet), Internet
Pallorium (PallTech Online) services are divided into three areas: the electronic mail system, which links all users (800 investigative/security professionals); the bulletin board system, which provides a forum for the free exchange of information among all approved subscribers (public or private law enforcement only); and the investigative support system, which provides investigative support to approved users. PallTech's searches include aircraft record locator, national financial asset tracker, bankruptcy filings locator, business credit reports, consumer credit reports, NCOA trace, criminal records, national vehicle records, current employment locator, NYC registered voters by address, court and governmental jurisdiction identifier, ZIP Code locator and more searches in the US, Canada, Israel and Hong Kong. New products of addresses and personal information for all states total more than five billion records.

Paragon Document Research, Inc.

PO Box 65216, St Paul, MN 55165
Toll-free phone: 800-892-4235; Phone: 651-222-6844; Fax: 651-222-2281
Web site: www.banc.com/pdrstore   **Email:** pdrinc@quest.net
Founded: 1990   **Parent Company:** PDR Inc   **Memberships:** NAFE, NALA, NPRRA, MSBA
Clientele Restrictions: Signed agreement required for subscriber rates; casual requests permitted
Proprietary Databases or Gateways:
Database Name: **Pdrlog; Termination Database**
  Uniform Commercial Code (US)
Special Distribution Methods to Client: Database, Disk, Lists/Labels, Microfilm/Microfiche
Paragon Document Research's services include searches throughout state and county levels nationwide covering UCC and federal and state tax Liens, corporate documents, Bankruptcy filings, judgment searches, past and present litigation, searches for ownership of, and liens on DMV reports, aircraft/watercraft and vessel searches, assumed name searches, and name reservations. Registered Agent Services and weekly tax lien bulletin orders can be requested online through www.banc.com/pdrastore. Turnaround time is 48-72 hrs; some exception on MN UCC searches, terminations included from 1996 forward.

Plat System Services Inc

12450 Wayzata Blvd #108, Minnetonka, MN 55305-1926
Phone: 612-544-0012; Fax: 612-544-0617
Web site: www.platsystems.com
Founded: 1961
Clientele Restrictions: Casual requesters permitted for free trial, but license will be required.
Proprietary Databases or Gateways:
Database Name: **PropertyInfoNet™**
  Addresses/Real Estate/Assessor (MN-Minneapolis/St Paul and nearby counties)
Special Distribution Methods to Client: Database, Disk, Internet, Lists/Labels, Publication/Directory

Plat System Services has a variety of services available including online services updated weekly, PID directories published annually, commercial sold reports monthly, residential sold reports monthly, custom reports updated weekly, and other monthly reports such as contract for deeds, and commercial buyers and sellers reports. They also offer mailing lists and labels, diskettes updated weekly, printed PLAT maps and PLAT books updated semi-annually. They provide computerized county plat maps.

Property Data Center Inc

7100 E Bellevue #110, Greenwood Village, CO 80111
Phone: 303-850-9586; Fax: 303-850-9637
Web site: www.pdclane.net
Founded: 1984   **Memberships:** NPRRA, REIPA, DMA, NAR
Clientele Restrictions: Casual requesters permitted

Proprietary Databases or Gateways:
Database Name: **Real Property Assessments, Taxes**
  Real Estate/Assessor (CO)

Database Name: **Owner Phone Numbers**
  Addresses/Telephone Numbers (CO)

Special Distribution Methods to Client: Disk, Internet, Lists/Labels
Property Data Center's PDC database includes more than two million real property ownership and deed transfer records for the metro Denver area, plus counties of Adams, Arapahoe, Boulder,Clear Creek, Denver, Douglas, El Paso, Eagle, Elbert, Jefferson, Larimer, Mesa, Pitkin, Pueblo, Summit, Weld. Customized databases are accessible by owner, location, and indicators such as property value. They specialize in lender marketing data, new owners, sold comparables, mapping data and direct mail lists.

PROTEC

PO Box 54866, Cincinnati, OH 45254
Toll-free phone: 800-543-7651; Phone: 513-528-4400; Fax: 513-528-4402
Branch Offices: Indianapolis, IN, 317-632-4264; **Cold Springs**, KY, 999-241-2992
Founded: 1964   **Parent Company:** World Search Group, Inc   **Memberships:** ACFE, EPIC, ICA, NCISS, WAD
Clientele Restrictions: Casual requesters permitted

Proprietary Databases or Gateways:
Database Name: **Consta-Trac**
  Addresses/Telephone Numbers (US)

Special Distribution Methods to Client: Dial-Up (Other than Internet), Software
PROTEC has 35 years of concurrent exposure to the information highway, beginning its database system in 1979 using its own information. Since that beginning, they have remained unique in responsible information gathering, being useful in fraud detection and factual data gathering. Their newest and most successful database is "CONSTRA-TRAC" - a master compilation of over 700 record systems and special use cross-check histories from individuals, businesses, societies, and public record data.

Public Data Corporation

38 East 29th St, New York, NY 10016
Phone: 212-519-3063; Fax: 212-519-3067
Web site: www.pdcny.com
Founded: 1988
Clientele Restrictions: Casual requesters permitted

Proprietary Databases or Gateways:
Database Name: **Public Data**
  Real Estate/Assessor, Environmental, Litigation/Judgments/Tax Liens and Uniform Commercial Code (NY)
Special Distribution Methods to Client: Disk, Email, Magnetic Tape

PDC maintains an online database of 60 million NYC real estate and lien records which are updated daily. Record include deed and mortgage recordings, bankruptcy judgments, federal tax liens and UCC filings. Searches can be ordered and received by email thru the company's web site at www.pdcny.com.

Public Record Research Library

PO Box 27869, (206 W Julie Dr #2), Tempe, AZ 85285
Toll-free phone: 800-929-3811; Phone: 480-829-7475; Fax: 480-829-8505
Web site: www.brbpub.com   **Email:** brb@brbpub.com
Founded: 1989   **Parent Company:** BRB Publications Inc   **Memberships:** PRRN, AIIP, AALL, SIIA
Clientele Restrictions: Casual requesters permitted
Proprietary Databases or Gateways:
Database Name: **PRRS**
    Addresses/Telephone Numbers, Legislation/Regulations (US)
Special Distribution Methods to Client: CD-ROM, Database, Disk, Internet, Lists/Labels, Publication/Directory
The Public Record Research Library is a series of in-depth databases formatted into books, CDs and online. BRB is recognized as the nation's leading research and reference publisher of public record related information. The principals of the parent company are directors of the Public Record Retriever Network, the nation's largest organization of public record professionals. Over 26,000 government and private enterprises are analyzed in-depth regarding regulations and access of public records and public information. The Public Record Research System (PRRS) is available on CD, the Internet and as a customized database.

Questel Orbit

8000 Westpark Dr, Ste 130, McLean, VA 22102
Toll-free phone: 800-326-1710; Phone: 703-442-0900; Fax: 703-893-5632
Web site: http://plpatprd.questel.fr/plpat/jsp/en/login.jsp   **Email:** help@questel.orbit.com
Branch Offices: Paris, FR, 33 (0)1 55 04 52 00   **Parent Company:** Questal Orbit-France Telecom Group
Clientele Restrictions: License Agreement Required
Proprietary Databases or Gateways:
Database Name: **QPAT-WW**
    Patents (US, International)
Special Distribution Methods to Client: Dial-Up (Other than Internet), Internet
Qpat-WW has the full text of all US patents since 01/01/74, along with most European patents since 1987. Access is available through a subscription service.

Rapsheets.com

PO Box 3663 (193 Jefferson Ave), Memphis, TN 38173
Phone: 901-523-1561; Fax: 901-526-5813
Web site: www.rapsheets.com/index.html   **Email:** webmaster@rapsheets.com
Founded: 1999   **Parent Company:** The Daily News
Clientele Restrictions: Casual requesters permitted.
Proprietary Databases or Gateways:
Database Name: **rapsheets.com**
    Criminal Information (AL, AZ, AR, CO, CT, FL, GA, IL, IN, ID. KS, KY, MI, MN, MS, MO, NC, NV, NJ, NY, OH, OK, OR, SC, TN, TX, UT, VA, WA)
Special Distribution Methods to Client: Dial-Up (Other than Internet), Email, Internet
The Daily News offers a variety of searches, many of them free or a small fee; rapsheets.com is a fee service. The Daily News specializes in information searches in the Memphis, TN area, and Nashville, including statewide MVRs for a fee. Rapsheets.com allows subscribers to access criminal records in most states.

Realty Data Corp

1325 Franklin Avenue, Garden City, NY 11530
Phone: 516-877-8715; Fax: 516-877-8724
Web site: www.realtydata.com   **Email:** customerservice@realtydata.com
Founded: 2000   **Memberships:** REIPA, ALTA, TAVMA, NYSLTA, MISMO, NACRC
Clientele Restrictions: Agreement required.
Proprietary Databases or Gateways:
Database Name: **RDC Database (www.realtydata.com)**
   Real Estate/Assessor, UCC, Litigation/Judgments/Tax Liens, Bankruptcy, Environmental (NY)
Special Distribution Methods to Client: Internet
Realty Data Corp. (RDC) is a B2B e-commerce aggregator of data that delivers online automated real estate data to the real estate and financial services industries. RDC has developed a proprietary system that has the ability to conduct "intelligent" searches, currently combing through more than 150,000,000 records. RDC clients can order and receive complete on-line customized property reports and images 24/7 without the hassle of record examiners or the inaccuracy of the manual process. Data can be retrieved for any person, property or owner in New York County, Kings County, Queens County and Bronx County, NY. Limited information is available Suffolk and Richmond counties of New York and in some counties in Michigan. Images are available from counties in fifteen other states.

Record Information Services Inc

PO Box 894, Elburn, IL 60119
Phone: 630-365-6490; Fax: 630-365-6524
Web site: www.public-record.com   **Email:** jmetcalf@public-record.com
Founded: 1993
Clientele Restrictions: Casual requesters permitted
Proprietary Databases or Gateways:
Database Name: **IL Records, New Homeowners, Mortgages/Foreclosures**
   Litigation/Judgments/Tax Liens, Real Estate/Assessor, Mortgages, Foreclosures (IL)
Database Name: **Bankruptcies**
   Bankruptcy (IL)
Database Name: **Business Licenses, News Incorporations**
   Licenses/Registrations/Permits (IL)
Special Distribution Methods to Client: Database, Disk, Email, Internet, Lists/Labels, Software
Record Information Services provides complete and timely public record data that is delivered through state-of-the-art technology. Custom reports are available upon request. They provide local document retrieval in NE Illinois counties.

Records Research Inc

PO Box 19300, Sacramento, CA 95819
Toll-free phone: 800-952-5766
Web site: www.recordsresearch.com   **Email:** recre@recordresearch.com
Founded: 1981
Clientele Restrictions: Signed Agreement Required
Proprietary Databases or Gateways:
Gateway Name: **RRI MVRs**
   Driver and/or Vehicle (CA, US)
Special Distribution Methods to Client:
Records Research (RRI) specializes in providing California motor vehicle reports (MVRs) to insurance and related industries. Driving histories and vehicle reports are available online, allowing instant response to client requests. Overnight service available. They offer a variety of searches including plate, VIN, automated name index, soundex searches, and financial responsibility reports. RRI offers MVRs from all other states with a 24-48 hour turnaround. RPI offers a wide range of other public record services including corporate and property searches. Clients must establish a commercial account with the state, which RRI will be happy to help expedite.

Rental Research Inc

30504 Pacific Highway S., Federal Way, WA 98003
Toll-free phone: 800-654-4936; Phone: 253-838-9545; Fax: 253-838-9445
Web site: http:/www.researchinc.net   **Email:** research@researchinc.net
Founded: 1978   **Memberships:** PRRN
Clientele Restrictions: User agreement.

Proprietary Databases or Gateways:
Database Name: **Tenant History Database**
  Tenant History (WA)

Gateway Name: **COIN**
  Criminal Information (AZ, ID, OR, WA)

Gateway Name: **Equifax, Trans Union**
  Credit Information (US, WA)

Special Distribution Methods to Client: Email, Gateway via Another Online Service, Internet

Rental Research Inc. (RRI) is the oldest (over 22 years) and fastest (4 minute reports) tenant screening company in Washington. They offer an array of online and offline reports for Tenant Evictions, employment screening, criminal records, backgrounds checks, credit reports. Over 10,000 users in five western states. Since 1978 they have created the largest database of eviction records available, all with serving you in mind. Now offering internet service.

Research Archives.com Legal Documents Library

c/o Beard Group, PO Box 4250, Frederick, MD 21705
Phone: 240-629-3300; Fax: 240-629-3360
Web site: www.researcharchives.com   **Email:** info@researcharchives.com   **Parent Company:** Beard Group
Clientele Restrictions: Subscription required.

Proprietary Databases or Gateways:
Database Name: **Legal Documents Library**
  Bankruptcy (US), Addresses/Telephone Numbers (US), Vessels (US), Corporate/Trade Name Data (US)

Special Distribution Methods to Client: Internet

ResearchArchives.Com is a powerful research tool for legal and business professionals. A convenient, fast and inexpensive online resource for copies of material contracts and agreements involving virtually all public companies in the United States. They have over 20244 bankruptcy documents and are adding 2,000 more every month. Also, data on troubled companies and serials.

Richland County Abstract Co

POB 910, Wahpeton, ND 58074-0910
Phone: 701-642-3781; Fax: 701-642-3852
Founded: 1922   **Memberships:** ALTA, MLTA, NDLTA
Clientele Restrictions: Casual requesters permitted

Proprietary Databases or Gateways:
Database Name: **Judgment & Tax Liens**
  Litigation/Judgments/Tax Liens (MN, ND)

Special Distribution Methods to Client: Disk

Richland County Abstract specializes in providing real estate information for the states of Minn. and North Dakota.

San Diego Daily Transcript/San Diego Source

2131 Third Ave, San Diego, CA 92101
Toll-free phone: 800-697-6397; Phone: 619-232-4381; Fax: 619-239-5716
Web site: www.sddt.com   **Email:** tran@sddt.com
Clientele Restrictions: Casual requesters permitted

Proprietary Databases or Gateways:
Database Name: **San Diego Source**
  Litigation/Judgments/Tax Liens and Uniform Commercial Code (CA)

Gateway Name: **US Bankruptcy Court Filings**
  Bankruptcy (CA)

Database Name: **Home Sales, Com. Real Estate, Leases**
  Real Estate/Assessor and Addresses/Telephone Numbers (CA)

Special Distribution Methods to Client: CD-ROM, Database, Email, Lists/Labels, Publication/Directory
The San Diego Source is a leading California web site for public record information and business data. Site visitors can perform customized searches on one or more than fifteen databases. Links with Transcripts Online are provided.

SEAFAX Inc

PO Box 15340, Portland, ME 04112-5340
Toll-free phone: 800-777-3533; Phone: 207-773-3533; Fax: 207-773-9564
Web site: www.seafax.com
Founded: 1985
Clientele Restrictions: Casual requesters permitted

Proprietary Databases or Gateways:
Database Name: **Business Reports**
  Credit Information (US)

Special Distribution Methods to Client: Internet
Seafax is the leading source of food industry-specific information, thus a valuable credit reporting resource to manage your exposure. Using Seafax, decision-makers access timely and accurate information 24/7. More than 1200 food producers, processors and distributors use Seafax services to minimize rick, save time and maximize profits using products like Supersearch to perform company, date or geography searches, or business report services like Seafax Credit Appraisal & Risk Index, bank & trade references, and unique financial data. Their Bankruptcy Creditor Index allow the identification of unsecured creditors of bankruptcies, receiverships and assignments. Other products include Agriwire and Agriscan Bulletin.

Search Company of North Dakota LLC

1008 E Capitol Ave, Bismarck, ND 58501-1930
Phone: 701-223-1848; Fax: 701-223-1850   **Email:** mkautzma@btinet.com
Founded: 1984   **Memberships:** PRRN
Clientele Restrictions: Casual requesters permitted

Proprietary Databases or Gateways:
Database Name: **North Dakota Records**
  Addresses/Telephone Numbers, Litigation/Judgments/Tax Liens, Licenses/Registrations/Permits, Criminal
    Information and Bankruptcy (ND)

Database Name: **ND UCC**
  Uniform Commercial Code (ND)

Special Distribution Methods to Client: Email, Lists/Labels
They will provide any and all city, county, state, or federal record searching or filing in North Dakota. Over 15 years of experience in all aspects of public record searching, retrieval, or filing. Their database, which is not availabe online, has been compiled from over 16 years of prior record searches. Access to this database is restricted to ongoing clients.

Search Network Ltd

Two Corporate Place #210, 1501 42nd St, West Des Moines, IA 50266-1005
Toll-free phone: 800-383-5050; Phone: 515-223-1153; Fax: 515-223-2814
Web site: http://searchnetworkltd.com   **Email:** lharken@searchnetworkltd.com
Branch Offices: Topeka, KS, 800-338-3618; Fax: 785-235-5788

Founded: 1965   **Memberships:** NPRRA, PRRN
Clientele Restrictions: Casual requesters permitted
Proprietary Databases or Gateways:
Database Name: **Search Network**
  Uniform Commercial Code (IA, KS)

Special Distribution Methods to Client: Dial-Up (Other than Internet), Lists/Labels, Microfilm/Microfiche, Publication/Directory
In business since 1965, Search Network provides full service public record search information. The company maintains an on-site UCC database for Iowa and Kansas. Same day searches and copies are available as well as personal filing service for UCC and corporate documents. Since 1980, they have offered direct online access to their databases of UCC filing/records information in Iowa and Kansas

Silver Plume

4775 Walnut St #2B, Boulder, CO 80301
Toll-free phone: 800-677-4442; Phone: 303-444-0695; Fax: 303-449-1199
Web site: www.silverplume.com   **Email:** sales@silverplume.com
Founded: 1989
Clientele Restrictions: Signed Agreement Required

Proprietary Databases or Gateways:
Database Name: **Insurance Industry Rates, Forms and Manuals**
  Legislation/Regulations (US)

Special Distribution Methods to Client: CD-ROM, Internet, Magnetic Tape
Silver Plume is the leading provider of insurance-related reference and research material. Receive material in one subscription on CD-Rom or online.

SKLD Information Services LLC

720 S Colorado Blvd #1000N, Denver, CO 80246
Toll-free phone: 800-727-6358; Phone: 303-820-0888; Fax: 303-260-6391
Web site: www.skld.com   **Email:** sales@skld.com
Founded: 1961   **Memberships:** ATLA, DMA, National Association of Mortgage Brokers
Clientele Restrictions: Casual requesters permitted but Agreement Required

Proprietary Databases or Gateways:
Database Name: **New Homeowners List, Deeds, Loan Activity, Notice of Demand**
  Real Estate/Assessor (CO-14 counties)

Special Distribution Methods to Client: Database, Disk, Magnetic Tape
SKLD Information Services maintains a complete database of public record information from documents recorded in 14 County Recorder offices in Colorado since 1990. Information is available to enhance existing databases, create new homeowner mailing lists, report on real estate loan transaction information, and mortgage marketing data. With archived county recorded documents and plat maps in their in-house microfilm library, SKLD can provide quick turnaround time for document and plat map retrieval. Reports available include: real estate loan activity reports, warranty deed/trust deed match, trust deed report, owner carry reports, notice of election and demand, and new homeowners lists.

Softech International Inc

13200 SW 128th St #F3, Miami, FL 33186
Toll-free phone: 888-318-7979; Phone: 305-253-9696; Fax: 305-253-1440
Web site: www.softechinternational.com   **Email:** reid@softechinternational.com
Branch Offices: Chicago, IL, 312-654-8045; Fax: 312-654-1285
Founded: 1996
Clientele Restrictions: Casual requesters permitted; agreement required.

Proprietary Databases or Gateways:
Gateway Name: **MVRs**

Driver and/or Vehicle (AL, AR, FL, GA, ID, IL, IN, MS, NJ, NY, NC, OH,, TN, TX, UT)

Special Distribution Methods to Client: Email, FTP, Gateway via Another Online Service, Internet

The provide MVR and registration information via the internet, real time.

Software Computer Group Inc

PO Box 3042, Charleston, WV 25331-3042

Toll-free phone: 800-795-8543; Phone: 304-343-6480

Web site: www.swcg-inc.com/courts.htm   **Email:** info@swcg-inc.com

Founded: 1975

Clientele Restrictions: Casual requesters permitted

Proprietary Databases or Gateways:

Gateway Name: **Circuit Express**

   Criminal Information, Litigation/judgments/Tax Liens (WV)

Special Distribution Methods to Client: Dial-Up (Other than Internet), Internet

The Circuit Express product brings civil and criminal public information records from the Circuit Courts in West Virginia to you online. You can locate cases by name or case filing type. Not all counties are available. Fees include a sign-up fee, and monthly fee with connect charges. There is an additional system for magistrate courts; however, this service is only available to government agencies.

Software Management Inc - eCCLIX

2011 Cobalt Ave., Louisville, KY 40299

Toll-free phone: 800-466-9445;; Fax: 502-266-9445

Web site: http:www.softwaremanagementinc.com   **Email:** sales@softwaremanagementinc.com

Founded: 1984

Clientele Restrictions: Signed Agreement required.

Proprietary Databases or Gateways:

Database Name: **CCLIX-OptiMA and CCLIX System**

   Real Estate/Assessor, Litigation/Judgments/Tax Liens, Uniform Commericial Code (KY)

Special Distribution Methods to Client: Internet

Software Management offers eCCLIX, the searchable internet version of CCLIX, a database produced for and used by the KY County Clerks for their electronic imaging and filing. Several Counties are available to non-government subscribers on eCCLIX. Available data includes real estate, liens, UCCs, marriage, and tax assessor records.

Southeastern Public Records Inc.

208 W Chicago Rd #4, Sturgis, MI 49091

Phone: 616-659-8131; Fax: 616-659-1169

Web site: www.publicrex.com   **Email:** jimbarfield@msn.com

Founded: 1993

Clientele Restrictions: Casual requesters permitted

Proprietary Databases or Gateways:

Database Name: **Michigan/Georgia Public Records**

   Addresses/Telephone Numbers, Bankruptcy, Litigation/Judgments/Tax Liens (GA, MI)

Special Distribution Methods to Client: CD-ROM, Database, Dial-Up (Other than Internet), Disk, Email, Internet, Magnetic Tape, Software

Southeastern Public Records can deliver bulk data up to 3,000,000 records within 48 hours of verifying customer specifications. Smaller batches of data available in 1 to 48 hours if needed. Verification of any judgment, tax lien, or bankruptcy at its original place of filing in all covered areas. All data is recorded from its original source by one of our certified collectors on software developed by us for that particular purpose. Our databases contain 15 years of historical data in Michigan and 10 years in Georgia. Our key personnel include: a full time onsite Internet/web specialist; full time onsite database development specialists; several full time personnel with extensive knowledge of legal recording, mortgages, major credit bureaus, and all civil public records at all levels.

State Net

2101 K Street, Sacramento, CA 95816
Phone: 916-444-0840; Fax: 916-446-5369
Web site: www.statenet.com
Branch Offices: Washington, DC, 202-638-7999; Fax: 202-638-7291; **Tallahassee**, FL, 850-205-7710; Fax: 850-205-7714;
Springfield, IL, 217-522-1188; Fax: 217-522-1195
Founded: 1978
Clientele Restrictions: Casual requesters permitted
Proprietary Databases or Gateways:
Database Name: **State Net**
  Legislation/Regulations (US)
Special Distribution Methods to Client: Dial-Up (Other than Internet), Internet, Publication/Directory
State Net delivers vital data, legislative intelligence and in-depth reporting for people who care about the actions of government. Based in Sacramento, CA, they were created by legislative experts who invented a computerized tracking system that has evolved into what they feel is the nation's leading source of legislative and regulatory information. State net monitors 100% of all pending bills and regulations in the 50 states and Congress. Successful government affairs managers from small state associations to giant Fortune 500 companies rely on them to report activity on their issues in the 50 states. Backed by a three-decade commitment to providing fast, accurate legislative information. State Net publishes a variety of online and print publications.

Superior Information Services LLC

300 Phillips Blvd #500, Trenton, NJ 08618-1427
Toll-free phone: 800-848-0489; Phone: 609-883-7000; Fax: 609-883-0677
Web site: www.superiorinfo.com   **Email:** lmartin@superiorinfo.com
Founded: 1987   **Memberships:** NPRRA, ICA, ACA, REIPA, PRRN   **Clientele Restrictions:** None reported
Proprietary Databases or Gateways:
Database Name: **Superior Online**
  Litigation/Judgments/Tax Liens and Bankruptcy (CT, DC, DE, MD, MA, ME, NC, NH, NJ, NY, PA, RI, VA, VT)
Database Name: **Corporate Files**
  Corporate/Trade Name Data (NY, PA, NJ)
Database Name: **UCC Files**
  Uniform Commercial Code (PA, NJ)
Database Name: **Real Property**
  Real Estate/Assessor (US)
Gateway Name: **People Finder**
  Addresses/Telephone Numbers (US)
Special Distribution Methods to Client: Dial-Up (Other than Internet)
Superior Information Services is an online public record provider. In addition, we provide Nationwide Corporate Services, and Core Data Services, as well. Currently, we provide online public records through our new product, Superior Online PLUS, as well as our existing product, Superior Online. With Superior's new National property file you can access forty-eight states of data with just one search. You can now access Criminal Data when using Superior Online PLUS. Registered users can search criminal records in 27 U.S. states - including NJ and NY. A number of data sources are used to ensure as complete a dossier as possible. In addition, this search tool gives you the ability to download the information - allowing you to customize reports for your investigative needs.

Tax Analysts

6830 N Fairfax Dr, Arlington, VA 22213
Toll-free phone: 800-955-3444; Phone: 703-533-4400; Fax: 703-533-4444
Web site: www.tax.org   **Email:** cserve@tax.org
Founded: 1970
Clientele Restrictions: Casual requesters permitted

Proprietary Databases or Gateways:

Database Name: **Exempt Organization Master List**
  Corporate/Trade Name Data (US)

Database Name: **The Tax Directory**
  Addresses/Telephone Numbers (US)

Database Name: **The OneDisc,TAXBASE**
  Legislation/Regulations (US)

Database Name: **TAXBASE, The Ratx Directory**
  Foreign Country Information (International)

Special Distribution Methods to Client: CD-ROM, Disk, Internet, Publication/Directory

Tax Analysts is a nonprofit organization dedicated to providing timely, comprehensive information to tax professionals at a reasonable cost. They are the leading electronic publisher of tax information. The Exempt Organization Master List contains information about more than 1.1 million not-for-profit organizations registered with the federal government. The Tax Directory contains information about 14,000 federal tax officials, 9000 private tax professionals and 8000 corporate tax professionals. Online databases include daily federal, state and international tax information as well as complete research libraries. Some products are available on DIALOG & LEXIS.

Telebase

1150 First Ave #820, King of Prussia, PA 19406
Toll-free phone: 800-220-4664; Phone: 610-945-2420; Fax: 610-945-2460
Web site: www.telebase.com
Founded: 1984   **Parent Company:** Dun & Bradstreet   **Memberships:** SPA/IIA
Clientele Restrictions: Casual requesters permitted

Proprietary Databases or Gateways:

Gateway Name: **Brainwave, I-Quest**
  Corporate/Trade Name Data, Addresses/Telephone Numbers, News/Current Events, Credit Information, Trademarks, SEC/Other Financial,Foreign Country Information (US)

Gateway Name: **LEXIS-NEXIS CaseLaw @AOL**
  Litigation/Judgments/Tax Liens (US)

Gateway Name: **Dun & Bradstreet @ AOL**
  Credit Information, Addresses/Telephone Numbers (US)

Special Distribution Methods to Client: Dial-Up (Other than Internet), Gateway via Another Online Service, Internet

Telebase, part of Dun & Bradstreet, offers company information from Dun & Bradstreet, corporate hierarchy information from LexisNexis and premium company and industry profiles from Datamonitor. Information Services are designed for people with little or no online searching experience and provide easy access to business information for sales prospecting, market analysis, competitive intelligence, product development, and other research. Several thousand sources, from over 450 databases, are available including credit reports, financial reports, company directories, magazines, newspapers, newswires, industry newsletters, etc. For a list of distribution partners visit www.telebase.com.

Tennessee Anytime

Toll-free phone: 866-886-3468; Phone: 615- 313-0300
Web site: www.tennesseeanytime.org/main/online/index.html
Founded: 2000
Clientele Restrictions: Premium services require registration

Proprietary Databases or Gateways:

Gateway Name: **Free Services**
  Corporate/Trade Name Data,Trademarks, Uniform Commercial Code, Real Estate/Assessor (TN)

Gateway Name: **Premium Services**
  Driver and/or Vehicle (TN)

Special Distribution Methods to Client: Internet

Tennessee Anytime, the official website of the State of Tennessee, is a gateway to a myriad of state information and services. Many free services are available, as well as "premium services' which require fees and registarion. A TennesseeAnytime subscription allows you to easily access Tennessee's eGovernment Online Services.

Tenstar Business Services Group

315 S College #245, Lafayette, LA 70503
Toll-free phone: 800-960-2214; Phone: 337-234-9933; Fax: 337-235-5318
Web site: www.tenstarcorporation.com   **Email:** tenstarco@aol.com
Branch Offices: Baton Rouge, LA, 800-864-5154; Fax: 225-273-8987; **Jackson**, MS, 800-864-5154; Fax: 225-273-8987; **New Orleans**, LA, 800-856-8515
Founded: 1989   **Parent Company:** Tenstar Corporation   **Memberships:** ACE, RPA, NAPPS, NPRRA, ACA, PRRN
Clientele Restrictions: Casual requesters permitted.
Proprietary Databases or Gateways:
Database Name: **ACB-1**
   Addresses/Telephone Numbers, Bankruptcy, Corporate/Trade Name Data, Criminal Information, Education/Employment, Litigation/Judgments/Tax Liens, UCCs, Real Estate/Assessor, Social Security Numbers, Tenant History, Wills/Probate, Workers Comp (LA, MS)
Datebase Name: **ACB-1**
   Criminal Information (permissible users only) (MS)
Gateway Name: **ACB-2**
   Credit Information, Driver and/or Vehicle (LA, US)
Special Distribution Methods to Client: CD-ROM, Dial-Up (Other than Internet), Disk, Email, FTP, Magnetic Tape
Tenstar specializes in research, retrieval, recording, corporate services, notary services, abstracting, process service, litigation support, paralegal services, court reporting, investigations, risk management and claims adjusting, and business office services. Add'l services not listed above are Tenant histories, and Wills/Probate records. Services statewide in LA, MS. All 64 Louisiana parishes researched in about 48 hours; 72 hours for Mississippi.

Texas Driving Record Express Service

7809 Easton / 7399 Gulf Freeway Plaza, Houston, TX 77017
Toll-free phone: 800-671-2287; Phone: 713-641-5252; Fax: 713-641-5252
Web site: www.txdrivingrecordexpress.com
Founded: 1992   **Parent Company:** Ernest L Calderon dba CATS
Clientele Restrictions: License Agreement Required
Proprietary Databases or Gateways:
Gateway Name: **Certified MVRs**
   Driver and/or Vehicle (TX)
Special Distribution Methods to Client:
Texas Driving Records Express provides driving records statewide in 1-7 days, also original/state-certified documents for ticket elimination, restoration of Texas driving privileges from TX Dept of Public Safety, employment requirements, current addresses.

The Official Providers Source

4500 S 129th E Ave, Tulsa, OK 74134
Toll-free phone: 800-331-9175; Phone: 918-664-9991; Fax: 918-664-4366
Web site: www.providerssource.com   **Email:** jeriw@dacservices.com
Founded: 1981   **Parent Company:** Total Information Svcs, Inc.   **Memberships:** SIIA, SHRM, AAMVA, ATA, PRRN
Clientele Restrictions: Signed agreement required, must be ongoing account
Proprietary Databases or Gateways:
Database Name: **Transportation Employment History; Drug/Alcohol Test Results, Security Guard Employment History; Drug/Alcohol Test Results, Security Guard Employment History**
   Education/Employment (US)

Gateway Name: **Driving Records**
  Driver and/or Vehicle (US)

Gateway Name: **20/20 Insight**
  Criminal Information (US, CD, International, VI, PR)

Database Name: **Claims and Injury Reports**
  Workers Compensation (AR, FL, IA, IL, KS, MA, MD, ME, MI, MS, ND, NE, OH, OK, OR, TX)

Special Distribution Methods to Client: Dial-Up (Other than Internet), Internet

They have serviced employers and insurance businesses for more than 16 years, providing employment screening and underwriting/risk assessment tools. CDLIS contains summary information on more than 6,000,000 drivers. Customers request information by PC and modem via toll-free lines. Computer access is available through networks and mainframe-to-mainframe connections. Customers may call or fax requests to their service representative toll-free.

The Search Company Inc

25 Adelaide Street East #720, Toronto, Ontario, CD M5C 3A1
Toll-free phone: 800-396-8241; Phone: 416-979-5858; Fax: 416-979-5857
Web site: www.thesearchcompany.com   **Email:** info@thesearchcompany.com
Founded: 1993
Clientele Restrictions: Must be ongoing account

Proprietary Databases or Gateways:
Database Name: **Property Ownership & Tenant Data**
  Real Estate/Assessor (Canada)

Special Distribution Methods to Client: Dial-Up (Other than Internet), Email, Software

The Search Company covers 2 distinct markets: 1) Canada wide public record retrieval; 2) Litigation related asset and corporate background reporting with or without a full narrative report, with analysis and opinion regarding the advisability of litigation.

Thomas Legislative Information

101 Independence S.E., Washington, DC 20540
Web site: http://thomas.loc.gov   **Email:** thomas@loc.gov   **Parent Company:** Library of Congress

Proprietary Databases or Gateways:
Database Name: **Thomas**
  Legislation/Regulation (US)

Special Distribution Methods to Client: Internet

Although technically a government site, we have posted in this section due to the tremendous information available to the public. Free Internet access to legislative information (including bill summary, status, and text), congressional record, and committee information. A giant plus is the ability to search by bill number or by key word/phrase.

Thomson & Thomson

500 Victory Rd, North Quincy, MA 02171-3145
Toll-free phone: 800-692-8833; Phone: 617-479-1600; Fax: 617-786-8273
Web site: www.thomson-thomson.com   **Email:** john.giaquinto@t-t.com
Branch Offices: Antwerp, Belgium, 323-220-7211; **Montreal, Quebec**, CANADA, 800-561-6240; Fax: 514-393-3854
Founded: 1922   **Parent Company:** The Thomson Corporation   **Memberships:** INTA, SIIA, AALL
Clientele Restrictions: Casual requesters permitted

Proprietary Databases or Gateways:
Database Name: **TRADEMARKSCAN**
  Trademarks and Foreign Country Information (US, International)

Database Name: **Worldwide Domain**
  Foreign Country Information (US, International)

Gateway Name: **Site Comber**
  Patents (US)

Database Name: **US Full Trademark Search, Site Comber**
  Trademarks (US)

Database Name: **US Full Copyright Search**
  Licenses/Registrations/Permits (US)

Database Name: **US Title Availability Search, The deForest Report for Script Clearance**
  Corporate/Trade Name Data (US)

Special Distribution Methods to Client: CD-ROM, Dial-Up (Other than Internet), Internet

Thomson & Thomson is a world leader in trademark, copyright and script clearance services, with over 75 years of experience and offices in the US, Canada, Europe and Japan. Accessing trademark records from more than 200 countries, T&T analysts provide reports to help clients determine if their proposed trademarks are available for use. Clients can perform their own trademark searches via Thomson & Thomson's TRADEMARKSCAN online databases. Thomson & Thomson also provides a complete offering of equally impressive copyright, title and script clearance services to help manage and protect your intellectual property assets.

Thomson Research Services

1455 Research Blvd., Rockville, MD 20850
Toll-free phone: 800-874-4337
Web site: www.thomsonfinancial.com   **Email:** researchcenter@tfn.com   **Founded:** 1978
Clientele Restrictions: Casual requesters permitted

Proprietary Databases or Gateways:
Database Name: **Global Access**
  SEC/Other Financial (US)

Database Name: **Thomson Research**
  News/Current Events, Trademarks, Environmental, Legislation/Regulation, Litigation/Judgments/Tax Liens (US)

Database Name: **Thomson Research**
  Bankruptcy (US)

Special Distribution Methods to Client: CD-ROM, Email, Internet

Thomson Research Services (TRS), formerly known as FDR and Disclosure, is a nationwide research and retrieval company founded over 30 years ago. Research can be done, on a state and federal basis, at any court or agency around the country. Court services include monitoring for new cases as well as obtaining filings in existing cases. TRS also has an extensive in-house collection of bankruptcy documents as well as other types of agency filings including FERC, DOT, & FCC. Securities and Exchange Commission documents, dating back to 1968, can be ordered from our research centers and delivered same day.

TitleSearcher.com

333 Industrial Park Rd, Piney Flats, TN 37686
Phone: 423-538-1900; Fax: 423-538-1919
Web site: http://auth.titlesearcher.com/ts/ts.asp   **Email:** support@titlesearcher.com
Founded: 1998   **Parent Company:** Business Information Systems
Clientele Restrictions: Online registration preferred.

Proprietary Databases or Gateways:
Database Name:
  Real Estate/Assessor, Litigation/Judgments/Tax Liens (TN)

Special Distribution Methods to Client: Internet

They offer subsciption access to over 40 Tennessse county recording offices, also a limited number of counties in Virginia and North Carolina. They offer a pay per search plan as well as a standard monthly sub.

TitleX.com

PO Box 4010 (502 E Kolstad), Palestine, TX 75802-4010
Phone: 903-723-2072; Fax: 903-723-2443
Web site: www.titlex.com   **Email:** information@titlex.com   **Founded:** 2000

Clientele Restrictions: Casual requesters permitted.
Proprietary Databases or Gateways:
Database Name: **titleX.com**
   Real Estate/Assessor (TX)

Special Distribution Methods to Client: Internet

TitleX's online search site allows users to search land-based records with speed, efficiency and cost effectiveness via the internet. They retreive content from the County Clerk. If the County Clerk is not digital, they partner with a digital title company in that county to retrieve the content. They specialize in Texas, allowing free searching of 28+ counties, plus Yakima Cty WA.

TML Information Services Inc

116-55 Queens Blvd, Forest Hills, NY 11375
Toll-free phone: 800-743-7891; Phone: 718-793-3737; Fax: 718-544-2853
Web site: www.tml.com   **Email:** edarmody@tml.com
Founded: 1985   **Memberships:** AAMVA, IIAA, NAPIA, NETS
Clientele Restrictions: Signed agreement required, must be ongoing account

Proprietary Databases or Gateways:
Gateway Name: **Auto-Search (Immediate MVR)**
   Driver and/or Vehicle (AL, AZ, AR, CT, DC, DE, FL, ID, IL, IN, KS, KY, LA, MA, MD, ME, MI, MN, MS, NC,
      ND, NE, NH, NJ, NY, OH, RI, SC, TN, TX, VA, VT, WI, WV)

Gateway Name: **Title File**
   Driver and/or Vehicle (AL, FL, SD)

Gateway Name: **Driver Check**
   Driver and/or Vehicle (AL, AZ, CA, CT, FL, ID, KS, LA, MD, MI, MN, NE, NH, NY, NC, OH, PA, SC, VA, WV)

Gateway Name: **Driving Records**
   Driver and/or Vehicle (US)

Special Distribution Methods to Client: Dial-Up (Other than Internet), Internet

TML Information Services specializes in providing access to motor vehicle information in an online, real-time environment. Their standardization format enables TML to offer several unique automated applications for instant access to multiple states' driver and vehicle information, including a touch-tone fax-on-demand service and a rule-based decision processing service for driver qualification for car rental. TML has online access to more than 200 million driver and vehicle records in more than 30 states and expects to add several more states soon. No third party use; professional license required.

tnrealestate.com

PO Box 1375, Murfreesboro, TN 37133
Phone: 615-907-8231
Web site: www.tnrealestate.com   **Email:** sales@tnrealestate.com   **Founded:** 1996   **Parent Company:** Kal Software LLC
Clientele Restrictions: Free limited access, also standard and enterprise subscriptions

Proprietary Databases or Gateways:
Database Name: **www.tnrealestate.com**
   Real Estate/Assessor (TN)

Special Distribution Methods to Client: Internet

Tnrealestate.com provides free and subscription level access to all 95 Tennessee counties. Information includes tax assessor files and other collected sales. Search by multiple fields or produce mailing lists, download results in text, perform statistical analysis and much more.

Trademark Register, The

2100 National Press Building, Washington, DC 20045
Phone: 202-347-2138; Fax: 202-347-4408
Web site: www.trademarkregister.com   **Email:** trademarks@erols.com   **Memberships:** ITA, SLA, NPC,

Proprietary Databases or Gateways:
Database Name: **The Trademark Register**
   Trademarks (US)

Special Distribution Methods to Client: Internet, Publication/Directory

The Trademark Register is an annual volume consisting of over 3 million active trademarks in effect with the U.S. Patent and Trademark Office and international marks from 1884 to present. It was first published in 1958 when it contained approximately 200,000 registered trademarks. Each trademark entry gives the date of registration or filling date, international class, registration or serial number. On January 1, 2003, the USPTO began production of a new process known as the Trademark Daily XML Process. The Trademark Weekly Text File (TWTF) will be discontinued March 31, 2003. This database and online service will be discontinued December 31, 2002. Please note that the company and database are for sale

Trans Union

PO Box 2000, Chester, PA 19022
Toll-free phone: 800-888-4213
Web site: www.transunion.com
Founded: 1969   **Memberships:** SIIA
Clientele Restrictions: Signed agreement required, must be ongoing account

Proprietary Databases or Gateways:
Database Name: **Trans Union Credit Data**
   Credit Information (US)

Special Distribution Methods to Client: Dial-Up (Other than Internet), Software

Trans Union is a primary source of credit information and offers risk and portfolio management services. They serve a broad range of industries that routinely evaluate credit risk or verify information about their customers. Their customers include financial and banking services, insurance agencies, retailers, collection agencies, communication and energy companies, and hospitals. They have strong relationships with every large and most medium and small credit grantors throughout the nation. Trans Union operates nationwide through a network of our own offices and independent credit bureaus. They also have many subsidiaries and divisions in the U.S. and abroad. The needs and desires of our customers and consumers directly shape Trans Union's products and services design. They have a competitive stance based on the highest levels of quality coupled with unmatched levels of service.

Trans Union Employment Screening Services Inc

6111 Oak Tree Blvd, Cleveland, OH 44131
Toll-free phone: 800-853-3228; Phone: 216-615-7600; Fax: 216-615-7666
Web site: www.tuess.com   **Email:** tuess@tuc.com   **Parent Company:** Acxiom
Branch Offices: Chicago, IL, 312-258-1717; Fax: 312-466-7992; **Atlanta**, GA, 770-613-2871; Fax: 770-409-2312
Founded: 1967   **Parent Company:** Trans Union LLC   **Memberships:** SHRM, ASIS, NEPHRA, NAC
Clientele Restrictions: None reported

Proprietary Databases or Gateways:
Database Name: **TRUSST (Tracking Residences using SSN Trace)**
   Addresses/Telephone Numbers (US)

Gateway Name: **Credit**
   Credit Information (US)

Gateway Name: **TransUnion**
   Driver and/or Vehicle, Workers Compensation (US)

Special Distribution Methods to Client: Dial-Up (Other than Internet), Disk, Email, Lists/Labels, Software

With accuracy in mind, Trans Union (Acxiom) engages in no third party handling whatsoever. 100% of their background investigations (including in-person/real time criminal record searches) are completed directly by Trans Union associates and court record researchers to eliminate the risk of error which often results from the transfer of information. Trans Union is a full service company offering Social Security traces, motor vehicle records, criminal searches, employment verifications, education verifications, license verifications, Workers compensation records, civil court action records at the local/state and county levels, drug testing, and character references. Utilizing the resources of both Trans Union Corporation and the marmon Group, Trans Union continues to be a leading power in the industry. Our experienced management team, associates and dedicated customer service staff have enabled Trans Union to set industry standards while adapting to the ever-changing needs of our business partners.

UCC Direct Services – (Formerly AccuSearch Inc)

PO Box 3248, 2727 Allen Parkway, 10th Fl, Houston, TX 77253-3248
Toll-free phone: 800-833-5778; Phone: 713-864-7639; Fax: 713-831-9891
Web site: www.uccdirect.com **Email:** info@uccdirect.com
Branch Offices: Sacramento, CA, 888-863-9241; Fax: 916-492-6655; **Austin**, TX, 800-884-0185; Fax: 512-323-9102; **Chicago**, IL, 847-853-0892; Fax: 847-853-0893
Founded: 1985 **Memberships:** NPRRA
Clientele Restrictions: License required
Proprietary Databases or Gateways:
Database Name: **AccuSearch**
  Corporate/Trade Name, Uniform Commercial Code (TX, CA, PA, IL, WA, OH, OR, MO)
Database Name: **AccuSearch**
  Bankruptcy (CA, IL, TX)
Special Distribution Methods to Client: Dial-Up (Other than Internet), Internet
UCC Direct - formerly AccuSearch - provides immediate access to UCC, corporate, charter, real property and bankruptcy search services via the Internet. Instantaneous access is available for each online database listed. Each online or over-the-phone search is followed by same-day mailing or faxing of the search report. They also performs any of the above searches for any county or state nationwide. Their Direct Access system allows multi-page, formatted reports which eliminates print screens, and selective ordering of UCC copies. Their new service iLienOnline integrates your UCC filing and search & retrieval activities, allowing you to do everything in one place - faster, easier, with more accuracy than ever before.

UCC Direct Services – (Formerly Intercounty Clearance Corporation)

187 Wolf Rd, Albany, NY 12205
Toll-free phone: 800-342-3676; Phone: 518-453-4020
Web site: www.intercountyclearance.com **Email:** information@intercountyclearance.com
Branch Offices: New York City, NY, 800-229-4422; Fax: 212-594-1304; **Hartford**, CT, 860-525-9238; Fax: 860-525-9280
Founded: 1935 **Memberships:** NPRRA **Parent Company:** CCH Legal Information
Clientele Restrictions: Must be ongoing business account.
Proprietary Databases or Gateways:
Gateway Name: **Intercounty Public Records Portal**
  Uniform Commercial Code, Corporate/Trade Name, Real Estate/Assessor Data, Aviation/Vessels,
    Licenses/Registrations/Permits, Litigation/Judgments/Tax Liens (US)
Special Distribution Methods to Client: Dial-Up (Other than Internet), Disk, Email, Internet
Formerly Intercounty Clearance Corporation, UCC Direct Services provides nationwide UCC and corporate services. They have experienced employees in each of the major metropolitan counties of New York. Their services include traditional and online UCC and corporate document retrieval, preparation (PowerLegal.com), online UCC database searching, online tracking/management of units of statutory representation, and corporate forms library.

Unisearch Inc

1780 Barnes Blvd SW, Tumwater, WA 98512-0410
Toll-free phone: 800-722-0708; Phone: 360-956-9500; Fax: 360-956-9504
Web site: www.unisearch.com
Branch Offices: Sacramento, CA, 800-769-1864; Fax: 800-769-1868; **Salem**, OR, 800-554-3113; Fax: 800-554-3114; **St Paul**, MN, 800-227-1256; Fax: 800-227-1263
Founded: 1991 **Memberships:** NPRRA, NRAI, PRRN
Clientele Restrictions: Casual requesters permitted

Proprietary Databases or Gateways:
Database Name: **WALDO**
  Uniform Commercial Code, Litigation/Judgments/Tax Liens (CA, WA)
Special Distribution Methods to Client: Dial-Up (Other than Internet), Email, Internet, Microfilm/Microfiche
Unisearch is online with dozens of states' UCC and corporate databases, providing instant access to current information. Often, they provide document copies within 24 hrs. In areas where computer access is not yet available, Unisearch offers a complete range of UCC and corporate services, including national and international Registered Agent service. Additional branch offices are located in Hilliard OH (877-208-7193) and Reno NV (800-260-8118).

United State Mutual Association

4500 S 129th E. Ave., #200, Tulsa, OK 74134
Toll-free phone: 888-338-8762; Phone: 918-280-4088; Fax: 912-828-9141
Web site: www.usmutual.com   **Email:** corporate@usmutual.com
Founded: 1996   **Parent Company:** Total Information Services Inc.   **Memberships:** ASIS, SHRM, NRF, NACS, FMI
Clientele Restrictions: Agreement required
Proprietary Databases or Gateways:
Database Name: **National Theft Database**
  Criminal Information, Addresses/Telephone Numbers (US)
Special Distribution Methods to Client: Automated Telephone Look-Up, Dial-Up (Other than Internet), FTP, Gateway via Another Online Service, Internet
USMA provides reports from a mutual and proprietary database containing documented incidents of theft. USMA's Theft Database contains the employee theft and shoplifting data of thousands of retail stores across the country. The database was established in 1996 when ten regional mutual associations combined the theft data of member-retailers into a single, national database. The 20/20 Database contains the results of more than 5-million criminal record searches. The database includes the results of previously requested criminal background searches from USMA and her sister companies. Applicant searches against this database provides member companies with a powerful tool that helps improve the quality and efficiency of the employment screening process. USMA is one of the single most comprehensive sources of employment screening products for human resource and loss prevention professionals. They provide unique access to background screening for retailers through automated phone, fax, web, dial-up and state-of-the-art call center services.

US Corporate Services

380 Jackson St., Ste 418, St Paul, MN 55101-3899
Toll-free phone: 800-327-1886; Phone: 651-227-7575; Fax: 651-225-9244
Web site: www.uscorpserv.com   **Email:** info@uscorpserv.com
Branch Offices: Portland, OR, 877-415-1822; Fax: 503-443-1056
Founded: 1966   **Parent Company:** Dolan Media Co   **Memberships:** NPRRA
Clientele Restrictions: Casual requesters permitted
Proprietary Databases or Gateways:
Database Name: **MN Secretary of State Records**
  Corporation/Trade Name Data (MN)
Database Name: **WI UCCs**
  Uniform Commerical Code (MN, WI)
Special Distribution Methods to Client: Dial-Up (Other than Internet), Disk, Lists/Labels, Publication/Directory, Software
US Corporate Services is a full service UCC, tax lien, judgment, litigation and corporate search and filing firm. Their optical image library of Minnesota enables them to provide custom reports to their clients. They have nationwide correspondent relationships. Their turnaround time is 24-72 hours. They will invoice monthly; projects are generally billed by the number of names searched.

US SEARCH.com

5401 Beethoven St, Los Angeles, CA 90066
Toll-free phone: 800-877-2410; Phone: 310-302-6300; Fax: 310-822-7898
Web site: www.ussearch.com/wlcs/index.jsp   **Email:** corporate@ussearch.com
Founded: 1995   **Memberships:** PIHRA, SHRM
Clientele Restrictions: Casual requesters permitted

Proprietary Databases or Gateways:
Gateway Name: **US Search**
  Addresses/Telephone Numbers, Corp/Trade Names, Vessels, Bankruptcy, Real Estate/Assessor, Aviation (US)

Special Distribution Methods to Client: Dial-Up (Other than Internet), Email

US SEARCH.com is one of the leading public record providers on the Internet. In addition to comprehensive locate and background reports on people and businesses, US SEARCH.com also provides nationwide data on Corporate & Limited Partnerships; Uniform Commerical Code; Employer ID Numbers; Bankruptcies, Liens and Judgments; Death Records; Real Property; Watercraft; Aircraft and Pilots. US SEARCH.com also offers On-Site Civil and Criminal Records Checks.

US Title Search Network

1370 Hazelwood Dr.#200, Smyrna, TN 37167
Phone: 615-223-5420; Fax: 615-223-5424
Web site: www.ustitlesearch.com   **Email:** webmaster@ustitlesearch.net   **Parent Company:** ProGResS, Inc.
Clientele Restrictions: Subscription required; free demo available.

Proprietary Databases or Gateways:
Database Name:
  Real Estate/Assessor, Litigation/Judgments/Tax Liens (TN)

Special Distribution Methods to Client: Internet

They offer online access via their subsciption service to indexes and images for 22+ TN county recording offices.

USADATA.com

292 Madison Ave, 3rd Fl, New York, NY 10017
Toll-free phone: 800-599-5030; Phone: 212-326-8760; Fax: 212-679-8507
Web site: www.usadata.com   **Email:** info@usadata.com
Founded: 1995
Clientele Restrictions: Casual requesters permitted

Proprietary Databases or Gateways:
Gateway Name: **Marketing Portal**
  Corporate/Trade Name Data, Addresses/Telephone Numbers, Real Estate/Assessor (US)

Special Distribution Methods to Client: Email, Lists/Labels, Software

USADATA.com's Marketing Information Portal (www.usadata.com) provides fast, easy access to the information you need to make critical business decisions. They provide mailing lists, research reports, consumer info, and helpful information gathering solutions. They draw data from the top names in syndicated consumer data on both a local and national level, including Mediamark Research Inc (MRI), Scarborough Research, Arbitron, Acxiom, Competitive Media Reporting (CMR) and National Decision Systems (NDS). Marketers, planners and media buyers can order reports on a pay-per-view basis from the website, or subscribe to unlimited Internet access.

USAScreening.com

7326 27th St W, #C, University Place, WA 98466
Toll-free phone: 800-568-5665; Phone: 253-565-9109; Fax: 253-566-1231
Web site: www.usascreening.com   **Email:** jim@verifacts.com   **Memberships:** NACM, NASA, NARPM
Clientele Restrictions: Signed Agreement Required

Proprietary Databases or Gateways:
Database Name: **Statewide Criminal Records**
 Criminal Information (AK, AZ, AR, CO, CT, FL, GA, HI, ID, IL, IN, KY, MI, MS, NC, NY, OH, OK, SC, TN, TX, UT, VA, WA)

Special Distribution Methods to Client: Email, Gateway via Another Online Service, Internet
USAScreening.com is the human resource site for your hiring needs. They use only the newest Internet technologies to provide quality information in a fast, easy-to-use process. Social Security searches nationally. In California, they retrieve criminal records in counties of Los Angeles, Riverside, and San Diego.

Utah.gov

68 S Main St #200, Salt Lake City, UT 84101
Toll-free phone: 877-588-3468; Phone: 801-983-0275; Fax: 801-983-0282
Web site: www.utah.gov/　**Email:** info@e-utah.org　**Parent Company:** Utah Electronic Commerce Council
Clientele Restrictions: Many free service, but must be ongoing account for premium services
Proprietary Databases or Gateways:
Gateway Name: **TLRIS/MVR**
 Driver and/or Vehicle (UT)

Gateway Name: **Business Entity List**
 Corporate/Trade Name Data, Addresses/Telephone Numbers (UT)

Gateway Name: **UCC Filing Data**
 Uniform Commercial Code (UT)

Gateway Name: **License Data**
 Licenses/Registrations/Permits (UT)

Special Distribution Methods to Client: CD-ROM, Database, Email, FTP, Internet
Utah.gov is the State of Utah's gateway providing a single access point, to all electronically available government information and services, to businesses and citizens via the Internet. Through Utah.gov, online users search the following databases: Business Entity, Principals, Business Name Availablity, Vehicle Titles, Leins and Tregistrations, Driving Records, Registered Notaries, and UCCs. In addition, online users can renew vehicle registrations, register a business name, buy hunting and fishing licenses, download offical forms, and access hundreds of government information sources and much much more. For more information, visit the web site at www.utah.gov.

Verifacts

5889 S. Greenwood Plaza Blvd. #201, Greenwood Village, CO 80111
Toll-free phone: 800-568-5665; Phone: 303-302-1930; Fax: 303-662-1608
Web site: www.verifacts.com　**Email:** jim@verifacts.com　**Parent Company:** Rentport Inc.
Memberships: NACM, NASA, NARPM, NMHC, NAA
Clientele Restrictions: Casual requesters permitted for criminal or eviction searches w/ credit card
Proprietary Databases or Gateways:
Gateway Name: **Statewide Criminal Records**
 Criminal Information (AK, AL, AZ, AR, CA, CO, CT, FL, GA, IA, ID, IL, IN, KS, KY, LA, MD, ME, MI, MN, MO, MS, NC, NH, ND, NJ, NM, NY, OH, OK, OR, PA, RI, SC, SD, TN, TX, UT, VA, WA, WI)

Gateway Name: **Eviction/Unlawful Detainers**
 Litigation/Judgments/Tax Liens (AK, AZ, CA, CO, ID, KY, NV, OR, PA, TX, VA, WA)

Gateway Name: **Registered Sex Offenders (included with criminal searches)**
 Criminal Information (AK, AZ, CT, FL, GA, HI, ID, IL, IN, KS, KY, MI, MS, NC, NY, OH, OK, SC, TN, TX, UT, VA, WA)

Special Distribution Methods to Client: Email, Gateway via Another Online Service, Internet
Verifacts, a division of RentPort, Inc., is one of the nation's most technologically advanced screening services. Verifacts provides nationwide criminal coverage; credit reports which are color-coded, easy-to-read, and include risk-score information; Social Security searches; national terrorist database search capability; registered sex offender

searches which include pictures of the offender in most states; and eviction searches. Scored credit reports are available through CreditRetriever, RentPort's online applicant screening and scoring product.

Virginia Information Providers Network

1111 East Main Street #901, Richmond, VA 23219
Toll-free phone: 877-482-3468; Phone: 804-786-4718; Fax: 804-786-6227
Web site: www.vipnet.org   **Email:** webmaster@vipnet.org   **Founded:** 1996
Clientele Restrictions: Signed agreement required, must be ongoing account

Proprietary Databases or Gateways:

Gateway Name: **VIPNet**
  Driver and/or Vehicle, Vessels, Legislation/Regulation (VA)

Gateway Name: **Health Professionals (free)**
  Associations/Trade Groups (VA)

Gateway Name: **State Employment Verification**
  Education/Employment (VA)

Special Distribution Methods to Client: Internet

The Virginia Information Providers Network was created by the state of Virginia to streamline and enhance the ways in which citizens and businesses access government information. VIPNet Premium Services includes access to state services including motor vehicle records, boat records, a value-added bill tracking service, state employment verification, and licenses health professionals data. VIPNet also provides an extensive range of free services for the public, including online election results, legisaltive tracking, and review of attorney disciplinary actions.

Vision Appraisal Technology

44 Bearfoot Rd, Northboro, MA 01532
Toll-free phone: 800-628-1013; Phone: 508-351-3600; Fax: 508-351-3798
Web site: www.visionappraisal.com   **Email:** marketing@visionappraisal.com   **Founded:** 1975
Clientele Restrictions: Casual requesters permitted.

Proprietary Databases or Gateways:
Database Name: **various New England Municipalities**
  Real Estate/Assessor (CT, ME, MA, NH, RI)

Special Distribution Methods to Client: Internet

Vision Appraisal Technology is a provider of state-of-the-art assessing (CAMA) software and real estate appraisal services in the NE USA. They provide real Estate appraisal services to New England municipalities and assessing software to assessing jurisdictions throughout the USA.

Vital Records Information

925 Cypress South, Greenwood, IN 46143
Web site: http://vitalrec.com   **Email:** Corrections@vitalrec.com

Proprietary Databases or Gateways:
Gateway Name: **vitalrec.com**
  Vital Records, Genealogical Information (US)

Gateway Name: **vitalrec.com**
  Foreign Country Information (International)

Special Distribution Methods to Client: Internet

Although primarily a links list, vitalrec.com is a gateway to extensive information, especially geneology.

VitalChek Network

4512 Central Pike, Hermitage, TN 37076
Toll-free phone: 800-255-2414
Web site: www.vitalchek.com   **Email:** vitals.comments@vitalchek.com
Clientele Restrictions: Casual requesters permitted

Proprietary Databases or Gateways:
Gateway Name: **VitalChek**
  Vital Records (US)

Special Distribution Methods to Client:
VitalChek Network has a sophisticated voice and fax network setup to help people acquire certified copies of birth, death and marriage certificates and other vital records. Some online ordering capabilities are included, but records are retruned form the states. VitalChek provides a direct access gateway link from participating agencies at the state and local level.

West Group

620 Opperman Dr, Eagan, MN 55123
Toll-free phone: 800-328-9352; Phone: 651-687-7000; Fax: 651-687-7302
Web site: www.westgroup.com
Founded: 1872   **Parent Company:** Thomson   **Memberships:** SIIA
Clientele Restrictions: Casual requesters permitted

Proprietary Databases or Gateways:
Database Name: **West CD-ROM Libraries**
  Legislation/Regulations (US)

Database Name: **Westlaw**
  Environmental, Legislation/Regulations, Corporate/Trade Name Data, Uniform Commercial Code (US)

Special Distribution Methods to Client: CD-ROM, Dial-Up (Other than Internet), Internet
West Group is one of the largest providers of information to US legal professionals. West Group includes renowned names such as Barclays, Bancroft Whitney, Clark Boardman Callaghan, Counterpoint, Lawyers Cooperative Publishing, West Publishing and Westlaw. Westlaw is a computer-assisted research service consisting of more than 9,500 legal, financial and news databases, including Dow Jones News/Retrieval. West Group produces a total of more than 3,800 products including 300 CD-ROMs.

Western Regional Data Inc

PO Box 20520, Reno, NV 89515
Phone: 775-329-9544; Fax: 775-324-1652   **Email:** wrdi@accutech.com
Founded: 1984
Clientele Restrictions: Casual requesters permitted

Proprietary Databases or Gateways:
Database Name: **WRDI's Lead Focus, Property Search**
  Real Estate/Assessor (NV)

Special Distribution Methods to Client: CD-ROM, Disk, FTP, Lists/Labels
Western Regional Data (WDRI) gathers assessor data from 3 counties (Washoe, Douglas & Carson) in Northern and resales the data in several media formats. The cumpany also supplies maps for th Washoe county area.

Westlaw Public Records

P.O. Box 64833 (620 Opperman Dr), St. Paul, MN 55164
Toll-free phone: 800-328-4880
Web site: www.westlaw.com   **Email:** admin@WESTPUB.COM   **Memberships:** NPRRA
Clientele Restrictions: Casual requesters permitted

Proprietary Databases or Gateways:
Database Name: **Bankruptcy Records**
  Bankruptcy (US)

Database Name: **Corporations and Partnerships**
  Corporate/Trade Name Data (US)

Database Name: **Lawsuits, Judgments, Liens**
  Litigation/Judgments/Tax Liens (US)

Database Name: **Professional Licenses**
  Licenses/Regist./Permits (AZ, CA, CO, CT, FL, GA, IL, IN, LA, MA, MD, MI, NJ, OH, PA, SC, TN, TX, VA, WI)

Database Name: **Real Estate, Liens & Judgments**
  Real Estate/Assessor, Litigation/Judgments/Tax Liens (US)

Database Name: **UCCs**
  Uniform Commerical Code (US)

Database Name: **Watercraft Locator/Aircraft Locator**
  Aviation/Vessels (US)

Database Name: **Business Finder/People Finder**
  Addresses/Telephone Numbers (US)

Gateway Name: **Motor Vehicle Records**
  Driver and/or Vehicle (AK, AL, CO, CT, DC, DE, FL, IA, ID, IL, KY, LA, MA, MD, ME, MI, MN, MO, MS, MT,
    ND, NE, NH, NM, NY, OH, SC, TN, UT, WI, WV, WY)

Special Distribution Methods to Client: Dial-Up (Other than Internet), Internet

Westlaw Public Records combines and links public records and courthouse documents with information from private sources to address the relationships between corporations, people and their assets. Banks, financial service companies, corporations, law firms and government agencies across the nation use their online and document retrieval services to obtain background data on businesses, locate assets and people, retrieve official public records and solve business problems. Westlaw Public Records was originally founded by a practicing attorney and a computer systems expert acquainted with the needs of government, legal and corporate customers.

Editor's Tip: Visit www.publicrecordsources.com for updated
information about these and other companies.

Additional sources/ companies that provide online record services exclusively from government entities are listed among the Government Online Sources by state in Section II pages 77-405.

Appendix

The Appendix Includes:

Trade Associations–A list of trade associations connected to the public information industry and their web sites.

Editors' Choices – 11 Great Web Sites–A short list of web sites to visit and use.

Trade Associations

There are many trade associations related to the public records industry. Below you will find a list of many of these associations. The companies profiled in our Private Database Vendors Section (beginning on page 407) are often members of one or more of these associations.

Acronym	Organization	Web Site	Members
AALL	American Assn of Law Librarians	www.aallnet.org/index.asp	4600
AAMVA	American Assn of Motor Vehicle Administrators	www.aamva.org	1500
AAPL	American Assn of Professional Landmen	www.landman.org	7000
ABA	American Bar Assn	www.abanet.org/home.html	417000
ABA (2)	American Banking Assn	www.aba.com	470
ABFE	American Board of Forensic Examiners	www.acfe.com	12000
ABI	American Bankruptcy Institute	www.abiworld.org	6500
ABW	American Business Women	www.abwahq.org	80000
ACA	American Collectors Assn	www.collector.com	3500
ACFE	Assn of Certified Fraud Examiners	http://cfenet.com	20000
AFIO	Assn of Former Intelligence Officers	www.afio.com	2500
AICPA	Assn of Certified Public Accountants	www.aicpa.org/index.htm	330000
AIIP	Assn of Independent Information Professionals	www.aiip.org	750
AIPLA	American Intellectual Property Law Assn	www.aipla.org	10000
ALA	American Library Assn	www.ala.org	56800
ALTA	American Land Title Association	www.alta.org	2400
AMA	American Management Assn	www.amanet.org/index.htm	70000
APA (2)	American Psychological Assn	www.apa.org	155000
APG	Assn of Professional Genealogists	www.apgen.org	1000
ASIS	American Society for Industrial Security	www.asisonline.org	40000
ASLET	American Society of Law Enforcement Trainers	www.aslet.org	7000

Acronym	Organization	Web Site	Members
ASSE	American Society of Safety Engineers	www.asse.org	35000
ATA	American Truckers Assn	www.trucking.org	4100
ATLA	Assn of Trial Lawyers of America	www.atlanet.org	56000
CII	Council of Intl Investigators	www.cii2.org	
DMA	Direct Marketing Assn	www.the-dma.org	4500
EAE	Environmental Assessment Assn	www.iami.org/eaa.cfm	3500
EMA	Employment Management Assn	www.shrm.org/EMA	4200
EPIC	Evidence Photographers Intl Council	www.epic-photo.org	1000
FBINAA	FBI Natl Academy Assn	www.fbinaa.org	17000
IAAI	Intl Assn of Arson Investigators	www.fire-investigators.org	9000
IAHSS	Intl Assn of Healthcare Security & Safety	www.iahss.org	
IALEIA	Intl Assn of Law Enforcement Intelligence Analysts	www.ialeia.org	1000
IIAA	Independent Insurance Agents of America	www.iiaa.org	300000
INA	Intl Nanny Assn	www.nanny.org	
INOA	Intl Narcotics Officers Assn	www.ineoa.org	
INTA	Intl Trademark Assn	www.inta.org	4200
ION	Investigative Open Network	www.ioninc.com	500
IREM	Institute of Real Estate Management	www.irem.org	8600
LES	Licensing Executive Society	www.usa-canada.les.org	4700
MBAA	Mortgage Bankers Assn of America	www.mbaa.org	2700
NALS	NALS...the Association of Legal Professionals	www.nals.org	6000
NAC	Natl Assn of Counselors	http://nac.lincoln-grad.org	500
NACM	Natl Assn of Credit Managers	www.nacm.org	35000
NAFE	Natl Assn of Female Executives	www.nafe.com	150000
NAFI	Natl Assn of Fire Investigators	www.nafi.org	5000
NAHB	Natl Assn of Home Builders	www.nahb.com	197000
NAHRO	Natl Assn of Housing & Redvlp Officials	www.nahro.org	8500
NAIS	Natl Assn of Investigative Specialists	www.pimall.com/nais/nais.menu.html	3000
NALA	Natl Assn of Legal Assistants	www.nala.org	17000
NALFM	Natl Assn of Law Firm Marketers	www.legalmarketing.org	1000
NALI	Natl Assn of Legal Investigators	www.nali.com	800
NALSC	Natl Assn of Legal Search Consultants	www.nalsc.org	130
NAMSS	Natl Assn of Medical Staff Svcs	www.namss.org	4000
NAPPS	Natl Assn of Professional Process Servers	www.napps.org/napps.htm	1100
NAPIA	Natl Assn of Public Insurance Adjustors	www.napia.com	
NAR	Natl Assn of Realtors	www.realtor.com	805000
NAREIT	Natl Assn of Real Estate Investment Trusts	www.nareit.org	1080

Acronym	Organization	Web Site	Members
NARPM	Natl Assn of Residential Property Managers	www.narpm.org	1400
NASA	Natl Assn of Screening Agencies	www.n-a-s-a.com	25
NASIR	Natl Assn of Security & Investgt Regulators	www.nasir.org	90
NAWBO	Natl Assn of Women Business Owners	www.nawbo.org/nawbo/nawbostart.nsf	3000
NCISS	Natl Council of Investigation & Security Sevices	www.nciss.org	
NCRA	Natl Court Reporters Assn	www.verbatimreporters.com	23
NCRA	Natl Credit Reporting Association	www.ncrainc.org	
NDIA	Natl Defender Investigator Assn	www.ndia-inv.org	32000
NFIB	Natl Federation of Independent Businesses	www.nfib.org	650
NFPA	Natl Federation of Paralegal Associations	www.paralegals.org	15000
NFIP	Natl Flood Insurance Program	www.fema.gov/nfip	600000
NFPA	Natl Federation of Paralegal Assn	www.paralegals.org	
NGS	Natl Genealogical Society	www.ngsgenealogy.org	
NHEMA	Natl Home Equity Mortgage Assn	www.nhema.org	240
NHRA	Natl Human Resources Assn	www.humanresources.org	1500
NICA	Natl Insurance Claims Assn	www.gonatgo.com	
NLG	Natl Lawyers Guild	www.nlg.org	6000
NPPRA	Natl Public Record Research Assn	www.nprra.org	375
NSA	Natl Sheriffs' Association	www.sheriffs.org	20000
PBUS	Professional Bail Agents of the United States	www.pbus.com	800
PIHRA	Professionals in Human Resources Assn	www.pihra.org	3500
PRRN	Public Record Retriever Network	www.brbpub.com/prrn	700
REIPA	Real Estate Information Providers Assn	www.reipa.org	
SCIP	Society of Competitive Intelligence Professionals	www.scip.org	6500
SFSA	Society of Former Special Agents of the FBI	www.socxfbi.org	7800
SHRM	Society of Human Resources Management	www.shrm.org	65000
SIIA	Software & Information Industry Association	www.siia.net	1200
SILA	Society of Insurance License Administrators	www.sila.org	
SLA	Special Libraries Assn	www.sla.org	14000
USFN	US Foreclosure Network	www.usfn.org	
WAD	World Assn of Detectives	www.wad.net	

Editors' Choices — 11 Great Web Sites

Acronym Finder –
A comprehensive database of acronyms, abbreviations, and initialisms.
    http://www.acronymfinder.com/

Crimetime Publishing – Home of Robert Scott's *Investigator's Little Black Book*
    http://www.crimetime.com

Domain Name Search – Great tool from VeriSign
    http://www.netsol.com/cgi-bin/whois/whois

FindLaw – Great overall legal reference site
    http://www.findlaw.com

Newspaper Links – You can even make your own newspaper
    http://crayon.net/using/links.html

PI Magazine – Jimmie Mesis has made this magazine an industry standard
    http://www.pimagazine.com

Sexual Offender Links – Includes excellent article on Megan's Law
    http://www.sexoffender.com/search.html

Social Security Number Verification Search – and it's free!
    http://www.usinfosearch.com/Free_ssn_search.htm

Translation Sites – English to ? – or ? to English!
    http://babelfish.altavista.com

Unclaimed Property – Free lookups for each state database that is online
    http://www.unclaimed.org

US Post Office – ZIP +4 Look-ups
    http://www.usps.com/ncsc/lookups/lookup_zip%2b4.html

Notes

Notes